John

The Mahler Compan.

The MAHLER Companion

EDITED BY

Donald Mitchell & Andrew Nicholson

OXFORD

UNIVERSITY PRESS

OXFORD

UNIVERSITY PRESS

Great Clarendon Street, Oxford OX2 6DP

Oxford University Press is a department of the University of Oxford
It furthers the University's objective of excellence in research, scholarship,
and education by publishing worldwide in

Oxford New York

Auckland Bangkok Buenos Aires Cape Town Chennai
Dar es Salaam Delhi Hong Kong Istanbul Karachi Kolkata
Kuala Lumpur Madrid Melbourne Mexico City Mumbai Nairobi
São Paulo Shanghai Taipei Tokyo Toronto

Oxford is a registered trade mark of Oxford University Press
in the UK and in certain other countries

Published in the United States
by Oxford University Press Inc., New York

© Donald Mitchell and Andrew Nicholson 1999

The moral rights of the authors have been asserted

Database right Oxford University Press (maker)

First published 1999

First published in paperback 2002

British Library Cataloguing in Publication Data

Data available

Library of Congress Cataloging in Publication Data
The Mahler companion / edited by Donald Mitchell and Andrew Nicholson.
p. cm.
Includes bibliographical references (p.   ) and index.
1. Mahler, Gustav, 1860–1911.
I. Mitchell, Donald, 1925–   .   II. Nicholson, Andrew, 1948–   .
ML410.M23M232   1999   780.92—dc21   98–45827

ISBN 0–19–816376–2 (hbk)

ISBN 0–19–924965–2 (pbk)

3 5 7 9 10 8 6 4

Music origination by
Figaro, Oxfordshire
Typeset by Hope Services (Abingdon) Ltd
Printed in Great Britain
on acid-free paper by
Antony Rowe Ltd.
Chippenham, Wiltshire

To Edward R. Reilly

in admiration and affection

PREFACE TO THE PAPERBACK EDITION

My co-editor, Andrew Nicholson, and I make our acknowledgements below, but I should like to make a personal acknowledgement of my own regarding Andrew's contribution. Without his patience and skill, the task of assembling and collating the multiple revisions, additions, and corrections which form part of this first paperback edition of the *Companion* would have been beyond my reach, at least within any time-scale that made sense to ourselves or our publishers. I am most grateful to him.

And now an apology. Owing to an inexplicable lapse of memory on my part, the hardback edition of the *Companion* omitted to mention Mahler's Piano Quartet movement of 1876 and two songs dating from 1880. Happily, readers will find at the end of this present volume the gap filled by a newly commissioned essay by Jeremy Barham, to whom we owe particular thanks for delivering his text within a very tight schedule.

Almost every reviewer of the book quite properly mentioned this omission, but the majority of our critics, and some readers, did much more than that; they brought to our attention not only factual errors but also, in what proved to be *in toto* a richly varied commentary, encouraging evidence that we had at least succeeded in some of our aims. One of these aims—a pioneering effort, I believe—was to attempt to tackle seriously the history of the reception of Mahler's music worldwide, to place the composer in a global perspective, and thereby throw light on why his music enjoys such an extraordinary international reputation today. (Popularity on this scale brings its perils as well as its rewards, a point to which I shall return.) We are, then, indebted to our critics for the seriousness of their approach.

There was a single exception to that general seriousness: a review of a grotesque parochialism, worth mentioning only because it emanated from Vienna—indeed, from the International Gustav Mahler Society itself. Mahler would surely have appreciated such an irony: parochialism of this kind was a phenomenon with which he was all too familiar.

We hope, of course, that the *Companion* in its new format will accompany fresh legions of Mahler voyagers and explorers as the new century progresses, and, most importantly, that it may offer useful insights into how his music should be heard, that is, performed. To my mind, this issue of interpretation is a crucial one, the more so as Mahler's popularity— the frequency of performances, the torrent of recordings—seems unlikely to abate. My anxiety, if I may poach from Trollope, about the way we hear Mahler now led me to conclude an address I gave at the MahlerFest in Boulder, Colorado, in January 2001 with these words and thoughts:

... I have not attempted to disguise my resistance to the false beautification of Mahler, to smoothness; the application of cosmetics; to routine; to blandness; to the reduction of the shock that is so often integral to his aesthetic. I most earnestly hope that younger generations of Mahler students, scholars, analysts and critics, indeed all who have direct contact with Mahler's genius, will unite and campaign to find a way, perhaps through the collaboration of a sympathetically inclined institution, to build this vital bridge of communication between analysis and interpretation. It could form a brilliant future area of Mahler studies which would also attract much public attention. Unless that happens, I am fearful of a future when Mahler may be performed not one whit less than he is now, but when, in the wake of a thousand performances of this symphony or that, members of the audiences might be heard asking themselves, homeward bound, 'I wonder what all the fuss was about?'

I am confident that our team of collaborators will be judged by readers to have come up with at least some of the answers to that vital question.

D.M.

ACKNOWLEDGEMENTS

During the preparation of this volume we have enjoyed the generous co-operation of a number of people and institutions. In particular we should like to express our gratitude and thanks to the following: the late Joseph Albrecht; Richard Alston (Diss); Chris Banks (The British Library); Paul Banks (The Britten-Pears Library); Eileen Bell (The Britten Estate); Andrew Bennett (Bristol); George Biddlecombe (The Royal Academy of Music, London); Herta Blaukopf (Vienna); Birgit Heinemann (Gürzenich Orchester/Kölner Philharmoniker, Cologne); Renate Hilmar-Voit (Vienna); Joe Hollings (King's College, London); Gilbert E. Kaplan (The Kaplan Foundation, New York); Henry-Louis de La Grange (Bibliothèque Gustav Mahler, Paris); Graham Lloyd (Worcester); the late Anna Mahler; Marina Mahler (Spoleto); the late William Malloch; Lesley Marshall (Camden Library Services); Knud Martner (Copenhagen); Colin Matthews (London); David Matthews (London); Graham Melville-Mason (London and Prague); O. W. Neighbour (London); Edward R. Reilly (Poughkeepsie, New York); Peter Righton (Diss); H. C. Robbins Landon (Rabastens); Gail Ross (The Kaplan Foundation, New York); Alan Rusbridger (Guardian Newspapers Limited); Morten Solvik (Vienna); Stewart Spencer (London); Henriette Straub (Amsterdam); Marion Thorpe (London); Rigbie Turner (The Pierpont Morgan Library, New York); Ian Venables (Worcester); Timothy Webb (Bristol); and Judy Young (The Britten Estate). We should also like to thank most warmly Jill Burrows for the index and our editors at Oxford University Press: Bonnie Blackburn, Helen Foster, and in particular Bruce Phillips whose encouragement has meant so much to us. Finally, a special debt of thanks to our contributors for their patient collaboration.

D.M.   A.N.   1999

ADDITIONS AND ACKNOWLEDGEMENTS
(paperback edition)

We would draw the reader's attention to new material on pages 235, 325, 337, 406, 408, 436–7, and 564. Additional items of bibliography have also been incorporated into 'Sources', on pages 609–25. We should like to thank Richard Alston, Jeremy Barham, Graeme Downes, Michael Kennedy, Henry-Louis de La Grange, Stephen McClatchie, Eveline Nikkels, Edward R. Reilly, Peter Righton, Stan Ruttenberg, Roger Savage, and Vin Tyndall for helping us with enquiries, and our contributors for undertaking further scrutiny of their chapters. We should also like to thank our editors at Oxford University Press, Julia Bryan Chukinas and, especially, Michael Wood, for their encouragement and co-operation.

D.M. A.N. 2002

CONTENTS

LIST OF ILLUSTRATIONS

NOTES ON THE CONTRIBUTORS

KENJI AOYAGI studied musicology at Tokyo University of Fine Arts and Music. He is Assistant Professor of Music at Kurashiki Sakuyo University and specializes in music of the late nineteenth and twentieth centuries.

JEREMY BARHAM studied music at the Universities of Durham and Surrey, writing his doctoral thesis on the relationship between Mahler's music and late nineteenth-century German philosophy. He has taught at the University of Surrey and is currently Lecturer in Academic Studies at Trinity College of Music in London. He is a regular contributor to *Music & Letters* and is editor of *Perspectives on Gustav Mahler* (forthcoming).

INNA BARSOVA studied musicology at the Moscow Conservatoire and was Professor of Music at the Nizhni Novgorod Conservatoire. She is now Professor of Music at the Moscow Conservatoire, and has published on Mahler, Wagner, and Soviet music of the 1930s.

LEON BOTSTEIN is President and Leon Levy Professor in the Arts and Humanities, Bard College, New York. He is music director of the American Symphony Orchestra and editor of *The Musical Quarterly*.

PETER FRANKLIN taught at the University of Leeds before taking up his current post of Reader in Music at Oxford University. He is the author of *The Idea of Music: Schoenberg and Others* (1985), *Mahler Symphony No. 3* (1991), and *The Life of Mahler* (1997), and writes on twentieth-century European music, opera, and Hollywood film music.

PAUL HAMBURGER is a pianist, writer, teacher, and translator. He worked with the English Opera Group and the Glyndebourne Opera, and was on the staff of the BBC from 1962 to 1981. He coaches singers and accompanists at the Guildhall School of Music and at seminars throughout Europe, and has published on Mozart, Chopin, and Britten.

STEPHEN E. HEFLING studied at Harvard and Yale Universities. He taught at Stanford, Yale, and Oberlin College Conservatory, and is now Professor of Music at Case Western Reserve University. He has published articles on Mahler, and is the editor of *Mahler Studies* (1997) and of a volume of the Mahler *Gesamtausgabe*.

HENRY-LOUIS DE LA GRANGE is the biographer of Mahler and a Mahler scholar whose services to the Arts and music have been honoured in France, Austria, and England. Born in 1924, he studied music under Yvonne Lefebure and Nadia Boulanger in Paris, and later at Yale University, before becoming a music critic writing for a number of American and French journals. Since 1953 he has devoted himself almost exclusively to Mahler, researching his life and work, lecturing on him throughout the world, and organizing festivals and exhibitions. In 1986 he founded the Bibliothèque musicale Gustav Mahler in Paris, which houses one of the richest archives of the composer. Three volumes of his projected four-volume biography of Mahler have so far appeared; the second volume, published by Oxford University Press in 1995, was greeted with wide critical acclaim and received the Royal Philharmonic Society Award.

Colin Matthews is a composer of many large-scale orchestral works (including two cello concertos) and much instrumental music (including three string quartets), and is currently Associate Composer with the London Symphony Orchestra. He worked as assistant to Benjamin Britten in the 1970s, and collaborated with Deryck Cooke on the Performing Version of Mahler's Tenth Symphony.

David Matthews is a composer whose many orchestral, chamber, and vocal works include four symphonies and seven string quartets. He collaborated with Deryck Cooke on the Performing Version of Mahler's Tenth Symphony, and has written a number of articles on twentieth-century music as well as a study of Michael Tippett (1980).

Wilfrid Mellers read English, then Music at Cambridge University, where he continued to teach both subjects before becoming Staff tutor in Music at Birmingham University. From 1960 to 1964 he was Mellon Professor of Music at the University of Pittsburgh, and in 1964 became the founding Professor of Music at the University of York, where he remained until his retirement in 1981. His many publications include major studies of Couperin, Bach, Beethoven, Vaughan Williams, and American music, and smaller books on Grainger, Poulenc, the Beatles, Bob Dylan, and women jazz-singers.

Donald Mitchell was born in 1925. Two composers have been central to his writings on music, Gustav Mahler and Benjamin Britten. His three studies of Mahler, *The Early Years* (1958), *The Wunderhorn Years* (1975), and *Songs and Symphonies of Life and Death* (1985), are among the enduring monuments of the postwar Mahler literature. In 1997 he edited for the Royal Concertgebouw Orchestra, Amsterdam, a monograph on Mahler's Fifth Symphony, *New Sounds, New Century*, to which he contributed a unique analytic interpretation of the work. The full version of that text is published here for the first time. He is Trustee Emeritus of the Britten–Pears Foundation and Life President of the Britten Estate. He was founder Professor of Music at the University of Sussex (1971–1976), was visiting Professor at King's College, London, and is currently visiting Professor at the Universities of Sussex and York. He was awarded the Gustav Mahler Medal of Honour of the International Gustav Mahler Society in Vienna in 1987, and was appointed CBE in 2000.

Andrew Nicholson is Research Fellow in Romantic Studies in the English Department at Bristol University and has had a lifelong passion for Mahler. He is the editor of *Lord Byron: The Complete Miscellaneous Prose* (1991) and of facsimile editions of Byron's *Don Juan*, *Beppo*, and other of his poems. At present he is editing the letters of John Murray to Byron.

Eveline Nikkels studied music and philosophy at the University of Utrecht. She lectures widely on Mahler and the *fin de siècle*, and has a particular interest in the influence of Nietzsche on Mahler's music. She is Secretary of the Dutch Mahler Society and has organized many conferences on the composer in the Netherlands.

Gérard Pesson studied musicology at the Sorbonne and is a composer of a number of award-winning works. He is the director of the Conservatoire of Vitry-sur-Seine and founding editor of the contemporary music review *Entretemps*. He has contributed articles on music to a variety of journals in France and has a special interest in music and society in the work of Proust.

Edward R. Reilly studied music history at the University of Michigan, and taught at Converse College and the University of Georgia before becoming Professor of Music at Vassar College. He has written on Mussorgsky, Johann Joachim Quantz, and eighteenth-century performance practice, and has published many articles and chapters on the life and music of Mahler. His book *Gustav Mahler and Guido Adler: Records of a Friendship* appeared in 1982.

PETER REVERS studied musicology, psychology, and philosophy at the Universities of Salzburg and Vienna, and taught at the Universities of Vienna and Hamburg before becoming Professor of Music at the University of Graz. He is the editor of the critical edition of Mahler's *Lieder und Gesänge* (1992), and his publications include books and articles on Mahler, twentieth-century music, East Asian music, and Sibelius.

MORTEN SOLVIK studied music at Cornell University and the University of Pennsylvania, and wrote his doctoral thesis on the cultural context of Mahler's Third Symphony. He is currently a freelance musicologist in Vienna, where he lectures at the College of Music and Dramatic Art and the Institute of European Studies. He has written on Schubert, Mahler, and other nineteenth-century musical topics.

JOHN WILLIAMSON is Reader in Music at the University of Liverpool. He has written articles and chapters on Mahler, Strauss, Wolf, and their contemporaries, and is the author of *The Music of Hans Pfitzner* (1992) and *Richard Strauss: 'Also sprach Zarathustra'* (1993). He is currently researching a book on Eugen d'Albert.

ABBREVIATIONS

Adorno, *Mahler*	Theodor W. Adorno, *Mahler: A Musical Physiognomy*, trans. Edmund Jephcott (Chicago and London: University of Chicago Press, 1992)
Alma Mahler, *Memories*	Alma Mahler, *Gustav Mahler: Memories and Letters*, trans. Basil Creighton, ed. Donald Mitchell and Knud Martner (4th edn., London: Sphere Books, 1990)
GMWL	*Gustav Mahler: The World Listens*, ed. Donald Mitchell (Haarlem: TEMA Uitgevers, 1995)
HLG(E)	Henry-Louis de La Grange, *Mahler*, i (London: Gollancz, 1974); *Gustav Mahler*, ii: *Vienna: The Years of Challenge (1897–1904)* (Oxford: Oxford University Press, 1995)

HLG(F)	Henry-Louis de La Grange, *Gustav Mahler: chronique d'une vie*, 3 vols. (Paris: Fayard, 1973–84):
	
	  i. *Les Chemins de la gloire (1860–1900)*, 1973
	  ii. *L'Âge d'or de Vienne (1900–1907)*, 1983
	  iii. *Le Génie foudroyé (1907–1911)*, 1984

Mahler, *Briefe* (1924)	Gustav Mahler, *Briefe, 1879–1911*, ed. Alma Mahler (Berlin and Vienna: Zsolnay, 1924)
Mahler, *Briefe* (1982)	Gustav Mahler, *Briefe*, ed. Herta Blaukopf (Vienna and Hamburg: Zsolnay, 1982)
Mahler, *Selected Letters*	*Selected Letters of Gustav Mahler*, trans. Eithne Wilkins, Ernst Kaiser, and Bill Hopkins, ed. Knud Martner (London: Faber, 1979)
Mahler, *Unknown Letters*	*Mahler's Unknown Letters*, trans. Richard Stokes, ed. Herta Blaukopf (London: Gollancz, 1986)
MDS	*Mahler: A Documentary Study*, comp. and ed. Kurt Blaukopf, with contributions by Zoltan Roman (London: Thames and Hudson, 1976)
Mitchell, *EY*	Donald Mitchell, *Gustav Mahler: The Early Years*, rev. and ed. Paul Banks and David Matthews (London: Faber, 1980)
Mitchell, *SSLD*	Donald Mitchell, *Gustav Mahler: Songs and Symphonies of Life and Death* (London: Faber, 1985)

Mitchell, *WY*   Donald Mitchell, *Gustav Mahler: The Wunderhorn Years* (London: Faber, 1975)

NB-L, *Erinnerungen*   *Gustav Mahler in den Erinnerungen von Natalie Bauer-Lechner*, ed. Herbert Killian (Hamburg: Karl Dieter Wagner, 1984)

NB-L, *Recollections*   Natalie Bauer-Lechner, *Recollections of Gustav Mahler*, trans. Dika Newlin, ed. Peter Franklin (London: Faber, 1980)

Introduction

ANDREW NICHOLSON

This *Companion* comprises a collection of original essays on Mahler written especially for the occasion by Mahler scholars from various parts of the world. The aim has been to address all aspects of his life and work—symphonies, songs, and song-cycles, his conducting activities and aesthetic development—and to set these within the cultural and political context of his time. In addition, an attempt has been made to follow the fluctuations of his fortunes and influence in those countries with which he was associated or where his music has become a firmly established part of the repertoire: America, Austria, France, Germany, Holland, Japan, Russia, and England. The volume has thus sought to fulfil a need we felt to exist in Mahler literature for a comprehensive guide and handbook to the composer which would appeal to the interests of the student, specialist, and Mahler enthusiast alike.

When the project was first mooted and invitations issued, contributors were merely asked to discuss their given topic with as little technical jargon as possible and to write in such a manner that the volume might be accessible to both the musicologist and non-professional, although not unsophisticated, reader. No particular line of argument was prescribed. Now that the chapters are all assembled, however, it appears to me that a common thread can be perceived running through them; or rather, that a latent unifying metaphor seems to suggest itself, which I should like, if I may, to articulate and elaborate briefly by way of introduction.

A recurrent motif in the poetry of Hölderlin, one of Mahler's favourite poets,[1] is that of a sailor or 'boatman' ('Schiffer') regaining the safe harbour of his own shores after a perilous voyage on the seas. 'Die Heimath' ('Home') opens with just such an image: a boatman, contentedly 'turning to the river's calm / From distant isles, his harvest all gathered in'. Like the boatman, the poet imagines himself returning home from his lonely wanderings, but—unlike him—with a harvest of 'gathered sorrow' and in the vain hope of finding

---

I should like to thank my colleague Andrew Bennett in the Department of English at Bristol University for reading through this introduction and making valuable comments and suggestions.

[1] In a letter to Alma of 15 Dec. 1901, Mahler wrote that Hölderlin was 'one of my favourites among poets, and men. He is one . . . of the truly great' (Alma Mahler, *Memories*, 215).

solace for 'love's sufferings' amidst his family and the familiar scenes of his youth. Yet he bears with him the knowledge that

> This grief, the grief of love, will be slow to heal,
>   Of this no lullaby that mortals
>   Chant to give comfort will now relieve me.
>
> For they who lend us heavenly light and fire,
>   The gods, with holy sorrow endow us too.
>   So be it, then. A son of Earth I
>   Seem; and was fashioned to love, to suffer.[2]

Mahler too sought just such a homecoming, and he too bore within him the same knowledge: no 'lullaby' of mortal origin, no worldly comfort, could assuage the 'holy sorrow' with which the gods had endowed him as a creative artist destined to love and suffer for the very privilege of that 'heavenly light and fire' (Horace's 'divinae particulam aurae', one might say).[3] Thrice homeless, as he frequently lamented,[4] he had no homeland to which to return. He had to *create* one—out of that very love and suffering he harvested; and, like Yeats's 'Soul', *his* had to 'clap its hands and sing, and louder sing / For every tatter in its mortal dress'.[5] This is the truth of his music: it is his homeland, his dwelling-place.

At the same time, however, and by contrast, no music is more peripatetic than Mahler's: it seems so often to be going somewhere, journeying, as if in quest of something—an answer, a solution—indeed, as if in quest of that very homeland where all striving ceases and antinomies are resolved. Hence it continually oscillates between the two poles of becoming and being, kinesis and stasis, striving and rest—even, one might hazard, diaspora and promised land—Andante (the distinctively Mahlerian Andante) and Adagio marking the twin gestures of both its *process* and its *goal*. As he himself said to his friend and future Boswell, Natalie Bauer-Lechner, in August 1896:

'In the Adagio, everything is resolved into quiet "being"; the Ixion-wheel of appearances has at last been brought to a standstill. But in the fast movements, the Minuet and Allegro (and even in the Andante, according to my tempi) everything is flow, movement, "becoming". So, contrary to custom—and without knowing why, at the time—I concluded my Second and Third Symphonies with Adagios: that is, with a higher as opposed to a lower form.[']'[6]

Perhaps the best examples that spring to mind are, on the one hand, 'Die zwei blauen Augen' ('The two blue eyes')—the fourth and final song of his earliest song-cycle, *Lieder eines fahrenden Gesellen* (1884)—which attempts to bridge the gap between the individ-

[2] Friedrich Hölderlin, *Poems and Fragments*, trans. Michael Hamburger (3rd bilingual edn., London: Anvil Press, 1994), 138 and 139.

[3] Horace, *Satires* 2. 2. 79: 'a particle of the divine spirit'.

[4] ' "I am thrice homeless," he used often to say. "As a native of Bohemia in Austria, as an Austrian among Germans, and as a Jew throughout all the world. Everywhere an intruder, never welcomed" ' (Alma Mahler, *Memories*, 109).

[5] W. B. Yeats, 'Sailing to Byzantium', stanza 2.

[6] NB-L, *Recollections*, 67.

ual and what Adorno calls 'the world's course',[7] yet remains in the world of diaspora, exile, and wandering; and, on the other, his loveliest song of all, 'Ich bin der Welt abhanden gekommen' ('I am lost to the World'), one of the five Rückert poems he set to music in August 1901. This achieves a perfect sense of surcease—Schopenhauerian 'will-lessness', stasis—and bears assured testimony to Mahler's rejection of the world of 'becoming' (Andante) and his embracing of being-in-song, his true homeland:

> I am dead to the world's commotion
> and at peace in a still land!
> I live alone in my own heaven,
> in my love, in my song.[8]

But this is not to suggest escapism. On the contrary, it evinces something profoundly instructive about Mahler's art—and something which he shares with kindred creative artists. As Hölderlin puts it in another poem, 'In lieblicher bläue' ('In lovely blueness'): 'poetically, man dwells on this earth'.[9] This is the very phrase to which Heidegger addresses himself in his Bühlerhöhe lecture of 6 October 1951, prompting his meditation on language—the creative Word, 'the poetic'—as 'the basic capacity for human dwelling':

When Hölderlin speaks of dwelling, he has before his eyes the basic character of human existence.... [T]he phrase 'poetically man dwells' says: poetry first causes dwelling to be dwelling. Poetry is what really lets us dwell. But through what do we attain to a dwelling place? Through building. Poetic creation, which lets us dwell, is a kind of building. ... *Man dwells in that he builds*[.][10]

The *act* of making, of 'building'—the very *process* of creativity itself—is the true 'dwelling', the existential homeland of being, for the poet and composer alike. 'Gesang ist Dasein' ('Singing is Being'), exclaims Rilke in the third of his *Die Sonette an Orpheus* (1923), upon which Heidegger again elsewhere comments: 'This . . . is Being itself. To sing the song means to be present in what is present itself. It means: *Dasein*, existence.'[11] And as our own poet Byron—in whom Mahler, had he known anything about him, would have found a surprisingly sympathetic fellow-traveller on many more counts than this— put it in 1816:

> 'Tis to create, and in creating live
> A being more intense, that we endow
> With form our fancy, gaining as we give
> The life we image, even as I do now.

---

[7] Adorno, *Mahler*, 8; a term which, despite its Hegelian ancestry, Adorno borrows from Mahler himself: 'weltlich' Getümmel' ('worldly tumult'), bars 17–18 in the vocal line of the final movement, 'Das himmlische Leben', of the Fourth Symphony.

[8] 'Ich bin der Welt abhanden gekommen', stanza 3; translation taken from Deryck Cooke, *Gustav Mahler: An Introduction to his Music* (London: Faber, 1980), 75.

[9] *Poems*, 714 and 715.

[10] Martin Heidegger, *Poetry, Language, Thought*, trans. Albert Hofstadter (New York: Harper & Row, 1975), 214 and 227.

[11] Ibid. 138.

What am I? Nothing; but not so art thou,
Soul of my thought! with whom I traverse earth,
Invisible but gazing, as I glow
Mix'd with thy spirit, blended with thy birth,
And feeling still with thee in my crush'd feeling's dearth.[12]

The self-presencing of the poet, his 'Dasein', the identity of his 'being' with that which he is at the moment creating, is trenchantly emphasized and sustained throughout the stanza by the present tense and the images deployed; indeed, every poetic effect and almost every word serves to contribute to the sense of immediacy, of 'being' in 'making', 'dwelling' in 'building'. This is precisely Mahler's position and what he expresses so eloquently in 'Ich bin der Welt abhanden gekommen'. To put it succinctly: he is saying he 'exists', both for himself and for us his audience, *in* and *through* his music; there is no 'being' outside that narrative.[13]

Is all this, however, just a personal journey, a goal or accomplishment for the poet or composer alone, or is there some promise in it, a prescription even, for all mankind? 'Do *we*', Heidegger asks with emphasis in his lecture, 'dwell poetically?'[14] Evidently not, at least not all the time. But again Hölderlin provides an answer: 'Yes. As long as kindliness ['Freundlichkeit'], which is pure, remains in [Man's] heart.'[15] Taking 'Freundlichkeit' quite literally to be Hölderlin's 'magnificent translation for the Greek word *charis*' ('kindness', or 'kindliness', that 'calls forth' or 'begets' kindness), Heidegger observes: 'Freundlichkeit' 'has come to the dwelling being of man, come as the claim and appeal of the measure to the heart in such a way that the heart turns to give heed to the measure.'[16] In other words, *we* 'dwell poetically' insofar as we respond to, answer the call into 'kindness' or 'kindliness'— the 'appeal of the measure'—with which the poet or composer bids to us. As Byron has it: 'the heart must / Leap kindly back to kindness'.[17]

And Mahler? If the 'higher' form of which he speaks to Natalie Bauer-Lechner is achieved and expressed most poignantly and *lyrically* in 'Der Abschied' of *Das Lied von der Erde*—

Whither I go? I go, I wander in the mountains,
I seek rest for my lonely heart!
I journey to the homeland, to my resting-place;
I shall never again go seeking the far distance.
My heart is still and awaits its hour![18]

---

[12] *Childe Harold's Pilgrimage*, Canto III, stanza 6.

[13] A salutary reminder, if one were necessary, cautioning us against falling into what might be called the 'biographical fallacy'—interpreting works of art in terms of their creator's biography; or, conversely, reading his biography *into* his work—to which Mahler and Byron (both intensely 'personal' artists) have frequently been exposed, and against which Adorno so warmly inveighs (*Mahler*, 23–5). Carl Dahlhaus addresses the same issue with exemplary clarity and rigour in his *Ludwig van Beethoven: Approaches to his Music*, trans. Mary Whittall (Oxford: Clarendon Press, 1991), esp. ch. 1.

[14] *Poetry*, 227.

[15] *Poems*, 714 and 715.

[16] *Poetry*, 229; Heidegger refers us specifically to line 522 of Sophocles' *Ajax*: 'For kindness it is, that ever calls forth kindness' (ibid.).

[17] *Childe Harold's Pilgrimage*, Canto III, stanza 53.

[18] *Das Lied von der Erde*, 'Der Abschied', Figs. 53–7; translation taken from Cooke, *Mahler*, 113.

—then the whole trajectory from 'lower' to 'higher', from Andante to Adagio, 'becoming' to 'being', is articulated most *dramatically* in epic and universal terms as a paradigm and promise for all mankind in the Eighth Symphony; Mahler's own commentary on the closing scene from Goethe's *Faust* and why he felt compelled to set it to music being especially pertinent in the present context. In a letter to Alma of June 1909 he writes:

It is all an allegory to convey something which, whatever form it is given, can never be adequately expressed. Only the transitory lends itself to description; but what we feel, surmise but will never reach (or know here as an actual happening), the intransitory behind all appearance, is indescribable. That which draws us by its mystic force, what every created thing, perhaps even the very stones, feels with absolute certainty as the centre of its being, what Goethe here—again employing an image—calls the eternal feminine—that is to say, the resting-place, the goal, in opposition to the striving and struggling towards the goal (the eternal masculine)—you are quite right in calling the force of love.[19]

This 'mystic force', 'the force of love', mediating between the 'masculine' compulsion to strive and desire and the 'feminine' harbour of respite, repose, redemption, corresponds exactly to Hölderlin's 'Freundlichkeit' and Byron's 'kindness', and applies with equal propriety not only to the Eighth Symphony but to Mahler's entire oeuvre.[20] The infinite compassion that emanates from his music, inviting us to enter its topography in a spirit of reciprocal sympathy, is perhaps the strongest claim his works make upon us and the reason why we seem to hear in them an ageless and unending narrative—the 'still, sad music of humanity'.[21]

If music is Mahler's homeland, then his house has many mansions—to which the variety and scope of the following chapters, exploring its parameters and fostering influences, testify. Such diversity in unity perhaps best reflects Mahler's output itself, which might justly be said to consist of discrete parts forming a coherent whole: not the monochrome of a uniform, but—like Byron—the 'tartanry' of a Scottish plaid.[22]

---

[19] Alma Mahler, *Memories*, 320–1.

[20] In this connection, it is remarkable that Giya Kancheli's recent composition, the hauntingly beautiful *Exil* (1994)—itself suggesting music as homeland—is cast as a five-movement song-cycle for soprano, flute, strings, and tape recording, opening with a setting of Ps. 23 and followed by three 'secular' poems by Paul Celan and one by Hans Sahl, thus combining both the human and the spiritual dimensions of the Eighth Symphony with the lyricism of *Das Lied von der Erde*. This can be heard on CD ECM New Series 1535 447808-2 (1995).

[21] William Wordsworth, 'Lines written a few miles above Tintern Abbey', line 92.

[22] I adopt and adapt this delightful shorthand term to suggest the unity of a *pattern*, or unified multiplicity, from Angus Calder's chapter ' "The Island": Scotland, Greece and Romantic Savagery', in id. (ed.), *Byron and Scotland* (Edinburgh: Edinburgh University Press, 1989), 135 and 148.

Additional note My analogy between Byron and Mahler is neither wilful eccentricity nor mere self-indulgence: both artists belong to all climes and all ages, and although they may not speak a common tongue they share a common language and express the same sensibility. Certainly, my own experience of the one has been enriched by my experience of the other; and it would be a grateful pleasure to me to feel that others might be similarly affected. Should the reader care to take up any canto of *Don Juan*, he or she would soon discover that the formal procedures and narrative strategies deployed by Byron—the juxtaposition of contrasting elements, mixing of styles and genres, the distribution of episodes, plurality of voices, and ventriloquism of the narrator—are features we recognize instantly as characterizing Mahler's music.

I

Gustav Mahler's Vienna

LEON BOTSTEIN

1. Mahler and Vienna

Gustav Mahler lived in Vienna for extended periods twice in his life; first between the ages of 15 and 23, from 1875 to 1883 (the year he moved to Kassel), and then between the ages of 37 and 47, from 1897 to the end of 1907, during his tenure at the Vienna Opera.[1] Mahler's ties with Vienna, however, went well beyond these dates of actual residence.

After 1875, and perhaps already in Mahler's early adolescence, Vienna functioned as the decisive cultural reference point for his creative life. From the moment of his departure from Vienna in 1883, Mahler's ambition was to return there and to win fame and recognition within the complex politics and daunting traditions of the city's artistic life.

[1] Mahler visited Vienna on his way to and from New York during the years 1908–11. He died in Vienna in May 1911. Few subjects have been so meticulously researched and shrewdly interpreted as the career and life of Gustav Mahler. The late 20th-c. enthusiasm for Mahler has coincided with a rediscovery of *fin-de-siècle* Vienna as a decisive source of 20th-c. art and culture. More than twenty years have elapsed since the first major English-language study of the roots of modernism in Vienna by Allan Janik and Stephen Toulmin, *Wittgenstein's Vienna* (New York: Simon & Schuster, 1973). The evocation of the names of Wittgenstein, Freud, Mahler, Klimt, Otto Wagner, and Schnitzler, as well as the figures from science such as Ernst Mach, has by now become a cliché of a mythic multi-faceted Viennese *Gesamtkunstwerk*, as have the many descriptions of the so-called 'gay apocalypse' of *fin-de-siècle* Vienna. The reader, therefore, is encouraged to consult the many well-written standard accounts of Mahler's Vienna in English and German that, it is hoped, this chapter will not duplicate. Likewise, the biographical and critical literature on Mahler is extensive, ranging from Henry-Louis de La Grange's three-volume work and Donald Mitchell's multi-volume sequence to smaller single-volume works, including such books as Hermann Danuser's *Gustav Mahler und seine Zeit* (Laaber: Laaber-Verlag, 1991) and Karl Josef Müller's *Mahler: Leben, Werke, Dokumente* (Munich: Schott, Piper, 1988). What has characterized the Mahler literature is the meticulous detail and the loving and often combative enthusiasm to get everything just right. This chapter attempts neither a contribution to nor a summary of these biographical efforts. Likewise, on the matter of Vienna, the reader is referred to Carl Schorske's *Fin-de-siècle Vienna: Politics and Culture* (New York: Knopf, 1980) and the French and German catalogues from the 1987 exhibition *Traum und Wirklichkeit: Wien 1870–1930* (Vienna: Eigenverlag der Museen der Stadt Wien, 1985) as the starting point. Two more recent works bear mentioning. First, there is the fine essay by Paul Banks, 'Fin de Siècle Vienna, Politics and Modernism', in Jim Samson (ed.), *The Late Romantic Era* (Englewood Cliffs, NJ: Prentice-Hall, 1991), 362–88, and the essay collection *Die Wiener Jahrhundertwende*, ed. Jürgen Nautz and Richard Vahrenkampf (Vienna: Böhlau, 1993), which contains recent bibliographical references.

As the crucial social and cultural context for Mahler's achievements, the metropolis might well be understood metaphorically as the indispensable scaffolding that accompanies the construction of any monumental structure.[2] Scaffolding, by definition, is temporal and temporary. To subsequent generations of listeners and admirers, the specific scaffolding for Mahler's work retains little evident residue. Despite its importance in the genesis of the musical work, with the passage of time—apart from obvious references (some quite ironic) to Viennese popular dance and song—the representations of the city and its influences become harder with the passage of time to reconstruct from the music itself.

Nevertheless, an adequate characterization of Vienna as Mahler and his Viennese audiences might have experienced it ought to reveal clues about the composer's creative process (particularly his perception of the audience) and insights into his music. This essay is an effort to reconstruct the network of platforms and points of access to Mahler's work—the fabric of elements specific to Vienna—which were crucial to Mahler and evident to his contemporaries.

One of the most often repeated remarks made by Mahler himself concerned his sense of perpetual foreignness and political dislocation. He had been a Bohemian (i.e. Czech) in German-speaking Austria, an Austrian in Germany, and a Jew throughout the world.[3] He tried to offset this apparent sense of conventional ethnic and political homelessness through an intense psychological engagement with Vienna. Younger contemporaries facing a similar predicament, including the writers Joseph Roth (1894–1939) and Franz Werfel (1890–1945), attached themselves instead to the idea of the Habsburg monarchy and its symbol, the Emperor Franz Joseph.[4] A poignant indication of Mahler's lifelong focus on Vienna as the decisive forum for his own work as composer and conductor was the particular sense of triumph he felt in 1901 at being able to conduct the première of his first major composition, *Das klagende Lied* (which had failed to win the Vienna Conservatoire's coveted Beethoven prize in 1881), as the then world-famous Director of the city's Imperial Opera.

During the last years of Mahler's life, from 1908 to 1911, when he was based primarily in New York, Vienna and its musical and cultural life continued to lure him. One reason for this was that Alma Mahler's social and familial ties were in Vienna. Mahler's American sojourn—for all its economic benefits and artistic virtues—never resulted in the kind of attachment to America that Antonín Dvořák developed during his American stay a little more than a decade earlier. Moreover, at the time he left for New York, Mahler knew that despite the controversies surrounding him in Vienna, the role he had come to play in that city would not and could not be duplicated elsewhere. We should be cautious about viewing Mahler as bereft of a stable connection to a place and its people, since he was linked to and part of Vienna's culture and traditions.

---

[2] The metaphor of scaffolding is taken from a comment made by Karl Czerny about Beethoven's use of extra-musical elements in his process of composition.

[3] See Mitchell, *EY*, 2.

[4] Like Mahler, Roth and Werfel, both born Jews, came to Vienna: Roth from Brody in Galicia and Werfel from Prague.

On a superficial level, posterity has taken Mahler's accomplishments and the opposition he engendered during his ten-year tenure at the Vienna Imperial Opera and used them as metaphors for a reductionist picture of how twentieth-century modernism came into being in *fin-de-siècle* Vienna. Particular myths about Mahler's relationship to the Viennese and his reception in Vienna have served as benchmarks and analogues for a simplified characterization of the circumstances allegedly faced by many of Mahler's famous Viennese contemporaries: Gustav Klimt, Arnold Schoenberg, Adolf Loos, Egon Schiele, and Sigmund Freud. A soap-opera-like account of how Vienna spurned Mahler, failed to appreciate him, and offered a debilitating conservative resistance to his music and conducting has become standard fare and is even cited to illuminate apparent divergences and similarities in the Viennese careers later in the twentieth century of Leonard Bernstein, Lorin Maazel, and Claudio Abbado.[5]

Despite the continual rehearsal in the scholarly literature on Mahler of the hostile treatment he received in Vienna, the truth is somewhat different. At the time of the *fin de siècle* Mahler was easily one of the city's few authentic celebrities, with many more admirers than detractors.[6] The editorials in the *Neue Freie Presse* lamenting his departure and the famous open letter of appreciation dated 11 May 1907, signed by virtually everyone of importance in Viennese life—from the arch-conservative, *echt*-Viennese piano manufacturer Ludwig Bösendorfer, to distinguished sceptics like Heinrich Schenker, and admirers like Stefan Zweig and Arthur Schnitzler—are indicators of how lionized Mahler was. He was neither neglected nor unappreciated. No doubt his prominence, his Jewish heritage, and his links with modernism made him a controversial figure in a city with a self-conscious civic pride in its own connoisseurship of music and a political life in which the Jewish question was a recalcitrant and dominant issue.

Indeed the most notorious opposition to Mahler came from overtly anti-Semitic circles. The day-to-day music criticism directed against him in the years 1897–1907 was unexceptional, run-of-the-mill newspaper criticism. It was motivated largely by allegiances to particular singers and local grievances about casting and management style at the Opera. No respected Viennese critic doubted Mahler's musical and conducting gifts.

Sharp controversy in the history of criticism is usually a sign that the target is worthy enough to be a vehicle for the critic's own vanity. The extraordinary and powerful and not the mediocre and routine draw the worst and most sustained fire.[7] This was the case with

---

[5] See e.g. Meryle Secrest, *Leonard Bernstein: A Life* (New York: Knopf, 1994), 306–9.

[6] Mahler's protégé Oskar Fried published in *Pan* the following, shortly after Mahler's death in 1911: 'you were, Gustav Mahler, while you lived, hated and abused'. The indispensable basis for this view has been the notion that the treatment Mahler received during the ten years he worked in Vienna, from 1897 to 1907, was hostile. This idea has been immortalized by the scene of Mahler's admirers gathered at the railway station in 1907 to see him off. Vienna, a city of petty critics and a philistine public, had driven its greatest genius from its midst. Klimt is said to have uttered a single word, *vorbei* (it's over). See HLG(F) iii. 175.

[7] See e.g. two reviews in Vienna's weekly journal *Neue Musikalische Presse* during Mahler's tenure: 6 July 1902 (vol. 11, no. 27, pp. 369–70); and 12 Oct. 1902 (vol. 11, no. 41, p. 513). One might compare the treatment Theobald Kretschmann received. He was a cellist in the Opera orchestra, a composer and conductor, and Kapellmeister in the Votivkirche. His concerts were routinely dismissed on account of their poor quality. Kretschmann wrote a useful two-volume memoir entitled *Tempi Passati* which is also critical of Mahler. In general, music historians place too much emphasis, even in so-called 'reception history', on the evidence provided by newspaper critics in the task of characterizing the musical life of the past.

Mahler. He thrived and succeeded in Vienna, drawing encouragement and inspiration from what he encountered there even from the opposition. Vienna was to Mahler what the light and landscape of Provence were to Cézanne.

2. Politics and Civic Culture

Vienna was the cultural, administrative, and political centre of the Habsburg Empire during the nineteenth century. It was a dominant commercial presence and a magnet on account of the economic opportunities it seemed to promise the largely rural population of the Empire. The combination of sustained rural population growth and increased agricultural productivity after 1848 in the Empire generated a flow of people to its leading cities, particularly Vienna.[8] As a result, throughout Mahler's lifetime, Vienna grew rapidly. During the late 1850s, a few years before Mahler was born, a period of substantial migration to Vienna from within the Empire began. The Bohemia and Moravia of Mahler's childhood supplied a large percentage of the migrants. Vienna's demographic growth intensified as the century wore on.

In the last four decades of the century, the population of Vienna increased at a rate of nearly 4 per cent a year. Between 1857 and 1890 the number of inhabitants in the city more than doubled, from under 600,000 to over 1,300,000. More than half of this explosive growth came from migration. In 1850, 57 per cent of Vienna's population had been born in Vienna, in 1869 only 45 per cent, and in 1890 just under 35. This shift from native-born to immigrant residents within the span of a few decades was the crucial social background to the cultural politics of the city that Mahler encountered first in 1875 and in which he became engulfed at the end of the century.

The first signs of the impending social transformation of Vienna coincided with the great Imperial project for the redesigning and developing of the city which began in 1857. The old walls surrounding the inner city and separating it from the outlying districts would be demolished. In place of the walls, the Ringstrasse was created—a massive curved grand boulevard (3,750 metres long and 56 metres wide) on the open space just outside the old walls called the Glacis. Eventually, the Ringstrasse became flanked on both sides by imposing public buildings and elegant residences.[9]

This programme of urban renewal, similar in significance to Baron Georges Eugène Haussmann's rebuilding of Paris, reshaped and redefined the city.[10] It is not surprising that the combination of demographic and physical changes provoked a powerful political and

---

[8] See David F. Good, *The Economic Rise of the Habsburg Empire, 1750–1914* (Berkeley: University of California Press, 1974) and A. Hickman, *Wien im XIX. Jahrhundert* (Vienna: Alfred Hölder, 1903).

[9] See Schorske, *Fin-de-siècle Vienna*, and Elisabeth Springer, *Geschichte und Kulturleben der Wiener Ringstraße* (Vienna: F. Steiner, 1979).

[10] For comparison, see David H. Pinckney, *Napoleon III and the Rebuilding of Paris* (Princeton: Princeton University Press, 1958).

cultural counter-reaction, and inspired a compelling nostalgic myth of a lost 'old' Vienna, *Alt-Wien*. Although the balance within the Viennese population shifted in favour of those born elsewhere, ethnic diversity within the migration limited the prospects for the emergence of a distinct cultural coherence among the newly arrived Viennese. In this context, the confrontation between the rapidity of change and the majesty and power of the city as symbol of Imperial traditions and dynastic unity created a dynamic in which symbols of local historical authenticity gained in prestige and allure for newcomers and native-born residents alike.

The celebration of idyllic local virtues—presumably characteristic of a bygone era before 1857—formed the core of the Viennese cultural conceits Mahler encountered first in 1875 and again in 1897. During the last thirty years of the nineteenth century, new residents of Vienna not only willingly embraced sentimental prejudices that, in their evocation of a romanticized past and a vanished world, mirrored a construct of the quintessentially Viennese character, they also helped to generate an elaborate and commercialized myth of an endangered pre-modern Viennese tradition. The nostalgic prejudices which evolved after 1857 were crucial to the definition and distillation of a widespread Viennese identity and *Weltanschauung* at the turn of the century. The profound changes in people and places in Vienna created a radical and novel myth of authenticity. The authenticity celebrated by that myth was seen as perpetually at risk. Yet it never existed. Insofar as myth approximated history, only an extreme minority (e.g. Eduard von Bauernfeld, Schubert's friend and a distinguished writer, 1802–90) qualified. Precisely the rarity of the genuine symbol of *Alt Wien* made the cult of authentic pre-modern Viennese sensibilities so appealing to new inhabitants of the city. It offered a common ground for allegiance and identity among a diverse group of foreigners in which few held any priority in terms of legitimacy.

In the first instance, during the years immediately following 1857, political conservatives, representing the presumed simple tastes and wholesome mores of the Biedermeier epoch and the years before 1848 (which were actually a time of considerable economic distress for the Viennese), sought to discredit the economic and social changes that were under way. By the end of the 1870s, liberalism, in its nineteenth-century form, with its explicit emulation of English civic ideals (e.g. representation within a constitutional monarchy) and economic life (e.g. joint-stock companies, entrepreneurship, the factory system, and the free market), came to be viewed with suspicion. It was identified with the new. A spontaneous conservatism and resistance to the changes of the early Ringstrasse years, palpable during the 1860s and 1870s, would evolve later in the century into the novel and radical reactionary movement of Christian Socialism which dominated Viennese politics at the end of the nineteenth century.

The codification, so to speak, of the familiar and commonplace image of Vienna—one that remains with us today, particularly among tourists—began in earnest during the 1860s in response as well to the deterioration in the international power and prestige of the Habsburg Empire of which Vienna was the capital. Johann Strauss II's *The Blue Danube* waltz (commissioned by the Men's Choral Society of Vienna) was written in 1867. Strauss's audience at that time was caught in a web of explosive events: the Habsburg monarchy had just been defeated by Prussia at Sadowa; the economic boom of the 1860s—the so-called *Gründerzeit* (the 'founding era' of rapid commercial and industrial change)—was at its peak; the constitutional structure of the Empire was altered fundamentally, leading to an internal political liberalization and the creation of a 'dual' Monarchy in which Hungary assumed a more autonomous role.

The immediate success of *The Blue Danube* was due in part to the fact that it suggested disillusionment with the present through a subtle and indirect musical evocation of a magical bygone past. The shimmering sense of temporal, psychic, and physical distance between past and present—between aspiration and reality—was immediately audible in the opening bars. The dreamy, bitter-sweet elegance of recurrent appearances of the thematic material was characteristic of Strauss's skill in using techniques of repetition in music to suggest the experiences of daydreaming, musing, and remembering. The surface of the alluringly sentimental both signalled and camouflaged doubt, fear, and despair regarding contemporary events.

The key to Strauss's success (and one reason for Mahler's attraction to Strauss-like material as subjects for irony and contrast) was an unspoken compact with his Viennese audience. The aspect of his work that communicated candid self-criticism and satire remained discreet, demanding only tacit recognition. The affectionate mix of accessible humour, elegance, irony, and vitality suffusing Strauss's scores and the texts he used both masked and mirrored the curious mix of pessimism and pride which made up Vienna's late nineteenth-century civic ethos.

Johann Strauss II (himself a descendant of Jewish forebears who had migrated to the city and converted to Catholicism) was easily the most successful musician in the city's history. One of the very last public events Brahms made the effort to attend was a Strauss première which took place in the spring of 1897, less than a month before Brahms died.[11] As the musicologist Guido Adler (1855–1941), Mahler's friend (and Eduard Hanslick's successor as Professor of Music History at the University of Vienna), observed on the occasion of Strauss's death in 1899, Strauss's music—at home, in outdoor public spaces, and dance-halls—provided a rare common ground in Vienna for the display of aesthetic and civic virtue. All the residents of the city, irrespective of the level of their musical sophistication, their social class, religious conviction, or nationality, seemed to love the music.[12] All members of the Vienna concert audience had Strauss's music in their ears. No single individual—let alone family—did so much to define the image of a city locally and internationally as Johann Strauss II, alongside his father, and brothers.

[11] On 13 Mar. 1897 Brahms, already visibly ravaged by liver cancer, was determined to attend the opening of Strauss's *The Goddess of Reason* (*Die Göttin der Vernunft*). He sat in Hanslick's box but left, exhausted, before the end. See Max Kalbeck, *Johannes Brahms*, iv/2 (Berlin: Deutsche Brahms-Gesellschaft, 1915), 507.

[12] See Guido Adler, 'Johann Strauss', in *Biographisches Jahrbuch und deutscher Nekrolog*, iv (1902), 27–33. This is the final version of a speech Adler gave in memory of Strauss on 6 June 1899 at the University.

No subsequent Viennese composer in the popular genres of song, dance, and operetta would ever approximate the range and depth of critical and popular acclaim within the city achieved by Strauss, even though his massive oeuvre of song, dance, and stage-works became the model for subsequent *fin-de-siècle* exploitations of the legend of old-fashioned Viennese virtues. Part of the magic of *fin-de-siècle* Viennese popular and commercial entertainment—for example, of *Opernball* (1898) by Richard Heuberger, a protégé of Brahms—derived from the continuation of the tradition of combining arrogance and conceit with sharp irony and self-criticism. Pride and doubt remained unique Viennese allies. Given the social strife, economic distress, and intolerance in Vienna during Mahler's lifetime, the city's legendary *Gemütlichkeit* (cosiness and camaraderie) was at risk. Even the natural beauty of Vienna's environs was threatened by demographic and industrial expansion.

A deceptive mix of reaction and innovation followed the cultural resistance to the changes of the 1860s and 1870s. The career of Anton Bruckner, who came to teach in Vienna in 1868, is a case in point. Bruckner's provincial manners—in speech (his use of dialect), dress, and even culinary taste—made him an ideal symbol in Vienna of old-fashioned native local virtues, even though he came from Linz. He became famous in Vienna not only as the antipode of Brahms, but as a standard-bearer in a campaign against the influence of the Jews and foreign ideas, against industrial and cosmopolitan values and bourgeois liberal secularism.[13]

Despite this ideological linkage in the Vienna of the 1880s and 1890s, Bruckner's music appealed (more than the music of Brahms) to a progressive younger generation—Mahler and his friends Rudolf Krzyzanowski (1859–1911) and Hugo Wolf (1860–1903). Admiration for Bruckner's music, considered independently of its uses and abuses in local politics, made these young enthusiasts often reluctant allies of the readers of the city's most rabidly reactionary political press, the *Vaterland* and the *Reichspost*.[14]

The irony was that the mythic and superficial anti-modern character of Viennese self-identity was tailor-made for those migrants from within the Empire, even Jews, who sought to find routes to an identification with local traditions. The local musical cultures offered an accessible and convenient opportunity. The struggle for psychological survival among new residents of the city encouraged acceptance of an inherently exclusive myth of authenticity, precisely because those who came by that authenticity naturally were the exception. As the anti-Semites knew all too well, the combination of an overbearing anti-Semitism and an alluring local aesthetic culture only accelerated the drive among Jews to acculturate. The premises of cultural assimilation were, however, at odds with the economic

[13] See Renate Grasberger and Erich Wolfgang Partsch (eds.), *Bruckner — skizziert: Ein Porträt in ausgewählten Erinnerungen und Anekdoten* (Vienna: Musikwissenschaftlicher Verlag BNM, 1991), esp. 11–58; and the quite revealing collection of images and caricatures from Bruckner's Vienna years collected in Renate Grasberger, *Bruckner-Ikonographie. Teil I. Um 1854 bis 1924* (Graz: Akademische Druck- und Verlagsanstalt, 1990).

[14] See Johannes-Leopold Mayer, 'Musik als gesellschaftliches Ärgernis — oder: Anton Bruckner, Der Anti-Bürger. Das Phänomen Bruckner als historisches Problem', in Franz Grasberger (ed.), *Anton Bruckner in Wien* (Graz: Akademischer Druck- und Verlagsanstalt, 1980), 75–160; also Margaret Notley, 'Brahms as Liberal: Genre, Style, and Politics in Late Nineteenth-Century Vienna', *19th Century Music*, 17 (1993–4), 107–23.

realities. These realities demanded, for newcomers, an embrace of entrepreneurial competition and modern practices in conflict with Vienna's backward artisan traditions. Vienna's scepticism vis-à-vis progress and modernity was not totally a new invention. It actually predated 1857, going back to the era of Ferdinand Raimund's 1826 satire 'Der Bauer als Millionär'.

The writers and musicians who themselves were migrants to the city understood well, as only outsiders might, the dynamic of ambivalence, nostalgia, and parody within the evolution of the civic cultural identity of Vienna during the last quarter of the nineteenth century. The myth of a continuum of cultural practices foreign to the mechanical and rational present and unique to Vienna, dating from before 1848—including the waltz, the polka, and the quadrille, for example, and the satirical use of differing national stereotypes in the theatrical farce—became the indispensable means of communication within and among the city's highly stratified and varied social structure. During the mid-1890s, one popular satirical weekly, the *Wiener Caricaturen*, featured a regular column entitled 'What Nestroy would have said, had he lived long enough to witness certain things'.[15]

In this sense, the late nineteenth-century Viennese operetta took its cue from the way the theatre functioned as a public forum for civic self-definition and criticism in pre-1848 Vienna. In the Biedermeier epoch political censorship created the context for the development of Viennese comedy. Towards the end of the century the contemporary ethnic and social conflict came to play the dominant part in setting the context for the comic element.

The commercialization of the dance, folk song, and operetta during Mahler's lifetime— these heirs to the distinctly Viennese entertainments and theatrical precedents from before 1848 written by Johann Nepomuk Nestroy and Raimund—was accomplished by men, who like Mahler, came to Vienna from within the Empire. Leo Fall came from Olomouc, Franz Lehár from Komáron (Hungary), Leo Stein from Lemberg (now Lvov, Poland), the comic actor Alexander Girardi from Graz, and Emmerich Kálmán from Siófok (Hungary).[16] They each exploited the need to fashion new variants of well-established civic symbols clearly identifiable and accessible to the continuing stream of migrants. Outsiders at the margins of old Viennese society, they played a crucial role in using music and theatre to refine and expand the very cultural centre from which they feared exclusion.[17]

Two forms of expression could most easily bridge the obvious differences in class, religion, and ethnicity which dominated Vienna: music and comic language, particularly in

---

[15] See e.g. *Wiener Caricaturen*, 13/8 (19 Feb. 1893), 2.

[16] Leo Fall (1873–1925) was among the most successful operatic composers of the generation of Franz Lehár. He had been a student at the Vienna Conservatoire. Franz Lehár (1870–1948) was himself best known for his operetta *The Merry Widow*, which received its première in 1905. Leo Stein (1861–1921) originally studied law and worked as a civil servant. He collaborated with Kálmán, Lehár, and also Oskar Nedbal (1874–1930), the Dvořák pupil and distinguished Czech musician who also experienced considerable success in Vienna as an operetta composer using 'exotic',

non-German materials. Alexander Girardi (1850–1918) was the most famous comic actor of Mahler's day. He, like Guschelbauer (see below), came to symbolize the true Viennese character. Emmerich Kálmán (1882–1953) was perhaps the most distinguished operetta composer after Lehár. His *Gypsy Princess* (*Die Csárdásfürstin*) was premièred in 1915.

[17] Leon Botstein, *Judentum und Modernität: Essays zur Rolle der Juden in der deutschen und österreichischen Kultur, 1848 bis 1938* (Vienna: Böhlau, 1991).

the journalism of satire and in light theatre. Indeed the cultural artifice, self-satire, hypocrisy, irony, and intolerance on and off the stage that surrounded the dramatic social, economic, and political changes of the last four decades of the nineteenth century made a profound impression on Mahler. His insight into the dynamics of Viennese cultural politics—particularly the resentments between the old and new inhabitants, the exploitation of nostalgia for what was old by the parvenus of Vienna and the popular glorification of Vienna and its habits and character—are reflected in the complex layers of allusion, parody, and irony one can find in his music.

In Mahler's music a critical and searching mirror is held up to the local Viennese audience. The fact that the music of Richard Strauss, despite virulent criticism, fared somewhat better in Vienna than Mahler's in the years between 1897 and 1907 reflects the extent to which the Viennese audience sensed that they, in particular, were being challenged and goaded by specific criticisms in Mahler's music directed at their habits and tastes in a manner more trenchant and serious than they were accustomed to.

Furthermore, the suggestions that Mahler's music represents a unique interaction between classical and modernist elements, that Mahler brought a tradition of symphonic and Lieder writing to a historically logical conclusion, and that he influenced the course of twentieth-century musical innovation, all evoke the seemingly contradictory dynamics of Viennese politics and culture. Even Mahler's intense attachment to the natural landscape paralleled the bitter-sweet Viennese nostalgic love of a pre-industrial environment. Nature became a symbol of opposition. It demanded defence and celebration precisely at the moment the survival of a pastoral landscape near the city as a refuge from the consequences of so-called modern progress was in danger. Grinzing and Heiligenstadt, the areas that Beethoven and Schubert had known as the countryside, had become more urban than rural. Even the legendary Vienna Woods were increasingly under siege by the city's industrial and residential expansion.

This Viennese ambivalence towards the new, rooted in an allegiance to a vanished landscape, inspired a strident Austro-German defence of Vienna's position as a leading city of German culture and people. Since 1815 the Habsburg Empire found itself outflanked consistently by Prussia in its bid for political leadership among German-speaking peoples. By 1871, the fate of the Habsburg Empire as a second-tier power dependent upon Prussia had been sealed. Imperial Germany, dominated by Protestant Prussia, would hold sway over multi-ethnic Catholic Austria until 1918. Among the currents Mahler first encountered in the Vienna of the 1870s, therefore, was a pan-German, anti-Habsburg political and cultural movement as well as an Austro-German pro-Catholic nationalism.

For the Viennese, these larger historical events and the polyglot population growth made it clear that both the unique source of hope and the fatal flaw of the Empire was its ethnic, linguistic, and religious diversity. The Empire was not a modern nation-state but a dynastic entity. Mahler arrived as a student less than a decade after the 1867 pro-Hungarian, anti-Czech compromise that created the Austro-Hungarian 'dual monarchy'. He worked and lived in the city throughout the struggles over language policies, the rights of the Czech and Polish minorities, and the crises on the southern border of the Empire. He also witnessed the gradual dismantling of an antiquated and exclusive electoral system and the extension of the franchise to adult males. In the transition from absolutism to a more democratic constitutional monarchy, Mahler also encountered the darker side of modern mass politics in Vienna: the growth of anti-dynastic nationalisms and the politics of intolerance, particularly towards Jews.

The Imperial city, Vienna, was the mirror *in nuce* of the Habsburg Empire's unique dilemmas. Despite the sense of fragility that beset the Empire after 1871, the idea persisted that the Habsburg Empire could become a model for a United States of Europe, a federal multi-ethnic state. This remained the dream of Franz Werfel, Alma Mahler's third husband.[18] Yet the barrier to the realization of this dream was that the administrative habits and cultural heritage of the Habsburg monarchy and Vienna, particularly since the reforms of Joseph II (1741–90) in the 1780s, were tied inextricably to German language and culture. This in turn only emboldened the nationalist movements among the Poles, Hungarians, and Czechs within the Empire during the second half of the nineteenth century.

Between 1875 and 1911 the struggle between Austro-Germans and the other nationalities of the Habsburg Empire was enacted in a violent fashion, not only in its streets but in the Imperial Parliament in Vienna. Mahler's work might be considered speculatively as paralleling this tension between the German and the non-German in the Empire. His music can be heard as an experiment in how an essentially German musical tradition might assimilate various non-German musical elements as part of a self-critical formalist strategy.

Mahler's mode of appropriation of elements from within his environment was distinctly Viennese. Identifiable fragments and allusions to the sounds and noises of the streets and the countryside in his work were integrated in contexts clearly tied to German cultural musical practice: to the forms of the Lied and the symphony. German and Slavic elements from Bohemia and Moravia, local Viennese materials as well as well-known German folk poetic and musical sources were assimilated within Mahler's compositional logic. In Mahler's music, observers have located a project to transform and transcend nationalism within an explicitly German cultural paradigm. This project ran parallel to the failed political history experienced by both the city and the Empire during Mahler's lifetime.[19]

In 1872, three years before Mahler came to Vienna, Karl Weiss, the city's archivist and librarian (who played an infamous role as a critic of the eclectic historicist aesthetics of the first major Ringstrasse building, the 1869 Opera House—the very stage on which Mahler

[18] See Franz Werfel, *Twilight of a World*, trans. H. T. Lowe-Porter (New York: Viking Press, 1937).

[19] See e.g. Henry A. Lea, *Gustav Mahler: Man on the Margin* (Bonn: Bouvier, 1985), 29–42, 91–116.

[20] The controversy over the Opera's design was typical of how the struggles of politics in post-1857 Vienna were fought with the symbols of culture and art. Mahler, owing to

his encounter with Vienna in the 1870s and early 1880s, was keenly aware of such precedents for the kind of serious battles he himself was to encounter after 1897. He eventually resigned his post. But one of the architects of the Opera House, Eduard van der Null, took his own life in the wake of the criticism of his design.

would later make his greatest contribution to Vienna's cultural life),[20] published a history of the city. In it he expressed the Viennese ambivalence about the role of the city in an Empire and a world facing modern politics and a social structure congruent with modern commerce, industry, and science:

Both political developments and the cultural life of the city show that Vienna has entered an important era in its history. For a millennium, like a lush island in the midst of a large river of East European migration of peoples, Vienna, although frequently threatened by greedy neighbours, never relinquished its fight for German culture and mores. So too today the city aims to preserve its old greatness and splendour. Although aware of the difficulties brought about by the insecure political situation of the Empire, and the jealousy and competition of other blossoming cities, the citizens of the city are more and more convinced that the promise of the future will only be secured when they trust in their own strength and only if they bolster the city with the tools of spiritual progress. For a decade now, this conviction has guided the education and training of the young, concerns for the health of the population, the development of commerce and industry, and all efforts to beautify the city and make it more comfortable. May the seeds of hope yield golden fruits. Just as Vienna was once the fortress against the onslaught of barbarism from the east, may it be in the future the focal point of a flourishing German cultural life; the arsenal of learning and progress, in which the emperor and the empire forge the weapons for their fight against their enemies.[21]

This Austro-German amalgam of progressive and reactionary idealism was an indispensable precondition for the success of the radical, anti-liberal Viennese politics of Christian Socialism and Karl Lueger (1844–1910) in the 1890s. Lueger became the city's mayor almost at the same time that Mahler was appointed to the Opera. When Mahler came as a student in 1875, the Viennese government was dominated by anti-clerical liberals, exemplified by Cajetan Felder (1814–94), Vienna's mayor from 1869 to 1878. When Mahler returned in 1897, the city government was in the hands of anti-liberals led by Lueger committed to a pro-Catholic, German-centred, anti-capitalist, and aggressively anti-Semitic platform.[22]

Perhaps no phenomenon reveals more succinctly the interrelated evolution of Viennese politics and culture from the early 1870s to the late 1890s than the Viennese cult surrounding the memory of Franz Schubert. A monument to the composer was dedicated in 1872. Its base was designed by the greatest neoclassical Ringstrasse architect, Theophil von Hansen, who designed Vienna's famed Musikverein which housed the Conservatoire where Mahler studied. The monument was a gift of the leadership of the Men's Choral Society, which included progressive industrialists and professionals such as Nikolaus Dumba (1830–1900).[23] The monument's iconography celebrated the universal and humanist power of music.

[21] Karl Weiss, *Geschichte der Stadt Wien* (Vienna: R. Lechner, 1872), 388.

[22] Karl Lueger had himself once been a liberal. In 1875 he was elected as a liberal to the Gemeinderat (city council).

[23] Dumba was a textile manufacturer and a leading citizen who was a patron of the arts, an avid collector of art, a choral singer, and active in the Men's Choral Society and the Society of the Friends of Music. He was a great Schubert enthusiast and commissioned Gustav Klimt to paint the now destroyed wall paintings 'Music' and 'Schubert at the Piano' for his music room.

In contrast, the centennial Schubert celebrations of 1897 became an ideological battleground between the liberal heirs of the 1872 monument initiative and Lueger and his followers. The Christian Socialists sought to make of Schubert a native-born Viennese symbol of a unique anti-modern local tradition of artisan and rural Austro-German culture. Schubert seemed an ideal vehicle for an assault on the cultural tastes of the liberal cosmopolitan middle class of Vienna—including its visible contingent of Jews—with whom Brahms was closely linked and whom Mahler would exemplify.[24]

Lueger's radical and reactionary rhetoric and his deft manipulation of a conservative nostalgia for the era which preceded economic rationalization, industrialization, and demographic cosmopolitanism revealed, however, just one side of 'handsome Karl', Vienna's most charismatic political figure. During the years Mahler was at the Imperial Opera, Lueger, as Mayor, spearheaded Vienna's long-delayed but remarkable modernization of transport, sewerage systems, water supply, and public facilities. His favourite architect was none other than the great Otto Wagner (1841–1918) whose apartment houses, institutional buildings, and railway stations helped shape the distinct modernist architectural aesthetic of turn-of-the-century Vienna. Once again, in Vienna reactionary politics and progressive aesthetics flourished side by side.

3. People and Spaces

Given Vienna's significance as a destination for migrating peoples, it is not surprising that the Vienna to which Mahler returned in 1897 was a city of young people. During the late 1890 and early 1900s—the years when Mahler was at the Vienna Opera—over half the city's population was under twenty-five years of age. During his student days, approximately 27 per cent of the population of Vienna had been born, like him, in Moravia, Silesia, or Bohemia. Of the Jewish population of Vienna in 1880, 15 per cent had migrated from Moravia and 15 per cent from Bohemia. Vienna was the chosen destination for peoples from provinces to the north—Poles and Czechs. Czech, Polish, and Yiddish were the major secondary languages of Mahler's Vienna, the largest minority in Vienna during the late nineteenth century being Czech by birth.[25]

Mahler's enthusiasm as a student for Austro-German cultural trends, particularly the attraction to Nietzsche and Wagner (which ran parallel to his friendship with the writer Siegfried Lipiner), took place in a city where reminders of his own provincial origins were

---

[24] See John W. Boyer, *Political Radicalism in Late Imperial Vienna: Origins of the Christian Social Movement, 1841–1897* (Chicago: University of Chicago Press, 1981), and *Culture and Political Crisis in Vienna: Christian Socialism in Power, 1897–1918* (Chicago: University of Chicago Press, 1995).

[25] The statistics are from the standard work in this field: Marsha L. Rozenblit, *The Jews of Vienna 1867–1914: Assimilation and Identity* (Albany, NY: State University of New York Press, 1983).

a regular part of daily life.[26] At the Conservatoire in 1875—Mahler's first year—192 of the 648 students who enrolled came, like him, from outside Vienna but from within the Habsburg Empire. In 1895, a quarter of the Conservatoire students were Jewish. Two decades earlier, the percentage was perhaps under twenty but still proportionately significant.

The Moravian and Bohemian Jews of Vienna, in contrast to their co-religionists from Galicia, were an elite, and were somewhat more dispersed throughout the city than other foreign Jews. Bohemian Jews in particular avoided the most Jewish district of the city, the second district, Leopoldstadt. They were rather more affluent than other Jews and, like Mahler's father, quite Germanophilic, and oriented towards German culture. The ambition to make a career in music in Vienna by its very nature demanded an allegiance to German culture.

Furthermore, most Jews from the Czech lands were immune, unlike their Polish Jewish counterparts, to the exhortations of Slavic nationalist rhetoric. The 'Young Czech' nationalists of the late nineteenth century left little or no constructive impression on Moravian and Bohemian Jews. The Czech Jews who came to Vienna used German as a primary language. In contrast, the Czech immigrants to Vienna, who made up between 25 and 30 per cent of the immigrants to the city, spoke Czech.[27]

Considering the magnitude of the Jewish migration to Vienna from within the Empire during the mid- and late 1870s, there was little that could endear even the German-speaking Jews from Bohemia and Moravia to the existing Viennese Jewish community which had developed between 1815 and 1867. Even though the older Jewish community feared most the poverty-stricken Jews from Galicia who became the model for the anti-Semitic caricature of all Jews, Mahler, as a student, was more likely to be welcomed as a young gifted artist by wealthy patrons of the Conservatoire than by the official Jewish community as a co-religionist in search of support.[28]

Most Jews native to Vienna in the late 1870s abhorred the immigration and the culture of the Ostjuden in part because of the increase in anti-Semitism that occurred after the Crash of 1873.[29] On 9 May 1873, nine days after the opening of the 1873 World Exposition in Vienna, the stock market collapsed after a period of sustained speculation, particularly

[26] See William J. McGrath, *Dionysian Art and Populist Politics in Austria* (New Haven: Yale University Press, 1974).

[27] The situation was somewhat different in Prague during the last quarter of the 19th c. There Jews were caught in between a majority Czech and minority German cultural and linguistic nationalism. See Hillel J. Kieval, 'Jews, Czechs and Germans in Bohemia before 1914', in Robert S. Wistrich (ed.), *Austrians and Jews in the Twentieth Century* (New York: Macmillan, 1992), 19–37.

[28] See Klaus Hödl, *Als Bettler in die Leopoldstadt: Galizische Juden auf dem Weg nach Wien* (Vienna: Böhlau, 1994), 115–67; for the best general study, see Robert S. Wistrich, *The Jews of Vienna in the Age of Franz Joseph* (Littman Library; Oxford: Oxford University Press, 1989).

[29] The reader who is interested in gauging the attitude of the older-established Viennese Jewish community to incoming Jews should consult first G. Wolf, *Geschichte der Juden in Wien (1156–1876)* (Vienna: A. Hölder, 1876; repr. 1974); then the turn-of-the-century point of view found in Sigmund Mayer, *Die Wiener Juden: Kommerz, Kultur, Politik, 1700–1900* (2nd edn., Vienna: R. Löwit Verlag, 1918); and last, Hans Tietze, *Die Juden Wiens: Geschichte, Wirtschaft, Kultur* (Vienna: E. P. Tal & Co., 1933; repr. 1987). See also Walter R. Weitzmann, 'The Politics of the Viennese Jewish Community, 1890–1914', in Ivar Oxaal, Michael Pollak, and Gerhard Botz (eds.), *Jews, Antisemitism and Culture in Vienna* (London and New York: Routledge & Kegan Paul, 1987), 121–51.

in railway stocks. Investors, small and large, were ruined. The many accusations of fraud which followed in the wake of the collapse were directed at prominent Jewish financiers. A long, nearly twenty-year period of economic stagnation began, which ended the boom of the 1860s.[30]

Mahler had little or no contact with the official Jewish community, with the possible exception of Salomon Sulzer (1804–90) the great Cantor (whose son Joseph Sulzer played cello in the Philharmonic under Mahler), whose reputation extended well beyond the Jewish community.[31] How familiar Mahler was with Jewish ritual music as practised in Vienna, and particularly the distinctive Vienna ritual shaped by Sulzer, remains unclear.

Despite the growing numbers of Jews in Vienna, the city was unmistakably and proudly Catholic. Over 80 per cent of the population was Catholic. The churches, from the medieval Stephansdom and the 1739 Karlskirche to the newer ones, such as the extravagant neo-Gothic Votivkirche (whose exterior was finished in 1868, but which was still being worked on while Mahler was a student) and the 1861 Altlerchenfelderkirche, designed by Eduard van der Null, dominated the urban landscape. The church hierarchy played a decisive role in the schools and in city politics.

An important part of the work of Guido Adler (who was also born a Jew in Moravia) involved collaboration with the Church in projects designed to improve church musical practices through the contributions of modern scholarship. Viennese religious devotion included a distinctly theatrical component. Every Viennese knew of the magnificent annual Corpus Christi procession that culminated in the Emperor praying before an open-air altar in the middle of the street. On Gründonnerstag (Maundy Thursday), Franz Joseph washed the feet of the poor in a semi-public ceremony. After the Emperor and the Mayor of the city, the Cardinal of Vienna was the most significant power in the political and cultural daily life of Viennese citizens.

The staunchly Catholic character of Vienna lent particular significance to the dramatic increase in the relative strength of the city's Jewish population. The striking expansion in the number of Jews living in Vienna was the most important demographic and political factor in the city's history during Mahler's lifetime. By the time he returned to Vienna, the traditional role played by the small numbers of elite Viennese Jews of the Biedermeier period—primarily in finance—had been supplanted by the varied activities of a population of Jews ranging from pedlars and members of the working classes to a new breed of tradespeople, entrepreneurs, professionals, academics, journalists, and artists.

The rapid ascent (including in some cases ennoblement) of the Jews and their increased visibility within the cultural life of Vienna after 1875 was perhaps most grotesquely captured by Richard and Cosima Wagner's notorious fantasy of 1881. That year, a major

---

[30] See Jutta Pemsel, *Die Wiener Weltaustellung von 1873: Das gründerzeitliche Wien am Wendepunkt* (Vienna: Böhlau, 1989), 77–83.

[31] See Hanoch Avenary (ed.), *Kantor Salomon Sulzer* und seine Zeit: Eine Dokumentation (Sigmaringen: J. Thorbecke, 1985); and Joseph Sulzer, *Ernstes und Heiteres aus den Erinnerungen eines Wiener Philharmonikers* (Vienna and Leipzig: F. Eisenstein, 1910).

theatre—the Ringtheater—burned down, killing over 400 people. Wagner responded with some glee and casually imagined the rebuilding of the theatre, the staging of Lessing's *Nathan der Weise*, and then the burning of the theatre again. He knew that the highest percentage within the Viennese audience for theatre and music was of Jewish origin, particularly in a theatre like the Ringtheater where tickets could be bought on a first-come, first-served basis (as opposed to events where subscriptions could be passed on from generation to generation, as in the cases of the concerts of the Society of the Friends of Music and the Vienna Philharmonic).

Vienna's Academic Wagner Society had more than its fair share of Jewish members, a fact that led the more virulent anti-Semitic Viennese Wagnerites to create a rival group in 1889, the Neuer Wagner Verein, explicitly free of Jews, to which Anton Bruckner lent his name.[32] The symbolic role played by the Jews of Vienna in musical politics was sufficiently extreme as to tarnish even Brahms's image in the city during the 1880s and 1890s. To those who were sympathetic to Hugo Wolf's virulent anti-Brahms criticism published in the *Salonblatt* in the mid-1880s, Brahms was not merely a symbol of the tastes of a politically liberal social class, and a reactionary counterweight (aesthetically speaking) to progressive Wagnerism. He became suspect as a philo-Semite and a North German outsider in Vienna, and as an artist with too many Jewish acquaintances and friends, the musicians Ignaz Brüll (1846–1907), Julius Epstein (1832–1918), and Karl Goldmark (1830–1915) among them. Brahms played a role in bringing Mahler back to Vienna by recommending him for a post at the Imperial Opera. He had been impressed by Mahler's conducting during the latter's tenure at the Budapest Opera in the 1880s. In turn, Mahler never participated in the polemical attack on Brahms characteristic of many of his pro-Wagnerian contemporaries.[33]

Mahler's complicated relationship with his Jewish birth has been the subject of considerable speculation. When he registered at the Conservatoire in 1875, and after completing his *Abitur*, at the University in 1877 he identified himself as a Jew. When he returned in 1897, he came as a Catholic, having converted as a matter of expediency: as a Jew he would not have been able to obtain the post of Director at the Opera. In this, Mahler was not an exception: advancement frequently required conversion. The largest proportion of Viennese converts from Judaism consisted of highly educated people—professionals, musicians, writers, and artists. Moreover, for individuals such as Karl Kraus (who converted to Catholicism), and Arnold Schoenberg (who converted to Protestantism), conversion seemed to offer the possibility of escaping some of the external and internal consequences of being Jewish.[34] During the last years of his tenure at the Opera, Mahler lived in Wieden, the Fourth District, near the Belvedere, where the percentage of Jews was

---

[32] See Margaret Notley, 'Bruckner and Viennese Wagnerism', in Timothy L. Jackson and Paul Hawkshaw (eds.), *Bruckner Studies* (Cambridge: Cambridge University Press, 1997), 54–71.

[33] See Leon Botstein, 'Brahms and Nineteenth-Century Painting', *19th Century Music*, 14 (1990), 154–68; and Notley, 'Brahms as Liberal'.

[34] It is interesting to note that Karl Kraus (1874–1936), one of the most significant intellectual and literary figures of the turn of the century, was born in Bohemia of wealthy Jews who moved to Vienna when he was three years old. Schoenberg's parents came from Szécsény and Prague.

under 5. Yet the total number of converts remained very small. Conversion continued to be the exception. In 1900, 559 Jews converted in Vienna, 0.004 per cent of the Jewish population.

Despite his conversion, there was no doubt in anyone's mind in Vienna that Mahler was a Jew. Jewish identity was no mere matter of an individual's theological practices or convictions. In the eyes of Jews and anti-Semites alike, it was a matter of birth, race, and nation, as well as faith. Understood in these terms, the Jewish presence in Vienna (and for that matter in Budapest, where Mahler's success in the 1880s was discredited by opponents as a conspiracy engineered by the large Jewish population of the city) increased from less than half of 1 per cent in the Vienna of Schubert's day, to around 5 per cent in 1862 when Brahms settled in the city, to over 10 per cent when Mahler left for Kassel in 1883. The Vienna in which Mahler died comprised over 175,000 Jews; the city he first encountered in 1875 comprised only about 55,000.

In terms of the social structure of the city, Mahler, as a student, was part of the 3 per cent of the population identified as students. Fifty-five per cent of the population of Vienna in 1875 consisted of workers in either modern factories or larger artisan workshops. Despite the enormously rapid economic growth experienced during the 1860s and early 1870s, by Western European standards Vienna was still somewhat old-fashioned. The dominant mode of production was the artisan workshop. Eleven per cent of the city's population were artisans who owned their own businesses. Six per cent could be classified as capitalists—bankers, large landowners, and industrialists. Twenty-one per cent of the population were domestic servants and related service personnel. Less than 5 per cent of the population possessed any form of higher education, which, in the system of that time, meant Gymnasium and University. The predominant tone of the city in popular culture was set by the independent artisan class and those workers whom they employed. This group was either native to Vienna or drawn from German-speaking, outlying districts of Lower Austria and provinces to the West.[35]

The rapid population growth of Vienna created a housing shortage in the city which remained almost unabated until the First World War. This shortage was not the result of the lack of building-work, but rather a constant lag, exacerbated by cyclical financial crises, between population growth and construction.[36] Rents were high and most apartments were small. In 1900, 30 per cent of Vienna's population had changed residences within the year, and only 10 per cent were in a place they had lived in for a decade. Most had no separate bathroom and only 20 per cent had one within the same building.

What Vienna did possess was extensive public spaces, including parks and open areas near the centre, and a by now legendary tradition of eating and drinking establishments—

[35] See Maren Seliger and Karl Ucakar, *Wien: Politische Geschichte, 1740–1934*, ii. (Vienna: Jugend & Volk, 1985), 739–82. The best study on the rise of Christian socialism and the decline of liberalism is Boyer, *Political Radicalism in Late Imperial Vienna*.

[36] Peter Feldbauer, *Stadtwachstum und Wohnungsnot: Determinanten unzureichender Wohnungsversorgung in Wien 1848 bis 1914* (Vienna: Verlag für Geschichte und Politik, 1977) and Roman Sandgruber, 'Alltag des Fin de Siècle—Wiener Glanz und Elend', in *Das Zeitalter Kaiser Franz Josephs, 2. Teil, 1880–1916, Glanz und Elend*, ed. Harry Kühnel (Vienna: Nö Landesmuseum, 1987), 138–51.

inns and coffee-houses—where individuals could gather, linger, and, if they were writers, even work. The Prater was Vienna's most famous park, offering entertainment ranging from carriage- and horse-racing for the elite to amusement-park fare for the working classes.

The long-standing inadequacy of private spaces in the city had an even more important legacy, however. Vienna was supremely a city of clubs and associations. Citizens organized themselves around activities which brought them out of their homes. In 1910, for example, there were over three hundred bicycle-riding clubs in the city alone. No doubt bicycling, a *fin-de-siècle* rage in Vienna, was a unique fad.[37] Mahler (who did not belong to a bicycle club) liked to bicycle for pleasure and exercise.

Other associations formed through shared occupations, interests, political allegiances, and, more important, active avocations, were common among all strata of society, from the exclusive Jockey Club, the Schubertbund—a singing club dominated by schoolteachers— to the numerous all-male and mixed singing clubs scattered throughout the city. At the turn of the century, the Viennese were in the habit of getting together in groups on a regular basis, particularly from September to June.

In terms of musical life, the Gesellschaft der Musikfreunde, the Wiener Männergesangverein, and the Singakademie were the city's most prestigious voluntary musical associations. But in every district and within each smaller community there were clubs and associations of musical amateurs. The Viennese choral tradition was widespread and remarkable at the *fin de siècle*. Johann Herbeck, Franz Mair, and Eduard Kremser were three of the most significant choral conductors and arrangers active during Mahler's lifetime. They were leaders in a form of music-making for lay people that brought into one social forum everything from folk songs, patriotic hymns, and comic material to sacred music and secular high art. These groups took themselves very seriously. Yet the celebration of the sociable and easy-going Viennese character—including touches of humour and irony—constituted a common thread in Viennese choral singing.

The Vienna of 1875, in terms of its physical appearance, was a new city. The Conservatoire building, the Musikverein, in which Mahler studied, had been opened in 1870, just five years before he enrolled. The Imperial Opera House, in which he first witnessed full-scale productions, was just one year older. Vienna's most important small concert hall (seating just under 600), the Bösendorfersaal, had been opened in 1872 (albeit in a renovated old building). The south railway station, built in neo-Renaissance style, was finished only in 1873. The north railway station was only a decade old and the west railway station just five years older.

The Ringstrasse was still a novelty. The new City Hall was under construction, and the foundations had just been laid for the neoclassical Parliament building designed by Hansen. The University, in which Mahler had enrolled briefly, was not located on the

---

[37] Roman Sandgruber, 'Cyclisation und Zivilisation: Fahrradkultur um 1900', in Hubert Ch. Ehalt, Gernot Heiss, and Hannes Stekl (eds.), *Glücklich ist, wer vergißt—? Das* *andere Wien um 1900* (Vienna: Böhlau, 1986), 285–304. See the parody of the cycling craze in *Wiener Caricaturen*, 14/46 (18 Nov. 1894), 5.

Ringstrasse but still at its old quarters within the inner city. Construction was already under way on the new University on the Ringstrasse by the mid-1870s. Designed by Heinrich Ferstel in a neo-Renaissance style, it was completed in 1884. The new stock exchange on the Ringstrasse, also designed by Hansen, opened in 1877.

What would have impressed the young Mahler most was not only the new monumental public buildings along the Ringstrasse, but also the number of elegant apartment houses surrounding them. Into these new and spacious homes moved aristocrats, bankers, and industrialists. In 1875 the new neighbourhood of the Opera and Vienna's Musikverein had the effect of bringing together both the traditional 'high' and 'second society' of Vienna: the minutely differentiated aristocracy (high aristocracy, finance aristocracy, and ennobled civil servants) and the upper strata of the bourgeoisie. The legendary strict and rigid protocol of the Habsburg court vis-à-vis the nobility of one's birth set a tone for the city as a whole. Among the upper classes, distinctions in terms of rank, age, and origin of title were rarely overlooked.

These privileged residents of Vienna were not only possessors of power, both economic and political, they were also the very people who formed the audience at concerts. The old inner city, including the Ringstrasse, made up the First District. At the *fin de siècle*, most of its residents were affluent, and just under 20 per cent were Jews—the most prosperous and acculturated members of the Viennese Jewish community.[38] They and their non-Jewish neighbours, together with individuals of comparable social and financial standing from the very few other affluent neighbourhoods, comprised the audience that filled the 1,600 seats in the main hall of the Musikverein on a regular basis. Access to top-quality professional performances of theatre and music was itself a relatively rare privilege. The Burgtheater, Vienna's new main theatre, which opened in 1888, had only 1,300 seats.[39] The Imperial Opera House was the city's largest hall and could accommodate 2,500 people.

The Musikverein, in which Mahler and Hugo Wolf studied, had been funded by a peculiar mix of private philanthropy and state support, including a lottery. The individual benefactors constituted a veritable 'Who's Who' of Viennese society, ranging from members of the Imperial family, high-ranking aristocrats (Schwarzenberg, Liechtenstein, Pallavicini, and Hohenlohe) to relative newcomers to the city. Numbered among the benefactors were well-known wealthy Jewish families (e.g. Rothschild, Wertheim, Schey, and Todesco), leading industrialists (e.g. Lobmeyer, Thonet, Dumba), and professionals (e.g. Franz Egger (1810–77), a jurist born in Laibach [Ljubljana] who helped to spearhead the effort to finance the new Musikverein), many of whom were active in the Men's Choral Society as well. The politics of the non-aristocratic patrons were largely liberal. Egger, for example, in 1870 explicitly asked the Viennese to emulate the enlightened support of voluntary institutions characteristic of English men of commerce. Furthermore, the membership lists of

[38] See Elisabeth Lichtenberger, *Wirtschaftsfunktion und Sozialstruktur der Wiener Ringstrasse* (Vienna: Böhlau 1970).

[39] The ratio of available seating to the size of the population, including Vienna and its environs, is a significant and sobering fact about the role of performance and high culture as such in the life of the city. The capacity numbers do not include the room for standees, who were often students.

the Society of the Friends of Music, whose home was the Musikverein, were a reliable indicator of the type of person who would be in the seats of concerts sponsored by the Society and by the Vienna Philharmonic.[40]

It may be hard to imagine how much less anonymous and open, and how much more exclusive and limited audience membership in public concert life was at the end of the last century. The performing artist who was a resident of Vienna knew a strikingly high proportion of those in the audience personally. Despite repeated attempts during the 1890s to expand orchestral concert life, access to concerts remained restricted in Mahler's lifetime. Mahler did not live to see the construction of Vienna's second major concert hall, the Konzerthaus, which opened in 1913.[41] A second concert orchestra in Vienna came into being only during the first decade of the twentieth century.[42] Yet, although the population of the city grew by nearly one million between 1872 and 1890, no additional concert hall— with the exception of the small Ehrbar Hall on the Mühlgasse in the Fourth District, opened by Friedrich Ehrbar, the Viennese piano manufacturer—had been constructed during the period.[43] Improved education and transport made the potential audience even larger than the number of inhabitants might suggest. The late nineteenth century witnessed expansion and improvement in music education in the schools. Lending libraries, instrument and sheet-music companies, and even concert agencies were growing and lucrative enterprises.[44] In the 1890s there was considerable debate on the need to encourage exposure to the musical traditions among the working classes as a matter of civic virtue and moral education. One of Mahler's severest critics, Robert Hirschfeld (1857–1914), played a significant role in the struggle to democratize access to art music and concert life in the city by organizing concerts in outlying districts.[45]

The Viennese traditions of music-making and dancing, therefore, were not maintained, in Mahler's lifetime, by concert-going. Dancing and dance halls played a significant role in sustaining musical life. But the most important source was the making of music by the residents of the city themselves. The guitar, the harmonium, the zither, the piano—in their

[40] This matter is covered in Leon Botstein, 'Music and its Public: Habits of Listening and the Crisis of Musical Modernism in Vienna, 1870–1914' (Ph.D. diss., Harvard University, 1985).

[41] Friedrich C. Heller and Peter Revers, *Das Wiener Konzerthaus: Geschichte und Bedeutung 1913–1983* (Vienna: Wiener Konzerthausgesellschaft, 1983), 9–27.

[42] See Ernst Kobau, *Die Wiener Symphoniker: Eine sozialgeschichtliche Studie* (Vienna: Böhlau, 1991), 11–23, and Margaret Notley, '*Volksconcerte* in Vienna and Late Nineteenth-Century Ideology of the Symphony', *Journal of the American Musicological Society*, 59 (1997), 421–54.

[43] Friedrich Ehrbar (1827–1905) had been a friend of the Steinway family and produced the other respected modern piano in Vienna in addition to the Bösendorfer. The piano never competed effectively outside Vienna but held its own in the city. Ehrbar was a friend of Brahms, Hanslick, and Ignaz Brüll.

[44] By the 1890s the concert-agent business—which was often allied with publishing and instrument selling—was in full swing. Vienna was obviously a major destination for visiting performers. With the exception of a visit of the Meiningen Orchestra under Hans von Bülow in the 1880s, and a group from Budapest in the 1890s, the age of visiting orchestras had not yet dawned. The Music and Theatre Exposition of 1892 in Vienna, at which Tchaikovsky performed, was a watershed. It heightened demand and the awareness of the need to expand the city's concert life.

[45] See Elisabeth Riz, 'Robert Hirschfeld: Leben—Wirken—Bedeutung', in Friedrich C. Heller (ed.), *Biographische Beiträge zum Musikleben Wiens im 19. und frühen 20. Jahrhundert*, i (Vienna: Österreichischer Kunst- und Kulturverlag, 1992), 1–80.

various sizes and configurations, including mechanical devices which simplified the need for technique—and singing were the popular mediums of musical expression.

Much of the material for intimate home use and music-making at larger social gatherings came not only from traditional sources—so called folk music from regions outside Vienna passed on by families and communities—but from a new genre of popular music. Vienna was a city of street and folk singers of its own. In the *fin-de-siècle* period the best known was Edmund Guschelbauer (1839–1912), whose many hit songs earned him the honour of being buried, ten months after Mahler, at the expense of the city. Not surprisingly, at the turn of the century Viennese popular music mirrored the social composition of the city. It ranged from the Schrammel tradition of pseudo-folk chamber music, to Jewish secular music, the operetta, and the modern eclectic hit song which drew on or imitated folk sources. New immigrants to the city continued to emulate and augment local traditions well into the 1920s.

Mahler's music, insofar as it was written with the contemporary Viennese audience in mind, was itself a critical reflection on the growing lure of the facile rhetorical conventions of popular song, operetta, and dance at the turn of the century. By using so-called folk and popular materials in a far less commercial manner, within the framework of classical symphonic form and Wagnerian notions of musical drama, Mahler confronted a slowly widening gulf between Vienna's popular musical culture and the traditions of its concert halls. In effect, he challenged the arrogance of superior taste maintained by conservative concertgoers by highlighting recognizable so-called 'banal' musical elements. At the same time, in the spirit of Beethoven and Liszt, he demonstrated the power of the concert-hall traditions of musical transformation by revealing the potential inherent within the seemingly limited materials of ordinary, everyday musical culture.

Mahler was certainly aware of the fact that during the last quarter of the nineteenth century, Jewish and Slavic elements altered the Viennese dialect and the popular culture of the city. This fact was not lost on Viennese conservatives intent on preserving an authentic Austro-German heritage. Rudimentary musical literacy may have been more widespread than even language literacy. Commentators on Mahler's music have noted the significance of the popular musical environment of Mahler's rural and small-town childhood.[46] The sounds he encountered in the streets of Vienna during the 1870s and late 1890s may present a closer link to the complex mixture of elements that grace the surface of many of his works. Too little emphasis in the scholarly literature on *fin-de-siècle* Vienna has been placed on the evolution of street language and dialect, as well as on the vital world of popular culture, ranging from operetta to street fairs, in order to gauge the influence of these elements on modernism in Viennese high art literature and music.[47] Furthermore, the

---

[46] See Vladimir Karbusicky, *Gustav Mahler und seine Umwelt* (Darmstadt: Wissenschaftliche Buchgesellschaft, 1978).

[47] A brilliant example of how the culture of *fin-de-siècle* Vienna can be understood from the perspectives of religious communities and popular culture can be found in Philip V. Bohlman, 'Auf der Bima/auf der Bühne—zur Emanzipation der jüdischen Popularmusik um die Jahrhundertwende in Wien', in Elisabeth Th. Hilscher, Theophil Antonicek, and Ottmar Wessely (eds.), *Vergleichend-systematische Musikwissenschaft: Beiträge zu Methode und Problematik der systematischen, ethnologischen und historischen Musikwissenschaft* (Tutzing: Hans Schneider, 1994), 417–49.

public audience for popular entertainments, while much larger than that for opera or concert music, included the elite patrons of the Burgtheater, Hofoper, and Musikverein.

The Vienna Mahler knew was a city addicted to the theatre. Max Reinhardt, Stefan Zweig, Arthur Schnitzler, and Martin Buber all testified eloquently in their childhood memories to their love of the theatre and the prominence actors and theatre politics maintained in Vienna. The stage and the various genres of theatre had been crucial dimensions of Viennese public life since the mid-eighteenth century. The Viennese heritage of Baroque theatricality in sacred ritual had its secular offshoots first in the Imperial patronage of opera and drama in Mozart's day and later in the more generalized Viennese love of spectacle, including the amusements of the Prater.

Mahler's success at the Opera was in part a result of his capacity to render opera a truly dramatic experience, particularly with the aid of modern lighting techniques and set designs. His audience was essentially the same audience that went to see Josef Kainz act in the classic and contemporary repertoire at the Burgtheater or attended operetta performances at the Theater an der Wien. In 1906 Vienna had at least thirteen theatres with full season schedules of professional quality.[48]

4. Literacy, Aesthetic Taste, and Politics

Except for the working classes, an important route for Viennese music-lovers to musical culture—apart from active amateurism—was reading about music. *Fin-de-siècle* Vienna was a city of newspapers and journals. In addition to the main German-language daily papers (e.g. *Neue Freie Presse, Neues Wiener Tagblatt, Das Fremdenblatt*), there were papers and periodicals for every section of the community, whatever their political, ethnic, or religious persuasion, many with their own music reportage. Most people read more than one publication. Music-lovers had access not only to specialized publications from Vienna, such as the weekly *Neue Musikalische Presse*, but also to other German-language, popular music periodicals, each of which reported on concerts in the major cities, new books, and sheet music, and published short biographical sketches, extensive reviews of new works, and serialized essays on pedagogy and theory.

The prominence of journalism in the culture of Vienna during Mahler's lifetime is perhaps best exemplified by the power exerted over public opinion by the *feuilleton*, a type of short polemical essay which became renowned as emblematic of Viennese journalism. The classic *feuilleton* appeared in the bottom half of the front page of the daily press, below a black line, and frequently ran onto the second page, below the black line. Masters of this

---

[48] Josef Kainz (1858–1910) was the leading male classic dramatic actor of Vienna during Mahler's tenure at the Opera. In Mahler's student days, Friedrich Mitterwurzer (1844–97) had been the dominant stage personality. *1906. Neuer Theater-Almanach*, ed. Genossenschaft Deutscher Bühnen-Angehöriger, 17 (Berlin, 1906), 571–92.

form of writing in the Vienna Mahler knew included Ludwig Speidel (1830–1906), Theodor Herzl (1860–1904), the founder of the Zionist movement, and Eduard Hanslick (1825–1904).[49]

Not surprisingly, the very power and prestige attained by journalism in Vienna inspired a lively satirical counterpart. During the second half of the nineteenth century, journalism offered a new outlet for the Viennese tradition of humour. In Mahler's day, magazines such as *Figaro*, *Kikeriki*, *Floh*, and *Bombe* presented a mix of cartoons, jokes, gossip, and commentary. Viennese humour, long before the *fin de siècle*, had perfected the techniques of irony, merciless satire, and subtle parody.[50] At work was the flexibility of the Viennese dialect and its pithy expressions. The *feuilleton* inspired its mirror image, the short satirical essay designed for journalistic publications. The great nineteenth-century Viennese satirists with whom Mahler would have been familiar were Ferdinand Kürnberger (1821–79), Daniel Spitzer (1835–93), and Karl Kraus. Politics, people, religion, literature, music, art, architecture, and journalism itself were the targets.[51]

Journalism was perhaps the most powerful influence on music and the politics of culture in *fin-de-siècle* Vienna. Most of the arguments held in middle-class homes about Mahler's appointment in 1897 or departure in 1907—or about Wagner's concerts in Vienna in the mid-1870s—would have been conducted by individuals who never attended a single concert or opera performance by Mahler or Wagner. Talk about the politics of art in Vienna was much like the talk in which individuals nowadays engage about electoral politics and foreign policy. Direct contact with the events or the actors in them was not required. Reading about them was sufficient to generate informed opinion.

Since journalism was a key force in Mahler's Vienna, music criticism had a crucial function as an educative instrument. It was linked more with the purchase of sheet music than with attendance at concerts. Beginning in the 1890s, the Vienna Philharmonic commissioned Robert Hirschfeld to write explanatory and descriptive programme notes to help the audience follow and comprehend the concerts. This itself was a sign of the weakening of earlier traditions of musical literacy and a new reliance in musical culture on reading about music.[52]

---

[49] For an example of the significance of journalism see the brief article on Mahler in the 7 Oct. 1897 issue of the *Illustrierte Zeitung*, a weekly published in Berlin and Leipzig (No. 2832, vol. 109), p. 477, which announced his Vienna appointment. The *feuilleton* set the standard for the short journalistic essay form in all types of Viennese publications. Front-page placement was actually the exception. See Herbert Zeman, 'Österreichs literarische Welt von der Jahrhundertwende bis zum Ersten Weltkrieg (1880–1918)', in *Das Zeitalter Kaiser Franz Josephs*, 185–99, and Walter Obermaier, 'Von Daniel Spitzer zu Karl Kraus: Witz und Satire in den letzten Dezennien der Donaumonarchie', ibid. 200–4.

[50] The origins of turn-of-the-century Viennese humour date to the pre-1848 era and to theatre, particularly the work of Nestroy. The mix of farce and biting political and social commentary, including self-ridicule—which frequently eluded the censors before 1848—now became widespread in Vienna during the last quarter of the 19th c.

[51] It is interesting to note that Kürnberger was a favourite of Richard Strauss and Ludwig Wittgenstein; Spitzer of Johannes Brahms and his biographer, the Viennese writer and critic Max Kalbeck; and Kraus of Arnold Schoenberg.

[52] See e.g. Busoni's biting observation from 1907: 'I begin to realize that the ruin of the Viennese, as regards their attitude to art, comes from newspaper criticism (*Feuilletons*). This systematic daily reading (for half a century) of *causeries* on art, witty and superficial, *short*, and all turning on an obvious catchword, has destroyed for the Viennese their own power of seeing and hearing, comparing and thinking with any seriousness.' Cited in Edward J. Dent, *Ferruccio Busoni* (1933; repr. London: Eulenberg Books, 1974), 160.

Since a high percentage of the audience that Mahler encountered throughout most of his career in Vienna was made up of individuals who either knew each other or of one another, the auditorium itself became an accurate mirror of the competing cultural and political groupings within the educated classes of the city. Attendance at a concert or an opera placed the individual in the position of having to display significant allegiances through his or her reaction to the events at hand. These allegiances would be noted and recognized by people who knew who one was. In this basic sense, going to the theatre and concerts was a political act. Anonymous ticket buying and the absence of communication with other concert-goers were rare occurrences.

The only regular exception would have been tourists, for whom, however, access to the concerts as described in the textbooks on music history would have been extremely difficult to procure. Practically all the seats at concerts of the Society of the Friends of Music and of the Philharmonic were reserved on a membership-subscription basis that was passed on from one generation to the next. The Baedeker and other guides to the city of the late nineteenth century and *fin-de-siècle* describe Eduard Strauss's popular Sunday and holiday concerts at the Musikverein and mostly summer outdoor and hotel- and restaurant-based entertainment involving military bands and dance bands.[53] Although Vienna in the 1870s was the third largest city in Europe, after London and Paris, it lagged behind them in most categories, including concert life and tourism. This was because the economic and industrial modernization of the Habsburg Empire had started later and advanced less rapidly and less thoroughly before 1900.

In the 1860s, a boom time for the monarchy, a sense of progress and modernity helped to raise the hopes of the city. Two events distinguished the Vienna that Mahler discovered in the mid-1870s and mirrored the character and consequences of the brief period of optimism: the World Exposition of 1873 and the *Festzug* (Celebratory Parade), which marked both the completion of the Ringstrasse and the silver wedding anniversary of the Imperial couple in 1879.

The Vienna Exposition of 1873 was an international world's fair celebrating primarily industry and commerce. Like similar events in the twentieth century, it produced a much-needed infrastructure of hotels and transport.[54] Students of Mahler's generation enjoyed these residual benefits. In anticipation of the 1873 Exposition, the city government sought to improve the street-lighting and water and sewerage systems of the city, which, by Western European standards, were antiquated. The massive Exposition was situated in the Prater. The Vienna organizers had hoped it would do as well as the Paris Exposition of 1867, which drew eleven million visitors; but, as only slightly over seven million people came, it was considered a disaster—despite the many benefits it brought. The causes for its failure were the stock-market crash and the cholera epidemic in the summer and autumn of 1873.

---

[53] See e.g. the information contained in the following two guidebooks: Julius Meurer, *A Handy Illustrated Guide to Vienna and Environs* (2nd edn., Vienna: A. Hartleben, 1906) and Karl Baedeker, *Austria-Hungary including Dalmatia* and *Bosnia: Handbook for Travellers* (10th edn., Leipzig: Baedeker, 1905).

[54] See Pemsel, *Die Wiener Weltaustellung*, 75–83.

The failure of the Exposition and the Crash of 1873 left an indelible mark on Viennese culture and politics. The stock-market speculation, the get-rich-quick schemes, and the confident imitation of English-style economic and political liberalism within the government and cultural elite of Vienna became objects of virulent criticism and satire. Modern Viennese political anti-Semitic agitation received an essential boost.[55] The 1873 Crash caused considerable distress in terms of employment and economic hardship. Although the city recovered somewhat by the end of the decade, a full-scale economic recovery did not occur until the mid-1890s, on the eve of Mahler's return to the city.

Nevertheless, one permanent residue of the 1873 Exposition was an increase in tourism. Vienna became a tourist attraction for museum-goers, nature-lovers, and music-lovers. The cultural reputation of the city and the prominence of its University in medicine and science were international. The search for up-to-date medical advice drew distinguished visitors. The very year Mahler returned also marked the start of Mark Twain's long stay in Vienna. What drew Twain to Vienna was music and medicine: consultations with physicians of international repute and the great piano pedagogue Theodor Leschetitzky, who taught Twain's daughter.[56]

Historians have become accustomed to a historical account of Vienna that identifies the birth of a new style of reactionary politics with the 1873 Crash and the subsequent decline of liberalism in the later 1870s. However, Lueger's Christian Socialism was the logical outcome of the fears already evident in the era of so-called liberal hegemony in Vienna of the 1860s: the ambivalent attitude towards the migration to the city, the physical destruction of the old city, and the aesthetics of new construction, as well as the new methods of business and commerce.

On 27 April 1879 the *Festzug*, involving over ten thousand participants, took place along the entire length of the Ringstrasse. Designed by Hans Makart (1840–84), the city's most influential painter and later president of Vienna's Union of Visual Artists, it was made up of groups of crafts and guilds marching in units. Each group was dressed in historical costume. The parade was a secularized version of a sacred public ritual, an expression of the taste of the age for the monumental and the theatrical, all with Makart's characteristically extravagant sense of gesture, scale, and colour.

Among Hans Makart's staunchest admirers were Richard and Cosima Wagner. In 1875 the Wagners were in Vienna (a city he had left in the early 1860s, having enjoyed little success there) for what were to become Richard Wagner's legendary concert appearances, and they visited Makart's studio.[57] The 1879 parade epitomized the taste for aestheticized historical fantasy that dominated the 1870s. The success Wagner enjoyed in the 1870s and

[55] The classic study is Peter Pulzer's *The Rise of Political Anti-Semitism in Germany and Austria* (rev. edn., Cambridge: Halban, 1988).

[56] See Carl Dolmetsch, *'Our Famous Guest': Mark Twain in Vienna* (Athens, Ga.: University of Georgia Press, 1992).

[57] See Cosima Wagner's *Diaries*, ii: *1878–1883*, ed. Martin Gregor-Dellin and Dietrich Mack, trans. Geoffrey Skelton (New York and London: Harcourt Brace Javanovich, 1980), 773; for a very pro-Wagner account of Wagner's relationship to Vienna, see Max Morold, *Wagners Kampf und Sieg: Dargestellt in seinen Beziehungen zu Wien*, 2 vols. (Zurich: Almathea-Verlag, 1930).

1880s was due in part to the extent to which his work appeared consistent with the aesthetics of Ringstrasse architecture and the canvases of Makart. Makart was, in Wagner's
view, his painterly ideal.

Among the many floats that made up the parade was one representing the railways.
Makart staged the procession so that the railway employees, clad in Italianate Renaissance
outfits, some on foot, some on horses, were carrying not spears or lances but poles and flags
with railway symbols on them. At the centre of the railway groups was an elaborately carved
neo-Baroque, gold, altar-like wooden platform drawn by horses, in which one could discern (amidst the Baroque depiction of wings and pseudo-Michelangelo carvings) fragments and outlines of modern industrial items associated with the railway. Rational
modern progress was clad in the garb of history and tradition.

The *Festzug* was emblematic of the Vienna Mahler knew as a student. An imagined history was evoked in architecture and painting to camouflage the radical transformation that
modernity brought about. Alternatively, in what to many appeared to be a gesture of essentially corrupt and eclectic historicism, Vienna, in its new architecture, had appropriated to
itself the external styles of the past through which to display a confidence in progress. The
post-1857 Viennese ambivalence about past and present, therefore, took the shape of
modernity clothed as mythic history. The present was hidden beneath a façade of history
transformed on an industrial scale: the past became grander, larger, and modified by modern technologies ranging from plumbing and heating to the lift.

The year Mahler left Vienna, 1883, was the year in which Wagner died. One year later, in
October 1884, Makart died. These two figures had dominated the high-art cultural life of
Vienna in the 1870s. The decade had begun with the highly controversial Viennese première of *Die Meistersinger*. Bruckner, Brahms, Ignaz Brüll, and Karl Goldmark were the
leading composers in the city.[58] Anton Romako (1832–89) was perhaps the city's most original living painter, whose portraits were suggestive of the work of a younger generation of
painters. Between 1879 and 1892 Gustav Klimt, his brother Ernst, and Franz Matsch
(1861–1942) would maintain a common studio. The 23-year-old Mahler left Vienna with
convictions typical of other young, ambitious contemporaries: an enthusiasm for Wagner
and Bruckner and a taste for Makart-style spectacle imbued with spirituality. Nietzsche,
Jean Paul, an early Romantic nationalism oriented towards Germany, and a wistful bitter-
sweet love of Nature as the antidote to the harshness of the modern city were part of the
intellectual baggage Mahler carried with him from Vienna after his first period of residence.

5. Cultural Politics at the Turn of the Century

By the time Mahler returned to Vienna in 1897, the city's transformation was essentially
complete. The major Ringstrasse building projects were concluded. The city government

---

[58] Both Brüll and Goldmark were Jews who died in Vienna. Brüll was born in Moravia and Goldmark in Hungary.

was in the hands of the Christian Socialists. The demographic balance within the city would not change significantly until after the First World War. Nearly two decades of economic stagnation had finally been reversed.

The pattern of Habsburg history—despite many domestic and foreign crises—took few decisive turns between 1897 and 1914, with the exception of the universal franchise introduced in 1907. This gave the socialist movement a role in politics that it had previously played only indirectly. By the autumn of 1897 both Bruckner and Brahms had died. The leading figure of the new in music, even for the Viennese, was Richard Strauss.

It was in the period 1897 to 1911, the year of Mahler's death, that the best-known dimensions of *fin-de-siècle* Viennese culture made their appearance. Yet chronological correlations and physical proximities do not imply causality or even linkages. The publication of Freud's *Interpretation of Dreams* (1899), the construction and dedication of Olbrich's Secession building (1897) and Otto Wagner's two finest structures, the Postal Savings Bank of 1906 and the sanatorium at Steinhof of 1907—let alone the paintings of Klimt, the poetry of Hofmannsthal, the criticism of Karl Kraus, the plays of Arthur Schnitzler, and the prose writings of Peter Altenberg and the 'young Vienna' circle—may evoke an image of a unified culture of which Mahler was a part. But what do these aspects of Vienna really have to do with Mahler's life and work after 1897?

Despite the intense literary and philosophical interests of his youth, after 1897 Mahler became connected primarily with the *fin-de-siècle* Viennese world of the visual arts. Unlike Richard Strauss or Arnold Schoenberg, he did not collaborate with or set the texts of contemporary writers.[59] In this way he may have sought to insulate himself from the intensification of the day-to-day cultural politics that preoccupied his Viennese colleagues. The debates over issues of personal ethics and political ideology—including anti-Semitism—in Vienna were powerfully delineated in Schnitzler's classic novel *Der Weg ins Freie* (1903). Mahler the artist kept such issues at arm's length. He read Dostoyevsky and Nietzsche; but in his music, as far as his setting of texts was concerned, he distanced himself from Viennese literary modernism, remaining instead attached to early nineteenth-century German romanticism.

On the other hand, he allied himself with contemporary Viennese painters and the Secession movement. In part, this was the result of his relationship and marriage with Alma, who was the daughter and step-daughter of two of the best-known Viennese painters, Emil Jakob Schindler (1842–92) and Carl Moll (1861–1945). The Molls were part of a close circle of artists, designers, and architects, including the legendary Josef Hoffmann (1870–1956), who would design the Moll house in Vienna.

At the Secession Beethoven exhibition of 1902, the centrepiece of which was Max Klinger's massive statue of Beethoven, Mahler conducted a fragment from the Ninth Symphony arranged for a reduced ensemble. Gustav Klimt also participated, producing his

---

[59] The setting of Hans Bethge's texts in *Das Lied von der Erde* can of course be considered an exception to this observation. But Mahler's return to Goethe and Rückert is more to the point. See Mitchell, *SSLD*, 55–73 and 128–9.

greatest of friezes, the 'Beethoven Frieze'.[60] The exhibition was an attempt at creating a totally integrated visual environment: each room and every wall was carefully designed, lit, and decorated. This fascination with the notion of 'the total work of art' (*Gesamtkunstwerk*) was clearly derived from Wagnerian aesthetics. Among Mahler's most celebrated and controversial achievements in Vienna after 1897 were his new productions and reinterpretations of Wagner. He abolished the traditional cuts that Hans Richter had introduced, darkened the hall, and commissioned two prominent Viennese artists associated with the Secession, the Hagenbund, and later the Wiener Werkstätte, Heinrich Lefler (1863–1919) and Alfred Roller (1864–1935), to design new sets.

Roller's designs for Mahler's Wagner and Mozart productions were revolutionary. Gone were the Makart-like painted backdrops. Instead, subtle effects of colour, light, and dark were deployed. The full three-dimensionality of the stage was exploited. The scene design eschewed the conventions of simplistic naturalism and replaced them with novel visual symbols evocative of modernist aesthetics. By using the innovations of turn-of-the-century Viennese design and painting, Mahler succeeded in the one area in which Wagner himself had failed to be original: the visual dimension of music drama.

Within the Viennese worlds of art, design, and literature in the years between 1897 and 1911 there were essentially two distinct and competing factions, each claiming authenticity as avant-garde and modern.[61] The first group was centred around Klimt and the Secession. In part inspired by the Scottish Arts and Crafts movement of Mackintosh and by French Impressionism, these visual artists overtly rejected the historicism celebrated by the architects and painters of the Ringstrasse era. In its place came *Jugendstil*, a kind of decorative modernism. A colourful and intricate aestheticized lyricism and psychological realism emerged in painting. The Viennese painters, designers, and architects allied with the Secession—Klimt, Koloman Moser (1868–1918), Olbrich, and Hoffmann, for example—met with extraordinary and almost immediate success among the patrons and audiences of Vienna. 30,000 visitors attended the 1901 Secession exhibition; and by 1900 Klimt's fees had risen to 35,000 crowns for a single portrait.

Critics linked the Secession artists to the so-called 'young Vienna' writers active in the 1890s. Hermann Bahr (1863–1934; he later married the great soprano Anna von Mildenburg whom Mahler brought to Vienna), the prolific dramatist and essayist, became an outspoken advocate of this group of new Viennese writers and the Secession artists. The 'young Vienna' writers made the literary life of the Viennese coffee-house famous. They published in the newly founded journals of cultural criticism, the *Wiener Rundschau* (1896–1901), *Die Zeit* (1894–1904), and the *Neue Revue* (1893–8), and also in art publications associated with the Secession.

---

[60] Marian Bisanz-Prakken, *Gustav Klimt. Der Beethovenfries: Geschichte, Funktion und Bedeutung* (Salzburg: Graphische Sammlung Albertina, 1977), 9–30 and 175–9.

[61] The most reliable attempt at providing an overview of the several groups in Vienna and their interrelationships is to be found in Edward Timms, *Karl Kraus: Apocalyptic Satirist, Culture and Catastrophe in Habsburg Vienna* (New Haven: Yale University Press, 1986), 3–29.

Arthur Schnitzler was perhaps the oldest, most distinguished, and best established of the new wave of writers. Hugo von Hofmannsthal was its young 'wunderkind', an early master of poetic lyricism. This literary movement included Richard Ber-Hofmann (1866–1945), who later became a Zionist, and Stefan Zweig. Like the artists of the Secession, these individuals also met with considerable local success and notoriety, despite their own affectations of radicalism. Schnitzler's plays, for example, became both extremely popular and objects of State censorship. What linked these writers to the Secession was the emphasis on subjective psychological perception, rather than naturalistic or realistic representations of everyday life. There was, too, an obsession with subtle detail and the sensuous beauty of form and technique. The short work of poetry and prose—not the long novel, or the massive multi-act drama—became the main vehicles of literary expression.

The mid-nineteenth-century Viennese mix of nostalgia and pessimistic detachment which accompanied the heyday of historicist aesthetics resurfaced at this time, particularly in the theatre. The psychological drama, with its focus on attitudes towards sexuality and conflicts in personal and family relationships, manipulated both sentimentality and irony through the element of shock. Fundamental questions of politics and philosophy were sacrificed for an aesthetics of subjectivity.

The striking success of these writers and artists with the critics and the public at the turn of the century generated a counter avant-garde, a competing group of radical younger writers, artists, and musicians, many of whom opposed the Secession and its allies. They took issue with what they perceived as the careerism, the self-indulgent aestheticism and subjectivism of Bahr, Schnitzler, and Klimt. They saw little crucial difference between the inflated claims of the modernists and those of their predecessors. They believed the reigning assumptions about the relationship between art and life, artist and public, aesthetics and ethics, had yet to be challenged.

The influence of this group on the later twentieth century proved to be profound. At its centre was Karl Kraus. If Bahr was the spokesman for the first faction, Kraus was the undisputed conscience of the opposition. His journal *Die Fackel* (the Torch), which began publication in 1899, relentlessly sought to expose the hypocrisy, smugness, and deceit of not only the older generation of established Viennese journalists, but the new self-styled modernists. Kraus first gained local fame in 1897 when he published his pamphlet *Die demolierte Literatur*, which pilloried the pretensions of the coffee-house society of writers and intellectuals. Amongst his allies were the architect Adolf Loos (1870–1933), the young Arnold Schoenberg, and, to some extent, the expressionist painters Egon Schiele and Oskar Kokoschka. Other significant figures of turn-of-the-century Vienna shared many of Kraus's views on art and life and *fin-de-siècle* Viennese modernism. They included the musical analyst Heinrich Schenker and the writers Otto Weininger (1880–1903) and Peter Altenberg (1859–1919).

The idea of language as the 'mother' of thought was central to Kraus's thinking. His crusade against his fellow writers and painters focused on the need to rescue art and language from trivialization, abuse, and corruption. Corruption meant the thoughtless employment of language as an instrument of commerce (as in journalism); as the vehicle of deception (in politics); and as a mere literary device divorced from ethical concerns (as in the work of the 'young Vienna' writers).

It is not surprising, then, that it was Kraus and those allied with him in *fin-de-siècle* Vienna who exercised the greatest influence on Ludwig Wittgenstein. Wittgenstein's determination to understand language, conserve but also delimit its capacity to express the truth was in part inspired by Kraus. Language was no mere instrument of decoration.

If the Viennese writers and artists associated with Hermann Bahr were obsessed with sensuality divorced from politics, Kraus and his group were committed to the idea that epistemological and ethical truth and therefore the improvement of society were crucial factors in matters of art.

Kraus observed that the charge of philistinism and provincialism levelled at the ascendant Viennese bourgeois taste of the 1870s and 1880s could be applied equally to the turn-of-the-century embrace of the Secession and the new generation of writers. Historicism and *Jugendstil* were merely different expressions of the reduction of art to mere style—an alluring camouflage designed to spin illusions of beauty over a flawed, hypocritical, and painful world. Kraus regarded the focus on sensuality and sexuality by both Schnitzler and Klimt as exploitative, designed to titillate, but devoid of a larger moral purpose. Those sympathetic to Kraus in Vienna called for a redemption of creativity from commercialism. The dominant premise of Viennese culture came under attack: the distance between art and any progressive social, ethical, or political project. Kraus's views were shared not only by radical modernists, but by the few remaining exponents of the principled and nostalgic Viennese conservativism of the early 1860s.

In formalist terms, many of this second faction of younger Viennese artists and writers—Kraus, Loos, and Schoenberg in particular—articulated a basic distinction between structure and surface, function and façade, style and idea. The Secession movement and the 'young Vienna' crowd were thus seen as guilty of focusing on surface, façade, and style, and hence, merely on ornament and decoration. Art and substantive thought, for Kraus, could not, ultimately, be separated.

The purpose of music, therefore, was not to encourage the habit of concert-going as a form of escape from everyday life or a vehicle for subjective delusion and sensual pleasure. Its mission was to rescue the souls of the public from hypocrisy, self-deception, commercial exploitation, and ethical corruption. Respect for the logical integrity and autonomy of musical materials—in the sense of classical formal procedures—was highly valued by both Schoenberg and Schenker. Following Kraus, they argued that an ethical sense of epistemological integrity demanded that music should not be cheapened. The task was to electrify the consciousness and thus the conscience of the listener.[62]

---

[62] See e.g. Heinrich Schenker's essay 'Das Hören in der Musik', and his review of Mahler's performance of and changes to Beethoven's Ninth Symphony, in Hellmut Federhofer (ed.), *Heinrich Schenker als Essayist und Kritiker* (Hildesheim: G. Olms, 1990), 96–102 and 259–68.

The favourite targets of this second faction of Viennese writers and artists were the pur-
veyors of popular commercial music, sanctimonious journalism, smug middle-class moral
discourse, and the attempt to obscure the lies inherent in modern life through art. If the
enemies of Kraus and his followers were obvious, so were their heroes. In this sense, within
the context of Vienna, Kraus's radicalism was quite conservative. He aligned himself with
an older Viennese tradition of satire and scepticism. He admired Nestroy and Offenbach,
and the satirist Kürnberger, whilst distancing himself from the provincial Viennese conservatism which dismissed all things foreign and new.

Fundamental innovation which led to new ideas was celebrated. Adolf Loos admired the
American architecture of Louis Sullivan because it responded to genuine changes in urban
life, and the materials and technology of construction. Likewise Kraus championed the
work of Frank Wedekind for its matter-of-fact directness, its striking ethical clarity, and its
integrity with respect to sexuality. Modern, functional clothing from England seemed
preferable to the stylized class-specific sartorial tastes of Vienna. Unlike Schnitzler and
Zweig, Kraus had little use for psychoanalysis and the work of Freud. He defended Oscar
Wilde, and praised Richard Wagner both as a composer and theorist, in part because of
Wagner's merciless attacks on philistinism and his views on the central role art should play
in society.

Given the ideological differences and the links between Mahler and the Secession, the
circle around Kraus and Loos included many individuals who were critical of Mahler.
Kraus and Altenberg, for example, were admirers of Robert Hirschfeld, whom Mahler
scholars have long demonized as a second-rate, jealous, nonentity of a critic. Altenberg,
Kraus, and Schenker harboured doubts about Mahler as both a composer and a conduct-
or. His music seemed too melodramatic and ornamented, too lush and committed to obvious sensual effects. His conducting stressed the surface drama and colours rather than the
internal logic of, for example, a Beethoven symphony. At the same time Kraus defended
Mahler against the provincial and philistine criticism of local conservatives. In contrast,
Bahr and the group around Klimt and Schnitzer embraced Mahler wholeheartedly as a
comrade and kindred spirit.

The public opposition to Mahler at the *fin de siècle* was chiefly provincial Viennese, dominated by philistine anti-Semites and the political right wing. This fact alone created a common front of support for him among the followers of the Secession, Hermann Bahr, and
those of Kraus and Loos. However, the fissures within Vienna, between new and old, and
among the new, would not disappear with Mahler's departure in 1907. The furore over
Adolf Loos's design for the Michaelerplatz Goldmann und Salatsch building opposite the
old Hofburg in 1910 was far more bitter and far-reaching than the 1907 controversy surrounding Mahler.

Mahler's difficulties were more analogous to Klimt's 1900 and 1901 encounters with the
University faculty and government bureaucrats over the paintings entitled 'Philosophy'
and 'Medicine' for the new University building. Despite these public controversies, Klimt
retained a large following in the city. The resistance encountered by Loos in 1910 and by

Schoenberg at concerts of his music in 1907, 1908, and 1913 reflected a profound Viennese rejection of Loos's and Schoenberg's construct of modernism. That criticism carried with it more than the traditional Viennese political overtones of resentment and hostility to the outside world. Indeed, the work of Loos and Schoenberg was far more radical and overtly defiant in its challenges to conventional taste than that of Mahler and Klimt.

The architectural designs of Otto Wagner provide the closest Viennese analogy to the work of Mahler both as a composer and as a conductor.[63] Both men stood somewhat apart from the two competing cultural factions of *fin-de-siècle* Vienna. Wagner's buildings possess a lush detail and a sense of scale and grandeur, thereby linking his work to the large-scale historicism of the nineteenth-century Ringstrasse painters and architects. At the same time, his sense of scale and historical precedent is consistently subordinated to a search for the modern, realized as an organic outgrowth of references to the past. In contrast to many Ringstrasse buildings, there is an exacting coherence between façade and interior design in his work. The decoration is original and linked to the structure. Modern building techniques are employed. The signal achievement of this union between modernity and a decorative tradition reveals Wagner's originality and genius.

Likewise, in a Mahler symphony one finds surface elements of folk song and references to street music, to the waltz, and to the military band. These untraditional materials are placed side by side with conventional musical subjects. They are all integrated into a musical structure which consistently draws on tradition—Beethoven, Berlioz, and Bruckner—but remains distinct. The historical reference points, such as debts to the harmonic practice and sonorities of Richard Wagner, remain audible but are subordinated to an unmistakably modern style that emerges from experimentation with formal structure and instrumental colour. As in the great Otto Wagner buildings, eclecticism becomes the impetus for formal innovation. Modernity is framed by the fragmentation and transformation of tradition. Originality is achieved without the wholesale destruction of past precedents.

As a point of comparison, in the writings of Karl Kraus the future is secured by the almost puritanical rejection of late Romanticism. In the service of the ethical necessity to use language to rescue modernity from hypocrisy and self-deception, a pre-Romantic, almost neoclassical economy of style is favoured. In this context, it is not surprising that Heinrich Schenker thought that Mahler's performances of Beethoven betrayed too much of an instinct for finding in Beethoven a Wagnerian story-line. This, for Schenker, seemed a concession to the contemporary listener's inability to follow deep musical structure. Despite the near-universal praise lavished on Mahler's productions of Wagner, there was a fear, not among reactionaries but among modernists such as Kraus and Altenberg, that an aestheticized trivialization of Wagner was taking place. To them, the Mahler–Roller

[63] Despite the enormous support that Wagner received, he, like Mahler, experienced his disappointments, particularly in his attempts to realize the most modernist tendencies of his work. On Viennese architects contemporary with Mahler, see Peter Haiko, 'Viennese Architecture 1850– 1930', in id., *Vienna 1850–1930: Architecture* (New York, 1992), 8–25. On the specific issue that stymied Otto Wagner, see Peter Haiko, *Otto Wagner und das Kaiser Franz Josef-Stadtmuseum: Das Scheitern der Moderne in Wien* (Vienna: Historisches Museum, 1988).

productions had the appearance of a decorative Klimt portrait or the over-ornamented interiors of Josef Hoffmann.

Mahler himself consciously sought to ally himself with the new generation. During his last years in Vienna he became the patron of Alexander von Zemlinsky and Schoenberg. Although he had doubts about radical modernism, he had no doubt about the authenticity and idealism of Schoenberg. In 1904 Mahler accepted the honorary presidency of a new group of composers, the Vereinigung Schaffender Tonkünstler, a splinter group organized by Schoenberg and others to challenge the musical establishment. At public concerts in 1907 he was a visible defender of Schoenberg against the critics and the public who took offence at the younger man's music.[64]

But all this was not enough to convince Karl Kraus to sign the famous letter of 11 May 1907, nor to endear Mahler and his music to Ludwig Wittgenstein, even though Wittgenstein's favourite contemporary Viennese musician, the conservative Josef Labor (who was blind), *did* sign the 1907 letter.[65] As the examples of Kraus and Wittgenstein indicate, the modernism of *fin-de-siècle* Vienna encouraged a profoundly anti-Romantic tendency which remained suspicious of the scale, intensity, and emotionalism of Mahler's music and performances.

When Mahler resigned his post at the Opera in 1907, he, like Otto Wagner, was as much an emblem of an artistic and social establishment as he was viewed a rebel. Radical conservatives regarded him as the ultimate personification of a Jewish cosmopolitanism which for decades had been destructive to native Viennese sensibilities. When the Viennese historian Eugen Guglia lamented in 1892 that the *Gemütlichkeit* of the Viennese was under siege and the joyful exterior of Viennese public life had been damaged, he tacitly held the cultural contribution of a new population of Vienna responsible.[66]

Mahler's prominence and success fifteen years later in 1907 vindicated the reactionary cultural pessimism which argued that Vienna's true Austro-German heritage had been supplanted by a foreign element. In contrast, when right-wing, anti-Mahler critics sought to praise modest local talents such as the young Josef 'Pepi' Hellmesberger (1855–1907), who was chosen to succeed Mahler at the Vienna Philharmonic in 1900, they were actually lamenting the loss of their own cultural hegemony within the city.

Like Otto Wagner, Mahler and his wife were at the centre of a powerful cultural circle which included Julius Korngold (the music critic of the city's leading newspaper), the wealthy patrons of art, and the majority of the elegant reading public who attended theatres and concerts. Otto Wagner dominated the Viennese architectural scene and trained and influenced a generation of architects. Mahler became an inspiration for a new generation of performers and composers in Vienna.

---

[64] The Schoenberg–Mahler relationship demands closer scrutiny, particularly on the matter of Schoenberg's estimate of Mahler's music, as opposed to his unqualified admiration for the man.

[65] The most complete study of Mahler's relation to the Vienna Opera is Franz Willnauer's *Gustav Mahler und die Wiener Oper* (2nd rev. edn., Vienna: Löcker, 1993).

[66] See Eugen Guglia, *Geschichte der Stadt Wien* (Vienna: F. Tempsky, 1892), 301.

Enthusiasm for Mahler in *fin-de-siècle* Vienna was, in this sense, more significant than the criticism of him. His directorship at the Opera represented the glorious apogee of an alliance between audience and conductor. His concerts at the Vienna Philharmonic and his productions at the Opera set standards for the favourite pastime of Vienna's elite: enjoying with smug confidence and comfort the 'classical' tradition, from Mozart to Wagner.

No doubt the Viennese were far less interested in Mahler's own music. But they were not much interested in new music in general. When Mahler left Vienna in 1883, the historicist bias in musical taste amongst audiences was visible but not dominant. By the time he left in 1907, the distance between the audience and the modern composer characteristic of the later twentieth century had become overt and harder to bridge. Mahler the interpreter made contact with the conventional audience. His own music represented—much as did Richard Strauss's *Salome* (whose 1907 Viennese première provoked severe criticism)—music of a future that exceeded the bounds of proper taste.[67] Schoenberg saw in this criticism of Mahler's music the symptoms of debased public taste.

It is ironic that Mahler died in 1911, just at the moment when his rival and contemporary Richard Strauss articulated a new stylistic direction in *Der Rosenkavalier*. Strauss solved the problem of the audience–composer relationship by turning further away, after *Elektra*, from the task of developing a distinct twentieth-century musical language.

Despite his feeling that he was poorly appreciated and grossly misunderstood, Mahler achieved the ambitions of his youth. The immigrant Jew triumphed at the centre of Viennese culture. He achieved something that would elude Schoenberg and Anton von Webern but not Alban Berg, who cherished the memory of Mahler and remained close to Alma. Berg emerged the heir of Mahler. Like Mahler and Otto Wagner, in terms of both his music and subsequent reception, Berg found an original modernist voice in the appropriation and transformation of tradition without sacrificing evident and audible links to the culture of his immediate surroundings.

[67] See Robert Hirschfeld, 'Feuilleton: "Salome" von Richard Strauss', in *Wiener Abendpost*, 26 Mar. 1907, pp. 1–2, and Guido Adler, 'Musikalische Kulturprobleme unserer Zeit', *Neue Freie Presse*, 17 Dec. 1906, pp. 1–4. The Vienna production was by a visiting company from Breslau. Mahler had sought to produce the opera but was blocked by the censors. Both friends and enemies of Mahler took exception to what they heard at the Vienna première of *Salome*.

2

The Earliest Completed Works: A Voyage towards the First Symphony

JOHN WILLIAMSON

The first period of Mahler's career as a composer (juvenilia apart) opened with a cantata, *Das klagende Lied,* and ended with a symphony. The former was the 'first work in which I really came into my own as "Mahler" ';[1] the symphony was the work that established (not without uncertainties) which genre would be most associated with his name. Whether the period possesses any kind of unity within these extremes is problematic. Later creative phases in Mahler's career have been characterized by such labels as 'Wunderhorn Years' or the 'Instrumental Trilogy', which generalize from the dominant poetic source or genre without undue simplification. For the years between 1878 (when the text for *Das klagende Lied* was written) and 1888, the traditional date for his discovery of *Des Knaben Wunderhorn,* there is no comparable generalization; even 'pre-*Wunderhorn*' will not quite do in view of the uncertainty as to when exactly Mahler discovered that famous collection of folk texts.[2] To the period belong a number of important works but also lost and unfinished projects, some of which had connections with works which survived. To write the history of these years as a gradual approach to the First Symphony, the work which quotes from *Das klagende Lied,* the song 'Hans und Grethe', the lost incidental music to Scheffel's *Der Trompeter von Säckingen,* and the song-cycle *Lieder eines fahrenden Gesellen,* is perhaps to surrender rather supinely to historical determinism. *Lieder eines fahrenden Gesellen* has always lived a robustly independent life in the concert hall, and *Das klagende Lied* has acquired a similar status since the Mahler revival of the 1960s. It is also arguable that *Das klagende Lied* is closer in many details to the Second Symphony than to the First. Nonetheless, the First Symphony is in many ways a work of musical summation, in which elements which had accompanied Mahler from his Conservatoire days found a firm expression in a programmatic and literary context that stands for a different kind of sum-

---

[1] Mahler, *Selected Letters,* 200.
[2] For information on Mahler's discovery of *Des Knaben Wunderhorn,* see Mitchell, *WY,* 117–19; also Alma Mahler, *Memories,* pp. xxv–xxvii.

mation equally characteristic of the composer. Writing the history of Mahler's earliest completed works is inescapably a voyage towards one of the most original 'First Symphonies' of the nineteenth century.

Das klagende Lied

Posterity has endorsed Mahler's verdict on *Das klagende Lied*, that it was his first fully characteristic work, even if it has not been able to reconstruct completely the genesis and history of the cantata. Whether it was first conceived as an opera is a matter over which leading Mahler experts disagree (Donald Mitchell's relegation of a hypothetical early operatic version to the status of 'myth' is still open to dispute).[3] Mahler's own account of its importance (given to Natalie Bauer-Lechner in 1898) has been shown to be at fault in some particulars. The work's failure to win the Vienna Conservatoire's Beethoven Prize in 1881 (not 1880 as was long thought) was not the reason why he was forced to take up a theatrical career.[4] But that it failed because its radical nature displeased a conservative jury (which included Brahms, Goldmark, and Richter) is plausible (it also failed to impress Liszt, an acknowledged leader of the progressive school). Mahler followed the modern, Wagnerian trend in writing his own poem for the cantata. Most experts agree that title and theme stem from a folk tale by Ludwig Bechstein, though elements also come from tales by the Brothers Grimm and possibly from a dramatic poem by Martin Greif entitled *Das klagende Lied*, which was performed at the Vienna Conservatoire in 1876.[5] So widespread is the subject of Mahler's poem in folk and ballad literature, so individual is his interpretation, that La Grange is justified in asserting that Mahler went beyond immediate literary inspirations to investigate deeper sources.[6] The result was numerous changes to Bechstein's subject, the most substantial of which was to replace the rivalry of a brother and sister with that of two brothers for the hand of a queen. The elder and darker brother murders his sibling, but a passing minstrel manufactures a flute from one of the younger brother's bones, which sings the story of the murder. The minstrel takes the bone flute to the wedding feast for the elder brother and the queen, where its narration leads to an all-engulfing catastrophe. Whether the theme of fraternal rivalry was rooted in the circumstances of Mahler's own childhood, and in particular in the trauma of his brother Ernst's death, is a matter for speculation. At least one part of the poem (which was completed on

---

[3] For a modified statement of the operatic origins of *Das klagende Lied*, see HLG(F), i. 947–8; for Mitchell's opinion, which is now widely accepted, see *EY*, 144–5, and *WY*, 56.

[4] NB-L, *Recollections*, 116; see also Mitchell, *EY*, 145–50, and HLG(F), i. 126–9.

[5] Mitchell, *EY*, 141–4; HLG(F), i. 945–7; the most recent

comments on Greif (which largely discount his influence on Mahler) may be found in Edward R. Reilly, '*Das klagende Lied* Reconsidered', in Stephen Hefling (ed.), *Mahler Studies* (Cambridge: Cambridge University Press, 1997), 34–5.

[6] HLG(F), i. 946.

18 March 1878) exists in more then one version, but nothing in the history of the text supports clearly the assumption that the work began its life as a projected opera.[7]

As with several later works by Mahler, *Das klagende Lied* had a far from easy genesis. It was intended to be in three substantial and self-contained parts.[8] Interruptions dogged the work, both personal and professional. Just as the First Symphony was to quote extensively from other works by Mahler, so the cantata fed on a near-contemporary song, 'Im Lenz', which was drawn upon for the section in the cantata's original second part ('Der Spielmann') which begins with the words 'O Wunder, was nun da begann'.[9] The short score of 'Der Spielmann' was completed on 21 March 1880, and that of the whole work on 1 November 1880. After its failure to win the Beethoven Prize, it waited until 17 February 1901 for its first performance, The reasons for this delay are fairly self-evident. That Mahler's confidence was shaken by the judgement of the Viennese Jury can hardly be doubted. Its length and forces (involving four soloists and off-stage band as well as chorus and orchestra) were also problematic (though he was to exceed both in later works). Mahler responded to these problems in a characteristically complex and painstaking process of revision, beginning in Hamburg in 1893. The first part (and with it, the bass soloist) was cut and the titles for the two remaining parts ('Der Spielmann' and 'Hochzeitsstück') were omitted.[10] The off-stage band had a chequered existence, first dropped, and then restored in 1898 when the possibility of publication seemed likely. The first performance took place in Vienna, sharing a programme with Wagner's *Faust Ouvertüre*. The original first part ('Waldmärchen') enjoyed a curious half-existence in Czech and Austrian radio performances of the 1930s, until it was finally released for general performance in 1970. Only on 7 October 1997 was it heard for the first time in its true context, with 'Der Spielmann' and 'Hochzeitsstück' in their 1880 versions.[11]

In spite of the uncertain composition history of the cantata, most Mahler authorities have agreed that *Das klagende Lied* in 1880 already inhabited a sound-world that is recognizably Mahlerian. Inevitably this sound-world and the orchestral terms in which it was couched are of central concern to Mahlerians. The two most obvious starting points are Bruckner and Wagner. At the time of writing *Das klagende Lied*, Mahler certainly knew one score by Bruckner intimately, the Third Symphony.[12] Bruckner may have discussed other

---

[7] For the *Ballade vom blonden und braunen Reitersmann* (a version of 'Waldmärchen'), see Hans Holländer, 'Unbekannte Jugendbriefe Gustav Mahlers', *Die Musik*, 20 (1928), 807–13 at 807.

[8] This very first version of *Das klagende Lied*, edited by Reinhold Kubik, was published in 1997 by Universal Edition, Vienna, in association with the International Gustav Mahler Society (Supplement, vol. 3, in the critical edition of Mahler's works).

[9] For the relationship between *Das klagende Lied* and 'Im Lenz', see Reinhold Kubik, '*Das klagende Lied*, Sources and Versions', in *Mahler the Revisionist*, Programme Book of the Symposium held at the Bridgewater Hall, Manchester, 7 October 1997, 8–16, 20; also Reilly, '*Das klagende Lied* Reconsidered', 31–2.

[10] There is some evidence that Mahler did not immediately decide to omit 'Waldmärchen'; see Kubik, '*Das klagende Lied*, Sources and Versions', 19.

[11] The changes made to 'Der Spielmann' and 'Hochzeitsstück' are not insubstantial and deserve more extensive treatment than can be given here. They affect music and text; see Reilly, '*Das klagende Lied* Reconsidered', 48–52; also Kubik, '*Das klagende Lied*, Sources and Versions', 20–6.

[12] [Mahler and Rudolf Krzyzanowski made a piano-duet arrangement of Bruckner's Third Symphony which was published in 1880. See Mitchell, *EY*, 67–8 and 193, and Mitchell, *WY*, 68–9. Ed.]

works (including the Fourth and Fifth Symphonies, which he finished revising in 1878) with the young Mahler. Echoes of his music certainly found their way (along with much Wagner and some Brahms) into the one completed symphony by Mahler's friend Hans Rott, a work that in turn had extensive influence on the later Mahler. But it is safest to assume that the Third Symphony was the most likely source for such Brucknerian elements as are to be found in Mahler's cantata.

A musical event of major importance in Mahler's Viennese years was his discovery of *Götterdämmerung*, which he experienced in the company of two other friends, Hugo Wolf and Rudolf Krzyzanowski (Alma Mahler is the source of the well-known story of their expulsion from lodgings as a result of a vigorous performance of the trio which ends Act II).[13] Whether this discovery was made through a performance (the first Viennese *Götterdämmerung*, which Mahler attended, took place in 1879) or through prior study of the score is impossible to determine. What can be said with safety is that the second half of the 1870s saw several opportunities for Mahler to become acquainted in detail with Wagner's operas, including *Tannhäuser* and *Lohengrin* in November 1875, when Wagner himself attended and Hans Richter conducted. Donald Mitchell has maintained that Mahler was probably initially influenced by such earlier works of Wagner as these and that all 'musical evidence points to his comparatively late assimilation of . . . late Wagner'.[14] But for Mitchell, late Wagner means '*Tristan* and *Parsifal* in particular', and there must be room for speculation that a work such as *Götterdämmerung*, stylistically the closest of the *Ring* cycle to the grand opera of Wagner's earlier years, left some mark on Mahler's cantata. Certainly the presence of what may be thought of as 'German Romantic Opera' as opposed to full-blown music drama helps to explain the character of *Das klagende Lied*, both musically and dramatically.

The opening of 'Der Spielmann' adheres to a characteristic musical gesture of the nineteenth century, the prolonged orchestral crescendo that opens most of Bruckner's symphonies and is found in Beethoven, Schubert, Wagner, and Liszt. The opening viola tremolo is possibly something that Mahler learnt from Bruckner (if he knew the openings of the Second or Fourth Symphonies); the bare harmonies implied by cellos and woodwind may also derive from Bruckner, as they are used in a similar way in the opening theme and woodwind background of his Third Symphony. Bruckner's context is more animated in the details of the texture, but the slow harmonic rhythm of his opening paragraph is not unlike Mahler's static prelude. In Mahler's crescendo, muffled drums are the only instruments added to those mentioned for over twenty bars, and no instrument rises above *piano* until five bars before Fig. 2. Any sense of progression is caused by the settling of the bass into a regular rhythmic tread and an insistence on rhythm rather than melody in the woodwind. With the entry of muted horns and trumpet fanfares comes a rhetorical broadening and triplets invade the bass line, suggesting for a couple of bars the Bruckner rhythm of duplet plus triplet (which Mahler can hardly have failed to notice in Bruckner's Third Symphony).

[13] Alma Mahler, *Memories*, 63–4.   [14] Mitchell, *EY*, 52–3.

The climactic chord of C minor is held for ten bars before evaporating in a scurry of basses which, like the entire opening, looks forward to the beginning of Mahler's Second Symphony.

It is difficult in this striking beginning to disentangle Brucknerian and Mahlerian elements, if only because the material is so simple. Bruckner would certainly have made a more elaborate melodic statement in such an opening. Mahler's later fondness for 'sound-sheets', static planes of harmony in which motifs and figurations create a sensation of melodic life below the surface, is certainly prefigured here, though the First Symphony takes such inspired inertia to altogether more radical lengths.[15] Where Bruckner and Mahler seem to meet is in the degree to which they suppress the full force of the orchestra so that its entry at the climax will seem the more overpowering. If Mahler's music is to be 'novelistically' interpreted as Adorno suggests, here is the orchestral equivalent of such fictional openings as those to *Eugénie Grandet* and *Germinal*, in which the steady accumulation of incident is replaced by a static block, the size of which, and the expectations it arouses, being such that a mere push causes a swift move to a climax or catastrophe.[16] Rhetorical crescendos of this kind, on analysis, seem to move by a series of spans, usually structured by harmonic shifts of various kinds. Mahler in this opening spends rather too much time on the tonic triad, suggesting a lack of experience in handling large-scale form. But this is part of his ability to create music out of atmosphere as much as out of themes or carefully structured tonal arguments. In his first major work, Mahler discovers how much may be suggested by commonplace 'precompositional' elements—a fanfare, a rhythm, a tremolo, and (at Fig. 3) the kind of hollow strokes in the bass which would later launch the last song of *Das Lied von der Erde*.

However fascinating it may be to assess the element of Bruckner in this opening, there is another much more obvious comparison to be made between the openings of 'Der Spielmann' and of the original Part I, 'Waldmärchen'. In the latter, *tremolandi* and fanfare elements are also interwoven in a crescendo, but in a rather more complex and Wagnerian harmonic web. 'Waldmärchen' begins with an enigmatic progression that dissolves into *Tristan*-esque harmonies that would suggest a more detailed knowledge of late Wagner than Mitchell allows. Mahler does not sustain this manner, and both 'Waldmärchen' and 'Der Spielmann' come closer after they reach their first climax. The impression of the two openings is quite clear, however, and illustrates how the influences of Wagner and Bruckner might have affected the young Mahler. 'Waldmärchen' seems relatively undigested because the opening plunges into the rhetoric of music drama without any kind of frame. 'Der Spielmann' opens in a way that Warren Darcy has termed 'creatio ex nihilo'.[17] One uniform colour compounded of a plain C minor and a small repertory of

[15] For the idea of a sound-sheet, see Monika Lichtenfeld, 'Zur Klangflächentechnik bei Mahler', in Peter Ruzicka (ed.), *Mahler: Eine Herausforderung* (Wiesbaden: Breitkopf & Härtel, 1977), 121–34; an English definition of the term is attempted in John Williamson, *The Music of Hans Pfitzner* (Oxford: Oxford University Press, 1992), 275–6.

[16] Adorno, *Mahler*, ch. 4.
[17] Warren Darcy, *Wagner's 'Das Rheingold'* (Oxford: Oxford University Press, 1993), 62–86.

characteristic figures creates a clear sensation of the beginning to a narration. The original Part I seems to begin *in medias res*, the original Part II announces the start of a fairy tale. Mahler's instinct to suppress 'Waldmärchen' served him better than those conductors of the present day who restore it in what Donald Mitchell has referred to as 'the illegitimate, unlovely mix of both versions'.[18]

There are many elements in *Das klagende Lied* which resist categorization in either Brucknerian or Wagnerian terms but occupy territory common to both. Thus Bruckner's massive unisons are frequently recalled in the cantata, as at Fig. 30, which suggests the style of the finale of the Fourth Symphony, but also Wotan's spear. The ensuing *fortissimo* horn motive has the monumental ring of a Brucknerian *Urthema*, though it functions throughout the cantata as a leitmotiv. The recurring patterns of overlapping fanfares, however reminiscent of the barracks at Iglau, suggest similar moments in Bruckner, though those that open 'Hochzeitsstück' might also have been shaped by the off-stage fanfares near the start of Act II of *Lohengrin*.[19] Already these reminiscences are being incorporated into Mahler's personal voice. This is as much a matter of context as musical style. The music associated with the minstrel of the title is of unmistakably popular character, as at Fig. 6, which suggests less Wagner and Bruckner than Schubert and Bruckner. Again specific works come to mind. The pacing bass and the melodic gestures with their *portamenti* up to the sixth degree of the scale are reminiscent of the polka in the finale of Bruckner's Third Symphony. The immediate juxtaposition of this material with the preceding paragraphs founded on fanfares is a Mahlerian trait in the making, however, as is the distorted shape in which this material appears after Fig. 18, a grimace that instantly conjures up the macabre tale that the minstrel is about to hear from his flute of human bone.

[18] Donald Mitchell, '*Das klagende Lied*: Mahler's Opus 1', revised typescript of essay in *Mahler the Revisionist*, Symposium, 7 October 1997.

[19] One of the more striking revelations of the 1880 score of *Das klagende Lied* is that an off-stage ensemble (trumpets, timpani, and cymbals) appeared also in 'Der Spielmann' in an episode that corresponds to Figs.14–16 of the revised score. Kubik ('*Das klagende Lied*, Sources and Versions', 20–6) notes that its C major clashes directly with the C flat major of the main orchestra, though the effect is complicated by a pedal F in the bass. Without the band, the passage evokes *Tristan und Isolde* (F-A♭-C♭-E♭ is one important form of the 'Tristan' chord', as at the climax of the Prelude to Act I). But the combination of two different streams of music is also evocative of the fanfares of Act II of *Lohengrin*, which cut across the orchestra's chromatic F sharp minor with the purest D major. But whereas Wagner juxtaposes elements, Mahler combines them and accentuates the contrast by placing orchestra and band in different metres (4/4 against 3/4), a feature which Donald Mitchell has compared to the introduction of the off-stage band in the finale of the Second Symphony ('*Das klagende Lied*: Mahler's Opus 1'). The band's C major is a fleeting effect, a chord rather than a fully-fledged tonality, and hardly qualifies as polytonality in the sense that it is used in referring to music of the 20th c. A later episode in 'Hochzeitsstück' (also cut in the revised version) achieves a similar effect but in rather more complex manner, by bringing in the C major of the band against a fading chromatic spasm in the orchestra (again over a pedal with clear reference to the harmonic world of *Tristan und Isolde*). Both passages resist conventional analysis if only because of Mahler's obvious intention that the two musical streams should not coalesce into a single harmonic field. They are perhaps the most extreme examples in early Mahler of that radical polyphony that has sometimes been compared to Ives; see Robert P. Morgan, 'Ives and Mahler: Mutual Responses at the End of an Era', *19th Century Music*, 2 (1978/9), 72–81. Not the least curious aspect of both passages is the manner in which late Wagnerian harmony is combined with collage techniques that seem more suited to simpler material. Almost equally intriguing is the suggestion that the earlier version of *Das klagende Lied* seems more indebted to late Wagner in Mitchell's sense than the revision, which brought it more obviously into the harmonic world of the '*Wunderhorn*' symphonies. Knowledge of the earlier version clearly will lead to a certain amount of rethinking of Mahler's musical development.

'Der Spielmann' is the most impressive part of *Das klagende Lied*. It possesses a better dramatic frame for music then 'Waldmärchen' in the form of a narration within a narration. The original first part seems excessively bound to the stanzas of the text and to a recurring refrain (based on a descending scale heard also in 'Der Spielmann' after Fig. 16, and in the closing bars of 'Hochzeitsstück'). 'Hochzeitsstück', though undeniably effective, is the part of the score upon which the hand of Wagner and Romantic opera lies heaviest. It is more of a blind alley in Mahler's music, though, like 'Waldmärchen', it has a pre-echo of the First Symphony. Its operatic quality is most directly evident in the off-stage band, a device that Mahler more than any other composer was to transfer to the symphony orchestra. In *Das klagende Lied*, the band's hectic fanfares and festal music stand for the framework of normality against which a tragedy is to be played out. In later works, Mahler diversified this in ways that recall the practice of Busoni in the opera house. In *Doktor Faust* and elsewhere, Busoni claimed to be enlarging the possibilities of opera by suggesting a backcloth of normality to the bizarre incidents and magical apparatus of his drama.[20] With Mahler, off-stage music seems variously to suggest the world of 'beyond' (symbolized at times in horn calls or church bells), the indifference of the world of normality or nature (symbolized in cowbells), or an ironic counterpoint of the two.

The manner in which Mahler employs the off-stage band is as important as the musical style, which at times is in the broad diatonic vein that Wagner had employed in festive passages both in his earlier works and in *Götterdämmerung* (particularly in Act II). The music at Fig. 45, an evocation of joy and splendour, illustrates this in the sustained inner parts, the haze of trills and *tremolandi* in upper strings, and the binding arpeggios of the harp. Elsewhere Mahler resorts to stock operatic gestures, as at two bars before Fig. 48, when a chromatic spasm in the strings foretells a later moment of crisis in the narrative (Fig. 68). Mahler's first major work is thus very much a reflection of a range of progressive influences that would have been accessible to a young composer even in the Vienna of the 1870s. His use of the orchestra has a traditional basis and this is inextricably bound up with harmonic and contrapuntal factors. But already there are numerous signs of his later style. In the section between Figs. 54 and 57 of 'Hochzeitsstück', there are no devices that would not be found in his predecessors: shimmering textures created by string harmonics, *tremolandi* and arpeggios in the harps, bariolage, woodwind filigree, and trills supporting horn and alto solos. If this is compared with such passages as the section after Fig. 32 in the first movement of the Seventh Symphony, a line of development can be perceived from the cantata to the much denser scoring of the Seventh. The texture in the cantata is a flat wash waiting for richer detail than Mahler provides; the instrumentation of the symphony suggests the interlacing of several different ensembles, each with its own music. Such shifts of perspective tend to occur not within but between sections of *Das klagende Lied*, as when the harsh minor chords of the bone flute's song slice into the pastoral of 'Der Spielmann' (before Fig. 25) or into the increasingly apocalyptic events of the wedding feast (Fig. 72 of 'Hochzeitsstück').

---

[20] Ferruccio Busoni, *The Essence of Music and Other Papers*, trans. Rosamund Ley (New York: Dover, 1965), 75.

Ex. 2.1. Comparison of (*a*) 'Hochzeitsstück', Fig. 81 (simplified) with (*b*) First Symphony, 4th movt., bb. 25–30 (simplified)

The most apocalyptic gesture of all links 'Hochzeitsstück' momentarily to the First Symphony. The chromatic cry of 'Weh!' at Fig. 81 appears twice in the Symphony's finale (at Fig. 4 and before Fig. 31). But in the cantata (Ex. 2.1(*a*)) it is a momentary pause before the final collapse of the work into the gloomy coda; in the symphony (Ex. 2.l(*b*)), it is part of an extended moment of tension which is differently resolved on each occasion.

Lieder und Gesänge, Vol. 1

Das klagende Lied maps out essentially three directions for the remainder of Mahler's first creative period. The operatic residue finds an increasingly tenuous existence in the third song of *Lieder eines fahrenden Gesellen*. Bruckner's influence becomes increasingly hard to find, save in radical transformation in the First Symphony. Popular idioms lead the most vital existence in the first volume of *Lieder und Gesänge* (1880–3) and the other songs of *Lieder eines fahrenden Gesellen*. The three directions are united in the First Symphony, where the popular elements prove by far the most important until the finale; there Mahler attempts to rework the apocalyptic elements of *Das klagende Lied* in symphonic terms. The result is hardly his most consistent symphony, but is nonetheless startlingly original.

Symphonic elements are created out of sound-sheets (in the outer movements), recomposed songs, popular idioms, fanfares that have been thoroughly integrated into Mahler's own idiom, and an apparatus of recurring figures, motives, and themes. *Lieder eines fahrenden Gesellen* gives the clearest idea of how such a co-ordination of disparate elements came to be achieved, but *Lieder und Gesänge* also illustrate the manner in which Mahler worked towards a style in which Bruckner and Wagner were diluted to vanishing point.

More than one commentator has noted that the songs of *Lieder und Gesänge* (originally entitled simply *Fünf Gedichte / Komponiert von Gustav Mahler*), though written for voice and piano, seem constantly to be on the verge of an orchestral style.[21] This is particularly obvious in 'Frühlingsmorgen' in the passages which depict lark, bees, and crickets, but also more intangibly at the words 'Steh' auf, Langschläfer', where a descending melodic figure is passed between voice and piano with the kind of echoing effect to be seen on a more protracted scale in the trumpet solo of 'Blumine' or the post-horn episode of the Third Symphony (though it also seems to glance unmistakably at Fig. 45 of 'Hochzeitsstück').[22] Moments in 'Erinnerung' seem to demand the liquid sounds of clarinets in thirds (an invitation accepted in both of Luciano Berio's orchestrations of this song). The setting of the 'Phantasie' from Tirso de Molina's *Don Juan* instructs the pianist to imitate the sound of a harp while contemplating performance with a real harp in a footnote. For its companion 'Serenade' from the same source, Mahler imagined the possibility of performance with wind instruments. The piano accompaniment, unusually for Mahler, reveals the outline of simple four- and five-part writing, suggesting strongly that the published text is a reduction to two staves of a compact ensemble (comprising perhaps oboes, clarinets, bassoons, and horns). The few spread chords suggest less pianistic effect than the kind of clumsiness that arises from such a reduction. Such passing clumsiness is common to Mahler's piano accompaniments throughout his career and may also be seen fleetingly in 'Hans und Grethe', the song with the clearest links to his other projects of the period.

Written originally in 1880 as 'Maitanz im Grünen', 'Hans und Grethe' famously provides a foretaste of the First Symphony's Scherzo in its piano motives and stamping bass (Ex. 2.2). Before that transformation from song into symphonic movement took place, however, Mahler may have attempted to incorporate the song in his fairy tale opera *Rübezahl* (on which he seems to have worked certainly between 1879 and 1883 and possibly later). Although no music for this has survived, the libretto quotes some words from the song in one chorus.[23] Mahler's intentions for the song accord both with its character and the general style of the music of the period. In its libretto *Rübezahl* suggests an attempt to rediscover the world of pre-Wagnerian German Romantic opera (though La Grange has pointed out some details that are also Wagnerian).[24] The combination of folk tale and magic

---

[21] See Mitchell, *EY*, 201–2 and 307.

[22] Ibid. 64–8.

[23] Ibid. 310 and 312. Not all Mahlerians are convinced that 'Hans und Grethe' was to be incorporated in *Rübezahl*; see Renate Hilmar-Voit, *Im Wunderhorn-Ton: Gustav Mahlers sprachliches Kompositionsmaterial bis 1900* (Tutzing: Hans Schneider, 1988), 255–7. In her account even the provenance of the surviving libretto pages is uncertain; the question of whether they are a Mahler autograph or a later copy by Alma is deliberately left open.

[24] HLG(F), i. 925–6.

Ex. 2.2. 'Hans und Grethe', bb. 1–19

suggests the world of Weber, E. T. A. Hoffmann, and Flotow, all of whom at various times turned to the story. That Mahler tackled the subject confirms an impression also to be gained from *Das klagende Lied* and *Lieder und Gesänge*, the sensation of deliberate anachronism which hangs over his first period, a sensation that is reinforced in the Schubertian plot of *Lieder eines fahrenden Gesellen*. The need to connect with a pre-Wagnerian musical past is not peculiar to Mahler (among his contemporaries Pfitzner revered Lortzing and Marschner as well as Weber, while Humperdinck's two principal stage works—*Hänsel und Gretel* of 1893 and *Königskinder* of 1910—stem at least as much from early Romantic models as Wagner). It is one of the strongest undercurrents among

German composers in the final decades of the nineteenth century and may suggest that the crushing influence of Wagner is to be seen at least as much in the manner in which composers sought to evade his example as in outright imitation of it. 'Hans und Grethe' is the most obvious case of an *alfresco* style in Mahler's songs involving modified strophic construction, diatonic melodies and harmonies, and four-square rhythmic periods. Chromaticism is confined to isolated moments, such as the Schubertian move to the flat side of the tonic (A flat in relation to F) near the climax of each strophe. The vocal part's alternative top Cs sit rather oddly with this cultivated rusticity but do not contradict the overall impression.

The tight control that Mahler exerts upon chromatic episodes is noteworthy in the other songs. In 'Frühlingsmorgen', he again prefers the Schubertian resort to the key of the flattened submediant (E flat in G major) as the main tonal excursion of a song otherwise lacking in significant modulation. 'Erinnerung' seems to be the main exception in that it has a more extensive use of chromaticism and structural modulation to the extent that it moves over its whole course from G minor to A minor; love awakens songs which come with the pangs of love so that songs in turn awaken love. But even this striking departure from tonal norms motivated by a literary conceit is not without Schubertian precedent, and songs such as 'Fahrt zum Hades' and 'Auf der Donau' (particularly the latter) seem more convincing models for Mahler's practice here than the instances in Schumann and Mussorgsky that Mitchell mentions.[25] To set against the chromatic episode with its expressive Wagnerian descent at the word '(Liebes-)klagen' (Ex. 2.3), there are also passages which move in the simplest diatonicism. This is confirmed in the archaisms of the Tirso de Molina settings, especially 'Phantasie', which has a modal flavour through its constant leaning to the dominant rather than the tonic at cadence points. Indeed the final bar of tonic is one of the few moments in any work by Mahler where he seems to lack the courage of his own convictions: here was a place which demanded an 'open' ending on the dominant rather than a tacked-on cadence.[26]

In *Lieder und Gesänge*, the tensions of *Das klagende Lied* are simplified into stylized gestures. While the pre-Wagnerian elements in the cantata dissolve into folk idioms, the tragic elements are to be found in the sighing appoggiaturas that punctuate 'Erinnerung' and (to a lesser extent) 'Serenade'. Mahler's distinctive tones are apparent in both, and also perhaps in two revealing details from 'Phantasie'. The world of the 'Wunderhorn' songs seems to be foretold in the whining repetitions of 'die Herzen' and in the combination of dominant harmony and Phrygian (flattened) second in bars 7–8 (Ex. 2.4). Stylized archaisms are often evident in mature Mahler, though curiously they are not treated as masks for the composer's own personality. Rather Mahler seems to sense the emotional power locked up in the clichéd gesture or tag and strives to release it on a larger scale. In

---

[25] Mitchell, *EY*, 222–4, 265–6, and 321, on which last page, last line, for DM¹ read DM².

[26] Songs which close on dominants or modally are not uncommon in Schumann (e.g. 'Im wunderschönen Monat Mai'; see Mitchell, *EY*, 223–4) and Wolf (e.g. 'Im Frühling' from the latter's Mörike set). Mahler himself later provided an even more striking example in 'Der Schildwache Nachtlied'. See also p. 72 and n below.

Ex. 2.3. 'Erinnerung', bb. 28–41

Ex. 2.4. 'Phantasie', bb. 7–16

his songs, such release seldom imperils the sense of structure imposed by the poem; in his symphonies, the strains and release of tension frequently seem alarmingly out of scale, a feature of his First Symphony in particular that has excited comment from Adorno and others.[27]

---

[27] Adorno, *Mahler*, 4–5.

Lieder eines fahrenden Gesellen and the First Symphony

The years in Kassel (1883–5) channelled the energies of Mahler's first compositions gradually towards the symphonic in two works, the lost incidental music for Scheffel's *Der Trompeter von Säckingen* and the song-cycle *Lieder eines fahrenden Gesellen*. Whether Mahler began to compose the symphony itself in Kassel in 1884, as some early Mahlerians suggested, is rather doubtful. When Fritz Löhr spoke of its 'beginnings' reaching back to 1884, he may only have been speaking of the satellite works, *Der Trompeter* and the song-cycle. Other sources suggest that its origins may go even further back, though all agree that the bulk of the work as it is now known was written in 1888.[28] The lack of any significant compositions in the years 1886–7 suggests that Mahler may have been working on the symphony in an earlier version than that first performed on 20 November 1889 in Budapest. An extended genesis would be compatible with the long process whereby both the First Symphony and *Lieder eines fahrenden Gesellen* (in its orchestral form) reached their final shape. At the Budapest première, the symphony was in five movements, the second being 'Blumine', later identified (at least in its beginnings) with a serenade from *Der Trompeter von Säckingen*. It retained this shape in subsequent performances in Hamburg (27 October 1893) and Weimar (3 June 1894). Not until a Berlin concert in 1896 (16 March) was the work performed in its familiar four-movement version. The theme from *Der Trompeter* thus played a constant part in the performance history of the First Symphony for some eight years. In earlier Mahler authorities there are also suggestions that music from *Rübezahl* was reused in the first movement of the symphony; La Grange has noted that the language of the *Rübezahl* libretto resembles lines from Mahler's poems from *Lieder eines fahrenden Gesellen*.[29] There is a considerable temptation to assume that Mahler's abortive and lost projects contributed towards his symphony in the manner that Berlioz's early works (such as the recently recovered *Messe solennelle)* provided ideas for several later, more characteristic pieces such as the *Symphonie fantastique*. Short of some major discoveries by Mahler researchers, this is liable to remain in the sphere of unprovable speculation. The case of *Lieder eines fahrenden Gesellen* is a much more tangible example of how Mahler gradually approached the writing of a symphony through the medium of a song-cycle on the most threadbare of myths.

The early history of Mahler's song-cycle is not without considerable problems relating to chronology (when was the cycle orchestrated?), musical content (it was originally to include six songs, not four), and text (which suggests a knowledge of *Des Knaben Wunderhorn* before 1888).[30] While all of these have a bearing on the cycle itself and in performance (particularly with piano), they remain tangential in any discussion of the cycle's relationship with the First Symphony. Donald Mitchell has suggested that some of the

---

[28] For the possibility of the symphony's having been begun in 1883, see Edward R. Reilly, *Gustav Mahler and Guido Adler: Records of a Friendship* (Cambridge: Cambridge University Press, 1982), 123; see also Mitchell, *EY*, 119 and 205 for an undated sketch for the scherzo; Fritz

Löhr's comment may be found in Mahler, *Selected Letters*, 400.

[29] HLG(F), i. 295.

[30] See above, n. 2.

cycle's music may actually have been orchestrated for the first time in the symphony.[31] Certainly Mahler recomposed the music of the cycle very carefully to fit its symphonic context. The text of the cycle is intriguing in that it compresses a tale of unrequited love into a series of Romantic attitudes. Although its resemblance to the themes of Schubert's two Müller song-cycles is fairly obvious in general, Mahler discards most of the circumstantial detail, the mill, brook, and huntsman of *Die schöne Müllerin*, the more inhuman cast of *Winterreise*, in favour of a small repertory of obsessive images.[32] Apart from the beloved and her two blue eyes, most of these belong to the world of *Lieder und Gesänge*, images of birds and flowers set against the burning dagger of grief. As a result, the contrast between an unalloyed diatonicism and a chromatic language of despair takes on a sharper form than in the earlier songs. 'Ich hab' ein glühend Messer' is the most pungent expression of frenzied grief in the cycle, but it, too, pauses to dream in the fields and to gaze into the heavens. The protagonist still sees the two blue eyes there, but the music for a moment swallows grief in the stillness of a musical pastorale with horn fifths and pedal effects. The sense of music becalmed which is to be found in many pages of 'Waldmärchen' and 'Der Spielmann' halts the headlong rush of the song to its catastrophe. The songs on either side expand this motionless music of nature into longer tableaux, each of which found its way into the First Symphony.

In creating the exposition of the First Symphony's opening movement, Mahler drew entirely on 'Ging heut Morgen über's Feld', a song in three strophes with a tonal structure that moves from D to B major. In reshaping it for symphonic use, he carefully worked into it a tonal structure based on D and A majors, the traditional tonic and dominant areas of the sonata-form exposition. The first subject group of the symphonic movement, although it begins with the main theme of the song and in the same key, actually owes more to the third strophe of the song than the first. The music of bars 84–108 (the continuation of the first subject) uses music from the concluding B major part of the song. Its first strophe is not used until bar 108 of the movement, when it appears as the second subject, transposed from the D major of the song to A major. Mahler follows an older classical practice in using the same head-motive (that sung to 'Ging heut Morgen über's Feld') for both subject groups but in different keys and with different continuations (corresponding to the so-called monothematic exposition of Haydn and, less frequently, Mozart). The impression therefore arises of a conventionally structured exposition, though it is created from a song that follows an unconventional tonal pattern. In the song, the drift from D to B is part of a dissolution into Nature that carries an increasingly regretful charge. The movement, on the other hand, points towards a conventional symphonic plot that only gradually takes on a much more radical appearance.

By contrast, the funeral March of the Symphony lifts the concluding strophe of the fourth song of *Lieder eines fahrenden Gesellen* more or less bar for bar and uses it as a

---

[31] Mitchell, *WY*, 246.

[32] Susan Youens, 'Schubert, Mahler and the Weight of the Past: *Lieder eines fahrenden Gesellen* and *Winterreise*', *Music & Letters*, 67 (1986), 256–68.

central episode (bb. 82–112). In her study of Mahler's use of songs and elements of songs in his symphonies, Monika Tibbe has noted that the melody of this episode is strongly folk-like, made up of melodic steps with occasional leaps: 'The melody for the most part is written homophonically in two or three voices in a narrow compass, and is continually accompanied by the same rhythm.'[33] Yet, as Tibbe notes, there are occasional chromatic and contrapuntal additions that stand outside the folk idiom as evidence of a more self-conscious creative personality. Between bars 96 and 102, the oboe shapes the descending chromaticism of 'Erinnerung' into a lamenting fall that colours the predominant diatonicism without disturbing the incessant drone of the bass (Ex. 2.5). The release of 'Waldmärchen' has shown that clearly recognizable elements of this episode had been invented by Mahler to evoke the forest landscape in which the younger brother fell asleep. In a passage which in retrospect strikes the Mahlerian as curious, the specifically diatonic music of the episode is combined, *inter alia*, with the music for 'Steh' auf, Langschläfer' in 'Frühlingsmorgen' (which thus achieves the curious distinction of being used in one work to depict falling asleep and in another as an awakening call).[34] The semantic of the episode thus develops from cantata to song-cycle; the music stands for a sleep of oblivion from which the blond hero of the cantata never wakes, but in which the hero of the cycle forgets the pain of life. Even grief is transfigured along with love, world, and dream. Significantly there is no equivalent to the oboe's lamenting line in the cantata, yet its plangent minor enclave within the prevalent major seems one of the most characteristically Mahlerian features of both the song and the symphonic movement. The fundamentally narrative sequence of events in the cantata is replaced with a much more layered approach in the later works, and in the layering resides the typical Mahler tone.

Ex. 2.5. First Symphony, Funeral March, bb. 96–102 (oboe)

---

[33] Monika Tibbe, *Lieder und Liedelemente in instrumentalen Symphoniesätzen Gustav Mahlers* (Berliner Musikwissenschaftliche Arbeiten, 1; Munich: Musikverlag Emil Katzbichler, 1971; 2nd edn., 1977), 80.
[34] See above, n. 22.

Ex. 2.6. First Symphony, Funeral March: (*a*) motive of bb. 109–12 (flutes) compared with (*b*) canonic theme

The transfer of the episode from song to symphony leaves a tiny loose end. In bars 110–12, flutes sound a motive that belongs to earlier events in the song but not at first sight to the funeral march (Ex. 2.6(*a*)). The join is suggestive of the way in which the First Symphony seems to have assembled its pre-existing elements. Yet in the context of the movement, the motive is not inappropriate. Its first three notes sound the same ascending scale degrees as the canonic theme of the march (Ex. 2.6(*b*)), a lucky chance that probably ensured the motive's survival. Rhythmically, too, it is not inappropriate in a funeral march.

The song from *Lieder eines fahrenden Gesellen* with least relevance in orchestral and thematic terms to the First Symphony is the first, with its melodic, harmonic, and orchestral colouring derived from Czech folk music. This, however, is probably the most intriguing song of the cycle on account of its sharp differentiation between the lively dance music of the woodwind and the lament of voice and strings. It is redolent of the layering of orchestra and off-stage band in *Das klagende Lied* but now transferred within the orchestra. Only in the orchestral version is the sensation of two intersecting planes of musical events effectively carried out, and it points towards experiments of greater complexity in several of the later symphonies. It is difficult to think of a comparable effect in the First Symphony save in the more conventionally theatrical use of off-stage fanfares. In this song at least, *Lieder eines fahrenden Gesellen* seems the more advanced and daring work.

The links between the song-cycle and the First Symphony are so strong that it is tempting to assume that the two works are also linked in content beyond the purely musical. Here the evidence is complex and hardly conclusive, but nonetheless intriguing, suggesting that the symphony took the music of the song-cycle but expanded its content into a wider context than an unhappy love affair. This is hardly the place to review the various forms that the programmatic hints and titles for the First Symphony took; they have been set out in detail by Mitchell and interpreted semantically by Floros.[35] It is sufficient to note that Mahler for a time avoided using the term symphony for the early performances, using 'Symphonic Poem' and the ponderous hybrid 'Tone poem in symphony-form'. The five-movement disposition of the work made it highly unlikely that anyone would confuse it with the symphonic poems of Liszt (most of which dated back to the mid-century) or the tone poems of Strauss (which were beginning to make their appearance). Although the term 'Symphony' was finally applied in Berlin in 1896, the Hamburg description of 'Tone poem in symphony-form' is quite a shrewd assessment of the work's intentions, since its form undeniably resembled a symphony while its content aspired to the poetic in senses that Schumann and Liszt would have understood. The withholding of a programme at the Budapest performance reinforced the parallel in some ways, since earlier composers of the nineteenth century had frequently allowed a programme to act as stimulus to composition and then withheld details to avoid the charge of having written illustrative music. But some details in Mahler's music have an almost cinematographic vividness: the sense of landscape at the start, the assorted dances of the Scherzo, the folk-music parodies of the funeral march, and the numerous fanfare passages. It is hardly surprising that poetic interpretations appeared quickly in print, such as that of August Beer in his review of the première, whose comments seemed to Floros to reflect Mahler's own thoughts.[36] Mahler's programmatic explanations of the 1890s reflect the lack of understanding with which the symphony was greeted in Budapest; to clarify his expressive intentions he fell back on the language of literary Romanticism.

Common to most of the programme drafts is the title *Titan*, usually taken to refer to the novel of that name by Jean Paul (Richter). But although Mahler was frequently quizzed as to the situations from the novel that might have inspired the title, he never went beyond the remark to Bruno Walter that the character of Roquairol influenced the funeral march.[37] The title, 'Blumen-, Frucht- und Dornenstücke', was used to group the first three movements into a single part in the programme at Hamburg and Weimar and this too refers to Jean Paul, specifically his novel *Siebenkäs*; even the title 'Blumine' for the second movement hints at Jean Paul's *Herbstblumine*. But no exact significance for these titles is to be

[35] Mitchell, *WY*, 158–9; Constantin Floros, *Gustav Mahler: The Symphonies*, trans. Vernon Wicker (London: Scolar, 1994), 29–32.

[36] Floros, *Gustav Mahler: The Symphonies*, 31.

[37] Bruno Walter, *Gustav Mahler*, trans. James Galston (New York: Vienna House, 1973), 137–8; see also Floros, *Gustav Mahler: The Symphonies*, 31–2.

found in the Mahler literature beyond suggestions as to Jean Paul's fondness for loosely structured form, which one writer on Mahler has interpreted as the forerunner of depth psychology and surrealism.[38] The events of Mahler's symphony make this a tantalizing clue, since it specializes in the apparent *non sequitur*, most obviously at the entry of the funeral march, a moment so out of character with what has gone before as to alter radically the perception of the whole symphony up to that point. Its subtitle in Hamburg, 'ein Todtenmarsch in "Callot's Manier" ', refers in its own way to Romantic models. Although the author of *Fantasiestücke in Callot's Manier* was E. T. A. Hoffmann, there remains a tiny link to Jean Paul in that he wrote the preface to the first edition of 1814.[39] The significance of the seventeenth-century engraver Jacques Callot to Hoffmann's collection of stories and essays was provided by Hoffmann himself, however, and helps to illuminate not only his intentions but possibly also Mahler's. Beginning with a reference to Callot's 'strange and fantastic pages', Hoffmann goes on to praise the wealth and colour of his 'most heterogeneous elements': 'No master has known so well as Callot how to assemble together in a small space such an abundance of motifs, emerging beside each other, even within each other, yet without confusing the eye, so that individual elements are seen as such, but still blend with the whole.'[40] The characteristics of Callot which Hoffmann most admired are 'exuberant fantasy' (which goes beyond any conventional rules), a 'uniquely vigorous physiognomy' which amounts to 'a certain romantic originality', and an irony that 'derides man with his paltry works and endeavours'. This is achieved by setting 'animal and man in conflict', an idea which may have brought the theme of the huntsman's funeral (as depicted by Moritz von Schwind) to Mahler's mind. Certainly he treats that subject (which is only mentioned in the Weimar programme) in the spirit which Hoffmann sees in Callot, employing 'grotesque forms' with the apparent intention (if the comparison with Roquairol is any clue) of revealing 'to the serious, deeper-seeing observer all the hidden meanings that lie beneath the cloak of absurdity'.[41]

Discontinuity, irony, and the grotesque are the characteristically Romantic modes whereby Mahler creates his singular symphony. By comparison, the other titles are less rich in associations, though that used for the first movement, 'Frühling und kein Ende', was interpreted in Hamburg and Weimar as an awakening of Nature that foreshadows the Third Symphony. The blanket title for the second part, 'Commedia humana', and that for the finale, 'Dall'Inferno al Paradiso', are conventional images that only take on resonance in the light of later works where the human comedy is more explicitly depicted (as in the 'Fischpredigt' of the Second Symphony). The dominant impression of Mahler's programmes is to reinforce the early Romantic strain common to all the works of his first period (and which continues into his discovery of *Des Knaben Wunderhorn*).

[38] Vladimir Karbusicky, *Gustav Mahler und seine Umwelt* (Darmstadt: Wissenschaftliche Buchgesellschaft, 1978), 70 and 80.

[39] David Charlton (ed.), *E. T. A. Hoffmann's Musical Writings: 'Kreisleriana', 'The Poet and the Composer', Music*

Criticism, trans. Martyn Clarke (Cambridge: Cambridge University Press, 1989), 31 and 51.

[40] Ibid. 76.

[41] Ibid. 76–8.

In the familiar four-movement version of the First Symphony, the element of discontinuity and irony emerges the more clearly for the absence of 'Blumine', which over-extends the pastorale-idyllic strain in the first movement. As with *Das klagende Lied*, Mahler's instinct to curtail was correct; while the occasional performance of the five-movement original is justified as an insight into the work's history, the revised score deserves to retain its status as the authoritative text. The character of the work in large measure depends on the manner in which Mahler reorientates traditional forms, especially in the outer movements. Not all writers on the symphony have favoured retaining the traditional categories of sonata form as a means of illuminating Mahler's procedures. But they still have a place if Helmuth Osthoff's emphasis on the extreme nature of the contrasts in the work (particularly in the third movement) is borne in mind.[42] In the first movement, the most curious aspects are the extent of the repeated introduction, the dwarfing of exposition and recapitulation, and the huge climax that emerges from nowhere. There are many examples in earlier symphonies, sonatas, and chamber works (particularly from late Beethoven onwards) of introductions which recur before or during the development section. What is unusual about Mahler's use of this device is its length. Equally curious is the tonal function of the double introduction. As in many classical symphonies, the introduction holds the key in suspense by its adherence to dominant harmony, represented in unusually extreme form by octave As sounded in a haze of harmonics at the start. So protracted a sounding of the dominant (which is recognized as such on occasions, as at the horn song at bar 32), makes the eventual entry of the 'Gesellen' theme in D all the more recognizable as the start to an exposition. But having modulated to A major in almost textbook fashion for the close of the exposition at Fig. 12, Mahler then resorts to the haze of A (less densely scored) to prepare D major once again at great length. The repeated introduction is not an exact recurrence, and the entry of the low pedal on F at Fig. 13 is a moment of intensification which corresponds to the introduction of new thematic material in the cellos (bb. 167 and 169–71). Mahler's exposition is largely lacking in thematic contrast, and the repeated introduction prepares for the emergence of new material (b. 221) in the development. Nonetheless, the scheme involves two extensive preparations of the tonic (three if the exposition repeat is observed) and a double image of the awakening of nature. This again corresponds to Mahler's later practice in the first movement of the Third Symphony, where the emergence of spring involves several returns to the inertia of the start. Effectively the exposition is experienced as a lyrical episode between two static tableaux.

Adorno spoke of a similar phenomenon in relation to the end of the movement. In his famous discussion of the climax and recapitulation he dignified the huge outburst at bar 352 as the 'breakthrough' of the introduction's shadowy world beyond the curtain of As, a moment of revelation that short-circuited the recapitulation; its correct sequence is disrupted (the new material from the repeated introduction precedes the 'Gesellen' theme) and the whole dwindles to the status of a mere epilogue.[43] Sonata form here becomes less

[42] Helmuth Osthoff, 'Zu Gustav Mahlers Erster Symphonie', *Archiv für Musikwissenschaft*, 28 (1971), 217–27 at 224.
[43] Adorno, *Mahler*, 4–14.

a schema for a movement than a collection of sub-genres that participate in a radical rethinking of the symphonic concept. In place of the motivic logic and development characteristic of such composers as Brahms, Mahler creates a series of startling contrasts. The music that prepares the breakthrough (which loses its quotation marks in Adorno as it moves from colourful metaphor to material category) is traceable to motives in the repeated introduction. But the harsh minor which emerges at bar 305 does not seem to grow naturally out of the context. Although we know that it is actually from the finale, this retrospective recognition does not legitimize its presence here; it should always be something of a shock in performance, a foretaste of the considerably greater shocks that the later movements have in store. It is thus not merely the shadowy 'beyond' of the introduction that breaks through in the first movement; the spiritual torments of the symphony's second half are also presented and set in immediate juxtaposition with the breakthrough itself.

The first movement effectively reunites the three streams leading away from *Das klagende Lied*. The operatic climaxes of the cantata, with the final Wagnerian apocalypse as the most extreme example, have survived their reduction to the more intimate scale and relatively conventional rhetoric of 'Ich hab' ein glühend Messer' and have acquired a new sharpness of contour while losing all operatic characteristics. It is not a paradox to say that it is the out-of-scale climax that announces the true scale of the work. In the introduction, the slow pulse of the typical Brucknerian opening is turned into a genuine suspension of movement, whose lengthy inertia is the balance to the apocalyptic 'breakthrough'. Between these extremes, the categories of sonata form are invaded by song-like material with a mildly popular flavour. The latter is intensified in the scherzo and rendered grotesque in the march. The combination is no longer dependent on a folk ballad. Mahler's symphonies from now on incorporate the voice episodically (apart from the Eighth Symphony and *Das Lied von der Erde*); his music no longer depends on the word for extended form. A keen sense of fantasy assembles 'an abundance of motives' in defiance of convention and presents them with a 'uniquely vigorous physiognomy'.[44] In a sense the whole symphony is 'in Callot's style'.

Ex. 2.7. First Symphony, 4th movt., bb. 370–5 (simplified)

C maj.: I (=V of F min.)   D maj.: I

[44] See above, n. 41.

The finale is similarly cavalier in its handling of the sonata. The violent paragraphs of the first subject group are recapitulated in a scurrying *pianissimo* and lead directly into the climax of the first movement. The extended second subject is repeated before the first, but as a half-recollected fantasy. Above all, the tonal scheme departs radically from the norm, beginning in a violent F minor that leaps to D major through a progression (Ex. 2.7) as monstrously unexpected as that between the last two of Beethoven's 'Diabelli' Variations. That tonal motion has already been suggested in the climax of the first movement and is heard later in the coda of the finale. Again, the idea of a half-remembered experience hangs over the work, as if something unthinkingly encountered was being rethought, in terms at first half, then wholly, understood. The theme of the symphony's introduction returns as a chorale that Natalie Bauer-Lechner described in 1900 as an overcoming in death.[45] This does not quite tally with Mahler's own elucidations to her at roughly the same time.

Originally, Mahler had called his First Symphony 'Titan'. But he has long ago eradicated this title, and all other superscriptions of his works, because he found that people misinterpreted them as indications of a programme. For instance, they connected his 'Titan' with Jean Paul's. But all he had in mind was a powerfully heroic individual, his life and suffering, struggles and defeat at the hands of fate. 'The true, higher redemption comes only in the Second Symphony.'[46]

Remarks about the Second Symphony by Mahler tend to confirm this contrast between the earthly drama of the First and the redemption of the Second.[47] Whether this should cause us to view the triumph of the close of the First Symphony as a more temporal overcoming than Natalie suggests is coloured by Mahler's own use of 'Dall'Inferno al Paradiso' as a title for the finale, but it is perfectly natural to consider these images (more cliché than Dante) as metaphors for the highs and lows of an earthly human comedy. However Mahler intended the last movement's progression to paradise to be viewed, the two inner movements represent more completely consummated experiences. In the scherzo, the idioms of 'Hans und Grethe' return with more individual thematic material, and Mahler begins his long obsession with revealing the ancestry of the waltz in the Ländler. The earthiness of the latter has its profile sharpened in the brittle timbres of a deliberately rustic woodwind, who are encouraged to raise their bells in pursuit of a coarser tone to balance the raucous and frequently stopped (or muted) brass tone. The trio sets this against an idealized waltz material whose elegance reveals an alarming streak of the grotesque in the *portamento* and *glissandos* of the strings. When Mahler sets waltz and Ländler in opposition to each other, as here or in the Fifth and Ninth Symphonies, it becomes difficult to distinguish the elements of parody from the ideal. Neither Mahler's nor Natalie's programmatic elucidations help with this problem, indeed they seem to imply that the essence of this scherzo is the expression of an unalloyed positivism.[48] It is only through the experience of Mahler's later scherzos that this revelling in the energy of folk idioms seems to have something about it that is larger than life. Nonetheless, the First Symphony's scherzo is the first of those move-

---

[45] NB-L, *Recollections*, 240.   [46] Ibid. 157.   [47] See Mahler, *Selected Letters*, 180.
[48] See e.g. NB-L, *Recollections*, 239–40.

ments (of which the scherzo of the Fifth is the largest) in which the energy of the dance is a metaphor for the life force of an all-encompassing universe.

The strain of the grotesque or the fantastic that is already present in the scherzo dominates the march. Whether the listener keeps the image of the huntsman's funeral in mind is in a sense irrelevant to the experience of the three types of music in this movement. Again the act of placing two quite distinct parodies alongside a vision of life without pain is the truly original facet of the movement regardless of stylistic discrepancy. The incessant canon on 'Brüder Martin' could hardly be a more potent image of 'the world's sorrow . . . with its sharp contrasts and hideous irony'.[49] In resorting to so tangible an image, Mahler renders such factors as style and taste irrelevant. In true Romantic fashion, the ironizing symbol attacks the more rationally considered requirements of musical ceremonial. When the vulgarities of the 'Bohemian' band enter at Fig. 5, the irony becomes the sharper as Mahler for once comes close to melodic idioms that suggest the world of Central and Eastern European Jewry, elements of whose music scholars have chased in his works without firm conclusion since Max Brod's celebrated article.[50] Mahler's music has become part of the contemporary experience to such an extent that this episode stands out by its evocation of a vanished world. It is now impossible to listen to such music without a reminder of the pain of its grotesque parody. It is at once a drastic contrast with the 'Gesellen' episode and a justification for the chromatic lamentation in the oboe with which Mahler decorated the diatonic music from 'Waldmärchen'.[51] The funeral march transcends the merely programmatic with its conventional talk of heroes and their sufferings and wrestling with fate. Its vulgarity is a touchstone. It is the most extreme form in the symphony of Mahler's capacity for writing a music that functions as a kind of metaphor. Its content is not a reflection of operatic or folk origins (which remain as a kind of residue within the material). Rather, it stands for an ironic questioning which sees the 'hidden meanings that lie beneath the cloak of absurdity'.[52] The history of Mahler's works in performance in the twentieth century has added to that stock of meanings in ways that only reinforce the remarkable contrasts and juxtapositions of which they are created. Whatever the programmes that Mahler envisaged for his First Symphony, history has provided the funeral march's 'banalities' with a subtext that extends beyond the symphony to areas of experience that can no longer be said to lie outside the framework of art and aesthetics.

[49] Ibid. 240.

[50] Max Brod, *Gustav Mahler: Beispiel einer deutsch-jüdischen Symbiose* (Frankfurt am Main: Ner-Tamid Verlag, 1961), 20 and 30.

[51] The first recording of the original version of *Das klagende Lied* in three parts was made in 1997 by soloists, Hallé Orchestra and Choir, conducted by Kent Nagano (Erato 3984-21664-2). The documentation which accompanies the recording represents a significantly revised version of the Programme Book published on the occasion of the première of 7 October 1997 at Bridgewater Hall, Manchester, the contributors to which were Herta Blaukopf, Reinhold Kubik and Donald Mitchell.

[52] Charlton (ed.), *E. T. A. Hoffman's Musical Writings*, 76–7.

3

Mahler and *Des Knaben Wunderhorn*

PAUL HAMBURGER

Throughout the nineteenth century composers of the German Lied entered into an ever-deepening relationship with their chosen poetry. What in the Lieder of Haydn and Mozart had often been fortuitous, though fortunate, encounters between a poetic and a musical sensibility took the form of a stable marriage of minds in the cases of Schumann/Heine, Schumann/Eichendorff, Wolf/Mörike, Wolf/Goethe—and even Brahms/Daumer. The *Gesamtkunstwerk* of Wagner—with its unity of words, music, and stage—became the ideal of an artistic generation emulating the growing organization and effectiveness of commerce and the sciences. Mahler, the great opera conductor who wisely refused to compose operas under the shadow of Wagner, needed and acquired, from Nietzsche and other sources, a supply of poetico-philosophical energy in order to create symphonies which were (as he said to Sibelius in Helsinki in 1907) 'like the world . . . all-embracing'.[1] In the realm of the lyrical miniature too, an energizing, unifying force was needed. A well-planned oeuvre of about fifty songs, paralleling the vaster edifice of the ten symphonies, could not have been founded on casual premises. Mahler turned to two poetic sources: first, the folk verses of *Des Knaben Wunderhorn* (on which his own texts to *Lieder eines fahrenden Gesellen* are closely modelled), which are associated with Symphonies 1–4; and second, the lofty poetry of Friedrich Rückert, which accompanied him from *Kindertotenlieder* to *Das Lied von der Erde*.

The title *Des Knaben Wunderhorn* ('Youth's Magic Horn'), refers to the frontispiece of the first volume (1806), which shows a boy on a horse holding a hunting-horn over his head. Though this points to the opening poem of the volume, a better image of the entire book's Romantic range is furnished by Moritz von Schwind's famous painting of a recumbent youth lifting up a kind of cornucopia from which myths and legends might be flowing. *Des Knaben Wunderhorn* is a collection of folk poetry, gathered by the poets Achim von Arnim (1781–1831) and Clemens Brentano (1778–1842) during their journeys on the Rhine and its tributaries, published in Heidelberg (then the centre of the Romantic move-

---

[1] See Erik Tawaststjerna, *Sibelius*, ii: *1904–1914*, trans. Robert Layton (Berkeley and Los Angeles: University of California Press, 1986).

ment in German literature) in 1805, and in an enlarged edition—running to some thousand specimens—in 1808.

These books of folk poetry represent the apogee of a movement which, distrusting the Age of Enlightenment and the dire political consequences arising from its enforced rationality, sought refuge in the demotic, the anonymous, the quaint, and the mystical. Taking the poetry of Ossian and Bishop Percy's *Reliques of Ancient English Poetry* as their models, the German Romantics reacted against the influence of French culture—particularly the Encyclopedists, and the upheavals of the Revolution and the Napoleonic wars—in the hope that a return to national wellsprings would speed the far-off unification of Germany. In his theoretical writings, the poet, collector, and translator Johann Gottfried Herder (1744–1803)—perhaps the most articulate voice of the nascent *Sturm und Drang* movement—distinguished between *Naturpoesie* and *Kunstpoesie*, the poetry of Nature and the poetry of Art, deeming the former superior and preferable to the latter. Even the young Goethe, during his Strasburg days, proudly announced to Herder in 1771 that he had lately 'plucked songs from the mouths of little old ladies'. Thirty years later, in 1806, when he had become Germany's greatest classicist and an Olympian figure, he reviewed the publication of *Des Knaben Wunderhorn* in terms partly nostalgic, partly condescending, and partly teasing. He opined that every family in German lands should own a copy, keeping it where they kept their cookery books and hymnals, and dipping into it at regular intervals in the certainty of finding a text to suit any mood. More seriously, he suggested that the piano should be its repository for musicians to match the poems to old tunes, or to invent new ones, so that in time the little volume would fulfil its purpose and return, enlivened by music, to the people.

But the future of the *Wunderhorn* collection did not turn out quite as Goethe had anticipated. It was not the amateur who became interested, but the professional composer—Schumann, Mendelssohn, Brahms, and above all Mahler. These craftsmen, and indeed intellectuals, extracted the *Naturpoesie* from the texts, clothing it in an attractive mixture of populism and sophistication, and thus reaching it out to the educated and mostly well-to-do middle classes.

It was a known fact, already exposed by the more 'scientific' brothers Grimm, that in their editing Arnim and Brentano had not scrupled to appropriate so-called folk poetry from identifiable, printed sources, nor had they had any compunction in telescoping discrete verses into manufactured units, often tuning down the roughness of the (vernacular) vocabulary and in fact interspersing verses entirely of their own making. Yet these, to a modern philologist, nightmarish shenanigans, actually helped in arousing the interest of nineteenth-century composers who, while welcoming the occasional verbal awkwardness or logical non sequitur left untouched by the editors, would have baulked at the uncouthness of the unadulterated originals. For their own part, the two collectors—who were also considerable poets in their own right—would have countered the reproach of 'cheating' by insisting that their overriding aim had been to revive the *Volksseele* slumbering in the breast of all good Germans, and that their communication had to be pegged at the level of easy receptivity on the part of the ordinary reader—a principle not unlike the practice of twentieth-century PR men. Brentano, the better poet, had wanted to split the publication into a North German and a South German part, so as to cater for the different ethos of each area; Arnim, however—scion of an old Prussian *Junker* family—disagreed with the idea as being detrimental to the book's pan-German propaganda drive. But they were at one in their urgent wish that by reading, reciting, and singing these poems German resistance to the Napoleonic armies should be stiffened. The years of publication of the small and the large collection, 1805 and 1808, span the complete subjugation of Austria and Prussia by Napoleon. The first *Wunderhorn* edition—though dated 1806 on the title-page—actually appeared in September 1805, a few weeks before the disastrous defeat of the Austrians at Austerlitz on 2 December 1805.

What, then, was the attraction of the *Wunderhorn* poems for Mahler? It was their mixture of realism and fantasy, the commonplace and the extraordinary, the tragic and the humorous, the coy and the glum—qualities found in neighbouring poems as well as sometimes cheek by jowl within a single poem. This evoked an instant response in a mind whose sophistication yearned for the balm of simplicity; an acute intelligence in matters not only artistic but also practical, longing for the healing touch of instinctiveness. The cosmopolitan in Mahler, the self-made man of high ambition and inflexible morality, was confronted here by an imagery outside his high-principled daily conduct as a creator and conductor. He was charmed by the book's naive insistence on stereotypes, its humour, in turn sensitive, pawky, sarcastic, and eerie, its saga-like inconsequentiality in matters of plot, cause, and effect, and even choice of grammatical tenses and unannounced shifts in the speaking voice. Add to this the many stories describing a soldier's life with cruel realism and again with compassion, the portraits of youngsters insecure or insolent in their first love, the birds that can talk, the fishes that listen, the rings that float in water, the bugles that blare out of graves, and you have a book of fairy tales to be set to music by a child of genius.

In his book *Gustav Mahler: The Wunderhorn Years*, Donald Mitchell has a closely argued chapter dealing with the difficulty of dating the two dozen *Wunderhorn* settings. He also speculates on Mahler's first acquaintance with the book. These are the facts: during his conductorship at Leipzig (1886–7) Mahler met Hauptmann von Weber, grandson of Carl Maria, the composer, and was shown Weber's sketches for a comic opera, *Die drei Pintos*, which Mahler subsequently reconstructed and completed. In the Weber household he was shown a copy, much used by the children, of *Des Knaben Wunderhorn*, and, as Mitchell says, became aware of 'the musical potentialities of the *Wunderhorn* texts'.[2] But there is evidence that Mahler had known the collection since early days, further borne out by the fact that in *Lieder eines fahrenden Gesellen*, which precedes the first *Wunderhorn* settings, Mahler's own verses lean closely on some specific *Wunderhorn* texts.

---

[2] Mitchell, *WY*, 115.

The Songs for Voice and Piano

The first batch of nine *Wunderhorn* settings dates from 1887–91; unlike the twelve later settings (1892–6), they are for voice and pianoforte, though the orchestral intentions of this great orchestrator, the sounds perceived by his inner ear, are ever-present. Together with five earlier songs based on different poetry, these nine *Wunderhorn* songs were published by Schott of Mainz in February 1892 as *Lieder und Gesänge für eine Singstimme und Clavier*, the words 'aus der Jugendzeit' being added to later editions to distinguish these fourteen songs from the subsequent orchestral *Wunderhorn* settings as well as from *Kindertotenlieder* (1901–4) and the five Rückert songs (1901–2).

As there is no particular performance order in this set, and certainly no story line running through the assembly of diverse characters, I shall discuss the songs as they appear in most editions. English titles and some line translations are taken from Deryck Cooke's outstanding and concise *Gustav Mahler: An Introduction to his Music* (London: Faber, 1980).

'Um schlimme Kinder artig zu machen' (To teach naughty children to be good)

This little homily in Swabian dialect is delicious music, with its comically plodding hoof-steps and crudely Alpine harmony sharpened up by 'knowing' dissonances: but will it convert a naughty child? The friendly toff on his (almost hobby) horse coming before the castle asking the chatelaine whether her children are good or naughty is more credible to adults than to kids, with his 'ku-ku-kuk, ku-ku-kuk' interspersing his queries; and that's where the fun lies. It is a very regular two-strophe song, the prancing introduction also serving as interlude and, writ large, as postlude. So the mother's rejoinder that the children 'are wicked, are wicked—they won't obey their mother', as well as the knight's predictable refusal to give any goodies to such disobedient children, becomes a put-up job, again delighting the grown-ups, but teaching no lesson to children until such time, that is, when they might have offspring of their own. Meanwhile, they may be amused by the stuttery bass quavers of the piano part coming as close as can be to the oompah, oompah of a bass tuba.

'Ich ging mit Lust durch einen grünen Wald' (Happily I walked through a green wood)

It is amazing what atmosphere a great composer can conjure up with a simple D major arpeggio and bits of the D major scale (see Ex. 3.1).

Within eight bars we take in the depth of the wood (in the bass), the height of the trees (in the rising triad), the walker pricking up his ears, and, in the piano's twiddly bits, the birdsong. Inspiration continues in the coyly mysterious turn to the parallel minor,

Ex. 3.1. 'Ich ging mit Lust durch einen grünen Wald', bb. 1–10

particularly fetching on 'when no one is in the street, then come to me', and in the third verse, 'Are you asleep or awake, my child?'. These phrases should be sung with the smiling insouciance of a happy lover, bouncing his knuckle, in *siciliano* rhythm, against the beloved's door.

Owing to folkloristic (deliberate?) carelessness in matters of punctuation, the second stanza may cause confusion: after the swain's exhorting the nightingale to sing to the girl, she herself, across the missing quotation marks, invites the boy to visit her when darkness has fallen ('Komm schier . . . ', 'schier' being an old form of 'bald', i.e. 'soon').

Performers of this song should transport us to a sleeping village in midsummer, nestling among the hilly, moon-dappled pinewoods. Nor should the fourth, final strophe turn ominous in any way: the unchangingly serene music tells us that despite the girl's sleeping through her lover's gentle knocking, there will be another night, another meeting.

'Aus! Aus!' (Finished! Finished!)

This half-tearful, half-mocking farewell of a boy raring to march out of town with his comrades, and a sad girl fearing to lose her lover for ever, is the first of several military 'confrontations' between a headstrong youth with itchy feet and a disconsolate girl. The boy's oft-repeated words 'Today we'll march, hurrah, hurrah, in May so green! Tomorrow we'll march through the high gate!' are set to a crude, callous trumpeting motive ('Keckes Marschtempo' is indicated), and his later assurance that 'our love is not yet finished', sung softly against the continuing drumbeats of the left hand, sounds pure bunkum. Nor are the girl's protestations, to be sung 'kläglich' ('plaintively'), to be taken quite at face value. She avers that she will enter a nunnery in a sobbing, chromatic harmony that is a parody of deep, lasting grief.

'Starke Einbildungskraft' (Strong Imagination)

This little half-serious, half-teasing exchange between two teenagers (the boy goes under the charming diminutive of 'Büble') calls to mind the sparring couples found in many of the Tuscan *rispetti* on which Wolf's *Italian Songbook* is based. The girl starts, poutingly voicing her disappointment: 'Hast gesagt, du willst mich nehmen, sobald der Sommer kommt.' There is a pun here on 'nehmen', meaning (decently) to propose marriage and (more crudely) to tumble a lass—an ambiguity absent in the English 'to take'. So when the Büble, in answer to her reproach that he hasn't 'taken her', replies 'How should I take you when I already have you all the time', he is equivocating, yet turns insolence into compliment by assuring her that whenever he thinks of her he feels he's already with her: marriage bells are ringing though as yet in the distance.

Mahler's superscription 'Sehr gemächlich, mit humoristischem Austruck' ('very leisurely, with humorous expression') tells the pianist to observe the many mock-bumptious staccato marks, accents, and dynamic changes. The singer is faced with the tricky task of changing from girlish to boyish petulance, without sounding downright offensive in either. It can be done!

'Zu Straßburg auf der Schanz' (On the Ramparts of Strasburg)

As Donald Mitchell points out,[3] this is of a type very characteristic of Mahler in his vocal as well as symphonic output: the slow farewell song or funeral march. The species, sharing strong emotional and structural features, begins with 'Die zwei blauen Augen', the final song of *Lieder eines fahrenden Gesellen*, and proceeds via the present song to 'Nicht Wiedersehen', and then to both 'Wenn dein Mütterlein' and the final lullaby of *Kindertotenlieder*, and even to parts of 'Der Abschied' in *Das Lied von der Erde*.

Here, however, we have a relatively simple example of the kind, remarkable chiefly for the piano's imitation of the 'Schalmei', the chalumeau or herdsman's pipe, which lures the homesick soldier into swimming the Rhine by night. There is also the imitation, in the left hand, of the military drums that accompany his capture, his conviction as a deserter, and the march to his execution. Mahler explicitly instructs the right hand to play 'like a

---

[3] Mitchell, *WY*, 125–6 and 144–6.

chalumeau', and notes for the left: 'In all those low trills the sound of muted drums is to be imitated by means of the pedal', a clear indication that he was moving towards a song form with orchestra.

There is also the curious turn to the major towards the end when, as in the much later 'Revelge', the man addresses his comrades as 'Brothers' who 'pass by unheeding' or, as in the present case, 'see me today for the last time', the major mode, combined with the inexorable marching rhythms, standing for the doomed man's touching recognition of the mute sympathy and powerlessness of his brothers-in-arms.

Like all the songs of this genre, 'Zu Straßburg' asks for a high baritone with a technique solid and flexible enough not to buckle under the extreme and varying demands made by Mahler's copious annotations of the voice part, not least of which is the *pp* head voice needed for the ghostly final section.

'Ablösung im Sommer' (The Changing of the Summer Guard)

This fantastic fairy tale of a song was, during 1895–6, to become the material for the Scherzo of the Third Symphony, Mahler's pantheistic hymn which, in a programmatic draft he later discarded, he called 'The Happy Life, a Midsummer Night's Dream (not after Shakespeare)'. Appearing between 'What the flowers of the meadow tell me' and 'What the child tells me', this particular movement was to be called 'What the cuckoo tells me'.

And indeed, the cuckoo is prominent in the song. Having collided with a willow tree, he has fallen to his death, which is a pity, for who should now pass away the time for us all summer long? But wait, there is Frau Nightingale waiting in the wings, with a wing and a song. She will be an admirable substitute; and once the short-winded, cackling noises of the cuckoo in the voice and his clodhopping in the accompaniment have gone, then the prima donna appears, warbling her trills and runs in bushes, just like Thomas Hardy's nightingales in his poem 'Proud Songsters', who 'pipe, as they can when April wears, as if all Time were theirs'. Yet like Britten in his setting of 'Proud Songsters', Mahler too puts most of the coloraturas into the pianist's glittering treble line (Ex. 3.2).

'Scheiden und Meiden' (Farewell and Forgo)

Together with two songs from Volume I to words by Leander, this was performed in Budapest on 13 November 1889 by Bianca Bianchi, a distinguished member of Mahler's Budapest Opera team, who was 'very discreetly accompanied by Director Mahler at the piano . . . to lively applause, and with Mr Mahler was repeatedly called back'. Thus wrote the critic of the *Pester Lloyd*.[4] While a little critical of supposed discrepancies between words and music in the other songs, the same reviewer found that in 'Scheiden und Meiden' the 'right note is struck . . . ; this is kept in the manner of a genuine folk-song, and

---

[4] Quoted in Mitchell, *WY*, 156.

Ex. 3.2. 'Ablösung im Sommer', b. 47

only at the end is one a little distracted by the artistically handled vocal part which, almost *alla concertante*, floats up two octaves'.[5]

Clearly he refers here to the four times repeated top Gs (hardly two octaves!) on the word 'Ade!', which actually form the peak of the climactic coda. The eventful compression of the song is dictated by the urgency of the early morning canter of the three riders out of town, past the window of the singer's sweetheart. In this crowded space Mahler manages to accommodate three moods: one a bold farewell gesture towards the girl while the hooves

⁵ Ibid.

Ex. 3.3. 'Scheiden und Meiden', bb. 21–8

thunder on in relentless dotted rhythm (see Ex. 3.3); one reflecting on the words 'Yes, to say farewell and forgo causes pain!', where the dotted rhythm momentarily ceases; and another, *with* the rhythm but in a muted piano in the tonic minor, first clothing the words 'If then we have to part . . .', then, rather eerily, 'the child in the cradle says already farewell'. Needless to say, this song asks for an accomplished singer who can speedily react to its quick-changing moods.

'Nicht wiedersehen' (Never to meet again)

This is another of the sombre marching songs mentioned in connection with 'Zu Straßburg' above. Moreover, it is what the Germans call 'eine Moritat'; a lugubrious street ballad of so ominous an opening that its tragic end is foreseen at once. The boy takes leave of his sweetheart; but when, as promised, he returns the following summer, he is told she was buried three days ago, killed off by grief and tears. So far the song has been a heavy-hearted march in C minor, but at this point, in the manner of folk poetry, direct speech enters into the boy's plaint, and this soon effects a change of the music into a C major, which is, if anything, even more heart-rending than the preceding minor. Here the boy goes to the churchyard and asks his darling to open her grave to him for a last farewell.

This could have turned out a cloying tear-jerker, but such is Mahler's economy of means that the bitterness, far from swamping the listener, has to be extracted by him, sucked out, as it were, from the sparse, potent chromatic chords.

'Selbstgefühl' (Self-assurance)

A quaint final song, taking a sarcastic swipe at a hypochondriac. Speaking in the first person, the odd fellow says: 'I don't know what's the matter with me. I'm not ill and I'm not well. I'd like to eat, but nothing tastes good. I have some money, but don't care for it. I'd like to marry, but can't stand the bawling of children. Only today I asked the doctor, and he said "I know quite well what's the matter with you—you are a fool!" Ah, that's it, then!' And, as often when an imaginary sufferer is given the label of a complaint, he feels better at once. Mahler's musical humour is up to it; after the querulous grouses depicted in the form of a rather crazy, tottering Ländler, the relief of the 'patient' is made obvious by a fatuous bleat and a few skips in the air.

The Orchestral Songs

The second group of ten songs from *Des Knaben Wunderhorn* spans the years 1892–8. The first five were originally entitled 'Humoresken' (see below, p. 189 and p. 339 n. 5) and included 'Wir geniessen die himmlischen Freuden' which was to become the finale ('Das himmlische Leben') of the Fourth Symphony, which itself—at an early planning stage— was thought of by Mahler as a 'Humoreske'. This last song, together with the two late and substantial *Wunderhorn* songs, 'Revelge' and 'Der Tamboursg'sell', composed in 1899 and 1901, are discussed elsewhere in this volume in the context of the relevant symphonies. The ten songs were first published by Josef Weinberger in Vienna in 1900.

The ten songs dealt with here were conceived with orchestral accompaniment, although Mahler's own playable and publishable pianoforte versions always preceded his eventual scoring for a chamber orchestra of varying constituents. Nor are the pianoforte versions mere props for study: as Donald Mitchell tells us, there is in the Berlin Staatsbibliothek a manuscript 'of the voice and piano versions of some of the best known of the *Wunderhornlieder*, in Mahler's own hand', often containing metronome marks that do not appear in the printed scores.[6]

Although it means missing out on Mahler's miraculous orchestrations, performances with pianoforte accompaniment are thus perfectly viable. Relating to the full score like a master drawing to the subsequent oil painting, they have the advantage of clarifying the weave of the leading, subsidiary, and contrapuntal lines, and a good pianist should be able

---

[6] Mitchell, *WY*, 423–6.

to imply by tone and phrasing much of the orchestral timbres. Besides, orchestral performances are often slapdash for lack of rehearsal time, and/or palpable disagreement
between singer and conductor, whereas voice-cum-piano performances are usually better
prepared.

'Der Schildwache Nachtlied' (Sentry's Nightsong)

This eerie dialogue between a soldier on sentry duty, stubbornly sticking to his post, and
his girl—or is it just a phantom?—holding out the blandishments of love, is one of
Mahler's most gripping military songs. Written for fairly large orchestra, which, however,
is used economically in chamber groupings, the cheerlessness and obstinacy of the soldier is rendered by brass, woodwind and timpani, and an array of percussion instruments,
while the invitations of the girl tempting him to a tryst in the rose garden, in the green
clover, are given to cor anglais and clarinet and muted strings. In his third speech, the
sentry, half-crazed, rejects the girl's commendation of trust in God's help by pronouncing
God the supreme warlord, a king, an emperor under whose command he acts. Example
3.4 shows the quite frightening climax of the song, where the brass brays and the percussion snarls. It needs a superb singer-actor to change from this to the disembodied
banks of mist of the final page, '. . . forlorn, a sentry sang it at midnight . . .'. But an oper-
atically schooled baritone should be able to cope with what Mahler, here and in other
'duets', certainly meant to be a one-voice effort.[7] On the other hand, the fashionable
farming out between two voices also has some merits, the chief being that these songs
become more accessible to a public conditioned by the plausibility of stereo recordings
and modern opera productions. (Original key B flat major.)

'Verlor'ne Müh' (Wasted Effort)

Another wee-lass/wee-laddie confrontation, like 'Starke Einbildungskraft'. She makes
him tempting offers: 'go and see our lambkins? nibble some sweets from my pocket? Also,
my heart is for the taking, will you help yourself?' But every time she gets the brush-off:
'Stupid young thing, I don't want you!' Yet, as in the earlier song, the Ländler rhythm,
comfortably rolling along in an almost unbroken A major, garlanded by little rustic fiddle
figures, precludes too serious a view of this song. Even the boy's rudeness does not come
over aggressively, but more as if cocking a snook at her (Ex. 3.5). In the manuscript of
Mahler's little collection of *Wunderhorn* versions with piano mentioned above, there are
some metronome marks. This song has quaver = 132, which makes it very cosy, sunny,
laid-back. (Original key A major.)

---

[7] The view very strongly expressed by Donald Mitchell (*WY*, 260 n. 34). As a coach, ambitious to stretch my singers, I agree; as a Mahlerian propagandist, I don't. Mitchell also writes about this song's arresting close on the dominant in his chapter 'Mahler and Smetana: Significant Influences or Accidental Parallels?', in Hefling (ed.), *Mahler Studies*, 110–21. See also p. 49 above.

Ex. 3.4. 'Der Schildwache Nachtlied', bb. 65–76

Ex. 3.5. 'Verlor'ne Müh', bb. 23–35

'Trost im Unglück' (Consolation in Misfortune)

Like 'Verlor'ne Müh', this quarrel between the sexes—here a hussar and an older, self-reliant girl—has its predecessor in 'Aus! Aus!' of the earlier collection. They lay into each other with a will—perhaps to deaden the pain of parting? He is saddling his horse with obvious determination, telling her that he loves her only from foolishness, and the sooner he's off, the better. To which she retorts that he is wrong if he believes himself a fine specimen of manhood, and that she too was a fool to have fallen for him. But the last word is his, and it's really hurtful: he's ashamed of her when in company.

In this charming set-to, he has the wilder music, with strings scraping their bows up and down in a choppy 6/8 rhythm, and side drum, triangle, and timpani going full blast. This song too has an authentic metronome mark, crotchet = 100, which, though a little brisk, is fine, as long as Mahler's 'Etwas mäßiger' ('A little slower'), as appears in the piano version, is observed. *Her* music, while not being exactly gentle, is petulant rather than insulting, and the instruction 'in a weepy tone' makes the hidden feelings behind the brazen words very clear. (Original key A major.)

'Wer hat dies Liedlein erdacht?' (Who made up this little song?)

Mahler's metronome marking of quaver = 160 gives me pause. Many of his songs are habitually taken too fast by sundry conductors, but even the worst speedmongers would not let this countrified, yodelling ditty hurtle along at such a lick. I humbly submit that the composer made a mistake when handling his metronome on this occasion. I myself—and most conductors—would be happy to amble along at quaver = 144.

As in some other *Wunderhorn* settings ('Das irdische Leben', 'Des Antonius von Padua Fischpredigt'), Mahler here sets up a lilting semiquaver chain winding its way round the (mainly) quaver movement of this 3/8 Ländler, and whose curves, trailing up and down, follow every change of mood.

The text of this song has been written off as 'charming nonsense', 'a children's fable'—but on closer inspection, it is not all that incoherent. Let us search out the implications. It is obviously about a lad whose sweetheart has 'gone astray', at least for the moment. He stands at the foot of the hill, looking up at the 'high house', or castle or manor, noticing his girl looking out of the window (the harmony tells us how pretty she is). But (a baffled, dissonant C#) she is not at home there. In fact (ha! that explains it) she is the innkeeper's daughter. But does daddy ply his trade in the village? Oh no, he and his charming daughter live 'on the green heath', out there where the riff-raff and the smugglers meet (great, swinging bass line, overlaid by fancy-free, hollering coloraturas).

So she has moved in with the squire, has she? The lad stands there bamboozled, almost admiring such cheek. But then, in a new, calmer key, he flops and bleats: 'My heart is so sick'—and, trying to jolly her along: 'Be a sport, and make it well!' And then, over a chromatically urging bass, he blurts out a whole catalogue of her supposed powers: her rosy lips can cure the sick, can even revive the dead. Yet that's enough now of self-abasement; with Mahler returning to the home key, the lad returns to the basic fact of her falsehood. So who has told him (and probably the village) this story of common laxity? Three geese have brought it over the water—and there they come flying in, with repeated wing-beats in the music, and stretching out their necks in a series of seven hissing top Fs, over a menacing chromatic bass, whistling their story to anyone who cannot sing it (i.e. behave properly) (see Ex. 3.6). And who are these geese, two grey and one white? Why, they are the populist

Ex. 3.6. 'Wer hat dies Liedlein erdacht?', bb. 77–85

version of the three Greek furies pursuing the guilty; and perhaps not the least of their threats is that they'll 'bite the girl in the leg', as is done more usually in German folklore by the stork announcing pregnancy. (Original key F major.)

'Das irdische Leben' (Earthly Life)

Another song with a continuous ostinato of semiquavers, but in character very different from the last. This is another 'Moritat', making us foresee the tragic end right from the start. A mother is trying to comfort her hungry child with the prospect of food, first after reaping, then after threshing, then after baking; but when at last the bread is baked, the child lies dead on the bier. Here, the unquiet, unceasing figuration stands for earthly labour and its inevitable futility; one could almost say that this catastrophe befalling an innocent child points to humanity tangling up its lines of communication with the Holy Spirit.

The singer needs two voices, one for the child's recurring, and ever more anxious 'Mother, oh mother, how hungry I am! Give me bread or I shall die!'; another voice for mother making promises, first soothing, then on the same notes, with increasing inner anxiety—not unlike the words of the father in Goethe's (Schubert's and Loewe's) 'Erlkönig'.

The scoring of this song is masterly: all the strings, except the pizzicato double basses, are divided, so there are eight constantly entwining strands of semiquavers, *con sordino*, rising and dipping in a texture called by Mahler 'Unheimlich bewegt' ('With sinister agitation') (see Ex. 3.7). At the last outcry of the child, the arpeggios of the middle strings, now frighteningly marked *pp – ff – pp*, span almost two octaves, and at the child's death a shattering climax is reached, only to subside rapidly into the mechanical indifference of the mill-wheels. (Original key E flat major.)

'Des Antonius von Padua Fischpredigt' (Antony of Padua's Sermon to the Fishes)

This scathing, and again humorous homily against the fallibility of man, mirrored precisely in the aquatic tribes, was to become in extended form the Scherzo of the Second Symphony. Again, in both works, the unifying element is the ostinato or perpetuum mobile, a stream of unending semiquavers which here, however, is neither rustic nor (until the end) menacing, but stands for the glitter of the many fish-heads peeping out of the water as the shoals listen to the holy man's sermon.

St Antony of Padua (*b.* 1195 at Lisbon, *d.* 1231 near Padua) was a famous Franciscan missionary and preacher, called a 'hammer of heretics' in his lifetime and later declared a Doctor of the Church. In this poem he finds the church empty, and goes to the river to preach instead to the fish. At this point, the flowing motive of the violins is taken over by two clarinets glittering in thirds as the sun plays upon the assembling congregation. And now begins the list of visitors and their besetting sins: the gluttonous carps, the pugnacious pikes, the amorous eels, and of course the backsliding crabs! The orchestra, with much wind and string exchanges, becomes a wallowing kettle of fish, whilst a smooth and

Ex. 3.7. 'Das irdische Leben', bb. 1–5

smarmy change to the tonic major, with the help of triangle and whip, highlights the fact that the pleasure the throng derives from the sermon is merely aesthetic. The crowd becomes ever more satisfied, while a tipsy overblown clarinet pokes fun at them. Eventually the penitential preacher ends on a grim C minor pedal-point; the fish disperse, the pikes to their thieving, the eels to their loving, the carps to their gorging. 'The sermon was splendid, but all remain as they were.' And as the holy man turns in dismay there is a distinct whiff of sulphur and brimstone in the air (Ex. 3.8). (Original key C minor.)

Ex. 3.8. 'Des Antonius von Padua Fischpredigt', bb. 157–69

'Rheinlegendchen' (Little Rhine Legend)

A fantastic story of lovers reunited by a smiling Fate. A shepherd grazes his flock by the Neckar and by the Rhine; sometimes his girl is with him, sometimes he is alone. He knows she's gone into service—but where? The music, in comfortable Ländler-time again (in Mahler's manuscript quaver = 132, which feels perfect), speaks of a verdant landscape, with pretty sheep in it, and a lad who's utterly fed up with his uneventful life. Bored with kicking pebbles around (those oft-repeated Es in the left hand, with their lazy grace notes), he tempts fate by throwing his golden ring into the river; the harmony is static while he lifts his arm, but moves on again at once as the ring, against all physical laws, 'flows down the Neckar, flows down the Rhine'.

Now things happen in a rush. Important stages are skipped in the manner of folk poetry: a fish gulps down the ring; the fish (caught, presumably) arrives on the king's table (king of where?); the king (has he filleted the fish?) holds up the ring, and kindly monarch that he is (white-bearded, surely!) asks, 'And whose, pray, might this be?'. And now Mahler uses a zoom lens, in and out, twice: modesty holds the girl against the wall where she stands with other serving wenches, in a *molto ritardando, piano crescendo* paragraph; but at the following *a tempo, subito piano*, and once more, *ritardando* and *molto ritardando, and* again, *a tempo*, she detaches herself, flies towards the high table, and stammers 'This ring is mine!' 'Of course, m'dear', we imagine the king saying, 'You have leave to return this to your friend!' And lifting her heel on two eagerly accented violin notes, the girl is off, skipping over hill and dale to be reunited with her boyfriend. No wonder this delightful gem had to be repeated at its first performance in Hamburg in 1893. (Original key A major.)

'Lied des Verfolgten im Turm' (Song of the Prisoner in the Tower)

Like 'Der Schildwache Nachtlied' and 'Wo die schönen Trompeten blasen', this is a military song in the form of a dramatic dialogue. Again, it can be performed as a duet or by a single singer, preferably by a man since it is easier for *him* to fine down his voice to *her* tone (is she an apparition?) than it would be for *her* to find the crude aggressiveness with which the prisoner utters the words 'Our thoughts are free, for who can divine them . . .?', spat out in an attempt to hold on to a vestige of sanity. Again, Mahler's orchestra is in full war cry, in a 12/8 movement that rattles along in curt *siciliano* rhythms interchanging with howling woodwind scales. The resultant abrasive textures are glued together by the sustained chords of the four horns.

The girl, to be imagined standing outside, close by the wall—or indeed existing only in his head—sings seductively of summer, 'a happy time up there in the high wild mountains'. But turning back to the minor mode and the military noises, the man breaks in, emphasizing his obsessive thoughts. Once more, this time in an even more beguiling B flat major, the relative major of the tonic minor, the girl holds out to him her vision of freedom and love. He begins to find these ideas dangerous to his hard-held mental independence since they cannot be turned into reality, and so he has to ward them off more strongly, now to thumped-out, repetitive chords of the full band. On her third attempt, however, the girl goes too far: 'My love, you sing as gaily here as a bird sings in the meadows. I stand forlorn at the prison gate; would I were dead, or else with you; oh, must I mourn for ever?' With this reproach she shatters the golden cage of rational self-preservation which he has attempted to interpose between himself and the dank prison walls. To an accompaniment which insanely insists on the rigidity of the barlines, as if they were bars of iron, the prisoner declares himself rid of irksome love: 'From now on, in my heart, I am laughing and joking. And so let it be, our thoughts are free!' It needs a great artist, perhaps someone who has sung Wozzeck, to make this great song palatable to an audience. (Original key D minor.)

'Wo die schönen Trompeten blasen' (Where the Splendid Trumpets are Sounding)

This dialogue between a girl and her ghost lover was one of five Mahler song first performed in 1900 in Vienna, when the redoubtable critic Eduard Hanslick wrote a perspicacious review, calling Mahler an enemy of the conventional and customary, and praising his extraordinary delicacy and masterly technique.[8] 'Wo die schönen Trompeten blasen' is perhaps the best introduction to Mahler's *Wunderhorn* style in its peculiar mixture of naivety and sophistication. Indeed, Mahler was represented by this one song alone in certain anthologies of Lieder in the 1920s.

Muted horns, oboes, and clarinets in *pianissimo*, like the distant noises of war, set the scene as the girl dreams of her lover. Half awake she wonders who is knocking so gently at her door, and hears his reply, 'It is your own true love, arise and let me in to you.' Here the music magically changes from punctuated rhythms to long, mellow legato lines, from wind to string textures. Although we are not yet told that the speaker is the ghost of a fallen soldier, the sweetness and ardour of this passage, including a disembodied *pianissimo subito* towards the end, hints at the presence of the supernatural. Now the girl gets up, opens the door to him and welcomes him, to one of the most wide-stepping yet searingly beautiful modulations in all music (see Ex. 3.9). Her words of welcome are a gentler, more feminine version of his speech, in the new, velvety key of G flat. As the truth of the situation dawns on her, she begins to weep, and he tries to comfort her, back in D major, in his soft, exalted ghost voice. But the true state of things can no longer be staved off: to the sound of muted trumpets and horns, he relives a past battle fatal for him, in the demotic present tense: 'I'm going to war on the green heath, and there, where the splendid trumpets are sounding, there is my home of green turf.'

Unfortunately, this passage is sometimes conducted and sung so sluggishly that it is like wringing out a crumpled handkerchief soggy with tears. Yes, remote it should be, but crisp and bright as is the mask worn by War over his true features. (Original key D minor.)

---

[8] See Mitchell, *WY*, 430–1.

Ex. 3.9. 'Wo die schönen Trompeten blasen', bb. 72–93

'Lob des hohen Verstandes' (Praise of Lofty Intellect)

Donald Mitchell draws our attention to a lecture on Mahler given by one of his principal sopranos (and lovers), Anna Bahr-Mildenburg, who presented Mahler with an early edition of *Des Knaben Wunderhorn* from her grandfather's library. He wrote to her: 'You cannot realize how delighted I am with the charming book. It is so beautiful that its contents are almost new to me, and I am in danger of setting one or another Lied to music for the second time. This would then be your fault . . . Immediately, I composed a merry little Lied which I shall call "Lob des hohen Verstandes".'[9] Mahler's original title was, however, an ironic 'Lob der Kritik'. Throughout his life, he suffered much from the attentions of the cloth-eared fraternity, and the recollection of the song in the introductory flourish to the artfully contrapuntal finale of the Fifth Symphony may be a swipe at those who prefer the cuckoo's song to the nightingale's.

The orchestra here has the usual four horns and two trumpets, but is the only one in the *Wunderhorn* songs to use a trombone and tuba, much needed to poke fun at the pomposity of the donkey. For it is old Jackass himself who is to judge a singing competition dreamt up by the cuckoo and the nightingale (a crackpot idea from the start). The cheeky, whistling, and pecking noises of the staccato solo woodwind sound like a whole forest on a bright morning, and lightly accommodate the cuckoo's sly suggestion that the donkey with his large ears will be a judge of acute critical faculties. And, of course, the donkey is delighted to be asked. In a syncopated passage for the brass he appears pompously to hitch up his gown like counsel in court. Bidden to sing, the nightingale pours out its enchanting strains, depicted in agile, warbling flute and oboe writing. But the donkey is utterly bewildered: 'Too hard for me! Too hard for me! Hee-haw! Hee-haw!' Yet when the cuckoo holds forth in his wonted, stencilled pattern, consisting of 'thirds, fourths, and fifths' (here the peasant poet quite innocently quotes the workaday terms for intervals as if they were the ultimate in musical profundity), the donkey feels in the presence of a like-minded spirit. The music stops for a moment while he doles out faint praise to the nightingale, and starts up again in a braying, bucking rhythm as he turns to compliment the cuckoo on his attainments. To the words 'So says my lofty intellect . . . I make you out the winner, the winner. Cuckoo! Cuckoo! Hee-haw!', the score puts on a happy, foolish grin, and the singer has the satisfaction of forgetting for once 'la voce' and enjoying the animal noises demanded of him. (Original key D minor.)

[9] Quoted in Mitchell, *WY*, 255.

Additional note The editors commend to the attention of readers and to performers of the *Wunderhorn* songs the following volumes published by the International Gustav Mahler Society, Vienna: *Fünfzehn Lieder, Humoresken und Balladen aus Des Knaben Wunderhorn für Singstimme und Klavier*, ed. Renate Hilmar-Voit with Thomas Hampson (Sämtliche Werke, 13/2b; Vienna: Universal Edition, 1993); and *Des Knaben Wunderhorn: Gesänge für eine Singstimme mit Orchesterbegleitung*, ed. Renate Hilmar-Voit (Sämtliche Werke, 14/2; Vienna: Universal Edition, 1998).

4

Todtenfeier and the Second Symphony

EDWARD R. REILLY

The Manuscripts

The manuscripts for Mahler's Second Symphony provide one of the most extensive, if still far from complete, records of the genesis of any of Mahler's compositions. At the same time they reflect the long and curiously discontinuous gestation of the work as a whole, and the highly intuitive nature of Mahler's approach to composition.

The unusual chronology of the work is well documented. The first movement was composed in an extraordinarily short period of time in 1888. It was apparently begun simultaneously with or shortly after the completion of the First Symphony (then still thought of as a tone poem in two parts) in Leipzig in January of that year.[1] An incomplete preliminary draft (actually something between preliminary draft and the beginnings of draft full score), now in the Jewish National and University Library in Jerusalem, is dated 8 August 1888, which places some of the important group of preliminary sketches in the Österreichische Nationalbibliothek before that time.[2] A complete fair copy of the full score, which is substantially different from the draft, followed very quickly and is dated 10 September 1888. This manuscript, now in the Sacher Foundation Collection in Basle, still preserves some features that differ from the movement as we know it, and calls for a much more modest orchestra.[3] Significantly, the title-page shows that the movement was conceived as the first

---

[1] Jan. 1888 can be established from Natalie Bauer-Lechner's reference to Mahler's vision soon after the performance of his completion of Weber's *Die drei Pintos* in Leipzig, the first performance of which took place on 20 Jan. of that year. See NB-L, *Recollections*, 53; NB-L, *Erinnerungen*, 50.

[2] For more details on the manuscripts for the symphony, see Reilly, 'Die Skizzen zu Mahlers Zweiter Symphonie', *Österreichische Muzikzeitschrift*, 34 (1979), 266–85; id., the chapter 'A Brief History of the Manuscripts', in Gustav Mahler, *Symphony No. 2 in C Minor 'Resurrection' Facsimile*, ed. Gilbert Kaplan (New York: The Kaplan Foundation, 1986), 57–67; and esp. Stephen Hefling, 'The

Making of Mahler's "Todtenfeier": A Documentary and Analytical Study' (Ph.D. diss., Yale University, 1985), a revised version of which is forthcoming. The same author's 'Content and Context of the Sketches' appears in Gilbert E. Kaplan (ed.), *Mahler: The Resurrection Chorale* (New York: The Kaplan Foundation, 1994), 13–24.

[3] For fuller discussion of the distinctive features of the *Todtenfeier* manuscript, see Mitchell, *WY*, 269–70; Rudolf Stephan, 'Mahlers sinfonische Dichtung "Todtenfeier"', *Nachrichten zur Mahler-Forschung*, 13 (1984), 6–7; and Hefling, 'The Making of Mahler's "Todtenfeier"', 706–8, 737–55; and my review of the critical edition of the work in the Music Library Association *Notes*, 4 (1989), 832–45.

Pl. 4.1. Probably the initial sketch for the opening of the first movement of the Second Symphony, with the 'Hauptthema' and an insert to follow the first two bars on the top stave. Österreichische Nationalbibliothek, Musiksammlung, Mus.Hs. 4364, vol. I, fo. 3ʳ.

movement of a symphony. It is labelled 'Symphonie in C moll. / I. Satz.' (Symphony in C minor. 1st movement). At some uncertain point, no later than 1891, Mahler cancelled the first part of his original title (leaving the 'I. Satz'), and replaced it with the new heading 'Todtenfeier' (Funeral service, or Funeral rite), thus suggesting the transformation of the symphonic movement into a tone poem.[4] At the same time that he wrote the first movement of the symphony, he sketched the beginning of the second movement (see Pl. 4.2), but did not continue with its composition.[5]

The failure to continue work on the symphony reflects the advent of a major 'dry' period in Mahler's creative work. One can only speculate about the causes: the unsuccessful première of the First Symphony; the deaths of his father, mother, and sister Leopoldine in 1889; and the heavy demands of his position as Director of the Royal Hungarian Opera from 1888 to 1891, when he moved to Hamburg, may all have contributed to the creative hiatus. Whatever the case, he resumed compositional work only in 1892, with at least six and possibly seven songs in a new group of settings of texts from *Des Knaben Wunderhorn*. These prepared the way for a return to the Second Symphony in the summer of 1893, five years after the completion of the first movement.[6] During that summer Mahler completed the composition of the second movement, wrote the song 'Des Antonius von Padua Fischpredigt' and the third movement which is based on it almost simultaneously, and orchestrated the song 'Urlicht', which may have been written the preceding year.[7] Having completed what were to become the inner movements of the symphony, during the 1893–4 opera season Mahler prepared the fair copies of these movements and undertook a revision of the first movement, which involved a few structural changes and a considerable expansion and modification of the orchestration. A chronology of the dates found in the various manuscripts may be useful at this point:

8 August 1888. Mixed preliminary draft and orchestral draft of the first movement.

10 September 1888. Prague. Fair copy of the first movement, in a version that differs in orchestration and some structural points from later forms of the movement. At some point re-titled 'Todtenfeier'.

Hiatus of five years

8 July 1893. Voice and piano version of 'Des Antonius von Padua Fischpredigt'. Later described as a 'preliminary study for the Scherzo of the Second'.

---

[4] For a facsimile of the title-page, see the Kaplan facsimile cited in n. 2 above, p. 56; for both the title and final page of the music, see *MDS*, ills. 80 and 81. The 1891 date is established by Mahler's report of how he performed the work, under that name, for Hans von Bülow, in a letter to Friedrich Löhr of 28 Nov. 1891. See Mahler, *Selected Letters*, 138–9 and Mahler, *Briefe* (1982), 94–5. He also mentions it in letters dated 14 Oct. and 19 Nov. 1891 to his publisher Ludwig Strecker. See Knud Martner and Robert Becqué, 'Zwölf unbekannte Briefe Gustav Mahlers an Ludwig Strecker', *Archiv für Musikwissenschaft*, 34 (1977), 287–97.

[5] This page is also reproduced in Reilly, 'Die Skizzen', 275. Bauer-Lechner provides a vivid report about how Mahler picked up this beginning and continued to work on it. See NB-L, *Recollections*, 29; NB-L, *Erinnerungen*, 25.

[6] Mahler's return to composition may have been stimulated by the publication of his early songs by Schott in 1892. See the letters to Ludwig Strecker cited in n. 4 above.

[7] J. B. Förster, *Der Pilger: Erinnerungen eines Musikers* (Prague: Artia, 1955), 406, specifically indicates that the song was written in 1892.

16 July 1893. Draft full score of the third movement, labelled second.[8]

19 July 1893. Fair copy of the full score of 'Urlicht'.[9]

30 July 1893. Draft full score of the second movement, labelled fourth.[10]

1 August 1893. Fair copy of the full score of 'Des Antonius von Padua Fischpredigt'. Note that it *follows* the draft orchestral score of the third movement.

29 April 1894. Revised version of the first movement.

A few points may be noted. By the end of summer 1893 all the movements for the symphony existed excepting the finale, and Mahler already had in mind the possible use of a chorus in that movement.[11] With regard to the middle movements at that time (i.e. the summer of 1893) some important uncertainties remained. 'Urlicht' may not even have been considered as a part of the work until later. The title-page of the fair copy of the orchestral score shows that it was still thought of as the seventh song in the *Wunderhorn* series. One reliable source, Mahler's close friend J. B. Förster (1859–1951), indicates that Mahler decided to include it only after he had drafted the finale.[12] If that is the case, the alternative positions of the present second and third movements indicated in the manuscripts suggest that at a rather late stage Mahler experimented with different arrangements of the inner movements, with one possibly presenting 'Urlicht' between the third and the second movements. Such a sequence seems curious today, but Mahler's tendency to explore different possibilities in the ordering of his inner movements is well known.[13] Having progressed thus far, Mahler still remained uncertain about how to complete his work. The answer came to him in a brilliant moment of illumination which he experienced at the memorial service (*Todtenfeier*) for his idol, the great pianist and conductor Hans von Bülow (1830–94), on 29 March 1894. In contemplating death, Mahler intuitively perceived that the answer to it was life beyond death: resurrection. He later described the experience to the critic Arthur Seidl (1863–1928):

Whenever I plan a large musical structure, I always come to a point where I have to resort to 'the word' as a vehicle for my musical idea.—It must have been pretty much the same for Beethoven in his Ninth. . . . In the last movement of my Second I simply had to go through the whole of world literature, including the Bible, in search of the right word, the 'Open Sesame'—and in the end had no choice but to find my own words for my thoughts and feelings.

The way in which I was inspired to do this is deeply significant and characteristic of the nature of artistic creation. —

---

[8] This manuscript, which disappeared many years ago, was recently acquired by Robert O. Lehman, and is now on deposit at the Pierpont Morgan Library in New York City.

[9] This manuscript is now in the Stefan Zweig Collection in the British Library.

[10] This manuscript is still missing, but a description of it from 30 Nov. 1923 provides the date. See Reilly, 'Die Skizzen', 269.

[11] See the letter to Arthur Seidl, cited below.

[12] See Förster, *Der Pilger*, 406.

[13] See Mitchell, *WY*, 184–7 on the uncertainty of Mahler's ordering of the inner movements of the symphony. We know, from the copyist's manuscript in the Bruno Walter collection in the Library of the Performing Arts in New York City, that at one time Mahler considered placing the scherzo second. We also know from Bauer-Lechner and his correspondence that he was not entirely satisfied with his final decision to place the Andante second. See NB-L, *Erinnerungen*, 169 (not in NB-L, *Recollections*); Mahler, *Briefe* (1982), 278–80; and Mahler, *Selected Letters*, 268–70.

I had long contemplated bringing in the choir in the last movement, and only the fear that it would be taken as a formal imitation of Beethoven made me hesitate again and again. Then Bülow died, and I went to the memorial service. – The mood in which I sat and pondered on the departed was utterly in the spirit of what I was working on at the time. – Then the choir, up in the organ-loft, intoned Klopstock's *Resurrection* chorale.–It flashed on me like lightning, and everything became plain and clear in my mind! It was the flash that all creative artists wait for–'conceiving by the Holy Ghost'!

What I then *experienced* had now to be expressed in sound. And yet–if I had not already borne the work within me–how could I have had that experience? There were thousands of others sitting there in the church at the time![14]

As Guido Adler was later to point out, Mahler 'did not always arrive at the point' where he had to draw on the word.[15] But at this period in his life, and through the Fourth Symphony, the exploration of mixed orchestral and vocal genres was fundamental to his conception of the symphony. Later, in the Eighth Symphony and *Das Lied von der Erde*, that exploration took very different forms.

As a vivid description of this same day in Mahler's life by J. B. Förster makes clear,[16] Mahler set to work on his finale immediately. Using only the first two stanzas[17] of Klopstock's hymn, Mahler drafted the text for the entire finale in at least two different versions, the second expanding the first with the addition of the stanza beginning 'O Schmerz! Du Alldurchdringer!' (see App. 1 for the full text of the movement). The earlier of the two draft texts is also of special interest in that it shows Mahler already thinking in terms of the dynamic plan for the movement.[18] The sketches for the finale are much less extensive than those for the first movement, but they suggest that the entire opening choral setting of 'Aufersteh'n' may have come to Mahler more or less whole.[19] Other sketches are for various vocal and instrumental sections of the movement.[20] The recent appearance of several previously unknown manuscripts in dealers' hands suggests that still more may eventually appear, permitting scholars to trace the evolution of the movement in even greater detail. A sketch found among those for the second movement at Stanford University shows a few bars that serve as a link between the first and last movements, and raises the question

---

[14] From the letter dated 17 Feb. 1897. See Mahler, *Selected Letters*, 212–14 and Mahler, *Briefe* (1982), 199–202.

[15] See Edward R. Reilly, *Gustav Mahler and Guido Adler: Records of a Friendship* (Cambridge: Cambridge University Press, 1982), 41. For the original German text, see Guido Adler, *Gustav Mahler* (Vienna: Universal Edition, 1916), 50.

[16] See Mitchell, *WY*, 168–9 and Förster, *Der Pilger*, 404–6. A partial translation of the passage in Förster's work is also included in Norman Lebrecht, *Mahler Remembered* (London: Faber and Faber, 1987), 78–9. See also Förster's article, 'Aus Mahlers Werkstatt', *Der Merker*, 1 (1910), 921–4, which quotes the verses of Klopstock's hymn that are printed in the programme of Bülow's *Todtenfeier*.

[17] It should be noted that the programme of the Bülow memorial service contained only three of the hymn's many stanzas. Mahler used the first two.

[18] Both drafts of the text are reproduced in the facsimile of the autograph MS of the complete symphony, p. 49. Henry-Louis de La Grange (HLG(F) i. 1028–9) conveniently prints the two preliminary texts in parallel columns with the final text, but does not include the dynamic markings found in the Walter manuscript. I am indebted to Knud Martner for the information that Mahler's setting of the text is unrelated to the melody of the hymn actually sung at the memorial service.

[19] The two principal sketches of the chorale, belonging to G. Kaplan and R. O. Lehman and on deposit at the Pierpont Morgan Library, are reproduced in facsimile, and in transcriptions by Stephen Hefling, together with a related sketch now in private hands, in Kaplan (ed.), *Mahler: The Resurrection Chorale*.

[20] See Reilly, 'A Brief History of the Manuscripts', 62 and HLG(F) i. 1016.

whether Mahler already had some ideas for his finale, as the letter to Seidl quoted above suggests, before he discovered the Klopstock text and its poetic theme. The fact that the orchestral draft of the third movement already contains the violent episode that anticipates the opening of the finale also raises significant questions in this regard. Could Mahler have written an anticipation of a critical passage that he did not yet foresee? It seems most unlikely.

As indicated by the date given above for the revision of the first movement (29 April 1894), work on the outer movements proceeded simultaneously, a point which gains in significance when one considers the motivic connections between them. Progress on the finale is recorded in Mahler's cards and letters to his friends and family. Having arrived in Steinbach in June and settled down to work in his new composing cottage, he wrote to Friedrich Löhr (and in a very similar vein to his brother Otto) on 29 June: 'Beg to report safe delivery of a strong, healthy last movement of my Second. Father and child both doing as well as can be expected—the latter not yet out of danger. At the baptismal ceremony it was given the name "Lux lucet in tenebris." [The light shines in the darkness]'. On 10 July he reported to Arnold Berliner: 'The sketch is complete down to the last detail and I am just completing the score. − It is a bold work, majestic in structure. The final climax is colossal . . . '. And on 25 July, again to Berliner, he wrote: 'The last movement (score) of the Second Symphony is finished! It is the most important thing I have yet done.'[21] The reference to a score here is probably to a draft full score. The fair copy of the complete symphony carries the inscription: 'Beendigt am Dienstag, den 18 Dezember 1894 zu Hamburg' (completed on Tuesday, 18 December 1894, in Hamburg). This autograph, formerly in the collection of the Mengelberg Stichting in The Hague, is now on deposit at the Pierpont Morgan Library in New York. Its owner, Gilbert Kaplan, published a facsimile in 1986, generously making it accessible for study by all students and scholars.[22]

Performance History

The performance history of the new symphony began very soon after the completion of the fair copy. Richard Strauss, who had already helped arrange for a performance of the First Symphony at the festival of the Allgemeine Deutsche Musikverein in Weimar on 3 June 1894, asked to perform the first three movements of the Second Symphony on 4 March 1895 in Berlin. Mahler himself took over the rehearsals and performance. The critical response was negative in the extreme. It did not, however, prevent Mahler from undertaking a performance of the complete symphony in the same city on 13 December of the same

---

[21] All three of these letters are quoted in the facsimile of the Second Symphony, 72–4, which contains a comprehensive record of Mahler's references to the work in his letters.

[22] See above, n. 2. The distributor for the volume was Faber Music, London.

year. The critics were no kinder,[23] although the reaction of the audience (including many students and professional musicians with complimentary tickets) seems to have been enthusiastic.[24] Still undaunted, on 16 March 1896, once more with the Philharmonic Orchestra in Berlin, Mahler conducted a programme of his own works that included the First Symphony, the *Lieder eines fahrenden Gesellen*, and the first movement of the Second, entitled *Todtenfeier* for the first and last time in one of his own concerts.[25] Performances of the symphony thereafter were not frequent, and did not initially mark a turning point in Mahler's reputation as a composer; but the work did gain some critical attention and notice in one of the most popular concert guides of the day, the *Führer durch den Conzertsaal* by Hermann Kretzschmar (1848–1925),[26] and in a well-known work by Felix Weingartner (1863–1942), *Die Symphonie nach Beethoven* (also 1898). Further discussions appeared in 1902 and 1903, in the analyses of Ludwig Schiedermair (1876–1957), Ernst Otto Nodnagel (1870–1909), and Hermann Teibler (1865–1906).[27] The work seems to have held a special place in Mahler's affections. He programmed it at many critical points in his life. It was the first of his symphonies that he conducted in Vienna, and also the last (9 April 1899 and 24 November 1907). It was also the first of his works that he conducted in Munich,[28] in New York, and in Paris, and was selected for the 1903 music festival of the Allgemeine Deutsche Musikverein in Basle (15 June).

Publication History

The Second was also the first of Mahler's symphonies to be published. As was Mahler's custom already, he first had another fair copy of the score prepared by a copyist. In this case at

---

[23] See HLG(E) i. 319–21 and 345–7, reproduced in the facsimile of the symphony, 51–5. See also the much more sympathetic review of the performance on 13 Dec. 1895 by Ferdinand Pfohl, included in his *Gustav Mahler: Eindrücke und Erinnerungen aus den Hamburger Jahren*, ed. Knud Martner (Hamburg: Musikalienverlag Karl Dieter Wagner, 1973), 67–72.

[24] On the popular response to the Second Symphony at the Berlin performance on 13 Dec. see Justine Mahler's report to Bauer-Lechner in NB-L, *Recollections*, 42–3; NB-L, *Erinnerungen*, 39–40.

[25] One must remember, however, that Mahler was using his own revised score of the Second Symphony, not the manuscript that he had entitled 'Todtenfeier'.

[26] (3rd edn., Leipzig: Breitkopf & Härtel, 1898), i. 675–9. See also the review by Ferdinand Pfohl cited in n. 23 above.

[27] See Schiedermair, 'Gustav Mahler als Symphoniker', *Die Musik*, 1 (1901–2), 506–10, 603–8, 696–9; Nodnagel, *Jenseits von Wagner und Liszt* (Königsberg: Ostpreußischen Druckerei, 1902), 10–13; and id., 'Gustav Mahlers zweite Symphonie', *Die Musik*, 2 (1903), 337–53 (also reprinted

separately); and Teibler, *Gustav Mahler: Symphonie No. 2 in c-moll* (Musikführer No. 207; Leipzig: Hermann Seemann Nachfolger, n.d. [*c*.1902]). Of the subsequent studies of the work, those of Richard Specht, *Gustav Mahlers II. Sinfonie: Thematische Analyse* (Vienna: Universal Edition, 1916); Paul Bekker, *Gustav Mahlers Sinfonien* (Berlin: Schuster und Loefffler, 1921; repr. 1969); Rudolf Stephan, *Gustav Mahler: II. Symphonie C-moll* (Meisterwerke der Musik, 21; Munich: Wilhelm Fink Verlag, 1979); and Constantin Floros, *Gustav Mahler*, iii: *Die Symphonien* (Wiesbaden: Breitkopf & Härtel, 1985), 47–74, should be especially singled out.

[28] Bauer-Lechner (*Erinnerungen*, 168–71; not in *Recollections*) provides a valuable report on this performance and its aftermath, during which various aspects of the work and its programmes were discussed. Ironically, the growing popularity of the Second Symphony created false expectations among the critics when the Fourth Symphony was first performed in Munich. See NB-L, *Recollections*, 183–4; *Erinnerungen*, 203.

least two partial copies were prepared. The earlier, containing the first three movements, but with the scherzo placed second, is now in the Bruno Walter Collection in the Library for the Performing Arts at Lincoln Center, New York. It may have been used for Mahler's initial read-through of these movements in Hamburg, and bears on its cover the name of Karl Muck (1859–1940), who is known to have performed the entire symphony on several occasions, including its première in Boston. A second manuscript, in this case containing the entire symphony except for the 'Urlicht' movement, with corrections by Mahler, is now preserved in the Osborn Collection in the Beinecke Library at Yale University. Both manuscripts are the work of F. Weidig, Mahler's regular copyist in Hamburg. Even at this stage, important changes could be made. The opening timpani solo in the third movement and its later echo towards the end of the movement were added after the original fair copy of the full score had been completed.[29] The symphony appeared initially in printed form in a two-piano version, arranged by Mahler's close friend in Hamburg, Hermann Behn (1859–1927), who had helped defray the expenses for the performance of the symphony on 13 December. He undertook his arrangement in the same year, 1895, and it was published in the same month, December—though with the copyright date of 1896—by Friedrich Hofmeister in Leipzig.[30] At the same time the fourth movement, 'Urlicht', was published with a two-hand accompaniment. The same publisher issued the full score in February 1897. Both the piano arrangement and the full score were subsequently taken over by Josef Weinberger in Vienna in 1897.[31] In 1899 Weinberger also issued a new piano-duet arrangement by Bruno Walter.

As was his custom, Mahler continued to revise his work even after publication, often adjusting details of scoring and performance indications in successive performances. Several copies of the printed Hofmeister score with alterations by Mahler have been preserved. One, formerly belonging to Bruno Walter, containing changes in red ink not in Mahler's hand but certainly stemming from him, is in the Library of Congress (LC ML [*sic*] H43e/ No. 50). Two copies with the Weinberger imprint, but with the original plate number, preserve later revisions. Both are on deposit from Universal Edition at the Stadt- und Landesbibliothek in Vienna. The first is undated, but may have been used as the basis for the octavo study score issued by Universal in 1906[32] and subsequently reissued many times, including the wartime Boosey and Hawkes reprint of 1943. The second copy bears the inscription 'corrected and definitely approved/December 1907', and below that the notation 'September 1910/Mahler'.[33] This copy served as the basis for the full score issued by Universal in 1910, and was also one of the primary sources for the critical edition, edited by Erwin Ratz, published by Universal in 1970. The 1988 appearance of the *Todtenfeier*

[29] On the evolution of this timpani solo, see Mitchell, *WY*, 427–9.

[30] See Mahler, *Unknown Letters*, 21 n. 2 and 27 n. 4.

[31] *100 Years Remembered: A History of the Theatre and Music Publishers Josef Weinberger*, comp. and published by Josef Weinberger Ltd (London, 1985), 9, indicates that Hofmeister and Weinberger published the symphony jointly, but I have not been able to confirm this point.

[32] See Stephan, *Gustav Mahler: II. Symphonie*, 17.

[33] See my report in the Kaplan facsimile, p. 67.

form of the first movement, edited by Rudolf Stephan in the critical edition of Mahler's works, forms the most recent chapter in the publication history of the work.[34]

Todtenfeier and Programme Music

The very name *Todtenfeier* leads naturally to a consideration of the often discussed question of the programmatic aspects of the tone poem and the symphony as a whole. Mahler's own ambivalence about programmes in the earlier stages of his career complicates the question of how and to what degree one is to consider the programmes that he left on record. There can be no question that his works were intended to convey an emotional message: music was not for him an abstract art. In his earlier works (up to and including the Third Symphony, and to some degree even in the Fourth), he was not averse to providing his friends, and sometimes his audiences, with clues about the nature of the musical message. His programmes, however, did not precede actual composition. At most a general plan might be jotted down, as in the preliminary outlines for the Third, Fourth, and Eighth Symphonies. Significantly, none of these plans *determined* the final form of each work.[35] In the great majority of cases, Mahler's verbal descriptions emerged either during actual composition, as in the case of the Third Symphony, or after the completion of the work, as in the First and Second Symphonies. Thus he did not write music to convey some pre-existent narrative, but found verbal analogies to suggest the emotional content of the works. The music created its own programme or *programmes*—for Mahler was not especially consistent in this regard, and often provided quite different comparisons for the same work.[36]

In the case of the Second Symphony, three programmes are preserved, all dating from well after the completion of the symphony (see App. 2). The earliest is that found in Natalie Bauer-Lechner's recollections of Mahler in January 1896; the second, covering only the first three movements, is in a letter to the composer and critic Max Marschalk (1863–1940); and the third was written, reluctantly, and after he had publicly disavowed programmes, for a performance of the work in Dresden on 20 December 1901. The descriptions share some points—especially the detailed consideration of the finale in the first and last of these programmes—but are not identical. The first movement, for example, according to Bauer-Lechner 'depicts the titanic struggles of a mighty being still caught in

---

[34] Supplementary vol. 1 of the Critical Edition (Vienna: Universal Edition).

[35] See the tabulations of the titles for the various movements of the First and Third Symphonies in HLG(F) i. 970–1 and 1038–9 and the early plan for the Fourth Symphony, p. 1053. Similarly, the Eighth Symphony was originally planned quite differently from the final version.

[36] Stephen E. Hefling, 'Miners Digging from Opposite Sides: Mahler, Strauss, and the Problem of Program Music', in Brian Gilliam (ed.), *Richard Strauss: New Perspectives on the Composer and his Work* (Durham, NC: Duke University Press, 1992), 41–53, provides an excellent comparative approach of the differences between Mahler and Strauss in their attitudes to programme music. Guido Adler's early discussion of the subject is also still worth reading. See Reilly, *Gustav Mahler and Guido Adler*, 40–1.

the toils of this world; grappling with life and with the fate to which he must succumb—and his death'. In writing to Marschalk, however, a rather different perspective emerges:

I called the first movement 'Todtenfeier'. It may interest you to know that it is the hero of my D major symphony that I bear to his grave, and whose life I reflect, from a higher vantage point, in a clear mirror. Here too the question is asked: *What did you live for?* Why did you suffer? Is it all only a vast, terrifying joke?—We *have* to answer these questions somehow if we are to go on living—indeed, even if we are only to go on dying! The person in whose life this call has resounded, even if it was only once, must give an answer. And it is this answer I give in the last movement.[37]

Further differences appear in the descriptions of the Scherzo. In both the first and third programmes, however, Mahler draws attention to the powerful and unexpected outbreak at bar 465 as a 'shriek' or 'cry' of a soul in anguish. And although his final description of the third movement (see App. 2, sect. III) seems to be approaching a suggestion of the cynical mood of 'Des Antonius von Padua Fischpredigt', which served as its starting point, in none of his programmes does he mention the song.

Having succumbed to the temptation to explain his symphony verbally, Mahler soon learned that many listeners could not see beyond the programme. The reductive approach, after all, seemed to 'explain' everything. After a performance of the symphony in Munich on 20 October 1900, he took the occasion to repudiate the notion that he wrote music to a programme, and clearly distinguished this approach from that in which the composer draws upon words as a means of articulating his musical ideas, as in the final two movements of the Second.[38] For Mahler the music expressed infinitely more than any words could suggest. And thereafter, with a few exceptions such as the Dresden performance mentioned above, he took the unusual step of forbidding the use of programme notes, including thematic guides, at performances of his works, in the hope of forcing audiences to listen, respond to their own emotional reactions, and arrive at their own conclusions. This step probably irritated people, including critics, more than it helped them to find pleasure in the compositions. But Mahler's aim remained valid. Although the programmes offer some insights and points of reference, none of them is *essential* to a genuine understanding of the symphony.

More recently, several scholars have drawn attention to the possible influence of Adam Mickiewicz's poem *Dziady* (Forefather's Eve)—translated by Mahler's close friend Siegfried Lipiner (1856–1911) under the title of *Todtenfeier* and published in 1887—on the composition of the first movement.[39] Stephen Hefling, in an elaborate and suggestive study, has even tried to show that there are detailed correspondences between one major part of the poem and the symphonic movement. That the poem might have provided the stimulus for exploring some aspects of the emotional world of the first movement certainly remains a possibility, but the hypothesis, in my view, is almost entirely speculative. And as

---

[37] See below, App. 2, for the complete programmes. They are also reproduced in the Kaplan facsimile, pp. 43–6. The translation has been modified in the light of the original German text.

[38] See NB-L, *Erinnerungen*, 171 (not in *Recollections*).

[39] See Peter Franklin, ' "Funeral Rites"—Mahler and Mickiewicz', *Music & Letters*, 55 (1974), 203–8, and Stephen Hefling, 'Mahler's "Todtenfeier" and the Problem of Program Music', *19th Century Music*, 12 (1988), 27–53.

Hefling himself ultimately shows, the form of the work is not governed by the story of the poem. Rather the music has a life and form of its own.[40]

Bauer-Lechner reports another experience that may well have some bearing on the emotional roots of the first movement. After telling of a vision of a *Doppelgänger* that Mahler had during the composition of *Das klagende Lied*, she goes on to say:

> He had had another similar experience when he was working on the funeral march in the first move-
> ment of his Second. He saw himself lying dead on a bier under heaps of wreaths and flowers (which
> had been brought to his room following the performance of the *Pintos* [in January, 1888]). Frau
> Weber had quickly had to remove all the flowers from his sight.[41]

Finally, yet another factor pointing to the composition of the work independently of any pre-existing programme is the terminology found in the earliest sketches for the first movement in the Austrian National Library (see above). With one exception, Mahler's verbal inscriptions for his sketches are all technical in nature: 'Hauptsatz' (principal theme); 'Gesang' (melody—in this case a contrasting lyric theme); 'Schlusssatz' (concluding section); 'Mittelsatz' (middle section); and so forth.[42] The one exception is a theme headed 'Meeresstille' (calm sea), a label probably derived directly from Goethe's well-known poem 'Meeresstille und glückliche Fahrt' (Calm sea and prosperous voyage) since the theme seems to bear no musical relationship to Mendelssohn's overture or Beethoven's cantata of the same name. This descriptive term also shows no obvious connection to any of the programmes or to Mickiewicz's poem. Perhaps ironically, the theme does have a distinct musical relationship with the so-called slumber motive of Brünnhilde in *Die Walküre*, a connection that did not go unnoticed by contemporary commentators such as Herman Kretzschner in his *Führer durch den Concertsaal*.

Thus, while Mahler's programmes and the possible connection with Mickiewicz's *Dziady* are all stimulating and suggestive of Mahler's emotional and intellectual world, they do not ultimately 'explain' the work. The music conveys Mahler's emotional message, and ultimately permits a much wider range of interpretative 'meanings' than the programmes indicate. Mahler's own ironic comments on the final programme that he felt forced to produce should be kept in mind when this issue is discussed:

---

[40] In my opinion, Hefling does not really answer the question that he himself raises: why Mahler never refers to the poem in any of his programmes or in any of his discussions of the work with his friends. There was no reason that he should conceal this source; he would in fact have done his friend Lipiner a service by drawing attention to this work. Although the title *Todtenfeier*, the publication date of Lipiner's translation, and Mahler's undoubted familiarity with it are, taken together, highly suggestive, they do not actually establish a connection. As indicated above, we do not know *when* Mahler added the title to the fair copy of his manuscript, currently in the Sacher Foundation Collection. It could have been well after the actual composition. The draft at the Jewish National and University Library in Jerusalem is still inscribed '1. Satz', and thus, like the

sketches in the Nationalbibliothek in Vienna, contains no hint of such a connection at the time that the work was composed. Max Steinitzer, however, in his recollections of Mahler during his Leipzig period, already refers to the work as 'Totenfeier'. See *Musikblätter des Anbruch*, 2, nos. 7–8 (1920), 297, and Lebrecht, *Mahler Remembered*, 44. Thus the change of title may have taken place soon after the completion of the movement. One must also remember that the term need have nothing to do with poetry or drama. It was not uncommonly used for just the kind of religious memorial services as that for Hans von Bülow, where it appears on the programme.

[41] See NB-L, *Recollections*, 53; *Erinnerungen*, 50.

[42] See Reilly, 'Skizzen', 278–9.

. . . My Almschi! Justi [Mahler's sister Justine Rosé] did not tell you, then, that I only drew up the programme as a crutch for a cripple (you know whom I mean).[43] It only gives a superficial indication, all that any programme can do for a musical work, let alone this one, which is so much all of a piece that it can no more be explained than the world itself. – I'm quite sure that if God were asked to draw up a programme of the world he had created he could never do it. – At best it would be a 'revelation' that would say as little about the nature of God and life as my analysis says about my C minor symphony. In fact, as all revealed religions do, it leads directly to misunderstanding, to a flattening and coarsening, and in the long run to such distortion that the work, and still more, the creator, is utterly unrecognizable . . .[44]

The Musical Structure

The Second Symphony shares some of the formal and stylistic features of the First, but enormously expands the scale of that work. Like the earlier symphony (in its original form), the Second is in five movements, with the more dramatic outer movements enclosing three inner ones, which have to some degree the character of song and dance interludes. In both works, the greatest weight is given to the finale, and numerous motivic and thematic connections exist between movements, especially the outer ones. The interval of the fourth is a central unifying element in both works. And in both Mahler borrows from his own songs and from other musical sources. Yet differences are equally obvious. The use of texts in the two concluding movements provides a specific message of a kind not found in the First Symphony; and in each case the text also influences structure.

Before considering the form of each of the movements and the interrelationships between them, a few basic stylistic features suggested by Mahler's own sketches may be noted. The contrapuntal nature of Mahler's thinking and its relationship to harmonic background are made strikingly clear in the composer's sketch for the opening of the movement (see Pl. 4.1). Here in a single sketch he combines the elements that are initially divided into the two different thematic portions of his principal theme, the bass theme (bb. 1–17) and the woodwind theme subsequently presented in combination with it (bb. 18–43) (see Ex. 4.1(*a*) and (*b*)) in the final form of the movement.

Mahler's tendency to think in terms of contrapuntal combinations, the elements of which can be effectively presented not only simultaneously but also successively, is repeatedly reflected in the score. The contrapuntal lines also coexist within a harmonic framework which defines their effect in many different ways. In this case, the first twenty-five bars are projected against a tremolo upper G pedal which, as the fifth above the tonic, adds breadth, continuity, and tension to the theme. Both melody and harmony underline the strongly

---

[43] As the editors of Alma Mahler, *Memories* indicate (p. 398), King Albert of Saxony was meant.
[44] See ibid. 217–18 and Kaplan facsimile, p. 98.

Translation modified in the light of the German original: Alma Mahler, *Gustav Mahler: Erinnerungen und Briefe* (Amsterdam: Bermann-Fischer, 1949), 274–5.

Pl. 4.2. Probably the initial sketch for the beginning of the second movement, showing the opening theme combined with the cello counter-theme as they appear in the restatement beginning in bar 93. Österreichische Nationalbibliothek, Musiksammlung, Mus.Hs. 4364, vol. I, fo. 7ᵛ.

tonal character of the music. Mahler's use of tonic and dominant pedals is a recurrent feature of virtually all his symphonies. It is fundamental to the creation of his primary tonal areas and also to the establishment and varying modification of the pace of each section.

At the same time, both elements of this contrapuntal combination contain within themselves an almost inexhaustible supply of melodic and rhythmic motives that reappear in an extraordinary range of different incarnations, some immediately recognizable, others quite as certainly concealed. A brief examination of some of the motives that grow out of the *Hauptthema* (principal theme) that Mahler places at the head of the sketch already cited (see Ex. 4.2(*a*)) may serve simultaneously as an introduction to some of the principal thematic material of the first movement and to Mahler's handling of this material.

First it should be noted that the theme contains within itself two distinct and overlapping motives, the descending and rising fourth (a), the gapped rise of an octave (b), and the repeat of the fourth an octave higher, now in a dotted rhythmic form (a′). Another dotted figure using quaver and semiquaver, rather than crotchet and quaver, already appears in (b). Characteristically, since Mahler's music is constantly evolving and unfolding, he reserves a full presentation of this theme until the recapitulation of the first movement (bb. 334–7). Meanwhile elements of it appear in many guises. Motive (a) and its variant with the fourth moving down to the lower octave appear repeatedly in the opening bass theme (see Ex. 4.1(*a*)), and lead into the woodwind theme, which begins with a rhythmically augmented form of (b) and the return of (a) (see Ex. 4.1(*b*)). The rising fourth is then promptly followed by a matching fifth, reversing the pattern heard earlier in the bass. A series of brief illustrations from the earlier part of the first movement will serve to suggest a few further examples of Mahler's procedures in his handling of motives. In Ex. 4.2(*b*) the fourth in motive (a) of the *Hauptthema* is followed by a descending scale, reversing and filling in the chord outline of (b). The scale is subsequently also treated as a distinct motive, as in bars 37–8 of Ex. 4.1(*b*). These examples are a reminder that Mahler's material is often so basic in terms of intervals, scales, and chord outlines that it is not always possible to determine

Ex. 4.1. Second Symphony, sketch for opening of 1st movt.: (*a*) bb. 1–18; (*b*) bb. 18–43

Ex. 4.1. *cont.*

Ex. 4.2. Second Symphony, 1st movt.: (*a*) 'Hauptthema'; (*b*) bb. 27–8; (*c*) bb. 67–70

Ex. 4.2. Second Symphony, 1st movt.: (*d*) bb. 74–9; (*e*) bb. 80–5; (*f*) bb. 85–6; (*g*) bb. 103–7; (*h*) bb. 123–4 and 127–8; (*i*) bb. 129–30 (*Meeresstille*) and 133–4

to what degree he is consciously creating inner connections between his various themes and motives. Ex. 4.2(*c*) shows different rhythmic formulations of (b). In Ex. 4.2(*d*) the opening notes of (b) are reharmonized, using a new combination of the rhythmic elements heard earlier. In Ex. 4.2(*e*) motive (b) is contracted intervallically, and then expanded to its original pattern. Ex. 4.2(*f*) presents the opening notes of (b) inverted. Ex. 4.2(*g*) shows motive (b) followed by a chromatically descending sequential form of the preceding inversion. Ex. 4.2(*h*) illustrates different rhythmic forms of (a). Ex. 4.2(*i*) shows the so-called

Meeresstille (calm sea; see above) motive, combined with (a) and then with the inversion of the opening notes of (b).

From the preceding examples, it should be clear that rhythmic features—in this movement, especially the interplay of dotted and triplet figures—are virtually equal in importance to intervallic patterns in organizing and contrasting thematic material.

Mahler is also a master in building up large-scale dynamic relationships. The impact of his climaxes is effective very largely because he varies his dynamic scale with great subtlety, and does not overuse his maximum levels. As with Beethoven, dynamics are also closely linked to and reinforce harmonic shifts and the ebb and flow of harmonic tension.

Similarly, darkness and light, weight and transparency are constantly reflected in Mahler's orchestration. Compare, for example, the colouristic features of the opening themes (Ex. 4.1(a) and (b) above) and the transparency of the contrasting *Gesang* cited below in Ex. 4.3(b).

With some of these general characteristics of Mahler's style in mind, the organization of each of the movements of the symphony may now be considered, though inevitably in a summary fashion.

First movement

Allegro maestoso. 4/4 time. C minor

This movement is often described as being in sonata form; but it shows significant departures from what are thought of as the 'normal' patterns in that type of structure. The earlier *Todtenfeier* form of the movement also differs in some structural matters from the final version as well as in its orchestration and performance markings.

The three main divisions of the movement can be, and frequently are, equated with the Exposition, Development, and Recapitulation of sonata form; and as noted earlier, in his sketches Mahler did not avoid terminology associated with this form. In this movement, he approaches the form (as always) in his own distinctive way, especially in his tonal plan. In my view of it, each of the main divisions of this tripartite structure is subdivided into two main parts.

Exposition, Part 1 (bb. 1–62; opening to Fig. 4⁻²).[45] The extraordinary opening section of the movement and its striking separation and combination of two distinct contrapuntal lines has already been discussed and illustrated above (see Ex. 4.1(a) and (b)). The remarkable shaping of both lines is, I believe, unique in the symphonic literature up to Mahler's time. After a full cadence and a reiteration of the central descending and rising fourth (Ex. 4.2(a), motive a) accompanied by march rhythms, a brief, more lyrical theme (see Ex. 4.3(a)) leads quickly to the strongly contrasting melody labelled *Gesang* in Mahler's

---

[45] Bar numbers are found only in the Critical Edition of Mahler's works and those editions derived from it, such as the Philharmonia pocket editions. To aid students with older editions or reprints of them, in outlining major divisions of movements I have also included Figure numbers. As is customary, ⁻¹ indicates one bar before the Figure, and ⁺³ indicates three bars after the Figure.

Ex. 4.3. Second Symphony, 1st movt.: (*a*) bb. 43–6; (*b*) bb. 48–52 (*Gesang*)

sketches (see Ex. 4.3(*b*)), transforming the harsh world of the C minor funeral march into the sunfilled light of E major over a dominant pedal. This melody is also presented contrapuntally with an imitative theme in the horns. This kind of harmonic shift to a mediant level in the opposite mode (E from C major, but harmonized as E major rather than E minor) is not altogether without precedent, but how Mahler proceeds is thoroughly unexpected. He promptly rebuilds new tension with emphasis on the dominant of B major and then, after resolution, a startling modulation to E flat minor, by way of its dominant. The emphasis on E major and E flat minor in this section seems clearly prophetic of the tonal organization of the movement and even of some aspects of the symphony as a whole. After the cadence to E flat minor, the G♭ of the tonic chord is promptly replaced by G♮ unison and octave tremolos, which lead to the second part of the exposition.

Exposition, Part 2 (bb. 62–116; Fig. 4⁻²–Fig. 7). The preceding surprises are followed by still more. The key returns to the original tonic, C minor, and the opening theme returns. A new and highly abbreviated configuration of motives from that theme appears (see Ex. 4.2(*c*) above for a portion of the modified theme), and moves on quickly to a 'new' theme in A flat major (see Ex. 4.2(*d*)). Related to the middle motive (*b*) of the *Hauptthema* (see Ex. 4.2(*a*)), this theme gives substance to Mahler's remark (see above) that the hero being marched to his grave here is identical with the hero we encountered in the finale of his First Symphony (see the passage–beginning in bars 370–5 in that movement). Here this theme moves to another combination of motives, now over a G pedal. A descending, trudging march figure is combined with the rising intervallically contracted form of the central *Hauptthema* motive, which gradually expands to its original intervals (see Ex. 4.2(*e*) above). 'Dotted' descending scale figures[46] in the upper strings add a third element to the counterpoint, and explosive combinations of falling and rising dotted scales (already important in the opening section, bars 37–8 in Ex. 4.1(*b*)) move through D towards G minor and the concluding section of this part of the movement.

A quiet, descending chromatic ostinato, perhaps derived from the descending chromatic motive in bars 39–40 of Ex. 4.1(*b*), and rhythmically related to the march figure in the

---

[46] Mahler frequently replaces the dots in such figures with rests of the equivalent value in order to sharpen the articulation in performance.

Ex. 4.4. Second Symphony, 1st movt.: (*a*) bb. 80–2 and 97–103; (*b*) bb. 99–100 and 109–10

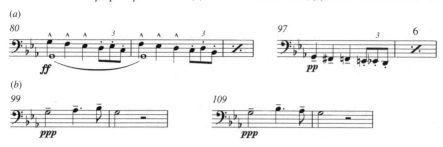

preceding passage (see Ex. 4.4(*a*)), forms the background to two forms of a new motive (see Ex. 4.4(*b*)).

The central *Hauptthema*'s motive (b) reappears, and moves on to a chromatic descending sequence using the three notes of the inverted motive (see Ex. 4.2(*g*) above) now presented over a diatonic version of the previous chromatic ostinato. The latter is reduced to a simple descending four-note scale figure, combined with the second version of the earlier new motive (see Ex. 4.4(*b*)). It is preceded by one of several important modal shifts between major and minor, with the trumpet moving from B♮ to B♭. A very stable G minor clearly seems to mark the end of the section.

Development, Part 1 (bb. 117–243; Fig. 7–Fig.15^{-1}). In a surprise equal to its first appearance, the *Gesang* (see Ex. 4.3(*b*)) reappears in C over a G pedal. The harmony, now linked with the descending-fourth motive and a descending scale, moves magically through F major to E major. While the strings sustain an E–B pedal, and present a smoothed-out version of the fourth, the cor anglais presents a new theme, inscribed *Meeresstille* by Mahler (see the first figure in Ex. 4.2(*i*)), subtly linked to the three-note descending motive previously heard towards the end of the preceding section (see Ex. 4.2(*g*) above). The two are then presented in counterpoint (see the second figure in Ex. 4.2(*i*)) and lead to yet another, more extended melody presented in thirds by the clarinets (see Ex. 4.5).

The horns join in with a new counter-theme of their own, and lead to a reappearance of the *Meeresstille* figure in a form similar to its first appearance, but again with new counterpoints. The skip up of a major ninth (B–C♯) is suddenly transformed into a minor ninth (B–C♮).

Against descending fourths in the flutes and an evenly flowing quaver figuration in the second violins and violas, a march-like dotted accompaniment figure, reminiscent of the

Ex. 4.5. Second Symphony, 1st movt., bb. 135–40

Ex. 4.6. Second Symphony, 1st movt., bb. 147–50

original march, appears (see Ex. 4.6). The pastoral tranquillity of the preceding section is replaced by the darker imagery of another death march, in E minor, with yet another 'new' dirge-like theme (see Ex. 4.7), projected in slow time values against the march rhythm associated with the opening theme.

Ex. 4.7. Second Symphony, 1st movt., bb. 151–4

Motives derived from the opening themes (see Ex. 4.1(*a*) and (*b*)) begin to reappear and are presented in new contrapuntal combinations, which form the beginning of an extended dynamic build-up that reaches its climax in bars 196–202.

A tonally unstable passage (bb. 164–74) leads to a reappearance of the 'heroic' theme (see Ex. 4.2(*d*) above) in D major. There follows a new contrapuntal arrangement of the contracted and then expanded version of the central motive from the 'principal theme' (see Ex. 4.2(*e*)), dotted descending scales from the main theme, and the descending chromatic ostinato (Ex. 4.4(*a*) above) in C sharp minor. The inversion of the opening notes of the central motive (see Ex. 4.2(*f*) above) follows, with much of the preceding passage then restated a semitone higher on D. The climax is marked by a dynamic pause (b. 196) followed by sweeping triplet descending chromatic scales, played *fortissimo*, still over D, but then moving back to C♯ and then unexpectedly to C♮, treated as the dominant of F.

Over the dominant pedal C, the *Gesang* theme (Ex. 4.3(*b*)) quietly reappears in the flute, and then in a different form in the strings and clarinets, leading once more to an unexpected harmonic turn to B major. The tension of the preceding section subsides in another extended quiet section, which introduces new variants of the descending form of the (*b*) motive derived from the 'principal theme' (bb. 227–9), and another theme that turns out to be a retrograde form of the *Gesang* in different rhythmic guises (bb. 229–31) below an F♯ pedal, which finally resolves to the tonic B *pianissimo*. Except for the timpani roll and bass drum beats (bb. 242–3), forward motion virtually ceases.

Development, Part 2 (bb. 244–329; Fig. 15–Fig. 20^{+5}). It is at this point that *Todtenfeier* differs most substantially from its revision in the Symphony. In *Todtenfeier*, the opening four bars of the original bass theme (see Ex. 4.1(*a*) above) reappear *fortissimo* in E minor. Then for twenty-four bars motives derived from this full theme are developed quietly in new combinations over a B pedal, which resolves to E, and then moves directly down to E flat, preparing for the following section (see bb. 253–79 in the critical edition of *Todtenfeier*).

In the final version of the movement, Mahler drastically reduces this passage to ten bars, and places it much more dramatically in the unexpected key of E flat minor. The violently stated opening five bars (*fff*) of the bass theme (bb. 244–8) are followed by five very soft bars, with strings moving down chromatically as a backdrop to a timpani motive that echos the end of the preceding bass theme.

Then, beginning 'sehr langsam', a new form of the passage which appeared in the first part of the development (bb. 147–63; see Exx. 4.6–7 above) in E minor, reappears in a sub-stantially modified form in E flat minor. Against the now double-dotted string figures, the original dirge theme (see Ex. 4.7 above) is this time preceded by a melancholy semitone motive (B♭–C♭–B♭) in the cor anglais. The theme itself (now in trumpet and trombone) is combined contrapuntally with motives from the main themes (Ex. 4.1(*a*) and (*b*)), and then moves on with a new continuation, a theme the beginning of which is derived from the famous *Dies irae* sequence depicting the Last Judgement, from the Requiem Mass (see Ex. 4.8). In his cantata *Das klagende Lied* Mahler had earlier made use of this opening motive. Made famous by Berlioz and Liszt, it was already established as a musical symbol for death. While the beginning seems threatening, the continuation becomes increasingly tri-umphant, and leads to a reappearance of the heroic theme (Ex. 4.2(*d*) above) and then quickly to the first of a series of climaxes (b. 291) with a strongly dissonant diminished ninth harmony (A♮–C♮–E♭–G♭–B♭, over E♭ and B♭).

Ex. 4.8. Second Symphony, 1st movt., bb. 270–7

The basic descending fourth from the 'principal theme' reappears in the brass (b. 304) in E flat minor and leads to a still more powerful climax that dissolves in a descending chromatic scale. The latter moves unexpectedly to a G in the basses, and to the reappearance of the expanding form of the central figure (b) of the *Hauptthema* (b. 320; see Ex. 4.2(*e*)). This motivic group, which had played such an important role in the first portion of the develop-ment, is here significantly reduced to a single presentation which prepares for the enormous build-up of harmonic tension in the four bars preceding the recapitulation (bb. 325–8).

The overwhelming tension generated by these chords and their resolution to the tonic C minor, with the restatement of the opening theme, leave no doubt about Mahler's contin-ued adherence to some aspects of traditional notions of sonata form. The familiar domin-ant preparation is now intensified to its maximum.[47] The partially chromatic descending scale that leads into the recapitulation reminds one of the earlier climax (bb. 189 ff.) and forecasts the end of the movement. Further surprises, however, remain in store.

[47] This passage attracted the attention of several of Mahler's contemporaries, as Bauer-Lechner reports (*Erinnerungen*, 169).

Recapitulation, Part 1 (bb. 329–91; Fig. 20^{+5}–Fig. 24). This part of the recapitulation is in fact a largely abbreviated version of elements from the first part of the exposition, now linked with the *Meeresstille* theme from the beginning of the development. The section begins not with the full bass theme, but with only bars four to six (see Ex. 4.1(*a*) above), at which point the complete *Hauptthema* enters, strikingly, for the first time in the form notated by Mahler in his sketch (see Ex. 4.2(*a*) above). The general course of the presentation of the remainder of the theme is similar to that of the exposition. It is clearly recognizable as a recapitulation, and fully re-establishes C minor as its tonal centre. At the same time numerous details, too many for discussion here, are altered. The continuation of the theme (see Ex. 4.1(*b*) above) leads to the reappearance of the *Gesang* melody (see Ex. 4.3(*b*)), once more in E over a B pedal. This time, however, E immediately becomes the dominant of A, with repeated appoggiaturas (F♯–E: b. 364) forming a new continuation of the theme. Variants of previously heard horn figures lead back to E and the reappearance of the *Meeresstille* motive, with the same counterpoint as earlier (see Ex. 4.2(*i*)). The passage that follows (bb. 372–83) is a very free and sensuous transformation of material heard in a parallel position at the beginning of the development. An intervallically contracted form of the *Meeresstille* motive, still in E major, leads to harmony that fluctuates between major and minor. G♯–G♮ in the horns dovetail with E♮–E♭ tremolos in the violins, which lead to the concluding section of the movement.

Recapitulation, Part 2 (Coda) (bb. 392–445; Fig. 24–end). Without further transition material, the final portion of the movement begins in C minor, with the chromatic form of the ostinato motive heard at the end of the exposition (see Ex. 4.4(*a*) above). The whole section remains rooted in C minor, and preserves the plodding tread of a dead march. Beginning with another version of figure (b) from the *Hauptthema* and its inversion (see Ex. 4.2(*e*) and (*f*) above), the section unfolds as a quiet, ghostly, and surrealistic configuration of motives drawn largely from the opening themes. Bird-like calls appear briefly and irregularly in the flute (bb. 404–7). The march continues, using both dotted and triplet motives from the opening themes, and a slow dynamic build-up dissipates almost immediately. Melodic fragments become increasingly brief, until they waver between only two notes, shifting from major to minor, at the end poignantly articulated as E♮ and E♭ in the oboe. The movement is brought to a close by a loud and emphatic descending chromatic scale which parallels those heard earlier in the movement, notably that leading to the recapitulation (without, however, the latter's harmony). Even this outburst subsides, with the progressively softer final unisons and octaves in the strings.

Second movement

Andante moderato. 3/8 time. A flat major

The form is that of a song in an A B A B-expanded A-extended pattern, with each return of A substantially varied, and the B sections creating a modal as well as a thematic and

Ex. 4.9. Second Symphony, 2nd movt., bb. 93–6

textural contrast to A. As clear and relatively straightforward as the overall form of this movement may be, its remarkable delicacy and subtlety should not be overlooked. It represents a very different side of Mahler's musical personality, one that was generally more appealing to his earliest audiences than were his more dramatic movements. The contrapuntal element is again very much in evidence, but in somewhat different ways from the first movement. Similarly, however, the main theme and its lovely cello countermelody (see Ex. 4.9)—which appears in the movement only with the second appearance of the main theme—clearly seem to have been conceived together though they were eventually uncoupled as the movement developed.[48]

In the intermediate contrasting sections, Mahler not only creates a striking change in mood and atmosphere through shifts to minor, but also through changes from homophonic to contrapuntal texture. Rather unusually, he uses imitative counterpoint, with a D♯ pedal, to establish a continuing triplet figuration in the strings (see Ex. 4.10), against which the winds present their themes. One of these themes emphasizes the central interval of the fourth (see Ex. 4.11) which both subtly and overtly links all the movements of the symphony. The interval, which appears in the second bar of the principal theme of A (see Ex. 4.9), stands out in B because of its opening position in the melody. The woodwinds create a strong con-

Ex. 4.10. Second Symphony, 2nd movt., bb. 39–41

[48] See above, Pl. 4.2, also reproduced in Reilly, 'Die Skizzen'.

Ex. 4.11. Second Symphony, 2nd movt., bb. 64–71

trast when they appear because the first A section is limited until its end to the strings. Only in the concluding variation of A do strings and winds combine to present the theme.

The movement also shows how far Mahler ultimately goes in moving away from the idea of simple variation of his thematic material. The return of the B section is in fact a substantially expanded development of the material in the first, emphasizing the dark atmosphere of these passages—the potentially threatening background for the delicate 'charm' of the main theme—which seem like anticipations of night-music movements and sections in the later symphonies. The concluding return of the opening theme, initially in pizzicato strings, is also substantially expanded, but now with a delicate sensuality. Hermann Kretzschmar, in his early commentary on the Second Symphony, noted that the main theme of this movement seemed closely modelled on the Waltz of Robert Volkmann's F major Serenade.[49]

Third movement

In ruhig fliessender Bewegung. 3/8 time. C minor
The opening (up to b. 138), a middle passage (bb. 380–404), and the conclusion (from b. 553) of this movement are derived, as noted earlier, from the orchestral *Wunderhorn* song 'Des Antonius von Padua Fischpredigt', an ironic and caustically sinister vision of the human condition. The endlessly varied species of fish listen attentively to St Antony and promptly return to their previous bad habits. The borrowed sections are associated, respectively, with the first six, the seventh, and the combined eighth and ninth stanzas of the poem.

The formula Introduction A B C A B X B A hardly suggests the motivic and tonal complexity of the movement. A more detailed but still very rough summary might take the following form:[50]

Introduction. Explosive timpani opening bars (bb. 1–7); see Ex. 4.12, reiterating the central interval of a fourth, linking all the movements in the symphony, in two different rhythmic positions.

[49] See his *Führer durch den Concertsaal*, 677. Stephan, *Gustav Mahler, II. Symphonie*, 48, makes the same point and illustrates it with the opening of the movement on p. 93. The caption for the latter mistakenly ascribes the composition to Robert Fuchs rather than Volkmann.

[50] In what follows, capital letters indicate the main divisions of the movement and correspond roughly to the formula given in the text. Italicized lower-case letters indicate the shorter subsections within the principal parts. After the introduction, the principal themes are cited in the examples that precede the subsections in which they first appear. The central key levels appear in the line below the subsections, with minor keys indicated by lower-case letters, major keys by capitals.

Ex. 4.12. Bars 1–7

A (bb. 6–189; Fig. 28^{+5}–Fig. 36^{-1}; see Ex. 4.13(*a*) and (*b*))

Ex. 4.13. (*a*) bb. 13–20; (*b*) bb. 68–75

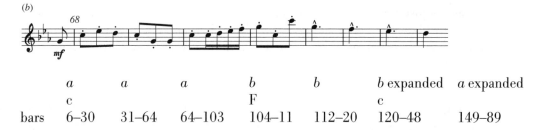

a	*a*	*a*	*b*	*b*	*b* expanded	*a* expanded
c			F		c	
bars	6–30	31–64	64–103	104–11	112–20	120–48	149–89

B (bb. 190–271; Fig. 36–Fig. 40^{-1}; see Ex. 4.14)

Ex. 4.14. Bars 190–8

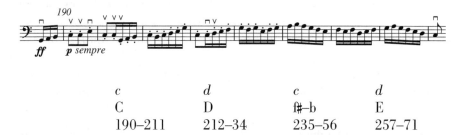

c	*d*	*c*	*d*
C	D	f#–b	E
190–211	212–34	235–56	257–71

C (bb. 272–327; Fig. 40–Fig. 43^{-1}; see Ex. 4.15)

Ex. 4.15. Bars 272–89

$$e \qquad\qquad e \qquad\qquad e$$
$$\text{E}$$
272–87   288–307   308–27

Transition (bb. 328–47); motives from *c*, especially its second form above
A (bb. 348–440; Fig. 44–Fig. 49^{+1})

$$a \qquad\qquad a \qquad\qquad b \qquad\qquad b$$
$$c \qquad\qquad\qquad\qquad\qquad \text{F}$$
348–67   368–406   407–28   428–40

B (bb. 441–64; Fig. 49–Fig. 50^{+8})

$$d$$
C over G pedal
441–64

X (bb. 465–80; Fig. 50^{+8}–Fig. 51^{-1}; see Ex. 4.16)

Ex. 4.16. Bars 465–6 (basic harmony)

'Shriek' forecasting the opening of the finale. B flat minor harmony over a C pedal. Descending scale leads back to a resumption of:
B (bb. 481–544; Fig. 51–Fig. 54^{-1})

c (with an echo of the	*e*+*c*	*c*
opening timpani solo)		
C	C	transition
481–99	500–21	522–44

A (bb. 545–81; Fig. 54–end)

elements of *a*, *b*, *c* combined
transition – c
545–81

The limitations of this kind of outline are immediately obvious when one hears the movement. Although the subsections identified with the same letter share thematic material, they never appear in the same guise. The same opening figures of each section, for example, are expanded in countless ways, melodic, rhythmic, textural, and colouristic. Contrapuntal additions and combinations are especially intricate. Parallel to the phenomenon noted earlier in relation to the sketches for the openings of the first and second movements—in which one part of a contrapuntal combination is presented alone, before it appears with its equally important counterpoint—in this movement Mahler initially presents simply the original accompaniment of his song (see Ex. 4.13(*a*)). Only in the passage corresponding to the third stanza of the poem (b. 64 of the song, and b. 68 of the movement) is the original vocal melody introduced in its orchestral guise (see Ex. 4.13(*b*)), presented by piccolo, clarinet, and bassoon. Meanwhile, the continuing semiquaver motion links each of the different sections of the movement, providing the background against which all the melodic and rhythmic contrasts take place.

The contrasts in mood created by the shifting thematic material and harmony reverse the emotional shifts in the preceding movement. While there the sunny main theme contrasts with the darker intervening sections, here the 'rather bitter-sweet humour' of the opening (as Mahler describes the mood of the song to Bauer-Lechner)[51] turns to the shimmering E major section (C in the diagram—the key is surely no accident), which begins with and is dominated by the trumpet solo (see Ex. 4.15).[52] The movement ends, as did the song on which it is based, with a clear and possibly intentional quotation from Schumann's ironic and melancholy song 'Das ist ein Flöten und Geigen' from his *Dichterliebe* (Ex. 4.17).[53]

Ex. 4.17. Schumann, *Dichterliebe*, no. 9, 'Das ist ein Flöten und Geigen', bb. 80–4

[51] See NB-L, *Recollections*, 32; *Erinnerungen*, 28. In his letter to Marschalk of 26 Mar. 1896, Mahler associates the movement with 'an eerie phantom state'. See Kaplan facsimile, p. 44.

[52] Mahler was clearly referring to this passage when he spoke to Bauer-Lechner in the following passage: 'But, even more strangely than in a whole movement or work, this unconscious, mysterious power manifests itself in individual passages, and precisely in the most difficult and significant ones. Usually, they are the ones which I don't want to come to grips with, which I would like to get around, yet which continue to hold me up and finally force their way to expression.

This has just happened to me in the Scherzo, with a passage which I had already given up on and omitted, but which I then inserted on an additional page after all. And now I see that it is the most indispensable, most powerful part of the whole movement.' See NB-L, *Recollections*, 31; *Erinnerungen*, 26. One may still see the insertion (*Einlage*) in the Kaplan facsimile, between bifolios 6 and 7.

[53] The connection was kindly brought to my attention by Dr Edward Kravitt. It is also noted by Glenn Watkins in *Soundings: Music in the Twentieth Century* (New York: Schirmer Books, 1988), 10.

Fourth movement

Sehr feierlich, aber schlicht. 4/4 time. D-flat major

As noted earlier, Mahler originally set this *Wunderhorn* text as a separate song, and apparently only at a fairly late stage decided to incorporate it into his symphony. One of several reasons for its inclusion was to provide the necessary contrast and change of mood and pace between the third movement and the finale, and also to allow the necessary musical time to elapse before the return of the 'shriek' of the third movement at the opening of the fifth movement. The single stanza is musically divided into three main sections following the opening invocation.

Invocation: 'O Röschen roth!' (bb. 1–2; see App. 1 for English translations of this and the remaining texts of the fourth and fifth movements of the symphony). D flat.

A (bb. 3–35; opening $^{+3}$–Fig. 3^{-1}). A brass chorale (unrelated to those in the first and last movements) serves as a prelude to the next three lines of text (see Ex. 4.18):

> Der Mensch liegt in grösster Noth!
> Der Mensch liegt in grösster Pein!
> Je lieber möcht' ich im Himmel sein!

The final line is repeated, and the concluding melodic phrase incorporates a transposed form of the opening of the chorale. Mahler subtly matches the rhythm of the poem with metrical shifts between 4/4 and 3/4. The section is rounded off with an oboe solo leading to a cadence in D flat.

B (bb. 36–49; Fig. 3–Fig. 5^{-6}). Marked 'Etwas bewegter', a new section is introduced by a B♭–F–B♭ ostinato in the harp (notated A♯–E♯)—once more stressing the fundamental

Ex. 4.18. Second Symphony, 4th movt., bb. 14–30

Ex. 4.19. Second Symphony, 4th movt., bb. 36–7

interval of the fourth—and a triplet figure in the clarinet, establishing a very stable B flat minor as the key (see Ex. 4.19). The single line 'Da kam ich auf einen breiten Weg', projected against this figure, is followed by a violin solo, with its own thematic material. With a direct shift to A major (soon changing to A minor), the flute takes up the violin solo as the accompaniment to the next line of the text: 'Da kam ein Engelein und wollt' mich abweisen.' The two-bar instrumental conclusion of the section, with the continuing flute melody, leads to a short transition (bb. 50–4). Over a descending bass (C♯–B♮–B♭) and dissonant harmony, the next line of the text, 'Ach nein, ich liess micht nicht abweisen', with its new melodic phrase, is presented and immediately repeated a minor third higher, creating the greatest harmonic tension thus far in the song. It leads to a further escalation of harmonic tension that is initially accompanied by a return to the thematic material of the A section.

A transformed (bb. 55–68; Fig. 5–end). A sequence, rising by semitones, presents the opening motive of 'Der Mensch liegt in grösster Pein' in a rhythmically diminished form, with the lines (see Ex. 4.20):

> Ich bin von Gott und will wieder zu Gott!
> Der Liebe Gott, der liebe Gott wird mir ein Lichtchen geben,
> Wird leuchten mir bis in das ewig selig Leben!

Ex. 4.20. Second Symphony, 4th movt., bb. 55–65

The end of the second line marks the end of the diminution, and a return to the original melody in its original slower time values and tempo. This very quiet return to the conclusion of the first part, and to the key of D flat, rounds off the movement with great delicacy. It is worth noting that all three of the middle movements end quietly. The ending here makes the opening of the following movement all the more earth-shaking.

This brief song serves as a prelude to the movement that follows, and with its sharp change of pace and tempo in relation to the preceding movement, shifts the mood from contemplation of this world to consideration of the next. Although we cannot be sure that Mahler knew it, another form of the 'Urlicht' text, more extended than that used here, links it directly with the Last Judgement.[54]

Fifth movement

Im Tempo des Scherzo. Wild herausfahrend. 3/8 time
The same 'shriek' heard in the third movement begins the movement with the same dissonant harmony (see Ex. 4.16 above), though new brass motives and fanfares are added that are to play a significant role in the later course of this enormous movement (see Ex. 4.21). This violent introduction subsides into the first main section, in C major, with a much slower tempo (Sehr zurückhaltend).

Ex. 4.21. Second Symphony, 5th movt., bb. 5–17

The finale, like the first movement, has sometimes been described in terms of sonata form. It does indeed contain elements of Exposition (after the Introduction, bb. 26–193; Fig. 2–Fig. 14), Development (bb. 194–417; Fig. 14–Fig. 27), and Recapitulation (bb. 418–764; Fig. 27–end). But even more than in the first movement, one wonders if the label does not conceal more than it illuminates. Notwithstanding Beethoven's Ninth, the scale and realization of Mahler's movement are unprecedented. Great clusters of motives are grouped in generally slow-moving sections, suggesting different time scales (but with important variations in motion) around an elaborate central quick march which develops and transforms motives heard earlier (bb. 194–324), and evokes Mahler's description: 'The earth trembles, graves burst open, the dead arise and step forth in [long] endless files.' (See Mahler's 1901 programme in App. 2.) A further development of contrasting material already heard in the first part (bb. 325–417) leads to a return to modified forms of several of the opening sections, in a new key sequence, unlike that found in any traditional sonata

---

[54] See my article 'Sketches, Text Sources, Dating of Manuscripts: Unanswered Questions', *News about Mahler Research*, no. 30 (Oct. 1993), 3–9.

form. These transformed sections move in turn (bb. 418–71) to the first vocal presentation of the 'Aufersteh'n' chorale (bb. 472–93), already fully prepared in many forms in the orchestra in earlier sections of the movement. The remainder of the movement consists of a mixture of some new material and transformed re-presentations of themes from the first part, reaching its climax in the appearance of the opening theme of the first main section in unison in the chorus, with the words 'Sterben werd' ich um zu leben!' in E flat major (bb. 696–711), the concluding key of the symphony, already anticipated in its minor form in the first movement.

A summary overview of this extraordinary movement follows:

Introduction (bb. 1–25). The 'shriek' from the Scherzo combined with new brass motives and fanfares (see Exx. 4.16 and 4.21 above).

Part I

A (bb. 26–42; Fig. 2–Fig. 3^{-1}). In spite of the written-out trills in the basses, both tempo and rhythmic motion are slow. Harmonic motion is also slowed with a C pedal throughout the section. A central descending fifth motive is gradually expanded with a rising scale and completed with two descending triplets (see Ex. 4.22), all of which appear in numerous guises throughout the movement.

Ex. 4.22. Second Symphony, 5th movt., bb. 27, 31–4

B (bb. 43–61; Fig. 3–Fig. 4^{+3}). Originally entitled by Mahler 'Der Rufer in der Wüste' ('The Crier in the Wilderness'), this section opens slowly with off-stage horns presenting an unaccompanied rising fifth motive that then continues to the upper octave and ninth (see Ex. 4.23). Triplet figures (see Ex. 4.24) dominate the remainder of the section, and are used in counterpoint with several additional motives. After the opening calls in F, the section continues once more over a C pedal, with some unexpected harmonic turns, and concludes with a descending chromatic motive reminiscent of the first movement and a bass drum solo that fades into complete silence (an interesting anticipation of procedures used in the first movement of the Third Symphony).

Ex. 4.23. Second Symphony, 5th movt., bb. 43–7

Ex. 4.24. Second Symphony, 5th movt., bb. 48–51

Ex. 4.25. Second Symphony, 5th movt., bb. 70–8

C (bb. 62–81; Fig. 4⁺⁴–Fig. 6⁺⁴). The *Dies irae* chorale used in the first movement (see Ex. 4.8 above) reappears in the woodwinds, accompanied by pizzicato strings. It now continues, however, with the first statement of the 'Resurrection' theme (see Ex. 4.25), that is, the theme which is later sung by the chorus, with the words 'Aufersteh'n, ja aufersteh'n wirst du', with triplet figures similar to those in B as accompaniment. Note that the opening of this theme inverts the downward turn of a whole tone of the *Dies irae* (C–Bb–C), with the consequence that the turn emerges in a rising version at a new pitch (F–G–F). Then more triplet fanfares appear over an F–C pedal. The key is F (minor and major by turns, or without a third).

B (bb. 82–96; Fig. 6⁺⁵–Fig. 7⁻¹). The triplet figures from the preceding B section, now combined with what is to become an increasingly important descending scale figure in the later stages of the movement (derived from the concluding triplets in Ex. 4.22 above), lead to a modified return of the off-stage horn calls of the 'Rufer'. The upper notes F–G–F now suggest the 'Resurrection' theme. Most of the section is over an F pedal-point, and the conclusion parallels that of the first B section, with its descending chromatic scales and timpani solo.

D (bb. 97–141, Fig. 7–Fig. 10⁻¹). The key shifts to B flat minor, the metre from common time to *alla breve*. New material, later to be associated with the text 'O glaube, mein Herz, O glaube: Es geht dir nichts verloren!', appears for the first time. Motives formed around falling and rising seconds (see Ex. 4.26) build, against a pattern of tremolo rising parallel thirds in the strings, to a powerful dynamic climax and then subside over an F–Ab pedal. After the preceding passages in which time almost seems suspended, creating a 'timeless' atmosphere, this section provides a striking return to a more urgent and 'regular' melodic and rhythmic style, and a more human (vs. heavenly) plane. The combination of this material with what precedes and follows it, is basic to the plan of the work.

Ex. 4.26. Second Symphony, 5th movt., bb. 97–109

C (bb.142–93; Fig. 10–Fig. 11⁻¹). The *Dies irae* chorale with its new 'Resurrection' continuation (see Exx. 4.8 and 4.25) reappears, beginning in D flat, now in the brass choir. Triplet
fanfares over a C pedal are expanded and combined with phrases from the chorale, the
descending figure heard in the preceding B section (see Ex. 4.22), and variants of the triplet
figures also used in B (see Ex. 4.24). These joyous outbursts gradually subside, and the
shifts between C and E flat harmonies heard at the end of the first B section are followed
by embellished descending chromatic scales, ending with a quiet timpani roll on C.
Combined with the bass drum and snare drum, the timpani then present a powerful
crescendo that leads to the middle section or 'development' of the movement.

Middle Section
E (bb. 194–324; Fig. 14–Fig. 21⁻¹). A Maestoso leads in two bars to an Allegro energico in
4/4 time and in the key of F minor. The whole section constitutes an unfolding quick
march, with dotted rhythms reminiscent of the first movement. It begins with the trumpet
and trombone motives first heard in the introduction and then apparently abandoned.
These two motives (see Ex. 4.21 above) recur at intervals throughout the section. In their
final climactic form, they appear triple *forte* in augmented form in B flat minor over an F
pedal (Fig. 20 or in bb. 310–13).

   Equally prominent throughout this development is the *Dies irae* figure in an immense
variety of shapes, both minor and major. At times it seems to struggle for supremacy over
the 'Resurrection' theme. One of the important motives from the first movement, that associated with the hero (see Ex. 4.2(*d*), in a form found in bb. 282–9 in the first movement)
reappears and is linked to the *Dies irae* (bb. 301–9 in the finale). Chromatic descending
scales at the climactic return of the introductory motives (bb. 310–13) are also reminiscent
of the first movement as well as quieter moments in the preceding sections of this movement (see the end of B and its later return). The pedal F at the end of this section leads without a break to the tremolo E♭–G♭ which begins the next main section.

D (bb. 324–417; Fig. 21⁻¹–Fig. 27⁻¹). This section constitutes an enormously expanded
development of the material first heard in the previous D section, now with the addition of
off-stage fanfares presented by trumpets accompanied by percussion. The principal key

that emerges is F minor, but many shifts in key and metre appear in the course of the gradually unfolding elaboration of the section. This part of the movement reaches its climax
with the eruption of its principal theme double *forte* in the trombones (bb. 379–94), building to a powerfully displaced G♭–C♮ ostinato in the basses (triple time units in 4/4 metre, bb.
395–9). This passage mounts in turn to the overwhelming final return of the introductory
motives (see Ex. 4.21) in the trumpets and horns (bb. 402–4): B–D–F♯ over a C♯ pedal, also
echoing the dissonant harmony of the introduction. The section then quickly subsides with
fanfares and a descending scale over the pedal. It leads to the third of the main divisions of
the movement, and a return to transformed presentations of some of the sections of the first
part.

Part I transformed
A (bb. 418–47; Fig. 27–Fig. 29⁻¹). C♯ is now transformed into D♭, and the descending-fifth
motive (see Ex. 4.22) reappears in the horns over the tonic pedal, now a semitone higher
than the C of the original presentation. With the slow tempo and a static pedal, Mahler re-
establishes the 'timeless' sense of the first presentation. Variants of the skip down now
make use of the interval of a fourth or a third in addition to the fifth; and the rising scale
that follows is now more clearly and consistently linked melodically and contrapuntally to
the descending figure heard in many of the sections of the first part of the movement (compare Ex. 4.27 with 4.22 above). Five beats of silence prepare for the next section.

Ex. 4.27. Second Symphony, 5th movt., bb. 426–30

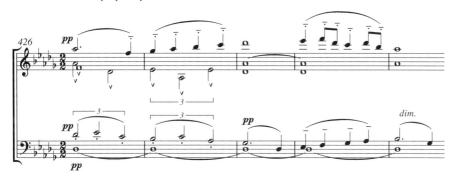

B (bb. 448–71; Fig. 29–Fig. 31⁻¹). Entitled 'Der grosse Apell' [*sic*] ('The Great Summons',
equivalent to the *Tuba mirum* in the text of the *Dies irae*) in Mahler's autograph, the section actually presents a transformed return to the music of 'Der Rufer in der Wüste' (see the
B sections of the first part). The off-stage rising-fifth horn call (see Ex. 4.23) is now also
heard a semitone higher: F♯–C♯ rather than F–C. The triplet figures previously heard in the
woodwinds are now appropriately presented by trumpets, which appear in a staggered
series of entries. Against them, a flute marked 'wie ein Vogelstimme', situated in the orchestra, creates a spatial as well as melodic and rhythmic contrast with the brass figures.
Combined with a piccolo, the birds become more voluble as the section proceeds. Their

Ex. 4.28. Second Symphony, 5th movt., bb. 472–9

highly irregular rhythmic figures, against the slow-moving harmonic background, once more suggest the 'timeless' plane. These are not the birds of death, but the heralds of the Resurrection. The hushed unisons, octaves, and fifths on C♯ and G♯ that conclude the section create a strong sense of anticipation. Treated enharmonically as D♭ and A♭, they prepare for the key of G♭ which follows.

C (bb. 472–559; Fig. 31–Fig. 39⁻¹). Marked 'Langsam' and 'Misterioso' the unaccompanied chorus enters *ppp* with the first stanza of Klopstock's poem (see App. 1 for the text). The key, G flat, is once more a semitone higher than the F minor of the first presentation, and the minor mode has been replaced by the major. The *Dies irae* motive has vanished and is now supplanted by the Resurrection form of the chorale, which after opening with the same initial phrase found in the instrumental version continues on a new path (see Ex. 4.28). Strings quietly join in, and towards the end of the stanza the soprano soloist detaches her line from that of the choral sopranos. The orchestra follows with fanfares similar to those in the parallel earlier section (B), now in counterpoint with the central theme from the A section (see Ex. 4.22, but this time with a skip of a third down, then the rising scale and concluding figure). Detached phrases from the chorale are then added. In general the dynamic scale is kept between *ppp* and *mf*.

The second stanza is introduced, once more by the unaccompanied chorus. It is a subtly rearranged variant of the first. In addition to a fresh harmonization, the notes of the melody are regrouped in shifting metres (2/4–3/4–4/4–2/4–3/4–2/4–4/4), a smooth but irregular flow that matches the accents of the verse. The orchestra again follows quietly, but not with the previous fanfares. Rather the two successively linked themes from A are now used in counterpoint with one another (see bb. 536–7). Shortly thereafter (in bb. 541–4), an octave displacement of the skip down of a fifth produces a form of the theme surprisingly similar to the *Gesang* of the first movement (see Ex. 4.3(*b*) above). The harmony remains largely static, with the tonic G flat strongly emphasized.

D (bb. 560–617; Fig. 39–Fig. 42⁻¹). Tremolo violas on B♭ and D♭ signal a shift to B flat minor and a return to the original material of D, now with the text of the third stanza sung by the alto solo. A short interlude, with the tremolo strings continuing, leads directly to the fourth stanza, sung by the soprano soloist. Its opening phrase suggests a transformation of the main theme from A, but it continues with motives largely from D. A harp glissando leads to the return of the chorale.

C (bb. 618–39; Fig. 42–Fig. 44⁻¹). The opening of the Resurrection chorale melody returns in B flat, with the tenors and basses in octaves and an inner pedal on F for the first two phrases. The choir breaks into a *forte* with the line 'Was vergangen, auferstehen', a new melodic continuation, and the trombones then bring the chorale to a full cadence in E flat. The choir re-enters *ppp*, with the concluding lines, 'Hör auf zu beben! Bereite dich zu leben!', but the cadence once more delays the key of the new world into which the symphony is entering: E flat. One further section reminds the listener of the struggle to conquer death.

F (bb. 640–71; Fig. 44–Fig. 46⁻¹). This section combines transformations of motives from the preceding sections, and a reference back to 'Urlicht' (bb. 660–7). This new development begins 'Mit Aufschwung' (with exaltation) with a sudden leap up a ninth in the strings, and a harmonic plunge away from E flat into a new passage of tonal instability. The soprano and alto soloists now present, without a break, the sixth and seventh stanzas (the last that Mahler added to his text) in a dialogue which mounts in tension until it reaches its climactic A flat (b. 664) in the soprano part. The melodic material seems to be largely transformed versions of the two final soprano phrases in the preceding D section (b. 602, 'O glaube . . .'), but linked at the words 'in heissem Liebesstreben' with a motive from 'Urlicht', where it appears, appropriately, with the words 'Ich bin von Gott und will wieder zu Gott' (bb. 55–8; see Ex. 4.20;[55] the motive that follows in bar 59 is also similar to that in bar 649). The final phrase quietly leads to E flat and the conclusion of the movement.

A (bb. 672–711; Fig. 46–Fig. 48⁻¹). The basses enter quietly with a repetition of the opening lines of the seventh stanza, but now with the melody of A as it has appeared in its numerous forms, with the descent of a third, fourth, or fifth, after the mid-section of the movement. The other voices enter in a quasi-imitative pattern and build to a climactic unison presentation of the A theme in augmentation, beginning as in its original form with a skip down of a fifth. The text, previously omitted in the solo dialogue, underlines as emphatically as possible the composer's central message: 'Sterben werd' ich, um zu leben' (see Ex. 4.29).

---

[55] See Mitchell, *WY*, 185, where the two passages are juxtaposed.

Ex. 4.29. Second Symphony, 5th movt., bb. 696–702

Ster - ben werd' ich, um zu le - - ben!

C+A (bb. 712–64; Fig. 48–end). The setting of the final stanza begins with a combined instrumental and choral presentation of the Resurrection chorale, with the melody in the brass. Forms of Ex. 4.29 (and its source, Ex. 4.22) soon reappear as counterpoints to the choral material. Then with the completion of the choral section, the instrumental coda presents and re-presents this theme in increasingly slower augmentations. Finally it is reduced simply to the original descending fifth with which it began, and then enlarged to the octave E♭ to E♭, against the background of a pure E flat triad. Heaven—or Nirvana—has been reached.

The impact of this movement and of the symphony as a whole in a performance faithful to the score is overwhelming, and its emotional power may in fact lead us to the conclusion that rational thought about the meaning of the work, and especially the implications of the texts of the two final movements, is superfluous. And I am not entirely convinced that Mahler himself would not have preferred such a response. Certainly what the music conveys goes far beyond what the words say. Nevertheless, some consideration of what the words both say and imply may throw some light on Mahler's thought. Clearly, in his use of the *Dies irae* motive and the *Wunderhorn* text, and in borrowing from Klopstock's hymn, Mahler was drawing from Christian tradition and established musical symbolism. But it also seems clear that he has attempted to remove these sources from any narrow form of dogmatic Christianity, and ultimately from any form of doctrinal religion. (Note his negative reference to revealed religions in his letter to Alma, cited above, p. 95.) The textual references are to 'God', never explicitly to Christ. And where the variant of the 'Urlicht' poem mentioned earlier[56] does connect the symbol of the rose with Christ, the *Wunderhorn* version used by Mahler does not. Fundamentally, however, unlike either a Christian or a Jewish God, the God implied by Mahler's text does not judge. Mahler seems clearly to have drawn on the Christian concept of the Last Judgement, and even to have modelled the implied sequence of events in his final movement along the lines of the Last Judgement as described in the *Dies irae* or other religious texts.[57] Ultimately, however, he removed all the

---

[56] See above at n. 54.

[57] At first the biblical lines in Rev. 21: 4 seem very close to Mahler's words in his third programme in their common compassion. Compare 'And God shall wipe away all tears from their eyes; and there shall be no more death, neither sorrow, nor crying, neither shall there be any more pain: for former things are passed away', with 'And behold: there is no judgement . . . no punishment and no reward! An almighty feeling of love illumines us with blessed knowing and being!' Or in the actual text of the sixth stanza of the poem: 'O Pain, thou piercer of all things, From thee have I been wrested! O Death, thou masterer of all things, Now are thou mastered!' But there is an essential difference. In the Bible, judgement has already been described in the preceding chapter: 'And whosoever was not found written in the book of life was cast into the lake of fire.' For Mahler, 'there is no judgement'.

inscriptions in his score that spell out these connections, perhaps realizing that his message went beyond a single creed. From this viewpoint, one may be reminded that the idea of some ultimate final judgement is not limited to Christianity, but is also found in many other religions, including Judaism and Islam. In Mahler's use of Klopstock's reference to 'Der Herr der Ernte' in his second stanza, although the expression has biblical roots, even a pantheistic God can be imagined. But what Mahler is essentially addressing are the very basic human fears of death and judgement (not just damnation, but judgement of the worth of one's life), and the need to feel that life has meaning. His answers are affirmations that *we* in our striving and in our love give meaning to our lives, and that we can transcend both death and judgement. Few more powerful expressions of such views, which suggest an outlook that goes beyond traditional sectarian beliefs, can be found in the history of music, and mark an attempt to find a response to the scepticism that has grown ever more potent in the twentieth century. But, perhaps ironically, one should not assume that these were Mahler's own personal convictions. Each of his symphonies is another (and a different) answer to the meaning of existence.

APPENDIX 1. TEXTS FOR THE SECOND SYMPHONY

Fourth movement: text from *Des Knaben Wunderhorn*

URLICHT

O Röschen rot!
Der Mensch liegt in größter Not!
Der Mensch liegt in größter Pein!
Je lieber möcht' ich in Himmel sein!

Da kam ich auf einen breiten Weg:
Da kam ein Engelein und wollt' mich abweisen.
Ach nein! Ich liess mich nicht abweisen!
Ich bin von Gott und will wieder zu Gott!
Der liebe Gott wird mir ein Lichtchen geben,
Wird leuchten mir bis in das ewig selig Leben!

PRIMEVAL LIGHT

O red rose!
Man lies in deepest need,
Man lies in deepest Pain.
Yes, rather would I be in heaven!

I came upon a broad pathway:
An angel came and wanted to send me away.
Ah no! I would not be sent away!
I am from God and will return to God.
The dear God will give me a light,
Will light me to eternal blessed life!

Fifth movement: text by Friedrich Klopstock (1724–1803) and Mahler.

Aufersteh'n, ja aufersteh'n wirst du,
Mein Staub, nach kurzer Ruh!
Unsterblich Leben! Unsterblich Leben
Wird der dich rief dir geben.

Rise again, yea, thou shalt rise again,
My dust, after short rest!
Immortal life! immortal life!
He who called thee will grant thee.

Wieder aufzublühn wirst du gesät!   To bloom again art thou sown!
Der Herr der Ernte geht   The Lord of the Harvest goes
Und sammelt Garben   And gathers in, like sheaves,
Uns ein, die starben!   Us who died.

O glaube, mein Herz, O glaube: O believe, my heart, O believe
Es geht dir nichts verloren!   Nothing is lost with thee!
Dein ist, was du gesehnt!   Thine is what thou hast desired,
Dein, was du geliebt,   Thine what thou hast loved,
Was du gestritten!   What thou hast fought for!

O glaube,   O believe,
Du wardst nicht umsonst geboren!   Thou wert not born in vain!
Hast nicht umsonst gelebt,   Hast not lived in vain,
Gelitten!   Suffered in vain!

Was entstanden ist   What has come into being
Das muss vergehen!   Must perish,
Was vergangen, auferstehen!   What perished must rise again.
Hör' auf zu beben!   Cease from trembling!
Bereite dich zu leben!   Prepare thyself to live!

O Schmerz! Du Alldurchdringer!   O Pain, thou piercer of all things,
Dir bin ich entrungen!   From thee have I been wrested!
O Tod! Du Allbezwinger!   O Death, thou masterer of all things,
Nun bist du bezwungen!   Now art thou mastered!

Mit Flügeln, die ich mir errungen,   With wings which I have won me,
In heissem Liebesstreben,   In love's fierce striving,
Werd' ich entschweben   I shall soar upwards
Zum Licht, zu dem kein Aug' gedrungen!   To the light to which no eye has soared.
Sterben werd' ich, um zu leben!   I shall die, to live!

Auferstehn, ja auferstehn   Rise again, yea thou wilt rise again,
Wirst du, mein Herz, in einem Nu!   My heart, in the twinkling of an eye!
Was du geschlagen   What thou hast fought for
Zu Gott wird es dich tragen!   Shall lead thee to God![58]

---

[58] Translation by Deryck Cooke, *Gustav Mahler*, 59–60, with minor emendations.

APPENDIX 2. THREE PROGRAMMES FOR THE SECOND SYMPHONY

I. Report by Natalie Bauer-Lechner, January 1896

[Quoting Mahler:] 'The first movement depicts the titanic struggles of a mighty being still caught in the toils of this world; grappling with life and with the fate to which he must succumb—and[59] his death. The second and third movements, Andante and Scherzo, are episodes from the life of the fallen hero. The Andante tells of love. The experience behind the Scherzo I can describe only in terms of the following image: if, at a distance, you watch a dance through a window, without being able to hear the music, then the turning and twisting movement of the couples seems senseless, because you are not catching the rhythm that is the key to it all. You must imagine that to one who has lost his identity and his happiness, the world looks like this—distorted and crazy, as if reflected in a concave mirror. — The Scherzo ends with the appalling shriek of this tortured soul.

'The "Urlicht" represents the soul's striving and questioning attitude towards God and its own immortality.

'While the first three movements are narrative in character, in the last movement everything is inward experience. It begins with the death-shriek of the Scherzo. And now the resolution of the terrible problem of life—redemption. At first, we see it in the form created by faith and the Church— in their struggle to transcend this present life. It is the day of the Last Judgement[60] . . . The earth trembles. Just listen to the drum-roll, and your hair will stand on end! The Last Trump sounds; the graves spring open, and all creation comes writhing out of the bowels of the earth, with wailing and gnashing of teeth. Now they all come marching along in a mighty procession: beggars and rich men, common folk and kings, the Church Militant [die ecclesia militans], the Popes. All give vent to the same terror, the same lamentations and paroxysms; for none is just in the sight of God. Breaking in again and again—as if from another world—the Last Trump sounds from the Beyond. At last, after everyone has shouted and screamed in indescribable confusion, nothing is heard but the long drawn-out call of the Bird of Death above the last grave—finally that, too, fades away. There now follows nothing of what had been expected: no Last Judgement, no souls saved and none damned; no just man, no evil-doer, no judge! Everything has ceased to be. And softly and simply there begins: "Aufersteh'n, ja aufersteh'n . . ." ["Rise again, yea, rise again"]—the words themselves are sufficient commentary. And' cried Mahler 'I absolutely refuse to give another syllable of explanation!'[61]

II. Letter from Mahler to Max Marschalk, 26 March 1896

Having stated 'Just as I find it banal to compose programme-music, I regard it as unsatisfactory and unfruitful to try to want to make programme notes for a piece of music', Mahler later concedes in this letter that it may be 'just as well if in the early stages' of a work's life 'the listener is provided with signposts and milestones on his journey—or rather, with a map of the heavens, so that he can get a picture of the night sky with all its luminous worlds'. . . .

---

[59] As noted by Peter Franklin in NB-L, *Recollections*, 231 and 232, the 'and' here was not found in the original German edition, but does appear in an excerpt published, when Bauer-Lechner was still alive, in *Der Merker* in 1913.

[60] This sentence is again derived from the article in *Der Merker* mentioned in the preceding footnote, but it also appears in the more recent German edition of the *Erinnerungen*.

[61] Quoted from NB-L, *Recollections*, 43–4 and 232; see also *Erinnerungen*, 40.

'Having said all that, I now feel some misgivings, as you will appreciate, in setting out to say anything about the C minor symphony. — I called the first movement "Todtenfeier". It may interest you to know that it is the hero of my D major symphony that I bear to his grave, and whose life I reflect, from a higher vantage point, in a clear mirror. Here too the question is asked: *What did you live for?* Why did you suffer? Is it all only a vast, terrifying joke? — We *have* to answer these questions somehow if we are to go on living—indeed, even if we are only to go on dying! The person in whose life this call has resounded, even if it was only once, must give an answer. And it is this answer I give in the last movement.

The second and third movements are intended as an interlude, the second being a *memory*! A ray of sunlight, pure and cloudless, out of that hero's life.

You must surely have had the experience of burying someone dear to you, and then, perhaps, on the way back some long-forgotten hour of shared happiness suddenly rose before your inner eye, sending as it were a sunbeam into your soul—not overcast by any shadow—and you almost forgot what had just taken place. There you have the second movement! — When you then awaken from that melancholy dream and are forced to return to this tangled life of ours, it may easily happen that this surge of life ceaselessly in motion, never resting, never comprehensible, suddenly seems *eerie*, like the billowing of dancing figures in a brightly lit ball-room that you gaze into from outside in the dark—and from a *distance* so great that you can *no longer* hear the *music*! Life then becomes *meaningless*, an eerie phantom state out of which you may start up with a cry of disgust. — There you have the third movement. What follows is certainly clear to you! — — —

What it comes to, then, is that my Second Symphony grows directly out of the First!'[62]

III. Programme written by Mahler for a performance in Dresden on 20 December 1901

Symphony in C minor

1st movement. We stand by the coffin of a well-loved person. His life, struggles, passions and aspirations once more, for the last time, pass before our mind's eye. — And now in this moment of gravity and of emotion which convulses our deepest being, when we lay aside like a covering everything that from day to day perplexes us and drags us down, our heart is gripped by a dreadfully serious voice which always passes us by in the deafening bustle of daily life: What now? What is this life—and this death? Do we have an existence beyond it? Is all this only a confused dream, or do life and this death have a meaning? — And we must answer this question if we are to live on.

The next 3 movements are conceived as intermezzi.

2nd movement—Andante: a happy moment from the life of his beloved departed one, and a sad recollection of his youth and lost innocence.

3rd movement—Scherzo: the spirit of unbelief, of presumption, has taken possession of him, he beholds the tumult of appearances and together with the child's pure understanding he loses the firm footing that love alone affords; he despairs of himself and of God. The world and life become for him a disorderly apparition; disgust for all being and becoming lays hold of him with an iron grip and drives him to cry out in desperation.

---

[62] Mahler, *Selected Letters*, 179–80; Mahler, *Briefe* (1982), 148–51.

4th movement Urlicht (alto solo). The moving voice of naive faith sounds in his ear.

> 'I am of God, and desire to return to God!
> God will give me a lamp, will light me unto the life of eternal bliss!'

5th movement.
[? . . . the cry of desperation starts up . . . ?]
    We again confront all the dreadful questions and the mood of the end of the 1st movement. —
The voice of the caller is heard: the end of all living things is at hand, the last judgement is
announced, and [all] the whole horror of that day of days has set in. — The earth trembles, graves
burst open, the dead arise and step forth in [long] endless files. The great and the small of this earth,
kings and beggars, the just and the ungodly—all are making that pilgrimage, [shuddering and (?) in
endless files]; the cry for mercy and grace falls terrifyingly on our ear. — The crying becomes ever
more dreadful—our senses forsake us and all consciousness fades at the approach of eternal judgement. The *'great summons'* is heard; the trumpets from the Apocalypse call [every body and every
soul];—in the midst of the awful silence we think we hear in the farthest distance a nightingale, like
a last quivering echo of earthly life! Softly there rings out a chorus of the holy and the heavenly:

    'Risen again, yea thou shalt be risen again!' There appears the glory of God! A wonderful gentle
light permeates us to our very heart—all is quiet and blissful! — And behold: there is no judgement.
— There is no sinner, no righteous man—no great and no small. — There is no punishment and no
reward! An almighty feeling of love illumines us with blessed knowing and being!⁶³

---

⁶³ Translation by Donald Mitchell, *WY*, 183–4. The
autograph of Mahler's text is reproduced in the same work,
pp. 179–82, and also in the Kaplan facsimile of the autograph score of the symphony, p. 40. The original German
text appears in printed form, with several slips, in Alma
Mahler, *Gustav Mahler: Erinnerungen und Briefe* (1949),
267–9. The bracketed passages in the translation are
crossed out in the autograph.

5

Mahler and Germany

MORTEN SOLVIK

Germany holds a place of particular importance in any consideration of Mahler's life and works. As a conductor, he gained much of his early experience honing his skills in Kassel, Leipzig, and Hamburg and earning a reputation as a talented musician. This period also brought him his first significant exposure as a composer. Ill-fated performances in Hamburg, Weimar, and other cities foreshadowed the many difficulties he would encounter in bringing his works before the public. Even after his career had taken him elsewhere, he returned to Germany often, mostly as a guest conductor giving concerts throughout the country. Perhaps most importantly, Germany represented a cultural heritage with which Mahler clearly identified—on a deeply personal level and as an artist and intellectual.

Mahler and the German Musical Theatre

Kassel (1883–1885)

Mahler began his first musical engagement in Germany as second conductor of the Royal Theatre at Kassel in the summer of 1883. Though he had already held a series of conducting posts in his native Austria (in Bad Hall, Laibach, and Olmütz),[1] the level of achievement in these provincial theatres remained rather modest. Kassel's larger orchestra and more sophisticated repertoire provided him with a much more professional setting in which to work. Despite these promising circumstances, it was not long before the aspiring young conductor encountered difficulties. The theatre was run under the strict management of Baron Adolph von und zu Gilsa, a decorated veteran of the Franco-Prussian War whose military style demanded absolute obedience. Mahler did not adapt well to such strictures of behaviour, as the record of disciplinary measures taken against him clearly demon-

---

[1] Laibach is the German name for Ljubljana, which today lies in Slovenia; likewise, Olmütz (Olomouc) is today a city in the Czech Republic.

strates. Worse still, the artistic standards of the theatre fell far below his expectations. Conducting mostly light operatic favourites[2] and struggling with an ensemble plagued by complacency, Mahler found little to satisfy his altogether loftier ambitions. Frustrated by the situation, he directed his resentment at his superior, Kapellmeister (First Conductor) Wilhelm Treiber: 'His Lordship the Court Conductor keeps all the classics for himself; he is the jolliest 4/4-beater I have ever come across. Naturally I am the "pigheaded young man" who absolutely refuses to receive initiation from him into the mysteries of art.'[3]

Such smugness seemed hardly befitting a man in his early twenties who could claim neither seasoned experience nor public acclaim. But Mahler, who was already becoming aware that his goals as a conductor lay far beyond the achievements of conventional opera houses, saw matters differently. Though his uncompromising standards and fanatic attention to detail sorely tested the nerves of the orchestra and singers, he felt entirely justified in upsetting traditions and ruffling egos in his pursuit of artistic excellence. In Kassel, these reforming efforts did not go unnoticed. Already in the first month of his tenure, local critics praised the results and pointed to the 'refined nuances' of his conducting.[4]

Despite such positive evaluations, the young conductor longed for more favourable conditions in which to work. A performance by the famed Meiningen Court Orchestra in January 1884 under Hans von Bülow only served to remind Mahler that far greater musical achievements were possible with more accomplished artists. The concert so impressed the young man that he immediately dispatched a letter to the maestro pleading with him to take him on as an assistant and to save him from his dreadful fate at Kassel.[5] Bülow rejected the plea and, in a coldly calculating move, passed the missive on to Kapellmeister Treiber, a revelation that could only have worsened Mahler's already troubled relationship with the Kassel Theatre.

In this first stormy season, Mahler also fell in love. Johanna Richter, a singer who had also recently joined the Kassel company, became the cause of endless torment and admiration. In attempting to express his emotions for his beloved, Mahler wrote a series of poems that would become the basis of his song cycle *Lieder eines fahrenden Gesellen*. Extensive quotations from the cycle would also appear in the First Symphony, another work that Mahler began during his Kassel years. A third work from this period, incidental music to Joseph Victor von Scheffel's highly popular drama *Der Trompeter von Säckingen*, has not survived.[6]

---

[2] The standard fare for Mahler included works by Nicolai, Flotow, Delibes, and others, although he did occasionally conduct more substantial works such as *Rigoletto*, *Robert le Diable*, and Gounod's *Faust*.

[3] Letter to Friedrich Löhr, 19 Sept. 1883; *MDS*, 169 (translation emended); see also Mahler, *Selected Letters*, 74–5.

[4] See e.g. the review of his performance of Gounod's *Faust* in the *Kasseler Zeitung*, 18 Sept. 1883. Mahler's tendency to take unconventional tempi stirred comment as well, though this habit would generate much greater debate in years to come.

[5] 'At the concert yesterday, when I beheld the fulfilment of my utmost intimations and hopes of beauty, it became clear to me that I had found my spiritual home and my master, and that my wanderings would come to an end now or never.' For the complete text of the letter, written on 25 or 26 Jan. 1884, see *MDS*, 170.

[6] Accounts reveal that some of the materials in this work appeared in the 'Blumine' movement of the original version of the First Symphony.

In the autumn of 1884 Mahler sensed that his position at Kassel was growing more precarious and prudently cast about for a new appointment. By December he had contacted the impresarios Angelo Neumann in Prague,[7] Max Staegemann in Leipzig, and Bernhard Pollini in Hamburg. All three would eventually offer him conducting posts, but it was Staegemann who acted first: Mahler was to begin a six-year contract in Leipzig in 1886. Though the arrangement called for only one more season at Kassel, this was not to prove possible. As the 1884/5 season came to a close, the animosity between Treiber and Mahler deteriorated into open conflict. Mahler, who had led a choral society in nearby Münden, had been invited to conduct the choir and the Kassel Theatre Orchestra at a festival in June 1885. As leader of the Kassel ensemble, Treiber took offence at being pre-empted by his subordinate and successfully used his authority to block the appearance of the orchestra. In spite of Treiber's efforts, Mahler managed to assemble a group of players, a choir of over 400 voices, and several prominent soloists to mount a performance of Mendelssohn's *Paulus*. The festival was a major public success; reviewers found Mahler's gesticulations on the podium somewhat overwrought, but most were truly impressed by the performance. One columnist concluded prophetically: 'we are convinced that he will have a great future as a conductor'.[8]

Mahler's coup at the summer festival considerably enhanced his standing in musical circles. Nevertheless, the intolerable conditions in Kassel forced him from his post and left him wondering with some anxiety what he would do until his engagement in Leipzig the following year.[9] Fortunately, negotiations undertaken with Angelo Neumann at the German Theatre in Prague secured him an appointment for the coming autumn. Though this engagement as 'second conductor' only lasted one season, Mahler was able to assume a prominent role in the running of the opera house. Eager to stay for a longer term, he was nevertheless forced by contractual obligations to go to Leipzig the following year.

Leipzig (1886–1888)

Mahler's return to Germany in the fall of 1886 at first proved extremely difficult. After his duties as *de facto* musical director in Prague he now found himself relegated to the position of subordinate conductor. The announcement at the Leipzig Municipal Theatre soon after his arrival, that the forthcoming *Ring* cycle was to be conducted exclusively by the first conductor, Arthur Nikisch, so infuriated Mahler that it prompted his resignation. Staegemann, however, refused to let the young conductor go, and when Nikisch became seriously ill later in the season Mahler unexpectedly had his chance to conduct the Wagner tetralogy. Audiences clearly approved of the replacement, as, eventually, did the critics, who especially praised Mahler's interpretation of *Siegfried*. Though resentful of his subor-

---

[7] Neumann first heard from Mahler when he himself was in the process of leaving his position at the Bremen Opera to become Director of the German Theatre in Prague.

[8] *Kasseler Journal*, 1 July 1885.

[9] For further reading on Mahler's years in Kassel, see Hans Joachim Schaefer, *Gustav Mahler in Kassel* (Kassel: Bärenreiter, 1982) and id., Heinz Rölleke, and Andrea Linnebach, *Gustav Mahler: Jahre der Entscheidung in Kassel, 1883–1885* (Kassel: Stadtsparkasse Kassel, 1990).

dinate position and ever on contentious terms with the orchestra,[10] Mahler was finally finding broad public support for his abilities.

At the end of Mahler's first season in Leipzig, Carl von Weber, grandson of the composer Carl Maria von Weber, approached the conductor with the fragments of a comic opera left unfinished at his grandfather's death. Though several attempts to complete *Die drei Pintos* had been made before (including a project begun by Meyerbeer), no one had yet assembled the work into a performable score. Mahler undertook the challenge and in the following months deciphered and orchestrated the sketches, filled in the many missing sections of the work with materials from lesser-known works by Weber, and even composed some numbers himself.[11] The première of the opera in January 1888 met with enthusiastic praise and prompted productions in Hamburg, Munich, Dresden, Kassel, and other cities. These performances considerably enhanced Mahler's reputation in Germany; what is more, royalty payments brought him appreciable financial reward.[12]

In this prosperous period of his life, Mahler found the inspiration to complete his First Symphony, a composition which at that time was conceived as a five-movement symphonic poem (later entitled 'Titan'). He wrote out the work in a matter of weeks in the early spring of 1888 while in the throes of an emotional involvement with the wife of Carl von Weber. Later that summer he completed the first movement of his Second Symphony, a movement that, for a time, he designated an independent symphonic poem with the title *Todtenfeier* ['Funeral rite']. The Leipzig period also saw the composition of the first of numerous songs with texts drawn from the folk-poetry collection *Des Knaben Wunderhorn*.[13]

Buoyed by his accomplishments, Mahler no doubt felt justified in demanding more say in the affairs of the Leipzig Theatre. When in May 1888 he became involved in a dispute with the chief stage manager (who, according to the protocol, was ranked higher than he), Mahler simply resigned and sought more propitious conditions elsewhere. After a brief summer engagement in Prague, he concluded a very favourable multi-year contract with the Royal Hungarian Opera House in Budapest.

Hamburg (1891–1897)

Mahler's third appointment in Germany followed three years later as unfavourable developments in Budapest's cultural politics prompted him to seek out another position. Though he finally accepted Bernhard Pollini's offer to join the Municipal Theatre of Hamburg as first conductor, it was difficult for him not to feel somewhat demoted in his

---

[10] Relations were so strained that the orchestra even filed a complaint with the City Council against Mahler's strictness as a conductor. See *MDS*, 177.

[11] See Dieter Härtwig, 'Notes on Gustav Mahler's Arrangement of Carl Maria von Weber's Opera Fragment *Die drei Pintos*', in *News about Mahler Research*, 37 (Autumn 1997), 3–11, and Birgit Heusgen, *Studien zu Gustav Mahlers Bearbeitung und Ergänzung von Carl Maria von Webers Opernfragment 'Die drei Pintos'* (Regensburg, 1983).

[12] After the première Mahler boasted with obvious pride to his parents that he was now a 'famous' man. See *MDS*, 179–80.

[13] It should be noted, however, that the *Lieder eines fahrenden Gesellen* also reveal textual similarities with *Des Knaben Wunderhorn*; see Gustav Mahler, *Lieder eines fahrenden Gesellen*, ed. Zoltan Roman (Sämtliche Werke, Kritische Gesamtausgabe, 14/1; Vienna: Josef Weinberger, 1982), viii and Donald Mitchell, *WY*, 117–19.

new surroundings. In Budapest he had enjoyed the privileges of directing the entire opera house; in artistic and governmental circles alike he was a well-respected personality whose productions had rescued the fortunes of the failing theatre.[14] In Hamburg he was again a subordinate, a 'Kapellmeister', with duties limited strictly to musical matters and with no direct say in broader artistic questions.

Mahler nevertheless had enough to do in his new position. A large standard repertory dominated by the works of Wagner, frequent performances, and a host of new productions (*Eugène Onegin*, *Falstaff*, and others) demanded virtually all his energies during the opera season. His performances found favour with the critics, especially in the period immediately following his appointment. Reviewers praised the 'ingenious conductor' for his ability to bring out the 'finest details' of operatic scores.[15] In Hamburg Mahler also came into contact once again with the esteemed conductor Hans von Bülow, this time making a far more favourable impression on the maestro. Bülow admired the younger musician's talents and called upon him to conduct in his famous Hamburg Philharmonic subscription series, a series that Mahler later led for the entire 1894/5 season. These concert appearances proved extremely valuable, for though Mahler had by now conducted in the theatre for more than ten years, he had had virtually no experience in the concert hall.[16] Bülow showed far less enthusiasm for the young man's compositions, however. The *Todtenfeier* movement of the Second Symphony, for instance, merely confounded the old master. Ironically, it was Bülow's own 'funeral rite' in 1894 that would inspire Mahler to bring the finale of this work to completion.

During these years, Mahler settled into the pattern of compositional activity that would characterize most of the rest of his life. In 1893 he spent his first summer in Steinbach am Attersee in Upper Austria, where the calm of the countryside allowed him to concentrate on his creative endeavours away from the rush of the opera house. The summers at Steinbach (1893–6) would see the completion of both the Second and Third Symphonies, further songs based on poems from *Des Knaben Wunderhorn*, and the orchestration of the song-cycle *Lieder eines fahrenden Gesellen*.

On the whole, Mahler remained on fairly good terms with the orchestra and opera house throughout most of his tenure at Hamburg. Occasional tiffs were not uncommon and his strict style of rehearsing bred discontent as always, but he had by now gained experience in handling such matters. His six-year stay in the Hanseatic port had far outlasted his tenure at any other institution thus far. Throughout this period, Mahler raised artistic standards in the theatre and discovered new talents among the singers. One of these, Anna von Mildenburg, who would also become romantically involved with Mahler, would become one of the leading Wagnerian sopranos of her generation. Despite his successes, however,

---

[14] For more information on this episode in Mahler's life, see Zoltan Roman, *Gustav Mahler and Hungary* (Budapest: Akadémiai Kiadó, 1991).

[15] See the articles by Carl Armbrust in the Hamburg *Fremdenblatt* and by Josef Sittard in the *Hamburgischer Correspondent* in the spring of 1891. Later reviews were at times much more critical, especially those by Sittard, who strongly objected to Mahler's quixotic tempi.

[16] As a theatre musician, Mahler led concerts on two religious holidays during the year and at certain ceremonies or rare benefit occasions; these performances took place in the theatre.

Mahler did not feel he had found his spiritual home in Hamburg. The situation worsened when a dispute with Pollini turned into a crisis in the autumn of 1896, yet Mahler, with characteristic foresight, had already begun the process of securing an appointment elsewhere. This time he had set his sights on the directorship of the Court Opera in Vienna, a position he had long coveted. Using all the political and artistic connections at his disposal and even converting to Christianity to avoid Viennese objections to his Jewish origins, he succeeded in returning to his homeland in April of 1897.[17] Mahler would often visit Germany as a conductor and composer after this, but he would never again return for a long-term professional engagement.

The Reception of Mahler's Works in Germany

Mahler achieved only modest success with his compositions during his appointments at Kassel, Leipzig, and Hamburg. For the most part, his reputation in Germany rested on his extraordinary abilities as a conductor. Only later in life and after rather inauspicious beginnings did he establish himself as a widely recognized composer.

The first performances of Mahler's orchestral works in Germany in the early 1890s left concert-goers deeply divided about the merits of his music. The composer had this to say on audience reaction to a performance in Weimar in June 1894:

My [First] Symphony was greeted on the one hand with furious opposition and on the other with the most unbridled approval. On the street and in the salons opinions collided in the most delightful manner![18]

While audiences demonstrated both for and against Mahler, critical opinion remained largely negative:

The amount of protean musical ideas appears small to me in comparison with the boundless formal expansion of the individual sections. I find the composer loses himself in mannerisms and trivialities which, in the end, evoke a feeling of discomfort.[19]

Such rejection deeply disappointed Mahler,[20] yet he was convinced of his own creative abilities and took an active role in promoting his works. In so doing, he demonstrated a keen awareness of the importance of good publicity:

[17] For further reading on Mahler and Hamburg, see Ferdinand Pfohl, *Gustav Mahler*, and Irmgard Scharberth, 'Gustav Mahlers Wirken am Hamburger Stadttheater', *Musikforschung*, 22 (1969), 443–56.

[18] Letter to Arnold Berliner, 5 June 1894; Mahler, *Briefe* (1982), 112 (my translation); see also Mahler, *Selected Letters*, 154.

[19] Review of the Weimar music festival by Otto Lessmann in *Allgemeine Musik-Zeitung*, No. 25 (22 June 1894); my translation.

[20] His frustration with unsympathetic listeners inspired the humorous caricature of his detractors in the sarcastic *Wunderhorn* song, 'Lob des hohen Verstandes', composed in 1896. See also his remark about the conductor Karl Muck's 'langohriges Urteil' ['long-eared verdict'] in a letter to Max Marschalk postmarked 6 Dec. 1896, Mahler, *Briefe* (1982), 185; the translation in Mahler, *Selected Letters*, 202 misses the point altogether.

Nothing would be more important for me than the presence at this concert of a representative of the Berlin press, and nothing would give me more heartfelt pleasure than to know that you, esteemed Sir, were among the auditors—and judges. . . .

Now at last I have the opportunity [to present my works]; nevertheless I am aware that I shall encounter strong opposition (and especially among the press) which could, in unfavourable circumstances, easily have the effect of blocking my access to the public, perhaps for years ahead.[21]

These efforts did not always bear fruit, but when critics finally did take a sympathetic view of his works Mahler was quick to express his thanks:

How much gratitude I felt, how important, yes how *necessary* it was for me after so much misunderstanding and philistinism to hear the voice of one who sees and comprehends; this you can easily understand when I tell you that I have experienced approval and encouragement for the first time in ten years.[22]

Mahler had not yet silenced the voices of opposition, but by the mid-1890s he had, in fact, become the object of growing interest in the musical world. The première of the Second Symphony in December 1895 brought him his first important success; from then on the musical press felt increasingly inclined to consider him a promising composer.[23] Mahler had by now also published his first compositions: a set of fourteen songs (for voice and piano) bound in three volumes that appeared in 1892.[24] The Second Symphony was published three years later in a four-hand piano arrangement by the composer's friend Hermann Behn; the full score of the symphony followed in 1897. It was during this period, too, that other conductors began performing Mahler's works. Arthur Nikisch, Mahler's one-time rival at the Leipzig Opera, gave the first public performance of the second movement of his Third Symphony on 9 November 1896. Other conductors soon followed: six performances of various movements from the Second and Third Symphonies took place in Germany over the next four months.[25] These concerts inspired both critical and popular praise and brought the composer considerable attention. Though Mahler objected that performances of such fragments misrepresented his compositional intentions,[26] he no doubt felt encouraged by the widespread interest in his works.

Despite these first modest successes, however, Mahler did not make a profound impact on concert life in Germany until after he had left Hamburg in 1897. At the Vienna Court

---

[21] Letter to the critic G. Davidsohn, 18 Oct. 1893; *MDS*, 197.

[22] Letter to Oskar Bie, 3 Apr. 1895, after a performance in Berlin the previous month of the first three movements of the Second Symphony; Mahler, *Briefe* (1982), 122 (my translation); see also Mahler, *Selected Letters*, 160. He had written a very similar letter to the critic Oskar Eichberg a few days earlier and later in the year began a long correspondence with the Berlin critic Max Marschalk; see Mahler, *Selected Letters*, 159 (Eichberg) and 172 ff. (Marschalk).

[23] Richard Batka, Ernst Otto Nodnagel, Ludwig Schiedermair, and Max Marschalk were among those who first supported Mahler in various publications.

[24] Published by B. Schott of Mainz; later entitled *Lieder und Gesänge aus der Jugendzeit*.

[25] Arthur Nikisch (Symphony No. III/movement ii) twice in Leipzig, Jan. 1897; Felix Weingartner (III/ii) in Hamburg, Dec. 1896 and (III/ii, iii, vi) in Berlin, Mar. 1897; Ernst von Schuch (II/ii, iii, iv) in Dresden, Jan. 1897; and Mahler himself (II/i, ii) in Leipzig, Dec. 1896.

[26] See e.g. Mahler's letter to Richard Strauss from the summer of 1901 in Herta Blaukopf (ed.), *Gustav Mahler, Richard Strauss: Correspondence 1888–1911*, trans. Edmund Jephcott (London: Faber, 1984), 53–4.

Opera and later at the Metropolitan Opera in New York, he used his considerable prestige as a conductor to appear in cities throughout Germany to promote his own works.[27] Twenty-seven of the thirty orchestral concerts he gave in Germany during this period featured at least one of his own compositions.[28] In fact, Mahler conducted his own works more often in Germany than in any other country, including premières of six of the eight symphonies that received first performances during his lifetime (No. 2 in Berlin, 1895; No. 3 in Crefeld, 1902; No. 4 in Munich, 1901; No. 5 in Cologne, 1904; No. 6 in Essen, 1906; and No. 8 again in Munich, 1910).[29] Two of these premières—those of the Third and Sixth Symphonies—took place at festivals organized by the German General Society of Musical Artists ('Allgemeiner Deutscher Tonkünstlerverein'). This forum, a self-consciously modern and 'German' union of composers, provided Mahler with the opportunity to present other compositions as well: the First Symphony in Weimar, 1894; the Second Symphony in Basle, 1903; and various orchestral songs in Graz, 1905.

While such engagements brought the composer into contact with a wide variety of orchestras, two performing bodies played an especially important role in presenting his music to German audiences: the Berlin Philharmonic and the Kaim Orchestra of Munich. At the turn of the century, Berlin ranked as a leading city of German concert life, and it is hardly surprising that Mahler should have set about establishing a reputation there already in the early 1890s.[30] Early performances by the Berlin Philharmonic of songs from *Des Knaben Wunderhorn* (some of which were first performed in Berlin),[31] the Second Symphony (world première 1895), *Lieder eines fahrenden Gesellen* (world première 1896), and the First Symphony (1896) were, in time, followed by concerts featuring virtually all of Mahler's major works.

The Kaim Orchestra, founded in 1893 by the literary historian Franz Kaim, attracted many talented conductors at the turn of the century. Mahler first directed the ensemble in 1897 and returned in 1900 to give a performance of his Second Symphony.[32] Impressed by the abilities of the players, he entrusted them with the world premières of his Fourth Symphony in 1901 and his Eighth Symphony in 1910.[33] In all, the Kaim Orchestra and the Berlin Philharmonic each gave over a dozen performances of the composer's works during his lifetime. It should be added that other German orchestras played Mahler's

---

[27] Mahler conducted most frequently in Munich and Berlin, but also appeared in a dozen other cities.

[28] Of concerts given after 1897; compiled from Knud Martner, *Gustav Mahler im Konzertsaal: Eine Dokumentation seiner Konzerttätigkeit 1870–1911* (Copenhagen: privately published, 1985).

[29] *Lieder eines fahrenden Gesellen* and various *Wunderhorn* lieder also received their premières in Germany; see below.

[30] See the letter to the Berlin critic Davidsohn cited in n. 21 above.

[31] 'Der Schildwache Nachtlied' and 'Verlor'ne Müh' on 12 Dec. 1892; 'Urlicht' was first heard at the première of the

Second Symphony (as the work's fourth movement) on 13 Dec. 1895.

[32] The Kaim Orchestra had already performed the second movement of this work on 3 Mar. 1898 in Vienna under Ferdinand Löwe.

[33] In 1908 the Kaim Orchestra reorganized as the 'Konzertverein München'; it was this ensemble that formed the core group of musicians that first performed the massive Eighth Symphony. For further reading on Mahler and the Munich orchestra, see Dietmar Holland, 'Gustav Mahler und die Muenchner Philharmoniker', in *Die Münchner Philharmoniker von der Gründung bis heute*, ed. Regina Schmoll Eisenwerth (Munich: Wolf, 1985), 183–206.

compositions as well,[34] and that many of these performances were led by conductors other than Mahler. Felix Weingartner, Arthur Nikisch, Ernst von Schuch, Bernhard Stavenhagen, Oskar Fried, Richard Strauss, and other early promoters of Mahler[35] collectively led more performances of his works in Germany during the composer's lifetime than he himself.[36]

Mahler's popularity as a composer grew rather slowly after 1897 but reached a decisive turning point with the première of the Third Symphony in 1902. Alma Mahler later recalled the stirring event:

The performance was awaited with breathless suspense, for the rehearsals had done something to reveal the greatness and significance of the work. A tremendous ovation broke out at the end of the first movement. . . . The enthusiasm rose higher with each movement and at the end the whole audience got up from their seats in a frenzy and surged to the front in a body.[37]

This widely celebrated triumph greatly promoted Mahler's standing as a creative artist in Germany. Voices critical of his works continued to be heard, but the general tone of reviews hereafter indicates a noteworthy shift away from the overriding scepticism so evident in earlier years. Later premières of works such as the Sixth and especially the Eighth Symphony generated intense interest in the musical press and were hailed as major cultural events.

In the wake of these successes, Mahler became something of a celebrity. His talents as a consummate conductor and gifted composer drew universal praise. Yet for all the acclaim bestowed upon him, he insisted that audiences and critics still largely failed to comprehend his creations. He had a point. Even the most flattering reviews reveal that contemporary perceptions of his works often hinged on superficial considerations:

An astounding instrumentation emerges, astounding too the sense of tone colour. And above it all reigns a conductor who inspires fear in every musician with his uncanny ear and knowledge of the score, who fascinates and sweeps away every member of the orchestra . . .[38]

More revealingly, critics hesitated to embrace Mahler as a truly great composer. For all their enthusiasm, most reviewers felt uneasy about the discrepancy between his unquestionable technical prowess and what they deemed to be a lack of thematic originality: 'Now Mahler's themes are certainly known to be quite varied and boldly sweeping, but this is not (at least not always) matched by their intrinsic value. One admires them, but one is not always inwardly moved or overcome.'[39] While carefully worded, this point of criticism

---

[34] Including, most notably, the Gürzenich Orchestra of Cologne, the Winderstein Orchestra of Leipzig, and the Königliche Kapelle and Blüthner Orchestra, both of Berlin.

[35] Others included Julius Buths, Josef Krug-Waldsee, Fritz Steinbach, Hans Winderstein, Hermann Kutschbach, Max von Schillings, and Artur Bodanzky.

[36] Mahler conducted his own works on just over thirty occasions in Germany, while other conductors led over fifty performances during the same period.

[37] Alma Mahler, Memories, 41. The press reacted with equal enthusiasm, one critic speculating that the concert might be an event 'of lasting significance in the history of modern music' (Krefelder Zeitung, 10 June 1902, midday edition).

[38] From a review after the première of the Sixth Symphony in Rheinisch-Westfälische Zeitung, 28 May 1906, evening edition.

[39] Ibid.

echoes with remarkable consistency the far less polite objections to Mahler's works voiced already at the beginning of his career.[40]

Empty praise and subtle condemnation confirmed Mahler's charge that fame had not brought him understanding. Other factors point to the same conclusion. Though his pre-mières could inspire adulation, his compositions did not take a permanent place in German concert programmes. His Fifth, Sixth, and Seventh Symphonies, in fact, passed rather quickly into obscurity. For a composer who once described his Second Symphony as a work that 'sounds as if coming to us from another world' and that 'plumbs the depths of human knowledge itself',[41] the far more mundane reactions of the listening public were bound to cause disappointment. Over the years, Mahler grew to distrust what he viewed as the fickle and superficial enthusiasms of musical fashion.[42]

After Mahler's death in 1911, the excitement generated by his public *persona* could not sustain a genuine interest in his musical output. Latent reservations about his composi-tional talents crept to the fore, and the composer's works eventually disappeared from the concert stage in Germany altogether. Mahler could have predicted this, yet he was confident that one day his works would find genuine widespread appreciation. More than half a century would pass before his vision would come true.

'Germanness' and the German Intellectual Tradition

A final aspect of Mahler's relationship to Germany concerns his sense of identity and his development as a thinker. It was German culture more than any other that influenced the formation of his reflections on self, life, and art. As with so many central Europeans at the turn of the century, Mahler's 'Selbstbild' relied on a complex web of religious, linguistic, and political components. The 'thrice homeless' Mahler was, in effect, a Bohemian-born Moravian Jew who grew up in a German-speaking enclave of the Austro-Hungarian Empire. The conflicting allegiances and prejudices this combination inspired left the artist with an acute, searching sense of self. Mahler ultimately found his spiritual home in music, but as he would already learn as a student in the Imperial capital of Vienna, even art had become inextricably linked to questions of politics and identity. In those heady days of youth he developed a deep sense of kinship with the German heritage espoused by Richard Wagner, an anti-Semitic, nationalistic aesthete and composer of undeniable genius. Such was the young man's enthusiasm that he failed to recognize the inherent contradictions of his convictions; he even joined a group of intellectuals that took a staunchly pro-German

[40] See the 1894 review of the First Symphony quoted in n. 19 above.

[41] Letter to Arnold Berliner postmarked 31 Jan. 1895. Mahler, *Briefe* (1982), 119 (my translation); see also Mahler, *Selected Letters*, 158.

[42] See e.g. Mahler's conversation with Peter Rosegger and Alma about the meaning of public success after the Austrian première of *Salome* in Graz, 1906. Alma Mahler, *Memories*, 98.

stance in the clash of interests that commonly flared up between German, Czech, Hungarian, Polish, and other nationalist groups.[43]

Tempered by his own reflections and experiences later in life, Mahler emerged as a far less politicized being, yet the German cultural tradition continued to make a profound impact on him as a thinker and artist. He saw himself, after all, first and foremost as a German composer whose explicit duty was to carry forth, even while challenging, the legacy of Beethoven, Brahms, and Bruckner. The composer's intellectual bent also reveals a creative mind immersed in the German literary tradition. The First Symphony, for instance, at one time bore the title 'Titan', a clear allusion to a novel of the same name by Jean Paul; likewise, the heading for Part One of the symphony—'Blumen-, Frucht- und Dornenstücke'—echoes the subtitle to *Siebenkäs*, another work by the same author. The third movement, 'Todtenmarsch in "Callot's Manier"', alludes to the *Fantasiestücke in Callots Manier*, a collection of stories and essays by E. T. A. Hoffmann. Other compositions by Mahler contain far less obvious literary associations, such as passing references linking Friedrich Hölderlin's 'Der Rhein' and Nikolaus Lenau's 'Der Postillion' to parts of the Third Symphony. Whether these novels and poems directly influenced the composer's musical imagination remains a point of discussion, yet Mahler's propensity, especially in his early works, to link word and music reveals a key aspect of his artistic thinking.

Mahler also borrowed literary texts for direct incorporation into his symphonies. The poem for the choral finale to the Second Symphony, though largely Mahler's own text, is based on Friedrich Gottlieb Klopstock's ode 'Aufersteh'n'. The Third Symphony uses the 'Drunken Song of Midnight' from Friedrich Nietzsche's *Thus Spoke Zarathustra*. Symphonies Two, Three, and Four all contain vocal movements drawn from *Des Knaben Wunderhorn*, while the second movement of the Eighth Symphony comprises a symphonic and choral realization of the final scene of Goethe's *Faust*.[44] Though far from complete, this list not only hints at the extent of written sources pervading Mahler's works, it also provides a revealing profile of the composer's interests as a reader. Mahler's borrowings from Jean Paul, Hoffmann, Hölderlin, Lenau, Klopstock, Goethe, Rückert, and Des Knaben Wunderhorn underscore the composer's lifelong fascination with past German masters and a rather conservative taste that eschewed the writings of many of his contemporaries.

The German tradition also informed Mahler's forays into philosophy. As already mentioned, to his mind the most important figure in the constellation of German thinkers was Richard Wagner. While Wagner's music dramas and his notion of the *Gesamtkunstwerk* (the complete work of art that integrated all forms of expression) influenced Mahler both as conductor and composer, his admiration for 'the Master' went far beyond purely musical matters. Wagner's activities as a writer on such topics as art, religion, and politics exercised a considerable influence on the intellectual debate of the late nineteenth century. His

[43] For Mahler's involvement with the 'Saga Society' and the so-called Pernerstorfer circle, see McGrath, *Dionysian Art and Populist Politics*, esp. chs. 3 and 4; see also Peter Franklin, *The Life of Mahler* (Cambridge: Cambridge University Press, 1997), 26–42.

[44] Note that these examples are drawn exclusively from the German literary tradition. Mahler also made use of sources as diverse as Dante, Greek mythology, and Chinese poetry.

philosophy blended artistic inspiration, religious mysticism, and German chauvinism into a manifesto for social and moral change. An entire generation of young idealists took Wagner with utmost seriousness, among them Mahler himself. After reading Wagner's attack on the consumption of meat in the essay 'Religion and Art' (1880), the young composer immediately became a vegetarian. Fully under the spell of Wagner's Utopian tract, Mahler wrote of his decision to a friend: 'I expect of it no less than the *regeneration* of humanity.'[45]

In general, Mahler's philosophical interests betray a persistent belief in a realm of being beyond the material world. He was intrigued by Wagner's claim that artistic inspiration provided privileged access to the inner essence of life itself. Wagner was not alone in formulating this point of view. The early works of Nietzsche, especially *The Birth of Tragedy*, and Arthur Schopenhauer's *The World as Will and Representation* espoused this aesthetic idealism as well. Not surprisingly, Mahler admired both philosophers.[46] He also enthused over such German idealists as Gustav Theodor Fechner (*Nanna oder Über das Seelenleben der Pflanzen*), Hermann Lotze (*Microkosmus*), and Friedrich Albert Lange (*Geschichte des Materialismus*). These thinkers, mostly forgotten today, attempted to synthesize an animistic, non-rational world-view with the mechanistic and material models of modern science.

The idea that the artist was blessed with a unique ability to perceive the world residing beyond physical appearances figured prominently in Mahler's conception of himself as a composer:

The need to express myself musically—in symphonic terms—begins only on the plane of *obscure* feelings, at the gate that opens into the 'other world', the world in which things no longer fall apart in time and space.[47]

For Mahler the act of composition constituted a retelling of this mystical vision. Ironically, it was also a desire to celebrate this fundamental belief in a domain that transcended natural phenomena that disquieted him, imbuing his character with a sense of unease that motivates perhaps the most telling and compelling quality of his music. From the hymn of resurrection in the Second Symphony to the evocation of eternity in *Das Lied von der Erde*, his works stand as a testimony to a lifelong pursuit of life's most fundamental questions. They are, as well, the artistic legacy of an individual who, for all his conviction, could not find redemption in his belief in an ideal realm. Trapped in a world-view that could no longer sustain its viability, Mahler revealed the profound tensions of his age, embodying at once the challenges of the 'modern' and the glorious achievements of a grand and dying tradition.

[45] Letter to Emil Freund, 1 Nov. 1880; Mahler, *Selected Letters*, 65.

[46] Although there can be no question that such works as *The Gay Science* and *Thus Spoke Zarathustra* held a certain fascination for the composer, he later distanced himself from Nietzsche. Nietzsche's later works, it must be remembered, departed radically from the lyrical, Wagnerian tone of his earlier writings.

[47] Letter to Max Marschalk, 26 Mar. 1896; Mahler, *Selected Letters*, 179.

6

Mahler and France

HENRY-LOUIS DE LA GRANGE

At first sight, there seems to be no conceivable connection between Mahler and France. As a composer of symphonies in the purest German tradition, as one of the foremost interpreters of Mozart, Beethoven, and Wagner, Mahler seems totally foreign to the Latin spirit, to the finesse, the self-restraint, and the nuances of French art. In literature as in music, from childhood on, Mahler steeped himself in the German classics and Romantics with all the fervour of a young Bohemian Jew who considered himself heir to a great German tradition, a missionary of German culture on Czech soil. No trace of French influence can be found in his early youth, his education, or his reading. What is more, the irresistible appeal of Wagner—his ideas, his theories, and even his prejudices—could only have turned him against France and things French, especially since the two groups to which Mahler belonged, the Conservatoire's Wagner-Verein, and later the vegetarian society founded by Victor Adler and Engelbert Pernerstorfer, soon adopted a pronounced pan-German stance. If Mahler did in fact speak some French, as is shown by a card he wrote to Alfred Bruneau around 1900, it must have been at school that he acquired a rudimentary knowledge of the language, at that time widespread in central Europe.

Mahler owed his first contact with French art to the theatre, and to circumstances independent of his own tastes and wishes. A conductor, particularly a conductor at the start of his career, is obliged to conduct the works chosen by his managers. And at that time, French operas were very popular in both Germany and Austria. In the provincial theatres where Mahler was first employed, the repertoire reflected not the intrinsic quality of the works but their popularity and even more the generally limited capacities of the performing companies. Light music played a major part, and especially the music of Offenbach, who twenty years earlier had been adopted by the Viennese with such enthusiasm that they brought him annually to the city to conduct his own works.

In Bad Hall, Laibach, and Olmütz, Mahler conducted *Orphée aux Enfers*, *La Vie parisienne*, *La belle Hélène*, *La Princesse de Trébizonde*, *Le Mariage aux Lanternes*, and *Les Géorgiennes* by Offenbach, as well as *La Fille de Madame Angot* and *Giroflé-Girofla* by Charles Lecoq and *Les Cloches de Corneville* by Robert Planquette. It was in Laibach, at the age of 21, that Mahler conducted his first French opera: Gounod's *Faust*, known in German-speaking countries by the far more appropriate title of *Margarethe*. The following year in Olmütz he scored one of his first successes conducting Meyerbeer's *Les Huguenots*, which he was required to learn in two or three days, or rather two or three nights, and he continued with *Robert le Diable* and *L'Africaine*. A faithful Wagner disciple, he had no particular esteem for French grand opera or for its leading exponent, Giacomo Meyerbeer. However, he eventually ended up defending this specifically French tradition against detractors, even in Vienna where in 1903 he revived *La Juive* by Halévy, whom he preferred to Meyerbeer, although that did not prevent him from also reviving *Les Huguenots*.[1]

In Olmütz he also conducted Méhul's *La Légende de Joseph et ses Frères*, which he described as a 'charming work possessing something of the grace of Mozart'.[2] But it was with another French opera that he had a real triumph in Olmütz, a triumph of great consequence for his future career. Karl Überhorst, chief stage director at the Dresden Opera, was so impressed by his performance of *Carmen*, staged under very primitive conditions, that he unhesitatingly recommended Mahler to the Intendant of the Kassel Theatre in Prussia, who immediately took him on.

In Kassel Mahler remained, against his will, the French opera specialist, broadening his repertoire with works that probably brought him no great satisfaction, such as *Le Roi l'a dit* by Leo Delibes and two operas by Adolph Adam, *Le brasseur de Preston* and *La Poupée de Nuremberg*. Later on, in Prague, he quickly convinced Angelo Neumann, the world-famous impresario, of his talent and his vocation as a theatre conductor with a performance of *Les Deux journées* by Cherubini, a work composed in the French style and first performed in Paris. At the German theatre in Prague, he was to prove to his cost that even Gounod was a composer to be reckoned with. He resigned his post rather than accept the tempi imposed on him for the ballet in *Faust* by the mistress of the *corps de ballet*.

After further enriching his French repertoire in Leipzig with works by Boieldieu and Auber, Mahler was appointed director of the Hungarian Opera in Budapest, where French music was also very popular. As well as the usual operas by Meyerbeer, Adam, and Auber, he put on Louis Maillart's *Les Dragons de Villars* (curiously titled in German *Das Glöckchen des Eremiten*) and *Mignon* by Ambroise Thomas, another familiar warhorse in Austrian and German opera houses of the time. But it was here in Budapest, and later in Hamburg, that Mahler could at last reveal his own taste by giving preference to Bizet's operas. He not only staged *Carmen* again, but also introduced *Les Pêcheurs de Perles*, which had never been performed on Austrian Imperial territory. In Hamburg, at the Stadt-Theater, where, though he could not choose the repertoire, he could at least decide who should conduct the various works, *Carmen* appeared frequently in the programme, nearly always conducted by him. Unfortunately, the stage sets and the productions were third-rate

---

[1] Mahler revived *Les Huguenots* at the Vienna Opera on 29 Sept. 1902. A speech he made during rehearsals in defence of the opera was reported shortly after his death in the *Fremden-Blatt* (21 May 1911, p. 17).

[2] HLG(F) i. 143; Mahler, *Briefe* (1982), 21.

and the orchestra was permanently overworked, which drove Mahler to despair. In October 1896 his friend and confidant Natalie Bauer-Lechner questioned him about *Carmen* as they were coming out from a performance that, for once, had pleased him. It is a wonderful work, she said, but would it not be better to avoid putting it on too often so as to avoid giving the public a surfeit of such 'spicy food'? 'That will never happen', replied Mahler, 'because of the wonderful scoring. This is one of the most meticulously worked-out scores that you can possibly imagine. When I am conducting, I observe and analyse all its subtle details; I am constantly learning something new from it, finding out how this or that effect is turned to the best advantage.'[3]

Mahler went still further when speaking to his friend the Czech composer Josef Bohuslav Förster, who asked him if he could borrow the score of *Die Meistersinger* to study the orchestration. Mahler, the devout Wagnerian, unhesitatingly replied that *Meistersinger* was 'badly orchestrated' (*schlecht instrumentiert*). He would send him instead the score of *Carmen* which contained 'not a single superfluous note' (*keine einzige überflüssige Note*).[4] Here we can see at first hand that he was consciously influenced by French composers such as Bizet in treating instrumental timbre in a freer and more original manner than most German composers.

Mahler's great interest in *Carmen* led him to explore Bizet's music further. He discovered the score of an unknown one-act opera, *Djamileh*, which he pressed the director of the Stadt-Theater into adding to the repertoire. Admittedly the libretto, inspired by a story by Alfred de Musset, was of no great worth, but the action's 'subtle psychological undertones' (*psychologisch tiefinnerliche Vorgang*) and the 'exquisitely refined' and 'delicate' orchestration (*schlanke Partitur*)[5] he found ravishing, especially because, once more, every note was directly to the point. Later, in Vienna, he again put on *Djamileh*; and in 1900, took advantage of the engagement of Marie Gutheil-Schoder, a highly talented singer who was also a first-rate actress, to freshen up the old production of *Carmen*.

In Hamburg Hans von Bülow (d. Cairo, 1894), Mahler's mentor and fervent admirer, bequeathed him when he died the conductorship of the Subscription Concerts. Mahler then took on the concert repertoire that soon became indispensable to him to 'shake the dust of the opera house from my feet'. It was thus that at the beginning of 1895 he had one of the key encounters of his life when he conducted the *Symphonie fantastique* by Berlioz. He brought to it such fire and excitement that the leading critics of the day blamed him for identifying himself too closely with a work whose 'ugliness' and 'strangeness' still displeased and shocked them. On 20 November 1898 when, with the Vienna Philharmonic, he again included the *Fantastique* in one of his programmes, the reviews, notably Hanslick's, were no less hostile, and Mahler railed against such absurd prejudice towards a score 'so full of originality and imagination'. 'Someone like me', he exclaimed, 'learns something new every time he conducts such a work, while the critics have the effrontery to condemn it out of hand on a single hearing!' (*Unser einer lernt immer neu beim Dirigieren*

---

[3] HLG(F) i. 584.   [4] HLG(F) ibid.; Förster, *Der Pilger*, 488.   [5] HLG(F) i. 715.

eines solchen Werkes, während ein Kritiker sich erfrecht, gleich beim ersten Anhören darüber den Stab zu brechen).[6]

In the United States, the *Fantastique* featured no fewer than eight times in his programmes with the New York Philharmonic, notably when the orchestra went on tour in New England at the beginning of 1910. Henry T. Finck, the noted critic of the *New York Post*, wrote that hearing him conduct this work was 'as hypnotizing as hearing Paderewski's famous interpretation of the Liszt Rhapsodies'.[7] In Boston, Olin Downes was overwhelmed by the 'appallingly effective' and 'nightmarish' 'March to the Scaffold': 'Like Berlioz, he lived in every phrase and measure, conducted as a composer would have done, with an enthusiasm for every note, a regard for each instrument, that was a sort of personal infatuation.'[8] The tone and content of such accounts make it clear that Mahler was a very great interpreter of the *Fantastique*. This comes as no surprise, for the influence of Berlioz on his own compositions was to prove durable and decisive, in more respects than are acknowledged even today.

Two orchestral works by Bizet were in Mahler's concert repertoire with the Vienna Philharmonic: the *Roma* Suite (pub. 1880), whose Austrian première he gave in 1898; and, later in New York, the first *L'Arlésienne* Suite (1872). But Bizet, who had died three months after the première of *Carmen* (1875), already belonged to the past. Mahler made contact with contemporary French stage music as well, starting in Hamburg, where he conducted premières of two operas by Alfred Bruneau, *Le Rêve* and *L' Attaque du Moulin*. At first he seems to have been somewhat startled by this music, which he said was 'very difficult but very interesting'. However, by the time he was Director of the Vienna Opera, he had come to like Bruneau's music sufficiently to write, in rather ungrammatical French: 'Dans notre Théâtre est toujours une place pour un nouveau oeuvre de vous' ('There's always a place for a new work of yours in our theatre').[9]

Appointed to Vienna in 1897, Mahler regretfully noted the great popularity of Jules Massenet's works at the Hofoper. He had in fact conducted the Hamburg première of *Werther* in the presence of the composer, who had attended the final rehearsals. Massenet was delighted with Mahler's conducting because, as usual when wanting to launch a new work, Mahler gave himself heart and soul to his task. God knows it was not easy for him in this case, for in his correspondence he described *Werther* as 'widerwärtigste Machwerk' (disgusting botch-work)[10] as 'an affront to Goethe'[11] and even as 'a crime for which anybody should be condemned to hard labour' (*für die einer ins Zuchthaus kommen solte!*).[12] To avenge himself upon a piece to which he was unwillingly devoting so much energy, he could only give it the nickname '*Mein Allerwerthester*', which is to say, 'my arse'.[13]

[6] Ibid. 752; NB-L, *Erinnerungen*, 127.

[7] HLG(F) iii. 624; *New York Post*, 7 Jan. 1910.

[8] HLG(F) iii. 652; *Boston Post*, 27 Feb. 1910.

[9] Undated card to Alfred Bruneau, *Revue internationale de musique*, No. 7 (Feb. 1982).

[10] HLG(F) i. 523; unpublished letter to Hermann Behn, dated in Behn's hand 4 Oct. 1895.

[11] NB-L, *Erinnerungen*, 42.

[12] Letter to Hermann Behn (see above, n. 10).

[13] Natalie Bauer-Lechner, unpublished manuscript entitled *Mahleriana* (Bibliothèque Musicale Gustav Mahler, Paris).

Of the French operas given first performances by Mahler throughout his long theatrical career, the most notable was undoubtedly Gustave Charpentier's *Louise* in 1903. For reasons which are not clear but which relate, perhaps, to the 'naturalism' of this 'roman musical', he hesitated for a long time before bringing to Vienna a work that had already been seen all over Germany. But in the end he changed his mind, and invited the composer to the final rehearsals and the first night. He freely complied with all the composer's wishes, and even postponed the première in order to make considerable changes to the staging. Charpentier's uncouth behaviour and his contempt for convention in no way shocked either Mahler or Alma, his wife. Charpentier was overwhelmed by the amount of work that had gone into the production.[14] However, although Mahler devoted much time and energy to it, this cannot be taken as proof of an affinity with French art, because he was always an ardent advocate of any work he had decided to perform. He eventually tired of *Louise*, as he had of Offenbach's *Contes d'Hoffmann* two years before, abandoning the podium to one of his assistants after a few performances.

At the time of the première of *Louise*, Mahler had already seen Paris, which he had visited with the Vienna Philharmonic in 1900. Unfortunately, this first journey—during which Parisians were introduced to the celebrated Viennese orchestra making its historic first tour—did not take place under auspicious circumstances: in June 1900 the Exposition internationale was in full swing. 'How completely incongruous', Mahler wrote to a friend, 'to be playing music for the French *at this time*! All the pointless turmoil around me is so upsetting that I haven't got a moment to enjoy the beauties of Paris. It is incredible how the whole thing boils down to a pack of fine phrases, lies, posturing. . . . There is only one word for it, Pfui! . . . I feel such a fool when I take up my baton! O! O! O! God knows how I will ever get rid of this feeling of disgust! I feel as if I had been prostituting myself!'[15]

As soon as he got out of the train, Mahler was alarmed to see his name written as 'Malheur' on the posters. 'A fine start', he groaned.[16] (He would no doubt have been even more mortified to see that eighty years later, his music having become extremely popular in France, the French were still having trouble placing the 'l' of his name after the 'h' rather than before it.) In 1900, concerts were held either in good conditions at the Théâtre du Châtelet, or at the Trocadéro. Unfortunately, it was in the latter vast hall, notorious for its terrible acoustics, that the opening concert of the tour took place. Some of the capital's best-known musicians and politicians were in the audience, notably Camille Saint-Saëns, Alfred Bruneau, the singer Victor Maurel, the parliamentary deputy Jules Roche, and the future prime minister Georges Clemenceau. Jules Massenet, Gustave Charpentier, and the writer Catulle Mendès joined later audiences for the concerts, whose programmes were exclusively made up of classical and Romantic works. Only the Scherzo from Bruckner's

[14] HLG(F) ii. 330; Alma Mahler, *Gustav Mahler: Erinnerungen und Briefe* (Frankfurt: Propyläen, 1971), 84.

[15] HLG(F) i. 883; unpublished letter to Nanna Spiegler, postmarked 22 June 1900 (Pierpont Morgan Library, New York).

[16] HLG(F) i. 879; Ludwig Karpath, *Begegnung mit dem Genius* (Vienna: Fiba, 1934), 151.

Fourth, and Goldmark's Overture *Im Frühling*, were there to represent contemporary Austrian music.

On the whole, the press was very favourable. At worst, some writers criticized Mahler's 'abuse of nuances' in classical works, his 'exaggerated polish', his tendency to 'discover an ulterior motive behind every note', or his 'never-ending search for contrast'. It was nonetheless acknowledged that the Viennese strings were superior to any in Paris, and that the Viennese displayed an 'exact discipline', 'obedient zeal', and 'sustained attentiveness' that were 'not always shown by French orchestras'.[17] Certainly some of Mahler's tempi caused surprise, and were unfavourably compared with those of Richter, but this was also the case in Germany and particularly in Vienna. His interpretation of the *Symphonie fantastique* was described as 'inspired', and the monthly magazine *Le Ménestrel* concluded a particularly favourable overall review with the judgement that the orchestra and its conductor had 'won the battle'.[18] If the prestige of the Vienna Philharmonic was thus fully recognized, the houses were only half full, as the Parisians and their foreign visitors already had too many distractions elsewhere. The takings were so inadequate that Mahler had to approach Baron Rothschild to pay the musicians' fares home.

The whole unfortunate experience left Mahler chiefly with memories of the few excursions he had been able to make to the outskirts of Paris: a long forest walk, for instance, from Versailles to Marly, on the track of 'the Louis (the Kings of France) and Napoléons'.[19] He had found the illuminations 'worthy of the Thousand and One Nights'. The French capital had immediately impressed him with its colossal size, and he had straightaway declared that: 'The difference between Paris and Vienna is as great as the difference between Vienna and Iglau.' He nevertheless expressed considerable bitterness on his stay as a whole:

'As I expected, for me Paris was nothing but a vast desert', he wrote to one of his friends. . . . 'The concerts left me with a dreadful hangover which I'll tell you about when we meet. Any music-making requiring deep inner concentration was necessarily out of place in such a turmoil. . . . As you can imagine, we poor *Musikanten* that we are wandered around like nightingales lost in the middle of a flock of sparrows. Even the most robust, coarse-stringed members of the Philharmonic couldn't rise above this utterly hostile background. And everything was overpainted in poster colours and splashed around by conscientious newspaper scribblers, as a pioneer expedition for "German" and "Viennese art". We were ashamed, and crept away with our tails between our legs.'[20]

Although he left France saddened by the failure of the tour, Mahler could not know that it was to have unexpected consequences and benefits for his personal life. One of the few consolations of his stay had been 'the enthusiasm of true friends of art'. In Paris, probably at the Austrian embassy, he had indeed made the acquaintance of two dedicated French music lovers. One was Colonel Picquart, hero of the Dreyfus affair, who had just emerged

[17] HLG(F) i. 880; Willy (as 'L'Ouvreuse') in *Comoedia*, Pierre Lalo in *Le Temps*.

[18] HLG(F) i. 882. Oscar Berggruen in *Le Ménestrel*.

[19] Unpublished letter to Justine Mahler, dated 18 June

1900 (Rosé Collection, University of Western Ontario, London, Ontario).

[20] HLG(F) i. 883; letter to Nanna Spiegler (see above, n. 15).

from prison after the trial of the famous case had been reviewed; the other was Paul Clemenceau, an engineer, a *polytechnicien*, and younger brother of the future prime minister. Both were bilingual, and steeped in German culture in all its forms. For both of them, music was one of the vital necessities of life and Mahler's Paris concerts had been a revelation. As it happened, Paul Clemenceau's wife was Austrian, the daughter of a liberal journalist, Moritz Szeps, a friend of Archduke Rudolph and founder of the *Neues Wiener Tagblatt*. In the course of a conversation, Sophie Clemenceau persuaded Mahler to get in touch with her sister Bertha Zuckerkandl on his return to Vienna. Bertha was the wife of a distinguished anatomist, and an art critic in her own right. Her salon was visited by leading Viennese artists, and in particular the Secessionists. In the autumn of 1900, Mahler thus made friends with the Zuckerkandls. He was not a regular visitor to their salon (nor to any other, for that matter), but he accepted an invitation to dinner there on 7 November 1901, an evening which was to be a turning point in his life. It was here that he fell almost immediately under the spell of a young Viennese beauty with a sharp mind and a quick tongue. Her name was Alma Schindler, and she was to become his wife.

The most important result of Mahler's ill-fated visit to Paris was that he had awakened in the two eminent members of the Paris intelligentsia mentioned above, Picquart and Clemenceau, an admiration and sympathy that were never to falter. When, in May 1905, Mahler was invited to conduct two concerts at the Strasbourg Festival, his two Parisian admirers came post-haste, bringing with them two of their best friends. In these unlikely circumstances a sincere friendship sprang up between Mahler and a group of Frenchmen whom Bertha Zuckerkandl nicknamed the 'Dreyfus Quartet' because they were all passionate Dreyfusards and all loved music with equal fervour. Apart from Clemenceau, soon to be appointed President of the Alfred Nobel factories in France, and the Alsatian Picquart, the quartet comprised the mathematician and *polytechnicien* Paul Painlevé, future prime minister, and Guillaume de Lallemand, a career soldier in spite of himself, whose main preoccupations were music and literature.

Strasbourg, the town where Mahler made friends with these four Frenchmen, was at that time under German rule. However, French culture was still important there, since a large part of the population and half the press were French-speaking. The Festival programme was divided between French and German music. Picquart came incognito from Paris, as Dreyfus had not yet been officially rehabilitated—nor had he been. From their first meeting, Alma was captivated by this exceptional man, a 'seraphic being' whose clear blue eyes, like a mountain stream, immediately convinced her that Dreyfus was innocent at a time when this was still open to doubt.[21] Picquart was already familiar with Mahler's symphonies, having played the four-hand piano reductions with Lallemand, so he was well prepared for the Fifth. The next day, after a performance of Beethoven's Ninth, the excitement of the public reached such a pitch that, as he tried to leave the hall, Mahler was engulfed by a crowd of hysterical admirers. He escaped with the help of his French friends,

---

[21] HLG(F) i. 669; Alma Mahler, *Erinnerungen*, 114.

who put him in a carriage and took him to a small tavern. That morning, the four of them had travelled in Goethe's footsteps to Sesenheim, an excursion Mahler had been unable to join because of a rehearsal. But at least they were able to talk together about the poet who throughout Mahler's life remained one of his favourite authors.

Ten months later, Clemenceau and Picquart went to Antwerp to hear Mahler once more conduct his Fifth Symphony. In the autumn of the same year, 1906, Mahler organized, especially for them, a 'secret festival' at the Hofoper conducted entirely by himself, with a programme consisting of major works in the German repertoire: *Fidelio*, *Figaro*, *Entführung*, and *Magic Flute*. On the evening of the last performance, which was to be *Tristan*, the culminating point of the week, Picquart received a telegram from Georges Clemenceau calling him urgently back to Paris to be Minister of War in the new Cabinet. According to Alma, he regretted all his life having missed Mahler's performance of what is probably Wagner's greatest work.[22]

Before moving on to the years of Mahler's life when he visited Paris almost annually, it is worth recalling that, in 1905, one of France's most famous writers, Romain Rolland, author of *Jean-Christophe*, the influential *roman-fleuve* about a musical genius (1906–12), and friend of Richard Strauss, was in Strasbourg. He attended Mahler's two concerts and gave a highly critical account of them, sparing neither the interpreter nor the composer. Mahler's Beethoven was to his mind 'neurasthenic', his 'incredible tempi' could only be described as 'a sin' (*un méfait*). According to Rolland, Mahler's performances betrayed 'the unfortunate hypnotic power of German force and brutality pulverizing a Viennese nature more given to reverie and gentle whimsy. This intensifies still more the impression of German heaviness'. His work 'strove to be colossal', and for the most part was 'empty'.[23] To understand this utterly negative point of view it must be remembered that the defeat of 1870 in the Franco-Prussian war had left terrible scars on France. Apart from Wagner, whom the French idolized in an almost masochistic manner, all composers from beyond the Rhine were taxed with their 'Germanic heaviness' and their obsession with the 'colossal'. Even Brahms was not fully recognized and accepted in France until much later during the Second World War.

Rolland's estimation of Mahler the symphonist was no more discerning. 'The melodies on which his works are built are rough-hewn blocks of mediocre quality, banal, imposing only through their massive proportions, and through the persistent repetition of rhythmic patterns, maintained with the obstinacy of *idées fixes*. . . . A lavish and strident bric-à-brac.' According to Rolland, Mahler was unable to escape 'the musical saturation to which his profession condemns him', and was ceaselessly assailed by 'alien thoughts crowding upon him from all directions'. This was also the main *leitmotif* of German criticism of Mahler at the time, which accused him repeatedly of filling his music with involuntary reminiscences and borrowings.

---

[22] HLG(F) ii. 958; Alma Mahler, *Erinnerungen*, 179.
[23] HLG(F) ii. 674; Romain Rolland, *Musiciens d'aujourd'hui* (Paris: Hachette, 1922), 185.

Romain Rolland was undoubtedly one of the most distinguished French musicologists and music critics of the time, and it is unfortunate that he should have thus failed to recognize Mahler's true stature as a composer and conductor. Luckily, among his younger colleagues in France, Mahler had already found at least one staunch supporter whose many essays and articles today make absorbing reading. In 1905, the year of the Alsace–Lorraine Festival, a slender volume of essays on painting and music by the young Swiss writer William Ritter, entitled *Etudes d'art étranger*, was published in Paris.[24] The longest article in it was devoted to Mahler, and it contained a description of the world première of the Fourth Symphony in Munich in 1901. At the final rehearsal, Ritter and his friend Marcel Montandon had 'heartily hissed' the new work, but a careful study of the score had subsequently changed their minds. In Crefeld, at the first complete performance of the Third Symphony the following year, Ritter was instantly won over, notably by the Finale, which he saw as 'perhaps the greatest Adagio written since Beethoven'.[25] In the years that followed, Ritter attended and reviewed several of Mahler's first performances, except that of the Eighth. Mahler, pleased to find such support in a world so often hostile to him, responded to Ritter's letters as early as 1902, and eventually met him in Munich in November 1906. Ritter's literary style can appear at first sight to be old-fashioned, with an almost baroque exuberance, but it nonetheless has extraordinary evocative power. A comparison of his articles with most of those written at the time shows that he was the first to understand the universal dimension of Mahler's music. Usually published in French magazines or papers, his eulogies sometimes provoked violent reactions, but at least they made Mahler's name known in Paris even before he had conducted any of his works there.

It was no doubt thanks to William Ritter and to the support of the Geneva composer Jaques-Dalcroze that in 1905 Mahler's music made its first appearance on the Paris musical scene. A modest appearance it was too, since it was not a symphony that was heard but an incomplete performance of *Lieder eines fahrenden Gesellen*, given on 26 February at a Lamoureux Concert conducted by Camille Chevillard, with Nina Faliero-Dalcroze, wife of Jaques-Dalcroze, as soloist. Although Gabriel Fauré, writing of this occasion in *Le Figaro*, praised the second song as 'a morning scene, fresh and fragrant', all the other accounts are inconsequential. 'L'Ouvreuse' (Emile Vuillermoz who, in 1905, was ghost-writing in *Comoedia* for Colette's husband, Willy) perpetrated some of his most biting puns at the expense of these 'pretentious bits of nonsense'.[26]

A few weeks later, a plan to perform the Fifth Symphony in the Alfred Cortot Concerts came to nothing—Mahler feeling that the rehearsal time proposed would be insufficient. In 1906, a young Viennese critic named Josef Reitler, living at the time in Paris, met with Gabriel Astruc, a young and dynamic impresario, to discuss the possibility of giving another Mahler performance at the Concerts Colonne. The Fifth was again suggested, then the Second, and finally the Third. Once again, however, these plans fell through because Mahler refused to accept a cut in the size of the orchestra for the occasion. He did not take

---

[24] William Ritter, *Etudes d'art étranger* (Paris: Le Mercure de France, 1905).

[25] Ibid. 269.

[26] HLG(F) ii. 665; 'L'Ouvreuse' in *L'Echo de Paris*.

these disappointments to heart, however, because he felt that his time had not yet come. 'I honestly doubt', he wrote to Reitler, 'whether France is at present a suitable milieu for my music and the thought of going to Paris to force upon people a kind of music that is found disconcerting even in my native country has quite frankly never occurred to me.'[27] A few weeks later he added, in another letter to Reitler: 'Getting away from here involves such great difficulties that it is only in quite exceptional circumstances—above all, only if I am assured of all the artistic requirements for a perfect realization of my intentions—that I could bring myself to come to Paris. And believe me, the time is not yet ripe! Let us wait another one or two years!'[28] On this occasion, Mahler proved astonishingly perceptive; for it was not until four years later, in 1910, that Paris first heard a work of his under his direction. Meanwhile his links with the French capital had strengthened, and he frequently stopped there *en route* to and from the United States.

Mahler and Alma did not visit Paris in 1908, but they were there twice in 1909, and for longer periods than on previous occasions. The first visit was in the spring and lasted about ten days. The occasion of this prolonged stay was a little family conspiracy hatched between Paris and Vienna. Carl and Anna Moll, stepfather and mother of Alma, had conceived the idea of commissioning a bust of Mahler from Auguste Rodin, who was then 70 years old and regarded as the greatest sculptor of his time. The prospect of sitting as model for hours at a time did not greatly appeal to Mahler, so he was told that the artist himself had expressed a wish to do his head. The ruse worked, and Mahler acquiesced. Paul Clemenceau served as intermediary, and managed to persuade Rodin to reduce his usual fee, which, at this stage of his career, was too high for Mahler's family.

In the spring of 1909 the Mahlers were invited to dinner by Georges Picquart at the Ministry of War. On arriving, they were not a little surprised to see, on each side of the main staircase, a double row of soldiers standing at attention in full dress uniform. A few days later, Picquart, having enjoyed their astonishment, greeted them by explaining that he had only conformed with the usual protocol for receiving crowned heads at the Ministry. As far as he was concerned, they both ranked with royalty. Picquart also intervened during this stay with the Prefect of Police so that husband and wife could attend a French performance of *Tristan* in his box. Unfortunately, in the middle of the second act, the Belgian tenor Ernest van Dyck (a former member of the Vienna Opera under Mahler's direction) abandoned his partner to bellow some of the most beautiful phrases in the love duet from the front of the stage. Mahler was so indignant that he stood up and walked out of the box without a word, leaving Picquart, the Clemenceaus—and the Prefect of Police—speechless with surprise.[29]

As Rodin had requested a few more sessions to finish the bust, Mahler came back and spent a few days in Paris in early autumn of the same year, arriving from Holland on his way to New York. At this time one of his symphonies, the First, had been introduced to Paris by José Lassalle, with the Munich Tonkünstler Orchestra. Lassalle was a Spanish conductor,

27 HLG(F) ii. 966; Mahler, *Briefe* (1982), 307.   28 HLG(F) ibid.; Mahler, ibid. 313.
29 HLG(F) iii. 482; Alma Mahler, *Erinnerungen*, 181.

born in France and living in Germany. Probably Mahler did not think much of him as a conductor since he left Paris some days before the concert. In fact this first performance was not regarded as much of an event by the Paris critics, who reviewed it briefly and merely expressed the wish to hear a Mahler work that was 'more characteristic'.

Their wish was granted the following year, Mahler having agreed to conduct the Orchestre Colonne in a performance of the Second Symphony. Meanwhile he had grown closer to France, and his knowledge of contemporary French music had increased, probably thanks to Paul Clemenceau and Guillaume de Lallemand, both friends of Debussy and Dukas. During his first Paris visit in 1909, Mahler studied a number of French scores, and chose some of them for his programmes with the New York Philharmonic. Besides Debussy's *L'Après-midi d'un faune* and three *Nocturnes*, he gave the New York premières of his two last orchestral *Images*, *Ibéria* and *Rondes de Printemps*, as well as performances of *L'Apprenti Sorcier* by Dukas and two works by Emmanuel Chabrier, *España* and *Ode à la musique*. According to Alma's memoirs, the only meeting between Mahler and Debussy took place in 1910, just before the concert at the Châtelet. Mahler's laconic comment on *Pelléas et Mélisande*, after hearing the work for the first time at the Hammerstein Opera in New York, has been reported by Alma and often quoted: apparently, he simply said that the music was 'not disturbing' (*Sie stört mich nicht*).[30] In my view, this tantalizingly enigmatic comment should in no way be taken as a definitive judgement, because Mahler often changed his opinions, and never clung to them when experience showed him that his initial judgement had been at fault. It should not be forgotten that, as early as 1907, before he left Vienna, he had included *Pelléas* among the new works to be produced at the Hofoper. If the first Viennese performance did not take place until three years later, it was because Mahler's successor, Felix von Weingartner, repeatedly postponed it.

Alma's account of the historic dinner at the home of Gabriel Pierné clearly implies that the meeting between Mahler and Debussy gave rise only to an exchange of polite and inconsequential remarks. Perhaps the language barrier was largely to blame for this lack of communication. Paul Dukas, Gabriel Fauré, Alfred Bruneau, and the Clemenceaus were present, but they seem not to have succeeded in enlivening the conversation. Dukas, sitting next to Alma, whispered unpleasant stories about Debussy's past in her ear. He invited the Mahlers to the Opéra-Comique the following evening, when his *Ariane et Barbe-Bleue* was being performed. Mahler went with Guillaume de Lallemand, and was sufficiently taken with Dukas's music to go backstage and congratulate him after the second act. Later he was glad he had not waited to do so until after the third, which bored him to death.[31]

The first Paris performance of the Second Symphony took place in 1910 thanks to the financial help of two competing organizations, the Société des grandes Auditions Musicales and Les Amis de la Musique. Both had been persuaded to sponsor the enterprise by a new Mahler admirer who was to prove both enthusiastic and tenacious, the young Italian composer, pianist, and conductor Alfredo Casella, who was then living in Paris.

[30] HLG(F) iii. 260; Alma Mahler Werfel, *Mein Leben* (Frankfurt: Fischer, 1960), 48.
[31] HLG(F) iii. 684; Alma Mahler, *Erinnerungen*, 199.

Edouard Colonne, conductor and founder of the orchestra which bore his name, died on 28 March, and there were fears that the concert of 17 April would have to be cancelled. Fortunately, his assistant Gabriel Pierné took over and, by the time Mahler arrived, had already begun rehearsals with the orchestra and chorus. The latter showed a lack of discipline characteristic of French groups; nonetheless Mahler praised the singers, regretting only that there were not enough of them—barely a hundred—to allow the symphony to make its fullest impact. He later expressed a lively appreciation of these 'professionals of excellent standard, far better than the Viennese'[32], all the more telling because he had rehearsed the Eighth Symphony with the Vienna Singverein and was thus in a position to make comparisons.

No effort was spared to make the Paris première of the Second Symphony an event of major importance in the capital. On Sunday 17 April, at 2.30 in the afternoon, a crowd of professionals and amateurs gathered in the vast Châtelet auditorium, which at the time seated almost three thousand. Once again, many well-known figures attended, notably Debussy, Dukas, Bruneau, André Messager, and Théodore Dubois. Alma Mahler later claimed she had seen Debussy, Dukas, and Pierné get up and leave in the middle of the second movement, an account that has many times been quoted. For my part, I have always found it extremely suspect, at least as far as Pierné was concerned; for the conductor of the Concerts Colonne could surely not leave the hall after having himself conducted the beginning of the concert. As for Dukas, the professional courtesy shown by Mahler in going to listen to his opera and conducting his *L'Apprenti Sorcier* in New York makes his departure seem equally unlikely. What is more, Dukas's kindness and courtesy were universally known and, indeed, a few days earlier, he had written a short tribute to Mahler which was destined to appear in a collection prepared by Paul Stefan on the occasion of Mahler's fiftieth birthday.

If neither Dukas nor Pierné left the hall, that still leaves Debussy unaccounted for. He was undoubtedly then living through a period of intense chauvinism, as was shown five months later when he refused to participate in the French Music Festival in Munich. What is more, *he* was certainly capable of being discourteous, even towards a colleague who had performed the *Nocturnes* and *Images* in the United States. Whether he showed it or not, he certainly reacted strongly against the Germanic nature of Mahler's art. Given that the only eyewitness report available was Alma's, I for years doubted whether he had in fact left the theatre, especially since Willy, who in his review was always searching for new opportunities to disparage Mahler, wrote only of the 'ironic smiles' of those who disliked the Second Symphony. Moreover, it seemed surprising to me that, on his return to Vienna, Mahler had never spoken to anyone of Debussy's departure. It was possible, of course, that he was never told of the incident at all. Mahler did say to Ernst Decsey, a few weeks later, that in general people had been 'full of kind attentions' in Paris. 'Only the artists' (and here Decsey tells us that Mahler named someone, but unfortunately declined to pass the name

---

[32] HLG(F) iii. 699; Ernst Decsey, 'Stunden mit Mahler', *Die Musik* (Berlin), 10/21 (Aug. 1911), 151.

on to posterity) 'had been envious, and had tried to make difficulties for him.'[33] Who can this 'envious' musician have been? Could Debussy perhaps have been jealous of Mahler the conductor, as he himself was certainly not a professional conductor, although he had occasionally conducted his own works? We shall probably never know. However, I was wrong to believe that Debussy had not left the hall; he did, as I later learnt from an unimpeachable source.

In the absence of William Ritter, detained in Switzerland at the time of the concert, a new voice appeared in the French press to support Mahler, a voice carrying more conviction than all the careful, diplomatic praise of the other critics. It was that of the organist and conductor Gustave Bret, founder of the French Société Jean Sébastien Bach. Having first outlined, in his article for *L'Intransigeant*, the total disagreement between Mahler's partisans and his enemies, Bret went on to claim that the audience at the Châtelet

had perforce to bow to a power which I believe only prejudice could deny. Whether it beguiles or repels you, whether it pierces your heart or makes you bristle, whether it moves you or leaves you cold, this power is there. . . . For myself, I know only one thing, and that is that I have been lost in admiration, profoundly moved, that I have vibrated in unison with each work—French, German, Italian, or Austrian—that reaches my heart. Tomorrow, perhaps, I shall ask myself why. For today, it is enough that I have been moved. This is my opinion; I allow others to have their own. My neighbour might perhaps have said: 'This Mahler fellow is just a fool!' . . . It's possible! But let's wait fifty years! I hope you will have that pleasure![34]

Although discouraged by Mahler's lack of success in France, before and after the Second World War, Bret collected Mahler recordings until his death in the 1950s. One day, by chance—some fifteen years after his death—his faithful secretary and librarian heard me on Radio France-Culture casting doubt on Debussy's departure, which no one until then had been able to confirm. At once she wrote to inform me that Bret, who had been on good terms with Debussy, had often told her how profoundly shocked he had been to see him leave the hall in the middle of the Second Symphony.

It has long been claimed that this first Paris performance of the Second Symphony was a dismal failure, but such a notion does not stand up to a close examination of the press at the time. Not only was each movement applauded in turn and with the greatest warmth, and not only did the concert end with a noisy ovation, but the French critics also showed infinitely more respect and comprehension than might have been expected. The leading critics—Robert Brussel in *Le Figaro*, Alfred Bruneau in *Le Matin*, Louis Schneider in *Gil Blas*, Arthur Coquard in *Echo de Paris*, Paul Souday in *L'Opinion*, and Amédée Boutarel in *Le Ménestrel*—expressed some reservations but wrote with the greatest respect and the most scrupulous courtesy. Some even praised Mahler's 'genius', others his 'beautiful, rich musical nature'.[35] Admittedly there were exceptions like Gaston Carraud who, in *La Liberté*, complained that Mahler's music lacked the power to move him; or like Willy who,

---

[33] Decsey, ibid.   [34] *L'Intransigeant*, 19 Apr. 1910.
[35] HLG(F) iii. 189; Jacques-Gabriel Prod'homme in *Paris Journal*.

in *Comoedia*, called Mahler a 'bluffer' (but Paris must have long since learnt not to take his *bons mots* very seriously); or again, like Camille Bellaigue who, in the *Revue des deux Mondes*, condemned Mahler's 'gigantic orgies of sound', and placed him 'far below Berlioz' whose heir he was; or finally, Jean Marnold who flatly claimed, in *Le Mercure de France*, that Mahler's 'Kapellmeistermusik' was 'devoid of the most minute interest'. Nonetheless, there were several other convinced Mahlerians in France from the very beginning—Darius Milhaud, for example.

The list of Mahler performances in France between the wars is brief; I have been unable to find more than ten between 1927 and 1945. These were: *Des Knaben Wunderhorn* (once), the Fourth Symphony (four times), the First (three times), and *Das Lied von der Erde* (twice). Much more could be said about the Mahler renaissance that began in 1960 (the centenary of his birth). True, it started slowly—as I should know, because I founded at that time an honorary committee consisting of certain prominent musical personalities. Most of them gladly supported my plans, but—alas—their influence proved almost nil on impresarios who feared that, with Mahler on the programme, the public would not come. Thus we succeeded in organizing just *one* concert that year, which included *Das Lied von der Erde*. Mahler's music did not really gain ground in France until after 1967—in which year the Ninth Symphony was at last performed in France, not once, but three times between April and June by Rafael Kubelik, Jascha Horenstein, and Otto Klemperer.

Yet it must be said that Mahler's early death was partly responsible for France's neglect of him. Had he lived longer, at least some of his symphonies would have reached the French public—aided by the spell of his own conducting. A second appearance had been planned for the spring of 1911, again with the Orchestre Colonne; but by then Mahler was on his deathbed. Unfortunately, I have been unable to discover which of his symphonies he had intended to conduct, but it was probably the Seventh. His death meant that, with a few exceptions, his works lay dormant in France for the next fifty years. The efforts of Camille Chevillard who, in January 1911, conducted the Fifth Symphony twice in one week and, in the autumn of the same year, a first performance of *Kindertotenlieder* with Marya Freund, were attempts too isolated to bear fruit. In the fifteen years from 1912 to 1927, Paris heard not a single note of Mahler, while the Sixth Symphony had to wait until 1966 for its French première!

To give some idea of Mahler's present popularity in France, I should like to conclude by mentioning the Mahler cycle given at the Théâtre du Châtelet in February, March, and April 1989. Fourteen different conductors, twenty-two concerts, the inclusion of rare scores like *Todtenfeier*, *Die Drei Pintos*, the Bach Suite, the two youthful volumes of songs orchestrated by Luciano Berio, the world première of the extraordinary Symphony by Hans Rott,[36] etc.; all this made the Festival one of the most comprehensive ever to be held,

[36] [Mahlerians owe a deep obligation to Paul Banks for his discovery and meticulous editing of Rott's Symphony in E major, which was first recorded in 1989 by Gerhard Samuel with the Cincinnati Philharmonia Orchestra (Hyperion: CDA66366). A slightly more deliberate, and equally distinctive recording has since been made by Leif Segerstam with the Norrköping Symphony Orchestra (BIS-CD-563, 1992). Ed.]

and surely one of the most successful. Everything was sold out, even concerts that were repeated; and one could sense an almost religious fervour in the attitude of the public— deep emotion being followed by outbursts of applause. More recently, another Mahler cycle at Lyon occupied not just one season, but eventually spread itself over three years— 1991–4. In a country which once seemed the least disposed to do him justice, Mahler has at last lost nothing by waiting.

7

Mahler and Debussy: Transcendence and Emotion

GÉRARD PESSON

Mahler and Debussy scarcely ever met. We do not have enough information to justify giving an account here of the celebrated dinner with Pierné aimed at bringing them closer together, or of the occasional anti-Mahlerian jest uttered in the presence of the Countess of Greffuhle. In the afternoon of 17 April 1910, at the Châtelet, Debussy is said to have left his seat during the performance of the second movement of the Second Symphony.[1] Some time before this Mahler told a *New York Tribune* journalist—somewhat formally, perhaps—that he 'admired' Debussy. Did they never exchange more than two or three words? Is there any more explicit way in which they could have avoided each other, wholly repudiated each other—as Schoenberg and Stravinsky were to do in later years—than by making up, in similar fashion, one-sided polite words of praise and rude remarks?

These two figures who do not touch at any point could be said to provide a near-perfect sketch of a Franco-German axis,[2] where any topic of discussion derives its flavour from the stilted generalizations which have long passed for serious critical judgement: Debussy, symbol of 'Frenchness' in all that this word connotes of clarity, transparency, and subtle implication; Mahler, exemplar of Germanic excess, rhetorical heaviness, epic inflation, Promethean gestures. We have to recognize that each of these clichés embodies some truth. The key to this clash of opposites is primarily a factual one. Debussy's France on several occasions displayed her mistrust of any movement that originated from across the Rhine, whether she wished to protect herself from them or whether she judged their teachings to be impossible to assimilate. In an early campaign the Société Nationale de Musique uttered

---

[1] These are, fundamentally, no more than items of gossip reported by Pierné (and dismissed as false by Ravel) to Alma Mahler, a link in the chain whose unreliability is well known. On this matter, however, and Mahler's pioneering introduction of late Debussy to his New York audiences, see above, Ch. 6, esp. pp. 148–50.

[2] The German nation, when it is taken to represent the whole, rather than only a *part* of 'Germanness'. ' "I am thrice homeless," [Mahler] used often to say. "As a native of Bohemia in Austria, as an Austrian among Germans, and as a Jew throughout all the world. Everywhere an intruder, never welcomed." ' Alma Mahler, *Memories*, 109.

its war cry—'Ars Gallica'—with the aim of holding back the tide of Wagnerism which had already engulfed one of its most active members, Vincent d'Indy. After a period of appeasement that corresponded with the period of mourning by the champions of César Franck, with Paris once more becoming—more or less until the arrival of Mahler in 1910—a musical centre of Franco-German détente (though this owed nothing to the customary proselytizing engaged in by Saint-Saëns, the French high priest of German national academic sterility), French 'sensitivity' again went into retreat. To Pierre Louÿs, Strauss's *Thus Spoke Zarathustra* seemed to weigh 'one hundred and twenty thousand tons'. Debussy, always a reliable barometer of these tendencies, wrote from holiday to Paul-Jean Toulet the following sally, which makes one shudder and says much: 'I would willingly offer up the nine symphonies of Beethoven, bound in Richard Strauss's skin, to be in Paris.'[3] The humour of M. Croche is, perhaps, less dubious, but one often senses in his fairly light-hearted banter the desire of the 'young French school' to ward off what is regarded as German arrogance. This feeling extends as far as Romain Rolland—nevertheless a fervent conciliator—who notes in his diary of 22 June 1898: 'Ho ho! I have an idea that Germany will not for much longer maintain the equanimity of the all-powerful. Giddiness has invaded its brain cells. Nietzsche, Richard Strauss, the emperor Wilhelm—there is Neroism in the air.'[4]

The most striking symbol of these two cultures, which strive to understand each other, which observe and mistrust one another, continues to be the lessons in French prosody that Romain Rolland poured out patiently upon Richard Strauss, making use of Debussy's *Pelléas et Mélisande*.[5] The reticence displayed by Strauss undoubtedly holds no validity for Mahler, but it lays bare the gulf his works never succeeded in bridging.[6] If 'information' about them got around, it carried no conviction. We know that Debussy consistently retreated into himself on this issue. The 1914–18 war, which had no use for his services, put into his head the project of restoring a national musical identity—represented by the sonatas which he signed as 'a French musician'. It is this Debussy—not the composer of the sonatas, which are masterpieces, but their national champion—who embarrasses us somewhat nowadays. We cannot reproach Mahler with anything comparable.

'Too Schubertian . . . and a Schubert too Viennese and too Slav', was the comment on Mahler's Second Symphony made by those who fled from the concert hall on that 17 April. A typically Parisian instance of cattiness, to which Mahler—embittered in all probability— replied that he had been 'charmed by the easy-going French attitude to life and by the beauty of its culture'.

These acidulous exchanges, these seductive little duels laid the foundations of an aes-

[3] Edward Lockspeiser, *Claude Debussy*, trans. Léo Dilé (Paris: Fayard, 1980), 369.

[4] *Cahiers Romain Rolland*, No. 3 (Paris, 1951), 118.

[5] Hoffmann, in his day, had learnt the same lessons from the operas of Lully and Rameau.

[6] 'What is false for a Frenchman is true for a German.' *Cahiers Romain Rolland*, 59.

[7] Mahler has quite recently paid the price of this by becoming a symbol of contempt, against which a campaign has been mounted to rehabilitate French musical values— in this case an 'anti-Mahler' campaign. It is amusing to note that, in the role of villain, Mahler has today replaced Wagner.

thetic clash of opposites[7] that even now offers little hope to, and carries no conviction for, the amateur music-lover—the indecisive traitor who is as deeply moved by *Das Lied von der Erde* as by *Pelléas et Mélisande*. The pages that follow will, therefore, in order to exorcize what we shall term the 'Châtelet Conspiracy' syndrome, reflect the manifest similarities between these two ways of thinking about music, these two expressions of genius, and the modernism which they anticipate.

When Claudel expressed regret that literature was becoming mired in lust and extravagant emotions, he delineated the area in which it is held that Debussy's music operates: a hedonistic art, rendered fragile by its wish to capture the passing moment; an art without a 'target', making a moral virtue of having no final purpose—what Adorno termed the 'Idea' in relation to Mahler. We can see quite easily that many of Debussy's own observations go a long way towards invalidating such a conclusion. Let us always be wary, however, of what is said about his music. By contrast with Mahler, Debussy makes use of several levels of 'sincerity', whether he is describing what he expects from a work—or from what might perhaps pass as a work of his own—or whether he is revealing his conception of poetry. The strategy he adopts—perhaps without premeditation—serves to cloud the issues. Just when we expect him to be 'modern' and to make no concessions, he preens his feathers like a sentimental dandy. In the midst of a characteristic outburst of sabre-rattling he will suddenly make a confession whose shamelessness makes us (wrongly) suspect his sincerity—and it is the *key* he is holding out to us.

The semantic analysis of this art-without-a-final-purpose is founded upon the Debussyan psyche, which is, at bottom, fairly close to Mahler's own: happiness forever trapped in the past turns the work into an occasion for mourning, a memorial that derives its air of resignation from a sense of failure. Its willingness to breach the conventional dynamics of musical language could thus be said to stem from a frustrated desire for something that existed in the past but is now no more. Both the discourse and the form in which it is embedded become fragmented as they evolve; what they represent in terms of feelings—a complex cycle of stimuli (the water jar plunged into the Vivonne river)—paralyses linear development. The resulting stylization of emotion, this 'fading', this 'shivering'— which are in truth signs of redoubled intelligence, acuteness, and precision—have always dragged in their train unavoidable questions about Impressionism. Like the symbolism we wish to see everywhere in relation to Debussy, like Mahler's *Jugendstil*, this is no more than a sign of the times that does not penetrate deeply into the heart of the work. A methodical analysis of the *Préludes* can convince us that Debussy's music is not impressionist in the same sense as Renoir's *Régates à Argenteuil*. The material exposed to view makes no play with illusion. As it develops, distinctive features are as prominent as colour.

The absence from Debussy's music of direction towards a stated goal has associations with what Jankélévitch has called poetic 'ecstasy' (in contradistinction to the 'trance' characteristic of Mahler's Germanness), and can be represented schematically by a term that German criticism had applied to *Pelléas et Mélisande*: the *vertical*. '[Debussy] makes us listen for three and a half hours to chords exclusively, and what chords! Sevenths, ninths, augmented fifths, and chords made up of six different notes. And all of these laid crudely end to end, with no transitions between them. The score resembles a cupboard belonging to a lover of complicated harmonies, a gallery of harmonic embryos.'[8]

Pleasure, therefore, has a category of its own: a harmony whose hedonistic powers have at all times—particularly since Rameau—been associated with the French tradition, and linked implicitly with its culinary genius. Observe the greediness of Strauss as he listens to the sugary harmonies of Charpentier's *Louise*! Within this sacrosanct categorization, refinement—perceived as a mannerism—is achieved at the expense of moral virtue. This 'art-of-the-instant', expressed in 'vertical' strokes, colourful but unprincipled, must atone for its shortcomings by weaving small or brief fragments into complex patterns.[9]

Like Mahler, Debussy is a beneficiary of history, reflecting the inheritance he took over during a time of nostalgia for lost stability that no process of restoration can—or should—bring back. The somewhat reactionary sense of despair he displays takes refuge in an innocence that bears witness to the absurdity of fate—like Mélisande's 'happy but sad'.[10] The same suffering, the same critical stance, the same dissatisfaction appear in Mahler's output, whose materials willingly endorse this anachronistic innocence, and seek to arm us against the world's pain. A certain anguish finds expression in these works, whether they depict victories or Dionysian festivities, which we may attribute—as Adorno does—to the dying traditions of the European century, whose disintegration stems, as with Mahler and Debussy, from depression and doubt. We shall return later to their habit of keeping themselves at a distance, the way in which they appear to hold their message in suspension, behaving like weathervanes in a changeable climate. A sense of failure surrounds, but also generates energy for, their enterprise. With Debussy—is his ecstatic mournfulness a *fin de siècle* phenomenon?—a progressive detachment and renunciation seem to underpin his wish to transmit a message about his diminished creative momentum. Weariness and lack of a sense of achievement meant that he never realized his poetic vision.[11] In contrast, Mahler's compositions convey a sense of strained impatience that may well be linked to the tight squeeze applied by the orchestral conductor to the musical material. Action wards off death; thus the grandiose Mahlerian structures pit themselves ruthlessly against the spirit of the age. With Debussy the opposite is true: energy is not a conqueror, the work does not risk the giddy heights. Something in the subtle equilibrium of his asymmetrical compositions retraces an age that has already vanished, mingling mystery with transparency.

The clarity we speak of, in connection with Debussy, and which may be interpreted as either propriety or insincerity, is closely linked to the pathos transmitted by his 'professional' style of composition and all that ensues from it. Contrast the *maturity* of Mahler

[8] *Die Signale*, 24 Apr. 1917. Romain Rolland, in his novel *Jean-Christophe*, calls it 'a factory of chords'.

[9] 'We scarcely dare to show spirit any more, fearing as we do that we lack grandeur.' Debussy, 'A propos d'*Hippolyte et Aricie* de Rameau', *Le Figaro*, 8 May 1908.

[10] A quotation from *Pelléas et Mélisande*, Act IV, sc. 4: 'Je suis heureuse, mais je suis triste.' Vladimir Jankélévitch, *Debussy et le mystère* (Neuchâtel: Baconnière, 1949), 140.

[11] Jankélévitch has commented on the 'geotropism' of his themes (their downward curve) as one effect of this depressed and negative state of mind(!).

against the *mastery* displayed by Debussy; compare Debussy's lofty repudiation of the amateurish, his miserly, subdued, aristocratic output, with the Mahlerian exertions,[12] the massive output of the *Sommerkomponist* whose time is running out, the victorious struggle of the Alpine explorer. For Debussy evidence of effort must be rubbed out, edges blurred, material thinned down (let us recall the disdainful words of praise of *Pelléas et Mélisande* uttered by Strauss in his box at the Opéra-Comique: 'it's very refined'). From this perspective he is—like Strauss himself—one of those exceptionally gifted people who absorb cultural influences, and return them, subtly and skilfully reshaped, to the artistic mainstream. Mahler's music, by contrast, spurns the smooth and harmonious effects of applying conventional techniques of composition. Not that he lacks skill. What he displays to a marked degree is a form of mastery which allows obvious and deliberate clumsiness to burst forth as though it were an intentional provocation. It is this that has permitted critics, on occasion, to associate him with Berlioz.[13]

For both men, the aesthetic implications of *discontinuity* in composition are relevant to their new vision of what they were seeking to achieve, no matter how eagerly they reached out towards a *Wholeness* to which their music bears witness. The quest for authenticity of feeling shows us how inaccessible is the global, all-embracing significance that all Debussy's music strives to 'exemplify', through a technique of fragmentation which appreciably enhances the emotional impact of the sound-web. For Mahler, it is the *narrative* function that seeks to embrace this significance. Disenchantment, reminiscence, regret for a lost golden age (often symbolized by the dream of an idyllic Greece in Debussy's case, and by a legendary Middle Ages in Mahler's), are caught up in the musical language of the subject matter, attaching it to the world, to the earth. Thus the unhappy experiences of the creative artist originate in the realm of the emotions; but at the point where Debussy comes to a halt—not that his music goes no 'further'—Mahler pushes us to the point of collapse, pits himself against the forces of the Universe, exploits every ambiguity of a language pressed to the limits of its meaning. The mysteries of what he seeks to communicate have their exact counterpart in Debussy: the withdrawal, the abandoned secret, the quest that has lost its objective—or, rather, revealed itself as its own objective (as in Proust's *Le Temps retrouvé*). Thenceforward, his communication sheds almost all its weight; it appears as a light imprint on the sands of language.

The specific meeting point of Mahler's and Debussy's music is Nature, the long poetic pathway that links the emotional with the spiritual, the direction taken by their idealism at its highest level. It is also the strategic point of anchorage for a dream of innocence

---

[12] Mahler always claimed to be a novice when confronted by new work (HGL(F) i. 902). 'When Debussy, on the occasion of the first Parisian performance of the Second Symphony, left the concert hall in protest, the sworn enemy of amateurishness behaved like a true specialist; the Second Symphony must have made the same impact on him as the paintings of le Douanier Rousseau in the midst of the Impressionists in the Jeu de Paume.' Theodor W. Adorno,

Mahler, une physionomie musicale, trans. J.-L. Leleu and T. Leydenbach (Paris: Éditions de Minuit, 1976), 36 (Eng. trans., 20).

[13] An astonishing parallel. It is Wagner that the ear of criticism has often heard in Debussy's music—an example of the narrowness of vision of the Franco-German axis. [For Mahler's admiration of Berlioz, and for Berlioz's influence on him, see Mitchell, *WY*, 333–7. Ed.]

which manifestly functions as an antidote to knowledge and technique. When Debussy recommends that, for the purpose of composition, one should listen only to the sea and the wind in the trees, his remark is both sincere and ambiguous (and only the lazy and the artistically pretentious will take it literally). It puts forward as an ideal an uncluttered mind, into which a new poetic vision could flow—'alchemy' as opposed to 'science'. In Mahler, too, one finds this same wish, simple-minded or poorly expressed at times, to escape from the constraints of technique, to make it spring forth anew in the purified atmosphere of the great heights. In more precise terms, we are concerned here with a process of *abstraction* which Mallarmé, anticipating Debussy, set in motion. The challenge to officially authorized knowledge, to doctrine, takes the form of a return to instinct, to that which emerges from the living forces of Nature—Dionysus vs. Faust. We may relish the horticultural imagery in one of Debussy's witticisms: 'Ultimately we must just cultivate the garden of our instincts and officiously trample on the flower-beds all symmetrically laid out with ideas in white ties.'[14] ('I don't know what I know', says Golaud.) In a quip that parallels Debussy's advice to 'return to Nature', Mahler told Bruno Walter during his visit to Steinbach that he need feel no obligation to gaze upon the Attersee and its cliffs: 'All of this you will find in my music. [It is] nothing other than the sound of Nature ['nur Naturlaut'].'[15] For Mahler as for Debussy, music echoes this 'unfolding of the world' of which Adorno spoke. It is a desperate attempt to decipher its mystery, an attempt that demonstrates how the exceptional transmutational power of music is firmly rooted in instinct. Innocence and purity can be attained only at the price of effort that is hidden from view. Believing as he does in the straightforwardness of instinct, Debussy often reminds us of Mahler in thought-provoking fashion. The following remarks, made during an interview given on the occasion of a performance of *Le Martyr de Saint Sébastien*, could come from any article by Mahler on the subject of *Des Knaben Wunderhorn*:

Who will ever know the secret of musical composition? . . . The sound of the sea, the curve of the horizon, the wind in the leaves, the cry of a bird—all these arouse in us a number of impressions. Then, all of a sudden without our willing it in any way, one of these recollections assumes an outward form and expresses itself in musical terms. . . . I loathe doctrines and their impertinences. That is why I wish to write my musical dream with complete detachment from myself. I want to sing my interior landscape with the naive candour of a child. This will always shock those who prefer artifice and lies.[16]

The gesture made by Mahler's music in the direction of the unattainable puts one in mind, metaphorically, of the Creation—which certainly does nothing to place his art in the realm of realism.

---

[14] Letter of 28 Aug. 1894 to Henri Lerolle; see *Debussy Letters*, selected and ed. François Lesure and Roger Nichols, trans. Roger Nichols (London: Faber, 1987), 73.

[15] HLG(F) i. 1034. 'Like a sound of Nature' ('Wie ein Naturlaut') is Mahler's specific indication at the opening of the first movement of his First Symphony.

[16] 'Est-ce une renaissance de la musique religieuse?', *Excelsior*, 11 Feb. 1911. Quoted by Stefan Jarocinski, *Debussy, Impressionism and Symbolism*, trans. Rollo Myers (London: Eulenburg Books, 1976), 96.

The act of decoding reality—'the way in which objective life intrudes upon subjective ideas and transforms the music into an Absolute that skims off all irrelevancies'[17]—brings in its train a poetic 'distancing' that can never be bridged. There is no greater proportion of 'genre' music in Debussy's works than in Mahler's; and their titles, renouncing the role of 'sworn-to-be-faithful translator' that he ascribes to painters, are somewhat deceptive—but more often simplistic—signposts.[18] The what-Nature-tells-me narrative of the Third Symphony does not represent any specific experience, and could apply, in any case, to many of Debussy's compositions, functioning as the code-words of an unseen speaker who dwells in the infinite, and who utters no more than a temporary message. 'Music is a mysterious mathematical form, the elements of which are linked to infinity',[19] and reflect in rhythm its 'shimmering immensity'. What one might pin down as symbolic in the work of Debussy, leaving aside the texts from which he borrowed, would become clearer if there were a more widespread belief that musical ideas and their expression are always closely connected: a belief he opposed in the interests of 'Nature and the imaginative'. Jarocinski links this type of approach with a decidedly Mahlerian notion put forward by the young Valéry, who saw the artistic ideal in a merger of the world that surrounds us with the world that haunts us within.[20] With Debussy, the imitation of Nature is Aristotelian, in the sense teased out by Heidegger: Nature's essential elements are *shaped*—not *reflected* as with Mahler. For Debussy, the imitation is not of Nature herself, but of the ways in which she operates: on the one hand a kind of alchemy which transmutes the model into a variety of shapes and textures; on the other a narrative thrust which transmits it, 'retrieves' it, enriched with pathos and feeling.

In this pact with Nature there is evidence of an attachment to the myth of completion, of coming back on one's tracks, that is not without consequences for thoughts about musical form. Mahler, without doubt more concerned than Debussy with issues of formal legitimacy, allows this preoccupation to speak for itself in the truly cathartic effort, for him, of composing a recapitulation. Incarnate in what is repeated, in what persists throughout a work, is the Idea; and Mahler's music is able to move towards it only when he presents us with an overall pattern, modelled on Nature, that incorporates within it repetitive echoes on a much smaller scale. For Debussy too, Nature is a 'lesson in development', a book which musicians do not consult often enough. His form is the arabesque, the 'most spiritual of all designs' according to Baudelaire.[21] Debussy seeks to tease out one 'law of instability' from the multitude of laws that are beyond human control. His pantheism inclines him most often towards doubt, and underpins the skilled and elegant manner in which he blurs all references to the specific, the unambiguous. For him Nature could well be the absence of

[17] Adorno, *Mahler* (French trans.), 108 (Eng. trans., 70). All our thinking about Mahler owes much to this thought-provoking book. It covers the entire field of Mahler's creative work so well that one would like to quote from it endlessly. In addition, the French translation is a masterpiece.

[18] Jankélévitch, alas, has founded 50% of his analyses on them.

[19] 'Considérations sur Le Prix de Rome au point de vue musical', *Musica* (May, 1903).

[20] Jarocinski, *Debussy*, 111–12.

[21] Charles Baudelaire, *Œuvres complètes* (Paris: Pléiade, 1956), 291.

God and the suspension of the Law, whereas for Mahler it is the supreme objective point of reference.

Over and above the questions about how it should be represented, Nature passes on to music something of its tissue, its flesh, its body. For Mahler and Debussy a dream of space is often associated with it. The boundlessness of Nature is reflected in the random multiplicity of voices to which the artist must give heed. The 'fragmentation', the 'scattering', of which Debussy speaks, constitute the specialized techniques needed to draw up a sound-map of this space, in which the music of the human world will find its orientation. It is curious to observe how, with Debussy and Mahler, music that is 'spontaneous', functional, 'innocent' is ascribed to instinct—and thus to Nature, to feeling—even when it can hardly be said to fall within this category. The account of the genesis of *Fêtes* is interesting in this respect:

A period of relaxation among the torches in the evening, in the woods... I saw from afar, through the trees, gleams of light approaching, and the crowd running towards the alley along which the procession was about to pass. And then... the resplendent horsemen of the Republican Guard, their weapons and helmets brilliant in the torchlight, and the bugles sounding forth their fanfares. And, at last, all these things fading away, becoming distan...[22]

In similar fashion, it was in a wood that Mahler heard the distant echoes of fairground music, in a combination of barrel organs, fanfares, wooden horses, male-voice choirs:

'Do you hear? *That* is polyphony if such a thing was ever heard', he cried, as he recalled childhood memories of the forest at Iglau. 'It is essential for music to resemble it in every particular. The themes must come from several different directions, and their melodies and rhythms be clearly distinguishable one from another. If this does not happen, all we have is a single score in several parts with a well-disguised homophony. It is the artist who must bring together the various elements, confer order on them and unify them into a single musical entity.'[23]

In both composers there is a profoundly creative impulse to express as fully as possible the whole universe of sound, and within its boundaries give shape to those tiny musical subjects placed there by Man, mingled with all that flows from Nature. With Debussy, structural divisions and the fragmentation of musical material determine in advance what shape the sound-map of space will take; it is the orchestral texture that provides its depth. Mahler, on many occasions, gives us a vision of wide perspectives, conveying his impressions of rural festival concerts by having distant fanfares played off-stage (*Das klagende Lied*, the last movement of the Second Symphony). Berlioz is unquestionably present in this desire of Mahler's to reshape the geography of the orchestra.

The fanfare has no rivals as 'the music of space'. Associated with the open air, with marching, it is always, for Mahler and Debussy, the distant summons that approaches or fades into the distance, the orchestral symbol of nostalgia itself—all its military energy, its power, its brilliance, reaching us in distorted form, like a vague memory. Mahler's experi-

---

[22] Lockspeiser, *Debussy*, 670 (analysis of the work discussed by Harry Halbreich).
[23] HGL(F) i. 902–3. [Cf. NB-L, *Recollections*, 155–6. Ed.]

ence of polyphony in the countryside cannot fail to remind us of the fanfares converging from different directions which Charles Ives heard in a clock tower, and which he incorporated in similar fashion in his symphonies;[24] but also, more widely, of the transcendentalist philosophy which he championed. We can undoubtedly detect, in the music of Mahler and Debussy, certain Emersonian characteristics: the exaltation of Nature, the expansion of mankind into infinite space, the clash between the individual human spirit (microcosm) and what Emerson calls the Oversoul (macrocosm). Mahler particularly, seen in the light of the pantheistic aspects of his idealistic vision, might seem to be an excellent example of transcendentalist Man, the 'self' as envisaged by Thoreau.

It is through references to Nature that we may trace in Debussy the threads of an idealism, of an Utopian vision, that are linked to the world of our experience. Amongst those at the turn of the century who reflected on the purpose of art and sought to free it from slavery to tradition, Kandinsky early understood what was at stake in Debussy's music and the role Nature played in it as a catalyst for subjective feelings, for exploration and, above all, for the transcendence generated by emotion. In his book *Concerning the Spiritual in Art* (*Über das Geistige in der Kunst*, 1911), he wrote:

The most modern musicians like Debussy create a spiritual impression, often taken from nature, but embodied in purely musical form. For this reason Debussy is often classed with the Impressionist painters. . . . But it would be rash to say that this definition is an exhaustive statement of Debussy's significance. Despite his similarity with the Impressionists this musician is deeply concerned with spiritual harmony, for in his works one hears the suffering and tortured nerves of the present time. And further Debussy never uses the wholly material note so characteristic of programme music, but trusts mainly in the creation of a more abstract impression.[25]

This analysis by Kandinsky—which, incidentally, bears witness to a level of perceptiveness far superior to that of contemporary writings about Debussy—very aptly reintroduces the concept of 'transcendence', a feature always ignored by critical language, which refers exclusively to the 'instinctual' and the 'primitive': a kind of prudishness that does no justice to the range of Debussy's output. For him, immodesty is the acknowledgement of pleasure, of the primacy of immediate delight in music as it is heard. In this respect he makes common cause with Mahler, sometimes giving with one hand the consolations of perceptible beauty, and with the other demanding stern discipline, intense effort—in turn, the fruits of emotion and a tribute to transcendence. In the music of both composers there is undoubtedly a schizophrenic conflict between expression and exploration, between the immediate moment and eternity, whose common denominator is the mystery of Nature, reaching out towards infinity.

For Mahler and Debussy, Nature is ultimately the pantheistic altar of their innermost feelings. In *Monsieur Croche* Debussy acknowledged that for him 'mysterious Nature had

---

[24] [For a comparison of Mahler's and Ives's use of polyphony, see Mitchell, *WY*, 169–71 and 373. Ed.]

[25] Wassily Kandinsky, *Concerning the Spiritual in Art*, trans. M. T. H. Sadler (New York: Dover Publications, 1977), 16.

become a religion. I think that no one clad in the robes of an abbot is closer to God . . . To be aware of the disturbing and all-powerful visions that Nature invites her ephemeral and alarming guests to gaze upon: that is what I call *prayer*'.[26] As for Mahler, the 'seeker after God', it is interesting to observe how he distances himself from the Dionysian atheism of Nietzsche, striving to reach beyond the conception of Nature as the immediately percept-ible, and arrive at its *essence*. As a disciple of Schopenhauer, he thinks of himself as 'an instrument played by the universe', 'a mediator of divine wisdom . . ., a high priest con-cerned, like Amfortas, to perform "das schreckliche Amt" (the fearful ceremony)'.[27] Nature, as a perceptual metaphor for the infinite, seeks out its own myth. Mahler wrote in a letter: '(We) forget that Nature includes the Whole . . . No one knows Dionysus'.[28] Here we see outlined the figure of Pan, celebrated by both musicians. Beyond their constant bor-rowing from neo-Hellenic symbolism, this reference to Pan recalls an earlier inspiration. The Third Symphony—truly an Arcadian cinemascope—is based on the myth of Pan. After he had rejected the Nietzschean title 'The Gay Science', Mahler thought of 'Pan, Symphonic Poems'. In the final version, the Introduction is still prefaced 'Pan awakes'. But these are no more than titles.[29] As a demiurge, Mahler took pleasure in playing with myth, and transmuting it into subjective and autobiographical forms in ways that often resemble those employed by Proust. With Debussy, myth is always associated with the awakening of desire, with the life of the faun as it is symbolized by its original voice: that of the syrinx, stirred into speech by the winds of summer. This flute, herald of unsatisfied desire, of bewitchment, has its counterpart also in German mythology with the legend of the Pied Piper of Hamelin, who rids the town of its rats.[30] We find a macabre twist to this myth in the singing bone of *Das klagende Lied*. The ancient Phrygian flute that awakened longing in its listeners becomes now the instrument which tells the truth, which gives an account of a brother's murder committed in the name of love (Pelléas/Golaud).

In *Das klagende Lied*, Mahler makes use of a legend that is not unrelated to Debussy's last work, *La Chute de la maison Usher*, which was left unfinished. The same juxtaposition of the sadistic with the oedipal (the evil brother kills the good one in order to steal the princess; Roderick Usher loves Lady Madeline, his sister, whom he buries alive); the same gruesome poetry: death itself returns to occupy the witness stand. These two dramatic pieces reveal a clear fascination for the darker depths of the unconscious, theories about which were in the process of development at the time. Fulfilling the demands of Nature—this 'fearful ceremony'—may be compared to a summons from the deep that appears to sig-nify, for Mahler and Debussy, both the resolution of their artistic endeavours and the explicit projection of a psyche characterized by a sense of *loss*. As facets of their poetic vision, nostalgia and regret for the past are linked to a form of morbid bewitchment con-

---

[26] Claude Debussy, *Monsieur Croche et autres écrits* (Paris: Gallimard, 1971), 302.

[27] HLG(F) i. 159.

[28] Ibid. 1034. See also the 'Dionysian interpretations' by Mahler of a text by Siegfried Lipiner (ibid. 893).

[29] [For a detailed discussion of Mahler's various revisions of the titles for the movements of this symphony, see Peter Franklin, *Mahler: Symphony No. 3* (Cambridge: Cambridge University Press, 1991), esp. 37–52. Ed.]

[30] It is strange how Nietzsche speaks of Dionysus as 'he who spirits away the rats of our consciences' [*Beyond Good and Evil*, para. 295, the 'pied piper of consciences'].

jured up by the eternal flux of Nature and all that it evokes. The music of both composers speaks of that which will never be again; it seeks to trap the fleeting moment within an illusory eternity of emotion, beneath the bright light of reminiscence; and this 'effort', for both of them, finds a welcome anchorage in the world of childhood—a state of past innocence, the true 'nature' of their subject matter. For Mahler and Debussy the world of childhood, the domain of the fairy tale, often resembles a harbour which protects them from the weather, and where they pile up, in miniature form, the consuming passions of an adult world which they have rejected. (These last will unleash themselves as soon as the forest—that mythical territory—has been left behind.)[31] This type of redemptive regression to childhood also manifests itself, in Debussy, in the shape of paternal fussiness. His *Children's Corner* is not only the playroom where he prattles away to himself; it is also the inkwell of youth from which he enlivens his writing.

In a striking passage, Adorno compares Mahler's work with that of Proust:

The girl in *Das Lied von der Erde* throws her secret lover 'long yearning looks'. Such is the look of the work itself, absorbing, doubting, turned backwards with precipitous tenderness, as previously was only the ritardando in the Fourth Symphony, but also like the gaze of Proust's *Recherche*, which came into being at about the same time . . . In both, unfettered joy and unfettered melancholy perform their charade; in the prohibition of images of hope, hope has its last dwelling-place. This place is in both, however, the strength to name the forgotten that is concealed in the stuff of experience. Like Proust, Mahler rescued his idea from childhood. That his idiosyncratically unmistakable, unexchangeable aspect nevertheless became the universal, the secret of all, he has in advance of all of the music of his time.[32]

We saw earlier that Mahler and Debussy often used the sounds of popular music to create an 'effect of Nature'. Often, this resort to a common corpus becomes a way of challenging conventional knowledge from the standpoint of innocence. These 'unadventurous songs', as Debussy called them, constitute a redeeming banality which can then be directly addressed. The great 'Frère Jacques' canon in the First Symphony makes play with extraordinary ambiguities of level. The song is so well known that it functions as a signpost; but it appears in perverted form, in the minor, orchestrated like a funeral march, but at the same time communicating a mood of exhilaration, the energy of awakening. 'Dormez vous?' ('Are you asleep?') One can understand how deeply this movement—because of its provocative orchestral oddities, among other reasons—scandalized the listening public. Its sarcastic message, announced initially as if it were no more than a form of teasing, unfolds itself sullenly, and by slow degrees wholly envelops the listener, who may then perceive it as an assault on him by a dogma—the scholastic rules governing the canon—which feels like a discordant metaphor for society as a whole. Similarly Debussy, in the trio of the 'Golliwog's Cake-Walk', dresses up the opening notes of *Tristan* in music-hall clothes. With

---

[31] We might emphasize here the symbolic theme of Mahler's imagination: of sylvan withdrawal to the assumed virtues of the mountain heights as an image of excessive effort and striving.

[32] Adorno, *Mahler* (French trans.), 211–12 (Eng. trans., 145–6).

Mahler, elements of the burlesque often emerge from such borrowings, which are always suffused with self-parodying energy and integrated with the work itself—how else may we interpret the circus fanfares of the first movement of the Third Symphony, except as fake 'borrowings', music that places quotations from itself between 'invisible inverted commas like grains of sand in the cogwheels of pure musical structure'?[33] In similar fashion Debussy, in the second section of *En blanc et noir*, devises the cantilena that comes to hover like a chorus from times of peace over the disasters of war ('For he who wishes ill to the kingdom of France is not worthy to have any virtue attributed to him').[34] The narrator splits into two people, the music begins to speak in a dialect characteristic of its earlier voice. For Debussy, popular music is by no means confined within the category of botanical curiosity to which it has been assigned by students of folklore; nor is it destined merely to attract admiring glances through a glass paperweight. A melodic fragment snatched from the revolving world, 'Nous n'irons plus au bois' ('We shall go to the woods no more'), begins to sing furtively in 'Jardins sous la pluie' and *Rondes de printemps*, through the medium of a cor anglais, the 'forgotten refrain of happiness' which made Swann weep. It is poetry joined by customary usage which gives these fragments their added human value, their emotional timbre.

The exoticism evoked by either Debussy or Mahler is only partially successful in conveying local colour. The pentatonicism of *Das Lied von der Erde* (making use of a scale highly characteristic of Debussy) turns the China of prints and engravings into an allegory (particularly in 'Von der Jugend'), which does no more than stylize its own reflection—like the Spain of *Ibéria*, a veritable battery of clichés where the only poetry to be found is in abstractions, in imaginary folklore. While popular song appeals to innocence, it is wisdom—the 'gaze into the distance'—that Debussy's exoticism seeks to invoke. He suggests that what counts as musical knowledge for us may be no more than infantile babble compared with music from faraway lands:

There have been, there are still, in spite of the disruptions brought about by civilization, delightful small societies whose people learned music as simply as we learn to breathe. Their concert hall is the sea's eternal rhythm, the wind in the leaves, and a thousand little sounds to which they listen with care without ever consulting arbitrary musical texts. Their traditions are rooted exclusively in ancient songs, mingled with dances, to which every individual, century after century, brings his respectful contribution. And yet Javanese music incorporates a counterpoint compared with which that of Palestrina is mere child's play.[35]

By integrating into his art materials that are external to it, or by constructing replicas of them, Debussy constantly challenges accusations against him of 'bad taste'. When he claims that the banalities of simple material may sometimes possess poetic power, he makes no concessions to vulgarity of any kind. This is a somewhat Attic standpoint—and one not shared by Mahler, who accepts, and knows how to reproduce, the vernacular qual-

---

[33] Adorno, *Mahler* (French trans.), 53 (Eng. trans., 32).   [34] Quotation from Villon placed at the head of the score.
[35] *Revue musicale S.I.M.*, 15 Feb. 1913.

ities of unsophisticated musical language.[36] Mahler always takes 'bad taste' for granted in this disturbing mixture of subject with object. Who is it that speaks the word 'I' in those hackneyed clichés taken from garrison life, in those fairground songs? As Adorno reminds us, the subject matter of Flaubert's *Madame Bovary* flickers to and fro in a similar way— 'prosaic material, sublime narrative'[37] (which also applies, incidentally, to the conversations that so languidly stir the kingdom of Allemonde in *Pelléas et Mélisande*, and whose provocative commonplaces have a poetry of their own). In both works a 'stylized' representation of the world is set against the stupidity and wickedness of Man. This representation makes us view his defects from a perspective that is critical without being dogmatic. As with Hieronymus Bosch's allegories, we do not always know, in Mahler's case, what is being condemned and what praised. In this vast fairground of the world every tune must be heard. Nonetheless Mahler—as reported by Schoenberg—defended himself against the charge of banality by saying that 'one ought not to look at the theme, but at what comes out of it'.[38] Moreover his genius, like Debussy's, is displayed in the way he appears to transform reality, the subject matter, even when it has its origins outside the work; and also in the way he deploys this poetry of reflection, turning it into a vision of the world—a characteristic common to every modern work that explores its environment and commands respect.

The particular skills shared in common by Debussy, Mahler, and Proust derive from a major upheaval in artistic form, a fundamental rethinking which brought about a new relationship between part and whole. The development of the musical text, the emergence of themes, the tailoring of detail to precise requirements—its 'orchestration'—all the modern principles of composition were absorbed into the tightly woven dialectic of emotion and transcendence, immediate, instant and final aim. At all times the style, the syntax, must be responsive to macro-structural requirements.

The positions occupied by Mahler and Debussy, both of them pioneers of this break with tradition, were, so to speak, at opposite ends of the same bookshelf. Mahler was to draw the dynamic energy for his work from the collapse of classical structures—'material that preceded criticism'—whereas Debussy would quarrel openly with inherited rhetoric. In the sense intended by Proust's Madame Verdurin, Mahler's music was less 'advanced' than Debussy's. The former plants its ambiguous language in ancient and well-tilled soil— resolutely tonal in sound (with every exception proving the rule), diatonic and pre-Wagnerian in compositional style (except for the slow movements, which are always more chromatic in character, as was also the case with Monteverdi), sometimes anachronistic in respect of materials. It even remains faithful to sonata form, though this came to be treated ever more unconventionally as Mahler's output developed. The transformation of traditional forms wrought by Mahler's music is harder to describe in technical terms (orchestration apart) than Debussy's modernism, in that it derives from a critical perspective on

[36] Raising such trivialities to the level of classical form had led to scornful condemnation by the Emperor of every bathing woman painted by Courbet. Thus, whether or not one is considered to be subversive is, as Mahler's experience teaches us, always a question of form.

[37] Adorno, *Mahler* (French trans.), 95 (Eng. trans., 61).
[38] Arnold Schoenberg, *Style and Idea*, trans. Leo Black, ed. Leonard Stein (London: Faber, 1975), 456.

the process of composition. From this perspective Mahler reviews its relationship to the musical ends to be pursued, and to the particular 'language' needed to achieve those ends—a complex area of debate, where questions about meaning, about historical context, turn into a game of words that has long perplexed the unsophisticated critic, and even today passes well over the heads of most ordinary admirers of Mahler. Debussy (and Proust, of course!) are also victims, on occasion, of misunderstandings that arise from this kind of debate. Mahler's Adagietto, Debussy's 'Clair de Lune' and Proust's 'Petite Madeleine' serve as iconic fly-papers that allow us to sort admirers of the creative artist into a number of different grades.

Modernism invariably connotes a break with the past. Mahler and Debussy achieved this in terms of form—for both of them this entailed abandoning structures inherited from earlier times. This reference to their break with tradition is not a retrospective interpretation after the event: the breach was intrinsic to their technique. Debussy often defined his musical aspirations in terms of a renewal of form and subject matter. 'What I should like to create is something looser, more fragmented, more nimble, more intangible, something that appears disorganized on the surface yet is methodical at bottom.'[39] These words are disturbing if we read them with Mahler's voice—especially that of *Spätstil* (late style). The apparent disorganization, the loosening, even the occasional contradictory orderliness, are true Mahlerian characteristics. The concepts of the 'intangible' and the 'fragmented' take us back to the opening bars of the Ninth Symphony (see below), the language of which assumes a variety of changing shapes from the outset, or to those floating thirds which provide a link between the mountain of the 'Abschied' and the hillocks of Debussy's 'Collines d'Anacapri'. These sounds, 'free yet coherent', give us an accurate impression of Mahlerian counterpoint, a turbulent flow that acknowledges no debt to conventional harmony, and sweeps freely into visionary chaos elements which more orthodox musicians commonly regard as crude or primitive.

Later on we shall rediscover 'fragmentation' in the orchestra; what this means in terms of form—discontinuity—is a feature of musical structure for both Mahler and Debussy. 'It is alternation that gives rise to form . . ., unity builds itself up across the gaps.'[40] Their joint mastery of agogics draws attention to one way in which form may be significantly varied. Every transition that is slowed down or speeded up in this way, its increasing or declining energy cushioned by the orchestration, raises questions about the meaning of form. In this respect, a change of metre resembles a weaving thread, which inverts the tempo and cuts across the entire structure of the work. A comparative study of the Ninth Symphony and of *Jeux* may serve to convince the reader of this.

Debussy's fascination with the art of understatement, to which his more enigmatic compositions bear witness (*La Mer*), turns his imagination towards the sketch, the work held in suspension. As with Mahler, when he makes use of classical form, the resulting material eventually becomes fragmented as subject matter interacts with timbre (the rondo form of

---

[39] Léon Vallas, *Claude Debussy et son temps* (Paris: A. Michel, 1958), 364.
[40] Adorno, *Mahler* (French. trans.), 24 and 55 (Eng. trans., 10 and 33).

'Dialogue du vent et de la mer'). The metaphor of painting could not apply to Debussy with greater relevance than in this matter of fusion of timbre and form, to which Boulez has given the name 'structural divisionism'. Mahler, the perfectionist, also lets his finest scores speak of infinity, presented in the shape of the 'unfinished'. The 'open end'—a characteristic of Berg's compositions—does away with the notion of a form that could embrace the Whole—not only that of a complete work, but also of the meaning that infuses it and makes it 'speak'. Often in Mahler's lieder or Debussy's *Préludes* the composer's intentions spill over the boundaries of form—appearing to prolong the work by posing problems of interpretation which put pressure on the listener to solve. Sometimes a knell sounds for this reaching out towards the infinite, the *Abgesang*: the bells at the death of Mélisande, the celesta which accompanies 'ewig' at the end of *Das Lied von der Erde*; and, in both works, the added notes which hold the harmony in suspension.

For both Mahler and Debussy, thematic development has one characteristic in common: the theme searching to escape from itself. Adorno introduced the concept of 'variant'[41] as the only way of explaining this transformational alchemy, which always pushes a theme of Mahler's beyond its first exposition, as if it could find no 'resting place'. The Andante of the Sixth Symphony offers us the supremely minimalist example of this thematic process: one phrase, divided into multiple brief periods, constantly changing its shape and shifting the emphasis of its accents. It turns upon itself, then seems to stretch out, to be regenerated, before at last taking flight. Mahler's themes, like those of Debussy, as they play with 'deviations' in this manner, affect the listener's memory in subtle, almost infinitesimal, ways, concentrating exclusively on feelings. At times the theme apparently seeks to 'make itself forgotten', in Paul Bekker's words. One does not know if its intended destiny is some kind of past existence which it tries to re-create (the Schoenbergian notion of the development that precedes the exposition).

The problem for Mahlerian analysis is how to pin down, in order to highlight it, the point beyond which the material can be reduced no further. As Adorno remarks, this search for the musical kernel is scarcely rewarding in Mahler's case (even if, by contrast, it is so with Beethoven), where thematic development is integrated into larger components that already outline the shape of the entire work (the theme as form itself). We find, nevertheless, in Mahler's later style, irreducible compositional 'cells', which have an integrative function comparable to those of *La Mer*.

With Debussy and Mahler alike, neither subject matter nor form abides by fixed rules. The music does not spell itself out unambiguously, whether it eliminates its own traces as it proceeds, or continually reshapes its constituents, putting their very identity at risk. The whole cannot be measured in terms of form or any of its constituent parts. This mastery of splitting, of division, is one of the clearest consequences of 'distance' in their art: a virtue symbolized by 'an ear oriented in the direction of faraway lands, an ear to which the remotest analogies and issues are already present, as they are to a narrative which is master of itself'.[42]

---

[41] [See Adorno, *Mahler*, 86 ff. Ed.]   [42] Adorno, *Mahler* (French trans.), 132 (Eng. trans., 87–8).

In the works of Mahler and Debussy 'exposition' no longer has any relevance as a concept. Any 'idea' that emerges has already absorbed into itself the potential for self-transformation. It makes no greater sense to think of exposition as an anchorage for memory before development takes place. In this respect, it is necessary to rehear and reread *Jeux*. The 'missing development' in this work amounts to a denial of exposition. One thing is always another thing, always different. If it returns it is no longer itself. This also helps us to appreciate the insoluble problem, in Mahler's case, of the recapitulation—now inflated by its own energy (the repeat is thus no more than a spark which reignites the narrative), now cut short by catastrophe, or whispered in the shadows, as in the finale of the Sixth Symphony. In ways such as these the structure itself takes shape from a work's expositional discrepancies.

This exposition held in suspension, this incomprehensible game in which it always reappears in different forms, triggers memory certainly (as it does an instant of perception), but also blurs its rational functions. Thus, what we hear of the Golaud theme, surreptitiously repeated in the fountain scene, or the theme of the Adagietto of the Fifth Symphony, brought back during the course of the Rondo-Finale, affects us primarily in terms of feeling. Precise recall does not feature prominently—it is, rather, kept in the background. With Debussy as with Mahler, the dominance of memories below the level of consciousness cuts across the linear progress of musical language in such a way that an intellectual grasp of these works, the feeling that one has 'understood' them, has stored every major part in them in one's memory, is hard to attain. Each seems like a world that has emerged from a universe.

The orchestra, for Mahler and Debussy, is not the clothing in which musical language is arrayed, but the domain of its frequent changes of meaning, where new relationships are developed, all of them of equal status—Adorno has spoken of 'integral composition'. Neither the role of harmony in the bass nor the layout required for it is consistently maintained (especially with Debussy). Counterpoint emancipates itself, the 'voices' are no longer precisely accountable in harmonic terms (particularly, in Mahler's case, in the Scherzo of the Fifth Symphony, the Rubicon of Mahlerian counterpoint). Exposition is no more than an instrumental figure, an 'idea' that has already been absorbed into the musical texture. At the start of the Ninth Symphony and of *Jeux*, the orchestra seems to come in behind the music, as if it had succeeded in giving the music utterance through a process of decipherment, touching on each individual note and recomposing each successive instant. In a sublime deflation of language, the music abandons every kind of grand gesture: it seems to stammer—not unlike those moments when it 'floats' in the 'Abschied'. In the opening bars of both scores we hear horns (acting as echoes), harp, and violas—shrewdly 'selected' in Debussy's case. The orchestrator takes great pleasure in giving every detail its own individual character, in deciding which instrument is to have a solo part, in dividing the desks, in arriving at decisions about harmony. The subtle devices used in the two *Nachtmusiken* of the Seventh Symphony (such as the guitar and mandolin in the second), or those in *Das Lied von der Erde*, as they single out a chamber ensemble from the larger orchestra, always allow us to 'hear' the silent space—those deliberate pauses in the score—of other 'virtual' orchestras.

Since thematic development is incorporated within the form of the work, orchestration must take into account the aesthetic implications of discontinuity. The fine stitching that ensues is located on the agogic fringes, where tempo is held in suspension, and ensures that one orchestral block succeeds another—both knitted together by the work's material. The music of the Scherzo of the Third Symphony flows into the suspended elegy of its trio, like a torrent filling a reservoir. The material settles down (in the strings) to let us hear the message of this trio, the music of which is identical with its instrument—the solo post-horn. Mahler's orchestration is coarser and harsher than Debussy's. Above all, it takes the risk of passing material from one orchestral section to another—a device which was to be much less successful with Schoenberg. After only one reading of the score (Figs. 7 and 8 of the 'Abschied'), how could one imagine that the transition of swaying thirds from harp to muted violas could possibly work? With Debussy, such 'transitions' are always masked by a form of inflection, an upbeat.

Orchestration is above all the art of dividing, of sharing. A classic view of the orchestra is that, beyond its function of disseminating many different voices, it is always bound to maintain the unity and coherence of musical discourse. Aiming as they do for a kind of salutary squaring-off, the operational principles underlying this viewpoint bear witness to a great fear of the void. In contrast, for Debussy the orchestra was the ideal vehicle for achieving the 'looseness' he dreamt of, the discontinuity (let us recall the 'space laboratory' of which he spoke). His orchestral sound, the colouring he gives it, stems in large measure from the divided strings, from the minutiae of their separate treatment—divided desks, selected soloists. With Mahler it is precisely this characteristic, as Paul Bekker has rightly observed, which often takes precedence over concern for colour. The timbres clash as though they were so many contour lines; conflicting dynamic forces gleefully plough their way through the web of sound, coming from individual desks, creating new timbres. Even more than Debussy, Mahler—no doubt one step ahead in this through his conducting experience—knows how to vary the equilibrium of different instrumental dispositions within the orchestra (*Kindertotenlieder*), and to 'take risks' with soloists (notably the emancipation of the trombone).

For Debussy and Mahler orchestration is not a matter of fixed technique, a question of precise tuning or adjustment. In their relationship with the orchestra there is always a vital element of conflict, as though there could never be a final version of the orchestral material. They touch it up incessantly. Even at the point of death Mahler asked, in a moment of sublime doubt, if he had not been mistaken in orchestrating as he did.

The practice of 'distancing' is the least explored aspect of Mahler's genius and the way it converges with Debussy's. There is in their art an obstructive impulse which stands in the way of completion, of transfiguration, and brings their work down to earth. It is as if they turn their backs on their own music, or dream, like Debussy, of composing it 'with the greatest possible detachment [from oneself]'. When Schoenberg puts forward the notion that there is, virtually, an author hidden away for whom Mahler is the spokesman, he is hinting at this 'absent-ness' from the work in hand—which may be seen as a matter of degree. 'Mahler', wrote Adorno, 'is a foreigner who speaks the language of music fluently, but with a discernible accent.'[43] It is through the light cast by disenchantment that we gain such a vivid picture of their works devoid of heroes—a picture which derives its clarity from what Freud called 'the phenomenal failure of the world'.

The beauty of the music they wrote, with its anticipation of modernism, is rooted in the 'sounds from a distance' which infuse it, sounds whose sources are hard to attain, and which are like a hoped-for dowry from inaccessible lands. The sense, in their work, of a perceived failure to achieve their aim, does not imply either a partial or total lack of real success; in simple terms, its presence holds their work in a state of uncertainty, not in the realm of insolent self-confidence and bursting-with-health affability that characterize the works of Strauss. In their music a feeling of *loss* finds expression, displayed by each composer in accordance with his way of interpreting nature. With Mahler, this feeling of loss is written into the telling anachronism of his materials and its mode of representation. With Debussy, it is like a condensed expression of regret for a vanished golden age, and of a wish to stop composing music. The hands of Mélisande are sick, as are also, on the threshold of death, those of Proust's Narrator, who is finishing his book in order to begin it. He 'thus promises what *could* be otherwise'[44] at the very moment when he understands that the essence of things has eluded him, is impossible to attain. This transcendence, whose lifeline has been severed, may well be the tenuous and subtle message which neither Mahler nor Debussy would have dared hope to convey.

Translated by Peter Righton

---

[43] [See Adorno, *Mahler*, 32. Ed.]   [44] Ibid. (French trans.), 16.

8

A Stranger's Story: Programmes, Politics, and Mahler's Third Symphony

PETER FRANKLIN

They are already so corrupted by programme music . . . that they are no longer capable of understanding a work simply as a piece of music! This disastrously mistaken attitude stems from Liszt and Berlioz. They, at least, were talented, and gained new means of expression in this way. But now that we have these means at hand, who needs the crutches any more?

> Mahler talking to Natalie Bauer-Lechner about critical misunderstanding of his Fourth Symphony in 1901 [*NBL*, 184]

Carolyn Abbate's reflections on *Todtenfeier*[1] have sharpened the focus of renewed interest in 'programmaticism' in Mahler's symphonies. She explains her particular interest in narrative voice, in meaningful disruptions and 'displacements', by suggesting that normative forms of technical analysis 'have one unfortunate critical effect: they emphasize how self-questioning, richer music (like Mahler's, like all opera) resembles music more ordinary'.[2] As Adorno's brilliant study of the composer begins to make a more tangible impact on Anglo-American scholarship,[3] the precise nature and extent of Mahler's far from ordinary richness in this respect has come to be regarded as central to the matter of his relation to modernism. The facts about the Third Symphony, about its descriptive titles, and Mahler's various philosophical and narrative glosses on the work are well established.[4] My concern here will be with how these 'facts'—enigmatic and in need of further interpretation as they often are—might be viewed within a broader, culturally orientated understanding of Mahler's historical significance. Questions arising from my opening quotation must first,

---

[1] Carolyn Abbate, *Unsung Voices: Opera and Musical Narrative in the Nineteenth Century* (Princeton: Princeton University Press, 1991), ch. 4 ('Mahler's Deafness: Opera and the Scene of Narration in *Todtenfeier*'), 119–55.

[2] Ibid. 152.

[3] First published in German as *Mahler: Eine musikal-* *ische Physiognomik* (Frankfurt am Main: Suhrkamp, 1960); for the English translation see Adorno, *Mahler*.

[4] They are set out in my Cambridge Music Handbook on the Third: Franklin, *Mahler: Symphony No. 3*. See esp. ch. 3, 'Genesis and design', 37–52, and App. I, which lists all the internal titles and annotations in the 1896 manuscript.

however, lead us to reconsider his position in the absolutist vs. programmaticist debate of the 1890s.

I

It is clear that Mahler came to reject the overt programmaticism of the Liszt- and Strauss-orientated 'New German' school with which he had been widely associated as a young man.[5] Much has been made of his semi-public renunciation of symphonic programmes following the 1900 Munich performance of the Second Symphony.[6] Insufficient attention, however, has perhaps been paid to the corresponding strength of his public commitment *to* programmaticism during the same period. The most famous of the programmes for the Second Symphony was written in 1901.[7] His First Symphony had been performed with elaborate programmatic explanations in 1893 (Hamburg) and 1894 (Weimar);[8] Henry-Louis de La Grange long ago pointed out that Mahler seems to have sanctioned Natalie Bauer-Lechner's explanation of that work's programme to Ludwig Karpath in 1900.[9] The gestation of the Third Symphony between 1893 and 1896 appears unequivocally to have been defined by the simultaneous development of structural plans and conceptual programmes that interpreted them. Lists of evocative movement titles, not musical analyses or thematic quotations, were what Mahler excitedly communicated to his friends as evidence of the work's progress towards completion in 1895–6.

Mahler's most considered statements on the issue of programmaticism almost invite selective summary as manifestations of a liberal concern for the listener to be free to construct his or her own verbally conceptualized 'inner programme' with only a minimum of guidance from the composer.[10] There can be no final word on this, however, and it would be my suggestion that contradictions in his expressed attitude reflect a historically significant tension between Mahler's behaviour in the public as opposed to the private sphere. This seems to have arisen from worry not to much about the possibility as about the politics of unguarded honesty in the public expression of matters personal, for all that his music seems (and seemed) striking for its consistent readiness to reveal the content of his inner life.[11] Mahler adopted a judiciously wary tone when discussing musical expression around the turn of the century for reasons that could be interpreted as bound up with matters of acceptance and assimilation; with constraints upon the outsider-achiever who sought power in a culture of which he was privately critical and in which he had been

[5] A direct, and implicitly derogatory, reference to the 'new German' school will be found in a letter of Jan. 1894 from Mahler to his sister Justine. See HLG(E) i. 290.

[6] See Franklin, *Mahler: Symphony No. 3*, 22–3.

[7] Alma Mahler, *Memories*, 213–14.

[8] See Paul Stefan, *Gustav Mahler: Eine Studie über Persönlichkeit und Werk* (Munich: R. Piper, 1920), 113–14.

[9] HLG(E) i. 748–9. A transcription and translation of Bauer-Lechner's letter to Karpath will be found in NB-L, *Recollections*, 236–41.

[10] See e.g. his letter to Otto Lessmann of 15 May 1894 in Mahler, *Briefe* (1982), 111–12.

[11] As he claimed to have done in his first two symphonies; see NB-L, *Recollections*, 30 (and see p. 231).

publicly marginalized as a Jew. A powerful explanation of this tension, reinvesting in the categories of Romantic aesthetics, is found in a late letter to Bruno Walter. Writing from New York in 1909, Mahler spoke of the visions and inner reality of dreams, whose evanescence 'is the deepest cause of the life of conflict an artist leads. He is condemned to lead a double life, and woe betide him if it happens that life and dream flow into one—so that he has appallingly to suffer in the one world for the laws of the other.'[12]

An interesting testimony to Mahler's lively concern, eight years earlier, to tailor his public image to the demands of the outer world is found in two letters written on his behalf by Bruno Walter to Ludwig Schiedermair on 6 December 1901.[13] Schiedermair had just published the first ever monograph on Mahler and was important to the composer as an enthusiastic critical proponent and programme-note writer. He had asked Mahler to explain the programmatic basis of his new Fourth Symphony. Walter explains in his first letter that Mahler was too busy to reply but had charged *him* with the task, hoping that the accompanying, more formal letter could be made public in full. This longer, 'public' letter certainly matches what we know of Mahler's informally developed approach to these questions, with all its contradictions. What amounts, in fact, to a revealing programmatic interpretation of the Fourth (it is here that we learn of the once-intended movement titles, like the Scherzo's 'Freund Hein spielt zum Tanz auf . . .') is prefaced with a lengthy sermon on the 'purely musical' nature of Mahler's symphonies. All the standard terminology of idealist aesthetics is employed:

No programme will lead one to an understanding of this work, nor any other Mahler symphony. It is absolute music ['absolute Musik'] and non-literary from beginning to end: a four-movement symphony, each movement organic in itself, and completely accessible to anyone who is responsive to subtle humour.[14]

Extra-musical questions are nevertheless teasingly invited by the reference to 'subtle humour', later associated more explicitly by Walter with the symphony's concluding song and the conception of it as a 'child's' answer to questions posed by the first three movements. (The song, 'Das himmlische Leben', had for a period in 1895 been intended to form the finale of the Third Symphony, with the title 'What the Child tells me'.)[15] Although Walter invites still further questions by using the word 'Heiterkeit' (much used by Nietzsche) to describe the Fourth's 'cheerfulness',[16] this humorous conception might still have been interpreted as evidence of Mahler's internalization of the Romantic construction of the classical style. Writers from E. T. A. Hoffmann to Wagner had linked 'naivety', 'play', and 'dance' in their descriptions of Mozart and Haydn: musicians dealing in a utopian perfection that 'modern' composers were perhaps able to reconstruct only as idyll, as irretrievably past or childlike. The Fourth Symphony might thus be read as a knowing (perhaps all too knowing) harbinger of the 'new style' of the purely instrumental,

[12] Translation from Mahler, *Selected Letters*, 346. The German text will be found in Mahler, *Briefe* (1982), 372.

[13] Bruno Walter, *Briefe 1894–1962*, ed. Lotte Walter Lindt (Frankfurt am Main: S. Fischer Verlag, 1969), 46–52.

[14] Ibid. 50.

[15] See Franklin, *Mahler: Symphony No. 3*, 45–50.

[16] Ibid. 51.

middle-period symphonies, in which Mahler seemed to respond to the anti-programmatic censure of his more conservative critics.

That censure Mahler may have come to see as implicit in the traditionally constituted project of symphonic composition, described so resonantly by Hanslick in his 1886 review of Brahms's fourth as 'the composer's severest test—and his highest calling'.[17] When Mahler frequently condemned tradition, he meant not the Great Tradition, but the sloppy, insufficiently idealistic tradition of performance practice, particularly in the theatre, with its over-used and under-rehearsed orchestras.[18] He rarely slandered the classical masters. There remains, however, the tantalizing evidence of the Fourth's conceptual or 'programmatic' relationship to the Third as a kind of epilogue to what Mahler also described as a 'perfectly self-contained tetralogy' of symphonies.[19] As the climactic and focal work of that tetralogy, the Third apparently had a vital synoptic role, cryptically signalled in the manuscript's movement titles that Mahler publicly reinstated in 1906 (although no edition of the score has ever included them).[20] Many other signs—publicized or concealed, both musical and 'extra-musical'—reflect Mahler's cultural-political affinities and allegiances in the period of the Third Symphony's composition and consistently compromise *its* claim to abstract, or 'absolute', status.

II

From its first complete performance at the Crefeld festival of the Allgemeine Deutsche Musikverein in 1902, all programmatic titles having been suppressed,[21] the Third seemed to resound with daring, even outrageous 'modernism' for both pro- and anti-Mahlerians alike. That meant New German programmaticism of the Straussian kind. Significant here was his apparently deliberate vulgarization of the musical high style through realistic or 'naturalistic' indulgence in common march tunes (even scored in military-band style in the first movement) and almost kitsch, sentimental melodies like the post-horn solo in the third movement. Innumerable related instances of deliberate nuancing, 'flavouring',[22] and ethnic voicing—particularly Jewish—were cited. There remained also the two literary associations that no programme suppression could avoid: the setting of Nietzsche in the fourth movement and, in the fifth, that of the 'Poor Children's Begging Song' ('Armer

[17] Eduard Hanslick, *Music Criticisms 1846–99*, trans. and ed. Henry Pleasants (London: Penguin, 1963), 243.

[18] Paul Stefan records a significant saying of Mahler's: 'Es gibt keine Tradition, nur Genius und Stupidität' ('There is no such thing as tradition, only genius and stupidity'). Stefan, *Gustav Mahler*, 61.

[19] NB-L, *Recollections*, 154.

[20] HLG(F) iii. 990, and Bekker, *Gustav Mahlers Sinfonien*, 358.

[21] They had been published in full in the programme for Nikisch's première of the symphony's second movement, as an independent item, in his Berlin concert of 9 Nov. 1896. See Franklin, *Mahler: Symphony No. 3*, 23–5.

[22] Theodor Adorno was to observe, in *Mahler: Eine musikalische Physiognomik*, 36 (Eng. trans., 23) that Mahler's tone had a bouquet-like 'aroma' by comparison with more orthodox, classically orientated music.

Kinder Bettlerlied'), from *Des Knaben Wunderhorn*. The latter movement might have been interpreted as celebrating decent Christian sentiments in a way that threatened no status quo; but Nietzsche had been the favourite philosopher of radical modernists in the 1890s, and *Also sprach Zarathustra* his most widely read book. Linked with the popular and conceivably political allusion of the first movement's main theme to Binzer's old fraternity song 'Wir hatten gebauet ein stattliches Haus',[23] this meant that the symphony was more than a little susceptible of a leftist, even socialist reading, explicitly made in 1904 by one Swiss critic.[24]

This needs comment and explanation, not least with respect to the role of Nietzsche, whom Mahler ostensibly rejected in the years immediately following the Third's completion. That rejection has led some to question the extent of his Nietzscheanism even at the time of the Third Symphony.[25] A change of heart could alternatively be seen as fitting in convincingly with his move from a radical modernist position to a more guarded and ostensibly 'conservative' one around 1900. This would still permit politicized interpretations of the Third like that by Dieter Schnebel, for example, and most fully developed in a historical context by William J. McGrath.[26] The latter's *Dionysian Art and Populist Politics in Austria* convincingly located the Third Symphony at the crossroads between the politicized aesthetics of the idealistic, leftist pan-Germanists of late nineteenth-century Vienna and the developing 'poetic politics' of a radical *völkisch* social democratic movement, whose ideas and techniques oddly harboured some of the seeds of National Socialism. Interpreted in this light, the Third seems to bridge contrasts and oppositions which were at the heart of political as much as cultural-aesthetic experience in Mahler's world. They met, perhaps, in Viktor Adler's 'unifying' conception of the May Day holiday, whose first celebration in Austria (1890) Alder later described as a 'Weckruf' ('Awakening call') to the working class.[27]

The Swiss critic who discerned a specifically socialist message in the Third would not have been surprised to learn that Mahler was moved to accompany a May Day procession in the Ringstrasse for a little way in 1905 (the same procession whose proletarian faces had supposedly infuriated Hans Pfitzner).[28] Even Richard Strauss seems involuntarily to have interpreted the first movement's march episodes as depicting a May Day procession to the Prater.[29] We know that Mahler still openly voted socialist in the 1901 elections,[30] but

[23] See Franklin, *Mahler: Symphony No. 3*, 81–2 and William J. McGrath, 'Mahler and Freud: The Dream of the Stately House', in *Gustav Mahler Kolloquium 1979*, ed. Rudolf Klein (Beiträge der Österreichischen Gesellschaft für Musik, 2; Kassel: Bärenreiter, 1981), 41–51.

[24] HLG(F) ii. 404.

[25] Joseph Marx, in *Betrachtungen eines romantischen Realisten: Gesammelte Aufsätze, Vorträge und Reden über Musik*, ed. Oswald Ortner (Vienna: Gerlach & Wiedling, 1947), 168, and Kurt Blaukopf, in *Gustav Mahler*, trans. Inge Goodwin (London: Allen Lane, 1973), 123–4, both question the 'Nietzschean' qualities of the fourth movement's setting of Zarathustra's 'Mitternachtslied'. On this specific question, see also Friedhelm Krummacher, *Gustav*

Mahlers III Symphonie: Welt im Widerbild (Kassel: Bärenreiter, 1991), 122–4.

[26] See Dieter Schnebel, 'Sinfonie und Wirklichkeit am Beispiel von Mahlers Dritte', in *Gustav Mahler: Sinfonie und Wirklichkeit* (Graz: Universal Edition, 1977), 103–17, and William J. McGrath, *Dionysian Art and Populist Politics in Austria* (New Haven and London: Yale University Press, 1974).

[27] McGrath, *Dionysian Art*, 222.

[28] Alma Mahler, *Memories*, 82.

[29] The source is Richard Specht, *Gustav Mahler* (Berlin: Schuster & Loeffler, 1913), 249.

[30] See *MDS*, 225. The candidate was Viktor Adler.

retrospective questions about the nature of his political ideas remain. Perhaps they are inaccessible to late twentieth-century conceptions of what a socialist or leftist position might sanction in the early 1900s. It is hard, for example, to overlook that curious 'interview' printed in the New York *Etude* in 1910 in which, under the general heading 'The Influence of the Folk-Song on German Musical Art', Mahler is quoted (in translation) as describing the American Negroes as descended from 'savages pure and simple', shortly adding: 'I cannot subscribe myself to the doctrine that all men are born equal, as it is inconceivable to me. It is not reasonable to expect that a race could arise from a savage condition to a high ethnological state in a century or two.'[31]

In fact the interconnection of these now apparently opposed attitudes is widely encountered in the intellectual history of the period. R. S. Hinton Thomas is one of a number of writers who have documented the way in which, in the 1890s, the often outspokenly anti-socialist and anti-democratic Nietzsche came to be embraced by liberals and socialists for his broadly critical stance.[32] Against the proto-Fascist tendencies manifest in a Nietzschean popularist like Julius Langbehn[33] might be set the representatively thoughtful engagement with Nietzsche of Heinrich Braun, subsequently Viktor Adler's brother-in-law and a friend of Mahler's intellectual mentor, Siegfried Lipiner. Braun was a socialist who found in Nietzsche valuable insights into the dangerous promptings of 'the masses' under capitalism. These he believed would be more fruitfully led by a Nietzschean 'Adelsmensch' ('noble man').[34] Many of those on the traditionalist right of the political spectrum nevertheless came to associate Nietzsche with anarchy and subversion.

Other case studies help to clarify this confusing picture. The German-Jewish writer Gustav Landauer, for example, followed an intellectual path in the 1890s that could usefully be compared with Mahler's.[35] Of anti-bourgeois, anarchist inclination, Landauer had discovered *Also sprach Zarathustra* in 1890, and had then written a novel, *Der Todesprediger*, about a man persuaded *away* from Marxist socialism by reading Nietzsche. Landauer later developed an idea of God as a projected image of what man himself aspires to become. By 1895 he had expressed a notion of the individual as but one element of an organic social whole, whose larger process of development subsumed the existential plight of its constituent parts. Increasing pessimism about tangible social change seems to have led Landauer ultimately to diagnose a general cultural decadence that turned him in the direction of such an ostensibly un-like-minded cultural critic as Max Nordau (1849–1923).

Mahler's ideas and those of the Budapest-born Nordau, author of *Die conventionellen Lügen der Kulturmenschheit* (1883) and *Entartung* (1892–3) and co-founder with

---

[31] The article is reprinted in Lebrecht, *Mahler Remembered* (London), 288–93; the quotation here comes from p. 292.

[32] R. S. Hinton Thomas, *Nietzsche in German Politics and Society, 1890–1918* (Manchester: Manchester University Press, 1983).

[33] Julius Langbehn (1852–1907) was author of the widely read, originally anonymous *Rembrant als Erzieher: Von einem Deutschen* (1890); an opponent of socialism, he envisaged the redemption of the German masses by a Nietzschean 'Führer'.

[34] See Hinton Thomas, *Nietzsche in German Politics*, 32–3.

[35] See ibid. 52–6.

Theodor Herzl of modern Zionism, have yet to be compared by scholars of the period.[36] Nordau's quasi-Nietzschean optimism, liberalism, and elitism were linked with an anti-religious standpoint that nevertheless led him to find greater consistency in conservative Catholicism than in critical Protestantism. Mahler could have shared Nordau's anti-Wagnerism no more than he could Nietzsche's (if Bruno Walter is to be believed),[37] but the invitation to further contextual study of his philosophical and religious beliefs is provocative. Equally interesting is the already mentioned 'conservative' context in which we may view some of Mahler's later interests. His favouring of Kant and Goethe over Nietzsche and Ibsen, for example, was widely shared by right-wing German nationalists.[38] Equally relevant, by way of comparison, is the trajectory followed by Mahler's and Lipiner's friend of the late 1880s, Richard Kralik (1852–1934).

Kralik's career followed an exemplary path.[39] In a sense it unfolded contradictions already implicit in the interests of the 'Saga Society', of which Mahler was briefly a member in 1881. These ranged around Wagner, from socialism to the mystical psychology of Lipiner's former teacher G. T. Fechner. Earlier than many of his friends, Kralik had followed the trend of early nineteenth-century Romantics away from active hope for political change in the 'real world' to an internalized and idealized utopianism that was rooted variously in notions of a mystic 'beyond' or of some primeval past. By the end of 1880 Kralik was dramatically converted to a kind of despairing nihilism that Lipiner only partially succeeded in modifying, to the extent of helping him to readmit the possibility of some transcendent, utopian otherness. This Kralik came to associate first with the world of Germanic sagas (hence his involvement with the 'Saga Society', for all its political leanings), then with the conservative, regeneration-seeking Catholic literary movement to which he devoted the later and most influential part of his creative life. Mahler's own, possibly pragmatic, conversion to Catholicism takes on an altered significance in the light of its conservative implications within a Catholic culture where a more radical move of the assimilated Jew might have been to convert to Protestantism.[40]

What emerges from all this is the clear possibility of contradiction and change in philosophical and aesthetic positions of the period. In Mahler's case we might further question whether he underwent an externally prompted change of perspective or an internal realignment of two contradictory yet complementary strata of attitudes. There are certainly earlier indications of a conformist, 'assimilationist' inclination. By the same token, Eveline Nikkels has interestingly argued the case for a persistent, underlying 'Nietzschean' strain

---

[36] A valuable account of Nordau's career will be found in Robert B. Pynsent, 'Conclusory Essay: Decadence, Decay and Innovation', in id. (ed.), *Decadence and Innovation: Austro-Hungarian Life and Art at the Turn of the Century* (London: Weidenfeld and Nicolson, 1989), 128–40.

[37] See Walter, *Gustav Mahler* (1973 edn.), 136.

[38] A significant example would be General Friedrich von Bernhardi, whose book *Deutschland und der nächste Krieg* (1913), an ostensibly 'Nietzschean' justification of the power of the state and universal military service, dealt admiringly with Kant, as founder of the Prussian sense of moral duty. See Hinton Thomas, *Nietzsche in German.*

[39] See McGrath, *Dionysian Art*, 87–105.

[40] See Michael Pollack, 'Cultural Innovation and Social Identity in *Fin-de-siècle* Vienna', in Ivar Oxaal, Michael Pollack, and Gerhard Botz (eds.), *Jews, Antisemitism and Culture in Vienna* (London and New York: Routledge and Kegan Paul, 1987), 65–6.

in Mahler's creative preoccupations right up to the last works.[41] The Third Symphony's complicated mediation between these two attitudes—of the critical, modernist outsider and the more guarded, assimilated conservative—begins to emerge almost as the subject matter of that work in a way that might both validate special interest in it in the canon of Mahler's symphonies and explain the extravagance and excitement with which he spoke about its completion in 1896. Did it dramatize an attempt to appropriate and colonize the dominant ideology of his culture under the banner of radical modernism? Or did it exemplify a grand form of what Marxist theorists might call 'false consciousness', apparently mediating an antinomy within that culture in the very act of selling out to the dominant ideology; to its vision of 'Nature' as diversely stratified but hierarchically organized by a power from on high?[42] Here the 'programmes' demand close attention, particularly as interpreted in the light of Mahler's reading of the period and in the context of some of the high-profile decisions he made after becoming Director of the Vienna Court Opera in 1897.

III

Mahler so arranged things that the first performance he conducted after his official appointment, little more than a year after completing the Third Symphony, was of a new production, on the Emperor's name-day (4 October), of Smetana's *Dalibor*.[43] This was in the midst of a gathering political crisis over the 'Badeni ordinances' in Bohemia, soon to erupt in Parliament and to conclude with martial law being declared in Prague on 2 December.[44] The sizeable and administratively dominant German-speaking minority in Bohemia had been outraged by the Bohemian and Moravian Prime Minister's ordinances giving equal official rights to the Czech language as to German. *Dalibor* had not hitherto been successful; and although Hanslick, in his favourable review of Mahler's production, felt able to discuss the musical and dramatic content of this Czech nationalist opera about a Czech national folk hero without any mention of contemporary events, Max Kalbeck, in the *Neues Wiener Tagblatt*, noted the fears 'expressed in some quarters' that the performance 'might be used for political purposes', adding 'one certainly saw people who would not normally come to the first performance of a new opera . . . very many Czech members of the Imperial Parliament were there'.[45] The anonymous 'German Austrian', who wrote to

[41] Eveline Nikkels, *'O Mensch! Gib Acht!' Friedrich Nietzsches Bedeutung für Gustav Mahler* (Amsterdam and Atlanta: Rodopi, 1989), esp. Sect. B III, pp. 122–200.

[42] Carl Dahlhaus's essay 'The Natural World and the "Folklike Tone"' throws light on aspects of this question with reference to Mahler. See Dahlhaus, *Realism in Nineteenth-Century Music*, trans. Mary Whittall (Cambridge and New York: Cambridge University Press, 1985), 106–14.

[43] See HLG(E) i. 454–6.

[44] A helpful synopsis of the relevant historical events will be found in Pynsent's 'Conclusory Essay' to *Decadence and Innovation*, 115.

[45] Hanslick's review is reprinted in Eduard Hanslick, *Die moderne Oper*, viii: *Am Ende des Jahrhunderts (1895–1899). Musikalische Kritiken und Schilderungen* (Berlin: Allgemeine Verein für Deutsche Literatur, 1899), 57–66. The extract from Kalbeck's article is quoted from *MDS*, 214.

berate the new Director for 'fraternizing with this anti-dynastic, second-rate Czech nation who are good for nothing but acts of violence against the German and Austrian State', may well have aroused grim satisfaction in Mahler, given his own Moravian–Bohemian roots and the fact that he had engaged in close consultation with the Czech National Theatre in Prague about his production.[46]

I would suggest that Mahler's audacious, even risky, conflation of artistic and political impulses in the 1897 *Dalibor* production characterizes his achievement in the first movement of the Third Symphony. Fairly precise questions about its ideological implications, given the previously discussed contradictions in his evolving outlook, might focus on one specific passage at Fig. 44. If we take Mahler at his word and read the movement as a hugely expanded, but fundamentally 'classical', sonata structure, we could describe this passage as coming after the midway point of an enormous 'development section', whose central crisis has been marked by a dramatic termination of the hitherto unstoppable momentum of the joyful march. Seven bars before Fig. 29 we reach what Adorno might have called a 'Durchbruch' or 'breakthrough'. Gestures of grand triumph sweep us off our feet in a surprise B flat major (the context is D major) before being contradicted by a shattering reversal that brings back introductory, or 'first group', material at Fig. 29 itself, contrasted in every way with the preceding music. This is the first of a series of displacements or rents in the musical fabric that Abbate would surely wish us to question interpretatively for their narrative implications. Further such disruptions occur at Fig. 32; but after Fig. 34 the indications in the score confirm that the affirmatively purposeful march material is 'returning' from 'the farthest distance', having been ousted from the symphonic arena by a music of Otherness, whose rhetorical portent was linked, in Mahler's explanatory glosses on the movement, with images of winter and stasis. Opposing it was the 'summer march' that grows out of the second-group material, labelled in the manuscript score 'Pan sleeps', the title-page heading having split the whole movement into an 'Introduction' ('Pan awakes') and 'Nro 1', entitled 'Summer marches in'.

This, then, was how Mahler interpreted the music's narrative: as juxtaposing two musical symbolizations of 'Nature'; the first is destructive, overpowering and impersonally Other in its fateful denial of growth and change; the second represents fruitfulness and growth, and acquires, as we have seen, those plebeian voices that, with or without the direct influence of Binzer's 'Wir hatten gebauet ein stattliches Haus', had led to Strauss's vision of May Day workers marching to the Prater. This dynamically personified image of the 'forces of nature' (crudely and dualistically pitted against, not evolved from, its 'other' image) is strikingly at variance with the artfully posed and costumed Bacchic revellers found in popular 'classical' history paintings of the period. One thinks, perhaps, of Alma-Tadema, whose models always look as if they had been drawn from the families of society aesthetes.[47] Even the fully awake

[46] *MDS*, 214.
[47] His 1889 painting *Eine Weihung an Bacchus* is a relevant example. Replete with Graeco-Roman objets d'art, its marble terrace by the sea is about to receive a procession of Bacchic celebrants whose elegantly balletic gestures nevertheless defuse any rowdiness threatened by the burning torches and high-held tambourines (the only other instruments visible are cymbals, flute, and aulos).

and enticing Pan whose face had looked out from the modernist art journal of that name, during the very years Mahler was writing the Third, was effectively inviting 'cultured' readers into a world of decorative luxury that had little to do with Mahler's 'rough children of nature' storming their way to heaven.[48]

All Mahler's allegorical, quasi-programmatic descriptions of this movement support the inference that the joyfully impetuous march of life represented for him a musical image of a positively interpreted 'nature'. Nietzschean optimism and a kind of idealistic egalitarianism meet in this march to rout the more negatively constructed, Schopenhauer-orientated Nature of the introductory music of the Will. This inference is interestingly elaborated in extra descriptive annotations found in Willem Mengelberg's first-edition conducting score. Added in Mengelberg's hand, their often bold clarity (given the conductor's reverence for Mahler and his intentions) suggest a possible origin in conversations with the composer. I present them here in italics against the page- and approximate bar-number at which they appear in that score; Mahler's own manuscript headings are included in capitals:[49]

[p. 1/bar 2:]	DER WECKRUF!	
[4/11:]		*tragic [tragisch]*
[15/132:]	PAN SCHLÄFT	
[15/139:]		*Slumbering/love [Schlummelt/Liebe]*
[15/140:]		*Love languishes [Schmacht Liebe]*
[16/148:]	DER HEROLD!	
		Cry/rough! [Schrei/roh!]
[17/166, solo trombone:]		*Proclamation by the Voice of Death*
		[Stimme des Todes ruft Predigt]
[59/496, over solo Vln:]		*Declaration of love [Liebeserklärung]*
[59/539:]	DAS GESINDEL!	
[68/538:]	DIE SCHLACHT BEGINNT!	
[72/605:]	DER SÜDSTURM!	
[73/608:] [in 1896 MS:]		*charge/storm forwards! [Vorwärts stürmen!]*
[89/787, over strings:]		*firm/wild (also 'vulgar') [fest/wüst]*
[96/832, before strings' 'Mit Schwung':]		*inspired [begeistert]*
[100/857:]		*Cry! [Schrei!]*

[48] *Pan*, edited by Otto Julius Bierbaum and J. Maier Graefe, was first published in Berlin in 1895. For Mahler's quoted comment see NB-L, *Recollections*, 59, and the longer version of the same passage in NB-L, *Erinnerungen*, 65.

[49] A parallel German/English listing of Mahler's programmatic titles and annotations in the 1896 manuscript appears in Franklin, *Mahler: Symphony No. 3*, App. I, pp. 91–9. Other movements in Mengelberg's score bear similar annotations, particularly the second movement, to which the stressed title *Was die Blumen erzählt* (What the *flowers* tell) is added. Adopting the same page- and bar-numbering system as here, the subsequent annotations are: [105/9:] *weiche Wiese Blumen* (delicate *meadow* flowers); [105/16:] *weich* (delicate, soft); [106, top left:] *sterben der Blumen* (*dying* of the flowers); [106, to asterisk marking Vln. 1 part, bars 27 ff.:] *Im Frühling plötzl. ein neues Leben* (spring, and

suddenly a new life); [107/44:] *lieb-duftig Blumen* (sweetly scented flowers); [109/71:] *Zigeuner* (gypsy); [114/117, under clarinet:] *sterben, verwelken* (dying, withering); [126/217:] *plötzlich: Wiese, Blumen* (suddenly: meadow, flowers); [132/267:] *Sterben der Blumen/leise klagen* (death of the flowers/gently lamenting); [132/267, over Glock. notes:] *Sterbeglöcklein/die Blumen sterben* (little death knell/the flowers die). The third movement bears the title (again the emphasis is Mengelberg's) *Was die Thiere des Waldes erzählen* (what the animals of the *forest* tell) and the direction [134, top right:] *Posthorn hinten aufstellen* (position post-horn off stage). The fourth movement ends with the direction *lautlose Stille* (soundless hush), while the fifth begins *Sehr naiif vortragen* (to be performed very naively). The only Mengelberg annotation in the sixth is the word *Zielemuziek* (Dutch: 'music of the soul') on p. 219, top right.

Here, then, the opposition is further glossed as one between death-orientated tragedy and the awakening of *Love*, reinforcing the conceptual link with the Finale ('Was mir die Liebe erzählt') that Mahler seems already to have made in August 1895, when describing the movement to Fritz Löhr as reaching out to the transcendent realm of angels and bells, where '*eternal love* acts within us'.[50] (In 1896 he would also describe the movement to Natalie Bauer-Lechner as becoming a bubbling flood torrent, rushing towards heaven (*zum Himmel*).)[51] What, then, of Fig. 44?

Just as the conceptual, implicitly political, meaning of this movement seems to grow clearer, we are introduced to strikingly characterized music, dominated by flutes, oboes, and screaming E flat clarinets. They slither about semitonally in trilled thirds in B flat minor, soon with deliberately 'crude' oom-pah accompaniment from horns and trombones ('roh!', one before Fig. 45). It is difficult not to assume that precisely this passage would have been amongst those heard as 'eastern', 'oriental', or even specifically 'Jewish' by Mahler's contemporaries.[52] The fact that we are structurally at the start of the final march span of the development section, including the extraordinary 'Battle begins' and 'Southern storm' episodes, leads us to assume that we have here Mahler's clearest and most natural-istic characterization of the milling 'mob' he had described to Natalie. The German word Natalie quotes is even added in his score annotation, 'Das Gesindel!' (the rabble), at Fig. 44. What thickens the plot is the fact that a section of *Also sprach Zarathustra* is entitled 'Vom Gesindel' (of the rabble)—one in which Zarathustra expresses his spiritual aspiration to fly away from and above the rabble, described as 'unclean', their grinning mouths bearing a 'repulsive smile'.[53] So deliberately does the music at this point seem to aspire towards grotesque effect that we begin to wonder whether the reappearance of the main 'Pan' march of summer at Fig. 48 signals another musical disruption and the return of an alter-native, more positively charged, musical voice—that of the victors in the coming battle (for all the problematic hiatus of the great 'recapitulation'). Are their opponents no longer the musically absent forces of life-denying winter but this crude musical mob of Fig. 44, whose role and characterization might thus prompt a nervous reinterpretation of the ideological message of the final part of this movement?

It grows more important to decide how 'Nietzschean' a reading Mahler was intending to invite here. Perhaps the answer lies precisely in the comparative *lack* of disruption or rent in the musical fabric at Fig. 48. The 'rabble' is surely drawn into the march in a community of purpose that is resoundingly celebrated at Fig. 49 ('Die Schlacht beginnt!' (the battle begins)). Their introductory cello and bass line from Fig. 43—in fact present in embryo at the earliest onset of the march material in the introduction (see p. 16, bb. 155–6, more explicitly p. 25, bb. 245 ff.)—here plays its part as a triumphant counter-melody, E flat clarinets and all ('cleaned up' and in C major), to the Binzer/'Weckruf' theme on the

---

[50] Mahler, *Briefe* (1982), 127.
[51] NB-L, *Erinnerungen*, 65.
[52] See Franklin, *Mahler: Symphony No. 3*, 21 and 29.
[53] Friedrich Nietzsche, *Thus Spoke Zarathustra*, trans.

R. J. Hollingdale (London: Penguin, 1961), 120. The German text of this section will be found in Pt. 2, Sect. 6 of *Also sprach Zarathustra*.

trombones. On this perhaps more convincing reading, the musical discourse suggests a critical revision or reinterpretation of Nietzsche, where earlier it had suggested a Nietzschean overcoming of Schopenhauer. The first movement of the Third thus takes its place not as a 'reflection' of 1890s Nietzscheanism but as a tangible *contribution* to it in specifically (if not 'purely') musical terms.

IV

To validate this politicized reading of the Third's first movement it has apparently been necessary to marginalize the recapitulation, which itself dislocates and disrupts the newly victorious progression of the marching rabble. They make it in the end, of course, but only after the movement's last surprise: the 'southern storm' is faded out and off-stage side drums suddenly announce the arrival of the initiating 'Weckruf' on eight horns, followed as before by the funereal music of Winter as Death. It is difficult to read the narrative implications of this strategy, which could certainly have helped to reinforce in Mahler's mind his happy discovery that the 'basic ground plan' of the classical masters lay behind the movement's modernist extravagances.[54] Exhilarating and yet at the same time confusing in performance, this recapitulation may mark an ambivalent reassertion of structural convention, comparable to the politic public stance with which Mahler increasingly sought to secure his final triumphant assimilation into Catholic conservative Viennese culture. The complex goal was to preach a new gospel of radical idealism from the Director's office of the Royal and Imperial Court Opera.

It is in the larger structure of the Third Symphony's 'Part Two' that the achievement of that goal is symbolically prepared in an evolutionary passage towards the resolution of ever grander, ever more extreme contrasts and oppositions. While the compositional process chronologically concluded with the most radical first movement—in which the contrast was between nothing less than Summer (as Life and all-inclusive Love) and Winter (as Death and threatening Chaos)—the symphony as a whole was protectively stabilized by that movement's relegation to an initial, self-contained 'Part One'. Innumerable reviews of the symphony testify to the judiciousness of that arrangement, whereby the anarchic implications of Mahler's stylistic transgressions were ultimately cancelled and transcended by the deliberately 'noble' Adagio, with its ostentatiously displayed Beethovenian pedigree. A 1930s critical essay on the symphony by the Viennese composer Joseph Marx demonstrates this point eloquently. Written at a time when Mahler was already comprehensively marginalized by official German criticism as a 'Jewish' composer (and thus constitutionally incapable of succeeding in the 'Germanic' form of the symphony), this essay contrasted the first and last movements as follows:

---

[54] See NB-L, *Recollections*, 66.

The mostly folk-like themes [in the first movement] are often abruptly juxtaposed so as to give somewhat intentionally scenic effects. These rise to an impressively strong climax in the closing march but . . . it doesn't convince. Above all, this whole first part seems somewhat roughly hewn, for all that one does not for one moment doubt the personal integrity of the composer. The way to this kind of popular-effects music is as difficult to find as it is easy to grasp; there is nothing to miss, but also nothing to discover. . . . The last part, 'What Love tells me', is a lyrical apotheosis. On hearing this piece one might extend the title to 'What love of melody and its great masters tells me'. It is Mahlerian in certain suspensions, turns of phrase, and unusual voice-leading which we have become accustomed to associate with his personal style from other works. Yet it is less individual than hitherto and bathes too much in the reflected light of those truly great ones, Beethoven and Wagner . . . the earlier movements are more truly his own, are children of his soul, while this last one seems to be dedicated to his enthusiasm for our great musical heroes [*Tonheroen*]. The effect, as indicated above, is one of apotheosis, yet also somewhat surprising; after much confusion we have found our way home to the classical temple of the purest art and are moved, stirred by the noble humanity, the highest aspiration of a man of genius.[55]

I have suggested that the play of oppositions and contrasts with which the symphony resounds included, both for Mahler and his audience, that between alternative constructions of the very nature of music in its social character—constructions that for the composer point on the one hand to an 'absolutist' concern for traditional formal models and, on the other, to a subversively 'programmatic' aspiration to heighten music's differentiating and concretizing expressive power. Marx reinforces this point in a way that is striking not least for his all but explicit drafting of the established interpretation of the Adagio (Mahler's 'higher' form,[56] consistently regarded by critics as containing the best and noblest music in the symphony) into an implicitly derogatory evaluation of it—and this at a time when popular culture would soon spring to his aid. In 1942 Irving Berlin's 'I'm dreaming of a white Christmas' prepared for the reclamation of the subsidiary theme of the movement (cellos, b. 8) as an example, by association, of 'low' musical manners. Cultural change and cultural continuity would thus collude in shifting interpretation of this music while contriving to reinforce what may have been the fundamental 'meaning' of the symphony. Marx's scorn of Mahler's failed aspiration to greatness might have found itself confirmed by Bing Crosby fans' attribution of sentimental emotionality to the 'White Christmas' theme in a recontextualized hearing of the Adagio. Perhaps Mahler had only temporarily succeeded in covering the tracks of his 'personal style' by playing the game of 1890s cultural politics, as reflected in then current notions of 'good' and 'bad' symphonic writing.

An all-too-human, heart-on-sleeve quality was in fact deliberately imparted by him to the Adagio theme at Fig. 1, where the 'peace' (*Ruhevoll*) of the chorale-like opening music is disturbed by rapid crescendo/diminuendo markings that presage the wide range of increasingly frenetic directions associated with derivations of the Fig. 1 theme later in the movement. Ripe for narrative disruption, it suggests a stream of precariously aspiring

[55] Marx, *Betrachtungen eines romantischen Realisten*, 166–7 and 169.   [56] See NB-L, *Recollections*, 67.

consciousness whose confidence is repeatedly lost in dramatic crises.[57] These allude to chaotic material from the first movement which blocks the music's culturally expected progress towards a triumphant conclusion. That triumph is, of course, achieved in the end, with grand processional theatricality and overwhelming volume of orchestral sound. The experience of the movement's closure relies upon the listener having interpreted its discourse in a double way: as sustaining the character of divine, revelatory euphony (signifying 'harmony' as collectivity, rightness, and order) while simultaneously unfolding a history of subjective individuality that successfully surmounts threatening narrative interventions.[58] It is for this reason that the closing pages are the most dangerously problematic of the whole work from a modern critical perspective. The very extremity of the effect Mahler strives for heightens our sensitivity to the meaning of the symphony concert itself as a social ritual. Its focus is a conductor who wields visible power over a body of players whose utmost effort he commands: to symbolize here the coming together of the human and the superhuman.[59]

No contextualized historical reading of the symphony as 'pure music' can comfortably separate this ending from other such conclusions in other works of the period that engage in grand resolution and closure. Perhaps it is precisely in Mahler's symbolic and narrative interpretations of the final movement that (to recall Abbate) we approach its special richness, its self-questioning particularity. His own image of the movement seems to have been that of a lens hovering above the rest of the symphony and gathering the rays of an all-enfolding eternal love,[60] as if in answer to the manuscript's epigraph prayer that 'no creature' should be lost.[61] Here at least we have evidence that it was Mahler's hope to produce a resolution that was redeeming, a homage to the Romantic notion of 'Classical' music, explicitly *interpreted* in programmatic privacy as an idealized goal where in public it might be left as a mysteriously numinous manifestation of some 'given', and describable, perhaps, only by that all too meaningful word 'absolute' (is it irrelevant that in English both music and monarchs have been thus characterized?). Given the debate about Mahler's private and public relationship with established religious faith, and the extent to which that relationship overlapped still broader social and political matters, a provisional clarification of the music's private meaning for Mahler may finally be approached only by questioning the

[57] Figs. 6–9, 19–21, and from Fig. 23⁻⁴ to Fig. 25.

[58] That the interventions allude to material and events from the first movement might lead to a consideration of these two movements as exemplifying 'expressive doubling' of the kind explored by Lawrence Kramer in 'Beethoven's Two-Movement Piano Sonatas and the Utopia of Romantic Esthetics' in ch. 2 of his book *Music as Cultural Practice, 1800–1900* (Berkeley and Oxford: University of California Press, 1990), 21–71. Mahler's habitual tendency to regard interior movements as interludes or 'intermezzi' would reinforce this interpretation.

[59] A critical interpretation of the social dynamics and meaning of the symphony concert is polemically elaborated by Christopher Small in his essay 'Performance as Ritual: Sketch for an Enquiry into the True Nature of a Symphony Concert', in Avron Levine White (ed.), *Lost in Music: Culture, Style and the Musical Event* (London and New York: Routledge and Kegan Paul, 1987), 6–32.

[60] The image is found in Mahler's letter to Fritz Löhr of 29 Aug. 1895; see above, n. 50.

[61] The epigraph in the 1896 manuscript of the Third Symphony, adapted from *Des Knaben Wunderhorn*, reads: 'Vater, sieh an die Wunden mein! / Kein Wesen lass verloren sein!' (Father, look upon my wounds! / let no creature be lost!).

precise nature of the 'blessed faith' which he claimed the movement attained and to which he gave the explicitly Nietzschean name 'Die fröhliche Wissenschaft'.[62]

It is significant that the books mentioned by Bruno Walter in his autobiography as having been recommended to him by Mahler in Hamburg (Walter was there from 1894 to 1896, the period of the Third's composition), included F. A. Lange's *Geschichte des Materialismus* (*History of Materialism*) of 1866. It was a book that Mahler returned to (Alma recalls reading it aloud to him in 1907),[63] as had Nietzsche, interestingly enough. Nietzsche first read it in the year of its publication and claimed to have reread it many times. Reminding us once more that problems of interpretation are in no way exclusive to music, characterizations of Lange's fundamental position in his long and much-revised *History* differ considerably. R. J. Hollingdale, in his 1973 study of Nietzsche, introduced it as having decisively persuaded the philosopher '*against* metaphysical presumptions' (my emphasis) and in favour of modern, ethical materialism.[64] Bruno Walter, on the other hand, described it as anti-materialistic: 'a classic work dealing with the oldest ailment of man's reasoning faculty. It put a definite end to any similar inclinations in my own thinking.'[65]

But was Lange's purpose ultimately to oppose or to explore the materialist world-view? So rich is his *History* that it can easily attract proponents of either position, as Lange himself recognized in the important second edition of 1873. In the opening paragraph of the first chapter, he characterized materialism as 'the physical conception of nature' which dominated early thought and 'remains ever entangled in the contradictions of Dualism and the fantasies of personification':

The first attempts to escape from these contradictions, to conceive the world as a unity, and to rise above the vulgar error of the senses, lead directly into the sphere of philosophy, and amongst these first attempts Materialism has its place.[66]

In 1873 he had added a note in which he observed that these words had been

directed, on the one hand, against the despisers of Materialism, who . . . deny it the possession of any scientific importance; and on the other against those Materialists who, in their turn, despise all philosophy, and imagine that their views are in no way a product of philosophical speculation, but are a pure result of experience, of sound common sense, and of the physical sciences.[67]

The subtle distinction in this warning points to one of Lange's central themes, which is his lively concern for what he calls 'the ideal side of religious life' which is otherwise

---

[62] The title of the book of 1882, rendered in Walter Kaufmann's translation as *The Gay Science*, in which Nietzsche adumbrated the themes of *Also sprach Zarathustra* (1883–5). It was explicitly appropriated as the title for the Third Symphony on the quarto-sheet list of movement headings that accompanied Mahler's letter to Fritz Löhr of 29 Aug. 1895. See Mahler, *Briefe* (1982), 128.

[63] Alma Mahler, *Memories*, 120.

[64] R. J. Hollingdale, *Nietzsche* (London and Boston: Routledge and Kegan Paul, 1973), 55 and 138.

[65] Bruno Walter, *Theme and Variations*, trans. James Galston (London: Hamish Hamilton, 1947), 93.

[66] Friedrich Albert Lange, *History of Materialism and Criticism of its Present Importance*, 2nd edn., trans. Ernest Chester Thomas (London: Kegan Paul, Trench, Trübner & Co., 1892), i. 3.

[67] Ibid.

inaccessible to people who reject 'everything that cannot be shown to the common understanding to be true'.[68]

This theme of Lange's *History* was what endeared it in particular to Mahler's friend Siegfried Lipiner and his circle in Vienna in the late 1870s and early 1880s. Its echo may be heard in Hamburg-period discussions with Mahler recalled by the composer and critic Ferdinand Pfohl.[69] What is equally important about Lange, however, is that a strong element in his judicious and complex critique is an opposition to culturally instituted religious dogma which extended to open anti-clericalism. Deeply worried by what he calls 'the terrorism of the hierarchy' whereby the organized religions dogmatically enforce 'superstitious fears',[70] and embracing what amounts to a kind of idealistic socialism, Lange's concern was for a continuing, enlightened philosophical debate inspired only by the 'ideal side of religious life'.[71] This opens directly onto the world of Lipiner, Nietzsche, and the Pernerstorfer circle in which the Third Symphony had both its musical and its conceptual roots. Few explanatory interpretations of the 'meaning' of that work's final movement could improve upon the following remarkable passage from the concluding section of Lange's *History of Materialism*, whose idealism is reflected and illuminated here in terms that clarify its complicatedly mediated socialism. They give voice, perhaps, to what is most grand and, with historical hindsight, most troubling about the 'blessed faith' which the Third Symphony achieved:

if the New is to come into existence and the Old is to disappear, two great things must combine—a world-kindling ethical idea and a social influence which is powerful enough to lift the depressed masses a great step forward. Sober realism, artificial systems, cannot do this. The victory over disintegrating egoism and the deadly chilliness of the heart will only be won by a great ideal, which appears amidst the wondering peoples as a 'stranger from another world', and by demanding the impossible unhinges reality.[72]

The whole symphony, in Adornian terms, might be interpreted as preparing a mighty 'Durchbruch'—a breaking-through to the celebration of the composer-conductor as the upstart stranger who has at last secured the reins of cultural power while hermeneutically redeeming the sounds of empowering 'culture'. One need hardly be surprised that Mahler's programmes for the Third became so cryptic and complex in their marriage of grand cosmological themes with figures and images from classical mythology. Their textual substance was reduced to a series of abstruse and highly literary titles which were in fact more judiciously tailored for public consumption than the music, whose exegesis they invite in coded terms. The detailed clarity of its meaning was, for more than technical reasons, 'inexpressible in words'. In throwing away the crutches of naive programmes we lay claim precisely to the self-questioning, vulnerably self-wrought richness of Mahler's music as meaningful discourse.

---

[68] Lange, *History of Materialism*, iii. 295.
[69] See Pfohl, *Gustav Mahler*, 21.
[70] Lange, *History of Materialism*, iii. 356.

[71] Ibid. 295.
[72] Ibid. 355 (translation slightly emended).

9

'Swallowing the Programme': Mahler's Fourth Symphony

DONALD MITCHELL

To Steuart Bedford

Man was made for Joy & Woe;
And when this we rightly know
Thro' the World we safely go,
Joy and Woe are woven fine,
A Clothing for the Soul divine;
Under every grief & pine
Runs a joy with silken twine.

William Blake, *Auguries of Innocence*

There is no contradiction between playfulness and pedantry; the one brings on the other.
. . . nothing tugs at the heartstrings so much as a quavering mechanical toy; think of the touching music boxes of bygone times.

Günther Grass, *Dog Years* (trans. Ralph Mannheim)

For the euphoria which we endeavour to reach . . . is nothing other than the mood of a period of life in which we were accustomed to deal with our psychical work in general with a small expenditure of energy—the mood of our childhood, when we were ignorant of the comic, when we were incapable of jokes and when we had no need of humour to make us feel happy in our life.

Sigmund Freud, *Jokes and their Relation to the Unconscious*
(trans. and ed. James Strachey, 1960)

I have just this minute received your letter and am delighted by the entrancing analysis of my Fourth. I hasten to reply at once, to tell you how touched I am at being so well understood. In particular, I find your approach to this work quite new and extraordinarily convincing. You actually say what had never before occurred to me whenever *I* had to say something about it. It now seems child's play, so obvious! One thing seems to me to be missing: did you overlook the thematic relationships that are so extremely important both in themselves and in relation to the idea of the whole work? Each of the first three movements is thematically most closely and most significantly related to the last.

Mahler to Georg Göhler, New York, 8 February 1911 (*Selected Letters*, 371–2)

Any exploration of the Fourth Symphony of Mahler has to confront the issue of the 'programme', not only in relation to this particular symphony but to its predecessors and successors. It is a complicated matter, made the more complicated, as we shall see, by Mahler's own complicated attitudes to it. But let me start with a characteristically pungent and provocative observation by Adorno, from his 1960 monograph on the composer, in which he writes:

Even the Fourth, with its overflowing intentions [Adorno has previously established the 'image-world' of childhood as the determining source of its materials], is not, however, program music. It differs from it not merely by using the so-called absolute forms sonata, scherzo, variations, song; the three last, extensive symphonic poems of Strauss also use these. Equally, even when he no longer had any truck with programs, Mahler cannot simply be subsumed under the practice of Bruckner or Brahms or even the aesthetic of Hanslick. *The composition has swallowed the program* [my italics]; the characters are its monuments.[1]

Adorno goes on to clarify what he means by his reference to 'characters' by making a comparison with the practice of Strauss. Mahler, he writes, 'does not subscribe to the program because he . . . [does not wish] . . . to fix the meaning of the musical figures by decree', while in Strauss, 'Characterization founders . . . because he defines the meanings purely from the standpoint of the subject, autonomously'. 'Mahler's medium', Adorno continues, 'is that of objective characterization':

Each theme, over and above its mere arrangement of notes, has its distinct being, almost beyond invention. If the motives of program music await the labels of the textbooks and commentaries, Mahler's themes each bear their own names in themselves, without nomenclature. But such characterization has a prospect of validity only insofar as the musical imagination does not produce intentions at will, does not, therefore, think out motives that express this or that according to a plan, but works with a musical-linguistic material in which intentions are already objectively present. As preconceived entities [Adorno has earlier identified some of these, e.g. 'The sound of the great drum [*recte* bass drum: Adorno of course writes 'Grosse Trommel'] . . . is as drums once seemed before the age of seven', while in the first movement's development 'The unison of the four flutes . . . does not just reinforce the sound. It creates an effect sui generis, that of a dream ocarina: such must have been children's instruments that no one ever heard'[2]] they are quoted, as it were, by the musical imagination and dedicated to the whole. The materials that achieve this are those called banal, in which meaning has generally sedimented, before the advent of the individual composer, and has been punished by forfeiting the spontaneity of living execution. Such meanings stir anew under the staff of composition and feel their strength.[3]

---

[1] Adorno, *Mahler*, 58.   [2] Ibid. 55 and 53.   [3] Ibid. 58.

For Adorno, of course, 'banal' bears a meaning entirely different from that of Mahler's early critics, who used it so often as a term of mindless abuse. I am not sure that 'banal', specifically in the context of the Fourth, is the word that I would use, though I can certainly see what Adorno was getting at. 'Innocence', or better still, 'a state of innocence', are what I would prefer, not only in relation to the symphony's musical ideas and images, the work's 'characters' as Adorno hears them, but to its eventually declared and explicit goal, its finale, the 'Wunderhorn' song 'Das himmlische Leben', the conscription of which to serve as the symphony's last movement has to remain an event of unique significance and fascination. There is nothing like it elsewhere in Mahler's oeuvre, and as I shall hope to suggest, much more is bound up with it than the novelty of Mahler's composing a symphony *into* a pre-existing finale, especially when that finale itself was a model of the unorthodox, a song for solo voice and orchestra. It is not my intention to rehearse here the long history of 'Das himmlische Leben' and its involvement in the creation of both the Third and Fourth Symphonies; the history is now both familiar and accessible.[4] Nor, for the same reason, shall I dwell, unless incidentally, on the evolution of the Fourth, for which an unusual number of preparatory programmatic, multi-movement schemes existed. It is sufficient for my purpose to remind readers that the song that was to be installed, virtually unamended, as the finale of the symphony had been composed in Hamburg in 1892. It was there on 26 April that Mahler brought to completion his 'Fünf Humoresken/"Wunderhorn-Lieder"' for voice and orchestra, among them 'Wir geniessen die himmlischen Freuden' (i.e. 'Das himmlische Leben'), which had been composed in its voice and piano version on 10 February and in its orchestral format on 12 March (see Ex. 9.1A).[5] The compositional substance of the song indeed remained unamended; on the other hand, Mahler was to make by no means insignificant instrumental retouchings and refinements, so that the version of the song we hear as the finale of the symphony varies in its orchestration from its original conception as an orchestral song (see Ex. 9.1B). A comparison of Ex. 9.1A with the corresponding passage in the symphony—the opening of the finale—makes clear the evolution of the orchestral sound that we are familiar with today when we hear the song in the context of the symphony.

In 1893, on 27 October, in Hamburg, Mahler included the song—its first performance—in the programme of a 'popular concert', along with two others of the original five 'Humoresken' and three further orchestral settings of 'Wunderhorn' texts. Finally, all these 'Wunderhorn' orchestral settings were gathered together and published as *Des Knaben Wunderhorn*, less of course 'Das himmlische Leben', which, by the time of publication (1899), had already been incorporated into the symphony. The Fourth itself was composed

---

[4] See e.g. Mitchell, *WY*, 311 ff.

[5] The manuscript full score of the five 'Humoresken' is in the possession of the Gesellschaft der Musikfreunde, Vienna. "Das himmlische Leben' in its original version as an independent 'Wunderhorn' song is included in the volume of the complete orchestral scores of Mahler's 'Wunderhorn-Lieder', published in 1998 by Universal-Edition, Vienna, in collaboration with the International

Gustav Mahler Society, edited with a full critical apparatus by Renate Hilmar-Voit and now forming Vol. 14/2 of the Society's Critical Edition of Mahler's works. I am grateful to Dr Hilmar-Voit for bringing to my attention the instrumental differences between the early and later version of the song that I have briefly illustrated in Exx. 9.1A and B (cf. Critical Edition, 14/2, pp. 55–87).

190 Donald Mitchell

Ex. 9.1A. A transcription from the autograph of the first two pages of 'Das himmlische Leben' in its original guise as the fourth of the five 'Humoresken' for voice and orchestra composed in 1892

Ex. 9.1B. The first two pages of 'Das himmlische Leben' as orchestrated by Mahler for the finale of his Fourth Symphony

across the turn of the century. The completion date for the symphony as distinct from the song was 5 August 1900, the date Mahler inscribed at the end of the slow movement (he got the date wrong, in fact, by one day, but his additional inscription of 'Sunday' tells us that it must have been the 5th on which he brought the first three instrumental movements of the symphony to their conclusion (the 6th—the date he inscribed—was in fact a Monday). I wish to concentrate on what, finally, Mahler himself concentrated on: the four-movement symphony that we know today as Mahler's Fourth. And that, necessarily, returns us to that striking observation of Adorno's that has been my point of departure, that in the Fourth, absolutely unlike its predecessors, the composition has swallowed the programme.

Most penetrating observations have an element of exaggeration about them, and to that rule the quotation from Adorno is no exception. It is undeniably the case that in the Fourth the programme has been 'swallowed' by the composition—perhaps 'suppressed by' or 'submerged in', though less arresting, might be a shade more accurate?—swallowed, that is, until, by analogy with Adorno's own concept, the 'programme' is disgorged in the shape of the song-finale. It is, furthermore—and this, to my mind, is one of the most interesting things about it—a *retrospective* enlightenment as to what the symphony, up to that point, has been all about; more than that, not only a retrospective act of illumination, but also an enactment and affirmation of the goal, we now come to realize, that all along has been the symphony's objective, the goal to which the 'characters', assembled in the first three movements, 'sonata, scherzo, variations' and freed, as Adorno has it, from their 'thing-like rigidity'[6]—have guided us, though to be sure what we arrive at is less a programmatic destination than the achievement of a state of mind, that idea of 'innocence' to which I have referred earlier.

This is a point to which I shall often return, but to emphasize the singularity of the solo song's function in the Fourth, it may be useful to remind ourselves how explicitly programmatic in outward conception at least the first three symphonies were.[7] After all, the First started life, without reservation, as a Symphonic Poem in two parts and five movements (1888), and a significant period was to elapse before the four-movement symphony we know today emerged (1896). For the Second (1888–94), Mahler at one stage provided a lengthy and elaborate programme; and indeed in an early printed edition of the symphony, Hermann Behn's arrangement of the Second for two pianos, four hands, published by Friedrich Hofmeister in Leipzig in 1896, we find installed there unequivocal 'programmatic' indications, e.g. at Fig. 74 in the finale, 'Der Rufer in der Wüste' (The Caller in the Desert), and at Fig. 96, a bold title—'Der grosse Appell' (The Last Trump)—forms the heading at the top of the first page of the great cadenza that precedes the chorus of Resurrection. In later editions, of course, all such programmatic clues or clarifications were expunged and Mahler's own detailed scenario, written originally in connection with a performance of the symphony in Berlin in 1901, categorically withdrawn. We must note, too, that for a time at least, while Mahler was still bringing the work to completion, he accorded quasi-

[6] Adorno, *Mahler*, 58.

[7] See also Donald Mitchell, 'Mahler I: "the most spontaneous and daringly composed of my works" ', a text accompanying the recording of the First by Riccardo Chailly and the Concertgebouw Orchestra on Decca 448 813–2 (1996). A fuller version of this text awaits publication.

independent symphonic poem status to the first movement, entitling it 'Todtenfeier' and indeed performing it himself as a work temporarily in its own right in a concert in Berlin on 16 March 1896, though spelling out in the programme that this was the first movement from a symphony in C minor. But we should not, because of this, hasten to identify the movement as a 'Symphonic Poem', as the title-page of its first publication (as Supplement (Vol. I) in the critical edition of Mahler's symphonies published by the International Gustav Mahler Society, Vienna) imprudently has it. It is more than likely in my view that Mahler added this title as a *continuation* of the scenario that is narrated in the First Symphony, i.e. to indicate that the protagonist—the hero—in the First was presumed by Mahler to have *died*, his demise to be solemnly celebrated in the first movement of the 'new' symphony (the Second), hence the inscription 'Todtenfeier' and of course the Resurrection that follows in the famous finale. This is something quite different from the conception of an independent 'symphonic poem', which I think 'Todtenfeier' never was.

Finally, there is the Third (1893–6), which evolved in its six-movement form only after Mahler had committed to paper a whole batch of movement titles in a variety of sequences in which the actual number of contemplated movements was also subject to change.[8] The work represents from many points of view the most elaborate and sophisticated of any of the 'programmes' that, before Mahler ruthlessly banished them—or attempted to banish them—from public knowledge, had formed an indispensable part of his aesthetic strategy; and part, too, of the means by which he clarified his intentions to his audience; or, to put it another way, a means of disseminating 'information' about a work in the interests of comprehensibility (it is in this light, bearing in mind a parallel with the 'Trauermarsch' inscription of the first movement of the Fifth, that we should consider the 'Todtenfeier' title).

Mahler's later antagonism to his programmes stemmed from a number of sources, some relatively superficial, some, I suggest, profound. There can be no doubt that he became increasingly exasperated by responses to his music which were seemingly conditioned or predetermined by the 'programmes'; far from clarifying the music or promoting intelligent discussion of it, they obscured it. A danger of programmes is that the listener, in seeking to hear the descriptive account, even when it is the composer who has provided it, does not hear the music. (Ultimately, Mahler's hostility to programmes was to extend to analysis of any kind; the idea of 'programme notes', it seems, was anathema to him. For example, when the Seventh was first done in Prague in 1908, the only information Mahler permitted to appear in the programme comprised the tempo (character) indications for the five movements, absolutely nothing else.)[9] Then there may have been a desire to distance himself,

---

[8] See Mitchell, *WY*, 187–94, *passim*; also Franklin, *Mahler: Symphony No. 3*, ch. 3.

[9] See, for example, the reproduction of the programmes for the Prague and Vienna premières, reproduced in the facsimile edition of the Seventh published by Rosbeek Publishers (Amsterdam, 1995), 41 and 67 of the volume of commentaries to which Edward R. Reilly and I contributed. The absence of a 'programme' was widely complained of by the work's early critics, e.g. Richard Batka, who wrote:

'Unfortunately, Mahler subscribes to the principle of the minimal programme. . . . I understand that the all-too-often literal use made by the audience of more detailed programmes would arouse the opposition of a composer like Mahler. But his refusal to provide even very brief hints concerning the meaning of, and the connection between, the individual parts of his work serves only to take us from misunderstanding to incomprehension' (45). See also below, pp. 199–201.

musically speaking, from his great contemporary, Richard Strauss, and to make the point, at least by the time his hostility to programmes had become explicit and he was retrospectively fighting a rearguard action to erase them, that while Strauss was undeniably the presiding genius of the symphonic poem, his—Mahler's—territory was the symphony.

There is a certain irony about this, to be sure. After all, Mahler himself, as I have just mentioned, began his life as a symphonist with one foot in the symphonic-poem camp. It is true, of course, and as subsequent events (i.e. successive revisions) were to prove, that all along there was a symphony awaiting its excavation, its release, from its symphonic-poem carapace; nor should it be overlooked that for an aspiring and ambitious young composer, still not out of his twenties, there was powerful motivation to hitch one's flag to the mast of the 'progressives' rather than enter a field—the Symphony—that was already crowded and where the competition, to put it mildly, was intense.

However, while the stripping out of the symphony from the initiating symphonic poem speaks for itself, so too does the continuing presence of the 'programme' in the ensuing symphonies, up to and including, though in a rather special way, the Fourth. It is not my purpose here to attempt a comprehensive exploration of the programmatic dimension of the first three of Mahler's symphonies. For one thing, the ground has been pretty well covered elsewhere; for another, it is self-evident that the idea of a programme, however varied its execution, was fundamental to the concept and creation of the early symphonies, that no amount of retrospective deprecation on Mahler's part could (or indeed, should) do anything to alter. If I omit at this stage specific reference to the Fourth, it is because I believe it represents a quite particular case, the natural but momentous consequence, if it may be stated thus, of what strikes me as the single most interesting and important feature of these so-called 'Wunderhorn' years (1888–1901 is my estimate): the tension generated by Mahler trying to pursue two opposed ideologies simultaneously, one dedicated to the path of the symphonic poem, to the programmatic idea, the other to the path, the tradition, of 'symphony', unpolluted by programmatic affiliations or associations.

This creative tension was never entirely extirpated from Mahler's formal thinking, his formal conscience—much to posterity's benefit let it be immediately said, since the competing aesthetic strategies gave rise to some of his most innovative music. The tension was the spring that kept the pendulum swinging between the two poles. There is no clearer instance of this than the first movement of the Second, the special formal profile of which—*pace* its 'Todtenfeier' entitling—surely indicated a bid to *abandon* the 'symphonic poem' territory occupied by its predecessor and undertake a big symphonic project: a 'Symphony in C minor', opening with a movement that was the first of Mahler's unequivocal affirmations of sonata form? Can we doubt that he revealed thereby his ambition to write a work in the Great Tradition? The monumentality of the gesture itself was an indication of the scale of the ambition. But what happened? The 'Symphony in C minor'—the work that Mahler's inscription (from 1888!) had originally implied—was never, perhaps, to materialize. What did, finally, emerge after a painfully long period of gestation, only did so—ironically—by courtesy of the 'programme', the dissemination of which he came later to regret. But there is no denying that it was fundamental to the continuation and comple-tion of the work that we know today as 'Mahler's Second'. Years of creative frustration and uncertainty interposed, while he was trying to find an answer to the question, 'how to con-tinue?'; and it was not until he found the 'programme' that he found the answer. No ques-tion here of the composition 'swallowing the programme'. The 'programme', at long last, was the indispensable means by which the composition came to be completed.

Among the group of Mahler's first three symphonies, it is the Second which unequivo-cally juxtaposes the concepts of symphony (the first movement) and symphonic poem (the sequence of ensuing movements). To be sure, the tension shows up again in the Third, in the first movement, where, as has so often been observed, a sonata scheme is to be discerned behind the elaborate programmatic concept. It is revealing, indeed, that Mahler clung to the skeletal sonata frame even when, as I have suggested elsewhere, it would surely have been more rational and convincing in terms of the given programme to have ditched it. But for Mahler, it seems, this foothold, or in this case, toehold, in the past, was a kind of certificate of immunity against total immersion in the aesthetic of the symphonic poem.[10] It is indubitably of significance as a piece of evidence when trying to assess Mahler's picture of himself. But does anyone, when experiencing the first movement of the Third, really 'hear' it as a sonata movement, as one certainly does the first movement of the Second? One hears it, surely, as the huge initiating stage in an evolving sequence of pro-grammes which culminates in the crowning, elevated, and elevating Adagio, representing, in Mahler's own words, 'What Love tells me'. We have made a long ascent, onwards and upwards, from the heaving introduction to the first movement, about which Mahler said to Natalie Bauer-Lechner in June 1896, 'It has almost ceased to be music; it is hardly any-thing but sounds of Nature. It's eerie, the way life gradually breaks through, out of soulless, petrified matter. (I might equally well have called the movement . . . "What the mountains tell me")'; and he continued: '. . . as this life rises from stage to stage, it takes on ever more highly developed forms: flowers, beasts, man, up to the sphere of the spirits, the "angels" . . . '.[11] And so on, and so on. There may have been an apparent surfacing of the symphony/symphonic poem dichotomy in the compositional histories of the First and Second Symphonies, but confronted by the Third at the time of its earliest performances it would have been hard—impossible, I suggest—to have predicted not only Mahler's aban-doning of the concept of the 'programme' but his hostility to its resurrection, even in those contexts where it had been fundamental to the creation of a specific work; the case of the Third is perhaps the most striking of all.

It would have been equally hard to predict that the ensuing Fourth would have taken the shape it did; for what it was to reveal, in absolute distinction from the preceding Third, was a marked preoccupation with the idea of 'symphony' from which, virtually, the 'pro-gramme' (at least in the sense that it is immediately identifiable as such in the Third) is

---

[10] See Mitchell, *WY*, 206–8, and Donald Mitchell, 'The Modernity of Gustav Mahler', in *Neue Mahleriana: Essays in Honour of Henry-Louis de La Grange on his Seventieth* *Birthday*, ed. G. Weiss (Bern: Peter Lang AG, 1997), 175–90.
[11] NB-L, *Recollections*, 59. See also Mitchell, 'Mahler's Creation Symphony'.

excluded (or 'swallowed', as Adorno has it); until, that is, we reach the finale, the 'Wunderhorn' song. Up to that point—and of course the act of *retrospective* illumination is an incomparable stroke of genius—up to that point, we have three perfectly articulated and constructed instrumental movements in 'so-called absolute forms, sonata, scherzo, variations' which—if we did not know otherwise—might well have culminated in a 'conventional' finale, a brilliant and engaging rondo, say; given the 'right' instrumental finale, i.e. one that fulfilled the thematic, motivic, and tonal implications—tonal, above all—adumbrated in the sonata-form first movement, we should have had not the work heralding the close of the period when Mahler and the 'programme' symphony were inextricably bonded, but the work that, so to say, established his credentials as a symphonist proper, and was to initiate the sequence of purely instrumental symphonies, Five, Six, and Seven. No one in his right mind would want a Fourth without 'Das himmlische Leben'; but that a Fourth might be so envisaged is a point worth making simply because it shows just how far at the turn of the century Mahler's *dependence* on the explicit programme had weakened; the new shape it was to take I shall want to discuss in relation to the Fifth. But the paradoxical truth about the Fourth is this: that it demonstrated how close Mahler was to the idea of 'symphony' in 1899–1900—is it not the case in the Fourth, indeed, of the idea of 'symphony' swallowing the *composer*?—while at the same time revealing his subtlest, most original, and most perfectly executed 'programme'.

Part of that perfection that 'Das himmlische Leben' vouchsafes is embodied in the fact that the song—unthinkable as a finale until Mahler brought it off—performs all the functions that were expected of a finale as the nineteenth century was on the brink of expiring. The song clarifies and justifies all that has preceded it, rounds off everything, tidies everything up, explicates what hitherto has been a shade inexplicable (not much of that, in fact, but perhaps those seemingly eccentric opening three bars, chinking sleigh-bells, chirruping flutes, the 'wrong' key, etc., etc., fall into that category until illumination dawns with the onset and evolution of the song). I have already sufficiently emphasized, I think, the unique act of fulfilment *plus* retrospection that 'Das himmlische Leben' represents, while not forgetting, naturally, that 'Wunderhorn' orchestral songs (or in the case of the Third, a setting of Nietzsche (the fourth movement), in addition to that of a 'Wunderhorn' text (the fifth)), had already been incorporated in two of the preceding symphonies. But if we examine their function in the contexts of the symphonies that contain them, we find it differs fundamentally from the role of 'Das himmlische Leben'. If it is 'Urlicht', the fourth movement of the Second, that we have in mind, then its function—apart from providing an absolutely obligatory intervening moment of repose after the agitation of the scherzo and before the unleashing of the epic theatre of the finale—is akin to that of a signpost, pointing the direction in which the symphony must travel, and anticipating its final destination; in short, playing its role as part of an evolving programme, a stage, a station, on the way to the eventual dénouement. The building of 'Wunderhorn' songs into the symphonies was a novel way of installing compact sources of information for the hypothetical traveller seeking enlightenment about the route he was following, as it were in the steps of the composer.

The orchestral songs in the Third function likewise. The Nietzsche setting, 'Was spricht die tiefe Mitternacht?', performs much along the same lines as 'Urlicht' in the Second, a moment for reflection, meditation, that also anticipates the symphony's dénouement, not only the final triumph of D major but the conquest, by incorporation, of the motive of verbally identified suffering from the Nietzsche setting—'Tief ist ihr Weh!' (the information process in action!)—into the great concluding Adagio; a recapitulation (at Fig. 20) that is surely meant to remind us of the suffering that necessarily precedes victory. But this event is not an example of the finale clarifying the song, but of the *reverse* process, the song acting as signpost to the finale, which will, as we shall hear for ourselves, come up with the answer to Nietzsche's question, 'What does deep midnight have to tell us?'

As for 'Es sungen drei Engel', the fifth movement of the symphony and a setting which shares the source and imagery of its text and much of its musical material with 'Das himmlische Leben'—which, it will be remembered, at one stage was envisaged as a potential finale for the Third—it does not so much clarify as represent a further stage in the evolving programme, evolving, that is, towards the sublime concluding Adagio, 'Was mir die Liebe erzählt' (What Love tells me). It is a movement to my mind that can only be understood, so marked is the contrast it offers to the movement to which it functions as a kind of prelude, as a reminder that before we can enter into and perhaps be redeemed by the spirit of Love, man must first aspire to or achieve—or at least hold intact within him—a condition of childlike innocence. This is a point of some significance; as I shall come to suggest, in the case of the Fourth, it is precisely towards the establishing of that condition that the thrust, the drive, of the symphony is dedicated, and made explicit, in terms of its techniques, tone, and style.

Little of any of that was comprehended by the work's first audiences. The symphony was first performed in Munich on 25 November 1901, when Mahler conducted the Kaim Orchestra; we may savour the irony that it was this work above all that was to be the agent of changed attitudes to Mahler in the years after the Second World War. Its relatively modest resources, and relative brevity, were also an influential factor; nonetheless it was the 'approachability' and 'appeal' of the Fourth that won it admiring audiences.

This was not at all Mahler's experience in 1901. In general, it is safe to say, the symphony was received with blank incomprehension and hostility. There were a few, very few, voices dissenting from the overall adverse judgement, and the majority seemed to think that they were the victims of a scandalous joke, of a hoax, even. Those who may wish to scrutinize for themselves the sorry parade of prejudice and ignorance—the critic of the Munich *Allgemeine Zeitung* of 26 November complained that the first movement of the Fourth was reminiscent [sic] of the Andante (the A flat Ländler) of the Second, while a further weakness was the similarity [sic] of the Scherzo to the first movement, 'too much like [the first]' in the critic's own immortal words—will consult the relevant and thorough documentation in Henry-Louis de La Grange's second volume.[12]

---

[12] See HLG(E) ii. 392–416.

Of greater interest is what some early critics of the symphony, whether favourable or unfavourable, had to say about the issue that directly concerns us—the 'programme'. Mahler's, by this time, explicit opposition to 'programmes' (or at least to the dissemination of information about them) only added to the confusion. As the critic of the *Münchener Zeitung* remarked, 'only a programme could possibly have "made the work's images and points of departure comprehensible to the listener". As it was, the Fourth repeatedly touched on the dubious genre [i.e. programme music] which, as the saying went, was "the only one not permissible".'[13] Likewise, the critic of the *Allgemeine Musik-Zeitung*, Karl Potgiesser, found it 'incomprehensible without a programme',[14] as did his colleague on the *Neue Musikalische Presse*, who wondered if Mahler 'was not simply making fun of his audience, since he even refused them the explanation and "programme" they so sorely needed'.[15] And so on, and so on. The critical reception of the work during the remainder of the tour was not one whit better. The strange, profoundly ironic truth was that not a single critic had observed the single most striking fact about the symphony, that it did indeed have a 'programme', but one that was not revealed until the song-finale spelled it all out, whereby the 'programme' that underpinned the symphony from its first note to its last was retrospectively made manifest. A further layer of irony was provided by the success 'Das himmlische Leben' occasionally enjoyed in comparison with the preceding movements. Here, at any rate, there was a modestly positive response, though it was emphasized that this of course was not a legitimate, serious symphonic finale; notwithstanding, it was a song that might be enjoyed in its own right. Did Mahler ask himself, one wonders, after the disastrous sequence of performances, if he had not been altogether too successful in composing a symphony which 'swallowed the programme' so consummately that in 1901 the climactic moment of revelation went unheard, unremarked by virtually everyone. There was, however, one exception, Max Graf, who heard the first Vienna performance of the Fourth on 12 January 1902 and wrote about it in the *Neues Wiener Journal*.[16] The reception of the work in Vienna was as hostile as it had been in Munich, and Graf was no less negative—indeed destructive—than his colleagues. There is something almost sublimely ironic, if not comic, about his launching a reproach that at the same time, though evidently unappreciated by its author (still in his twenties), precisely described the retrospective process which every other critic had apparently not noticed. 'This symphony', he declared, 'has to be read from back to front like a Hebrew Bible.' Given the tragi-comic history of the Fourth's reception, it seems entirely appropriate that one of the few genuine insights about the symphony should have been expressed (and intended) as an adverse comment. Graf himself was a Jew, so it may have been that Mahler was not offended by what may have been intended or at least understood as a good Jewish joke. In any event, wittingly or unwittingly, Graf's perception matched Mahler's own, who had remarked to Bauer-Lechner after a reading rehearsal of the Fourth in October 1901, 'In the last movement . . . the child—who, though in a chrysalis-state, nevertheless already belongs to this higher world—*explains*

---

[13] See HLG(E) ii. 400.   [14] Ibid. 401.   [15] Ibid. 402.   [16] Ibid. 475.

what it all means' [my italics].[17] (It is of no little interest in this context that in a letter to Weingartner from the autumn of 1901 he explained his opposition to a *vocal* work preceding his symphony because he wanted 'the appearance of the soprano to come as a complete surprise before the Finale'.)[18]

Adorno, as we have read above, places a good deal of emphasis on the roots of the Fourth, as he hears it, having their location in the events and experiences of our early years. 'Its image-world is that of childhood. . . . No father figures are admitted to its precincts. The sound avoids all monumentality, which had attached itself to the symphonic idea since Beethoven's Ninth.' Later, he continues, 'The *entire* [my emphasis] Fourth Symphony shuffles nonexistent children's songs together; to it the golden book of song is the book of life.'[19] And so on.

If, as I have suggested, we substitute a state or condition of innocence for Adorno's 'golden book of song', or any other of the many vivid metaphors he employs, we find ourselves not so far removed from Adorno's conceptualizing, providing, that is—and for me this is fundamental to our comprehension of what the Fourth is 'about'—that 'innocence' is acknowledged to be the symphony's goal, the *condition to which it aspires*, and which the finale, 'Das himmlische Leben', at the last moment, unveils.

The progression, or, rather, the possibility of the progression, is brilliantly contrived from the outset of the symphony, from the jingling sleigh-bells of the introduction and the beguilingly simple 'cut', i.e. character, of the ensuing first subject. But is the first movement in fact quite as simple, i.e. childlike, as Adorno would have us believe? One wonders, indeed, if the simplicity that he equates with childhood were not also a remarkable anticipation of an aesthetic that in the history of music in the twentieth century was eventually to be known as Neo-Classicism—'Der neue Klassizismus' that was the object of Schoenberg's derision in his identically entitled cantata of 1925 (Op. 28, No. 3). But Neo-Classicism in fact did not have to await the advent of Stravinsky and Hindemith, or for that matter of Schoenberg himself, who had pursued his own form of Neo-Classicism, less immediately assimilable (audible) than, say, Stravinsky's, but no less part of his creative strategies in the Twenties and Thirties. We often discuss or think about Neo-Classicism as if it were wholly a matter of 'style', of explicit references to the manners of the past; and to be sure the 'past' must be integral to any attempt at defining the concept of Neo-Classicism. There is, however, another approach, another perspective, which perhaps transcends the issue of style or manner as the prime means of 'reviving' the past. It manifests itself, rather, as an awareness of the evolution of an established form to that critical point in time at which our hypothetical composer himself begins to work at extending the chosen form— the symphony, say—and, thereby, its pre-existing history. In short, the *history of the form itself* then becomes a subject of the composer's discourse.

---

[17] NB-L, *Recollections*, 178. There is a further remark of Mahler's to Bruno Walter in 1902 recorded by Bauer-Lechner which should be read in the light of his comment from 1901: 'They [the public] don't really know *what* to do with this one: *which end* [my italics] should they start gobbling it up from?' (ibid. 185).

[18] HLG(E) ii. 394.

[19] Adorno, *Mahler*, 53 and 55.

I use the word 'critical' advisedly, because it was at just such a critical moment that Mahler (our composer unmasked!) was, so to say, suspended between two centuries and the two symphonies which it is my business to survey, the latter of which, the Fifth, was to mark a fresh departure, something for which the composer himself, perhaps to an unexpected degree, found himself unprepared. In the Fourth, on the other hand, where he had encountered none of the difficulties (in the sphere of instrumentation in particular) that were to haunt him as he undertook successive revisions of the Fifth, there is, interestingly enough, not a sense of a new start, no hint of an experimental initiative (the finale excepted), but more a conscious reference to past practice, past styles even; to form, above all, and to first-movement sonata form, emphatically so. Indeed, it is surely a brilliant dimension of the symphony's first movement that in the wittiest and most sophisticated manner, Mahler seems to hold up for our inspection an 'innocent' age in the history of the symphony, though only to show that any kind of literal return to the past is no longer possible, that there has to be both renewal and innovation if the past is not to petrify. It is thus that I read the unique telescoping (or overlapping) technique that Mahler applies to a critical moment in the form of the movement, the recapitulation. This is what I wrote in 1975:[20]

But it is in the first movement of the Fourth Symphony that Mahler offers us the most brilliant and sophisticated example of his telescoping technique; rightly so, because in this case the technique is pressed into service at a highly important formal moment: the recapitulation in an elaborate sonata movement (at Fig. 18). Because of the 'formality' of the movement, Mahler's treatment of it is all the more riveting. This is a well-known passage in the symphony and one of which Mahler himself was clearly proud. He remarked about it to Bauer-Lechner that the audience would only discover later 'how artful [kunstvoll] it is'.[21] The artfulness rests in the ingenuity with which Mahler manipulates his telescoping principle. We recognize the principle involved just as soon as we hear the way in which Mahler recapitulates the principal theme [see Ex. 9.2]. We drop into the tonic, G major, but the theme itself is picked up in mid-flow. In characteristic Mahler fashion, what he recapitulates is not in any case the first statement of the principal theme from the exposition but the varied repeat of it (see two bars after Fig. 1 *et seq.*), which, in the recapitulation, he surrounds with a whole nest of fresh motives (see, however, the lower strings, one bar after Fig. 18, where the principal tune persists). It is with bar 3 of the principal theme, in fact, that the recapitulation opens; and . . . precisely as in the Minuet [of the Third Symphony], the thematic recapitulation has started on the 'wrong' side of the double bar at Fig. 18.[22] If one looks back to the point of climax of the development (at Fig. 17) and then at the ensuing lead-back to the recapitulation, one finds not only the 'missing' opening bars of the principal theme in an augmented version (bars 234–8) that carries one right up to the double bar and proves to dovetail precisely with the continuation of the melody (bar 3) with which the recapitulation so surprisingly opens, but also the introductory motives (cf. bars 1–3) which in the exposition precede the main tune.[23] At bar 225, flutes and sleighbells reintroduce the very opening idea of the symphony, and thereafter, and before the double bar is reached, all the introductory motives are recapitulated in a mosaic-like pattern of motivic combinations, as well as

---

[20] See Mitchell, *WY*, 322–4.   [21] NB-L, *Recollections*, 183.   [22] See Mitchell, *WY*, 318–22.
[23] See ibid. 366 n. 10.

Ex. 9.2. Fourth Symphony, 1st movt.: overlapping technique at recapitulation

the principal tune's opening bars; and to all this Mahler adds a nice touch of symmetry by using the version of the introductory motives that actually opens the development (Fig. 8) and now returns to close it (bars 233–8), while at the same time serving in a recapitulatory role. This is altogether an amazingly elaborate passage, the more so when one remembers that this subtle recapitulatory process also has to work smoothly and effectively as part of a transitional process, in which the development winds down and in which we are finally led back through an ingenious modulatory scheme[24] to the tonic and the recapitulation proper. 'Kunstvoll' indeed, and certainly a more complicated compositional exercise than the Minuet in the Third Symphony. Nonetheless, it was in that 'simple' movement that the essential principle underpinning this complex construction in the Fourth Symphony was first outlined.

I notice that when I came to continue that text I did not fail at least to raise the issue of Neo-Classicism, while not pursuing it very far:

Undoubtedly the complexity of this passage was part of the aesthetic game that Mahler was playing in his Fourth Symphony: an outwardly simple-minded, even backward-looking symphony (an early manifestation of neo-classicism?), that creates a peculiar world of its own by contradicting, in developments of a demanding complexity and sophistication, the anticipations of simplicity and guilelessness that the very opening of the work seems to arouse (though only momentarily).

Now, however, I believe that greater weight and consideration should be given to it, as an early example, indeed, of what Adorno himself describes as 'Musik über Musik' (music *about* [my emphasis] music).[25] For all its urbanity and playfulness, is this first movement not saying to us in fact that there can *not* be a return to the 'simplicities' of the past (they were never that, of course) at any level, formal, thematic or tonal, while at the same time saluting the certainties, the symmetries, the proportions—though none of these was invariably so—of Classicism? Typical of Mahler that his gesture to the past should simultaneously incorporate patent and elaborate innovations (cf. Ex. 9.2 above) that, so to speak, turn the past on its head, in order to make the very point that at this critical juncture in the history of the symphony, innovations were obligatory if the form—and its future—were to remain alive and kicking. In the first movement of the Fourth, then, Mahler was in a sense bidding farewell to the ideals of Classicism, rather than reasserting them as models that might service the future of the form.

Thus the Fourth, to my mind, represents a manifestation of Neo-Classicism peculiar to Mahler himself, an awareness of and reflection on the role he himself and his work(s) in progress might play in the still evolving history of the idea of the symphony. The Fourth, or one significant dimension of it, spells out the impossibility of rolling history back or complacently attempting to continue in the line of—wake of, rather—the Great Tradition. We should remember too that the symphonies that preceded the Fourth, all three of them, exploited the still new and intriguing concept of the 'programme' symphony; and that it was in the Fourth that Mahler, so to say, turned his back on programme music (while at the

---

[24] See Mitchell, *WY*, 366 n. 11.

[25] See Theodor W. Adorno, *Philosophy of Modern Music*, trans. Anne G. Mitchell and Wesley V. Bloomster (London: Sheed & Ward, 1973), 181–4.

same time, as I have already suggested, creating his most perfect example of the genre). Goodbye to an illusory golden past, goodbye to the illusions of the 'programme'. The Fourth quite remarkably proved to be the vehicle of change, the symphony in which the ground was cleared to make way for the new symphonic initiatives of the first decade, the Fifth and its successors; the symphony too in which some of the most conspicuous features of Mahler's later orchestral manner were anticipated.

All of this, however, does not argue against the basic concept of the 'innocent' and the 'childlike' which I believe to be the *fons et origo* of the symphony's inspiration, though I stress again that this must not be approached as a static concept but a mobile one, as a journey from Experience to Innocence.[26] In this sense, the first movement is all Experience. To be sure, Adorno has a point in his promoting the 'image-world . . . of childhood' as a defining influence on the character of Mahler's themes, the often bright colours of their instrumentation, the choice of percussion, etc., etc. There is indeed something of the celestial nursery to be discerned, obligatorily so in the light of what the finale is to vouchsafe. But there is nothing very childlike or naive about the organization of the first movement's recapitulation, while the intense and intensive polyphony that we encounter throughout the movement, and in its development section in particular, is hard to read as a manifestation of 'childhood' or the 'childlike'; or if so, then this is an exceptionally clever, knowing child, playing an exceptionally sophisticated game.

This last factor is of quite special importance, for in fact it is in the first movement of the Fourth that for the first time in a Mahler symphony we are confronted by a show of that hyperactive motivic counterpoint which, in the succeeding instrumental symphonies, was to be a hallmark of his 'new' polyphonic orchestral style. As we shall see, this technique was to land Mahler in no end of trouble, about which he himself was unusually forthcoming; for example, as late as February 1911—almost a decade after the symphony's completion—he was writing to Georg Göhler from New York, 'I have finished [*sic*] my Fifth—it had to be almost completely re-orchestrated. I simply can't understand why I still had to make such mistakes, like the merest beginner. (It is clear that all the experience I had gained in writing the first four symphonies completely let me down in this one—for a completely new style demanded a new technique.)[27]

That 'new style', although Mahler himself did not amplify the statement nor point to any precedents, has always been assumed to be the onset of the polyphony that characterizes the symphonies (but not only the symphonies) from the Fifth onwards; and surely rightly so—after all, Mahler himself in 1904 in a letter to his publisher had remarked on the difficulty of getting every last detail right in 'such a very polyphonic' work as his Fifth.[28] But as Adorno remarks, it was in the first movement of the Fourth that 'he writes counterpoint for the first time in earnest, although polyphony did not dominate the imagination of the

---

[26] I capitalize Innocence and Experience henceforth to remind readers that my use of these concepts in relation to the Fourth derive from William Blake, i.e. his *Songs of Innocence and Songs of Experience: Shewing the Two Contrary States of the Human Soul*, published in 1794.

[27] See Mahler, *Selected Letters*, 372.
[28] See HLG(E) ii. 801.

earlier pieces'.[29] How odd, then, and to some significant degree inexplicable, that the Fifth was plagued by such problems when the first copious manifestation of the new contrapuntal style, the new polyphonic thinking, had been executed with such remarkable clarity in the first movement of the Fourth, and with seeming ease; like the rest of Mahler's symphonies, the Fourth was also the subject of pretty continuous revision, but on nothing like the scale of the obsessive revisions of the Fifth. There is not a commentator on the Fifth who, parrot-like, does not echo the established opinion that 'new style' meant a new preoccupation with counterpoint, while remaining seemingly oblivious to the fact that the 'new style' was adumbrated, however improbably, in the first movement of the Fourth. It is true that our apprehension of the movement's polyphonic profile does nothing to help explain why it was that Mahler found himself in such a predicament when coming to realize the polyphony of the Fifth. If anything, indeed, it heightens the enigma, about which I shall have more to say in my chapter on that symphony. But a failure to perceive that the new contrapuntal thinking was, so to say, launched in the Fourth, is to diminish the pivotal role the symphony plays in the evolution of his compositional resources and techniques. There can be no doubt that the overt contrapuntal features of the first movement were widely *mis*understood as a means of jokey reference to the past; so much emerges from many of the notices of the work's first performances. We can reinterpret it in our own day as an early signal of a revived Classicism yet to materialize, though the motivation for Mahler's salutation, as I have suggested, was probably somewhat distinct from that of his successors, the later proponents of Neo-Classicism proper. But much more seriously and illuminating, the Fourth's polyphony we now realize was an intimation of the new polyphonic style that was to service, virtually without exception, Mahler's music thenceforth.

But it was not only counterpoint that was a signpost to innovations to come. Scarcely less significant was another dimension of the work altogether, though one clearly related to the burgeoning contrapuntal component, which brought in its wake the obligation to achieve clarity of articulation: a marked reduction in the orchestral forces involved (no trombones or tuba). Adorno has not failed to take note of the new dispensation: 'The means are reduced, without heavy brass; horns and trumpets are more modest in number. No father figures are admitted to [the symphony's] precincts. The sound avoids all monumentality, which had attached itself to the symphonic idea since Beethoven's Ninth.' And he continues: 'The reduction of the orchestra caused the symphonic writing to approach chamber-music procedures, to which Mahler, after the alfresco quality of the first three symphonies, returned again and again, most markedly in the *Kindertotenlieder* . . .'.[30]

It was *Kindertotenlieder*, one might claim, that finally gave birth to the idea of the *chamber orchestra*, an event of no little consequence for the future of twentieth-century music,

[29] Adorno, *Mahler*, 54.

[30] Ibid. 53. Some comparative figures: whereas in the Fourth Mahler uses 4 horns and 3 trumpets, his First had required 7 horns, 5 trumpets (+ 3 trombones and bass tuba); his Second, 10 horns, 6–10 trumpets (+ 4 trombones and bass tuba); and his Third, 8 horns, 4 trumpets (ideally 6 + 4 trombones and bass tuba). Numbers, when Mahler is involved, cannot tell anything like the full story, and in each of the Fourth's predecessors one can locate passages and textures of a chamber-musical character. But the Fourth represents a defining stage in Mahler's progress towards the concept of a chamber orchestra.

and again a topic to which I shall return in the ensuing chapter. But its foreshadowing here
in the Fourth, in the symphony's very constitution, has to be spelled out in order to
heighten the work's peculiar status and achievements, and to remind us of its singular history, greeted by scorn and mockery on its first airing and then, decades later, earning a reputation as the most accessible and approachable of the symphonies. How wonderfully
ironical that it was this symphony above all that fired the enthusiasm of many of those
hearing a Mahler symphony for the first time, an enthusiasm only made possible by its
relative accessibility—even amid the constraints of war in the 1940s—an accessibility
itself facilitated of course by the deployment of (relatively) slender orchestral resources;
while that, in turn, as I have suggested above, represents to us one of the symphony's most
original and, in Mahler's terms, forward-looking gestures. Represents *now*, I should have
written, in the light of everything we know about Mahler today. But it says something about
the symphony that it could speak so directly, eloquently, and expressively in virtually the
total absence in those far-off days of anything like the contextual information we have
ready to hand, not to speak of the torrent of performances and flood of CDs.

There is no doubt in my mind that Adorno was correct in identifying the childlike as one
of the most important stimuli, both symbolic and sonorous—that is, as image and sound—
to Mahler's imagination. But exaggeration blunts the sharp point he is making. A symbolic
representation of childhood, of the childlike, we may all agree, was obligatory at an early
stage in the symphony if the narrative were to culminate, in the finale, in the unveiling of
Innocence; and indeed Mahler wastes no time at all in making the point himself in the very
first three bars of the first movement: the jingling bells and repetitive patterns in the woodwinds are akin in their bright, arresting simplicity to a musical box, a bit of nursery equip-
ment, the machinery of which, however, is imperfectly synchronized. Was that perhaps
what Mahler had in mind when organizing the slight but calculated rhythmic confusion
that attends the winding down of the introduction, the flutes marked 'ohne rit.', the last beat
of the clarinets marked 'poco rit.', while the upbeat in the violins to the first statement of
the first subject and the establishment of G major is also marked 'Etwas zurückhaltend' (i.e.
'poco rit.')? Clearly, this is what he wanted to happen, this teasing dis-synchronization; but
in fact it is only in a very recent edition of the symphony, incorporating Mahler's very last
corrections made, probably, between October 1910 and May 1911—an invaluable note of
which was kept by Erwin Stein—that his wish is made adequately explicit (cf. this introduction as it appears in the first publication of the work in 1902 with its parallel in the corrected edition of 1995, forming part (Vol. IV) of the critical edition of the symphonies
supervised by the International Gustav Mahler Society, Vienna).

The choice of ideas to initiate the symphony cannot have posed much of a problem for
Mahler. These were ready to hand in the already existing finale, the song, 'Das himmlische
Leben' (it is not only the symphony itself that has to be read backwards but also the
chronology of its composition). What Mahler had to be mindful of was not to divulge *too
much Innocence too soon*; hence, no doubt, the exceptional brevity of this introduction.
(The only comparable example of extreme economy is the introduction to the first

movement of the Ninth and even that runs for a bar or two beyond the three bars of the Fourth, the briefest of all the composer's introductions.)

It is exactly in this manipulation of balance and proportion, in keeping the symphony's goal in his sights, setting up the objective, but avoiding a premature dénouement, that we encounter the very considerable and conscious art—artifice might be the better word here—Mahler brings to this first movement. In short, Innocence has to be signposted, but then held in check and subjected to the challenge of Experience. It is the conflict between those two prime areas of the human condition—and the resultant tension—that forms the principal business of the first movement, a tension that is skilfully sustained by Mahler across the whole span of the symphony until its final dispersal in the finale's closing stanza.

In this respect, we do well to note, the Fourth behaves virtually as does every other Mahler symphony, its predecessors and successors. For example, the overall concept of the Fifth was to be entirely different, as we shall see. But the narrative *process* is there, unmistakably, and in all important respects identical with that of the Fourth, i.e. the basic conflict articulated at an early stage and a significant indication vouchsafed of a possible (probable), albeit still distant, resolution of the drama. It is always the finale, without exception in Mahler's oeuvre, that clinches the narrative, unfolds the dénouement; and the ultimate dénouement of the Fourth, which will make final sense of the B minor musical-box introduction that I have described above, is of course the last stanza of 'Das himmlische Leben'—'Kein Musik is ja nicht auf Erden . . .'—floated on a sublime E major (from Fig. 12).

Already, I suggest, there is sufficient to encourage us not, as it were, to swallow Adorno whole (leaving on one side the question of the programme); as is often the case with the best of critics, perhaps necessarily and fruitfully so, the overestimation of one dimension of a work, important and illuminating though that may be, leads him or her to underestimate one that may be equally (or perhaps even more) important. Adorno zooms in on Innocence, thereby excluding Experience; all the odder, one may think, since he shows himself to be alert to many of the novel features of the Fourth that I believe run counter to the images (or practices) of childhood, and which I believe to belong incontrovertibly to the sphere of Experience.

A case in point is the explosion of counterpoint in the Fourth, something that Adorno was quick to observe while seeming not to have sufficiently recognized the specific role it plays in the contest between Innocence and Experience; how, so to say, it emerges at its most potent and challenging in the first movement in that crucial section, the development, where Mahler explores areas of feeling and expression the farthest *removed* from Innocence. The development, indeed, demands separate scrutiny in its own right and I shall turn to it in a moment. But in any event counterpoint alone does not exhaust a list of features that decisively contribute to the interplay between the opposed ideas out of which conciliation will eventually emerge. After all, what sort of resolution or dénouement would it be, if challenge, contrast, and opposition had not preceded it?

So, in pursuit of our qualifications of Innocence, we have to add to our list such things as the elaborate, 'knowing' treatment of critical formal junctures in a sonata-form movement with a long musical history behind them, and which depend for their effect on a kind of tacit complicity between the educated, historically minded listener and the historically minded composer, e.g. the lead-back to the recapitulation in the first movement that my Ex. 9.2 above illustrates; the shift towards a chamber-orchestral style that Mahler was soon to establish in *Kindertotenlieder* and the late Rückert settings,[31] his 'Kammermusikton' as he was himself to describe it; the explicit references to a spirit of Classicism by no means confined to the forms Mahler expounds, e.g. 'textbook' sonata form in the first movement, 'textbook' variations in the third, but extending also to the very configuration of themes, motives, textures and, not least, rhythm, e.g. in the first movement, Figs. 2–3, Figs. 19–20, and the movement's very last four Allegro bars, remarkable anticipations, one might think, of the Neo-Classicism with which the first half of our century has made us familiar; these are like neoclassical windows opened up in the façade of the symphony. Nor should one overlook an often unblemished assertion of the diatonic, as if, say, *Tristan* had been temporarily erased from the historical record.

All of this, the sheer sophistication and technical virtuosity of it, seems to run significantly counter to Adorno's surely too exuberant and indiscriminate categorizing of the symphony, its ideas, its 'characters' and characterizing sonorities, as having their origin in the 'image-world . . . of childhood'. At the same time we should not fall into a similar trap ourselves, thereby underrating the importance of the role of childlike imagery in the symphony as a whole. But it would count for little if it were not for the context of Experience, from which indeed Innocence has to be seen to be—heard to be—at last extrapolated.

If there is an agenda that appears not to have claimed Adorno's full attention, then it surfaces unmistakably and audaciously in the first movement's development section, from Figs. 8 to 18, about which there is nothing very childlike in character or seraphic in mood. On the contrary, what we encounter here, after the relatively benign exposition, is what might be described as distinctly unsettled weather, accompanied by constant fluctuations of temperament and temperature. There is no other part of the symphony comparable to this abrupt destabilization of the prevailing mood; to respond adequately to this remarkable music, we have to fall back on words like 'doubt', 'anxiety', 'scepticism', 'irony', 'agitation'—again, a vocabulary remote from the texts of an imagined 'golden book of song'[32] belonging to childhood that Adorno suggests is the Fourth's generating source.

For the song Mahler sings in his development is a very different kind of song. His manipulation, distortion, and distending of his invention surface in ever new and intricate counterpoints, projected, more often than not, in startlingly unpredictable instrumental combinations; some of these—they form a continuous array between Figs. 8 and 16—unequivocally reverse the 'classical' relationship between winds and strings. There have been plenty of precedents for this calculated dis-balance in earlier symphonies, of course;

---

[31] And not only in the Rückert song-cycle and songs I mention here, but also in at least some of the 'Wunderhorn' settings. See the section on 'Mahler and the Chamber Orchestra' in Ch. 10, where I examine some of the statistical—and other—implications of the historic 'Lieder-Abend mit Orchester' that Mahler conducted in Vienna on 29 Jan. 1905. The first half of the programme was made up exclusively of 'Wunderhorn' songs.

[32] Adorno, *Mahler*, 55.

perhaps one becomes particularly conscious of it here because of the no less calculated tribute he seems to pay to Classicism in the Fourth in so many of its parameters, and perhaps more specifically because the exposition, relatively speaking—everything is relative in Mahler!—has been homogeneous in texture. But with the onset of the development at Fig. 8, a radically different sound-world manifests itself.

The very first eight bars of the development initiate the shift away from anything recognizable as classical homogeneity of orchestral sound; we hear nothing but woodwind, bells, solo horn, and solo violin! We are borne back—which was of course Mahler's intention—to the complex of motives and identifying instrumentation with which the symphony was launched in bar 1. But any illusion we might have that we are to embark on a further exploration of the guileless naiveties of the introduction and the generally affirmative, shadowless character of the ensuing exposition—all G major and D major but for a five-bar recall (bb. 72–6) of B minor along with the introduction (what follows is a seeming 'classical' repeat of the exposition which is then cut short (no second subject!))—is shattered by the path the development pursues. I have already mentioned the dazzlingly varied, eccentric textures, from which the strings are often absent or relegated to a subordinate role; woodwind and brass predominate. When the strings do participate, on a highly intermittent and selective basis, their function is to contribute yet another means of articulating and colouring the web of motivic polyphony that is the development's *raison d'être*. If one needs to isolate one single example in the development that embodies a sound-world as remote as one could get from the 'noise-fields' of infancy that Adorno seems to have had (too much) in mind, then we need look no further than, say, bars 160–7 and their restatement in bars 200–8: first time round repeated high chords in the flutes, *p*, accompanied by muted trumpets and cymbal strokes (with the soft stick); second time round, the high chords repeated, *pp*, distributed among flutes, oboes, and clarinets (clarinet 2 in E flat), while harp harmonics, *f*, punctuate and articulate the soft vibrations of the cymbal. On both occasions, the chords function as interpolations—interruptions—in the midst of ceaseless motivic variation and fragmentation and no less ceaseless motivic counterpointing, though naturally enough, because (second time round) we are approaching the climax of the development—when E flat minor and F minor are not so much replaced as ejected by a robust C major—the motivic activity (vertical and horizontal) becomes ever more intense and elaborate. To be sure, the music withdraws from this encounter with foreboding and agitation, and unequivocally reasserts its 'optimism'. But for a significant stretch of musical time we have, so to say, been suspended over an abyss.

These specific passages in the development cannot be left without one further comment on the extraordinary ingenuity with which Mahler expounds his materials. For a start, why this emphasis *here* on the three repeated chords? That these repetitions derive, rhythmically and motivically, from the main theme of the 'himmlische Leben' melody (see, for example, the opening bars (clarinet) of the finale) must of course be part of any answer. But perhaps a little less obvious is, on reflection, their clear relationship to the first bar of the second subject (at Fig. 3); whereupon it will be recalled that the expected restatement of

the big D major tune in the (only seeming) repeat of the exposition was never to materialize. True to past practice, Mahler compensates for what is apparently 'missing' in one spot
by resuscitating it, albeit in disguised form, in another. Hence the development's concentration on a derivative which continuously, once it has been remarked, is heard to evoke
the omitted second subject. (The precedent for this may be found in the first movement of
the Second Symphony.)[33]

I have referred above to the development's withdrawal from foreboding and its eventual
reaffirmation of the symphony's 'optimism'; and it is precisely at the climax of the development, and in an exuberant C major, that the reversion is made. This is a critical passage (Figs.
16–17) from many points of view, not least Adorno's, for whom this climax is 'an intentionally infantile, noisily cheerful [noise-]field . . . the forte growing increasingly uncomfortable
until the retransition [the lead-back] with the fanfare.'[34] It seems to me, however, that he
once again overstates one dimension at the expense of all else. For example, it is here for the
first time that the thematic source and eventual thematic goal of the symphony is spelled
out—proclaimed *fff*—by the solo trumpet, simultaneously combined, however, with a whole
nest of related motives (cf. Figs. 2–3), not excluding the repeated-note (chord) motive which
has attained such prominence in the development and now continues to enjoy a high profile,
but one stripped of its former expression of anxiety. Moreover, while it is perfectly true that
this brilliant climax serves as a kind of apotheosis of the calculated naivety which is an essential part of the symphony's aesthetic, we should not fail to remark the ingenuity of the counterpointing, a demonstration, surely, in this prime location that, in the Fourth, counterpoint
does not necessarily belong to the torments and trials of Experience but can also wear the
face of Innocence. The polyphony here represents the obverse of that which has held sway
between Figs. 11 and 16; thus it is that one compositional principle assumes two contrasting
roles in the evolution of the narrative, and contributes to the interplay between the opposed
poles of Innocence and Experience. If counterpoint is one of the 'characters' involved, then,
it seems, 'characters' can from time to time change sides.

How, then, are we to read that C major climax and the trumpet tune? Has Mahler, so to
say, given the game away, arrived prematurely at his dénouement? I think not. For a start,
the projection of the 'himmlische Leben' tune, forcible though it is, is but one motivic
strand in a complex of motives; as we shall hear, when Mahler does finally release the
melody in its entirety, it not only uncoils itself in a wholly relaxed way—there is no sense
of it having to justify its existence—but comprises virtually the total experience the symphony has to offer at this (still distant) point, by when everything will have been stripped
away, pared down and simplified. It is an extensive melody that embodies the symphony's
resolution, that tells us, retrospectively, all we need to know about what has preceded it;
and its consummatory E major indicates that the C major of the development's peak, no

[33] See Donald Mitchell, 'Mahler's Longest Journey', the
note written to accompany Claudio Abbado's recording of
the symphony with the Vienna Philharmonic on DGG 439
953–2, released in 1994.

[34] Adorno, *Mahler*, 54.

matter its motivic/thematic importance, its triumphalism even, could not possibly be taken to represent to us that the 'conflict', the tension, was near to being solved; least of all did Mahler intend us to read that *C major* as his symphony's eventual tonal destination. In any case, while this critical passage is certainly not wanting in confidence, its staying power is limited; at Fig. 17^{+4} there is an intervention—the famous fanfare, which is followed by the overlapping lead-back I have described above to the recapitulation by way of F sharp minor, B minor, and *E minor* (bar 229 *et seq.*).

I emphasize E minor because the sleigh-bells we hear at the beginning of the development (Fig. 8) indisputably function, as I have already mentioned above, as a recall of the movement's introduction, and, along with it, the introduction's own B minor (bar 102 *et seq.*). Eight bars later, 'classically' enough, it is in E minor that the development really gets under way; whereupon one becomes acutely conscious of what might be described as the movement's *double tonic*; there is not only G, as it were, to be accommodated, but also E, in both its minor and major mode.

This is a fundamental aspect of the first movement, and—eventually—an issue—i.e. G or E?—that is fundamental to our understanding of the work as a whole and its narrative. It is a feature of the Fourth about which the New Zealand Mahler scholar, Graeme Downes, has written exceptionally well in his 1991 doctoral thesis,[35] and especially so in relation to the character and organization of the first movement's development. He suggests that the 'tonal direction' of the development becomes 'crucial to the question of overall tonicity. G major could be confirmed if another strong structural dominant is reached, but on the other hand, the failure to provide such a dominant could place G's tonicity in jeopardy'. He continues:

The first sign that the development section might take the latter course is the return of the sleigh-bell introduction. Not that this is disruptive in itself, but here it begins to assert its tonal independence and, in so doing, realizes a different tonal function that has remained latent up until this point. Specifically, B minor functions as the dominant of E: not as a modal colour subsidiary to the tonic G major. Here it is strengthened by a stronger modal implication thanks to the tonicizing leading note in the solo violin part, which therefore implies B minor more strongly than B phrygian, thus avoiding the modal connection with G.

Very quickly the development section establishes the key of E, which will ultimately be the work's tonal destination. But it is not merely a case of beginning the development in the relative minor of G. The development section here is the most unusual Mahler has written so far in his career, in as much as it avoids any goal-oriented drive towards a preparatory dominant and subsequent resolution to the tonic. In other words the development ends up as a disconnected structural unit, one which begins and ends in E minor no less. . . . In terms of the local tonal context, the return of G major [at the recapitulation] is entirely gratuitous. So the muted articulation of the structural outlines that Mahler achieves with his thematic dovetailing [Ex. 9.2 above] actually points out a more serious situation—namely the growing crisis over the tonicity of G.

---

[35] Graeme Alexander Downes, 'An Axial System of Tonality Applied to Progressive Tonality in the Works of Gustav Mahler and Nineteenth-Century Antecedents', Ph.D. thesis (University of Otago, Dunedin, 1991), 143–59.

Such a claim may seem far-fetched at first sight, but it is nevertheless a fact that the development fails to establish a goal-oriented structural dominant that seeks to tonicize G.[36]

Dr Downes has much more to say that is illuminating; those who wish to pursue his line of thinking should consult his thesis. What captured my attention—and indeed my imagination—was his clear recognition that this development section was not only the 'most unusual' that Mahler had yet written but 'a disconnected structural unit', an analytic insight that I think spells out in another way what I have already remarked upon as the development's unique detachment, its decoupling almost, from the movement's—the exposition's—principal concerns. Dr Downes adduces a tonal strategy that I believe supports what I have written about at length above: that the virtually self-contained development explores territories that the exposition has not led us to expect. Above all, its failure to confirm a 'goal-oriented structural dominant', combined with its own structural independence, beginning and ending in E minor, makes one acutely conscious of the competing claims of the symphony's 'alternative' tonic, E; not only of its eventual status—as Dr Downes observes, the 'latter stages of the work will effect [the] transition whereby E becomes the tonic'[37]—but of the role it plays in the overall narrative of the symphony, the 'character' allotted it by the composer.

If I can put a gloss of my own on what Dr Downes has to say about E, then it seems to me entirely appropriate that at this first-movement stage of the symphony it is E *minor* that, by association, comes to represent the impact of Experience on Innocence: in short, it is the disconcertingly restless, uneasy character of the development that defines for us what, in terms of tonal symbolism, E minor embodies. That it may eloquently represent unmitigated lamentation is revealed in the third movement, the Adagio, in which, after the first unfolding of the theme in a serene G major, there follows at Fig. 2 a long lament initiated by the oboe in E minor, music which again anticipates significant features of Mahler's later style, of *Kindertotenlieder* in particular, from which, in bars 80–1, Mahler *seems* to make a quotation (cf. the opening bars for the voice in the cycle's second song, 'Nun seh' ich wohl, warum so dunkle Flammen'). However, if—as important research[38] has suggested—'Nun seh' ich wohl' post-dated the symphony, i.e. was composed in 1904, then it must be that the song took as its point of departure the oboe lament from the slow movement of the symphony.[39] Whichever option may be thought to be correct, the result does not affect my argument: that the idea of mourning, of pain and suffering, are inextricably associated with the advent of E minor in the Adagio of the Fourth, thus retrospectively clarifying the function of the E minor that frames the development section in the first movement (everything in this symphony has to be read backwards!). This unmediated juxtaposition of G major and E minor that opens the Adagio articulates in its clearest guise the conflict, the spiritual drama if you like, that as I have already suggested is the work's *raison d'être*. Or as Dr Downes puts it succinctly from his own

---

[36] Ibid. 147–8.
[37] Ibid. 149.
[38] See Christopher O. Lewis, 'On the Chronology of the *Kindertotenlieder*', *Revue Mahler*, 1 (1987), Paris, Bibliothèque Gustav Mahler, 21–45.

[39] Odd if this were, in fact, the case: all Mahler's markings in bars 80–1 of the Adagio of the symphony go out of their way to indicate a 'quote'. Should we perhaps rethink—investigate further—the chronology of *Kindertotenlieder*?

perspective: it was clearly Mahler's aim in the slow movement 'to juxtapose the work's *main tonal combatants* [my emphasis]'[40]—I would only add, 'from the movement's very outset'.

The overall form of this Adagio has often been described as a double-variation form after the model of Beethoven's Ninth, but this is surely not the case? We have a theme, and then two chains of variations, *between* which is interpolated the lament, the first time round in E minor (and then extensively and agitatedly developed), the second time round in G (Phrygian) minor and again extensively and likewise developed.

It is in the second chain of variations (like the theme, both units of variations centre on G) that for the first time E *major* is energetically asserted, in the fast—Allegro subito—variation that precedes the even faster final variation in G. It is perhaps not without significance that this last and very short variation borrows its rapid figuration from its E major predecessor. E major, so to speak, is intensifying its infiltration, gaining the upper hand in its contest with its rival. But the moment of triumph is not yet; indeed, the closing section, based on the main theme, that follows the final variation must have led early audiences to believe that the Adagio was to be rounded off in the blissful G major with which it had opened. But the climax of the movement is still to come; a huge—*fff*—affirmation of an undiluted E major, from within which horns and trumpets triumphantly articulate that complex of motives, themes, and rhythms that we heard originally at—or, rather as—the climax of the first movement's development. But there it was in the 'wrong' key. The eruption of E major at last fulfils almost all the implications of its role as an alternative tonic that have been a fundamental part of the composer's tonal strategy since the symphony's initial handful of bars. It massively dispatches the E minor of the lament—and though E minor, inevitably and necessarily, continues to be a vivid presence in the song-finale, it is an E minor purged of its associations with pain and anguish—and proclaims unequivocally the vision of 'heavenly life' that is but a step, a song away. The continuity of the narrative that is enacted across the Adagio and ensuing song-finale is secured by the concluding D major chord of the slow movement functioning as dominant upbeat to the ensuing G of 'Das himmlische Leben'. The final attainment of Innocence, of freedom from the pains and tribulations of Experience, is still to come; and Mahler, with characteristic skill, reserves the very last moments of his symphony for his apotheosis of E.

There is another feature of the Adagio that I should like to mention before we come to that final stanza in the fourth movement. I have referred before to the systematic reduction in complexity of virtually all parameters of the symphony, of textures and forms in particular. This is an important part of the process by which, gradually, perhaps without our being always conscious of it, Mahler effects his evolving transition from Experience to Innocence across all four movements. The Adagio, I suggest, usefully illustrates the point. To be sure, Innocence and Experience are forcefully juxtaposed; but there is nothing like the elaborate and sophisticated 'mix' of contrasting moods that we have encountered in the first movement's unique development; nor any comparable display of the intricate polyphony that distinguishes the movement as a whole, though in the interpolated lament, in the G (Phrygian) minor version

---

[40] Downes, 'An Axial System', 154.

in particular (at Fig. 6), we are suddenly made aware of the linear preoccupations that were to surface around the turn of the century, and distinguish the textures of *Kindertotenlieder*, *Das Lied von der Erde*, and the Ninth Symphony. In bars 179–86 of the Fourth's Adagio, the long lines of the counterpoint, scored for solo woodwind and solo horn, open a window on a type of polyphony that was to become an identifying characteristic of Mahler's later and last style. (Cf., for example, *Das Lied*, 'Der Einsame im Herbst', Figs. 15–17.)

Appropriate enough, one might think in the light of all I have said, that these manifestations of counterpoint belong to the slow movement's lament, to the sector of Experience, to the plaintive minor mode (E minor, G (Phrygian) minor). On the other hand, the 'innocent' sector, the G major theme and variations, carries a rapturous simplicity to an extreme we have not witnessed before. This is especially true of the second chain of variations, from Fig. 9 onwards, which—but for a momentary passing shadow between bars 267 and 277— are of an artlessness that indeed has its roots in childhood: this is a kind of music that ingeniously evokes those simple sets of variations that are part of the experience of every child musician—especially aspiring infant pianists—for which reason, perhaps, the very figuration that Mahler introduces evokes, uniquely for him, the keyboard and the agilities required of young fingers. No doubt, too, it is precisely because this second variation chain attains an unprecedented simplicity of spirit that we find there (at Fig. 10), as I have already observed, the first accommodation, the first intimation, of the forthcoming avowal of E major, the symphony's terminus.

If I have chosen to concentrate on the Adagio, it is because the movement so aptly illustrates and represents the diminishing complication that we experience as the sequence of movements progresses. That I have said nothing about the Scherzo should not in any sense be interpreted as mute adverse comment. On the contrary it is a strikingly original and often very beautiful movement in its own right, one too from which one may well conclude that Experience, in the shape of the spectral solo fiddler, 'Freund Hein', has an important role to play, beckoning those who follow him 'to dance out of life into death'.[41] Mahler himself, it seems, in a conversation with Natalie Bauer-Lechner, referred to the 'screeching and rough-sounding' tone of the *scordatura* fiddle part, 'as if Death were fiddling away'.[42]

But what I wish to emphasize here is not so much the self-evident and perfectly explicit character of the Scherzo as its relatively simple *form*, a sequence of dances, i.e. three

[41] See my note on the Fourth in *GMWL*, 2.54–7, where I specifically mention (2.56) the covert references Mahler makes in the Scherzo to the contour of the melody of 'Das himmlische Leben' (cf. for example the passage between Fig. 9[+10] and Fig. 11[+13]).

[42] NB-L, *Recollections*, 162, who writes, 'He is altering the violin solo of the Scherzo by having the instrument tuned a tone higher, and rewriting the part in D minor instead of E minor', which prompts Peter Franklin to ask in an editorial note, 'Is Natalie mistaken here, or did Mahler originally conceive the Scherzo in E minor?' (ibid. 222). Professor Edward R. Reilly, to whom I am much indebted, confirms that the earliest MS known to him, a sketch in short-score format for the opening of the movement, 'clearly shows the key to be C minor'. It seems most probable, writes Prof. Reilly, 'that a slip was made in transcribing Bauer-Lechner's text, with E accidentally written instead of C'. I am also grateful to him for pointing out that while the short-score sketch is inscribed by Mahler '2. Satz', a later fair copy in full score of virtually the same passage is inscribed '3. Satz (Scherzo)', another fascinating example of the habitual uncertainties that attended the ordering of the middle movements of Mahler's symphonies; and yet, once the final sequence has been determined, one realizes that it was, after all, and from the start, the only possibility.

statements of the main scherzo section (and its repeats, second time round), into which are interpolated two trios (the second repeated). There are of course a hundred subtleties in Mahler's treatment of his ideas; but the generally straightforward character of the overall form is matched by invention and textures that on the whole are similarly uncomplicated[43] and certainly free of the polyphonic hyperactivity that crowds in on our ears in the first movement. If Experience *is* a presence in the Scherzo, then it must be attributed to the symbolic figure of Freund Hein, rasping away on his rustic fiddle (*?klezmer*).

And so to the finale, and to the finale's finale, the magical onset of E major that accompanies the setting of the last stanza of the 'Wunderhorn' poem:

Kein Musik ist ja nicht auf Erden,	There's no music at all on the earth
die unsrer verglichen kann werden.	Which can ever compare with ours.
Elftausend Jungfrauen	Eleven thousand virgins
zu tanzen sich trauen!	Are set dancing.
Sankt Ursula selbst dazu lacht!	Saint Ursula herself laughs to see it!
Cäcilia mit ihren Verwandten	Saint Cecilia with her companions
sind treffliche Hofmusikanten!	Are splendid court musicians.
Die englischen Stimmen	The angelic voices
ermuntern die Sinnen!	Delight the senses,
Dass Alles für Freuden erwacht.	For all things awake to joy.[44]

It is an extraordinary experience without parallel elsewhere in Mahler, this retrospective 'explanation' by the pre-existing 'Wunderhorn' song-finale of what the three preceding movements have been 'about', and why they took the shape they did; and in particular, as I believe Dr Downes to have very convincingly shown,[45] how, in the vocal last movement, E is finally established as the symphony's authentic tonic. Here again, the tonal organization of the finale retrospectively clarifies the emerging role of E, both minor and major, in the first movement and the Adagio.

As for the long journey from Experience to Innocence, how, so to say, is it left as the movement ends—as it has to do, naturally—on those low, repeated Es on the harp punctuating a low E, *ppp*, on the double basses, gradually dying away? A stroke of genius that an unadorned E should be the very last sound we hear. But no less inspired, surely, is the long-breathed, seamless melody, occupying virtually the totality of the last stanza's available musical space, a quietly rapturous celebration of a music that awaits us when Experience has been purged. Not Paradise, perhaps, but Innocence Regained; and by reserving that sublime melody for his final act of simplification, by his concentration on melody alone to bear the weight of the ultimate transformation, Mahler seems to return us to an age of innocence in music when (if I may echo Freud) such things were still possible.

[43] There is another ambiguous comment by Natalie in her memoirs in which she recalls Mahler revising 'the part-writing in the second movement', which had 'become too elaborate and overgrown—"like limbs with ganglia"' (NB-L, *Recollections*, 162). If this were indeed the Scherzo that Mahler was talking about, then it would seem he was himself conscious of the progressive diminution in textural complication that to my ears is a highly innovative feature of the symphony and one, again, that brilliantly relates to the 'programme' from a different angle of approach.

[44] Translated by Deryck Cooke.

[45] Downes, 'An Axial System', 156–8.

10

Mahler's 'Kammermusikton'

DONALD MITCHELL

Kindertotenlieder

Mahler's second orchestral song-cycle, *Kindertotenlieder*, composed over an unusually long period, overlaps with the Fourth,[1] Fifth, and Sixth[2] Symphonies, and, scarcely less important, with the last two settings of 'Wunderhorn' texts, 'Revelge' and 'Der Tamboursg'sell', and the four independent orchestral settings of lyrics by Rückert. There are many fascinating crossovers and revealing relationships between songs and symphonies from this period in Mahler's creative life; but it is probably in the area of *form* that we encounter the most important relationship between *Kindertotenlieder* and the surrounding and ensuing symphonies. It could be expressed, albeit crudely, like this: that as Mahler developed towards his last works there emerged a profound symbiotic relationship between his late songs and his symphonies, the songs evolving ever more symphonically— a striking case in point is that masterpiece of symphonic song, 'Der Tamboursg'sell' (see p. 232 and Ch. 11, pp. 236 ff.)—while his late symphonic thinking shows the influence of the innovative forms adumbrated in *Kindertotenlieder*. Mahler himself, one has to conclude, demonstrated this integral relationship in the very last years of his life by writing *Das Lied von der Erde*, the symphony that is also a song-cycle (or the song-cycle that is also a symphony, which was Mahler's choice of nomenclature). This concept of the formal relationships between songs and symphonies is embodied for me not only in the forms of individual songs and symphonic movements but also in the dominant idea of the 'frame', that is, the idea of a first movement outlining the start of a narrative or interior drama and a finale supplying the dénouement, the resolution of what has intentionally been left incomplete; an elaborate example of this practice we have already encountered in the case of the Fourth Symphony. Mahler's first song-cycle, the *Lieder eines fahrenden Gesellen*, certainly had unfolded a narrative, but a 'frame' there was not; in *Kindertotenlieder*,

---

[1] On the assumption that is, that the symphony, in its Adagio, quotes from the song-cycle's second song. See, however, Ch. 9 nn. 38 and 39 above, and pp. 213–14.

[2] See Mitchell, *WY*, 40–3 and 322–3.

however, 'frame' and narrative are virtually indissoluble, and were to remain so until the very end of Mahler's life, as indispensable, for example, to the form and total experience of the Tenth Symphony in *its* entirety as to the First (something we should never have known, by the way, if it had not been for Deryck Cooke's feat of creative scholarship in transcribing Mahler's composition sketches).

It is just this remarkable dimension, generated by the preceding symphonies, that constitutes a unique feature of *Kindertotenlieder*. Who could have predicted that an outwardly 'poetic' sequence of songs, narrow in focus—each song in its way a meditation on mortality, on the special poignancy of the loss of children—and seemingly devoid of the possibility of 'drama', of narrative progression, should in fact represent one of Mahler's subtlest and most sophisticated treatments of both 'frame' and narrative.[3] At this stage in the development of his phenomenal compositional techniques, *Kindertotenlieder* revealed the clearest indication of the coincidence of song-cycle and symphony, though in fact it is only in recent years that the unique characteristics of the work have been recognized.

It is helpful, I believe, to consider the 'frame' first, comparing the first song, 'Nun will die Sonn' so hell aufgeh'n', and the fifth, 'In diesem Wetter, in diesem Braus'. In the first song, the image—message—of the poet is ultimately one of hope: that the sun will after all rise again and disperse the darkness and shadows of the night. Mahler brilliantly mirrors the poet's imagery by purely musical means. He sets out by striking a note of mourning, of grief (D minor), and then, in the second half of the first stanza, moves gradually towards D *major*—the promise that the sun *will* rise; it is out of this initial alternation of minor and major, the accents of grief giving way to hope (or if not hope, then at least consolation), through this basic minor/major contrast, that the eventual 'goal' of the work is established. Mahler is careful not to establish D major at the end of the first song, as careful as he had been not to release too early the competing tonic, E major, in the Fourth Symphony, and as careful, as he was to prove to be again in the Fifth, to avoid a premature affirmation of D. The outcome in the first song had to remain open; and indeed it is to be the chief function of the finale to resolve the D minor/D major conflict, as we shall see.

The first song not only initiates the evolution of the frame—by implication there has to be a finale to complete it—but also discloses in its own method of formal organization a novel relationship with symphonic form, specifically first-movement sonata form. For the characteristic duality of that historic formal scheme—in Mahler's own time and in many of his own symphonies this continued to survive in the shape of emphatically contrasting first

---

[3] Perhaps it might be useful here to be reminded of my definition of the 'narrative idea' in Mahler, i.e. the practice of 'not ending up where one had started' which was developed by the composer 'across his symphonies, from first to last, into the concept of the "frame", where the finale not only lands us up somewhere else [Heaven, as it happens, in the Fourth, an ecstatic Void in *Das Lied*, acceptance (of death?) in *Kindertotenlieder*] but also brings to a conclusion what the first movement (or song) had, so to say, left unfinished in terms of narrative; and to the completion of the narrative Mahler added a further dimension, the resolution of a con-

flict, a drama, outlined in the first movement (or first song in the case of the song-cycles). Thus the *dénouement*, both musical and narratory, is kept for the very final stage. The tension between these two poles sustains the thread of continuity throughout the often varied intervening middle movements and songs.' See *GMWL*, to which I contributed an article on 'The Orchestral Song-Cycles', 2.120–2.139. It is from that text that these comments on *Kindertotenlieder* have been taken in a revised form. See also Mitchell, *SSLD*, 74–108.

and second subject groups, despite the tonic/dominant axis having been drained of its original form-building power—for that now disestablished complex of dualities, Mahler substitutes a fresh duality, the juxtaposition and alternation of D minor and D major,[4] while each of the four stanzas in the song also plays the role created for it by a novel application of sonata form to strophic song. To be precise, Stanza 1 = Exposition; Stanza 2 = Repeat of Exposition; Stanza 3 = Development; and Stanza 4 = Recapitulation. I cannot stress too strongly the evolution of this unique formal scheme from the preceding symphonies and their preoccupation with sonata form and its potential. If one wants proof of that, then look back no further than to the first movement of the Fourth, to the critical moment of the lead-back—a passage I have already dwelt on in detail in the preceding chapter (see above, Ex. 9.1). The overlapping technique we hear again in *Kindertotenlieder*, at exactly the same structural juncture, at the end of the first song's third, developmental stanza: while the lead-back is still continuing, the recapitulation begins (see Ex. 10.1 overleaf).

The consequences of these formal innovations were to be immense, and nowhere more so than in the planning and execution of Mahler's last song-cycle, *Das Lied von der Erde*, a work built on a vastly more elaborate and extended scale.[5] However, immediate confirmation of the direct influence of *Kindertotenlieder* in matters of form on *Das Lied* is brought to us by the very first song of Mahler's last song-cycle, the outline scheme of which follows precisely the pattern of Stanza 1 of *Kindertotenlieder*, i.e. Stanza 1 = Exposition; Stanza 2 = Repeat of Exposition; Stanza 3 = Development; Stanza 4 = Recapitulation. Small wonder that Mahler's elucidating subtitle for *Das Lied* was 'Eine Symphonie' for solo voices and orchestra.

Before I continue with the sequence of the songs contained within the 'frame' of *Kindertotenlieder*, i.e. Songs 2, 3, and 4, I think logic demands that we take first the finale, the fifth song, which completes the 'frame', and proves to function, I suggest, precisely as I have sketched out in my opening paragraphs. The first movement having set up the conflict and the possible 'goal' which might resolve it, the finale proceeds to do just that, with perfect formal logic. The formal and narrative parallels with the Fourth are compelling.

What Mahler does in the song-cycle's finale, the fifth song, 'In diesem Wetter, in diesem Braus', is to dilate the initial contrast with which we are confronted in the first song, the

---

[4] Mahler had long been preoccupied with the expressive and symbolic potentialities of major and minor. From his earliest years he had made use of the device, examples too numerous and too familiar to spell out here. But I believe it was in *Kindertotenlieder* that, for the first time, he introduced the novel idea of the minor and major modes of the same key functioning, effectively, not only to characterize and occupy what previously might have been thought to be the contrasting territories which were the special preserve of first and second subject groups, but also in terms of longer-range tonal organization to replace the discarded functions of tonics and dominants. A case in point is the Ninth Symphony, its first and last movements in particular, in which this process is carried to yet further and more elabor-

ate lengths, i.e. the D major/D minor complex of the first movement, and its symmetrical reflection, a semitone lower, the D flat major/C sharp minor complex of the finale. All of this makes the more pointed Mahler's 'textbook' procedure in the first movement of the Fourth, in which the second subject is allotted its proper dominant in the exposition (Fig. 3) and re-emerges in the tonic of the recapitulation (Fig. 20^{+1}). This show of tonal rectitude is of course part of the work's aesthetic strategy, a deliberate 'pedantry' which can also, as Günter Grass suggests, wear the guise of 'playfulness' (see the epigraph to Ch. 9).

[5] See Mitchell, *SSLD*, 173–205; and *GMWL*, 2.132–2.139.

Ex. 10.1. *Kindertotenlieder*, 'Nun will die Sonn' so hell aufgeh'n'

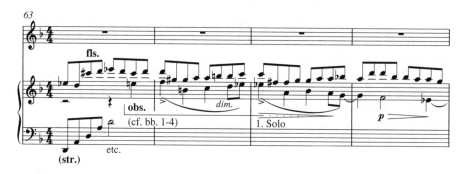

alternation of D minor and D major, on a greatly expanded scale. Indeed, the basic form of the finale is one huge, dichotomous strophe, the first part in a stormy D minor, from 'In diesem Wetter, in diesem Braus', the second part, from 'In diesem Wetter, in diesem Saus' (b. 99), a mitigating lullaby from which D major only very gradually emerges, finally to be established with and on the word 'ruh'n' (b. 119). The lost children have at last found peace, acceptance has been achieved: what was left an open question at the end of the first song has been answered. In a marvellous epilogue, the song of the solo horn reaffirms the attainment of what has been the work's goal, an unclouded D major. (The model for this postlude Mahler must have taken from Schumann, whose song-cycles are sometimes distinguished by a similar feature, an extended consummatory coda for the piano.)

I hope these comments on the 'frame' may make clear that it is through the first and fifth songs that we come to understand the 'story', the narrative, that this extraordinary cycle tells; some may be surprised by a suggestion that there is a narrative involved in so outwardly a 'poetic' work. And yet the truth is, surely, that a story is told each time the sun sets—and rises again? It is a recurring image that tells us something about the human condition, about the sunrise and sunset that are part and parcel of every single human life. In the last of the song-cycles, *Das Lied*, Mahler was again to pursue his constant preoccupation with matters of life and death—indeed, he was to do so until the sun set on his own life in 1911, with the Tenth Symphony left incomplete.

This might be the place, by the way, to clear up any misconceptions about an autobiographical interpretation of *Kindertotenlieder*. It is true that Mahler was to suffer the tragic loss of his elder daughter in 1907, but this was after the song-cycle had been composed. Nor, as some commentators have implied, was there a morbid, unnatural preoccupation on Mahler's part with the death of children. On the contrary, he transforms what might have been a topic too painful to dwell upon into an experience that is ultimately ennobling and itself transcendent, even of our sorrow at the loss of innocence, of lives intolerably abbreviated by the unpredictable and the unforeseen; that is what Mahler's 'storm' in the finale is about: it is an image of turbulent emotion—as in Britten's opera *Peter Grimes*—not a climatic event. Even so great a tempest of sorrow can be withstood; the psychic destruction caused by the 'storm' can be healed and at length accepted. The profound conciliation that Mahler's D major affirms at the conclusion of his finale is a philosophy to which he was to turn again in the finale of *Das Lied*.

The three songs that are contained within the frame in *Kindertotenlieder* are strongly contrasted, but at the same time each of them explores an aspect of loss; each unfolds a memory and a vision of the lost one or ones. The second, 'Nun seh' ich wohl warum so dunkle Flammen', reveals as its principal image eyes that now live on in the memory like stars burning in the night; in the third, 'Wenn dein Mütterlein', a father is constantly reminded of the void left by the loss of a daughter; the fourth, 'Oft denk' ich, sie sind nur ausgegangen', is again a memory, this time of the children who departed on a journey from which they were never to return; in an exultant, even ecstatic, coda (in E flat), the singer has a vision of the lost ones climbing ever higher, iridescent in radiant sunlight: 'Der Tag ist schön auf jenen Höh'n!'. But we have to live through the immediately ensuing storm of the first half of the fifth song before that vision is sublimely fulfilled.

Each of these interior songs, moreover, is strongly contrasted in orchestral treatment. The second, 'Nun seh' ich wohl', through-composed, with its passionately yearning appoggiaturas and prominent harp arpeggios, stands close in style and texture to the independent settings of Rückert texts but closest of all perhaps to the famous Adagietto (for strings and harp) from the Fifth Symphony, which, as I suggest in Chapter 11, is itself a 'song without words' for orchestra in the manner of the Rückert settings. All three songs are independent and each creates its own distinct world; but what must fascinate all students of Mahler are the common features of style, embracing both songs and symphonies, that lend this particular period its stylistic unity, a unity of techniques that Mahler developed and had at his disposal during the first decade of the new century. There is certainly no more convenient way of scrutinizing them than by observing how they function in Mahler's settings of Rückert, in the independent settings or *Kindertotenlieder*.

To conclude our survey of the three songs that form the middle part of the cycle, 'Wenn dein Mütterlein' and 'Oft denk' ich, sie sind nur ausgegangen', though inimitably Mahlerian in tone, traverse widely disparate historical traditions and styles. While the warm and glowing sixths of the horns at the opening of 'Oft denk' ich' vouchsafe resonances of, say, Brahms, the austere character of 'Wenn dein Mütterlein', where a long cor anglais solo is projected over a pizzicato bass, calls to mind, irresistibly, an aria or arioso by J. S. Bach, with the cor anglais playing a traditional obbligato role. Mahler was among the first to make overt gestures to the past, consciously to incorporate into his own work aspects of the history of music; on occasion taking distant predecessors, e.g. J. S. Bach, as models, using them as sources for his own creative innovations. Bach was a constant and profound stimulus to Mahler's imagination; but there were other composers too, representing a more immediate history, one of whom, Bedřich Smetana (1824–84), was bound up with the history of Mahler's own life and experience as a performing artist—as a conductor, that is, and yet more specifically, as a conductor in the opera house.

Many years ago now I isolated in *Kindertotenlieder* a melodic contour in the second song, 'Nun seh' ich wohl', that quite clearly had its origins in a virtually identical vocal contour from the entombment of the doomed lovers in the final act of Verdi's *Aida*.[6] A crucial contour, one might say, because, as I point out above (see pp. 213–14), it is also to be found in the E minor lament of the Adagio of the Fourth, either as a quotation from, or as an anticipation of, the song in question; and what unites all three manifestations of an identical contour is their common source in feelings (whether Mahler's or Verdi's) of pain, suffering, grief, and awareness of mortality.

This conjunction of musical imagery fascinated me at the time because it showed, on however a miniature scale, how Mahler's imagination might be serviced by external sources; how an identical dramatic or poetic situation might give rise to identical music; how, in the first instance, the idea might owe its origins to the hand of another creator altogether. This is not to diminish the transformation the idea would undergo, whereby it would attain its own unique Mahlerian character. But it memorably vouchsafes a glimpse of how a composer's set of distinctive responses may initially be shaped by ideas, by invention, other than his own, above all by specific ideas situated in specific contexts, which, albeit unconsciously, have made a quite specific impression on him. (They must also have exerted a quite special and profound *appeal*.) Opportunities thus to sink a tiny illuminating shaft into a composer's psyche are few and far between. This particular example enables us at least to understand why, yes, it had to be *that* idea that seized Mahler's imagination, and not another.

Smetana's operas were works that Mahler knew well and often had conducted himself. I have written elsewhere about possible meaningful influences of Smetana on Mahler, meaningful in the sense that I have just defined above, i.e. they extend well beyond the reach of explanation as casual or inadvertent reminiscence.[7] Thus a special savour was attached to uncovering the same influential contour that I had identified in *Aida*, in Smetana's opera *Dalibor*. Mahler conducted a celebrated production of the work at the

---

[6] See Mitchell, *WY*, 38–9. A further striking Verdi parallel has been brought to my attention by the kindness of O. W. Neighbour. See *La Traviata*, Act III, Violetta's aria, 'Addio, del passato' (A minor!), which clearly influenced the contour of the melody of the second trio (A minor!) of the 'Trauermarsch' in the Fifth.

[7] See ibid. 209, and Donald Mitchell, 'Mahler and Smetana: Significant Influences or Accidental Parallels?', in Stephen E. Hefling (ed.), *Mahler Studies* (Cambridge: Cambridge University Press, 1997), 110–21. See also p. 49 n. 26 above.

Vienna Opera in 1897, but of course had known the opera—indeed conducted it—long before then. Once again, it is not the replica of Smetana's idea (see Ex. 10.2, bb. 286–9) that is of principal interest, though it demonstrates how familiar Mahler was with the music of his great Czech predecessor. (It is a replication by the way that also embraces timbre and instrumentation, primarily plaintive woodwind in both instances.) What is significant—as in the comparable case of *Aida*—is again the conjunction of imagery. In Smetana's

Ex. 10.2. Smetana, *Dalibor*

Ex. 10.2. *cont.*

Dalibor, my Ex. 10.2 is generated by the mourning of Milada for her brother, the murdered Burgrave of Ploškovice. The idea stayed with Mahler and then took vital shape in the third song of *Kindertotenlieder*, 'Wenn dein Mütterlein', as Ex. 10.3 shows (cf. bb. 3–4, et seq.). It is singular indeed that two operas, one by Verdi, one by Smetana,[8] should have been influential in the making of Mahler's second song-cycle; singular, without doubt, but not surprising given the shared context of grief and sorrow. For in a very real sense, the choice of *musical* image had already been made for Mahler by his predecessors, before he began to compose his own sequence of threnodies.

The anatomy of the compilation of Mahler's musical imagery, especially, it would seem, in the field of mourning, is undeniably an absorbing topic. But it must give way to something, I think, of greater significance. I have mentioned above how, in the Fourth

[8] Parallels between Smetana and Mahler offer an enterprising student of Mahler—of both composers, perhaps—a valuable research topic that has still not been thoroughly explored. What I have written about Ex. 10.2 from *Dalibor* by no means exhausts the interest of this passage, where in fact one finds juxtaposed with the contour that has particularly claimed my attention a type of appoggiatura-laden, surging chromaticism (strings prominent!) that is also typical of *Kindertotenlieder* (e.g. the cycle's second song), albeit Mahler's version of this style is more sophisticated and refined than Smetana's. (See Ex. 10.2, b. 290 et seq.)

Ex. 10.3. *Kindertotenlieder*, 'Wenn dein Mütterlein', bb. 1–15

Symphony, the concept of the 'chamber orchestra' is already a presence: it became, one might say, in Mahler's hands, a combination of slender resources and counterpoint, both of which innovations are foreshadowed in the symphony. The very first ten bars of the opening song of *Kindertotenlieder* establish the new world of sound; we hear (voice apart), only one oboe, one horn, and two bassoons (strings and harp enter only at the end of the tenth bar: see also Ch. 11 n. 109). This was a revolutionary development, and it requires a note to itself.

Mahler and the Chamber Orchestra

On 29 January 1905 a remarkable concert took place in Vienna (and was repeated on 3 February).[9] It was advertised as a 'Lieder-Abend mit Orchester'—an 'Evening of Songs with Orchestra'—and it was given in the Kleiner Musiksaal—the small hall (also known as the Brahmssaal)—of the Musikverein. Three singers participated—Anton Moser (baritone), Fritz Schrödter (tenor), and Friedrich Weidemann (baritone)—and the orchestra, made up of members of the Vienna Philharmonic, was conducted by Gustav Mahler.

The programme consisted exclusively of Mahler's songs with orchestra (see Pls. 10.1 and 10.2). It included a number of his 'Wunderhorn' settings, among them two of the most recent that he had composed, 'Revelge' and 'Der Tamboursg'sell'. They were also to prove to be the last settings of 'Wunderhorn' poems that Mahler was to compose (see below). Indeed, he had already turned to a new poetic world of imagery and feeling represented by the lyrical poems of Friedrich Rückert (1788–1866). Two of Mahler's Rückert settings, now among the most celebrated of his orchestral songs—'Ich bin der Welt abhanden gekommen' and 'Um Mitternacht'—brought the programme to an end. But there was also another Rückert item on the programme, the first performance of *Kindertotenlieder*, composed between 1901 and 1904, in which Weidemann was the baritone soloist.

We can surmise from the programme announcement what Mahler was after. Something novel, to be sure: an evening of songs—a 'Lieder-Abend'—with a rather special kind of orchestra in place of the customary piano, performed in an acoustic and a hall appropriate to the intimacy implied by the title of the programme. The substitution was seized on by one of the critics attending the later Graz performance and used—inevitably—to make an *adverse* point:

In his *Kindertotenlieder* (to words by Rückert), Gustav Mahler has treated a subject that is in part related to [Otto] Naumann's [*Der Tod und die Mutter*, a large-scale choral work performed at the same Festival]; but there is no doubt that in his choice of resources he reveals himself the superior

---

[9] The programme was virtually identical with that of 29 Jan. but Marie Gutheil-Schoder (mezzo-soprano) joined the team of soloists and contributed a group of 'Wunderhorn' songs that included the première of 'Lob des hohen Verstandes'.

Pl. 10.2. The repeat performance of the 'Lieder-Abend' in Vienna, 3 February 1905, when the programme and soloists were slightly varied (Gutheil-Schoder had not participated in the first concert)

Pl. 10.1. The programme of Mahler's 'Lieder-Abend mit Orchester', Vienna, 29 January 1905

artist since, in order to stage this miniature domestic tragedy, he needs only a small orchestra and a single vocal soloist. It should be added that the merits and inwardness of Mahler's songs continue even today to provoke lively and heated discussion. And not without good reason. Far from warming their hearts, Mahler's new songs from *Des Knaben Wunderhorn* simply seem to have left their audiences hot under the collar.

In terms of their craftsmanship, each of these songs is a phenomenon unto itself, and there is no other orchestra that sounds like Mahler's chamber orchestra. Its characteristic qualities are its tearfully muted trumpets, its thrusting sforzati, its rattling side drums and so on. As an example of humour in music, the 'Fischpredigt des heiligen Antonius' is a collector's item with its leering thirds, its strokes of the switch [*Rute*] and bubbling cymbal tremolo [*Tschinellenwirbeln*]. These vocal character pieces reveal tremendous artistry in their execution; but in those places where the profundities of simple emotion are to be laid bare, not even the most sophisticated musical staging can hide the fact that the musical emotion often has little depth to it. Among all Mahler's songs, there is not one in which a great and impassioned idea pulsates from start to finish, as it does, for example, in Wolf's Suleika setting, 'Hochbeglückt in deiner Liebe', which positively burns with emotional fire. At the same time, there are some songs by Mahler that it is impossible to remember but which, at the same time, are impossible to forget. What an impression was left by 'Der Tamboursg'sell'! And by the *Kindertotenlieder*! The mere fact that Mahler has chosen such touchingly beautiful poems as the poetic basis for his songs would speak volumes for him and for the musician in him. But once again we have the same fussy instrumentation, which is no doubt a pleasure to listen to, but which seems so 'studied' and affected, often contradicting the naive and popular melodies that Mahler uses. One is left wondering whether the orchestra, however subtly it may be deployed, is really the best means of expression for the lied? Or is it not, rather, the piano, an instrument which, in its artistic way, merely hints at what the orchestra expresses more robustly? . . . Be that as it may: whatever objections one may have to Mahler and however much he may repel or fascinate his listeners, he has real personality and is one of the most complex figures ever to have existed. Whether vocal music will develop further on the basis of his art is something that no one can tell today.[10]

Well, at least the critic in question recognized the unique sound of Mahler's chamber-orchestral concept, something to which perhaps these days we pay too little attention, especially in the field of performance practice.

Mahler's radical reduction of his orchestral forces in *Kindertotenlieder* is self-evident in the areas of woodwind, brass, and percussion; they are spelled out by the composer. But what about the strings? We have no precise instructions from the composer, though surely the physical circumstances of the première serve as an indicator of the string forces for which he conceived the work. The choice of the Kleiner Musiksaal speaks for itself; and we know too that not only was the same hall used on 3 February for the repeat of the 29 January programme but that a similar chamber-music venue in Graz (the Stephaniensaal) was also chosen for the programme on 1 June, when Mahler was again the conductor (see Pl. 10.3).

---

[10] This (unsigned) article appeared in the *Grazer Tagespost*, No. 161, of 11 June 1905. The performance itself had been given on 1 June. Dr Renate Hilmar-Voit, whose seminal study I mention on p. 229, has been unfailingly generous in providing me with much of the information and illustrations on which this section of the chapter is based.

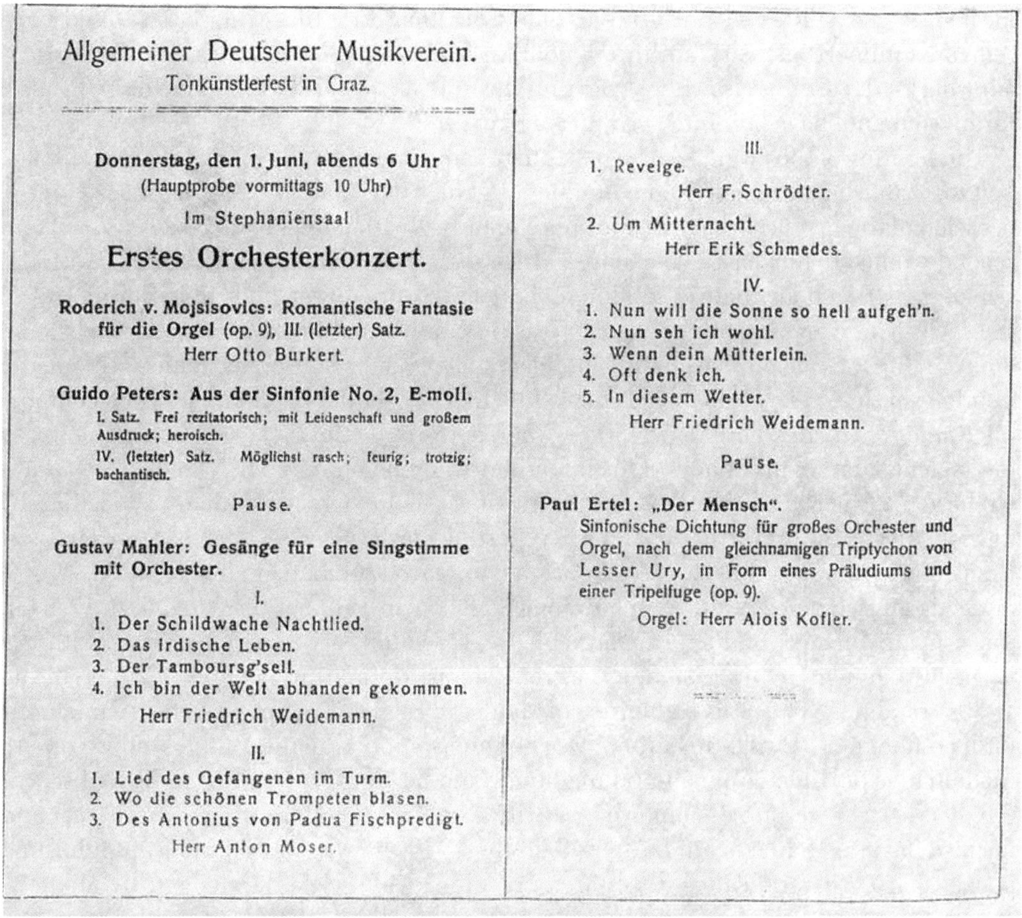

Allgemeiner Deutscher Musikverein.
Tonkünstlerfest in Graz.

Donnerstag, den 1. Juni, abends 6 Uhr
(Hauptprobe vormittags 10 Uhr)

Im Stephaniensaal

Erstes Orchesterkonzert.

Roderich v. Mojsisovics: Romantische Fantasie
für die Orgel (op. 9), III. (letzter) Satz.
Herr Otto Burkert.

Guido Peters: Aus der Sinfonie No. 2, E-moll.
I. Satz. Frei rezitatorisch; mit Leidenschaft und großem
Ausdruck; heroisch.
IV. (letzter) Satz. Möglichst rasch; feurig; trotzig;
bachantisch.

Pause.

Gustav Mahler: Gesänge für eine Singstimme
mit Orchester.

I.

1. Der Schildwache Nachtlied.
2. Das irdische Leben.
3. Der Tamboursg'sell.
4. Ich bin der Welt abhanden gekommen.
Herr Friedrich Weidemann.

II.

1. Lied des Gefangenen im Turm.
2. Wo die schönen Trompeten blasen.
3. Des Antonius von Padua Fischpredigt.
Herr Anton Moser.

III.

1. Revelge.
Herr F. Schrödter.

2. Um Mitternacht.
Herr Erik Schmedes.

IV.

1. Nun will die Sonne so hell aufgeh'n.
2. Nun seh ich wohl.
3. Wenn dein Mütterlein.
4. Oft denk ich.
5. In diesem Wetter.
Herr Friedrich Weidemann.

Pause.

Paul Ertel: „Der Mensch".
Sinfonische Dichtung für großes Orchester und
Orgel, nach dem gleichnamigen Triptychon von
Lesser Ury, in Form eines Präludiums und
einer Tripelfuge (op. 9).
Orgel: Herr Alois Kofler.

Pl. 10.3. The Graz Festival, 1 June 1905. The programme of the 'Mahlersoirée' in the Stephaniensaal

His consistent choice of a small hall, which only permitted the employment of a much reduced string band, has been fascinatingly illuminated by some recent and telling research by Renate Hilmar-Voit, who has enterprisingly investigated two Viennese archives in search of the sets of orchestral parts that Mahler might have used for his 'Lieder-Abend' in January 1905.[11] So far, it is only the parts for the 'Wunderhorn' settings that have come to light, together with those for one Rückert setting, 'Blicke mir nicht in die Lieder', for the performance of which, it seems, Mahler could have employed a maximum orchestra of thirty-six players![12] Parts for *Kindertotenlieder* and the other Rückert songs have to be

[11] See 'Symphonic Sound or in the Style of Chamber Music? The Current Performing Forces of the *Wunderhorn* Lieder and the Sources', *News about Mahler Research*, no. 28 (Oct. 1992), 8–12.

[12] The song is scored for a wind quintet —flute, oboe, clarinet, bassoon, and horn— harp, and strings (less double basses), for which reason it is possible that an even smaller number of strings would have participated in this song than

located, if they still exist. But it seems safe to assume that the string band would have remained numerically constant throughout, in *Kindertotenlieder*, at least, while perhaps allowing for departures elsewhere from the 'norm'. In any case, the size of the hall (the platform) would not have permitted significant expansion.

The scrutiny of the original string parts that had come to hand enabled Renate Hilmar-Voit to establish an average for the number of strings that Mahler might have used on the occasion of the first performance and subsequently: 8–10 players respectively for first and second violins; 6–8 violas; 4–6 cellos; 2–4 basses, a total that strongly contrasts with the size of the string body that we still too often hear in our concert halls in performances of the cycle. There are undoubtedly grey areas remaining, and further research needs to be done.[13] But we can be reasonably confident that Hilmar-Voit's speculations about the numbers of string players involved come close to what Mahler had in mind when composing *Kindertotenlieder*. Perhaps in future, when performing the cycle, we should attempt to implement what we now know of his intentions when he mounted his 'Lieder-Abend mit Orchester' in the Kleiner Musiksaal of the Musikverein in Vienna in January 1905, thereby introducing to the world his chamber-orchestral masterpiece. It seems, however, as if Benjamin Britten, without the benefit of statistics or research, had already, in the 1960s, perfectly apprehended Mahler's requirements. It was in 1966, at the Aldeburgh Festival, that I heard Britten conduct a remarkable interpretation of *Kindertotenlieder*, with the English Chamber Orchestra and, as baritone soloist, John Shirley-Quirk. Britten, in the 1930s, was among the earliest admirers of Mahler in England and possessed an ear famous for its refinement. At that time, there was no information available of the kind we owe to the initiative of Hilmar-Voit, and I thought it would be highly interesting to try to discover the precise string resources employed by Britten on the basis alone of his intuitive ear and his insights into Mahler's mind. After all, in the 1930s he was writing in his unpublished pocket diary, *Kindertotenlieder* 'restores my faith in life' (1935); 'cheered by Mahler's glorious *Kindertotenlieder*' (same year); 'Listen also for the 12th time to Mahler's peerless *Kindertotenlieder*' (same year); '. . . play Mahler's divine *Kindertotenlieder*. I feel it is worth having lived, if only for those little miracles' (1936); and finally, in the same year, 'Music that I think I love more than any other'.[14]

I cannot say that I was altogether surprised, given the discrimination of Britten's ear, by what I found: that the numbers of players he used almost exactly conformed to Hilmar-Voit's suggested averages. These were the figures for Britten in 1966: 9 first violins; 8 seconds; 4 violas; 5 cellos; 2 (!) double basses. I find them remarkable and convincing confirmation, arrived at through consideration of the score alone, of Hilmar-Voit's calcula-

Hilmar-Voit's 'average'. *Kindertotenlieder* apart, did Mahler perhaps adjust the size of the string body according to the individual needs of each independent song? See also *GMWL*, 2.127 and 129, where the statistics in respect of 'Blicke mir nicht' should be corrected.

[13] For example, there is an intriguing reference by Mahler in the context of his correspondence with Strauss

(see below, n. 16) to '*twenty-four* Philharmonic players', but this could not possibly represent a total, i.e. the final song of *Kindertotenlieder* alone requires minimal forces well in excess of that number.

[14] See also the section on 'Britten and Mahler' in Ch. 26 below.

tions extrapolated from the evidence available to her. Is it not high time that Mahler's performing practice in 1905, Britten's in 1966, and Mark Wigglesworth's in 1993,[15] should be widely adopted, with modification only when *Kindertotenlieder* is to be played in an acoustic larger than that envisaged by Mahler? With his own acute sensitivity to acoustic space he would surely himself have adapted his resources according to the needs of the particular occasion; but that does not mean that we should not ourselves be equally sensitive, whatever the occasion, to Mahler's explicit wishes, that is, continually to keep in mind the ideal acoustic space for which these songs were created.

The truth is that *Kindertotenlieder* represents what, for Mahler, was *his* form of chamber music—in his case, *vocal* chamber music, with a small, highly selective instrumental ensemble accompanying the voice. So much is confirmed by what Mahler himself wrote to Richard Strauss from Vienna in May 1905:

Dear Friend

I do not desire a 'special position' [i.e. the 'preferential treatment' Strauss mentions in the letter to which Mahler replies]! That would be a great misunderstanding on your part. Only a *small hall* for my songs that would be performed in the manner of *chamber music* [*Kammermusikton*]. — And just because I should not wish to take away an *evening*, I suggest a matinée. And in the interests of the *whole* it does not seem dignified to put on a few songs as the *conclusion* of a *Festival*. . . . Moreover, you yourself know best that I am not forcing myself upon you, and that I really am not vain. — Here, for artistic reasons (despite all the pressure of 'commercial' considerations), I have put on these songs only in the *small* hall [i.e. in the Kleiner Musikvereinssaal, in January], and they were only appropriate there. To perform them in a large hall to round off a Festival is *decidedly lacking in taste* and really would expose us to those reproaches!

Mahler goes on to add in a postscript:

. . . I suggested the songs, as they are less trouble to prepare, being a more modest gift. But as they *are* being performed, it must be done in appropriate style. So—only in the small hall!

That I should cut a better figure at a large festival concert is self-evident. So it cannot be ostentation on my part to prefer a matinée in the small hall. —

To round off the story, Strauss wrote to Mahler on 18 August: 'I have had enthusiastic reports of your songs in Graz from many friends . . .'.[16]

---

[15] See the Aldeburgh Festival Programme Book for 1966, pp. 27–9 and 52, and the programme for the London Philharmonic Orchestra concert conducted by Mark Wigglesworth, at the Royal Festival Hall, London, 7 Dec. 1993. On 26 May 1994 I contributed a lecture to the British Library's Stefan Zweig Series entitled 'Mahler's Chamber Music: His Late Orchestral Songs', an altogether wider investigation of his 'Kammermusikton' than is possible here. In a slightly amended form I read this same paper at Oxford on 31 Oct. 1995, as part of a series of seminars, 'Gustav Mahler and *fin de siècle* Vienna', convened by Daniele Reiber and James Ross.

[16] Mahler had his way, and when the 'Lieder-Abend' was repeated at Graz on 1 June 1905, as part of the Tonkünstlerfest des Allgemeinen Deutschen Musikvereins, the concert was given in the Stephaniesaal. The programme, substantially, was the same as its Vienna counterpart, but Gutheil-Schoder (a later addition) did not participate and the original team of male singers was joined by Erik Schmedes (tenor). The exchange of letters between Mahler and Strauss is to be found in *Gustav Mahler–Richard Strauss: Correspondence 1888–1911*, ed. Herta Blaukopf, trans. Edmund Jephcott (London: Faber, 1984), 77–82.

The Two Last 'Wunderhorn' Songs, 'Revelge' and 'Der Tamboursg'sell'

By 1905 Mahler had completed his *Kindertotenlieder* and independent settings of Rückert, and thenceforth, undeniably, when we are considering the interplay and interpenetration between song and symphony, it is the Rückert songs that play the role in the symphonies that had formerly been played by the 'Wunderhorn' songs, though the relationship now assumed new shapes, new orchestral sounds, and—in *Kindertotenlieder* above all— opened up new formal vistas. But the completion of the Fourth Symphony, and the shift— unequivocally anticipated in that symphony—in the succeeding trinity of symphonies, Five, Six, and Seven, exclusively to the orchestra (no orchestral paraphrases of songs, no vocal signposts), did not, in my view, mark the complete break with the 'Wunderhorn' past that it has so often been taken for; indeed, as I shall come to suggest in my discussion of the unique characteristics of the Fifth Symphony, the 'Wunderhorn' world that Mahler had made his own up to the turn of the century was still, after it, a potent creative force; it had not been abandoned so much as assumed new guises. In this crucial cross-centuries evolution, it was the two final 'Wunderhorn' settings, 'Revelge' (1899) and 'Der Tamboursg'sell' (1901), through which, in significant part, the transition to the 'new' symphonic manner was effected.

About the latter song, Mahler spoke at length to the invaluable Bauer-Lechner— Mahler's Boswell!—in the summer of 1901, adding the comment that 'he felt sorry for himself that he should have to write 'Der Tamboursg'sell' and the *Kindertotenlieder,* and he felt sorry for the world that would have to hear them one day, so terribly sad was their content.'[17]

As Mahler himself recognized, these are indeed tragic, ironic, sometimes desperate songs, both of them—I use these words advisedly—towering masterpieces and each of them a march, in the case of 'Revelge' a vocal march of epic proportions. There is nothing quite like this elsewhere in music, nor in Mahler's vocal music. We come to realize, moreover, that these last two 'Wunderhorn' settings reverse the hitherto established relationship of song to symphony: in 'Revelge' and 'Der Tamboursg'sell' it is symphony that is now fertilizing song. It is not at all fanciful to regard these extraordinary songs as the spiritual ancestors of the great opening march movements that distinguish the ensuing trinity of symphonies, Five, Six, and Seven.

The sheer scale of the songs speaks for itself, as does the high profile allotted the orchestra alone. Each song inhabits a unique sound-world,[18] a consequence of the orchestra's transformation into something approximating to military wind bands. Percussion is prominent. The strings themselves in 'Revelge' are used as a percussive resource, while in 'Der Tamboursg'sell' only the lower strings—exclusively cellos and double basses—are

---

[17] NB-L, *Recollections*, 173.   [18] See also Mitchell, 'Mahler's "Lieder-Abend": Many Songs, Many Orchestras'.

employed. The *intensity* of this music has few parallels, even elsewhere in Mahler. These final 'Wunderhorn' settings remind us of one central truth about his approach to his texts, that for him the poems were not artificial evocations or revivals of a lost age of chivalry and German Romanticism but, with the exception of a few genial, sunny inspirations, vivid enactments of *reality*, of sorrow, heartbreak, terror, and pain. The 'Wunderhorn' songs often tell a chilling truth about the human condition.

It is generally received opinion that the 'Wunderhorn' songs contributed fundamentally to the character and period of Mahler's first four symphonies, while it was the Rückert settings, albeit in a different way, which made a contribution of scarcely less importance to the character and period of the symphonies from the Fifth onwards. That was a view to which I subscribed, perhaps helped formulate, myself; and it remains largely true. But there is no doubt in my mind now that it represents an over-simplification, and in particular overlooks the peculiar complexities of the overlapping(!) that occurred during this critical phase of evolution. This is fascinatingly represented by a passage from 'Der Tamboursg'sell', one of the crowning glories of the 'Wunderhorn' world, which, on examination, unequivocally has its roots in the 'new' style that Mahler was developing in *Kindertotenlieder* and independent Rückert settings: not only a unique slenderness of sound but—counterpoint! Moreover, in 'Der Tamboursg'sell' it takes the canonic shape that is often at the heart of the counterpoint in *Kindertotenlieder* and the Rückert songs. In the remarkable passage I quote as Ex. 10.4 we have, so to say, stepped out of the 'Wunderhorn' world and—in compositional techniques, I must emphasize, *not* character—into the world of the Rückert songs. The point is clearly made if we compare Ex. 10.5 from *Kindertotenlieder* (song 1) with Ex. 10.4 from 'Der Tamboursg'sell'.

Everything—timbre, the slenderness of sound and refinement of instrumentation, the insistently canonic thinking—points to this singular coincidence of the 'Wunderhorn' and 'Rückert' worlds in these last 'Wunderhorn' settings. At the very time that he was, from one point of view, quitting that world, he was rethinking it in terms of the techniques that were to service the new world of song he was about to explore. As for the high profile allotted canonic formulations, it is not in *Kindertotenlieder* alone that we find striking examples. Some of the independent Rückert settings are rich in canonic activity, on a simple scale in 'Blicke mir nicht . . .', and on an elaborate, innovative scale in 'Ich bin der Welt . . .', the counterpoint of which directly anticipates the unique heterophonic polyphony of *Das Lied von der Erde* (see also Ch. 11, pp. 317 and 325 and n. 115). This is a huge subject in its own right. It must suffice for me to say here that in the evolution of the heterophony that was often to characterize—indeed, to revolutionize—Mahler's late contrapuntal style, an altogether logical developmental stage was the priority given to canonic thinking. Here too, then, there is further evidence of the signposts to later and radical events in Mahler's music that study of the two final 'Wunderhorn' songs, and of 'Der Tamboursg'sell' in particular, will reveal. It is entirely typical of Mahler that in the very songs that seemingly close the door on his 'Wunderhorn' period, he was at the same time opening a window on works to come as seemingly remote in style and contrasted in character as *Das Lied* (which,

Ex. 10. 4. 'Der Tamboursg'sell'

Ex. 10. 5. 'Nun will die Sonn' so hell aufgeh'n'

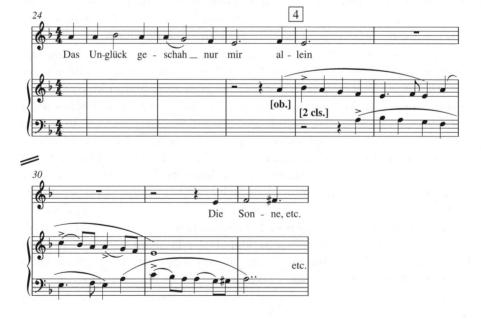

heterophony apart, is also rich in canonic incident!). Thus my Ex. 10.4 not only palpably 'belongs' to the mind that—I have no doubt—was already preoccupied with *Kindertotenlieder* but also to that same mind that was, four years later, to create *Das Lied*.

All this should make us cautious, as I have already remarked, about establishing clear lines of demarcation in pursuit of a tidy chronology. There were certainly shifts in textual sources, narrative preoccupations, and compositional techniques; but as I hope our scrutiny of the works, symphonies, and songs is beginning to show, there was no specific moment in the history of Mahler's creativity which one could describe as a condition of stasis. His oeuvre was always in a state of evolution, one thing beginning as another was ending, irrespective of genre or 'period'. 'Overlapping' which, as we have seen, surfaces not only in the first movement of the Fourth Symphony but also in the first song of *Kindertotenlieder*, at identical formal junctures, might well serve as a motto for the whole of this chapter; and indeed as we move into the final phase of it, and embark on an exploration of the Fifth Symphony, overlapping yet again must rivet our attention; for it is 'Der Tamboursg'sell' which proves to be the vehicle of transition to the new symphony's first movement, itself an epic 'Trauermarsch'. It is no more than the truth to claim, quite simply, that the last 'Wunderhorn' song from 1901 provides us with an upbeat to the symphony on which Mahler had started work in the same year, an upbeat both in general and in particular because, as we shall see confirmed by Ex. 11.1 in the next chapter, it is precisely an upbeat that is one of the features that distinguishes—and unites—the song that is a 'Trauermarsch' and the 'Trauermarsch' which is the movement with which the Fifth begins.

Additional note On pp. 226–35 above I raise the issue of 'Mahler and the Chamber Orchestra'. In this context it is fascinating to find that of a performance of Mozart's G minor Symphony conducted by Mahler at Carnegie Hall on 29 November 1910, the same occasion on which he conducted Elgar's 'Enigma' Variations (see p. 554 n. 4 below), the critic of the *New York Times* wrote: 'Mr. Mahler gave the audience a surprise. He had it played by a much reduced number of orchestral players, on the basis of eight first violins instead of the sixteen that make up the normal number of the orchestra. The other stringed instruments were reduced in proportion; some of the wind instruments were also lessened in number, but there were four flutes, though they did not always all play. The intention obviously was to give, as far as might be, the effect of such an orchestra as Mozart had in mind when he composed the symphony—an effect in which the wind instruments have a larger share than they have in performance of such works by the modern orchestra. But it may be doubted whether the results falling upon the ears of auditors in Carnegie Hall were such as were heard by listeners of Mozart's time; for they were those of a small orchestra in a large hall, instead of a small orchestra in a hall suited to its number. They were interesting results, however. The sonority was greater than was to be expected, and the quality of the orchestral color, with the increased proportion of the wind instruments, was no doubt new to many to whom the symphony has been a lifelong friend. It may be questioned whether this attempt was convincing to those who know the symphony as it is usually played in these days, or whether many will wish to hear Mozart's symphonic music hereafter in no other guise' (see Zoltan Roman, *Gustav Mahler's American Years: 1907–1911. A Documentary History* (Stuyvesant, NY: Pendragon Press, 1989), 415–16).

11

Eternity or Nothingness?
Mahler's Fifth Symphony

DONALD MITCHELL

To—and for—Riccardo Chailly

He was afraid she would ask him to explain something he had written, and he always winced at that—perhaps too timidly—for to his own ear the explanation of a work of art sounded fatuous.

Henry James, *The Lesson of the Master* (1892)

Part I

(i) 'Trauermarsch'; (ii) Stürmisch bewegt. Mit grösster Vehemenz ['Hauptsatz']

The 'Trauermarsch' and 'Der Tamboursg'sell'

As my Ex. 10.4 above has shown, and as I have already mentioned in the concluding sentence of the preceding chapter, the characterizing upbeat that distinguishes the last 'Wunderhorn' song, composed in July 1901, itself forms the no less characterizing and ubiquitous upbeat that is the distinguishing feature of the 'Trauermarsch' of the symphony. The song in fact comprises two funeral marches, the second appreciably slower than the first; it is virtually an independent Part II, an independence further emphasized by its own independent tonality and characterizing instrumentation: the first (vocal) march is accompanied by a military wind band, while the second emphatically introduces the strings. Here already is a manifestation of the dichotomy fundamental to the concept of the symphony, both its instrumentation and its narrative. In a typical gesture, Mahler, for Part II, forsakes the E minor of Part I, and shifts a whole tone downwards, to D minor. Thus the concluding march of the song is yet more sombre, yet darker, than its predecessor. The penultimate

Pl. 11.1. A page from Mahler's autograph full score of the Fifth Symphony. The passage comprises bars 351–8 (inclusive) of the second trio in the 'Trauermarsch'. Reproduced by kind permission of the Pierpont Morgan Library, New York (Robert Owen Lehman Deposit).

statement of the dead drummer-boy's last farewell, before night envelops him, his desperate 'Gute Nacht!', is launched, *fortissimo*, on the rhythm of the upbeat itself, returning the song in fact to the motive that was its genesis (bb. 4 and 156).

In the previous chapter I quoted Mahler's remark to Bauer-Lechner in August 1901 that shows how conscious he was of the burden of tragedy that both 'Der Tamboursg'sell' and *Kindertotenlieder* carried; an infinitely touching example I find it, of the artist's capacity (his need, perhaps?) to distance himself from his creations, to grieve for himself—that he is compelled to act as a vehicle of sorrow—and for the world that 'one day' would have to listen to the products of his grieving; and yet there is no hint of an option that might have relieved him of his burden to act, to create, to communicate, as spokesman for the suffering inherent in the human condition. Mahler's (I dare say) casual comment to Bauer-Lechner reminds us of how it is that the world itself learns *how* to suffer, from and through the work of artists, who suffer, without complaint for the most part, on the world's behalf.

It was on this same occasion, it seems, that he recounted to Bauer-Lechner how 'Der Tamboursg'sell' 'came into being':

[The song] occurred to him literally between one step and the next—that is, just as he was walking out of the dining-room. He sketched it immediately in the dark ante-room, and ran with it to the spring [adjacent to Mahler's land on the Wörthersee]—his favourite place, which often gives him aural inspiration. Here, he had the music completed very quickly. But now he saw that it was no symphonic theme—such as he had been after—but a song! And he thought of 'Der Tamboursg'sell'. He tried to recall the words; they seemed made for the melody. When he in fact compared the tune and the text up in the summer-house, not a word was missing, not a note was needed; they fitted perfectly![1]

It is a recollection, if accurate, that seems to anticipate a similar creative incident that was to occur a few years later: the first intimation of the music for 'Veni creator spiritus' in the Eighth, hurriedly written down in the absence of a full text which later proved to match up with the initiating musical genesis.[2]

But of more significance for our present purpose is the issue of chronology which the circumstances of the song's composition bring to the fore. It is already clear, I believe, from a comparison of Ex. 10.4 with Ex. 11.2, that 'Der Tamboursg'sell' and the opening 'Trauermarsch' of the symphony share the same world. My earlier quotation of a passage from the song's second march is sufficiently revealing; but if one juxtaposes the melody of the song's first march (Ex. 11.1) with the principal melody of the symphony's first movement (Ex. 11.2), from which I cite the march tune's second appearance (and expansion), the convergence is yet more striking. Moreover, while the first limb or contour of the march melody in either case adheres to the established pattern of a funeral march, each departs from that 'model' when embarking on its continuation or, as in the case of the song, a second (related) march is added by way of conclusion. In both cases, however, it is precisely

---

[1] NB-L, *Recollections*, 173. See also below, n. 10. On the specific significance of the Ballad form for Mahler, see *Additional note*, p. 325 below.

[2] See also Mitchell, *SSLD*, 523–6.

Ex. 11.1. 'Der Tamboursg'sell', bb. 1–30 (vocal score)

Ex. 11.2. Fifth Symphony, 1st movt., march melody

during the process of extension or addition that each march, in the song as in the symphony, incorporates references to a further prime source, the first song of *Kinder-totenlieder*: my Exx. 10.4 and 10.5 make this very point, the unique surfacing of the song-cycle's characterizing techniques in a 'Wunderhorn' context, thereby constituting what I designate Part II of 'Der Tamboursg'sell', while the evolution of the symphonic march, second time round, after its repeat of its basic march profile, itself seems to assume the character of the song's second march and, at the same time, even more closely approximates to the contours of 'Nun will' die Sonn' . . .'. Indeed, it is exactly this conscious or unconscious convergence that then logically permits the direct quotation from the song in which the final statement of the symphony's 'Trauermarsch' culminates, just before the onset of the first trio of the march at Fig. 15.

There are, then, three independent yet intimately related items for consideration,[3] each of which had a role to play in the critical period of transition following the completion of the Fourth Symphony: 'Der Tamboursg'sell', the first song of *Kindertotenlieder*, and the first movement, the 'Trauermarsch', of the Fifth, the movement which represented the first stage in a symphonic narrative in which, in my submission, the transition from the 'Wunderhorn' world to a new world, of which the move to settings of Rückert was emblematic, was accomplished. (I emphasize 'emblematic' because of course the innovations in form alone, not to speak of style, of manner, of technique, far outweigh the significance of setting fresh texts. There is no denying that the imagery of Rückert is something very different from the characteristic imagery of the 'Wunderhorn' anthology. But it would be simple-minded in the extreme to attribute Mahler's radical formal innovations, say, to his 'discovery' of Rückert. Other forces were at work; hence the critical importance of the Fourth, in which so much of the 'new' that was to come is anticipated. Nonetheless, 'Rückert' remains a useful shorthand to indicate the changes that were afoot.)

Everything, naturally, could be clarified if we were able to introduce into the jigsaw puzzle-like constellation of interrelationships a tidy chronological account of when the works, whether song, song-cycle, or symphony, were composed. First, some known dates and information of relevance. As my Table 11.1 shows, there are relatively few firm dates amid a quantity of information of probable chronological relevance. This is particularly true with regard to the detailed creative evolution of the symphony. What follows is inevitably largely conjectural; but it seems to offer, on the basis of our present knowledge, a reasonable account of when, and in what sequence, the Fifth came to be composed.

TABLE 11.1. CHRONOLOGY OF THE FIFTH SYMPHONY

1899	June/July	'Revelge', the first to be composed of the two last 'Wunderhorn' settings [see also 1901]
1900	5 August	Mahler completes the slow movement of his Fourth Symphony, thus bringing to a conclusion the symphony as a whole (the song-finale-to-be had been composed as an independent orchestral song (see Ch. 9, Ex. 9.1) in 1892). [See also Ch. 9 nn. 38 and 39 and Ch. 10 n. 1.]
1901	June/August	Mahler composes four of his independent Rückert settings, among them 'Ich atmet...' and 'Ich bin der Welt...'
	12 July	'Der Tamboursg'sell' composed in its voice and piano version
	25 July–10 August	'During these past few days, Mahler talked to me [Bauer-Lechner] for the first time about the work he is now engaged on, his Fifth Symphony, in particular the third movement, which he is writing at present' [NB-L, *Recollections*, 172]
	10 August	Mahler plays through 'Der Tamboursg'sell' to Bauer-Lechner, according to her diary [NB-L, *Recollections*, 173]

[3] There might be four if, as I speculate in Ch. 9 nn. 38 and 39 and Ch. 10 n. 1, further research on the chronology of the composition of *Kindertotenlieder* indicates a change in the relationship between the second song in the cycle and the slow movement of the Fourth Symphony, with its seeming 'quote' from, or reference to, 'Nun seh' ich wohl'.

TABLE 11.1. *continued*

1901	Summer[a]	*Kindertotenlieder*: three songs composed, among them 'Nun will' die Sonn' so hell aufgeh'n', the first song of the cycle
		Fifth Symphony: works (probably) on first three movements, i.e. the Scherzo (Part II) and the two movements of Part I ('Trauermarsch' and 'Stürmisch bewegt' [Allegro])
	end of year	Works on Adagietto (fourth movement)? [See below, pp. 315–17.]
	27 December	Announcement of engagement to Alma
1902	9 March	Marriage of Mahler and Alma
	Summer vacation (June–August)	'He had the sketches for his Fifth Symphony with him, two [*sic*] movements completed and the rest in their earliest stages' [Alma Mahler, *Memories*, 42]
		Fifth Symphony: Part III (movements four and five) completed
	Autumn	'He played me the completed Fifth Symphony' [Alma Mahler, *Memories*, 47]
1903	October	To initiate the publishing process, Mahler sends Alma's MS fair copy of the full score to Heinrich Hinrichsen, his publisher (Peters). His inscription to Alma ran as follows: 'Meinem lieben Almscherl, der treuen und tapferen Begleiterin auf allen meinen Wegen' Wien, Oktober 1903' ('To my dear Almscherl, the faithful and brave companion on all my journeys')
1904	Summer vacation (late June–August)	*Kindertotenlieder*: two further songs composed, the last and No. 2, 'Nun seh' ich wohl, warum so dunkle Flammen'. [See, however, 1900 and n. 3, above, and Ch. 10, p. 222.]
	September (Leipzig)	Publication by Peters of Study Score, the first printed edition of the symphony
	17 and 26 September (Vienna)	Two runs-through ('reading' sessions) with Vienna Philharmonic heighten Mahler's dissatisfaction with his scoring
		There was to follow a seemingly endless series of revisions that was to continue until the end of his life, though in fact the process had begun even in advance of the 'reading' sessions
	18 October (Cologne)	First performance of Fifth Symphony in Gürzenich concert hall (see Pl. 11.3 and 11.4)
	November	First edition of Full Score published, incorporating some of Mahler's revisions of Study Score
1905	13 March	First Hamburg performance of Fifth under Mahler. 'Brecher . . . told us . . . [the Scherzo] came first in order of composition' [Frau Dehmel's diary quoted in Alma Mahler, *Memories*, 92]
		At the general rehearsal on 12 March, Hermann Behn, a close musical friend of Mahler's, had made a note of the timings of the individual movements. Part I: $1 = 12''$; $2 = 15''$. Part II: $15''$. Part III: $1 = 9''$; $2 = 15''$. There was a pause of $2''$ between the 'Trauermarsch' and ensuing Allegro, a pause of $3''$ after the end of Part I and a pause of $3''$ after the Scherzo.[b]
1907	22 October (St Petersburg)	'By day I revised my Fifth Symphony' [Alma Mahler, *Memories*, 295]. See also pp. 524–5 below.
	9 November	The Fifth performed in St Petersburg
1908	(and after)	Constant revisions of orchestration of the Fifth [Alma Mahler, *Memories*, 143]

[a] No specific dates, but we know Mahler's vacation extended from early June until late August: these are generally assumed to have been his working months, compositionally speaking.

[b] See the 'Verbesseter Ausgabe' of the symphony, Vol. V in the Critical Edition published by C. F. Peters and the International Gustav Mahler Society, Vienna, ed. Karl Heinz Füssl (1988), p. iv. In 2001 the International Gustav Mahler Society, Vienna, announced for publication a new edition of the Symphony edited by Reinhold Kubik in association with Robert Threlfall.

First, we should bear in mind as a kind of backdrop to our consideration the singular fact that during the summer of 1901, more probably the early summer, Mahler was much preoccupied with the idea of death. Perhaps it was, as some have suggested, Mahler's nearmortal illness in February that made him peculiarly conscious of death as a neighbour.[4] On the other hand, the idea of death, above all as an imaginative source, had been part of his creative personality long before 1901; and again, can we really interpret *Kindertotenlieder* as a response to the sharp shock of being reminded of the possible and unpredictable immediacy of his own death? One must be cautious, in any event, to avoid the trap of confusing an artist's life and his art, while at the same time recognizing that, in this particular period, there was an altogether unusual *concentration* on the image of death in the works on which Mahler was currently engaged, varied though the genres were and widely differing in their modes of expression: *Kindertotenlieder*, 'Der Tamboursg'sell', the symphony's 'Trauermarsch'.

Questions of Chronology

Perhaps the best start on the chronology of the symphony can be made by focusing on the Scherzo, because it seems likely that this movement, which was to become Part II of the symphony, was the first to be completed.[5] For one thing, it is certain that Mahler had had a movement of this character in mind well before embarking on the Fifth, i.e. a Scherzo (in D major), entitled 'Die Welt ohne Schwere' (the world without gravity), had formed part of a draft programme for the Fourth, where it was located as a possible penultimate movement, preceding the 'himmlische Leben' finale.[6] We know for a fact that Mahler was working on the Scherzo between (early) June and 25 July because Bauer-Lechner documents a conversation with the composer in which he refers to it, describing it indeed in terms that almost precisely correspond to the title that formed part of the draft programme for the Fourth: 'Every note is charged with life, and the whole thing whirls around in a giddy dance…. There is nothing romantic or mystical about it; it is simply the expression of incredible energy. *It is a human being in the full light of day, in the prime of his life*' (my italics). Furthermore, in this same conversation, Mahler, it seems, told Bauer-Lechner that his new symphony was to be 'a regularly constructed symphony in four movements [*sic*], each of which exists for itself and is self-contained, linked to the others solely by a related mood'.[7] If that report is authentic, then it lends credibility to the supposition that the Scherzo was the first movement to be conceived, since it appears that even before the movement was completed Mahler still had no very clear idea of how the symphony as a whole was to be shaped (he could hardly have talked of a regular four-movement overall form if he had already had in mind, or in part worked on, two pairs of interdependent movements, i.e. Parts I and III of the symphony as we know it today).

[4] Notably La Grange; see HLG(E) ii. 367–9. See also Edward F. Kravitt, 'Mahler's Dirges for his Death', *Musical Quarterly*, 64 (1978), 329–53.

[5] See also n. 66 below.
[6] See Mitchell, *WY*, 138–9, and n. 67 below.
[7] NB-L, *Recollections*, 173.

There is one further bit of evidence that supports the view that the Scherzo was the first movement to materialize. This is a reference to be found in an excerpt from the diary of Ida Dehmel, the widow of Richard Dehmel, the German poet (1863–1920); it was Dehmel's poem 'Verklärte Nacht' that inspired Schoenberg's work of the same title. The Dehmels, it seems, were with the Mahlers in Hamburg in 1905, where the Fifth Symphony was performed on 13 March. Frau Ida wrote of the occasion:

This Fifth Symphony of his carried me through every world of feeling. I heard in it the relation of adult man to everything that lives, heard him cry to mankind out of his loneliness, cry to man, to home, to God, saw him lying prostrate, heard him laugh his defiance and felt his calm triumph. For the first time in my life a work of art made me weep, a strange sense of contrition came over me which almost brought me to my knees. The *Adagietto* may for me have lacked something, and in the last movement I noticed some check to the logical development. Nevertheless, this symphony is a masterpiece of the first rank, and at a second hearing it was precisely the last movement which engaged my passionate attention: I positively drank in every note. Mahler had warned me in advance that the Scherzo might seem obscure—no critic so far had known what to make of it. It was the Scherzo that made the strongest impression on you, as by the way it did on Brecher too, who told us it came first in order of composition . . .[8]

The 'Brecher' mentioned by Frau Ida was Gustav Brecher (1879–1940), the conductor, who collaborated with Mahler in the preparation of a new performing edition of Weber's *Oberon*.[9] He was a distinguished musician who had the opportunity to be close to Mahler and thus a source to be taken seriously, especially as he confirms what seems to be the credible chronology that may be extrapolated from Bauer-Lechner's recollections.

I believe, then, that everything points to the Scherzo as the first movement to be done, to be sketched out, perhaps while Mahler was still thinking of his new symphony as a four-movement shape. But to what next did Mahler turn his attention?

'Der Tamboursg'sell' again

At this point we must return to Bauer-Lechner's recollections and more specifically her memory of the composition of 'Der Tamboursg'sell'. This relevant excerpt has already appeared above; I shall only repeat here comments of particular relevance. Mahler, it seems, was searching for a 'symphonic theme' when what came to him was the march melody that proved then to be a song, the carrier of the text of 'Der Tamboursg'sell'. We know the song was written by 12 July 1901 (see Table 11.1), which means that Mahler in the weeks preceding that date, and on the assumption that he had brought the Scherzo to

---

[8] Alma Mahler, *Memories*, 91–2.

[9] Tragically, Brecher—a Jew—committed suicide with his wife in 1940, on board ship off the Belgian coast, while attempting to flee from the Nazi invaders. How ironic to reflect that Alma Mahler's stepfather, the Austrian painter Carl Moll (1861–1945), committed suicide for the opposite reason; he was known to be an anti-Semite and feared the liberation of Vienna by Russian troops as the Second World War came to an end, 'like a good many Viennese Nazis', as Alma herself remarks (Alma Mahler Werfel, *And the Bridge is Love* (London: Hutchinson, 1959), 274). Important information about Moll's tragic last years and hours can be found in G. Tobias Natter and Gerbert Frodl, *Carl Moll* (Vienna: Österreichische Galerie, 1998), the catalogue published to accompany the exhibition, 'Carl Moll: Maler und Organisator', at the Belvedere, Sept.–Nov., 1998.

completion (in outline at least), may have been seeking for the 'theme' (the crucial idea, perhaps?) that would get him going on the movements that remained to be composed; not only composed, but conceived.

All of this I hasten to emphasize must be speculative, until such time as more precise chronological information emerges (if ever). Meanwhile, we must do what we can with what the music tells us, often the best and most revealing source of all. It has always puzzled me a little that, according to Bauer-Lechner, when Mahler ran off to the spring with his new idea in his head, 'he saw that it was no symphonic theme . . . but a song!' I began to wonder, in fact, if it were not the case that 'Der Tamboursg'sell' and the possible setting of it had been stored away in Mahler's mind for who knows how long, and came, albeit unconsciously, to influence the contours and rhythm of the melody that surfaced in the summer of 1901 when he was in search of a 'theme' for his new symphony. This would account for what otherwise seems inexplicable, that the words, after the melody had been imagined, 'seemed made for the melody'.[10] But even if that did prove to be the case, the truth is, surely, that *it was the words that had given birth to the melody*, even if Mahler had not recognized the connection as he wrote the melody down.[11]

How the melody of 'Der Tamboursg'sell' came to take the shape it did is undeniably fascinating. But what is surprising, if Bauer-Lechner's recollection can be trusted, is Mahler's opinion—'no symphonic theme . . . but a song!'; perhaps not only surprising but amusing even, when one observes what I guess was the next creative step in the chronology of Mahler's summer activities, his embarking on the 'Trauermarsch' that was to form the first movement of Part I of the new symphony. Amusing, because—as I think I have already demonstrated by the juxtaposition of Exx. 11.1 and 11.2—the great march melody in the symphony is clearly a sibling of the song. If Mahler did indeed commit himself to the view that this type or character of theme was inherently alien to the concept of symphony, then he would have soon had to change his mind (eat his words would be the better metaphor, perhaps). For I have little doubt that once 'Der Tamboursg'sell' was, so to say, fulfilled and off the creative agenda, Mahler must have realized that the song, not only musically (that is to say, melodically) but also image-wise, provided him with the point of departure for

---

[10] Long after I had written this passage I was astonished to discover the following comment of Britten's, made in a broadcast interview with the Earl of Harewood in 1960. What he says goes a very long way indeed to confirm for me my guess about the sequence of creative events with regard to 'Der Tamboursg'sell'. This, as I have always supposed, is exactly how composers' minds work, whether they be a Britten or a Mahler: 'Quite often I find that I am in the mood for writing a song about a certain kind of subject or in a certain kind of mood, and I have even had in my experience the suggestion of a tune which would like to have words attached to it. I then look through volumes until I find such a thing, but nearly always, and I suppose this is where the subconscious comes in, it is a poem I've known, and I sus-

pect that that poem has been going on ringing in my subconscious, *and has produced the tune but I haven't been aware of it*' (my italics).

[11] For individual studies of 'Der Tamboursg'sell', see Susanne Vill, *Vermittlungsformen verbalisierter und musikalischer Inhalte in der Musik Gustav Mahlers* (Tutzing: Hans Schneider, 1979); Michael Johannes Oltmanns, ' "Ich bin der Welt abhanden gekommen" und "Der Tamboursg'sell"—Zwei Liedkonzeptionen Gustav Mahlers', *Archiv für Musikwissenschaft*, 43 (1986), 69–88, and Elisabeth Schmierer, *Die Orchesterlieder Gustav Mahlers* (Kassel: Bärenreiter, 1991), and ead., 'Between Lied and Symphony: On Mahler's "Tamboursg'sell" ', *News about Mahler Research*, no. 33 (Mar. 1995), 15–22.

the narrative that the new symphony was to unfold.[12] It is thus, I believe, that in this overlapping of the last 'Wunderhorn' setting with the 'Trauermarsch' of the symphony we can hear the 'Wunderhorn' tradition and influence sustained beyond the point where received opinion has it that the 'Wunderhorn' period ended, that is, with the Fourth Symphony. On the contrary, there seems to me to be good reason, as I suggested some years ago,[13] that the 'Trauermarsch' (not the trios!) might be regarded as an example of a wordless song for orchestra in his (late) 'Wunderhorn' manner. (In a work that is replete with singular symmetries and overlapping I shall have something to say later about the Adagietto in a similar context, though the movement owes its origins to Mahler's development of a quite different song style.)

The 'Trauermarsch'

The 'song' then that the orchestra sings in the 'Trauermarsch' is the same song—or a continuation and extension of it—that the doomed drummer sings in 'Der Tamboursg'sell'; and therein resides an overlapping with the long line of preceding 'Wunderhorn' songs which are specifically military in their imagery.[14] It was perhaps only appropriate, if somewhat grimly so, that the tradition should expire—but for its extension in the 'Trauermarsch'—in a song itself dedicated to the process of extinction. But having, I hope, established the relationship of 'Der Tamboursg'sell' to the new symphony, the next step must be to examine how this orchestral song functions as the initiator of the narrative that will unfold itself across the whole span of the symphony; above all to determine how Mahler sets up the basic conflict that the symphony must have resolved by the time it has ended, along with those indispensable indicators of the means, the mechanisms, by which that resolution will be achieved. As we shall see, the investigation of the narrative techniques involved mean that we have to take into account not only the 'Trauermarsch' but the succeeding A minor Allegro, 'Stürmisch bewegt. Mit grösster Vehemenz', the fast movement that constitutes the second part of the symphony's Part I.[15] It has often been suggested in the past that the bipartite concept of Part I represents a divorce of the idea of Exposition from the idea of Development, each process, in the opening two movements of the Fifth, occupying its own autonomous area. In a very loose descriptive sense, there is an element of truth in the observation. But as we shall see, in order to appreciate the unique

---

[12] Once again I must emphasize that any attempt to sort out the chronology of the Fifth's composition must be speculative. However, that the song was a prime source for the 'Trauermarsch' seems to me to be highly probable. Even if it proved otherwise—and I am not simply covering my tracks in the event of evidence surfacing that shows the reverse chronology to have been the case—it would make no great difference to the point of substance that I am trying to make, that is, it would leave unaffected the mutually influential and interdependent relationship between the two works.

[13] In a paper I contributed to the Rondom Mahler II Congress and Workshop, Rotterdam, May 1990, 'Mahler's "Orchestral" Orchestral Songs'. See also below at n. 97.

[14] e.g. 'Zu Strassburg auf dem Schanz'; 'Der Schildwache Nachtlied'; 'Lied des Verfolgten im Turm'; 'Wo die schönen Trompeten blasen', and of course 'Revelge', the first of the two last 'Wunderhorn' songs.

[15] Inscribed 'Hauptsatz' (main movement) by Mahler in his MS full score. However, this highly significant designation was not included in the first published edition of the symphony, nor thereafter.

characteristics of the Fifth we must be prepared to look at those old terms, Exposition and Development, in a new light.

Self-evidently, the 'Trauermarsch', through its song of sorrow, 'exposes' the theme of grief, of mourning, which is the symphony's starting point. The slow march makes its (brief) first appearance at Fig. 2, in the midst of the very grandly conceived ceremonial gestures which open the movement. At the start, of course, is the initiating fanfare for solo trumpet (see bb. 1–20), with which almost every commentator draws a parallel with the fanfare that intervenes at the height of the development of the first movement of the Fourth Symphony (at Fig. 17^{+4}). It is in the nature of fanfares to share common features, or so it seems to me; and the contexts in which the two fanfares are used are so very different that the parallel of the most obvious kind, of which we have heard most in the past, has struck me up to now as a distraction. It is a personal observation of Colin Matthews' that has made me change my mind, i.e. that the opening fanfare of the Fifth is launched on the same pitch—C♯—as its counterpart in the Fourth, a fact that is highly suggestive of a possible *narrative* relationship. The fanfare in the Fourth emerges at the very end of the development of the first movement, during which all manner of complexities, tensions, and confrontations have been revealed. The movement then returns to its state of grace and innocence; and eventually the symphony ends with a vision of 'heavenly life' (we are even permitted to hear in the last stanza of the 'Wunderhorn' song that is the symphony's finale the kind of music that awaits us if we are lucky: it will all be in E major). By recalling—or reviving—the fanfare from the Fourth—if that indeed were the case—was Mahler forcefully making the point that, albeit he had vouchsafed his audiences a glimpse of heaven at the end of the Fourth, the *larger* narrative that had underpinned his symphonic oeuvre from its outset—the established conflicts and combats—had by no means run its course?

There will be no disagreement, however, about the significance of Mahler's use of the fanfare at the beginning of the Fifth as an agent of overlapping. The Fourth, we may recall (see Ex. 9.1) is especially rich in examples of this compositional technique; and in this respect perhaps a further parallel can be drawn in the ways both fanfares perform in both symphonies: the fanfare in the Fourth not only signals the climax of the first movement's development but also the premature return of the recapitulation; indeed, while the ascending fanfare fades, the sleigh-bells make their unscheduled entry. Perhaps then, it is not altogether accidental that one of the most overtly dramatic and gripping examples of overlapping surfaces in this first movement of the Fifth, at a critical formal moment of transition at the end of both trios (of which more, much more, below): as each trio winds down, so too does the fanfare start up, puncturing the texture. The principle of simultaneity here—one event beginning even while another ends—is identical with the principle that we encounter in the Fourth (and before that in the Third); and it is this transitional technique, no less than the parallel in narrative imagery, that decisively unites the fanfares of the Fourth and Fifth.

The fanfare, it seems, has led us, quite naturally, into a consideration of the two trios. Quite naturally and also, as it happens, quite appropriately, since in fact the fanfare not only leads us, overlappingly, *out* of both trios, but also *into* each trio, though in this latter case there is no simultaneity involved: it is the unaccompanied and unadorned fanfare that functions as transition to the first trio (Fig. 7^{-3}) and also to the second (Fig. 15^{-7}), though here Mahler effects a surprising switch in instrumentation—the solo trumpet is eschewed and instead the rhythmic profile of the fanfare is transferred to the timpani, albeit a profile that conserves one of the intervals (a minor third) that is integral to the fanfare in its basic form. Mahler rarely introduces a surprise for the sake only of creating a surprising effect; and in this instance, as we shall see, the surprise of the timpani heralds an even greater surprise in instrumental colour. But we must give our attention first to the character of both trios and the calculated implications these interpolations have for the overall narrative of the symphony, from its beginning to its end.

Perhaps I may be allowed here to introduce an interpolation of my own, an enlargement of what I have already remarked on above, that this first movement of the Fifth has a successor in the second movement, the first 'Nachtmusik', of the Seventh, which again is basically a march with two trios, preceded by an initiating gesture comparable in its function, though distinct in character, to the fanfare and its forceful continuation at the opening of the 'Trauermarsch'.[16] But having said that, and having acknowledged that the Seventh's patrolling nocturne is one thing and the Fifth's funeral march quite another, what drives the radical contrasts between the movements is Mahler's treatment in either case of the trios. In the Seventh, the trios perform their traditional function, certainly providing serenade-like contrast with the enfolding march but as certainly never assuming responsibilities other than those that are properly theirs. They are trios that have no status as commentary; they are interludes, rather, relaxations of the steady pace of the march.

The Trios, their Function and Significance

The trios in the 'Trauermarsch', however, turn tradition on its head. They come as a shock, and were no doubt designed to shock us into an awareness of the symphony's principal issues and concerns, both dramatic and musical. The precipitating role played by these trios is to confront us with the symphony's main business, the struggle to overcome, to conquer, the image or threat of implacable mortality that the funeral march itself represents. This is an extraordinary *reversal* of the customary role that a trio plays. In place of relaxation or relatively simple contrast we have two eruptions of protest *against* the implications of the march, eruptions which at the same time constitute a music or musics in often desperate search for a resolution of, or solution to, the fateful conflict. If one had no more to suggest than this, it would already be apparent how profoundly Mahler has transformed the idea of the trio in this opening march. Never before, one begins to think, has it borne such a weight of feeling and narrative responsibility. For if these trios are a protesting commentary on the context in which they find themselves, they also perform developmental

---

[16] Something of Mahler's 'Wunderhorn' manner may linger on in the second movement of the Seventh doubtless because of its march character. But this is nocturnal music that is not bathed in a ghastly or ironic light, as is so often the case in the most typical of the 'Wunderhorn' military songs.

and expository roles. For example, the first (B flat minor) trio (IFigs. 7–11)[17] not only develops materials from the preceding fanfare and march sections, but introduces during its middle part (IFig. 9) an ascending theme (at IFig. 9^{+9}, G flat major) that is to recur in the second (A minor) trio (see IFig. 16, D minor) and, yet more importantly, in the ensuing (A minor) Allegro (see, for example, IIFigs. 7, D flat minor, and 12^{+9}, E flat minor). Thus the first trio combines expository and developmental roles, while the second both develops materials from the first trio while also functioning as a source of important themes and motives for the second *movement*. In short, if one is seeking processes which are identifiably 'symphonic' in character and execution, it is precisely in the trios of the 'Trauermarsch' that one locates them; it is thus that Mahler endows the 'trio' with an entirely new formal status and capability.

There is a further arresting feature of the trios which must claim our attention, perhaps the most crucial of all. Each trio, each in its own unique way, rehearses the drama that, at the outset, is the *raison d'être* of the symphony's narrative: the attempt to counter and, finally, to dispel the sorrow, grief, and mourning that the 'Trauermarsch' represents; each enactment of the basic conflict in each trio, however, ends in defeat, thus anticipating the defeat with which the second movement is to end. Necessarily so, of course, because if Part I of the Fifth were to end in consolation or triumph, we should have no need of the rest of the symphony. Likewise, there can be no possibility of either trio prematurely disclosing the means by which victory will eventually be achieved; this would put at risk the *coup de théâtre*—the chorale, which is the distinguishing feature forming the dramatic climax of the second movement, the stormy Allegro. At the same time, if the trios were to amount to more than local eruptions of frustration, pain, and indignation at the inescapable reality of non-negotiable death, they must, with a longer perspective in view, indicate at least the possibility of a goal, a dénouement, that will finally, in this symphony at least, reach an accommodation with the idea of mortality.

It was with characteristic ingenuity that Mahler solved the problem of premature disclosure in the trios. Each trio has somehow to suggest, as each does, the possibility of escape from the *douleurs* of the march, for there can be no—albeit obligatory—defeat if hope has not been created, thence to be suppressed. Thus the aspiring dimension of each trio is serviced by the aspiring theme that I have already mentioned in the context of discussing the first trio's expository role. But 'expose' as it may (IFig. 9^{+9}, G flat major), and anticipate though it may the aspiring function this same theme fulfils in the succeeding Allegro (e.g. IIFig. 12^{+9}), disclosure falls far short of revealing a goal that, if achieved, will mitigate the conflict and round off the narrative, when the torrents of protest captive in the trios will at last have run their course.

---

[17] IFigs. 7–11 = 'Trauermarsch', the *first* movement of Part I, the passage between Figs. 7 [Rehearsal Numbers] and 11. IIFigs. 7, D flat minor and 12^{+9}, E flat minor = the *second* movement of Part I, the Allegro, the passage beginning at Fig. 7, and next, the passage that begins 9 bars *after* Fig. 12. IIFig. 29^{-1} = the *second* movement of Part I, Fig. 29 *less* 1 bar; and so on. It is the complex relationship of movements I and II sharing the same numerical sequences for bar numbers and rehearsal numbers that makes it essential to precede each reference with a roman numeral to identify the movement.

Mahler brilliantly manipulates his long-term strategy by divorcing, at this stage in the symphony, his thematic and tonal strategies. To be sure, the aspiring theme will continue to aspire; but there is no unequivocal disclosure of the ultimate *tonal* goal—D major—that the conclusion of the finale will eventually and confidently confirm. It is true that even the most modest analysis will show a key scheme—C sharp (leading note) for the 'Trauermarsch' and A (dominant) for the ensuing Allegro—which, if nothing else, shows how conscious Mahler was, at one level, of preparing the long-term evolution of an ultimate D major; he clearly needed to have the sense of a logical scaffolding in place. Having said that, it seems to me that, in the music he actually went on to create in Part I, in all its eruptive and disruptive ferocity, he tested his scaffolding to destruction. We may intellectually be aware of the 'logic' underpinning the chaos, but I doubt if we hear it, or that Mahler wanted or expected us to hear it. Hence, in the 'Trauermarsch', neither trio affords us a glimpse of that destination, even when, as in the second trio, the critical moment of aspiration (^{I}Fig. 16 ff.), followed by defeat (^{I}Fig. 18, 'Klagend'), is enacted in a handling of sound that almost exactly parallels the comparable passage in the second movement, where D major is divulged and established (^{II}Fig. 29^{-1}), briefly held, and then—as if life itself were audibly drained out of the music—its texture and dynamics, the very density of the chords in the brass, thin out, fade into nothingness (^{II}Fig. 29^{+5}): the final moment of extinction comes with the onset of D minor and the shrill intervention of the woodwind, one of the interruptive gestures ('Cut-off', about which I shall have much more to say below) that are such a prominent—and dramatic—feature of the movement.[18]

The principle generating this procedure—which, as I have just described, is to give us, in the second movement, one of the most remarkable passages in all Mahler—is precisely adumbrated in the second trio at ^{I}Fig. 18, this time in the shape of a sustained chromatic slide conceived as a diminuendo.[19] The sound gradually fades and decays as step by step the slide descends and retreats from the initiating dissonance unleashed *fortissimo* in bar 369, the texture thins out, and we are so to say on the brink of silence (in the wake of collapse) until the intervention of the trumpet fanfare and resumption of C sharp minor remind us that while the trios may have revealed ample evidence of the search—of the need—for a solution to the spiritual crisis that the idea of mortality engenders in Everyman, they reveal no hint, musically speaking, of what that solution may prove to be.

As we have seen, we are to encounter the parallel collapse in the second movement, but this time with a vital difference: collapse the affirmation may, and fade to extinction, but not before the brief-lived, but unambiguous D major at ^{II}Fig. 29^{-1} (Mahler marks the bar with its up-rushing D major scale and D major triad, asserted *fff* in the brass, 'Höhepunkt')[20] has indicated unequivocally that, though we are by no means at the end of

---

[18] See Table 11.2A–C below.

[19] All too often underplayed these days by the composer's interpreters, as are so many comparable passages elsewhere in the symphonies. If a passage like this—the climax of the second trio—is not very carefully considered in terms of its novel dynamics and above all without thought being given to

its singular role in the drama of the symphony as a whole, and in particular as an anticipation of a critical event in the ensuing Allegro, then its significance will pass unheeded. If the interpreter does not comprehend it, then audiences certainly won't.

[20] See below, n. 55.

the search, D major is potentially the goal towards which the symphony must strive. It is this dimension, the assertion of an unequivocal tonality as potential target, that is conspicuous by its absence from the anticipatory collapse at the end of the second trio. It is, so to say, *Hamlet* without the Prince, and the more chilling, the more 'negative' in its impact, for that very reason.

A Collective of Orchestras: Instrumentation and Revisions

I may seem to have expended an excessive amount of attention on the two trios of the march; but in fact there has been relatively little comment in the past that has measured up to their importance; and that, if nothing else, I hope to have got across. How we hear those trios is fundamental to our apprehension of what Mahler was about in Part I of his Fifth. If I have concentrated on the 'collapse factor', it is because collapse is their point of consummation (if that is the right word). But by concentrating on this feature common to both trios I do not want to overlook the very significant and intriguing differences between them, especially those that distinguish the second trio from the first. Indeed, the very opening of the second trio introduces a sound-world that hitherto has not impinged on our ears. There is nothing surprising, one might think, in Mahler conjuring out of his hat one of those many independent instrumental constellations that go to make up the orchestra we think of as 'Mahler's orchestra'. (The plural—'Mahler's orchestras'—might be the more appropriate description of the resources deployed in any one of his symphonies, songs, or song-cycles.) The 'Trauermarsch' provides us with an example of the diverse orchestras involved in the march itself: for example, between ᴵFigs. 12 and 14, Mahler abandons the 'conventional' symphony orchestra and converts it, temporarily, into an authentic wind-and-percussion band, precisely the sonority that is associated with ceremonial funeral processions.[21] This vivid interpolation of wind-band instrumental colour is reserved for the final appearance of the principal march melody, preceding the second trio, the opening of which, after the obligatory dotted rhythm upbeat, introduces another and yet more radical change in instrumental constitution. What takes the stage is, basically, a string orchestra (it is unequivocally that, for the fifteen bars between ᴵFigs. 15 and 16), plus—from ᴵFig. 16 onwards—solo horn (such (soft) brass chords as there are—bars 345–8—simply fill out the harmony), and, from ᴵFig. 17, solo trombone(s), plus a pair of horns, effectively, for the two bars immediately preceding the collapse at ᴵFig. 18.

[21] The addition of a viola line (first for solo, then tutti) at ᴵFig. 13 in no way materially modifies the wind-band character of this passage. In fact, it is only there to guarantee and sustain the seamlessness of the solo trumpet's melody. Typical of Mahler's fanatically precise ear that, of the violas' nine bars, the first five are for a solo viola, while the remaining four are marked *tutti* ('with mutes'). The solo viola bars, naturally, form part of a dynamic scheme that nowhere exceeds *p*, while the violas tutti are summoned to participate in a texture culminating in the climax (with horns and woodwind) of the trumpet melody. Even so, the mutes, along with Mahler's fastidious distribution of his dynamics among the instrumental groups, ensure that there is no assertion of an *independent* string timbre to dilute the authentic wind-band sonority of this section of the march.

Pl. 11.2. Fifth Symphony, 1st movt., second trio: (*a*) first edition (1904 study score): bars 312–28. This version of the trio was recorded for the first time together with Mahler's revised version of the trio by Riccardo Chailly and the Royal Concertgebouw Orchestra in 1997 on the CD which accompanies *New Sounds, New Century* (see n. 26 below).

SYMPHONY NO. 5 (I)   37

(*b*) Revised edition (full score, 2nd edn., 1919): bars 312–28

1904 edn. (cont.): bars 329–43

38   SYMPHONY NO. 5 (I)

1919 edn. (cont.): bars 329–40

1904 edn. (cont.): bars 344–50

1919 edn. (cont.): bars 341–52

1919 edn. (cont.): bars 353–65

1904 edn. (cont.): bars 358–65

1919 edn. (cont.): bars 366–74

1904 edn. (cont.): bars 366–74

1919 edn. (cont.): bars 375–83

1919 edn. (cont.): bars 384–401

1904 edn. (cont.): bars 384–401

Furthermore, a scrutiny of the orchestral revisions that Mahler made to his Fifth—a huge subject in its own right[22]—shows him intent on stripping out from his first conception of the second trio all those instrumental redundancies and needless doublings, as a result of which it is a string-orchestral sonority, pure and simple, that magically materializes. This not only provides the maximum contrast to the heavyweight orchestral turbulence and rhetoric of the first trio (not to speak of the imposing funerary ceremony (the fanfare and the rest) with which the 'Trauermarsch' opens). If one studies Pl. 11.2, in which I juxtapose the first conception Mahler had of the sound of his second trio with a version that is close to what we currently hear performed in our concert halls or on disc, the paring-away process—in effect the extrapolating of an orchestra of strings alone from the larger orchestra that is the basic resource—is clearly exposed. The relevant pages from the first published edition (the study score of 1904) are faced in the main by the comparable pages from a later published edition, probably the second edition of the full score, published in 1919 and incorporating many of the revisions he made, unceasingly, to the symphony up to the time of his death. This bringing to bear of a micro-lens, so to say, on the string body is characteristic of Mahler's revisionary practice; one must always—while acknowledging that an important minority of his orchestral revisions derived from the changing acoustic environment in which he found himself performing his music—seek the profounder creative motive behind the façade of seeming practicality.

Was then his prime creative motive to find a way of establishing a radical contrast? Up to a point, yes; but beyond that there is also what one might call the anticipatory function of the second trio, which is part of the special role the trio is designed to play, both musically and narrative-wise. For a start, with the benefit of hindsight (which of course the very first auditors of the symphony did not have), this remarkable opening of a window on the string band cannot but strike us as a prefiguration of a kindred sonority to come (string orchestra plus harp) that is exclusively to service the symphony's fourth movement, the famous Adagietto; and since the Adagietto has now surfaced in the context of our discussion of the first movement's second trio, perhaps I may emphasize how underrated is Mahler's pioneering of a movement for (primarily) string orchestra in the frame of a large-scale symphony—representing, in fact, its only slow movement. A most unusual step to take, given the evolution of the symphony in the nineteenth century. Is there a meaningful precedent? I have not been able to uncover one.[23] I think we have to conclude that this novel isolation

[22] See Sander Wilkens, *Gustav Mahlers Fünfte Symphonie: Quellen und Instrumentationsprozess* (Frankfurt: C. F. Peters, 1989), and Colin Matthews, *Mahler at Work: Aspects of the Creative Process* (New York and London: Garland Publishing, Inc., 1989). See also Irene Lawford-Hinrichsen, *Music Publishing and Patronage: C F Peters, 1800 to the Holocaust* (Kenton, Middx.: Edition Press, 2000).

[23] No doubt someone will be able to produce a precedent from somewhere. But will it be relevant? For that reason I exclude the 18th c. as a possible or probable source. This is something different from suggesting that models for the character of the Adagietto may not have been stored away in Mahler's imagination, e.g. the Adagietto from Bizet's *L'Arlésienne* Suite No. 1 (1872), while the exploration by other composers towards the end of the 19th c. of the specific potentialities of the string orchestra, e.g. Grieg's brilliant *Holberg Suite* (first composed for piano solo (1884) but very soon emerging in its string orchestral guise (1885)), may well have stimulated Mahler's own interest in the medium. It is worth noting that there are significant stretches in the Ninth Symphony, in its first movement, e.g. Figs. 11–12[+13], where it is virtually a string orchestra that carries the weight of seething expression. Other instrumental sectors are intermittently involved but it is the timbre of the *strings*, virtuosically exploited, that is predominant.

Pl. 11.3. The cover of the programme for the première of the Fifth Symphony at Cologne on 18 October 1904, the first Gürzenich Concert

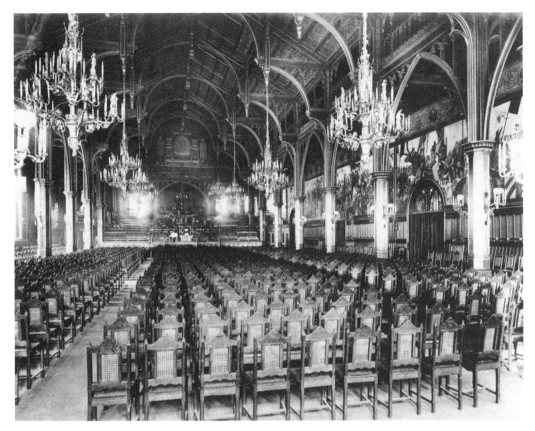

Pl. 11.4. The interior of the Gürzenich Hall, Cologne

of the strings as an independent string band owes most to the development in Mahler's own music of his concept of the orchestra as a *collective of orchestras*, including, it must be added, from the turn of the century onwards, the idea of the chamber orchestra.[24] There are essential things of course still to be said about the clear relationship of the Adagietto to Mahler's late orchestral song style, manifest in the settings of Rückert; and just because of that it is worth recapitulating here that, for Mahler, those songs represented his 'Kammermusikton' (see Ch. 10). I think in the context of the symphony, as it unfolds, the switch to the string orchestra (not to speak of the intimate, song-like character of the Adagietto, that Mahler seems to have recognized himself; see pp. 312–13 n. 97) created the atmosphere—perhaps illusion might be the better word—of a *chamber music conceived for the large concert hall*; and that in turn brings to mind Mahler's string orchestral arrangements of Schubert ('Death and the Maiden' string quartet (D. 810), the slow (variation)

[24] I have pointed out in the previous note how the string orchestra, as an entity, surfaces in the Ninth. So too, even more decisively, does the concept of the chamber orchestra, again in the first movement. See bars 376–98. See also *Additional note*, p. 235 above.

movement of which Mahler performed in Hamburg in his 1894/5 season) and Beethoven (the F minor quartet, Op. 95, performed in Vienna in 1899). These arrangements were greeted with incomprehension and hostility by their first audiences. To us, however, they are evidence of his preoccupation with string orchestral sound during those last years of the nineteenth century, a fascination that surely was to influence, at and after the turn of the century, his own forays in the medium.[25]

All of this, I suggest, speaks strongly for the impact the second trio makes in terms of contrast and anticipation; and as we have already seen, both these considerations raise the issue of Mahler's notorious revisions. After all, it was he himself who was writing in a letter as late as 8 February 1911, to Georg Göhler, from New York, 'I have finished [sic] my Fifth—it had to be almost completely re-orchestrated. I simply can't understand why I still had to make such mistakes, like the merest beginner. (It is clear that all the experience I had gained in writing the first four symphonies completely let me down in this one—for a completely new style demanded a new technique.)'[26] (See also Pl. 11.5 and Pl. 11.6.)

The few pages that I have chosen to illustrate the fresh sound that accompanies the opening of the second trio also clarify the general principles underpinning Mahler's revisionary practice, principles that we encounter time and time again not only in the Fifth but in later and—up to a point—preceding works. It is the volume, character, and extent of the revisions in the Fifth that are singular.

Pl. 11.2 (1904) perhaps what it was that Mahler had in mind when referring to himself as the 'merest beginner' when contemplating the errors of judgement he made in his orchestration(s) of the Fifth, at least in its early stages. The extirpation of the entire woodwind section from ¹Fig. 16 to ¹Fig. 17⁻⁴, for example, and again from ¹Fig. 17 for 8 bars, shows how ruthless he was in disencumbering himself of overweight textures—those dense, obscured, syncopated chords in clarinets and bassoons!—and doublings surplus to requirements; and if we scan the facing pages and note, as we proceed, his omissions and deletions, we can experience the very process by which he achieved the clarity and transparency of sound that was his objective.

---

[25] Nor should we exclude the first twenty-four bars of the opening of the Fourth Symphony's Adagio, though there is a distinction, I believe, to be made between string orchestral passages interpolated into a movement, as in the Fifth and Ninth Symphonies, and a third movement in a sequence of movements which opens with the string body and only after the obligatory break between movements. In the context of the Fourth and its Adagio, and, more specifically, its string-orchestral character, it is perhaps worth mentioning that already there are clear anticipations of the 'new' melodic style that was taking shape in Mahler's works around the turn of the century. For example, see in the Fourth's Adagio Fig. 2⁺⁵–Fig. 2⁺¹⁰ and Fig. 3⁺⁴–Fig. 3⁺⁸, both of which passages (violins) directly foreshadow the manner—the 'Ton'—of the Adagietto. It seems, then, that here too the Fourth shows itself to have been a vital stage in the evolution of the new style and new sound that were to be fully revealed in the Fifth and co-terminous settings of Rückert. So it was not only the polyphony of the Fourth that brought with it news of Mahler's future style, but also the profile (in the Adagio) of its melody. This makes the question of the 'quote' of *Kindertotenlieder* in the Adagio of the Fourth, the more intriguing. See Ch. 9 n. 39 and Ch. 10 n. 1.

[26] Mahler, *Selected Letters*, Letter 443, 372. For Göhler's own note on the revisions he incorporated into the score of the Fifth for his performance in Leipzig on 9 Jan. 1914 of a so-called 'new version' of the symphony, see Donald Mitchell and Henriette Straub (eds.), *New Sounds, New Century: Mahler's Fifth Symphony and the Royal Concertgebouw Orchestra* (Bussum: THOTH/Amsterdam, Royal Concertgebouw Orchestra, 1997).

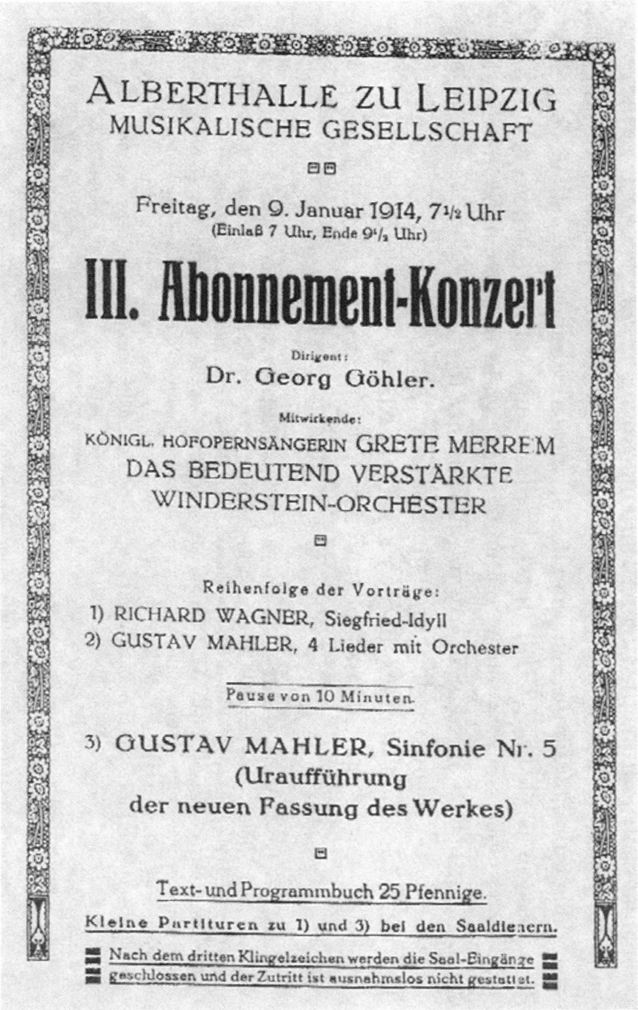

ALBERTHALLE ZU LEIPZIG
MUSIKALISCHE GESELLSCHAFT

Freitag, den 9. Januar 1914, 7½ Uhr
(Einlaß 7 Uhr, Ende 9½ Uhr)

III. Abonnement-Konzert

Dirigent:
Dr. Georg Göhler.

Mitwirkende:
KÖNIGL. HOFOPERNSÄNGERIN GRETE MERREM
DAS BEDEUTEND VERSTÄRKTE
WINDERSTEIN-ORCHESTER

Reihenfolge der Vorträge:

1) RICHARD WAGNER, Siegfried-Idyll
2) GUSTAV MAHLER, 4 Lieder mit Orchester

Pause von 10 Minuten.

3) GUSTAV MAHLER, Sinfonie Nr. 5
(Uraufführung
der neuen Fassung des Werkes)

Text- und Programmbuch 25 Pfennige.

Kleine Partituren zu 1) und 3) bei den Saaldienern.

Nach dem dritten Klingelzeichen werden die Saal-Eingänge geschlossen und der Zutritt ist ausnahmslos nicht gestattet.

Pl. 11.5. The cover of the programme for the performance of the Fifth Symphony in Leipzig on 9 January 1914 conducted by Georg Göhler, who had incorporated into the score many of the revisions of the performing materials Mahler had continued to make up to the time of his death

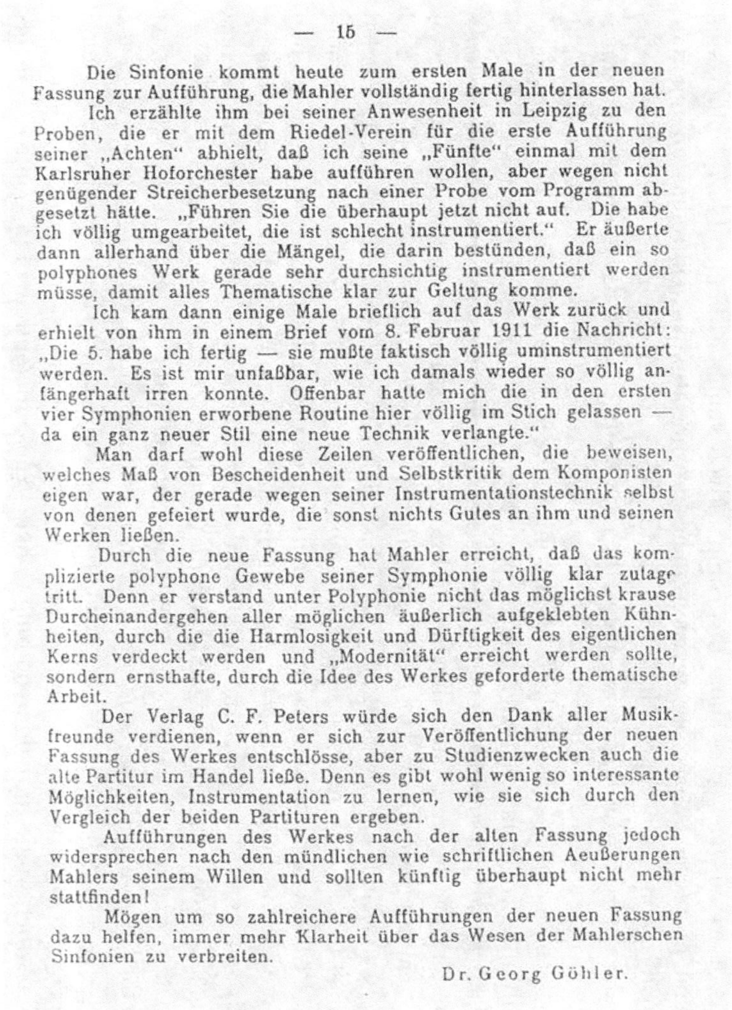

— 15 —

Die Sinfonie kommt heute zum ersten Male in der neuen Fassung zur Aufführung, die Mahler vollständig fertig hinterlassen hat.

Ich erzählte ihm bei seiner Anwesenheit in Leipzig zu den Proben, die er mit dem Riedel-Verein für die erste Aufführung seiner „Achten" abhielt, daß ich seine „Fünfte" einmal mit dem Karlsruher Hoforchester habe aufführen wollen, aber wegen nicht genügender Streicherbesetzung nach einer Probe vom Programm abgesetzt hätte. „Führen Sie die überhaupt jetzt nicht auf. Die habe ich völlig umgearbeitet, die ist schlecht instrumentiert." Er äußerte dann allerhand über die Mängel, die darin bestünden, daß ein so polyphones Werk gerade sehr durchsichtig instrumentiert werden müsse, damit alles Thematische klar zur Geltung komme.

Ich kam dann einige Male brieflich auf das Werk zurück und erhielt von ihm in einem Brief vom 8. Februar 1911 die Nachricht: „Die 5. habe ich fertig — sie mußte faktisch völlig uminstrumentiert werden. Es ist mir unfaßbar, wie ich damals wieder so völlig anfängerhaft irren konnte. Offenbar hatte mich die in den ersten vier Symphonien erworbene Routine hier völlig im Stich gelassen — da ein ganz neuer Stil eine neue Technik verlangte."

Man darf wohl diese Zeilen veröffentlichen, die beweisen, welches Maß von Bescheidenheit und Selbstkritik dem Komponisten eigen war, der gerade wegen seiner Instrumentationstechnik selbst von denen gefeiert wurde, die sonst nichts Gutes an ihm und seinen Werken ließen.

Durch die neue Fassung hat Mahler erreicht, daß das komplizierte polyphone Gewebe seiner Symphonie völlig klar zutage tritt. Denn er verstand unter Polyphonie nicht das möglichst krause Durcheinandergehen aller möglichen äußerlich aufgeklebten Kühnheiten, durch die die Harmlosigkeit und Dürftigkeit des eigentlichen Kerns verdeckt werden und „Modernität" erreicht werden sollte, sondern ernsthafte, durch die Idee des Werkes geforderte thematische Arbeit.

Der Verlag C. F. Peters würde sich den Dank aller Musikfreunde verdienen, wenn er sich zur Veröffentlichung der neuen Fassung des Werkes entschlösse, aber zu Studienzwecken auch die alte Partitur im Handel ließe. Denn es gibt wohl wenig so interessante Möglichkeiten, Instrumentation zu lernen, wie sie sich durch den Vergleich der beiden Partituren ergeben.

Aufführungen des Werkes nach der alten Fassung jedoch widersprechen nach den mündlichen wie schriftlichen Aeußerungen Mahlers seinem Willen und sollten künftig überhaupt nicht mehr stattfinden!

Mögen um so zahlreichere Aufführungen der neuen Fassung dazu helfen, immer mehr Klarheit über das Wesen der Mahlerschen Sinfonien zu verbreiten.

Dr. Georg Göhler.

Pl. 11.6. The last page of the lengthy programme note Göhler wrote for the occasion

But even as one writes about this comparatively simple example of how Mahler went about his revisions, *necessary* revisions to be sure, one also has to introduce an important qualification. Yes, of course Mahler was ridding himself here of a frank miscalculation, but at the same time the obligatory remedy, the radical surgery, was also motivated by a singular creative ambition, to upgrade the basic string-orchestra character of the trio almost up to the moment of collapse at ${}^{\mathrm{I}}$Fig. 18. This mix of the purely practical and an unprecedentedly inventive orchestral imagination seeking to make yet more explicit the materialization of a fresh body of sound is typical of his revising methods; one must always be on the lookout for their purely creative dimension. In short, for Mahler, revising and composing (or recomposing) were locked together in an inextricable association.

We must note too how careful he was in his striving for clarity, which necessarily entailed much paring away, not to lose essential motives but rather, to articulate them yet more clearly. For example, in the second trio, in its first orchestral format, the accompanimental motive in the divided violas, first emerging in bar 323 (${}^{\mathrm{I}}$Fig. 15^{+1})—this motive, rhythmically and intervallically,[27] has a fundamental role to play in the second movement, often as a means of energizing the long haul towards the summit of a climax (e.g. cf. ${}^{\mathrm{II}}$Figs. 26–7)— on its second appearance (cf. ${}^{\mathrm{I}}$bb. 345–51) was originally allotted (as Pl. 11.2 (1904) shows) to the bassoons. The bassoons, and the clarinets along with them, were to be excised, as I have already indicated; but the critical motive is transferred to the violas, thus sustaining the colour and character of their entry at ${}^{\mathrm{I}}$Fig. 15, while the clarinets' rhythmic punctuation, which would have done nothing to help expose the outline of the motive, is maintained by the second violins, *pp* and staccato, and functions, with perfect ease, as an accompanimental, undistracting, figure. Third time round (cf. ${}^{\mathrm{I}}$bb. 353–6), the winds have been restored and the motive heard in the penetrating oboes (as compared with the bassoons), along with (now for the first time) the clarinets' rhythmic punctuation. The motive in this passage, as Pl. 11.2 (1919) shows, has to compete with a cluster of other basic motives and themes simultaneously combined; although by now its importance has been aurally established, Mahler takes care, notwithstanding, to secure again its clear articulation (triple oboes), relative to the surrounding motivic polyphony.

This same passage also offers an interesting and typical example of what one might describe as Mahler's motivic instrumentation, i.e. heightening the profile of the motives

---

[27] The motive itself, while almost always retaining its identifying outline, contracts or expands intervallically according to need. Perhaps its point of initiation is located, as Graeme Downes has suggested ('An Axial System of Tonality', 164–5), in the very first gesture of the first trio, i.e. the upbeat plus succeeding bar at ${}^{\mathrm{I}}$Fig. 7, which already foresees the role it is to play in the second movement, again at an early initiating moment, ${}^{\mathrm{II}}$Fig. 1–8. It is a moment itself preceded by two bars (flutes, oboes, and clarinets) of the motive, the audibility of which Mahler, as I hope I will have shown, took so much trouble to secure at the opening of the second trio. The second movement confirms time and time again

how essential it was in the cause of long-term comprehensibility for the significance of this motive to be unequivocally established. Once more, a critical interpretative point that conductors should take on board. There is one last observation I should like to make. Mahler *himself* virtually draws our attention to this fundamental motivic bond between the first trio and the second movement by accompanying its first appearance at the onset of the trio with an explicit injunction to the conductor: 'Geigen stets so vehement als möglich!' (violins as forceful as possible!). It is precisely this form of words that he attaches to bar 8 at the opening of the second movement.

that go to make up a melody or theme by distribution of its constituent motives among a sequence of instruments. In the Fifth, unsurprisingly, it is the brass that is often involved. Consider, for example, the bars between [I]Figs. 16 and 18. The aspiring triplet theme (from [I]Fig. 16) is allotted in the first published edition (see Pl. 11.2 (1904)) to the horns (solo horn to begin with), and it is the horns that sustain the melody until [I]Fig. 17, when the trombones take over. Mahler's revision (see Pl. 11.2 (1919)) maintains the horns until bar 352, but thereafter—at bar 353, a climactic quotation of the anguished opening of the first trio (see below, pp. 277–8)—it is the solo trumpet that provides the bridge (an early rhythmic anticipation, in fact, of the motive that generates the ensuing Allegro, hence the spotlighting that the change of instrument secures) to the solo trombones, themselves conducting a motivic exchange; they also swap their directional thrusts (ascent and descent). This may be a simple example of the analytic instrumental thinking that was habitual for Mahler, but it also demonstrates how close was the association in his creative thought between motivic and instrumental texture. After all, in just two bars ([I]bb. 353–4), we have three levels of instrumentation—woodwind, brass, strings—and three levels of invention, each of which is distinguished by its own motivic profile, all of which are combined simultaneously, and all of which are directly related to some of the most prominent musical ideas of the forthcoming Allegro. Indeed, it is precisely this motivic group that initiates the second movement, and rounds it off. (Once again, any interpretation that purports fidelity to Mahler's intention must take account of the complex anticipatory and retrospective motivic networking that is the *raison d'être* of his motivic polyphony.)[28]

All of this, we may argue, is evidence of a composer intent on cleaning up, clearing out, what hitherto had been an overloaded texture. At the same time, as we can observe with fascination, the cleaning-up process also had the result of vastly extending the role of the string orchestra that, in Mahler's initial concept of his second trio, was confined to a first handful of bars. The orchestration of this particular passage would certainly have had to be amended; but that it came to be amended in the way that it did—therein lies the evidence of the hidden (creative) agenda that was ever the active collaborator in Mahler's revisionary practice.

A further remarkable feature of the Fifth, even allowing for the massive precedent that we find in, say, the slow introduction to the first movement of the Third Symphony, is the

---

[28] In the *first* trio too there is evidence of Mahler's constant refinement of the dynamics and distribution of his instrumental parts. For example, how crude the concluding three bars of the horn melody look—[I]Fig. 10⁻³—if compared with the revision of 1919: it is not only the redistribution of the melody among all six horns that one notes but the introduction of a vastly more complex range of dynamics, a recurrent feature of Mahler's revisionary practice. The observant reader will note too in [I]b. 210 the consequent excision of the doubling by the horns of the bassoons' descending figure. This was transferred to the trombones (as the 1919 score shows), but finally, it seems, Mahler indicated the excision of the transfer, committing instead the doubling of the bassoons to the cellos and basses, while an even later revision modified the lower strings' dynamics. (See the study score of the Fifth published as Vol. V of the Critical Edition, [I]Fig. 10⁻¹, though for an example of a more radical modification of dynamics, cf. [I]bb. 361–3 in the *second* trio in Pl. 11.2 (1904), basses, with Pl. 11.2 (1919), where we find the dynamics have not just been modified but precisely reversed!)

liberation of Mahler's writing for the wind, for the solo brass especially. The sheer *extent* of the materials entrusted there to the solo trumpet or solo trombone (not to speak of the virtuoso contributions from the horns, as a group) continues to astonish, however many times one hears the work. If there is a distinction to be made between his practice in this field in the Third and the development of his liberating instrumental techniques in the Fifth, it rests, I suggest, in this: that while the scale of the involvement of the wind in the introduction to the Third's first movement, and the potentialities of the individual instruments are innovatingly tested and exploited, the instruments are never, so to say, required to hijack the territory of another family of instruments altogether.

Something different happens in the Fifth.[29] For example, consider the very opening of the first trio, where, in brilliant, vibrant counterpoint to the torrent of protest from the

[29] Only the second trio of the 'Trauermarsch' is illustrated by Pl. 11.2. The attentive reader who cares to consult the first published edition (1904) of the score in full will notice that, while the solo for trumpet opens as a solo for the first six bars, the part is then allotted to trumpets 1 and 2, and then resumed again as a solo until ᴵFig. 8. At Fig. 10, however, it is a pair of trumpets that continues what from Fig. 9 has been a solo flight. Clearly what Mahler had in mind here was the approaching climax at bar 221 and empowered his trumpet line, with characteristic precision, according to the changing dynamics and densities of the orchestral texture. If one follows the evolution of the music from Fig. 10 to the peak of the climax at bar 221, it is obvious that he needed to keep a pair of trumpets at work to sustain the penetrative role of the trumpets in this crucial passage (bb. 211–227). We can guess that Mahler wanted the peak pitch in the contour of the trumpet melody not only to ring out but ring *through* the texture, a high point also dynamically speaking. The pair of trumpets is of course retained in the 1919 revision, but we note there (see Pl. 11.2) further refinements: a reduction, from bar 215 onwards, of the horns' doubling, from six horns to three; and, more significantly, for the first four bars after Fig. 10 the two trumpets are reduced to a solo player (evidence of a calculated intent that I shall have more to say about below). It is in this guise that we hear the passage today.

But there are other refinements and nuances of colour that warrant attention. For example, as will be found if the first trio in the 1919 revision is consulted, the six horns on their collective entry in bar 159 are marked 'gestopft', i.e. 'hand-stopped', whereas in the 1904 score no form of mute was indicated but the dynamic was *p*. In the 1919 score this is transformed into *ff*! Though the modification of the dynamics may appear to be dramatic, the effect of hand-stopping is to produce a horn sound which throws into contrast the high trumpet (which has embarked on its solo flight in bar 155) besides adding an uneasy colour to music that in any case is turbulent—'Leidenschaftlich. Wild.'—in character.

The sustained *p* euphony of the horns, as Mahler originally had them, would have padded out the middle part of the texture, conceivably masking or softening the sharp edge of the trumpets' articulation rather than providing in their own right a distinctive sonority. It is exactly this that hand-

stopping the horns accomplishes—no cushioning, filling out or absorption but, in Norman Del Mar's vivid words, 'the savage bite of the best hand-stopped notes'. (Mahler prepares us for this radical switch in timbre, as the 1919 score shows, by doubling the existing oboe part with hand-stopped horn pitches while deleting the then redundant second violin and viola parts (see ᴵFig. 7⁺⁵).)

It is clear that Mahler concluded that in the changed circumstances of the first trio's bars 155–64 the solo trumpet would not require further strengthening. I believe, however, that another factor may also have played an influential role. The Fifth, as I have suggested, is particularly rich in solo instrumental flights of many kinds: long, long arches of evolving melody, built out of motives, shuffled and reshuffled in ever new sequences. I believe that in entrusting these bold flights to a solo instrument and, above all, a solo*ist*, Mahler was not only enlarging and developing the scope of the instrument itself—what it could, technically, be pressed to deliver—but at the same time developing the technique of his players, not least perhaps testing their stamina, their nerves. There is a real difference in the spirit of a performance where the player, so to speak, is obliged to go it alone. The challenge creates its own characterizing tension which then forms an indispensable part of the musical idea itself, e.g. the opening trumpet melody of this first trio. It must remain speculation, inevitably, but I believe this sensitive and highly complex relationship between the performer and the composer, the latter bent on exploring his performers' capabilities to their limits, and beyond, was always part of Mahler's thinking, conscious or unconscious, when making his revisions. Thus when and wherever in the Fifth a solo role proved possible (perhaps only after Mahler had himself experienced the symphony in performance), he worked systematically, though always with high imagination, towards that end. This is not to say, however, that he failed to double up (or more) where the needs of his music made it obligatory. The passage I have already mentioned, ᴵFigs. 10–11⁻⁶, makes this very point. To sum up, what took a hand in the history of Mahler's revising practice was the complex history of the capabilities of performers and potentialities of instruments during his creative lifetime. Here is yet another example of his both making *and* documenting the history that is embodied in his scores.

strings, the first trumpet embarks on a huge, seamless, bounding solo that in other times would surely not have been conceived for the trumpet. Indeed, it is a passage that brings to mind a characteristic insight of Erwin Stein's with regard to the orchestration of one of Britten's operas: 'the fiddles', he wrote, 'do not play first fiddle in *Billy Budd*. Actually, the orchestral part of the first trumpet covers as many pages as that of the first violins, and the parts of the first woodwind players are still bulkier.'[30] Britten, in fact, was following in Mahler's footsteps in pushing back the boundaries of what was thought to be traditionally 'appropriate' to one instrument rather than another. However, in my view, it was undoubtedly in the Fifth that Mahler carried forward his liberation of the brass to a further critical stage, not only in the passage I have just mentioned in the first trio, but also in the second.

The Second Trio

A feature of the second trio—a consequence of the process of revisionary extrapolation that I have described above—offers us further proof of Mahler's liberation of the brass. For hardly has he established his string orchestra than we hear the first horn embark on the long melodic flight (from [Fig. 16) that I have already mentioned in a different context. But here I want to emphasize the concerto-like character that emerges along with the entry of the horn. 'Concertante' might be the more apt word; and that in turn should remind us of the role of the *Corno obbligato*—designated thus by Mahler himself—in the Scherzo, the third movement, comprising Part II of the symphony.[31] I remarked many years ago that if one were looking for the horn concerto that Mahler never wrote, then it is to be found here, in the Scherzo of the Fifth, the symphony which is particularly rich in *concertante* textures, in which the brass in particular predominate (not only the horn and trumpet, incidentally, but also the trombone). So it is, I suggest, that the horn entry in the second trio, sustained as a solo for twelve bars, anticipates the *obbligato, concertante* conception that we are later to encounter in the Scherzo. A window is opened on a style that, in fully-fledged form, is yet to be revealed; likewise, the second trio's anticipation that I have already mentioned of the string orchestra that is (predominantly) to service the forthcoming Adagietto.[32] (We note that in Mahler's earliest score (1904) the emphasis on the role of the horn was sustained from the end of the first horn's solo flight, when the third horn joins the first (b. 349),

[30] Erwin Stein, '*Billy Budd*', in Donald Mitchell and Hans Keller (eds.), *Benjamin Britten: A Commentary on his Works* (London: Rockliff, 1952; repr. Westport, Conn.: Greenwood Press, 1971), 199.

[31] I remember that at the first British public performance of the Fifth, at the old Stoll Theatre in London on 21 Oct. 1945 (!), when the London Philharmonic Orchestra was conducted by Heinz Unger, the orchestra's first horn, at the end of the second movement, took up his place (his seat) at the front of the platform, alongside—or close to—the leader of the orchestra. Thus the concerto parallel was spelled out visually. I had no idea if the conductor were following his own instinct or responding to a performance tradition of which he was himself aware. But in Willem Mengelberg's conducting score the following note is to be found: 'Das

Hornsolo immer hervortretend u. Horn beim I. Konzertmeister zu placiren als Solist.' (The first horn should always stand out and be placed as soloist at the front next to the leader of the orchestra.) It is possible, then, that this was a 'tradition' Mengelberg inherited from Mahler himself. See also Truus de Leur, 'Mahler's Fifth Symphony and the Royal Concertgebouw Orchestra', in Mitchell and Straub (eds.), *New Sounds, New Century*, 76–101.

[32] I am aware, naturally, that the composition of the Scherzo (probably) preceded the composition of the first movement and its second trio. But this does not affect my argument. It means merely that Mahler took account of the stylistic precedent the Scherzo represented when composing (and, above all, revising) the trio.

until Fig. 17. Thus the horn colour in 1904 was dominant for a total of twenty-one bars (solo for 12 bars). But his revision of the preceding four bars (349–52) continues to assert the combination of horns and strings. Horns I and II unite in exclamatory extensions of the solo horn's unfolding of the 'Ascent' theme (337 et seq.) from the first trio (203 et seq.), which theme is itself counterpointed (Fig. 16) with the solo flight of the trumpet that opened the first trio but is now transferred to the violins, while at bar 345 it is the strings that accompany the horns with the 'Ascent' theme! (Cf. Pl. 11.2 (1904) and (1919).)

The second trio, in short, is replete with anticipations of types and styles of music yet to come, in addition to the thematic and motivic anticipations that I have already touched on. But there is one anticipation that I have not so far mentioned which is one of the most important of all: along with the marked contrast in character and sound that the opening of the second trio brings is the first intimation of the second movement's principal tonality, A minor. There has been little to prepare us for this onset of a new tonal area, though one recalls that the very fanfare that initiates the 'Trauermarsch' culminates in an ascending A *major* triad ([I]b. 11); and thereafter a grand orchestral tutti asserts, though only very briefly, A (b. 13).[33]

I shall return to the issue raised by Mahler's move to a fresh tonality below; or, rather, when Mahler himself returns us to it, in the second movement itself and, crucially, towards the end of that movement, where I believe the implication of the A major triad in the fanfare that opens the 'Trauermarsch' audibly finds fulfilment, thus demonstrating its place in the narrative scheme and the long-term logic of Mahler's tonal symbolism.

However, this retrospective illumination still lies way ahead. I ventured to suggest at an earlier stage above that Mahler in Part I of his symphony divided his thematic and tonal strategies between the 'Trauermarsch' and its two trios on the one hand, and the ensuing Allegro on the other. One is struck, naturally, by the advent of A minor in conjunction with a radical change in texture and mood, but at this stage in the evolution of the symphony surely what commands our attention is the second trio's thematic profile? The opening melody for the violins could hardly offer a more vivid contrast to the turbulence of the first trio, or, one might think, a clearer contrast to the 'Trauermarsch' itself. That we should listen, however, *beyond* (or *beneath*) the outward appearance of contrast is indicated by the ubiquitous upbeat at [I]Fig. 15 (b. 322; see Pl. 11.2 (1904) and (1919))[34] that has hitherto always introduced and reintroduced the original march melody. In this context, it puts us on notice that what follows in the ensuing trio will be *march*-derived and thus *march*-oriented; and what in fact we hear from [I]Fig. 15 is a remodelled version of the

[33] Graeme Downes ('An Axial System of Tonality', 162) is one of those who comments on the significance of A emerging at this crucially early juncture. For him, the juxtaposition of C sharp minor and A major represents a further example of the 'axial relationships' that he believes to have been fundamental to Mahler's tonal strategy in his symphonies. I find his arguments entirely persuasive in the case of the Fourth, less so in the case of the Fifth. The strategy can be heard—experienced—by listeners to the Fourth, even if not accounted for in analytical terms. It is, so to say, *felt*. I wonder if the same can be said with quite the same conviction about the Fifth? Nonetheless Dr Downes has good points to make which warrant our serious consideration.

[34] See also Ex. 11.3 and related text on pp. 279–80 below; also p. 222 n. 6 above for a fascinating Verdi parallel.

'Trauermarsch', in a new orchestral guise—as remote as one could imagine from the regimental wind band that we have encountered at an earlier stage in the movement—a version, moreover, that accommodates, most intriguingly, the triplets that up to now have represented musical and narrative ideas opposed to the march, seeking escape from it, indeed. It is one of the rare passages in Part I where there is some identifiable suggestion that a mitigation of the march of sorrow may eventually prevail. But here again, Mahler is careful not to overplay his hand. Although the opening melody for violins, reflective, even gently melancholic in character, may seem to distance itself from its generating source, the march is with us as an unmistakable rhythmic presence from the start of the trio, from ^{1}Fig. 15 to, say, Fig. 16^{+11}, which, with the advent of A minor, the interpolation of the string orchestra, and the incorporation of the 'triplet factor' into the remodelled march melody, seems to establish a rare, if fragile, moment of calm. Here, certainly, A minor is not yet endowed with the characteristics of Mahler's habitually 'tragic' (the Sixth) or tormented (*Das Lied*, first movement) key; nor even does it portend the storm of nerves and agitation that A minor is to embody in the succeeding Allegro. (Once we have been engulfed by that storm at the beginning of the movement, the trio's A minor, in retrospect, inevitably takes on a new significance.) In any event, the march, remodelled though it may have been, has not been subdued. It has been submerged, rather. As Mahler's bass line asserts, the march continues to prowl through the second trio downstairs, even while, upstairs, in the violins' melody, it shows a new face. It is not, however, the bass alone that confirms that it is the march that we are hearing, but also Mahler's insistence that the second trio, *un*like the first, should throughout, but especially at its outset, maintain 'always the same tempo'—'Immer dasselbe Tempo', he directs—as that of the immediately preceding principal march section. In other words, a conflation of tempo + rhythm + bass combines to remind us that the 'contrast' the second trio vouchsafes at its beginning is more apparent than real; and as we shall see, the remodelled march, bearing its load of particular symbolic significance, has an important role—a multiple role, indeed—to play in the Allegro. The history of this one theme could be chosen to illustrate the highly complicated interrelationships, by means of exposition, development, and quotation, that exist not just between the two movements of Part I but between the two trios, and, in turn, their interrelationships with the march that frames them.

I have concentrated on the opening of the second trio, but what about the rest of the trio, which after all leads to the climax that I have already touched on above?[35] There is no doubt that the (relative) A minor calm of the trio at its start only heightens the awful intensity of the lament—a black hole, almost—into which (at ^{1}Fig. 18) the trio collapses.

The Triplet Factor and Unveiling of the 'Quotation Principle'

The 'triplet factor' has an important part to play in this process. It is useful perhaps to remind ourselves, before the opening of the trio persuades us otherwise, that the triplets

---

[35] See pp. 249–50.

have their origin in the fanfare that opens the 'Trauermarsch'. A triplet, indeed, is the first rhythmic unit we hear. Thereafter it becomes virtually a basic rhythmic *Leitmotiv*, saturating much of the invention of the first two movements and the trios of the 'Trauermarsch'. If the fanfare spawns triplets, so too does the immediate and agitated continuation of the violins' chromatic outburst at the very onset of the first trio (see [I]Fig. 7[+4] ff.). It is not really until a later stage, at [I]Fig. 9[+9], that the triplets become irrevocably associated with the idea of ascent, of 'aspiration', in a theme (in G flat, violins) that is to re-emerge in the second trio at [I]Fig. 16 (in D minor), but this time functioning not as a kind of contrasting 'second subject', the role it has played in the first trio, but as a triplet-related continuation of the second trio's opening A minor melody (the remodelled march). The thrust here of the 'triplet factor' seems to indicate an ascent that will climax on at least a glimpse of a resolution, however distant, which makes it all the more remarkable that the 'aspiring' triplets (cf. b. 352) are interrupted by a quotation, no less, of the cry of protest and anguish, *fortissimo*, that constitutes the opening bars of the first trio; as if to reinforce the authenticity of this interpolation, the violins' chromatic agitations are restated at their original pitch, a case of what is known these days as *pitch-specific*. The importance of this event can scarcely be overstated. It represents, in fact, the first unequivocal anticipation in the symphony of the 'quotation principle', the innovating technique that is to unite the pairs of movements in Parts I and III. That it should be first adumbrated by means of interaction and quotation between the trios of the 'Trauermarsch' puts beyond doubt their unique formal and dramatic significance.

    This unforeseen rupture-by-quotation raised to the status of a principle was something new in Mahler's art, an addition to his arsenal of musico-dramatic resources. At the same time it represents a radical development of a practice that he had long made his own, the reversal, reshuffling, and fresh combination of his themes and motives. As we have seen, the aspiring triplet theme in the first trio was in the first instance ejected by the turbulence of that trio's opening, to function as a mitigating contrast, almost, as I have suggested, like a 'second subject'. In the second trio, the chronology is reversed. What opened the first trio now interrupts—ruptures—the triplet invention that it had initially generated. The interruption, having made its dramatic appearance, now gives way, or so the casual listener might assume, to a resumption of triplet-inspired 'aspiration' (from [I]Fig. 17). But here again, and very typically, Mahler unfolds a nest of basic motives in a new combination. At the very beginning of the first trio, the violins' chromatic contours are simultaneously combined with the solo flight of the trumpet, itself generated by the symphony's opening fanfare. In the second trio, from [I]Fig. 16, the triplet theme, this time a flight of the solo horn, is simultaneously combined with a version of the trumpet's solo from the first trio, but transferred to the first violins. At [I]Fig. 17, when the triplet 'ascent' theme is resumed, this time by the solo *trombone*, the violins continue to counterpoint it with motives drawn from the trumpet solo (see [I]Figs. 7 and 16). The motivic web then exploits a fresh dimension, in the shape of a dialogue, an exchange, between trombones 1 and 2: the first having delivered its opening and ascending triplet limb (b. 357), it is answered by the second, in descending contra-motion, *its* limb based on motives from the solo trumpet (fanfare) flight. This exchange, which is also a development, is continued across twelve bars until at ^{I}Fig. 18, and after a final upward triplet thrust from the first trombone (bb. 367–8), the trio achieves its dynamic peak but only to collapse across the ensuing eight bars.

Thus it is that in the space of some fifty-five bars (the overlapping transition to the coda begins in bar 376) we encounter both quotation and interruption; the unfolding of themes in a reverse chronology; the concept of ascent and collapse; development; and intensive, intricate motivic work, leading to ever new sequences, combinations, and exchanges of motives, a complex polymotivic texture throughout, in which the composer's instrumentation acts as a creative partner, articulating all the information that we need to have if we are to decode and thereby comprehend the significance of this second trio. For it is here, in miniature, that the narrative, the inner drama, of Part I of the symphony is rehearsed and played out to its bitter, protesting ('Klagend') end.

There is one final revision that I want to mention, that of the ubiquitous upbeat that almost in its own right accrues to itself the status of a *Leitmotiv* throughout Part I of the symphony. It has a high profile, naturally, in the pool of motives on which the first trio draws for its thematic context (cf. e.g. ^{I}Fig. 7^{+2}, the first limb of the trumpet's solo) and functions likewise in the second trio, where it is all-pervasive from ^{I}Fig. 15 onwards. A presence, in fact, from the very first bar (^{I}Fig. 15^{-1}), where, as I have already pointed out above, it introduces the remodelled version of the march, appropriately enough, since it is to the (original) march that the upbeat properly belongs. What I did not mention was the combining of the upbeat with the timpani's final triplet, the triplet that forms what one might describe as the very first thing we hear as the symphony begins; in fact, this simultaneity has already been anticipated at ^{I}Fig. 7^{-1}, but there the (crotchet) upbeat and its tumultuous continuation anticipates, rather, the motive that is to dominate the second *movement* (^{II}Fig. 1-8). Indeed, the trumpet's triplets (^{I}Fig. 7^{-3}) have the character of opening up a fresh vista—which they do—while the timpani's triplets, perhaps because they are stripped of the 'heroic' associations of the instrument to which they properly belong, convey much more the idea (muffled drums) of a winding down. In any event, the return to the upbeat in its original form at the beginning of the second trio provides us with another example, albeit on a tiny scale, of Mahler's overlapping technique, the more intriguing because it combines—within the space of one bar—an end, the last bar of the lead-back into the second trio, with a beginning, the upbeat which introduces the trio itself, while the 'end' derives, as I have said, from the very beginning of the symphony itself.

I have used above the words 'upbeat in its original form', and indeed this is true rhythmically, as a comparison of my Pl. 11.2(1904) and (1919) shows. However, Mahler was to make a later revision of the upbeat which must have been overlooked, or had not yet been discovered, when the 1919 edition of the score was published. In the latest published edition of the symphony,[36] the upbeat appears as in Ex. 11.3, clearly articulating the A minor

---

[36] Vol. V in the Critical Edition, 39 (^{I}Fig. 15).

triad, in its second inversion. This is a revision, then, that yet more emphatically clarifies the onset of the 'new' tonality. A fine detail—cf. Fig. 15 in the 1904 and 1919 editions of the symphony—but, in its context, one that tells.

Ex. 11.3. Fifth Symphony, 1st movt., bb. 322–5

Problems of Instrumentation and Re-instrumentation and their Origin; the Paradox of Mahler's Loss of Nerve; his Revisionary Practice

Before we quit altogether the topic of Mahler's revisions—only a fraction of which I have had the space to touch on—it is essential at least to raise the question that is always asked in the context of any discussion of this symphony: why was it that Mahler seemingly lost his nerve, orchestrally speaking, when embarking on the composition of the Fifth? How was it that he came to feel, in words that I have already quoted above, a 'merest beginner' in his first orchestral conception(s) of the Fifth?[37]

From the start, consideration of this complicated matter has been influenced by Alma Mahler's highly coloured account of an early reading rehearsal of the symphony in Vienna conducted by her husband. This is what she wrote:

Early in the year [1904] there had been a reading-rehearsal with the Philharmonic, to which I listened unseen from the gallery. I had heard each theme in my head while copying the score, but now I could not hear them at all. Mahler had overscored the percussion instruments and side drum so madly and persistently that little beyond the rhythm was recognizable. I hurried home sobbing aloud. He followed. For a long time I refused to speak. At last I said between my sobs: 'You've written it for percussion and nothing else.' He laughed, and then produced the score. He crossed out the side drum in red chalk and half the percussion instruments too. He had felt the same thing himself, but my passionate protest turned the scale. The completely altered score is still in my possession.[38]

If we were to rely exclusively on an examination of the *extant* manuscript sources, there would be no option but to conclude that Alma got it wrong; it is an assumption that has been held by countless commentators, myself among them, that is, that what emerges from any such scrutiny is the very reverse of what she reports. Colin Matthews puts it succinctly in his 1977 thesis:

[37] Mahler's letter to Georg Göhler in 1911: see also above, n. 26. Göhler himself was interestingly to comment on Mahler's attitude, reporting that the composer told him *'the first version of the Fifth was never to be played again,* because it was badly orchestrated' (Göhler's emphasis). Mahler could not have put it more baldly. See Mahler, *Selected Letters*, 448.

[38] Alma Mahler, *Memories*, 73.

However much truth there may be in this engaging story, the evidence of the manuscript and the printed scores does not, unfortunately, bear it out. In fact the first edition of the score actually has very slightly more percussion in the first movement (to which Alma is surely referring) than the manuscript; while the second edition merely omits a mezzo-forte cymbal and two pianissimo bass drum strokes. The orchestral revisions are, however, all concerned with lightening and clarifying the texture—the first version was heavily scored, in places almost clumsily so, as if Mahler was unsure of how to deal with the middle-period change of style ushered in by this Symphony.

But what had escaped my notice—and I am indebted to Edward Reilly for bringing it to my attention—was a letter of Mahler's written on 27 September 1904 to his publisher, Heinrich Hinrichsen, the day after the second run-through of the Fifth in Vienna, in which he remarks: 'it was still necessary now and then to retouch a little. *The percussion in particular was certainly overloaded* [my italics], and would certainly have distorted the impression [made by the work].' Alma's recollection of the (second?) run-through—confirmed by no less an authority than the composer himself—reminds us that, though she may have had a penchant for exaggeration, her skills, memory, and musical intelligence should not be underrated. Is there a missing manuscript link—perhaps a percussion part—that was specific to the occasion of which Alma writes and has since disappeared? It seems probable. The fact remains, however, that while Mahler's revisions of the Fifth were voluminous and unceasing, it was not the percussion that consumed his time and skill but, as Dr Matthews remarks, and as I hope to have illustrated above, 'lightening and clarifying the texture': that was his principal concern. And Mahler's textural clarifications, at the heart of his revisory practice, not only addressed—as I think I have amply demonstrated—the question of relative 'weight' but were also intricately bound up with clarifying the symphony's narrative retrospections and anticipations, and the mosaic of its motivic content.[39]

The Need to Revise: What Created It?

There is no disputing the *need* for the revisions in the light of what the study score of 1904 tells us. But what created the need? That is the major question that seems to me never to have been satisfactorily answered. After all, it was hardly the case that Mahler had had to struggle to establish a consummate orchestral style and the techniques to serve it. There were notable stretches of music at which he had had to work hard to achieve what his imagination demanded, for example, the slow introduction to the first movement of the First Symphony. But consider briefly the stage in the evolution of his mastering of the orchestra he had reached before starting work on the Fifth. He had behind him not only heavyweights like the Second and Third but also, and more relevantly, the Fourth, in which, as I have suggested, we not only encounter the shift to a pronouncedly polyphonic-cum-motivic style but also the

[39] Matthews, *Mahler at Work*, 59. See also Eberhardt Klemm, 'Zur Geschichte der Fünften Sinfonie von Gustav Mahler: Der Briefwechsel zwischen Mahler und dem Verlag C. F. Peters und andere Dokumente', in *Jahrbuch Peters*, 1979, 9–116. For a clear exposition of the 'puzzle that never-theless remains', see n. 14 to Edward R. Reilly's contribution to *Gustav Mahler: Adagietto: Facsimile, Documentation, Recording*, edited by Gilbert E. Kaplan (New York: The Kaplan Foundation, 1992), 39–57.

shift to an emerging chamber-orchestral concept. Radical technical developments, both of these; and yet the novel Fourth was never subject to the uncertainties and consequent revisions that were to affect the Fifth. Even more extraordinary, as my chronological table clearly indicates, it was precisely at the time that the Fifth was on the drawing board that Mahler brought to fulfilment his 'Kammermusikton' in the two last 'Wunderhorn' songs, *Kindertotenlieder*, and four independent Rückert settings. One simply has to emphasize the oddity of this—Mahler floundering badly as he drafted the Fifth, having just imagined the innovative but perfectly realized orchestral textures of the Rückert songs. There is no easy explanation of this seeming paradox. How was it that having accomplished *Kindertotenlieder*, say, on the one hand, he felt himself on the other—as late as 1911!—to have undertaken the Fifth as 'the merest beginner'? The technical finesse of the one seems hard to reconcile with the defects of the other. I have no simple answer. That it was primarily a question of 'style'—the advent of the 'new' polyphony as is often suggested—I take leave to doubt. Even if one allows for the evolution of a 'new' component, this was a feature that had distinguished virtually each new symphony that Mahler had composed; and it had always proved the case that his compositional techniques had kept pace with his innovating imagination.

The Abandonment of 'Programmes'

I believe it was factors other than style (exclusively) that contributed to the undoubted crisis that Mahler experienced with regard to the Fifth. First, though probably the less important of the two factors I shall adduce, there was the swallowing of the programme in the preceding Fourth that I have already sufficiently described in Chapter 9, a step that may well have left him with a feeling of insecurity. To be sure, the rejection of the idea of the *overt* programme was a conscious decision, fiercely maintained in the years (and symphonies) to come. No matter that, as we shall see, the 'programme', having been successfully swallowed in the Fourth, was to resurface in the Fifth in a new guise—perhaps dis-guise might be the better description?—but this time as an eventful but wordless narrative generated solely by Mahler's manipulation of his musical materials, themes, motives, tonalities, forms. As the work progresses, its fundamental ideas acquire symbolic significance and evolving identities, and thus come to play the roles allotted them in the drama without their ever having been named.

This casting away of the props that the earlier 'programmes' had constituted—we should not forget that they had been devised initially to serve as instruments of elucidation—may well have left Mahler feeling somewhat exposed. It is possibly significant that he seemed himself peculiarly convinced (in his letters, for instance) that his Fifth was a symphony no one was going to be able to understand. Was this nervousness tied in, in some way, to his denying himself programmatic schemes, vocal movements, or movements composed 'after' songs? Now, so to say, Mahler's signposts had become exclusively soundposts.

This dumping of an overt programmatic dimension was, we may agree, part and parcel of Mahler's move away from synthesizing symphonies like the Second and Third (though the Eighth was to reinhabit the tradition) and his embarking, via the Fourth, on the trinity of purely instrumental symphonies, initiated by the Fifth. It has become virtually received opinion—perhaps even Mahler himself was influenced by it—that it was the critical distinction between the 'synthesized', i.e. mixed, genres and the 'pure', i.e. exclusively instrumental, concepts that was at the root of the crisis. But as I have suggested, the purely instrumental symphony was already significantly anticipated in the Fourth, without, it seems, initiating doubts in the composer's mind about his competence. Why the sudden loss of confidence? Of course in the Fourth there was the concluding 'himmlische Leben' finale to 'explain', 'elucidate', the preceding three orchestral movements. Of course in the Fifth, the 'programme' went underground, so to say. Was it, then, a combination of all the considerations I have so far outlined above that conspired to make Mahler stumble?

Matters of Life and Death

It would be senseless to deny the contribution these factors made to the crisis of 'style' that Mahler was to experience while composing the Fifth; however, by 'style' I do not mean the issue of polyphonic clarity, which I take to have been already established in the Fourth, but, rather, the inflection of the voice that Mahler chose specifically to serve the great issues of Life and Death—they deserve their capitals—that the Fifth and its successor, the Sixth, address.

It was particularly in Part I of the Fifth—the 'Trauermarsch' and Allegro—that Mahler's revising of his orchestration was most intensive; and it is precisely in Part I where the inner drama—the contest, if you like, between Life and Death—is adumbrated. Once we have comprehended what has been set in motion in Part I—that the trios are locked into, held captive by, the funeral march; struggle to achieve release in the ensuing Allegro; encounter implacable defeat; succeed eventually in their striving only through the genial mediation and mitigation of the finale, which, in turn, permits the materialization of the chorale— there is very little else that requires 'explanation'. What does, is the consistent overscoring of that very part of the symphony where instrumental clarity (and thereby formal and narrative clarity) was indispensable.

I believe that the factor that must be added to the others already adduced was the question of 'voice' or 'tone' (perhaps the German, 'Ton', more economically conveys what we mean by 'tone of voice'). How was the 'new' polyphonic style, already established in the Fourth, but there serving a very different narrative and aesthetic, effectively to function in the Fifth, a symphony which directly confronts the issue of mortality and man's battle with it?

There is no question that Mahler as an artist was no stranger to the idea of mortality. It had haunted him since his earliest years,[40] had been treated on an epic scale in the Second

---

[40] In the text I wrote for Chailly's recording of the First (see p. 194 n. 7 above) I give specific consideration to Mahler's suggestion that his hero in fact has died in the finale, to be memorialized and then resurrected in the Second.

Symphony, and, as we have seen, was a topic high on his creative agenda throughout the period of the Fifth's composition.

Hitherto, moreover, each approach to the idea of mortality had found its own sound-world, whether it was the unashamed theatricality and rhetoric of the Second or the unique intimacies of *Kindertotenlieder*, the last 'Wunderhorn' songs[41] and independent Rückert settings. When it came to the Fifth, however, the first step into the territory of the instrumental symphony with all the weight of 'tradition' attached to it, one is almost obliged to conclude that Mahler's nerve wobbled. But did it? One talks or thinks of 'tradition' but only if one forgets the breathtakingly original form that Mahler unfolds in the Fifth, innovative even by his own standards.[42] Amusingly enough, as I have already quoted (on p. 243), Mahler himself seems originally to have intended to conform to 'tradition', that is, to compose 'a regularly constructed symphony in four movements'. That ambition—and up to a point he had already done that in the Fourth, the 'regularly constructed' bit, quite consciously—was soon abandoned: the narrative drama that evolved as the Fifth progressed imposed its own overall form, as remote as one could imagine from classical precedents. Mahler, then, in the formal area, remained entirely true to himself, behaving exactly as one would have expected him to behave. When it came to the point, and whatever the pressures he may have felt himself under, and whatever the state of his nerves, there was no false obeisance to 'tradition'; which leaves us, still, with the paradox of the instrumentation, the strange miscalculations that, leaving on one side the category of refinements and motivic clarification that Mahler would have made anyway, even had there been no larger problem to circumvent, may be subsumed under the general heading of patent overscoring.

The explanation, surely, must reside in this first attempt to 'dramatize' in the 'new' context of the instrumental symphony the old preoccupations with Life and Death. For some reason, still not absolutely clear, Mahler's anxiety—*psychologically* rather than technically based?—led him blatantly to overscore, as if compelled to an excess of emphasis by his determination to match the challenge of the great issue of mortality with a comparably 'weighty' body of orchestral sound. A momentary aberration, perhaps, though the impact of it was long-lasting, unnaturally so, which suggests to me that it was more than 'technique' that was at stake. In any event, Mahler finally succeeded in rescuing his symphony from a false aesthetic that he had pinned on it, releasing thereby a work, the sound-world of which and the techniques that created it were perfectly integrated. The comparative exercise that is my Pl. 11.2 clearly articulates what was more a process of revelation than correction, the *release* of something that was already there, implicit, but which had been

---

[41] This is the place perhaps to remind ourselves of the unique orchestra Mahler assembled for 'Der Tamboursg'-sell': 2 oboes, 2 clarinets, bass clarinet, 2 bassoons, 2 horns, tuba, percussion (timpani, side drum, bass drum, tam-tam), voice, cello, and double bass (NB: lower strings only, throughout) and, in the second section of the song, 'Gute Nacht . . .', the unprecedented substitution of a *pair* of cor anglais for the oboes.

[42] See Colin Matthews, 'Mahler and Self-Renewal', in *Britten and Mahler: Essays in Honour of Donald Mitchell*, ed. Philip Reed (Woodbridge: The Boydell Press/The Britten-Pears Library, 1995), 85–8. There is not much to be gained from the pursuit of a 'classical' four-movement symphony in Mahler's oeuvre. The nearest approach that he made to that model was in the Sixth, the symphony that followed the Fifth, though the parallels cease to be of much significance as soon as the finale is reached.

distorted, exaggerated, at the early stage of its evolution. Undoubtedly, Mahler came to see this, but that did not prevent him from indulging in a long-sustained bout of self-laceration (did it ever end, in fact?). All the more reason, I suggest, for supposing that the 'regression' that Mahler found so dismaying—his becoming again 'the merest beginner'—had touched on a sensitive area that had its roots in the depths of the composer's psyche rather than his technique; or to put it another way, it was the former that led in this instance to his problems with the latter.

After the 'Trauermarsch'; the 'Hauptsatz' (Part I^2)

Mahler himself, as I have noted, considered the second movement of Part I to be the main movement of the pair that make up Part I.[43] Rightly so; the movement has to be—and has been—assessed as one of the most original of all Mahler's symphonic movements. It is indeed a unique concept. However, while it is certainly the 'Hauptsatz' of Part I—of the symphony as a whole, I would argue—it is only so because of its extraordinary relationship to the preceding 'Trauermarsch', on which, indeed, it is entirely dependent and from which, unequivocally, its unique formal character derives. I have already indicated the complex Exposition/Development layout that underpins this formal scheme, while the significant role played by the trios in the 'Trauermarsch' would almost alone single out the first movement as an altogether special achievement. But the truth is that the two movements of Part I are fundamentally interdependent, for which reason it makes no sense to approach them as separate entities, no more sense, in fact, than to consider a divorce of the finale from the preceding Adagietto; and in saying that, one has broached the topic of the larger symmetries that shape the Fifth, a topic that will arise naturally in the course of our further discussion.[44]

Not *Sonata Form but Discontinuity*

Nor does it make any more sense to attempt, as so many commentators still do, alas, to try to account for the singular character of the second movement of Part I in terms of sonata form, for example, Floros,[45] who writes that Paul Bekker 'was right when he spoke of the

[43] See above, n. 15.

[44] Inconceivable, of course, even to think of the finale as an independent item, let alone perform it. This does not hold true of the Adagietto which, in the old days, represented all that we were actually able to hear of Mahler in public along with the occasional song. Furthermore, the movement achieved a kind of independent status in Mahler's own lifetime, a suspect 'tradition' that was maintained after his death. However, there is surely now little justification for performing the Adagietto out of context, and none at all for imposing on it a lugubrious valedictory character à la Bernstein. All the more reason for performers who want to programme the Adagietto as a separate item to bear in mind what we now know of its probable history and its integral relationship to the ensuing Rondo: Part III of the symphony

is as much an integral unit as Part I. (See also below, pp. 307 and n. 80 and 308 ff.)

[45] Floros, *Gustav Mahler: The Symphonies*, 145–9. In this connection I commend to readers the thoughtful and refreshingly independent-minded account of the Fifth in Bernd Sponheuer's *Logik des Zerfalls: Untersuchungen zum Finalproblem in den Symphonien Gustav Mahlers* (Tutzing: Hans Schneider, 1978), 219–79. Dr Sponheuer in his outline of Part I^2, the unique formal significance of which he clearly recognizes, places alongside a column that describes the movement in conventional sonata-form terms a parallel column that is headed 'Peripetaler Verlauf' (peripatetic path), and articulates the movement's unpredictable and above all itinerant character. It offers an admirable corrective to Floros's narrow vision.

[movement's] "ingeniously organized sonata form" '. Floros is not content even with that unequivocal statement, and goes on to add, 'The movement is indeed cast in normal [*sic*] sonata form. It contains everything considered typical: the division into three main parts and a coda, the contrasting themes, a clear disposition of tonalities, and finally the thematic treatment in the development'—and so on, and so on. This is not to mock Floros; but to observe, rather, the danger attendant upon a myopia which leads, it would seem, to treating the movement—hearing it even—as a 'normal' sonata form, whereas the whole point of it, its uniqueness, is inextricably bound up with the 'Trauermarsch' and the role it plays in the ensuing Allegro, to which it contributes an unprecedented series of interpolations and interruptions. It is precisely in these quite astonishing punctuations and ruptures (to gloss Adorno's word, *Durchbruch*) that the genius of the movement resides; and it is, in my view, a clear apprehension of their function which must provide the basis for any meaningful analysis of the Allegro. To summon up a sonata scheme in this context is—grotesquely—to prevent us from hearing what Mahler was really up to.[46] Might it be argued that the composer himself suffered from the same misapprehension for which I chide Floros, since, in his autograph MS full score, he included repeat signs at the end of the section that Floros identifies as the 'Exposition'? These appear in the MS (in the Pierpont Morgan Library, New York, Robert Owen Lehman deposit) at I^2, bar 145, the double bar, five bars after Fig. 9, and were included in the first published edition (study score) of the symphony. Mahler himself was soon to get rid of the repeat, if indeed, in terms of rehearsal or performance, he ever gave effect to it; how could he ever have envisaged that this would have been a possibility in a movement the very *raison d'être* of which is embodied in the calculated discontinuity of the music, barely a bar of which, let alone a substantial section, is repeated? Once again, I believe the explanation for what is otherwise inexplicable rests in a curious recess of Mahler's creative personality. It would seem as if he needed to reassure himself by making this gesture that he had not, after all, altogether abandoned 'tradition'. It was a kind of guarantee of propriety, a means of self-assurance and -insurance. The more innovative the formal thinking, the more the need for a comforting sign of conformity, of orthodoxy. It is significant that exactly the same phenomenon was to recur in the case of the first movement of the Ninth, again one of the boldest of Mahler's formal schemes. The repeat signs are to be found in the Ninth's composition sketch but were again—as they had to be—deleted.

---

[46] This whole aspect of Mahler's sometimes uneasy consciousness of the obligations to be paid to the past I have tried to clarify in 'The Modernity of Gustav Mahler', 175–90. I must add here—because it has only just come to my notice as I prepare the final draft of this text—an exceptionally interesting article by Peter Gülke, 'The Orchestra as Medium of Realization: Thoughts on the Finale of Brahms's First Symphony, on the Different Versions of Bruckner's Sixth Symphony, and on "Part One" of Mahler's Fifth', *Musical Quarterly*, 80 (1996). The few pages (273–5) the author devotes to the Fifth strike me as making the most enlightening (and enlightened) approach to the analysis of Part I of the symphony that I have yet come across.

Interruptions, Quotations, Ascent/Collapse, and Cut-Off

It is my purpose in what follows to try to articulate the *means* by which Mahler achieves the brilliant, continuous *discontinuity* to which I have referred above. For that reason, it seems to me redundant to plod through the movement, listing every single instance when there surfaces a reference to, or development from, the 'Trauermarsch' and its trios. For one thing, this would be an endless task, given that the Allegro is virtually dedicated to a total development of the first movement (of its trios, in particular); and for another, it is those crucial gestures that act consistently as agents of interruption and collapse that should have first claim on our attention.

I believe these may be broken down into four principal categories, one of which is itself subdivided: Interruptions (which may also take on the character of a 'rupture', or 'break-through' as Adorno has it: see Table 11.2A, col. 5); Quotations, split between the March in its original form, which on one famous occasion functions also as Interruption (see col. 2), its remodelled version (see col. 4), and the theme and complex of associated motives I identify as Ascent (see col. 3); and—my col. 1—a persistent and consistently descending scalic gesture, the best description for which I can devise is Cut-off (an association with the process of guillotining is perhaps by no means inapposite). My three Tables A, B, and C attempt to represent the second movement in tabular form, from different angles of approach.

If there is one further 'quotation' by means of which Mahler himself makes the point that I have been making time and time again myself, it is, surely, the unique resurfacing in I^2, between bars 392 and 399, of the opening bars of trio 1 of I^1, though now in E minor, and not, as originally, in B flat minor (the unrelatedness of these two keys only further emphasizes the unprecedented character of this intervention).[47] It is as if Mahler goes out of his way to bring home to us, by the stitching in of this remarkable interpolation, the overwhelming importance of the *trios* of the March for the evolution of the second movement and, above all, for our comprehension of the drama of ascent and collapse that is enacted first in the trios of the March and then re-created in the ensuing Allegro. If this anticipatory dramatic role played by the trios is kept in mind as a constant *backdrop* to the events of the Allegro that I index variously in my tables, the patient reader—with score to hand!—may arrive, I believe, at a clearer picture of the unique formal and musical processes that generate the Allegro, one more faithful to the movement and more relevant than the improbable sonata schemes foisted on it by too many commentators.

The tables, I hope, and their implications, speak for themselves. It is not my intention to comment on them, beyond here and there isolating one or two special features. The most straightforward category, and certainly one of the most important and arresting in concept, is that which I have named Cut-off (Table A, col. 1). The gesture itself—a shrill cry of pain or despair—requires no further elucidation. However, it does require forceful projection by the woodwind, and a conductor who understands its unchanging function; it should freeze our blood each time it occurs, like a scream in the dark. Its contour may change a little, it

---

[47] See also pp. 277–8 above, 'The Triplet Factor and Unveiling of the "Quotation Principle"', where I discuss the significance of the 'quotation' of this identical gesture in I^1, trio 2.

Table 11.2. Cut-Offs, Quotations, and Interruptions

Table A

1. Cut-off	2. Quotations of 'Trauermarsch'	3. Quotations ('ascent') from trio 1 of 'Trauermarsch'	4. Quotations from trio 2 of 'Trauermarsch'	5. Interruptions ('collapse')
(1) I^2, from Fig. 5–8 to Fig. 5 (bars 66–73) Ww.*	(1) I^2, from Fig. 15 to Fig. 16 (bars 266–84) *March* + original tempo as in I^1	(1) I^2, Fig. 7, *Ascent* theme from I^1, trio 1 (Fig. 9–9 to bar 221). NB throughout the trio the pervasive intimations of simultaneous contrary motion, i.e. ascent and descent combined!	(1) I^2, from Fig. 5 to Fig. 7 (bars 74–116) *March*: theme (remodelled) + original tempo as in I^1 [NB cf. I^1, trio 2 from Fig. 15 to Fig. 16, bars 323–36]	(1) I^2 from double barline after Fig. 16 (bar 288). A flat section leading to
(2) I^2, from Fig. 9 to double barline (bars 141–6) Ww. and str.		(2) I^2, bars 222–33, *Ascent* theme combined with second quotation of (remodelled) *March* (see (6) in Table B)	(2) I^2, from Fig. 11^{+13} *Recit.* (slow), from which *March* (remodelled) emerges [Fig. 12, bar 213]; tempo as in I^1	(2) double barline (bar 316), attempt to establish A major and Chorale I
(3) I^2, from Fig. 11^{-1} to Fig. 11^{+10} (bars 176–86) Ww.		(3) I^2, bars 364–71, *Ascent* theme (see also (12) in Table B)	(3) I^2, from Fig. 20^{-4} to Fig. 21 *March* (remodelled), somewhat slower than tempo 1 of I^2 (i.e. see Fig. 18). For the source of its continuation (bars 362–Fig. 21) see I^2, Fig. 2^{+7} et seq., yet another example of Mahler's discontinuous continuity	(3) From Fig. 27 to double barline at Fig. 30 (bars 463–520), attempt to establish D major and Chorale II
(4) I^2, from Fig. 18 to Fig. 18^{+11} (bars 322–6) Ww. and str.		(4) I^2, bars 392–9, first quotation of opening bars of trio 1 of I^1; the continuation at I^2, Fig. 23 (bars 400–19) introduces the *Ascent* theme from trio 1 in combination with accompanimental motives first introduced in trio 2		
(5) I^2, from Fig. 30^{+1} to Fig. 31^{-3} (bars 521–6) Ww. and str.				

* The Cut-off is itself accompanied by a further punctuation in the shape of a diminished seventh chord delivered by the brass. (See horns and trumpets, bars 66–7.) Note in particular the dynamics and colour of the horns: what begins p, crescendos into a hand-stopped f at bar 66, thereby transforming the chord into a (vertical) snarl that presages the first Cut-off, a (horizontal) slash. This same punctuating chord recurs at all the succeeding cut-off points, with the exception of bar 176, i.e. at bars 141, 322, and 520. Bars 66–73 provide a model example of Mahler's exploitation in a highly compressed space of open and hand-stopped pitches by the horns, not only in sequence and juxtaposition (e.g. bars 69 and 70) but in simultaneous combination (bar 66).

TABLE B

CUT-OFF; QUOTATIONS; INTERRUPTIONS: classified by type and in order of chronological appearance

(1) First Cut-off (I^2, bars 66–73)

(2) First quotation of (remodelled) *March* (I^2, bars 74–116). Cf. I^1, trio 2, Fig. 15 et seq.

(3) First quotation (I^2, Fig. 7) of *Ascent* theme from trio 1 (origins—'triplet factor'—in I^1, bars 165–72, by which bars 203–10 are generated)

(4) Second Cut-off (I^2, bars 141–6)

(5) Third Cut-off (I^2, bars 176–86)

(6) Second quotation (I^2, from Fig. 12) of (remodelled) *March*, from bar 222 incorporating second quotation of *Ascent* theme (see (7) below)

(7) Second quotation (bars 222–33) of *Ascent* theme from trios 1 and 2 of I^1, combined with continuation of *March* (see (6) above)

(8) First quotation of *March* in its original form (I^2, Fig. 15, bars 266–84)

(9) First interruption (I^2, bars 288–316)

(10) Second interruption: Chorale I (I^2, bars 316–22)

(11) Fourth Cut-off (I^2, bars 322–6)

(12) Third quotation of (remodelled) *March* (I^2, bars 355–71), combined (bar 364 et seq.) with Third quotation of *Ascent* theme from trios 1 and 2 of I^1 (see also (7) above)

(13) First quotation (I^2, bars 392–9) of opening bars of trio 1 of I^1 (cf. bars 155 et seq.)

(14) Fourth quotation (I^2, bars 400–19) of *Ascent* theme from trios 1 and 2 of I^1 (cf. (12), (7), and (3) above)

(15) Third interruption: Chorale II (I^2, bars 463–520)

(16) Fifth Cut-off (I^2, bars 521–6)

(17) Coda (I^2, Fig. 33 to end)

TABLE C

CHRONOLOGICAL ORDER

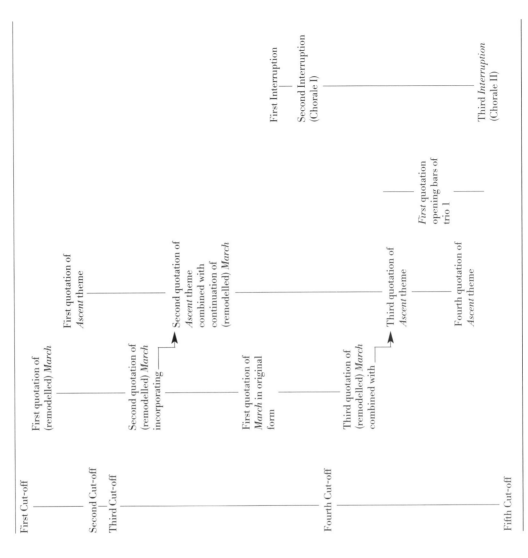

may be contracted or extended—its longest version runs to eleven bars (I^2, Fig. 11^{-1}), its shortest to four (I^2, Fig. 18)—but, after its first release at Fig. 5^{-8}, it is immediately recognizable, summing up, as it does, the proliferation of scalic figuration in hectic descent that has been a feature of the trios of I^1.

It is not my intention to pursue the retrospection principle even more thoroughly than the composer does himself in his symphony, and in the second movement of Part I in particular. But I cannot, in the context of our discussion of the evolution of the Cut-off gesture, avoid making one last observation. I have just mentioned above the interpolation of the opening bars of trio 1 of the 'Trauermarsch', sited, as Table A shows (col. 3, no. 4), well towards the end of the movement, approaching, in fact, the third and crucial Interruption, Chorale II (col. 5, no. 3; see also the chronological Tables B and C) which finally achieves D major, but only to lose it: it is the last Cut-off (col. 1, no. 5) that delivers the *coup de grâce*.

This sequence of events, one among many of the same type, variously put together but always leading to the same dénouement—collapse—encapsulates the *fons et origo* of Part I, both musically and dramatically. But overwhelming though this chain of quotation, interruption, and cut-off may be, we must not overlook, in the 'Trauermarsch', the first movement, the earlier quotation of the first trio's opening bars, to which I have already drawn attention on pp. 277–8 above. Almost as striking as the quotation itself (^{1}bb. 353–4) is the sequence of 'events' that follows it. First, a Cut-off (woodwind prominent, bb. 355–6), a nascent version, surely, of what is to be established later and elaborated as the dominating Cut-off that punctuates the Allegro; next, the 'ascent' theme, as *Hauptmelodie* in a polyphonic web of motivic allusions (bb. 357–68), a dialogue, no less, for two trombones, exchanging characteristic ideas that pull in opposite directions; and finally, the extraordinary climax at I^1, Fig. 18—'Klagend' (an explosion of sorrow),[48] woodwind and (hand-stopped) brass with their bells up, so Mahler orders—that provides the model, as I have suggested, for all the collapses into the abyss that follow.

This further instance (Mahler's doing, not mine) of the high importance of the opening bars of trio 1 and their dramatic development in trio 2—which affords an almost total glimpse of what is to come, of unflagging contrast between ascent and descent, triumph and collapse—together with the comparable sequence of events in the Allegro that I have already touched on—confirms, if nothing else, what I have been arguing so strenuously: the prime generative function of the trios of the 'Trauermarsch'. Who can doubt indeed, as Graeme Downes has pointed out,[49] that it is from the turbulent chromaticism of the opening of trio 1 that the principal theme of I^2, the Allegro (see b. 9–Fig. 2), evolves? Or that, ultimately, we may similarly ascribe the origins of the Cut-off gesture to the seething (but needle-sharp) chromaticism of the 'wild', insistently descending violins of the first trio in I^1? (It is no accident, Dr Downes makes clear, that in each case, the opening theme of the trio and principal theme of the Allegro are initiated by an upbeat spanning an eleventh in

---

[48] It is important to remember that 'Klagend' is not only an indication of sorrow but also an unleashing of protest, of complaint (e.g. 'Die klagende Partei' – the plaintiff), a fist shaken at fate.
[49] Downes, 'An Axial System of Tonality', 160–1.

the trio and a minor ninth in the Allegro, the latter to assume virtually the status of an intervallic leading motive as the movement unfolds.)

So much for the Cut-off column, its impact on, and some of its relationships to, the parallel columns. The March columns (cols. 2 and 4), again, are pretty straightforward in their
disposition. Readers may use them as a guide and draw their own conclusions as to the
validity or otherwise of what each column implies, i.e. the constant resurfacing of the
'Trauermarsch', in one guise or another (straight quotation or remodelled), so that its presence is never wholly dispersed or absorbed: our consciousness of mortality, it seems, is
always at hand. As col. 4 shows, the March most often emerges in its remodelled form (after
the precedent established in I[1], trio 1 (see above, pp. 276–7)), but there is once more a
unique moment that calls for our special attention; its uniqueness, indeed, is represented
by its having a column (col. 2) to itself. The musical incident this, in every respect, singular entry embodies is the surfacing of the 'Trauermarsch' in its original form (and tempo)
in a context that has not led us to expect its intrusion. On the contrary, at the double bar-
line (I[2], b. 265) the ascending intervallic upbeat, which has gradually expanded from bar
261 onwards, would seem to prepare us for a return to, say, figuration directly related to the
agitated principal theme of the Allegro. But instead, the leap from E♯ (b. 265) to G♯ and
thence to F♯ (a variant of the *Ur*-intervallic motive), together with the onset of B major, is
audaciously *interrupted* in bar 266. Mahler makes the interruption graphically visible by
interpolating *mid-bar* dotted vertical cut-off[50] lines from top to bottom of his score, at
which point the 'Trauermarsch' suddenly materializes, contradicting our thematic expectations. It is as if a door had shut on one orchestra, and opened on another, in another room
where the 'Trauermarsch' is still in progress. An unmistakably Ives-like event this,[51]
though perhaps more subtly conceived than if the American master had had a hand in it.
In contriving this extraordinary interruption-that-is-also-a-quotation, Mahler, albeit
unknowingly, was contributing a new page to the history of twentieth-century music.

Few interpreters, alas, as we move into the twenty-first century, show themselves to be
alert to the significance of the passage: the general run of conductors play *through* it, pay-
ing little attention to Mahler's dynamics and least of all, most times, to the *triple forte* that
Mahler demands for the proper articulation of the apex of the upbeat, without which there
is no arousal of expectation and thus no contradiction of it either. Nor, apparently, do the
composer's dotted lines impinge. Smoothness and unblemished continuity carry the day

[50] Cf. a similar dotted line in bar 322, to mark the release
of Cut-off no. 4. Mahler undoubtedly added this graphic
form of interruption to emphasize the significance of this
particular Cut-off, that it aborts the first attempt to establish
the chorale (in A, b. 316).

[51] It continues to surprise me that the Ives/Mahler conjunction has received relatively little serious attention, though
it is clear to me that the two composers often made a similar
response to the sound-worlds by which they were surrounded,
very different though those sound-worlds were. Nonetheless,
it was surely the case that both Ives and Mahler took a pioneering interest in multi-directional sound and the incorpora-

tion of the vernacular into their music—the deployment of the
one often brought with it the use of the other—and I find the
silence on the subject—which I aired as long ago as 1975 in
WY, 169–71, 280, and 373—baffling. The more welcome,
then, are two recent studies: Leon Botstein's 'Innovation and
Nostalgia: Ives, Mahler and the Origins of Modernism', in
Charles Ives and his World, ed. J. Peter Burkholder
(Princeton: Princeton University Press, 1996), 35–74; and
Robert P. Morgan's 'Ives and Mahler: Mutual Responses at the
End of an Era', in *Charles Ives and the Classical Tradition*, ed.
Geoffrey Block and J. Peter Burkholder (New Haven and
London: Yale University Press, 1996), 75–86.

and erase all possibility of Mahler's brilliant innovation making its full effect. I shall be
returning to this passage once more when I come to the final column, Interruptions (col.
no. 5), to which it might well be argued that this intervention by the 'Trauermarsch' also—
and quite properly—belongs.

I shall spend very few words indeed on the second of my Quotations columns (col. 3)
which lays out in sequence the genesis and evolution of the 'Ascent' theme (I can think of
no better shorthand description than this). If the reader cares to take the list in one hand
and a score in the other and follow the history of the theme from beginning to end, he will
find himself in possession of everything he needs to know as the composer himself tells it,
the best of all possible guides. The only caution I would enter is to avoid theme-spotting or
theme-counting (the danger inherent in numerical lists) and always take into account, in
this movement above all, context and location; a reasonably informed scrutiny of *where* a
quotation occurs, with an eye (and ear) trained on what has happened before and after it,
may help one to come up with an answer to the question, *why?*: that is, why *here*? I hope
that in this specific respect the layout of Table C may be helpful. It represents an attempt to
show how the particular events with which I have concerned myself are located and interrelated within the 'space' of the movement as a whole (something different, I think, from
the laundry lists which make up Table A, say).

As for 'Ascent', my description, like the theme itself, speaks for itself. We need only add, at
least in the context of this movement, that what ascends must also descend, or be cut off or
otherwise terminated; and it is certainly obligatory to keep those consequences and implications in mind when categorizing the theme: it soars, as it were, only to fall. Here again Mahler
goes out of his way to spell out the dichotomy—ascent and its obverse—simultaneously. I
have already mentioned one example of this—the solo trombones' duet-dialogue in I^1, trio
2, bars 357–68, which presents the 'Ascent' theme along with its directional opposite.[52] In
fact, the contrary impulse in relation to the 'Ascent' theme has already been adumbrated at
an even earlier stage, in trio 1, bars 165–72, and at the earliest stage in the evolution of the
theme itself (cf. the version of the theme that establishes itself later in the same trio at Fig.
9^{+9}). All of which goes to illustrate the symbiotic relationship between ascent and descent
with which the theme is identified from the start, and reconfirms yet again the almost manically anticipatory, indeed prophetic, role that the trios discharge.

What remains is the final column (col. 5), dedicated to Interruptions (and their collapse),
a short list, inevitably so, since the events both incorporate and effect their own termination and indeed bring Part I of the symphony to its close. The list, some may think, should
be shorter; and I confess to some doubt about the justification for including the A flat section (beginning at the double bar, I^2, Fig. 16^{+4}) as an interruption proper, on the same
scale, say, as the preceding intervention of the March.[53] On the other hand, this oddly

[52] See above, pp. 278 and 290.

[53] Dr Downes ('An Axial System of Tonality', 170–1)
locates a source for this passage in I^1, bars 243–5, oboes. A
typical instance, this, of a seemingly random counterpoint
acquiring later a special motivic or thematic significance.
The first movement of the Fourth is littered with like examples. See also my discussion of the apotheosis of the 'triplet
phenomenon' in the finale on p. 324 below.

swaggering, quasi-march episode undeniably strikes a new note even while—and perhaps because—the triplets that go to make up its profile recall, by association, the 'promise' of the 'Ascent' theme. It is, at the very least, a significant *remission*: is light, then, about to dawn, the promise of 'Ascent' to be fulfilled?

I noted earlier that the interpolation of the March was launched by the ascending leap of a ninth, thus contradicting our expectations of a resumption of the characteristic agitation of the Allegro's principal theme; and it is again that same preparatory gesture that initiates the A flat mini-march, thus furnishing a further contradiction of our expectation that this time round the Allegro will resume its pursuit of the conflict. But instead, there is this quirky switch to a more positive mood. It is of relatively short duration (some 20 bars), after which there follows a transition, based, in its last four bars, on the ubiquitous upbeat, which finally takes shape at the double bar (b. 316) as a leap from E natural to F *sharp* (317, and sustained for a semibreve), falling to E natural (again a semibreve). As we proceed, this sounds less like a forthcoming contradiction and more and more like a breakthrough; which, in fact, is exactly what happens: a triumphant A major is affirmed by strings, wood-wind, brass, and timpani—even the triangle is conscripted to take part with a celebratory (sempre *fortissimo*) trill. For a moment it seems as if the battle (or whatever) is over, mortality banished, and the tonic *major* of the Allegro unveiled as the goal after which Part I has been remorselessly seeking. But there is hardly time to be convinced, or indeed unconvinced by the breakthrough. For after two bars of assertion, the penultimate Cut-off intervenes (col. 1, no. 4)—at which critical point Mahler introduces another vertical dotted line mid-bar (322), an interruption in fact of an interruption (the aborted A major)[54]—and this time (same bar) the Cut-off is reinforced by—uncoils over—a diminished seventh chord (on A), brutally projected by the six horns, hand-stopped, bells up, for five bars, after which, at last, the *furor* of the Allegro is resumed. Typically, however, it is not the principal theme that returns but the ascending upbeat, which, after frantically repeating itself (from b. 325), finally succeeds in reuniting itself (333) with the principal theme from which it had become detached. And so on and so on. There is no more remarkable passage in the whole movement than this complex sequence of discontinuities, executed, notwithstanding, with ferocious logic. One comes to realize, retrospectively, that the postponed reunion of the upbeat with its rightful continuation has all along been part of Mahler's long-term tactical thinking. If the seemingly unpremeditated is to make its effect, it must, paradoxically, be minutely, even manically, organized.

A Chorale Collapses

Table B sets out the sequence of the events I believe to be of cardinal importance in the music that succeeds the penultimate Cut-off (a double-strength cut-off, as I have just suggested); and I have already touched on the special significance of at least one of those events, the spectacular quotation (at b. 392) of the opening bars of trio 1, of an importance

---

[54] See also above, n. 50.

comparable, in its different way, to the resurfacing of the March in its original form and tempo in I² at Fig. 15. In the light of what I have already had to say about the status acquired by the ascending upbeat as the Allegro evolves and in particular its role as an agent, a creator, of expectation, there is perhaps nothing very surprising about its reappearance at Fig. 26, once again screwing up the tension and preparing us—for what, exactly? After all, we have been through all of this before and landed up with the 'Trauermarsch' at Fig. 15; and again at Fig. 16, when the A flat mini-march was interposed; and again at Fig. 17^{+8}, when we were catapulted into the short-lived A major, almost immediately dispatched at Fig. 18 by the fourth Cut-off. What is afoot this time round? We are soon to know. Exiguous though the A major interruption was, it made its impact, a chorale, cut off—cut down—almost before it had announced itself; and when we hear the onset of D major at Fig. 27, jubilant string figuration, the noisy presence of the timpani, and above all a lot of ascending triplets that finally participate (from Fig. 28) in the adumbration of an unmistakable brass chorale, we may be forgiven for thinking that we are in the midst of a replay of Chorale I but this time with the probability of a final, positive outcome. This indeed is vouchsafed at bar 500, where D major is unequivocally affirmed—Mahler takes care to mark the bar 'Höhepunkt'.[55] But then something, to my ears, quite astonishing happens over the ensuing twenty bars. A sustained, graduated diminuendo sets in; the dynamics fade; D major loses its brightness; the mass of sound thins out; the orchestra itself, so to speak, packs its bags and steals away, so that by bar 512 all the strings have departed but for the cellos and double basses, all of the woodwind but for the bassoon and double bassoon, and all of the brass but for the horns who keep alive—just—a spectral version of the chorale until it expires altogether on a D played by the first horn only, *pianissimo*. What seemed to promise an unequivocal blaze of triumph has been reduced to a whisper, if not a whimper.[56] And with awesome logic, the fifth Cut-off (I², bb. 521–6) again provides the *coup de grâce*, to confirm, if confirmation were needed, that Chorale II, like its predecessor, has had its lifeblood drained out of it.[57] An analogy with the photographic process might be drawn here, but in reverse: we start with a full-colour print but are left with a negative.[58]

[55] It is not surprising perhaps that when Mahler came to compose the first movement of his Ninth, like the second movement of the Fifth, a form built systematically around the idea of ascent and collapse, he wrote above bar 308, after the tempo designation 'Pesante', the words 'Höchste Kraft' (maximum force). But he might just as well have followed the precedent, 'Höhepunkt', that we find in the Fifth (I², b. 500): the two bars in question both represent the climactic peak of a final ascent followed by a final collapse. I am much indebted to Henry-Louis de La Grange for drawing my attention to a remark of Mahler's, made to William Ritter, probably in Munich in 1910, with reference to the Ninth. 'Now', Mahler said, 'I am embarking on an entirely new path' (*Revue française de musique*, 10/7 (15 July 1912); in French, Ritter's recollection of what Mahler said to him runs like this: 'Maintenant je suis entré dans une voie toute nouvelle!').

[56] 'This is the way the world ends / Not with a bang but a whimper.' T. S. Eliot, *The Hollow Men* (1925).

[57] Incidentally, this passage provides for good measure a marvellous example of Mahler's overlapping technique. For as the Cut-off unfolds, its 'accompaniment' is made up of a diminished seventh chord (cf. bb. 322 ff., but this time *piano*: it too, at first, has been drained of its former power); the ascending upbeat (properly attached to its correct continuation), and the movement's opening, basic motive (see I², bb. 1–5 ff.). A typical instance of Mahler's passion for the simultaneous combination of ends and beginnings.

[58] The listener, however, will have to make all of this out for himself if the interpretation of the symphony does not do it for him, as it should. Conductors need to pay particular attention to the preview of the Allegro's final collapse that is disclosed in trio 2. An absolute commitment to Mahler's dynamics here, and in Chorale II, as it fades, would make a good start.

Another extraordinary moment in the symphony, this expiring of the chorale; and, I want to suggest, if we are listening correctly, it should also represent an extraordinary moment of déjà vu, quite in the manner of Proust. For what we hear—the recovery of a moment of lost time—is a recovery, replay, a re-enactment, not so much of the just aborted Chorale I, but of the similarly aborted climax of the second trio of the 'Trauermarsch'. Indeed, if one harks back—to time past!—to that passage in I^1, bars 368–76, it is immediately apparent that it is there that the model for the ultimate collapse of the Allegro has been set up. It is final proof of the long shadow thrown over the Allegro by the trios of the funeral march; and the recovery of our memory of it in its very first materialization must be an essential part of our experience of its later manifestation.

There are of course differences. The volume of sound, for example, is diminished overall, from *fff* to *p morendo*, by means of dynamics alone, not by the reduction of instrumental resources that is the radical procedure adopted in Chorale II. But the chief difference resides in the substitution of the nascent chorale for the trio's extensive chromatic slide. Mahler had no option but to find an idea, a concept, that could act as both agent and symbol, of affirmation, a gesture that might, eventually, reverse the slide dramatically articulated as the failing climax of the second trio.

It was not just a matter of confirming the D major that had been momentarily established and then withdrawn in the passage I describe as Chorale II. The concept also, from the start, had to incorporate a potentiality for ascent, the direction that would run contrary to the predominant directional thrust downward of the two trios of the 'Trauermarsch' and much of the Allegro. It was also obligatory to light upon an idea that could effectively affirm and then unaccountably fade, while leaving behind an impression, at least, that a possible means to secure and then enact the obverse of collapse had been disclosed.

Hence, surely, Mahler's choice of 'chorale' as the concept that would meet his needs. Too many words, it seems to me, have been expended in a variety of attempts to elucidate its significance for the composer and thereby, naturally, the significance it should have for us. For example, was Mahler (improbable thought) evoking the shade of his great predecessor, Anton Bruckner? (This, it seems, was Alma Mahler's opinion, which she apparently expressed to her husband; in any case she thought it a mistake.)[59] Was Mahler's intent religious, mystical even? Or was it, as some have suggested, a suspect strategy, to achieve too easily a crowning moment of triumph, triumphal*ism* rather than a genuine expression of joy?[60] On the whole, this last was Adorno's line of approach, who was a resolute *un*believer in the 'happy end' of the symphony, for reasons perhaps more to do with his own psychology (and psycho-politics?) than the facts of the music.[61]

It would be naive to imagine that Mahler was unaware of the weighty baggage of tradition, of various kinds, that the chorale, as an idea, carried; we must assume the contrary,

---

[59] See Alma Mahler, *Memories*, 47–8.

[60] Shades of the finale of another famous Fifth, Shostakovich's!

[61] There is an admirable summary of many of the varied responses to Mahler's deployment of the chorale in the finale of the Fifth in HLG(E) ii. 822–85. The major statement of Adorno's scepticism with regard to the Fifth will be found in Adorno, *Mahler*, 136–8.

that he was prepared to take advantage of its traditional affiliations and associations. But it is far more interesting and illuminating, I believe, to try to analyse those musical, even utilitarian, reasons why the chorale must have seemed to him to fit the bill precisely. In short, it was not the influence (or seductiveness) of tradition alone that made the choice of chorale as agent of resolution imperative.

Some of those reasons I have already touched on above, for example, directional thrust and the chorale's capability both to affirm and fade (and yet preserve its identity); but any scrutiny of the chorale's inherent properties must include two further items. First, what one might describe in the context of the music of Part I as a whole, the 'alien' character of the chorale, an intrusion—interruption, in truth—from another aesthetic, another world of musical ideas, another *vocabulary* altogether, which Mahler must have realized to be exactly what he was seeking for: it is in its 'otherness' that the strength of the chorale resides. In this respect, indeed, it seems to me to be more like an *objet trouvé* than a symbol of traditional values. (This may develop later, as a matter of natural course, in the finale, but is not manifest here.) Second, and yet more importantly, while the chorale here, on its first materialization, offers, *because* of its drastic abridgement, a potentiality for future expansion, that very same *truncation*, in the unique context of the drama that Part I of this extraordinary symphony rehearses, consummately *completes* the cycle of ascent–collapse that is Part I's *raison d'être*—not by breaking it but by representing it in its ultimate guise! After which, one may well feel (along with the composer), that there is no more to be said, no absolute imperative that further music (movements, even) should transpire.

The Coda of the 'Hauptsatz'

This is a major issue, to which I shall return in *my* coda below. Meanwhile, there follows one further brief burst of energy after the fifth Cut-off (I², Fig. 30) that very swiftly subsides into Mahler's coda (I², Fig. 33), itself an exceptional feat of orchestral refinement. The orchestra is much reduced; the brass muted (a mixture of mutes (trumpets) and hand-stopping (horns)); the dynamics, but for a solitary *sforzando*, never rise above *p*, while bleached, spectral fragments of some of the movement's principal motives are recalled as if overheard in a dream. The only constant rhythmic feature is the unvaried triplet figuration of the divided first violins, a conflation of fourths, for which Mahler indicates artificial harmonics, and an overall dynamic of *pp*. This thin, ethereal string sound forms a backdrop against which the motivic shards are articulated. The very last sequence of motives we hear (see Ex. 11.4) unites the ubiquitous ascending upbeat and its consequent falling away, a graphic reduction at this last moment of the movement's life to the basic contour of its overriding obsession: ascent and collapse.[62] A final touch of drained colour is provided by

[62] It was Hans Keller who was the first to point out that one of the leading themes in Britten's *Peter Grimes*—'What harbour shelters peace?' (Act I, sc. 2)—had its source in this theme of Mahler's. Britten had first heard the Fifth, a broadcast from Holland, in 1934. It was this symphony of Mahler's above all that was a major influence on Britten's opera of 1945, e.g. cf. his 'Storm' interlude with Mahler's Allegro in Part I. The contribution of the Fifth to *Grimes* is amply documented in Paul Banks (ed.), *The Making of 'Peter Grimes'*, vol. 2, Notes and Commentaries (Woodbridge, The

Ex. 11.4. Fifth Symphony. The last page of the coda in the 1919 score. A revision by Mahler of this page in which he further refined and clarified the *glissandi* in the concluding bars forms part of Vol. V of the Critical Edition of Mahler's works (Vienna, 1989), p. 115. A comparison provides a model example of his revisory practice: the goal was always maximum transparency.

the overlapping entries in the movement's closing bars of the ubiquitous ascending upbeat, detached from any immediate continuation,[63] allotted to solo strings—viola, then cello, then double bass—the upwards leap now transformed into a glissando, *p*. We hear it three times, like sighs, or exhalations of a last breath.

Reflections in the Shape of a Coda

It is just because of the perfect, albeit 'negative', conclusion that is achieved at the end of Part I, that a question remains uppermost in the mind during the interval that ensues— Mahler, as we can see, asks for a long pause, and conductors should observe this—before embarking on Part II: what is there left to say? Such is the extraordinary totality of the musico-dramatic experience that Part I unfolds, that one can feel (temporarily, in performance at least) that anything that follows has to be redundant.

No doubt this is an exaggeration; and I am not (I think) suggesting, at least not seriously, that Parts II and III are expendable. On the other hand, the very fact that this is an impression—more than that, a conviction—that is left with me in the wake of a convincing performance of the symphony, or immersion in the score, says something about the peculiar self-sufficiency of Part I, its unique form deriving from the interdependence of the two opening movements and the inspired obsessiveness and attention to detail with which the drama is worked out; one might, indeed, quite properly describe Part I as a kind of *monodrama* in two acts.

It did not, in fact, surprise me when I had the rare opportunity to hear Part I of the Fifth as an independent item in the course of an orchestral programme,[64] to have confirmed the unique, detached integrity of the 'Trauermarsch' and Allegro, making perfect sense as a musico-dramatic unit: in other words, one did not, as Berg (his *Wozzeck* interludes) hove into view, really miss the unheard rest of Mahler's symphony. At the same time—because *of course* one can not abandon Parts II and III—the very independence of Part I casts an illuminating light on our comprehension of the symphony as a whole.

I find here a parallel with the Sixth, interestingly enough to be the next symphony and the one that was to end in defeat, not triumph; and yet, as I have argued elsewhere, Mahler shows us, in the Sixth, by his rounding off the first movement in a brilliant A major, how the symphony might have concluded had, in fact, the tonic *major* proved to be its ultimate

Britten Estate/The Boydell Press, 1996), and in particular, by Mitchell, '*Peter Grimes*: Fifty Years On', 125–51.

[63] True to form—by which I mean Mahler, contrary to carefully calculated appearances (as here), always ensures that nothing integral is ever omitted—the upbeat is reunited in the last three bars with its rightful continuation, dispersed among the tuba (*morendo!*), harp, pizzicato cellos and basses, and a final stroke on the timpani, an A that Mahler marks *p* with an accent and an indication that this ultimate, isolated pitch must be perfectly tuned and clearly articulated ('gut stimmen!!').

[64] This was at the Aldeburgh Festival of 1995, for which I devised a concert made up of music that had actively influenced Britten in the composition of his opera *Peter Grimes*, the 50th anniversary of the first performance of which the Festival was celebrating. Among the composers represented were Berg, Shostakovich, and Mahler, the last by a performance of Part I of the Fifth, when the City of London Sinfonia was conducted by Steuart Bedford. See also the Programme Book for the 1995 Festival, to which I contributed a note, 'Contexts of Violence: The Sources of *Peter Grimes*', 91–6, and n. 62 above.

destination: 'this first movement . . . incorporates an alternative Sixth that was never composed'.[65]

The parallel of course is not exact. For one thing, the 'alternative' that Part I of the Fifth proposes is much more elaborately fulfilled and at far, far greater length. What indeed we have in the Fifth is virtually an independent 'symphony' contained within the overall form of the Symphony itself, a uniquely self-sufficient and self-generating stretch of symphonic music in two movements, of an originality without parallel (almost) elsewhere in Mahler's oeuvre, that consummately enacts and brings to *tragic* resolution the 'tragic' drama that the symphony *as a whole* is designed to deny. That affirmative denial, we have to believe, awaits us in the finale, and indeed has been prepared. Nonetheless, what the Fifth offers is not, as the Sixth does, a relatively brief glimpse 'of how the inner drama might have gone otherwise', but, rather, two independent 'readings', each complete in itself, each vouchsafing a reverse dénouement of the basic conflict, that is, ascent or collapse, but one of which, Part I, can either work in association with Parts II and III combined or be decoupled and function in isolation.

There is, then, I believe, a case to be made for the very occasional occasion when Part I of the Fifth might be heard as a separate entity with its own identity, strictly for the reasons that I have outlined above; I am not, absolutely not, suggesting some kind of eccentric dismemberment of the symphony. But while I think Part I of the Fifth is an entirely special case, and before I am accused of vandalism or worse, it is surely of some relevance to consider a possible precedent like the first movement of the Second (an earlier 'Trauermarsch') and supreme inventions still to come, like the finale, 'Der Abschied', of *Das Lied*—in effect Part II of that symphony—or the first movement of the Ninth, again huge stretches of symphonic music that in some sense, and despite their incorporation into individual symphonies, can leave a marked impression of downright self-sufficiency. The first movement of the Ninth for me is comparable, for the impression of an integral completeness it makes, to Part I of the Fifth; it is again virtually a one-movement symphony, and I would not object here either to an occasional performance of that movement in isolation. It is certainly not my ambition to start a new performing tradition; but if nothing else, this discussion may provoke us to speculate a little about how Mahler's music might have developed had he been spared to live, say, for another decade. The arbitrariness of his death is too often lost sight of, with the consequence that we 'read' the last works as if they

---

[65] See my note on the Sixth in *GMWL*, 2.71–7 and 74 in particular. The passage I have in mind is that from Fig. 42 to the end of the movement, where the onset of A major plus jubilating timpani, not to speak of the upward thrust of the second subject, the leading motive of which is recalled at this point, cannot but call to mind the aborted A major Interruption towards the end of the second movement of Part I of the Fifth (in the Sixth, the second subject playing the role of the chorale (Chorale I)) that in fact does not fully materialize in the parallel passage of the Fifth's Allegro until the later Interruption that momentarily establishes D (I²) bb. 488 ff.). As the conclusion of the Sixth's first movement proceeds, it increasingly takes on the character of a displaced cyclic recapitulation of first-movement materials (cf. for example, the recapitulatory C major gesture that crowns the finale of the Seventh Symphony (Fig. 293 ff.), for which the conclusion of the first movement of the Sixth was clearly a model) that in other circumstances might have brought the finale of the alternative Sixth, that I have referred to above, to a triumphant A major end. It is thus that Mahler's 'tragic' Sixth also informs us how an optimistic, conquering Sixth might have gone. (Colin Matthews believes that it is in fact the Seventh Symphony itself that represents Mahler's alternative to his Sixth.)

were the logical consequences of a pre-ordained fate. If there had been an 'alternative' *biography*, for example, had Mahler lived on to 1921 instead of dying in 1911, it is my guess, on the basis of those quite extraordinary independent movements that I have singled out (interestingly enough all of them first movements or Parts and, in one case, a finale), that his innovatory, formal thinking might have led him to the creation of new concepts of what might constitute a symphony; Part I of the Fifth, the finale of *Das Lied*, the first movement of the Ninth, contain the seeds—the intimations—of an evolution that, alas, was never to be completed, the results of which might have had a profound influence on the development of the idea of 'symphony' in our century.

Part II

(iii) Scherzo. Kräftig, nicht zu schnell

Chronology and Sketches

The very recent discovery of two further manuscript sources, one incomplete, though substantial, one more complete, for the composition of the Scherzo, is an event of extraordinary interest—where, all these years, have these manuscripts been?—and of exceptional significance for detailed study of Mahler's working methods.[66] What they do not give us, it seems, is any helpful information about chronology; there are no dates, while the paper is of a type in general use by Mahler over a stretch of years that included the composition of the Fifth. We must assume, I think, until fresh evidence suggests otherwise, that these manuscripts—surfacing for the first time in 1996—represent the sketches that Mahler would have had to hand, or under his hands, at the beginning of the summer of 1901, when he began seriously to work on the new symphony: I make the distinction because, taking into account the complex character of the new sources, it seems scarcely credible that the Scherzo plus the two movements of Part I could all have been completed in this first summer of work on the symphony; for instance, does the first (partial) set of newly discovered composition sketches belong to an earlier chronological stage? Were these sketches that he might have brought with him to Maiernigg, to work up and flesh out, as was his habit, during his summer vacation? I often wonder if the division of creative labour between summer and the rest of the year was quite as absolute as established opinion has it. If not, perhaps it was a first set of sketches for the Scherzo that accompanied Mahler to Maiernigg, at the beginning of his summer vacation in 1901.

---

[66] These are an addition to the magnificent Robert Owen Lehman deposit at the Pierpont Morgan Library, New York. I am much indebted to Edward R. Reilly for an early indication of the manuscripts' existence and whereabouts, though their provenance, it seems, has not yet been made known. See also Dr Reilly's 'The Manuscripts of Mahler's Fifth Symphony', in Mitchell and Straub (eds.), *New Sounds, New Century*, 58–63, where he discusses the newfound sketches in some detail.

In any event, we may safely assume that the Scherzo had been round and about in Mahler's thinking for a (relatively) considerable stretch of time, as is indicated by the inclusion of it—as a title—in a projected scheme for the Fourth Symphony, in six movements, the fifth of which,[67] ran as follows: 'Die Welt ohne Schwere, D-dur [D major] (Scherzo)'. In 1975 (*WY*, 139) I translated Mahler's title as 'The World without Care', a version that I think now conveyed no sense of the weight, the heaviness, that 'Schwere' implies (along with seriousness and severity); in any case, my own inadequate terminology might have been better spelled out as 'The World without Cares' which would at least have had the merit of not flatly contradicting Mahler's own description of the movement to Natalie Bauer-Lechner in the summer of 1901: 'There is nothing romantic or mystical about it; it is simply the expression of incredible energy [*unerhörte Kraft*]. It is a human being in the full light of day, in the prime of his life . . .'.[68] For Mahler, one might think already (with some disbelief), a remarkably shadowless, shadow-free, concept, a question to which we shall return. Meanwhile, still intent on decoding the title, we note Floros's—or his translator's, Vernon Wicker's—clever translation, 'The World without Gravity',[69] which accommodates the idea of a weightlessness of spirit and at the same time, of material things, 'Gravity' in its scientific sense; and—who knows?—given Mahler's interest in the physical sciences, it might well have been this meaning of 'Schwere' that attracted him to incorporate this word, and not some other, into his title.

The Character of the Scherzo

But more important than the title, which I guess Mahler would have formulated before he had a very detailed picture in his mind of how the music might eventually go, is the character of the music itself. Perhaps the first thing to observe, however, is the Scherzo's principal tonality, D major. There was surely an element of risk here, of a premature affirmation of a D major that from the outset of the symphony Mahler had envisaged to be its goal. We have seen how, at the end of Part I, we are left in no doubt that there is much ground still to be travelled before there can be any chance of a secure D major establishing itself. Does, then, the exuberant D major in which the opening Ländler of the Scherzo declares itself, constitute a misjudgement, or perhaps a puzzling paradox? In other words, is this, at this stage, where we ought to be?[70]

[67] Mahler's tentative numbering of the narrative scheme for a possible Fourth gives us *two* fifth movements, i.e. the movement that succeeds the Scherzo, 'Das himmlische Leben, G-dur [G major]', is also marked as No. 5 in the sequence of titles, though placed sixth and last. The outline scheme was first published in Bekker, *Gustav Mahlers Sinfonien*, 145. See also Mitchell, *WY*, 139, where I refer to the draft programme showing 'the dense intertwining of song and symphony characteristic of these 'Wunderhorn' years' and further, on 258–9 (n. 30), suggest that it 'must belong to the time when Mahler was engaged on the Third Symphony and still uncertain as to the exact disposition of the wealth of invention and creative ideas available to him.

Already, it seems, even before the final shape of one symphony was determined, the shape of another was materializing . . .'.

[68] NB-L, *Recollections*, 173.

[69] *Gustav Mahler: The Symphonies*, 111. Likewise, HLG(E) ii. 800. I have gratefully adopted 'Gravity' and use it throughout this chapter.

[70] Deryck Cooke, in *Gustav Mahler: An Introduction to his Music*, 82–3, takes the view that it certainly is: the Scherzo 'completely contradicts the nihilistic mood and minor tonality of practically everything that has gone before, by switching to the brilliant key of D major, and to an exploration of the joyfully affirmative view of life, both of

In attempting to answer that question we have to look back for a moment to Mahler's own concept of 'a human being in the full light of day, in the prime of his life', and remark that the movement he created, brimming over with energy though it may be, is in fact (and unsurprisingly) replete with extraordinary moments of darkness and frenzy which effectively undermine any conclusion we might reach that the Scherzo's D major represents the D that is (still) Mahler's—his symphony's—ultimate goal.

For a start, even the most cursory scan of the movement reveals a notable accumulation of minor keys, among them F minor, D minor, A minor, E minor, which, if one takes into account the nervous, shadowy, sceptical, even desperate music associated with these tonal excursions, makes one realize how impossible it is to reconcile the image of Cooke's 'joyfully affirmative view of life' or indeed of Mahler's, of 'a human being in the full light of day', with what some of the most significant music of the Scherzo is actually telling us.

Adorno, with his customary, if elliptical, economy, points to the Scherzo's novelty, that is, to Mahler's concept of it as a 'development-scherzo',[71] thus isolating what is so striking about it, what Adorno himself goes on to describe as the composer's labouring 'at the possibility of a symphonic unity arising from dances arranged serially as in a suite', a *trouvaille* 'without which, incidentally, Strauss's *Rosenkavalier* [1911] would hardly be thinkable'.[72] And not only *Rosenkavalier*, but also perhaps, and much more relevantly, Ravel's *La Valse* (1919–20)? It was surely Mahler who, in the Scherzo of this Fifth Symphony, was the first to deploy the waltz as an ironic icon, subjecting it to all manner of distortion and consistent reversal or contradiction of its traditional meanings? This, after all, is what happens in the waltz section (F minor) that develops, after the very brief beguilement of its opening bars (bb. 429 ff.: the double bar marks the end of the movement's central trio section), into a veritable dance of death, especially when, in bars 472–5 and again in 482–5, the *Holzklapper* (whip), *fortissimo*, takes over its rhythm (forcefully doubled by the trumpets)—the horrible rattle of bones—from the glockenspiel (cf. b. 462). It is precisely here, in the Scherzo of Mahler's Fifth, that the Viennese waltz, perhaps never an entirely virginal concept, finally lost its innocence.

Mahler, Goethe, and Schubert

We owe to Constantin Floros the restitution of a bit of fascinating information that was originally included in Richard Specht's early monograph on Mahler first published in 1905,[73]

---

which are to occupy the rest of the symphony. Thus the dark world of Part I is not gradually dispelled by a process of spiritual development: it is abruptly rejected [*sic*] in favour of a completely different attitude', etc., etc. As will emerge below, this is a view I do not share, one moreover that seriously underestimates the compositional skills Mahler demonstrates in avoiding just such a crude contradiction that would have fatally weakened the overall evolution of the narrative. To be sure (and fair), Cooke concedes moments of 'nostalgia' and 'haunting music full of sadness and loneliness'. But these he suggests 'have nothing emotionally in common with the despairing laments of the first part of the work . . . The scherzo is really a dance of life, evoking all the bustle of a vital existence, as opposed to the concentration on the inevitability of death in the funeral marches and ferocious protests of Part I.'

[71] Adorno, *Mahler*, 102.

[72] Ibid. 103.

[73] Floros, *Gustav Mahler: The Symphonies*, 153–4, and Specht, *Gustav Mahler* (Berlin, Gose und Tetßlaff, 1905), 44–5. But Specht also refers to Goethe's poem—in fact he quotes a line from it—in his second, large-scale monograph published in 1913, 290–1. The English translation I use is by Norma Deane and Celia Larner, in John Reed, *The Schubert Song Companion* (London: Faber, 1993), 47.

who drew his readers' attention to a close parallel between a poem by Goethe, 'An Schwager Kronos' (To Brother Time the Coachman), and the character of those parts of the Scherzo that have particularly interested me. In so doing, Specht specifically mentions Bruno Walter's perception that Mahler's Scherzo grew out of Goethe's poem; and given Walter's intimate association with the composer it must be highly probable that this was something that he had from Mahler himself.

What Specht does not mention (nor, oddly, does Floros) is the famous setting of the poem by Schubert (D. 369), similarly entitled 'An Schwager Kronos'. This would also certainly have been well known to Mahler; and I have no doubt that the conjunction of Goethe's text and Schubert's music offers us a source, a 'model', of some significance for the Scherzo of the Fifth. The song gallops along in 6/8 from beginning to end in an unmodified moderate tempo ('Nicht zu schnell') and in an energetic D minor. Before the double bar is reached, however, Schubert registers the impact of the poet's vision of faltering old age and advancing death in a turbulent chromatic interpolation, climaxing on Goethe's image of the 'dark gate of hell'. The 'gate', however, opens not on hell but on the postilion's cheerful horn signals that take over and round off the song in a brilliant, unqualified D major. The character of the narrative itself, which includes not only an unnerving vision of a 'dance of death' (Mahler's *Holzklapper*!) but also, we may think, a glimpse of 'a human being in the full light of day, in the prime of his life' (Mahler's words), plus the incorporation of the post-horn, plus—and perhaps most importantly—the song's tonality, seem to me good reason for including Schubert's song among the influential sources that contributed to the making of Mahler's Scherzo.

'An Schwager Kronos'	*'To Brother Time the Coachman'*
Spude dich, Kronos! Fort den raßelnden Trab! Bergab gleitet der Weg; Ekles Schwindeln zögert Mir vor die Stirne dein Zaudern. Frisch, holpert es gleich, Über Stock und Steine den Trott Rasch ins Leben hinein!	Hurry on, Time, on at a rattling trot! The road runs downhill, your dawdling makes things swim before my eyes. On at a brisk pace, over stick and stone, stumbling headlong into life!
Nun schon wieder Den eratmenden Schritt Mühsam Berghinauf, Auf denn, nicht träge denn, Strebend und hoffend hinan!	Now once more toiling uphill, out of breath—up then, no slacking, upward striving and hoping.
Weit, hoch, herrlich Rings den Blick ins Leben hinein, Vom Gebirg zum Gebirg Schwebet der ewige Geist, Ewigen Lebens ahndevoll.	High, wide, and glorious the prospect of life rings us round. The eternal spirit soars from peak to peak, full of intimations of eternal life.

Seitwärts des Überdachs Schatten   A shadowy doorway beckons you aside across the
Zieht dich an   threshold of the girl's house, and her eyes promise
Und ein Frischung verheißender Blick   refreshment. Take comfort! For me too, lass,
Auf der Schwelle des Mädchens da.   that sparkling draught, that fresh and healthy look.
Labe dich!—Mir auch, Mädchen,
Diesen schäumenden Trank,
Diesen frischen Gesundheitsblick!

Ab denn, rascher hinab!   Down then, faster down! See, the sun sinks. Before
Sieh, die Sonne sinkt!   it sets, before the marsh-mist envelops me in my
Eh sie sinkt, eh mich Greisen   old age, with toothless gnashing jaws and tottering
Ergreift im Moore Nebelduft,   limbs;
Entzahnte Kiefer schnattern
Und das schlotternde Gebein.

Trunkenen vom letzten Strahl reiß mich,   snatch me, drunk with the sun's last ray, a sea of
ein Feuermeer   fire boiling up before my eyes, blind and reeling
Mir im schäumenden Aug,   through the dark gate of hell.
Mich geblendeten Taumelnden
In der Hölle nächtliches Tor.

Töne, Schwager, ins Horn,   Blow your horn, brother, clatter on at a noisy trot.
Raßle den schallenden Trab,   Let Orcus know we are coming, so that mine host
Daß der Orkus vernehme: wir kommen,   will be there at the door to welcome us.
Daß gleich an der Tür
Der Wirt uns freundlich empfange.

                                            (trans. Norma Deane and Celia Larner)

The Character of the Scherzo Resumed: Retrospections and Innovating Anticipations

The reference to the postilion's horn in Goethe's final stanza inevitably summons up the
trio of Mahler's Scherzo, which in turn looks back to the post-horn trio in the Scherzo of
the Third Symphony; this is the only feature of the Scherzo in the Fifth that is unequivocally retrospective. For the rest, this 'development-scherzo'—Adorno's serial suite of
dances—very clearly anticipates, in form and treatment, Mahler's late scherzos, that is,
those of the Ninth and Tenth Symphonies, while those of the Sixth and Seventh pursue a
different function and in quite a different manner. They are indeed brilliant inventions,
pungently atmospheric—spooky—and profoundly idiosyncratic in character, as remote
from the traditionally energetic and energizing role of the 'classical' (dance-)scherzo as it
is possible to imagine. But the Scherzo of the Fifth is something quite else, for which
reason I believe Paul Bekker, in his magisterial study of 1921,[74] refers to it (p. 179) as
'Mahler's first traditional [*artgerechts*] Scherzo' and, a few pages on (p. 188), as 'Mahler's
first Scherzo in the classical spirit of a dance-piece [*Tanzstück*]'.[75]

[74] *Gustav Mahlers Sinfonien.* Why has this influential
study never appeared in English translation?
[75] Bekker goes on to state that in Mahler's later sym-

phonies this 'type' of Scherzo was not to return. But he oddly
overlooked the Scherzo of the Ninth, another 'dance-piece',
surely? And the type in fact was to emerge again in the

There is a further observation of Adorno's (pp. 102–3) that relates to wider issues: 'The structure of the movement', he writes, 'is itself governed by counterpoint' (likewise, he might have added, the second movement of Part I and the second movement of Part III). In isolating this fundamental feature that helps create the 'symphonic unity' of the Scherzo, he also reminds us how much the unity of the work as a whole owes to its cease-less counterpointing, despite the many different types of polyphony involved on a move-ment-by-movement basis. And that, in turn, reminds me of a relationship with the Fourth that has gone largely unremarked. There may appear at first sight to be an unbridgeable gulf between the Scherzo of the Fifth and the sophisticated sonata-form first movement of the Fourth, about which I have already said so much. But I want to suggest that in fact, set-ting aside the obvious differences in the two movements' forms and the character of the musical materials involved, the treatment of them in the Fifth's Scherzo derives from the composer's practice in the first movement of the Fourth. I am not just thinking of the coun-terpoint, though clearly much of the polyphony of the Fifth, as I have argued, can be heard as a logical evolution from the polyphony of the Fourth. Yet more striking, however, is the parallel in developmental and narrative strategy between the development section of the Fourth's first movement and the development(s) of Mahler's 'development-scherzo'. In short, we are unnerved by those developments in the Scherzo of the Fifth in precisely the same way and by precisely the same means—thematic distortion, unforeseen motivic com-binations, excursions into unsettled or unsettling tonal areas (often minor keys), shrill or hollow (e.g. the whip in the Fifth) instrumentation—that we encounter in the development of the Fourth's first movement. Indeed, taking into account that it is, for the most part, the most innocent-seeming of the Scherzo's materials, the waltz, that is subjected to the most intensive and sceptical 'development', is it all that far-fetched to ask ourselves if we do not have here another example of the confrontation between Innocence—of which the waltz, at its first appearance in B flat at Fig. 6, is the very picture—and Experience, that is so marked a feature of the first movement of the Fourth? It is, I submit, a technique and aesthetic strategy repeated here in the Scherzo of the Fifth for exactly the same reasons, that is, to ensure that the D major that the Scherzo 'affirms' is heavily qualified, just as the seemingly blithe and uncomplicated G major associations of the Fourth's first movement are subjected to critical developmental scrutiny. In both cases we are left, as the composer intends, with the conviction that there are still narrative and musical issues to be resolved before either symphony may be reckoned to have run its course.

I have briefly mentioned the trio's central episode and its retrospection: the obbligato horn here naturally recalls the post-horn solo in the Scherzo of the Third. But in one respect at least the trio vouchsafes a glimpse of Mahler's innovating imagination, the extra-ordinary passage for a quartet of horns (Fig. 10, bb. 270–8). There is good reason for this. The timbre of the horn is fundamental to the character of the Scherzo, and here we have a huge release of horn-sound, out of which, with perfect logic, emerges the obbligato horn,

Tenth, notably in the second of the work's two Scherzos, though of course in the 1920s Bekker would have had no way of knowing this.

Ex. 11.5. Fifth Symphony, Part II, Scherzo, bb. 271–7

blowing the melody of the trio—'Blow your horn, brother . . . ', as Goethe has it—and conducting an echo-like dialogue with differently constituted instrumental groups. Given the
concertante role that the horn has to play in the movement in its entirety, this great tumult
of horns that signals the onset of the trio could not be more apt. But what could never have
been foreseen, and continues to astonish—another testing passage for the conductor—is
the composer's articulation of his tremendous horn signal (see Ex. 11.5). He lays this out
for his four hornists as if it were a highly compressed canon or round (favourite contrapuntal forms for Mahler),[76] made up of overlapping *fortissimo* entries, each horn in numerical turn, all of them with their bells up, on a single pitch, F: in short a sustained unison,
across seven bars (Fig. 10[+1] ff.) that is also a canon. One must not overlook the systematic
detailing of the dynamics which permits each successive horn entry to be heard and then
add to the crescendo, which the obbligato horn joins first by stealth, i.e. *pp*, so there can be
no mistaking its participation as a fresh 'entry', and then, by matching the dynamics (in b.
278) with the *fortissimo* of horn 4, takes over in solo flight at the exact dynamic level at
which horn 4 relinquishes its entry. This is an exceptional passage by any standards, and
one which caught the ear of Mahler's successors, especially Berg[77] and Webern. After all,

[76] It is not just 'Bruder Martin' in the First Symphony that
I am thinking of but the setting of 'Die du grossen Sünde
rinnen' at Fig. 136 in Part II of the Eighth. See also Mitchell,
SSLD, 587–8 and nn. 51 and 54, 612.

[77] One only needs to look at the crescendo on a unison B
in Berg's *Wozzeck*, Act III, Fig. 110, to realize how deeply

indebted was Berg's famous Expressionist gesture to
Mahler's precedent in his Fifth. See also 'What is
Expressionism?' in Donald Mitchell, *Cradles of the New:
Writings on Music, 1951–1991*, ed. Christopher Palmer and
Mervyn Cooke (London: Faber, 1995), 219 ff.

is there not bound up in the intricacies of how Mahler lays out his unison, the idea of the rhythmic canon, not to speak of the systematic sequential ordering of dynamics as a prime parameter of the musical idea as a whole? This horn signal, then, succeeds in launching a retrospection by compositional means which clearly presage the future, a characteristic Mahler paradox one may think.[78]

The Scherzo brings to fulfilment one of the most striking aspects of the opening of the second trio in the first movement of Part I, where we first hear adumbrated the role of the horn as obbligato soloist,[79] the same trio that at its opening, as has been amply emphasized, introduces the concept of the string orchestra into the symphony as a sonority in its own right. This pregnant anticipation is now fully opened out, with the addition of harp, in the Adagietto which forms the prelude to the finale, and with it constitutes Part III. Thus the seminal second trio has an influential hand in both parts of the symphony that succeed Part I.

Part III

(iv) Adagietto Sehr langsam (v) Rondo-Finale Allegro

Larger Symmetries

These days it is scarcely a revelatory observation to point to the integral unit that the Adagietto and finale of the Fifth comprise; worth making again however, because it emphasizes one of the larger symmetries of the total form of the symphony that often goes unnoticed but in fact is one of the work's distinguishing features, especially in the context of Mahler's oeuvre as a whole: it is his only symphony in which the two pairs of movements (slow/fast) which form Parts I and III are conjoined by systematic inter-quotation, that is, in each case the second movement extensively quotes from the materials surfacing first in the first movement. A novel process, and one peculiar to the Fifth, for which reason it seems not at all inapposite to think of or refer to the work as Mahler's 'quotation' symphony. (The only other writer whom I know to have made this same point is Adorno, not in his monograph but in his Centenary Address, Vienna, 1960 (the 100th anniversary of Mahler's birth).)[80]

---

[78] There may also have been a different kind of retrospection involved in this passage. On the one occasion that I heard Smetana's opera *Hubička* in the opera house (in Prague), a work Mahler first heard in the 1880s and later was to conduct himself at Hamburg in 1895, the interlude for orchestra alone between Scenes 1 and 2 of Act II, representing night giving way to dawn in the shape of a continuous C major crescendo, very strongly evoked for me the horn unison in Mahler' Fifth. I think it not at all improbable that Mahler's signal had its distant origins in Smetana's interlude. As time passes I believe we shall uncover more and more instances of Mahler's debt to Smetana. See also Mitchell, 'Mahler and Smetana', and above, Ch. 10, pp. 222–6.

[79] A precedent for the obbligato horn in the Scherzo of the Fifth is to be found, however, in the Scherzo of the Fourth. Cf. e.g. Fig. 5[+4], where Mahler marks the first horn part 'sehr hervortretend' (very prominent). Many of the ensuing solo flights for horn in this movement directly anticipate the role of the obbligato horn in the Fifth.

[80] This—plus a new section, 'Afterthoughts'—was included in an English translation in Adorno's *Quasi una*

The Adagietto in and out of Context: Its Peculiar Reception and Performance Histories

It could well be that the famous Adagietto, the fourth movement of the symphony, the first movement of Part III, a prelude to the finale that at the same time is the symphony's only slow movement, might come out ahead in any attempt to identify the movement of Mahler's about which most has been written or which has stimulated most contention. It is not just that my description of it as the work's 'only slow movement' must immediately prompt the response, 'Yes; but *how* slow?', and thus raise an issue of interpretation that has engaged the attention of not a few students (and performers) of Mahler in recent years but—a yet more fundamental issue—how good is it, how faithful to—characteristic of— the creative personality whom we think we know, and whose 'truth' (his capacity to be true to himself) we think we can recognize from our experience of his music. In short, could— as some have thought—the Adagietto represent some sort of 'betrayal' by the composer of his own values and ideals?

Among the keenest sceptics is Adorno, who dismisses the Adagietto as 'shallow senti-mentality',[81] a movement that 'borders on genre prettiness through its ingratiating sound'. At the same time he recognizes the importance of its conception 'as an individual piece within the whole',[82] a point to which I shall return. An earlier adverse opinion Mahler was to receive by post from Richard Strauss, who wrote, after attending a performance of the Fifth in Berlin conducted by Nikisch in February 1905—'Your . . . Symphony again gave me great pleasure in the full rehearsal, a pleasure only slightly dimmed by the little Adagietto. But as this was what pleased the audience most, you are getting what you deserve.'[83] Mahler certainly got what, by now, he must surely have *expected* in the way of a critical reception of his new symphony, a chiefly negative response, but—*pace* Strauss— for the Adagietto, which won almost uniform public approbation.

Irony, one might think, attended Mahler in his life, it was not only a component of his music; and virtually a compound of ironies has been a feature of the Adagietto's history

Fantasia: Essays on Modern Music, trans. Rodney Living-stone (London: Verso, 1992). Adorno writes: 'Because of their vast scope Mahler was induced to construct entire symphonies on the principle of correspondence. In the Fifth, for example, the Funeral March is elaborated in the second movement parallel to a theme of the Adagietto in the finale, and between these two analogously structured parts [Parts I and III] the great Scherzo acts as a caesura' (p. 105). Edward Reilly (in conversation) has made an interesting further suggestion about the symmetries in the Fifth to which Adorno refers. If indeed it were the case that the first movement to be composed was the Scherzo (Part II), then the brilliance of Mahler's subsequent articulation of his tripartite total structure shows up in his concept of Part I as exclusively 'tragic' or 'negative' in character while Part III concentrates on the life-enhancing and positive. In short, Part I makes a proposition (thesis), which Part III counters with its opposite (antithesis), while the Scherzo mediates the transition from one to the other. One might think the thesis/antithesis pattern can be discerned not only in the 'analogously struc-

tured' Parts I and III, but in almost every parameter of the symphony's organization, e.g. 'Wunderhorn' imagery (Part I, 'Trauermarsch') is replaced by 'Rückert' imagery in Part III; and since it is specific sonorities we are talking about (there are no verbal clues!), the thesis/antithesis conjunction (or *disjunction*, better) unequivocally manifests itself in the wind band orientation of Part I[1] and the strings plus harp orientation of Part III[1]. One might discern the same 'pairing' at work even in the organization of the work's dynamics, e.g. compare the D major 'Höhepunkt' that Mahler locates towards the end of Part I[2] (b. 500)—a climax that *fails*— with a similarly calculated 'Höhepunkt' (though not inscribed as such by Mahler) in Part III[2], a D major climax (b. 731) that this time *prevails*.

[81] Adorno, *Mahler*, 51. Adorno's German, however, is more powerfully dismissive: 'kulinarische Sentimentalität' (German edn., 74), for which 'cooked-up' or 'dished-up sentimentality' might serve as an English equivalent.
[82] Ibid. 136.
[83] *Gustav Mahler–Richard Strauss: Correspondence*, 75.

since it was first heard in 1904. For a start, how ironic that a movement that was conceived as prelude or slow introduction to a succeeding finale, as the first part of an integral two-part unit (the two parts in a differently executed but similar organic association as the two parts of Part I), was soon to be detached from its natural continuation and fulfilment, to lead a kind of amputated afterlife as an independent item in the concert hall or broadcasting studio, or on a ten-inch shellac disc.[84] This strange performance history reflects the strange history of the reception of Mahler's symphonies, shaped as that was not just by the familiar difficulties that narrative forms and innovative language habitually encounter before the breakthrough into public comprehension, but also by political events and swings in cultural fashion. Mahler's music had to contend not only with the cataclysm of the First World War but the appalling political ideologies that held sway in Germany from the early 1930s until the end of the Second World War in 1945. This meant that there were large areas of the world in which Mahler's music was suppressed;[85] and where it was not suppressed, there were pitifully few performances because—to take Britain as an example—the dominant musical culture of the day, also in its way ideological rather than rational,[86] set its face against Mahler or, rather, closed its ears to him. The confidence of the adverse views expressed was only equalled by the ignorance of the music itself.

This is not the place to rehearse the generally sorry history of the reception of Mahler's symphonies between the two World Wars; there were of course brilliant exceptions, pairs of ears in England (Henry Boys's and Benjamin Britten's, for instance), in Russia (Ivan

[84] The first recording of the Adagietto was made in May 1926 by the Concertgebouw Orchestra conducted by Mengelberg and issued on the Odeon label, 0 8591. Interestingly, the title on the label runs as follows: 'Adagietto a. d. [aus der] V. Symphonie/II. Teil (Mahler)'. Bruno Walter's recording of the Adagietto with the Vienna Philharmonic Orchestra was made in 1938, on 15 Jan. In *GMWL*, 1.15, Truus de Leur, 'Gustav Mahler in the Netherlands', writes: 'The Adagietto [as a separate item] was to become one of Mengelberg's showpieces—witness the performances and recordings he made of it in later years.' Small wonder that in our very own time—the 1990s—the Adagietto has found a home in more than one 'compilation disc', along with other severed limbs and parts.

[85] An incident during a concert given in the Concertgebouw, Amsterdam, on 5 Oct. 1939 is a painful reminder of the ideology that was shortly to oppress Europe (we should recall that just a month earlier, on 3 Sept., a state of war had been declared between Germany and the United Kingdom). Carl Schuricht was the conductor of the Concertgebouw Orchestra in a performance of *Das Lied*, with Kerstin Thorborg and Martin Oehman as soloists. During a pause in the 'Abschied' a supporter of Germany and the Nazis shouted, 'Deutschland über alles, Herr Schuricht!', an intervention greeted with whistles and boos from the scandalized audience. Seven months later Holland was invaded and performances of Mahler's works banned, as they had been in Germany since 1933. I am indebted to Mr Pierre Geelen, of Aerdenhout in Holland, who drew my

attention to this incident. The intervention can clearly be heard on a CD that was issued in 1993 of Schuricht's performance (Archiphon, ARCH-3.1). The recording was originally discovered in the archives of Dutch Radio (NAA).

[86] e.g. Vaughan Williams's famous dismissal of Mahler: 'Intimate acquaintance with the executive side of music in orchestra, chorus, and opera made even [*sic*] Mahler into a very tolerable imitation of a composer' (Ralph Vaughan Williams, *National Music and Other Essays* (2nd edn., Oxford: Oxford University Press, 1987), 187). Or there was Julius Harrison's judgement, enshrined in a popular guide, *The Musical Companion*, ed. A. L. Bacharach (London: Gollancz, 1934) and many times reprinted. Having concluded that Bruckner's nine symphonies 'are in no wise worthy to rank with those of the great masters', he went on to add: 'Much the same can be said of the nine composed by Mahler; works of enormous size; interesting at times but laboriously put together and lacking that vital spark of inspiration that made Beethoven's nine the only nine springing direct from the nine Muses' (p. 237). I can not forbear a mention of Dyneley Hussey's memorable prediction, in the same compilation, p. 456, that 'It is not improbable that, of Mahler's music, posterity will cling to the songs and let the rest go.' Posterity, it seems, has taken its revenge on Harrison and Hussey rather than the composer. But their views, like Vaughan Williams's, were thoroughly representative of entrenched conservative opinion in the 1920s and 1930s.

Sollertinsky's and Dmitri Shostakovich's), and in the States (Aaron Copland's), that 'heard' Mahler quite otherwise. If I use quotes, it is because knowledge of his scores had to be obtained from reading them; performances, opportunities actually to *hear* the music, were few and far between. For which reason early recordings took on a quite special significance, among them, inevitably, those of the Adagietto, which was also, because of its relative brevity and slender resources, one of the few bits of Mahler that surmounted the culture barrier and was occasionally admitted into the concert hall.

The highly unusual history of this one movement from a Mahler symphony—which, remember, had been heard much more often in isolation than as an integral part of the symphony from which it had become unnaturally detached—has contributed, I believe, to the ambiguities and contradictions that seem still to surround its interpretation, even though, as our century comes to an end, that performance history has been reversed: it is now relatively infrequent to encounter the Adagietto without the symphony to which it belongs.

It is to the divorce of the Adagietto from the finale that I attribute the extremes in variation of tempo that have in recent years been the subject of so much critical attention. I do seriously wonder, for example, if the funereal tempo of Bernstein,[87] who on one celebrated occasion—the funeral of Robert [Bobby] Kennedy in 1968—performed the Adagietto in the spirit of a solemn valediction,[88] would ever have happened but for its promotion as an authentic slow movement by Mahler (the genuine article, of course, was often, and properly, very slow) that could stand alone; the hijacking of the movement—of the supposed emotion it represented, at least—surely reached its apogee when Visconti used the Adagietto in his film of Mann's *Death in Venice* (1971) as sonorous symbol of Aschenbach's nostalgia, frustrated passion, and hopeless longing: one might think, ironically, that the singular performance history of the Adagietto up to this point had been nothing but preparation for the iconic, cult status with which Mahler's prelude to the finale of his Fifth Symphony found itself lumbered as a result of the film.[89]

---

[87] More than 11 minutes in one instance. Slow enough, one might think, but this pales into insignificance when compared with such eccentricities as Scherchen's 15 minutes plus, or Haitink's 14 minutes (approximately). I choose these examples more or less at random. The field of contrasting tempi is exhaustively documented in Gilbert E. Kaplan's facsimile edition. (See also Table 11.1, p. 242 above, for the details of Mahler's Hamburg performance in 1905.)

[88] See Humphrey Burton, *Leonard Bernstein* (London: Faber, 1994), 373–4: 'Jacqueline Kennedy [the former President's widow] called Bernstein . . . to ask him to supervise the music for the funeral at St. Patrick's Cathedral in New York... . He persuaded the appropriate Monsignor at the cathedral to agree to the inclusion of the "Adagietto" movement for strings and harp from Mahler's Fifth Symphony... . It was, Bernstein recalled, a beautiful service. "The Mahler part of it was made more beautiful by the Kennedy children's procession up to the Altar carrying the Communion articles." ' There was an earlier occasion too when Bernstein had used the Adagietto to commemorate his

old teacher and patron, Serge Koussevitsky, who died in 1951. Burton tells us further (p. 532) that 'a baton and the score of Mahler's Fifth Symphony were placed in the coffin alongside the body'.

[89] See also Philip Reed, 'Aschenbach becomes Mahler: Thomas Mann as Film', in *Death in Venice*, ed. Donald Mitchell (Cambridge: Cambridge University Press, 1987), 178–83. A memorable exchange on Classic FM between the Rt. Hon. David Mellor and Vinnie Jones, reported in *The Guardian*, 9 Jan. 1998, was a disquieting reminder of the continuing currency of the association. In one of his comments to Vinnie Jones, football's 'hard man' as the paper put it, Mellor remarks: 'I want to tell you about a piece of music that I came across in a film called *Death in Venice*, about the love of a middle-aged man for the beauty of a young boy. They played the Adagietto, the slow movement of a Mahler Symphony. At the beginning of this film there is this gondola going across the lagoon into Venice. Every time I listen to this music I think about this film [*sic*]. And I am deeply moved by it [plays Adagietto] . . .'.

It is true that Mahler himself once, and once only, gave a performance of the Adagietto as an independent item in a concert that he conducted in Rome in 1907, in the Augusteo on 1 April, with the orchestra of the Accademia di Santa Cecilia; but it would be an error to think that this constituted a precedent that thereafter legitimized the dissolution of the Adagietto's marriage to the finale. Quite the contrary. Mahler's original intention when planning his programmes had been to perform the fourth and fifth movements—Part III— of his symphony as an integral unit. (I wonder what he might have made of my suggestion that we might, likewise, on occasion hear Part I as a self-sufficient item? See my Coda, above, pp. 298–9.) What seems to have prevented this plan coming to fruition was the mis- routing of the Mahlers' baggage when they were on their way to Rome—Alma spells this out in her memoirs—baggage that included Mahler's conducting scores and, presumably, orchestral material (of the Fifth, at least).[90] The scores and parts were recovered in suffi- cient time for Mahler to introduce the Adagietto into his second concert, along with Weber's overture to *Der Freischütz*, Tchaikovsky's *Romeo and Juliet*, and Beethoven's Seventh. Perhaps too these circumstances may have encouraged him to be cautious; the mediocre standards of the orchestra at that time might not have enabled it to rise to the challenge of the finale.[91] Incidentally, at an early stage in planning this sequence of two concerts for Rome, Mahler had considered including the Andante and Scherzo from the Second Symphony. He was not celebrated as a composer in Italy. Did he have it in mind when turning over his ideas for the programmes that he would be addressing audiences not only unfamiliar with his music but inhabiting quite another musical culture?

It has not been my intention here to go over all the ground that has been exhaustively documented in the facsimile edition, and explored above all in Paul Banks's pioneering article,[92] but, rather, to make a note of the extra-musical factors, socio-political, historical, and cultural, that have conditioned, I suggest, our reception of the Adagietto, the way we hear it; and then there is performance practice, past and present, which in turn conditions *what* we hear.

I prefer to concentrate on what seems to me to be important aspects of the Adagietto that have not been sufficiently recognized. First, the altogether exceptional incorporation into the symphony—'für grosses Orchester' as the title-page has it—of a movement for string orchestra and harp. This certainly represented a radical departure from tradition. Indeed, can one think of a precedent in the orchestral tradition, i.e. post-Beethoven, which is surely the only relevant tradition here? To be sure, the character of Mahler's Adagietto may have been influenced by Bizet's Adagietto from the first *L'Arlésienne* suite;[93] but by far the most significant precedents are to be found in the evolution of Mahler's own orchestral thinking, e.g. in the gradual deconstruction across his oeuvre of 'the orchestra' into an assembly of diverse orchestras and instrumental groups, the string orchestra among them.[94]

[90] See Alma Mahler, *Memories*, 117–19.
[91] See also HLG(F) iii. 20–6. An important fresh source of information regarding Mahler's Italian visit is *Mahler a Roma* (Rome: Accademia Nazionale di Santa Cecilia, 2000).
[92] 'Aspects of Mahler's Fifth Symphony: Performance Practice and Interpretation', *Musical Times*, 130/1775 (May 1989), 258–65.
[93] See also above, n. 23; and what about the 'Méditation' (intermezzo) from Massenet's *Thaïs* (Act 2)?
[94] See also above, nn. 23 and 24.

A 'Song without Words' for Strings and Harp

But the principal source for the sonority of strings and harp must be looked for in Mahler's own settings of Rückert, not only the four independent settings for voice and orchestra, but also *Kindertotenlieder*, where strings and harp often combine to colour—more than that, *incise*—the instrumental profile of a song. Think for example of 'Ich bin der Welt abhanden gekommen' or the second of the five *Kindertotenlieder*, 'Nun seh' ich wohl', where strings plus harp are at the very heart of the sound-world these songs inhabit. No matter, either, that while 'Ich bin der Welt . . .' belongs precisely to one of the summers when Mahler was working on his Fifth, the second of the *Kindertotenlieder*, 'Nun seh' ich wohl', might have postdated completion of the symphony. On the contrary, it is a chronology that helps make more emphatic the point that I want to make: that the late Rückert settings signify not only their marvellous individual selves but the onset of a late musical style[95] (new melodic contours as well as new sonorities) that spilled over into the symphonies, not only taking shape as the Adagietto of the Fifth but also generating (strings plus harp again) the remarkable lyrical effusions that constitute the second subjects of the first movements of both the Sixth and Seventh symphonies, not to speak of 'Die liebe Erde . . .' in the 'Abschied' of *Das Lied* (the very apotheosis, one might think, of strings plus harp). This was a point I made as long ago as 1980 in Grove/11, pp. 520–1.

The near relationship of the Adagietto to 'Ich bin der Welt . . .' has often been claimed. I take a different view, as I argue below, and believe that the mistaken claim has itself been a source of interpretative confusion. To the evidence in support of a reconsideration of the supposed 'parallels' between the songs I shall turn later (see p. 317), evidence that is of some relevance, too, to our speculation about the probable chronology of the symphony's composition. But for the present let me take the short step that will bring us to perhaps the most important of the issues to which the Adagietto gives rise: its status, that is, a 'song without words', a wordless Rückert song for orchestra alone, or, rather, for string orchestra and harp.[96]

The 'Right' Tempo

Once that step has been taken, which involves rejection of the image of the movement as principally elegiac and valedictory, other matters usefully fall into place, in particular the question of the 'right' tempo. I would prefer not to attempt to impose a duration deduced from past documentation and recordings—it should never be forgotten that there are occasions when the 'wrong' tempo in the right hands can convince, whereas the obverse does not—but instead to repeat what I said in a paper contributed to a conference in Rotterdam in May 1990.[97] After referring to Banks's *Musical Times* article, I continued:

---

[95] I use this term as Adorno uses it when describing *Das Lied* as 'one of the greatest achievements of a late musical style since the last Quartets [of Beethoven]'. See Adorno, 'Mahler: Centenary Address, Vienna 1960', in *Quasi una Fantasia*, 92.

[96] See also Adorno, *Mahler*, 22: 'the Adagietto, actually a song without words, is linked to "Ich bin der Welt abhanden gekommen" . . .', and below, n. 97.

[97] 'Mahler's "Orchestral" Orchestral Songs', Rondom Mahler II Congress and Workshop, Rotterdam, 1990. I am

He has a good deal to say about performance practice and refers especially to the widely differing tempi adopted for the Adagietto by various conductors, some very slow indeed—Hermann Scherchen takes 13′ 07″ over it—while others are relatively much more flowing—Mengelberg and Walter outstandingly are among those who linger the least, with durations respectively of 7′ 04″ and 7′ 57″. That sounds to me as if both Mengelberg and Walter had firmly in mind the song concept of the movement.[98] Because, if one accepts that, then the successful interpretation will be that which sustains the long melody as if it were written for the voice. No singer could possibly sustain Scherchen's tempo. Walter's and Mengelberg's tempi, on the contrary, are paced by that hypothetical singer. It's a point conductors might bear in mind, although I don't expect they will.

Or only, I would add in 1997, the most enlightened.

Mahler's 'Spätstil'

The status of the Adagietto as a 'song without words' for strings and harp is one thing; another and perhaps more important feature is its character, that is, that it belongs to the same act of creative imagination that in the summer of 1901 gave us four of the independent Rückert settings and three (possibly) of the *Kindertotenlieder* cycle. One can have no quarrel at all with Adorno's invocation of the term 'Spätstil' in relation to *Das Lied*; but in fact the first genuine intimations and anticipations of that epoch-making 'late style'

again much indebted to Henry-Louis de La Grange for acquainting me with an unpublished, unedited article on Mahler's songs by William Ritter, written in 1914. Ritter had attended a performance of the Fifth Symphony in Munich in 1910, when the orchestra of the *Konzertverein*, Vienna, was conducted by Ferdinand Löwe. Mahler, it seems, was present and was addressed (reprimanded?) by Löwe after the Adagietto had been heard in rehearsal, Löwe holding that there could be no other explanation of it but that it was 'a parody'. Mahler, it seems, stopped, looked at Ritter, and shook his head in a gesture of denial that Ritter interpreted thus (I quote from his French text): 'Cela prouve à quel point on est incapable aujourd'hui d'un chant simple. On ne sait plus que la sincerité peut encore exister!' ('That shows how everyone today has lost the art of a simple song. It is no longer thought possible that sincerity can exist!') While Ritter makes clear that this was his interpretation of Mahler's gesture, not Mahler's own words, we should not necessarily discount it as evidence of his thinking about the Adagietto. Mahler and Ritter were in the midst of a long conversation—an 'interview', according to Ritter—and it is certainly not impossible that the Adagietto had been a topic already touched on in some way, which allowed Ritter thus to 'translate' Mahler's sign of dissent into words.

In this same context, an entry in the diary of Elisabeth Diepenbrock, the wife of the composer, Alphons, dated 23 March 1906, is of special relevance and interest, in particular Diepenbrock's reception of the Adagietto as 'a love song'. Diepenbrock was a member of the circle of very close friends surrounding Mahler on his visits to Amsterdam.

23 March [1906]—Yesterday and the day before again Mahler's Symphony (the 5th). This time such an over-

whelming and wonderful impression. Sitting downstairs, where the sound is so bad, ruined everything the first time. Fons thinks it is so beautiful, so magnificent and regards Mahler as 'the only poet' of our time. At first he thought of the 5th as a step backwards after the 4th—but not any longer! The 'Trauermarsch' is magnificent and yesterday we were also deeply moved by the Adagietto. Fons thinks it is almost too tender, especially at first, he understands it as a love song; to me it seems more like a solace, a caress from above after the Scherzo's harsh reality [*sic!*]. Lien [Jas] experienced it likewise; she thought of her mother. [Eduard Reeser (ed.), *Alphons Diepenbrock. Brieven en documenten*. Volume 5. Amsterdam: Vereniging voor Nederlandse Muziekgeschiedenis, 1981, page 115.]

Lien [Eveline] Jas (1866–1951) was a close friend of the Diepenbrock family. I am most grateful to Henriette Straub (Amsterdam) for bringing this information to my notice.

[98] On the timings, see also above, nn. 87 and 92. In this same article, Dr Banks mentions a performance of the Fifth under Mahler in St Petersburg in Nov. 1907, on the occasion of which one of the orchestral players noted a timing of 7′ for the Adagietto. If this were accurate, or near accurate, then clearly Mengelberg and Walter, 'immediate disciples' of Mahler's as Banks remarks, were opting for tempi close or closer to Mahler's own than has been the case in many modern performances. A recent recording conducted by Boulez with the Vienna Philharmonic for Deutsche Grammophon (DG 453 416–2) which challengingly and perhaps rather surprisingly offers a duration of 10′ 59″.

unequivocally surface in the Rückert settings *c.*1901–4, while Adorno's own mention of Beethoven's late quartets in this context brings to mind (though evidently not to Adorno's) Mahler's own claim (see Ch. 10 above), that his late songs represented his 'Kammermusikton', his 'chamber-music manner' or 'tone of voice'. Thus, in one respect at least, the Fifth shares in the innovatory sound-world that was to be a distinguishing feature of his final decade.[99]

It was a future implicit in the late Rückert songs, of which, I continue to emphasize, the Adagietto was one, albeit minus a text by the poet himself, though as we shall see below, there is real probability that there *was* a (silent) sub-text linked to Mahler's courting of Alma Schindler, whom he was to marry on 9 March 1902; the engagement was announced on 27 December 1901.

Symmetries again

But before dwelling for a moment on the possible consequences for the chronology of the symphony's evolution if the association of the Adagietto with Mahler's courtship were shown to be likely, there is a point I wish first to make: that, irrespective of any identifiably autobiographical content or image, the very fact that we have here in essence a Rückert song for orchestra alone, asserts yet another of the remarkable symmetries that characterize, define, the Fifth as in no other symphony by Mahler. In short, whereas in Part I, a wordless 'Wunderhorn' song for orchestra alone, the Funeral March, serves as prelude to the ensuing movement and as source of that movement's 'quotations' ('interruptions') in Part III, it is again an orchestral song, the Adagietto, that serves as prelude, as source of the Rondo-Finale's contrasting episodes, thus demonstrating an even larger symmetry across the span of the symphony as a whole. These two orchestral 'songs' represent two sharply opposed styles, a brilliant consummation of the 'Wunderhorn' manner ('Ton') in the shape of the Funeral March that opens Part I, and an unmistakable intimation—evocation—of the late style that was increasingly to manifest itself in the later and last symphonies, in the shape of the Adagietto. Typical of Mahler, one might think, that the very symmetries in which is embodied the logic of the symphony's formal thinking, which provide the rational basis for the symphony's otherwise unique form, should at the same time represent an effortless transition from one creative phase to another, phases which in themselves represent two contrasting poles, two extremes, of the composer's creative imagination. If one thinks of 'Der Tamboursg'sell' as representing one extreme and, say, 'Ich atmet' . . . ', 'Ich bin der Welt . . . ', or 'Nun seh' ich wohl . . .' (from *Kindertotenlieder*)[100] the other, it would

---

[99] See also pp. 267–70 above, where I suggest that we can owe part of the development of Mahler's fascination with the potentialities of the string orchestra to his 'arrangements' of Schubert and Beethoven string quartets for string orchestra. It is significant, too, that one of the Beethoven quartets was a late masterpiece, Op. 95, in F minor; while it was certainly Mahler's intention to attempt a like arrangement of Op. 131, in C sharp minor, the last but one of Beethoven's quartets.

Critical editions of these arrangements by Mahler, by David Matthews and Donald Mitchell, were published in 1984 (Schubert) and 1990 (Beethoven) by Josef Weinberger, London.

[100] It matters, in my view, not at all if 'Nun seh' ich wohl . . .' were composed before or after the Adagietto. The song clearly belongs to the same mindset that generated the movement for strings and harp.

be hard to conceive a starker contrast; and yet it is the case that both these seemingly con-tradictory worlds of sound and images cohabit in the Fifth, indeed are fundamental to the symphony's narrative. Without the 'Trauermarsch' there could have been no beginning; without the Adagietto, no 'end', or at least not the finale that the Adagietto in fact enabled Mahler to compose and thus complete his narrative; and it is not the thematic bonding between the Adagietto and the finale that I have principally in mind.

The Fifth, a Pivotal Symphony

Meanwhile, we can ponder on the curiosity of received opinion in the past (including my own) that insisted on Mahler's having abandoned the incorporation of 'song' into his symphonies after the Fourth, while in fact it is precisely in the idea of 'song', albeit word-less orchestral song, that the *genre* innovatively lives on in the Fifth, and in the instance of the Adagietto, which we should hear—and perform—*in context*, that is to say with the co-terminous Rückert settings in mind, opens a window on the late style of Mahler's last years. In all of these ways, then, that I have touched on in this chapter, but in particular those relating to the character and function of the wordless orchestral songs, the Fifth has to be acknowledged as the symphony which acts as pivot between the period of the so-called 'Wunderhorn' symphonies and the period(s) that ensued; and one may savour the strange irony that it is the two songs for orchestra that are emblematic of the evolution that is con-ducted within the confines of the symphony itself, 'song', the very *genre*, the supposed dis-appearance of which was taken to represent Mahler's radical ditching of a convention he had established and made peculiarly his own.

As we shall see, this very process of style-transition, which one might think to be prin-cipally bound up with the evolution of new techniques, Mahler deploys as part of the evo-lution of his *narrative*; the continuity of it is a consequence of the introduction of the Adagietto as agent of a change in style. Style, in short, has become a tool of narrative. But before I come to that, there is the sub-text to the movement, the 'Alma dimension' one might name it, that calls for scrutiny.

The Adagietto's 'Alma dimension'

It was in the full score used by Mengelberg for his performances of the Fifth that the link of the Adagietto to Mahler's courting of Alma was first plainly stated. This is what he wrote:

This Adagietto was Gustav Mahler's declaration of love to *Alma! Instead of a letter* he confided it in this manuscript without a word of explanation. She understood and replied: *He should come!!!* (I have this from both of them!)[101]

This inscription has been the subject of commentary elsewhere, by Floros, for example, and Henry-Louis de La Grange,[102] Floros positive in his account, La Grange more sceptical.

---

[101] See also Mitchell, *SSLD*, 31. The first page of the Adagietto, marked up by Mengelberg as described above, is repro-duced in *GMWL* 1.25, and Mitchell and Straub (eds.), *New Sounds, New Century*.

[102] See Floros, *Gustav Mahler*, 154–5; HLG(E) ii. 816–17; and Kaplan, facsimile edn., 21–3 and 35–7.

It is true that the fact that nowhere in Alma's diary does she mention this incident, that is, her receiving the manuscript (what might that have been? a composition sketch? a preliminary draft of the score?) and her decoding of it (skilled musician that she was, Mahler's 'letter' would not have presented her with any problems), undoubtedly suspends a question mark. As La Grange remarks:

To my mind, however, some doubt remains about Mengelberg's story. It seems to me improbable that Mahler could have written two pieces so related in every way [i.e. the Adagietto and 'Ich bin der Welt . . .'] with such different meanings. I also find it highly improbable, if Mengelberg's story is true, that Alma should have failed to mention the true meaning of the Adagietto at some time during the half-century in which she survived Mahler. She was always very careful to record and preserve each one of her *Trophäen* ['Trophies'] and kept the autograph of 'Liebst du um Schönheit' [the song for voice and piano Mahler composed specifically for her in 1902] on her living-room wall in New York.[103]

On the other hand, I find it difficult to believe that Mengelberg made the whole thing up, and in particular am convinced by the authentic ring of his parenthetic, 'I have this from both of them!'

If I refrain from quoting the 'poem' that Mengelberg also wrote into his score—a text he envisaged accompanying the melody of the Adagietto—it is because I have no wish to lend further currency to a horrible, mawkish fabrication that can only shake one's confidence in his taste and judgement; but this is something different, I suggest, from his reliability when recollecting and recording what he claims to have been told by the composer and his wife.[104]

The case must inevitably remain open. But if what Mengelberg relates was basically accurate then there are at least two or three consequences of importance.

The first clearly raises the question of chronology: if the Adagietto were indeed a declaration of Mahler's love for Alma, then it must have preceded their official engagement, announced at the very end of December 1901. If that were so, then the Adagietto, in some shape or form—as a sketch of some kind?—must have been in existence at some stage between the summer and Christmas. The autumn and winter months were not, as we have

---

[103] HLG(E) ii. 817. But might it not have been the case that *she* at least told the story to Mengelberg *after* her husband's death? Much depends on the *date* on which Mengelberg wrote the ink inscriptions into his conducting score. A clear reproduction of the first page of the Adagietto may be found in *GMWL*, 1.25.

[104] However, this must have been on an occasion other than the première of the Fifth in Amsterdam on 8 Mar. 1906, when Mahler himself conducted the Concertgebouw Orchestra. Interestingly, the second half of the programme was devoted to the Dutch première of *Kindertotenlieder* and, finally, as coda, a performance of 'Ich bin der Welt . . .', yet another example of Mahler's 'thematic' planning of his programmes. As his wife had not accompanied him, the story must have been related to Mengelberg later, by the Mahlers jointly or separately ('I have this from both of them' would seem to imply the latter?). The inscription itself, in ink, along with the 'poem', is quite distinct in character and execution from the red and blue pencil marks of Mengelberg's that were plainly made in connection with his own first performances of the Fifth in Holland, also in Mar. 1906, but after Mahler's departure. The ink inscriptions suggest memories written into the score at a later date or dates, together with a related note written at the bottom of the page (it must have been at the same time). This reads: 'If Music is a language, then this is proof of it. He tells her *everything* in "*notes*" ["Tönen"] and "*sounds*" ["Klängen"] in: Music.'

Floros (*Gustav Mahler*, 155) makes much of the 'Gaze' *Leitmotiv* from *Tristan* that he discerns, much more clearly than I do, as a significant presence in the contours of the Adagietto's melody (in the movement's middle section, in particular). A conscious, knowing—if covert—'quote' from *Tristan*? I don't hear it. Nor, it seems, did Mengelberg, who would surely have remarked on it, if he had.

so often been told, periods when Mahler sat down to compose. I have already expressed a lurking doubt about our accepting this as a *total* prohibition, especially in the absence of so much sketched material that must have existed but has mysteriously disappeared and, on occasion, as mysteriously resurfaces (the newly recovered sketches for the Scherzo are a case in point). In any event, there can always be exceptions to any rule. Was, then, the Adagietto sketched during, say, the last six months of 1901? Was it a spin-off from the bout of song-writing that had occupied Mahler, along with work on his new symphony, in that year's summer months? Was it—even—an idea for a song that had not yet found its text, that Alma then proved to be? Speculation this, undoubtedly, but by no means wholly impossible. Mengelberg almost wrecks any confidence one might have in his veracity as chronicler by his perpetrating that abominable 'poem'. However, even if one discounts the whole Alma scenario, and with it the implied chronology, the important fact remains, that in the context of the symphony as a whole the Adagietto plays the role of a 'song without words', a 'song' in the manner of the Rückert Lieder that had preceded it. From this point of view, Alma is immaterial. The fundamental source of the song was Mahler's own Rückert manner, the new style that broke surface in 1901. (We may note too that later manifestations of the style, e.g. the second subject of the first movement of the Sixth, were also Alma-oriented.)

The Adagietto, another 'Ich bin der Welt . . .'?

Almost every commentator on the Rückert settings draws a parallel between the Adagietto and 'Ich bin der Welt . . .', Adorno, for example, and La Grange; indeed it is part of the latter's argument, consistent in its own terms, that just because the Adagietto and 'Ich bin der Welt . . .' inhabit the same spiritual world (of renunciation, of resignation) one must doubt the credibility of Mengelberg's suggestion that it was an avowal of human love, not a retreat from it.[105] The strict parallel between the songs, I believe, is based partly on reality, that is, that their respective codas ('closures' or 'liquidations' as current jargon would have it) are indeed very close in conception and execution, and partly on illusion, that is, too much has been read into the parallel between the closing sections, which, in turn, has been read *back* into performance practice, thus leading to those exaggeratedly slow, leave-taking misinterpretations of the Adagietto, in the manner of 'Ich bin der Welt . . .'. But the truth is, surely, that these are two highly individual songs (I am counting the Adagietto as one of them), distinct in their invention—where, for example, in the Adagietto is the pronounced pentatonicism of 'Ich bin der Welt . . .' or a sign of the latter's patent heterophonic thinking which unequivocally anticipates techniques Mahler was to deploy in *Das Lied*?—and thereby demanding distinctive tempi and interpretation. What they do share, undeniably, are the characteristic features of Mahler's emergent 'Spätstil', not only among themselves but with manifestations of that style yet to be composed, for example, as I have said before, the ardent second-subject groups in the first movements of the Sixth and Seventh

[105] See HLG(E) ii. 818.

Symphonies. It is by looking forward and then back that one can help oneself decouple the Adagietto from its distorting association with 'Ich bin der Welt . . .' and receive it instead in its own individual right as a typical example of the type of inspirations, invention, and sound-worlds with which Mahler was busy just after the turn of the century. It is hardly surprising that among the songs there should be parallels and cross-references; but if one insists on parallels there is much more to be got out of a comparison with 'Nun seh' ich wohl . . .', the second song of *Kindertotenlieder*, in its own way another avowal of love, though made (by the poet) in very different circumstances.[106]

A New Sonority Facilitating a Dénouement

No doubt the Adagietto will continue to generate discussion and disagreement. But on one feature of the movement, there must be wide agreement: that in the context of the symphony its novel sonority struck an entirely new note, to which I would add, emphatically, that it was also precisely *this* that was required if the symphony's narrative were to continue and reach a dénouement.

I do not need to recall the drama(s) enacted so comprehensively in the two movements of Part I, nor the uncompromisingly bleak conclusion that is asserted at the end of the Allegro. Likewise, I hope to have sufficiently indicated the problem (of his own making) that faced Mahler in the guise of his great central Scherzo in D and the dexterity with which he solved it, by his avoiding giving premature birth to an unclouded D that had to be kept in reserve for the finale and, when produced, prove to have retained sufficient vigour convincingly to bring the narrative to an end.

The Scherzo, with its emphatic inner tensions and contradictions, continued the drama of Part I, though on a much reduced scale. With the onset of the Adagietto, a new sound and new character are introduced—remember that in the grand overall design, the Adagietto replicates the functions, formal and thematic, of the opening march, the other 'song', in Part I, but in a style that could hardly be more powerfully contrasted to that of the 'Trauermarsch': a new sound and character, signifying that, after all, a resolution is possible, or if not a resolution, then at least a mitigation. We should feel, as the Adagietto slowly (but not sluggishly) unfolds, something akin to the poem by Stefan George set by Schoenberg as the finale of his Second String Quartet (Op. 10, 1907–8): 'Ich fühle Luft aus anderen Planeten' ('I feel an air from other planets'). In the context of Mahler's Fifth, the 'air' that his Adagietto exhales is comparable to the sense of an approaching new creative phase that is part of our response to Schoenberg's quartet. So it was that a new direction in his creativity provided Mahler with the means to embark on Part III and complete his symphony.

The enabling resource proved to be Rückert's poetry, and it must have come to Mahler as a heaven-sent intimation that rescue was at hand; for not only did he now have a wordless orchestral song (à la Rückert) to complement the wordless orchestral song (à la

[106] See also above, n. 100.

'Wunderhorn') of Part I and thereby service the ensuing Rondo, but, perhaps most importantly of all, the intermediary that would effect the substitution of human passion (whether or not Alma was the generating *raison d'être*) for the initiating rite of death, the march, in Part I, and thus open the door to what I can only describe as the humane preoccupations of the finale itself. In short, there was to be no more of the metaphysics of catastrophe but instead an affirmation of how, against the odds (Part I), however overwhelming, the individual spirit of man may after all survive (Part III): the interpolation of the Adagietto was the marker not only for the new style but also, in the context of the Fifth, for a radical switch in philosophy. It was that now newly defined goal that lent fresh impetus to the continuation of the narrative.

While the Adagietto may indeed strike a new 'tone', it also, almost literally so, strikes a new note, insofar as it explores a tonality, F major, that till now has not played an extensive role in any of the preceding movements: it is F *minor* that has made the majority of previous appearances. However, while the movement breaks new ground, at the same time it shows itself aware, in typical Mahler fashion, that there is still unfinished tonal business to be completed: between bars 63 and 72 there is an unequivocal, though undemonstrative, implication of a D yet to be conclusively affirmed, after which F resumes and brings this unique song to rest. The final goal, it seems, is now in sight and within reach.

The Rondo-Finale

Inevitably, debate will continue about the third and last part of the symphony, above all about the status of the Rondo. Adorno's notorious adverse judgement has already achieved wide currency: 'the Finale, fresh in many details and with novel formal ideas like that of the musical quick-motion picture ['wie der das kompositorischen Zeitraffers'], is undoubtedly too lightweight in relation to the first three movements. . . . Mahler was a poor yea-sayer. His voice cracks, like Nietzsche's, when he proclaims values, speaks from mere conviction, when he himself puts into practice the abhorrent notion of overcoming on which the thematic analyses capitalize, and makes music as if joy were already in the world. His vainly jubilant movements unmask jubilation', and so on, and so on.[107] An ideological rather than a musical judgement, one might think, though, alas, one that has undeniably influenced some celebrated interpreters of Mahler and their performances, of the Fifth's finale in particular.

The assumption that Mahler was incapable of affirming a humane belief in humanity, that he was unequal to the task or uninterested in it, for me has the ring of ideological intolerance—an ideologically rooted pessimism—about it. If nothing else, I hope my suggestion that Mahler did not abandon an intelligible strategy when undertaking the completion of his symphony, even while recognizing that it was his own genius that, in Part I, had created some of the problems he had to face in Part III, may at least aid our understanding of how it was he went about his attempt to solve them.

---

[107] See Adorno, *Mahler*, 136–7; German edn., 179–80.

Humour, I think even his most fervent admirers might concede, was not Adorno's strongest suit. Mahler, however, was a big enough and broad enough artist to know that humour, good humour that is, not just black humour (in which field he operated with a special expertise; indeed he may be said to have invented a special language for it), was part of the human condition and proper to a finale in which geniality and energy are to have a high profile, and much else besides, as I hope to show.

A 'Wunderhorn' Song Recollected

It is not inappropriate then that the Rondo's opening flourish (bb. 3–4 inclusive) is a literal quote from Mahler's 'Wunderhorn' song, 'Lob des hohen Verstandes' ('In praise of lofty intellect'), composed in the summer of 1896, a song (a competition between a nightingale and a cuckoo, of which a donkey is the judge and chooses—naturally—the cuckoo) that takes a knock at the critics; an alternative title for the song at one stage was 'Lob der Kritik'. Perhaps too, as I observed some years ago, the 'quote' may have had a special significance in relation to the movement that follows, a finale that was avowedly and artfully contrapuntal ('learned') in character. The quote, for sure, was aimed at the critics, 'daring the donkeys to fault his [Mahler's] contrapuntal art—and half expecting them to do just that, at the same time'.[108]

It is in the context of the satirical shaft aimed at his critics in the preludial quotation from the 'Wunderhorn' song that I interpret the final manifestation of 'learned' counterpoint in the Rondo's coda (from Fig. 34), where Mahler (tongue in cheek, perhaps, or at least smiling) puts the song quotation through its contrapuntal paces. I find it hard to hear this as a covert comment on the chorale, that its triumph (like the chorale in Shostakovich's Fifth) is not 'meant', is not to be taken seriously. On the contrary, this was Mahler trouncing his critics with a final flourish of contrapuntal ingenuity, genially capping a movement that is, indeed, all about counterpoint (of more than one species). In all of this one has to note that a further internal symmetry is introduced. While the 'Wunderhorn' and 'Rückert' styles are crucial to Parts I and III, in Part III itself, III^1 (the Rückert-like orchestral song without words) is complemented by III^2, which makes retrospective reference to an earlier 'Wunderhorn' song. Thus the juxtaposition of movements in Part III itself juxtaposes the 'song' parallels that hitherto have traversed Parts I^1 and III^1. Part III^{1+2} unites in sequence *both* song sources.

Mahler and Haydn

The variety of energetic counterpointing in fact raises an interesting issue in itself. Closely linked though it is by quotation to the preludial 'song', the finale can hardly be said to belong to the 'new phase' in Mahler's composing represented by the Adagietto. The counter-

---

[108] See Mitchell, *WY*, 261 n. 36 and 374–5 n. 30, where I refer to Mahler's irrational sensitivity about the adequacy of his contrapuntal technique. This might have been another motive for the quotation from the 'Wunderhorn' song, a kind of joke against himself, though his critics would have been unlikely to know of the history that gave rise to it.

point itself is quite distinct from the innovatory motivic polyphony of the Allegro, say, or that of the Scherzo. I have suggested way back that the new (polyphonic) style of the Fifth, to which Mahler himself referred, had already been significantly anticipated in the Fourth Symphony's first movement, in its development especially. But there was in the Fourth, besides this intimation of an innovatory counterpoint, an intimation of another style that was to become of huge significance in the twentieth century and was not to leave Mahler untouched, well beyond the confines of the Fourth and its chronological place in his oeuvre. It is in fact, if one may put it a shade paradoxically, to the anticipations of neoclassicism in the Fourth to which Mahler returns in the finale of his Fifth. There *is* something arrestingly 'classical' about the Rondo's principal sections and their industrious counterpointing, in which context Paul Banks, in conversation, made an observation of particular relevance to the topic of Mahler's classicizing. He drew my attention to the Haydnesque character of Mahler's invention in his finale, of the Rondo's principal sections, that is, and the contrapuntal activity they ceaselessly generate. Haydn is not a composer that one often

(*a*) Tchaikovsky's 'Manfred' Symphony, opening

(*b*) 'Manfred' Symphony, bb. 14 ff.

(*c*) Mahler's *Kindertotenlieder*, 'Nun will die Sonn' . . .', bb. 48–51

[see over, n. 109]

thinks of in association with Mahler; nor did he have much opportunity to conduct Haydn's music. The more remarkable, then, as Dr Banks went on to point out, that Mahler had conducted two performances of Haydn's 'Drum-roll' symphony (No. 103 in E flat)—the only occasions on which he conducted this symphony—in Vienna on 18 March 1900 and in St Petersburg on 29 March 1902, dates spanning a period in which the Fifth was put together. I think even a cursory juxtaposition of Mahler's and Haydn's finales bears out Dr Banks's insight, who did not allow to go unremarked the fact that both finales open with prominent contributions from the horns.[109]

The Quotation Principle again at work

One of the novel features that Adorno presumably had in mind when writing of 'quick-motion movie music' (which would be my translation of his 'kompositorischen Zeitraffers') is the speeded-up version of the Adagietto that serves as the contrasting episodes of the Rondo.[110] A brilliant idea this, maintaining the formality of the quotation principle while at the same time throwing fresh light on the Adagietto. This is an elegant, witty, compositional performance; and if there is any satirical or parodistic intention involved, it is of the gentlest, one might say, even, playful, kind, for example the subverting woodwind trills (flutes, oboes, clarinets) from Fig. 29 ff., and, in the bars immediately preceding this passage, the dynamic extremes Mahler calls for from *ff* to *pp* in the space of four bars. However, there is little hint of Mahler's habitual caustic tone of voice when demonstrating that some-

[109] It is a strange but illuminating coincidence that during this very same period Mahler also conducted Tchaikovsky's 'Manfred' Symphony, Op. 58, in Vienna on 13 Jan. 1901 and in St Petersburg on 23 Mar. 1902. These were the years during which not only the Fifth was composed but also the first group of *Kindertotenlieder*. As my music examples on p. 321 show, it was not only Haydn who may have been an influential model for Mahler in his new symphony, but Tchaikovsky, in the shaping of the new song-cycle. It is clear that one of the most memorable contours developed by the melody of the cycle's first song, 'Nun will die Sonn' . . .', owes its identity to the first movement of Tchaikovsky's symphony and his tormented hero. Moreover, Tchaikovsky's movement opens with woodwind alone (bass clarinet and bassoons: cf. Mahler's oboes, bassoons, and horn).

With regard to Haydn, it is of some interest that Georg Göhler, with whom Mahler, as we have seen, corresponded about his Fifth, mentions Haydn when writing about the finale in the exhaustive programme note he prepared for the performance of the symphony he conducted in Leipzig on 9 Jan. 1914. This was announced as the first performance of the so-called 'new version of the work' [Uraufführung der neuen Fassung des Werkes], for which Göhler had collated, in association with the publishers, C. F. Peters, very many (though, as it turned out, not all) of the revisions that Mahler had made ceaselessly up to the time of his death. These, however, had never been systematically incorporated into the published performing materials for the symphony. Hence the importance of Göhler's pioneering effort. The complete text of Göhler's note has appeared in *Muziek & wetenschap/Dutch Journal for Musicology*, 7 (1999), 65–74. His response to the Adagietto is perhaps of particular interest in the context of our discussion of this movement. Göhler first of all remarks that at the end of the Scherzo, the third movement, in the evolution of the narrative we are hardly further along the road than at the end of the second; he continues: 'Once again one must imagine a longer break before the third part of the symphony (4th and 5th movements). The noisy delights of the world were of no help. Peace, calm, consoling love alone ensure that the miracle happens. The fourth movement tells of this peace, this calm, of consoling, helping, kindly love, love that heals all wounds and restores to life the man who seemed to be dead to happiness and life, granting him the plenitude of the sunniest happiness.'

Finally, I am grateful to H. C. Robbins Landon for his reminder that it was Mahler who was responsible for one of the very earliest—if not the earliest—revivals in modern times of an opera by Haydn, *Lo speziale*, which he conducted in Hamburg (1895) and again in Vienna in 1899.

[110] It was surely this acceleration that Adorno had in mind, not as Floros would have it (Floros, *Gustav Mahler*, 157–8), the relatively orthodox variation by diminution of the chorale.

thing that one has assumed to be the case is abruptly stood on its head. This approach to the Adagietto returns us for a moment to a further reflection on the parallel that is so often drawn between the movement and 'Ich bin der Welt abhanden gekommen'. If it really were the case that both inhabit the same spiritual world (with all that that implies for tempo or expressive character), is it likely, possible, even, that Mahler would have risked seeming to trivialize what in those circumstances must have been conceived as another solemn revelation of his profoundest feelings about his life and his art? I take leave to doubt it.

There is much to admire as the finale proceeds in an atmosphere that is remarkably shadowless and free of the volcanic tensions of Part I. (One notices that the interpolations of the Adagietto in the Rondo never take on the character of interruptions; they are integrated variations, rather, of what we have heard before.) Does this mean, then, that ingenuity and geniality reign supreme? Does Mahler thereby risk blandness?

A Narrative Parallel with the Fourth?

To arrive at that conclusion would entail overlooking a parallel that, to my knowledge, has scarcely been remarked upon, with the narrative strategy that governs the evolution of the Fourth from its beginning to its end: the progressive reduction in complexity—of texture, of invention, of tonal excursions—in which refining process the inner drama of the work—the passage traversed from Experience to Innocence (see Ch. 9 above, pp. 209–13)—is embodied.

At least something of that same long-term strategy underpins the evolution of the Fifth, from the highly complex chromaticism, dissonance, and fractured textures of Part I (of the Allegro, in particular) to the (almost) unblemished diatonicism and euphony of Part III, a sustained assertion of D major. The final extrapolation of a resounding D is comparable in its own way to the affirmation of E major at the end of the Fourth. The acute difference lies in the fact that it is an *entire movement*, the finale itself, that is required in the Fifth to lend sufficient weight and authority to the final attainment of D. (Small wonder, in the light of the hard time D major has been given in the Allegro.)

Quite apart from this significant parallel in narrative strategies, it is intriguing to find a movement in the Fifth that overtly sustains the (neo)classicizing pursuits of the Fourth. Paul Banks's provocative suggestion that Haydn might have been an influential model opens up a highly interesting line of inquiry. In general, indeed, much more work needs to be done on the direct relationships between the music that Mahler was busy conducting and the music he was busy creating. There was a singular 'feeding' process in operation here that now warrants serious, systematic investigation.

It was Schoenberg who said there was still plenty of good music to be written in C major;[111] perhaps it might be claimed that Mahler was making that same point about D major already in the finale of the Fifth. The exceptional energy of the movement, which is one of its leading features, inevitably leads to that final act of reparation, no less, when the chorale that has twice been undermined by collapse in the Allegro of Part I, returns to

[111] See Dika Newlin, 'Secret Tonality in Schoenberg's Piano Concerto', *Perspectives of New Music*, 13 (1974), 137–9. (Our thanks to O.W. Neighbour.)

crown—to anoint—the dénouement of the finale. There is never any serious doubt that this time round the chorale will survive and make its joyful statement, a perfectly legitimate joy (or so it seems to me, *pace* Adorno); triumphant, yes, but free of triumphalism. Impossible in any event to put words to work when it is Mahler's untranslatable pitches that alone can provide the key to the 'parade sauvage' in which we ourselves, the world, Mahler, and his music, are all participants.[112] I find it moving in the Fifth that Mahler dumps transcendental solutions and instead offers as contra-assertions to collapse and catastrophe the consolations of human passion and mankind's unique capacity not only to find joy in a generally hostile world but to create it.

There is no question that in one major respect at least Mahler's finale departs from precedents established in the preceding symphonies: with the exception of the chorale there is no cyclic recall of materials from the two movements comprising Part I, which normally would bring with them a vivid reminder of the tensions, the fundamental conflicts, that have led to the creation of the work.

This is not to say that there are no moments of retrospection, of music that suddenly puts us back in touch with notable events that have occurred at earlier stages in the symphony. A telling but minor example breaks surface at Fig. 16 where for fourteen bars, and in the context of a reappearance of the Adagietto, the layout of the passage, for solo horn and the Adagietto's very own string orchestra, spirits us back to the opening of the second trio in I^1 (Fig. 15) and the opening of the Scherzo, from Fig. 1^{-1}, where the obbligato horn (for twelve bars) first embarks on its virtuoso, concerto-like solo flight, and again accompanied by strings alone (plus two solitary strokes on the triangle).

The 'Triplet Factor' Apotheosized

A major recall, however, is to follow in the finale between Figs. 21 and 23, where Mahler is limbering up for the materialization of the chorale. Once again we have a powerful affirmation of D and a further release of superabundant energy in a brilliant variation of the Rondo's principal theme. But it is the detailed features of the variation that are wholly remarkable and that seem to have gone unacknowledged but for the briefest of mentions by Paul Bekker.[113] What is so riveting here is Mahler's reintroduction of the *triplet* as a prime feature of his melodic invention at this point. We have not in fact heard triplets—the *triplet phenomenon*—on this torrential scale since Part I, where this rhythmic unit carried an ever-increasing load of imagery, becoming one of the immediately recognizable signifiers of Aspiration.[114] Its resurrection at this critical juncture in the finale, and the role it

[112] 'J'ai seul la clef de cette parade sauvage', Arthur Rimbaud, *Les Illuminations*, No. IV, 'Parade', final line ('I alone possess the key to this barbarous sideshow').

[113] *Gustav Mahlers Sinfonien*, 200.

[114] For parallel passages in Part I, Part I^{1+2}, see e.g. I^1, Fig. 9^{+9} ff., and in I^2, Figs. 12–13, or bars 356 (double bar) ff., or Fig. 23, from double bar to double bar at bar 428. The downward thrust of the triplets in the finale at Fig. 21 is of course bound up with the built-in direction of the Rondo's principal theme. But on this occasion the descending triplets are as elevating as their ascending precedents were signifiers of aspiration. Now at Fig. 21, the triplets are freed of aspiration and can celebrate having arrived at their goal without directional restraint; and in fact Mahler disseminates his joyous triplets in both descending and ascending forms.

plays in the creation of an almost incandescent web of polyphony, means that we have here a mini-celebration of all the aspiring music that heretofore has met with defeat. It is a unique apotheosis, in which Mahler lets loose any ties with 'classicism' and liberates a type of ecstatic counterpoint that presages his late contrapuntal style. So the finale of the Fifth too has its moment of disclosure of 'Spätstil'; and a tremendous moment it is.[115] A good case could be made for identifying it as the real climax of the finale and, no less, the moment when the symphony's initiating conflict is at last resolved.

The Chorale Recovered

After which there remains the recovery of the chorale, which proceeds, if one may put it thus, without a hitch from Fig. 32. On the other hand, is there one among us, on reaching Fig. 33 and its continuation at bar 730, who does not feel a tremor at the final statement of the chorale, especially at bar 740 ff.? One knows, of course, that this time round the chorale will not fade, will not have its life-blood drained from it, as was the case in the parallel passage in I^2, Fig. 29^{-2}–Fig. 30; and yet, even after the ultimate unison D has sounded (b. 791), one has to concede that one's memory of the chorale's fate in I^2 has not been entirely erased; nor could it be, nor perhaps should it be. Mahler might well have been of one mind with François Mauriac: 'Why are we always taught to dread annihilation? . . . The really awful thing is to believe, against all evidence, in life eternal! To live eternally would be to lose the refuge of nothingness.'[116] Perhaps the truth is that the Fifth draws its strength from its juxtaposition of those options: Eternity (after a secular fashion) or Nothingness.

---

[115] Moments of high emotion in late Mahler (there are many examples in *Das Lied* and the Ninth Symphony) bring in their train an identifiable type of 'ecstatic' counterpoint.

[116] François Mauriac, *Le Mystère Frontenac* (1933); *The Frontenac Mystery*, trans. Gerard Hopkins (Harmondsworth: Penguin Books, 1986), 172.

Additional note In his admirable study of the life and works of Theodor Fontane (*Theodor Fontane, Literature and History in the Bismarck Reich* (New York and Oxford: Oxford University Press, 1999), 11–12), Gordon A. Craig remarks on 'the great success Fontane had with his ballads', and continues: 'This method of telling a dramatic story in short stanzas with a striking or dramatic conclusion had, of course, been popular in Germany ever since the eighteenth century, encouraged in the first instance by Herder's interest in folk songs and attracting such poets as Goethe ('Der Erlkönig') and Bürger ('Lenore') in the Storm and Stress era and, in the Romantic period, Chamisso, Brentano, Eichendorff, and Uhland. In Fontane's day, both before and particularly after the 1848 revolution, interest in the ballad revived because, in an apparently inert society with nothing in particular to look forward to, people took refuge in stories about the past triumphs or, failing that, about dramatic events in the remote history of Germanic peoples, the Danes and the Norwegians, the English and the Scots.' No less tellingly he observes: 'In [Fontane's] view, ballads had to be composed—that is, written according to a logical scheme—but must, at the same time, appear to be natural and free of any literary artifice. Success depended also on the skillful use of suggestion, omission, and abrupt transitions, on mastery of the art of repetition, refrains, and leitmotiv, on an ability to create effects with a minimal use of means, and, above all, on color.' Professor Craig's words—'composed'!—might well serve as a remarkably precise description of the method and means that distinguish Mahler's many ballads, the generating source of which was, of course, *Des Knaben Wunderhorn*. Each of his settings is indeed a miniature drama; each has a distinctive colour; each combines extreme sophistication and simplicity; and each represents an encounter between the real world and historical fantasy. It should be no surprise, I suppose, that the genius of a composer so strongly driven by *narrative* should have seized on the potentialities of the *Wunderhorn* anthology, thereby raising to new heights the form's potentialities for the exploration of timeless and often bleak psychological truth while not forsaking the link with the Ballad's historical past. (See also pp. 238 and 244–6 above.)

12

Mahler and Holland

EVELINE NIKKELS

Mahler and Mengelberg

When we speak of 'Mahler and Holland' we might as well say 'Mahler and Mengelberg', because without Mengelberg the well-known Dutch Mahler tradition, still flourishing today, would never have arisen. Mengelberg introduced Mahler's works to Holland at a time when very few people believed in the composer's creative genius. Year after year he performed them until his audiences became thoroughly acquainted with them and realized their greatness.

How much Mahler actually meant to Mengelberg can be seen from an article Mengelberg published on 18 May 1926, fifteen years after Mahler's death, in the Dutch newspaper *Algemeen Handelsblad*, in which he surveyed the Mahler period which had begun during the 'Tonkünstlerfest des Allgemeinen Deutschen Musikvereins', held in Crefeld (Germany) in 1902:

About twenty-five years ago I received some printed scores to review. The name on their title-pages meant no more me than just an Austrian colleague.[1] Although their contents fascinated me immediately, the meaning of certain passages remained obscure; so I didn't feel compelled—as I did with the works of Richard Strauss—to study and play the music with my orchestra.

For some time the scores lay on my desk, and on occasion I went through them to try to familiarize myself with their details.

Although I did not succeed in appreciating the full beauty of such original music, I became increasingly aware of the extraordinary talent that spoke to me from the pages of these scores. So I took the first opportunity I could of hearing a Mahler work, and of getting in touch with the composer himself, by attending the Tonkünstlerfest in Crefeld in 1902, where he was to conduct his Third Symphony, and I came under his spell immediately. His manner of interpretation, his technical command of the orchestra, his way of phrasing and building climaxes were all that I, as a young conductor, considered ideal. Here stood a great master, who embodied exactly everything I myself,

---

[1] Mengelberg became chief conductor of the Concertgebouw Orchestra in 1895; Mahler was the Director of the Vienna Opera from 1897 to 1907.

still partly subconsciously, was striving for. And when I eventually met him after the concert I was so deeply moved that I promised to play his work as soon as possible in Amsterdam. But then it occurred to me that the composer's own expressive powers would be of great consequence in helping to understand such utterly new music. So I suggested that he himself should introduce his works to Amsterdam—an opportunity which he grasped with both hands.[2]

And so, in 1903, the intimate relationship between Mahler and Holland began, a relationship which persists to this day.

In the autumn of 1903 Mahler came to Amsterdam for the first time. He conducted his Third Symphony, and in the following year his First. To all those who participated, the way he interpreted his work was very interesting and instructive. *His rehearsals in particular established a precedent for our future performance practice of his music.* At these rehearsals he would analyse his works in the minutest detail, and explain his views on every single phrase. Thus we learnt exactly how he wanted his work to be performed. '*Das Wichtigste steht nicht in den Noten*', he used to say: the most important part is not in the notes. This was the clue both to his art and to his interpretation. And he never tired of rehearsing again and again. During rehearsals he was extremely temperamental and gave his utmost, which left him completely exhausted afterwards.

After his first visit to Amsterdam in 1903 Mahler returned to Holland on three further occasions, the last time in October 1909. Thus, within the short period of six years, he was guest conductor of the Concertgebouw Orchestra four times, with which he rehearsed and conducted the major part of his oeuvre: the first five symphonies, the Seventh, *Das klagende Lied*, and *Kindertotenlieder*. 'Indeed', wrote Mengelberg,

his rehearsals were very inspiring and we felt the music coming to life under his hand. His manner of conducting went further than just reproducing the score in sound; he frequently made alterations in his manuscripts according to the practicalities of performance and the demands of the acoustics. Many of these alterations were made especially for the Concertgebouw Orchestra and were incorporated into the printed score. My own scores are filled with numerous annotations and revisions made by Mahler himself during or after the rehearsals.[3]

Mengelberg made an arrangement with Mahler whereby he would rehearse a new work with his orchestra in advance, so that when Mahler arrived he had only to add the finishing touches before the performance itself.[4]

Before his arrival here in town I used to practise with the orchestra first and afterwards attend most of his rehearsals, writing down the statements he made, which often went straight to the heart of the music. Alphons Diepenbrock, a great admirer of Mahler's art, was often there as well, and, in his analysis of the Fourth Symphony, has recorded some of Mahler's poetical observations on the work. On the whole Mahler found our orchestra and the 'Toonkunst' choir enthusiastic and cooperative. He was delighted with the spirit that inspired us all and, no less, with the technical performances we achieved. The love that den Hertog and his boys' choir bore him was most touching (they had taken part in the Third Symphony). Mahler's major strength, however, lay in the magical power of his

[2] Willem Mengelberg, 'Bij de sterfdag van Gustav Mahler', *Algemeen Handelsblad*, 18 May 1926.
[3] Ibid.   [4] Alma Mahler, *Memories*, 246.

presence. His strong personality imposed its will on everyone, inspiring even those who resisted him to their greatest efforts. Of course there were people who did resist. Not everyone could accept the strenuous conditions and the extreme tension he created.

But in Mahler himself there was something that inspired love, and made both performers and public willing to cooperate and empathize with him. Such close contact with his audience allowed him to experiment: for example, to perform the Fourth Symphony twice on a single evening. This happened at a memorable concert in 1904, and was intended to give true music-lovers the chance to understand this novel work in greater depth. I don't doubt for a moment the impact it had at the time; and today, after more than twenty years, the Fourth Symphony is one of the best-known music works in Holland.

When I think of the significance of Mahler's music in our time the question arises: have those who considered Mahler *a passing phenomenon* in music history been proved right? I think I have to answer in the negative. Undoubtedly the number of countries where Mahler has received attention is still small, but one cannot deny that his music is being played more and more. In Austria, Germany, and Holland Mahler belongs among the great masters whose works are part of the standard repertoire. And in other countries too, people are beginning to sense the hidden power in his music that expresses the ideals and concerns of the present day. After the Amsterdam première of the Second Symphony in 1904, I delivered a speech in which I expressed my admiration for the composer in the following words: 'We have come to know a great genius, someone I should like to call the Beethoven of our time.' This statement provoked amazement and indignation. But, looking back today over the musical life of the past twenty years and at the part Mahler played in it, I would still reiterate what I said then; because, without wishing to draw a comparison between the two masters, I do sense a deep inner relationship between them: both held similar positions in the artistic and social life of their times and in the history of music.[5]

The Aftermath of the 'Tonkünstlerfest'

As a result of the 1902 'Tonkünstlerfest' in Crefeld, the year 1903 witnessed *two* performances of Mahler's Third Symphony in Holland in *one week* by two different orchestras and two different conductors. Martin Heuckeroth, the music director of the orchestra in Arnhem, conducted the first performance (and thus its Dutch première) in Arnhem on 17 October. Although it was very successful, as the press reviews reveal, it was overshadowed by the fact that the composer himself would be performing the work a week later. On 22 and 23 October Mahler conducted his Third Symphony in Amsterdam, followed on the 25th by a performance of his First Symphony. As we have seen, Mengelberg had carefully prepared the scores with his orchestra beforehand, and consequently Mahler felt he had rarely enjoyed his own music so much. He wrote to Alma on 21 October: 'Another rehearsal this morning. The orchestra were off their heads with delight. Its beauty fairly winded me.

---

[5] Mengelberg, 'Bij de sterfdag'.

I can't tell you what I felt when I heard it again. . . . It will be a fine performance. Better than at Crefeld.'[6] And fine it was, as Mahler wrote to Alma again two days later:

And now for yesterday evening. It was magnificent. — At first they were a little puzzled, but with each movement they grew warmer and when the contralto came on . . . the whole hall was gripped, and from then to the end there was the familiar rise of temperature. When the last note died away the tumult of applause was almost daunting. Everyone said nothing like it could be remembered.[7]

One of those attending the performance was Alphons Diepenbrock, a Dutch composer, friend of Mengelberg, and friend-to-be of Mahler. Diepenbrock would later turn out to be Mahler's strongest supporter in Holland after Mengelberg. After listening to the Third Symphony he wrote: 'I have the greatest admiration for Mahler; he is modern in every way. He *believes* in the future'; and again, 'Last week I met Mahler and he made a deep impression on me.'[8] Mahler himself was happy to make the acquaintance of this 'very interesting Dutch composer, who . . . composes very original church music', as he wrote to Alma.[9] From this time onwards Diepenbrock was to be included, at Mahler's particular request, in all the social events to which Mahler was invited.

The success story of Mahler and Holland continued the following year, 1904, when Mahler introduced two of his symphonies to the Amsterdam public: the Fourth on 23 October, and the Second on 26 and 27 October. On 20 October Diepenbrock's wife noted in her diary: 'Mahler is back in town'; and on the 23rd: 'A performance of the Fourth Symphony twice over: afterwards supper at the Mengelbergs. Mahler told us wonderful things about the essence of his music. Fons calls him Orpheus and says he has classical ideas about music.'[10]

For years it has been believed that at this double concert of the Fourth, Mahler conducted one of the performances and Mengelberg the other—as can still be read in an article on Mahler in Holland by Ian F. Finlay: 'On the occasion of the first performance of Mahler's Fourth Symphony in the Concertgebouw on 23rd October, 1904, the work was performed twice at the same concert, being conducted before the interval by Mahler and after it by Mengelberg!'[11] However, that Mahler alone conducted both performances is not only recorded by Mrs Diepenbrock but also by one of Diepenbrock's Latin pupils, Balthazar Verhagen, who wrote: 'On the memorable Saturday night of the 23rd October Mahler conducted his Fourth Symphony twice to a small but appreciative audience.'[12] During the first rehearsal of the Fourth, Mahler discovered a misprint in the score. Immediately he sent off a telegram to the publisher Ludwig Doblinger in Vienna to correct the error, because otherwise 'the whole world will play it with a wrong note.'[13]

[6] Alma Mahler, *Memories*, 247.

[7] Ibid. 249.

[8] Eduard Reeser (ed.), *Gustav Mahler und Holland: Briefe* (Bibliothek der Internationalen Gustav Mahler Gesellschaft; Vienna: Universal Edition, 1980), 10.

[9] Alma Mahler, *Memories*, 248.

[10] Reeser, *Gustav Mahler*, 14 ('Fons' was Elisabeth Diepenbrock's nickname for her husband).

[11] Ian F. Finlay, 'Gustav Mahler in Holland and England', *Britain and Holland*, 10 (1958), 85–90 at 86. In this, however, he was probably misled by Alma, who states that 'Mahler conducted the first time, Mengelberg the second, with Mahler sitting comfortably in the stalls to hear his own work played to him' (Alma Mahler, *Memories*, 73)—but she was not present at the occasion.

[12] Reeser, *Gustav Mahler*, 15.

[13] Ibid. 17.

Although there were still some strong attacks on his music, most of the critics were won over by the poetic and naive atmosphere of the Fourth. One of them even prophesied that 'this symphony will not only gain a chief place in the repertoire of the Concertgebouw Orchestra, but will also become a much beloved and popular work'.[14] And how right he was: of all Mahler's symphonies, this one was to be performed thirty-three times by Mengelberg over the period 1911–19.

In the meantime, on 26 October 1904 Mahler conducted the Dutch première of his Second Symphony in Amsterdam. It was understood much better than the Third, although the critics—as ever—were mixed in their response. Some of them found his music spell-bindingly original; others considered Mahler just a brilliant charlatan.

The next concert season (1905–6), Mahler was invited to conduct his Fifth Symphony in Amsterdam. Once again, however, it was another city, orchestra, and conductor which gave it its Dutch première: in Scheveningen, the Berlin Philharmonic Orchestra under August Scharrer performed the symphony on 30 June 1905. Mahler himself eventually conducted the Fifth—together with *Kindertotenlieder* and one Rückert song ('Ich bin der Welt abhan-den gekommen')—in Amsterdam on 8 March 1906. This was followed by performances of *Das klagende Lied* on 10 and 11 March.

Mrs Diepenbrock considered the Fifth a strange and capricious work—at least at its first hearing; and *Kindertotenlieder* met with incomprehension from the audience—perhaps because the songs were felt to be too sad. After each song crowds of people left the hall, which depressed Mahler deeply, although he did not show it in his letter to Alma of 9 March: 'The audience *very attentive*, the press positively glowing.'[15] It was Diepenbrock who translated the reviews for Mahler, and he may diplomatically have overlooked the adverse ones in order to put Mahler's mind at rest. At all events, the general tone of the crit-ics was now more positive: 'Mahler fascinates us, his music keeps us spellbound', said one; and again, 'His emotional outbursts are extreme but thrilling.' Only one critic continued to regard Mahler's music as 'a torture, full of unbearable noise and dissonances, in short *supermodern*'.[16] Very daringly, Mengelberg took the Fifth Symphony on a tour of seven concerts round Holland—at the last of which only the Adagietto was played together with *Kindertotenlieder*. In Rotterdam the public was lukewarm; but in the Hague there was considerable applause, perhaps because the work was already known to some who had pre-viously heard it in Amsterdam.

Over the next three years, only one performance of the First Symphony under Mengelberg and one of the Fourth under Diepenbrock took place. Plans to bring Mahler to Holland to introduce his Sixth Symphony fell through. Only in September 1909 did he find his way back to his 'second home', this time to introduce his Seventh Symphony. 'Holland again delights me beyond measure. . . . The orchestra is splendid and quite infatuated with

[14] See Eduard Reeser, 'Die Mahler-Rezeption in Holland, 1903–1911', in Rudolph Stephan (ed.), *Mahler-Interpretation* (Mainz: Schott's Söhne, 1985), 81–103 at 86.

[15] Alma Mahler, *Memories*, 273.
[16] Reeser, 'Die Mahler-Rezeption', 92.

me. It's a pleasure this time instead of hard work', he wrote to Alma.[17] He found the orchestra 'brilliantly rehearsed in advance', and not surprisingly: Mengelberg had worked on the symphony for a week, rehearsing mornings and evenings with the orchestra, which had never studied so difficult a score before! 'Thanks to Mengelberg's exemplary preliminary work the performance, conducted by Mahler himself, was an unforgettable experience', wrote one of the members of the orchestra. 'Mahler conducted his symphony almost without moving; he led the orchestra more with his eyes than with his right hand. . . . He toyed with the orchestra, and each player felt compelled to fulfil his part exactly as the great petty tyrant demanded of him.'[18]

At its first performance in Amsterdam on 3 October, the Seventh was received more warmly by the public than the Fifth had been. The fact that the press were invited to attend the final rehearsal evidently helped them to understand the work better. After the second performance on 7 October, public and critics alike were won over. Diepenbrock, however, was not entirely drawn to the work. As he wrote to his friend Johanna Jongkind:

In his Seventh there are many things that don't please me. There is no real Adagio. In the first movement one finds some of those divine moments, followed by beautiful, plaintive bird sounds. Also some typical Jewish things ('Sie wissen ja dass ich ein Jude bin'! ['You know that I'm a Jew']) . . . A Serenade—the fourth movement—indescribably charming, a declaration of love to the universe. The first three movements are all in a nocturnal atmosphere, as is the fourth—though it is mostly charming. The third movement is spooky—the second too, in some places, though we do hear Mahler's genial melodies as well. It is *not true* that he has 'repainted' Rembrandt's *Night Watch* in the second movement. He only mentioned the painting by way of comparison. The movement does represent a nocturnal tour, and he claims to have thought of a 'patrol' whilst composing it. But he says something different about it each time. What is certain is that it is a march with a fantastic chiaroscuro atmosphere—and this has led to its being compared with Rembrandt's painting. The same extraordinary colouring takes the imagination back to the past and conjures up a group of soldiers and lansquenets. . . . But the culminating point is the fifth movement in C major: the radiant sun breaks in—the night has yielded to the day.[19]

These 1909 concerts were the last Mahler conducted in Holland. The Concertgebouw Orchestra continued to play the Seventh on tour under Mengelberg. Perhaps from a sense of chauvinism, or possibly because there really was very little difference between the two, the critics generally agreed that Mengelberg's interpretation matched Mahler's.

Although Holland would never see Mahler again in his musical capacity, he was to visit Leyden—incognito—the following summer. As Donald Mitchell has pointed out: 'Towards the end of his life Mahler became increasingly anxious about his relationship to his wife and decided to consult Sigmund Freud.'[20] Alma herself relates how her husband realized that he had lived the life of a neurotic and decided (she writes 'suddenly', but actually he postponed the visit several times) to consult Sigmund Freud, who was then on holiday in

---

[17] Alma Mahler, *Memories*, 272. Mahler speaks of Amsterdam as his 'second home' in his undated letter of Oct. 1903 to Mengelberg (Mahler, *Selected Letters*, 273).
[18] Reeser, 'Die Mahler-Rezeption', 27–8.

[19] Ibid. 31–2. Diepenbrock's favourite piece of Mahler's music was the third movement of the Fourth Symphony.
[20] Alma Mahler, *Memories*, p. xvii.

Holland. From what Mahler said to him, Freud concluded that he had a fixation on his mother—just as Alma had one on her father. Moreover, a personal communication from Freud to Marie Bonaparte in 1925 contains a remark made by Mahler at their meeting which sheds light on his way of composing:

In the course of the talk [with Freud] Mahler suddenly said that now he understood why his music had always been prevented from achieving the highest rank through the noblest passages, those inspired by the most profound emotions, being spoilt by the intrusion of some commonplace melody. His father, apparently a brutal person, treated his wife very badly, and when Mahler was a young boy there was a specially painful scene between them. It became quite unbearable to the boy, who rushed away from the house. At that moment, however, a hurdy-gurdy in the street was grinding out the popular Viennese air 'Ach, du lieber Augustin'. In Mahler's opinion the conjunction of high tragedy and light amusement was from then on inextricably fixed in his mind, and the one mood inevitably brought the other with it.[21]

Had Mengelberg, Diepenbrock, or the critics known this story, they might have understood the characteristic 'conjunction of high tragedy and light amusement' in Mahler's music a little better. Of them all, I believe Diepenbrock came closest to appreciating what lay hidden deep down in Mahler's soul. The warm friendship, understanding, and admiration that he bore Mahler and his music resulted in a very moving obituary which he wrote in the weekly *De Amsterdammer* on 4 June 1911, two weeks after Mahler's death. It opens with a quotation from Mahler's Second Symphony ('O glaube, mein Herz . . . gelitten') and states that with his death a rare specimen of mankind had gone, a man not of this time, whom one encountered only in books. On the one hand he was an inwardly living composer, wrapped up in his dreams like the later Beethoven; on the other, he was a modern man, a man of the twentieth century, possessed—as Diepenbrock believed—by his *daimon*. Mahler believed in himself and went his own way, undeterred by other men's opinions. 'He did his work and gave us nine symphonies and fifty songs, asking in return no money, fame, or admiration but only love. And of this we gave him too little.'[22]

After Mahler's death Mengelberg took it upon himself to champion his friend's music, both in Holland and abroad, and he did so with success. Between 1911 and 1920 (the year of the Mahler festival), the Concertgebouw Orchestra gave 207 concerts, each of which included one or more of Mahler's works, beginning with the memorial concert on 7 September 1911, when *Kindertotenlieder* and the Fourth Symphony were performed. Moreover, not only the Amsterdam Orchestra, but also the Residentie Orchestra of The Hague and the Utrechts Stedelijk Orkest began putting more and more Mahler on their programmes, often at the special request of the public.

Now how did the press react to this stream of Mahler's music? As Rob Overman has shown in his article 'The Mahler-Reception in the Netherlands 1911–1920',[23] the

---

[21] Alma Mahler, *Memories*, p. xvii.
[22] Reeser, *Gustav Mahler*, 110.
[23] Rob Overman, 'The Mahler-Reception in the Netherlands 1911–1920', in *A 'Mass' for the Masses:*

Proceedings of the Mahler VIII Symposium Amsterdam 1988, ed. Jos van Leeuwen, Eveline Nikkels, and Robert Becqué (Rijswijk: Universitaire Pers Rotterdam, 1992), 68–77.

memorial concert of 7 September marked a sudden change in the attitude of the press. An analysis of the reception in the press yields the following results: the First and Fourth Symphonies, *Kindertotenlieder*, and *Das Lied von der Erde* were greeted with immediate enthusiasm and quickly became part of the standard repertoire. Opinions varied, however, about the remaining works. *Das klagende Lied* was unanimously recognized as the work of an obviously young composer; and while the Second Symphony found favour in Rotterdam and The Hague, Amsterdam still criticized it. The Third Symphony, so difficult to understand at its first hearing in Amsterdam, was now generally well received; but the three 'middle' symphonies, the Fifth, Sixth, and Seventh, continued to be criticized and enjoyed little sympathy. The Dutch première of the Eighth Symphony on 9 March 1912, conducted by Mengelberg, was as overwhelming an event as it had been at its world première in Munich on 12 September 1910 when Mahler himself conducted it. All Holland was there, including all the important critics, who applauded Mengelberg's masterful leadership of the 700 musicians on stage. The audience was ecstatic, but the hall was considered too small for such a colossal symphony. This leaves us with the Ninth, which was not performed by Mengelberg until 1918, for fear that the public would misunderstand it. And how right he was: the reaction of both audience and press was negative, and it was to be so again at the Mahler Festival of 1920. But on the whole, as Overman concludes, 'the opinions about Mahler had stabilized completely. Mahler had become one of the favourite composers of the majority of both press and public.'[24]

The 'Mahlerfeest' of 1920

When I gave you, my honoured and dear friend Mengelberg, the manuscript score of the Seventh Symphony of Gustav Mahler two years ago, I felt that Mahler himself would have agreed with this gesture of thanks to you. . . . You were not only one of the first to understand Mahler's art at a time when it met with so much hostility, you were also the first to dedicate yourself wholeheartedly to it. He always regarded you and loved you as his close friend, his unsurpassed interpreter, and even more as a strong, independent artist and human being. Once, after a concert at which you conducted the Fourth Symphony and which he attended, he said: 'I felt as if I had been standing there myself.'[25]

These remarkable words were written by Alma Mahler in the 'Gedenkboek Mengelberg' in 1920, on the occasion of Mengelberg's twenty-fifth anniversary as chief conductor of the Concertgebouw Orchestra. It had been rumoured that a gift of 100,000 guilders was to be raised for him. On hearing of this, however, Mengelberg announced that he would prefer instead to organize a series of concerts in which he could perform all Mahler's works and in which musicians from all over the world would be invited to participate. This was the

[24] Ibid. 73.   [25] *Willem Mengelberg Gedenkboek* (The Hague: Martinus Nijhoff, 1920), 109.

origin of the first Dutch Mahler Festival, which took place in Amsterdam between 6 and 21 May 1920. In nine concerts, Mengelberg conducted Mahler's nine symphonies, *Das klagende Lied*, *Das Lied von der Erde*, *Kindertotenlieder*, and Rückert Lieder with the Concertgebouw Orchestra, the Toonkunstkoor, and the singers Cahier, Durigo, Förstel, Hoffmann-Onegin, Noordewier, Reidel, Denijs, Duhan, and Urlus. In the mornings of the days between the big Mahler concerts, Mengelberg had organized concerts of modern chamber music and lectures on Mahler's music and personality, held in the small concert hall of the Concertgebouw.

One of the speakers at these lectures was Guido Adler, who spoke on Mahler's personality as an artist and a man. He told his audience that Mahler was fanatical and uncompromising where truth, life, and art were concerned; that he had indomitable will-power, but was generous in his friendships, and, though touchy, always kind and reliable—a rare mixture of willingness to oblige and domination.

For those who might regard Mahler even today as a pessimist, another speaker, Richard Specht, observed that all his symphonies exhibited an optimism, which was only now and then interrupted by pessimism; and that Mengelberg, who knew Mahler so well, had judged aright to end the Festival with the Eighth Symphony, because Mahler taught us that light and love are the basic instincts of mankind.

A third speaker, Alfredo Casella, spoke on the significance of the Festival: it was an occasion to get to know Mahler and to celebrate the anniversary of one of his greatest interpreters, Mengelberg. 'The essential meaning of this Festival is the affirmation of life, the positive and joyous life of continual creativity. No shadow of sorrow shall overcloud our feelings. In our jubilations we celebrate both the great works of the master and his illustrious interpreter; and each of us shall take away from here the memory of one of the most beautiful musical events of our time.'[26]

The prestigious assembly of foreign guests at the Festival—which included such distinguished names as Arnold Schoenberg and Paul Stefan—gave rise to the idea of founding an international Mahler Society. Accordingly, Schoenberg was commissioned to draft a circular letter to potential subscribers, which opened as follows:

Dear Sir, At the conclusion of the Mahler Festival in Amsterdam in May 1920 a *Mahler Society*—as proposed by the Mahler Festival Committee—was founded with Mrs. A. M. Mahler as the Patroness, Willem Mengelberg as the Honorary President; I myself have been installed as the President. Possibly the Mahler Society is going to be founded early in September.[27]

Schoenberg was also asked to draft the statutes of the society, but unfortunately this proved to be the very rock on which the whole project foundered. His idea of basing the Mahler Society in both Vienna and Amsterdam met with disapproval on the part of the Dutch Mahlerians, who wanted it to be based in Amsterdam alone. Furthermore, his motives were questioned by the Festival Committee, at which he grew indignant:

[26] *Mengelberg en zijn tijd*, no. 25 (1993), 10.
[27] Berthold Türcke, 'The Mahler Society', *Journal of the Arnold Schoenberg Institute*, 7/1 (June 1983), 29–93 at 39.

I am *deeply offended* with the manner in which my draft of the statutes for the Mahler Society was received. . . . *Do you have so little confidence in my friendship, gratefulness and reliability that you are not aware of my intention to do the best for you? . . .* Don't you have better impressions of me? And shouldn't I be offended, if I am gauged by such conventional standards as though I were an ordinary careerist and ambitionist? . . . shouldn't I be entitled to be treated differently?[28]

And he queried, with heavy irony, whether the society should not rather be called the 'Mengelberg Society', and so make it suspect of being a business enterprise. In his reply by telegram, Mengelberg tried to soothe Schoenberg, but still took a rather uncompromising position:

Your concept of establishing Mahler Society is all right in every respect; however we have a different concept in Holland. We want an absolutely international Mahler Society, in which America, England, France are as interested as Vienna and Germany. This is to serve the Mahler matter. Your statutes establish the whole thing according to your personal concept based on local—i.e. German, particularly Viennese—circumstances and aspects; this would be absolutely unacceptable for other nations—even Holland would not go for that.[29]

Although Schoenberg replied that despite their differences he felt sure they could come to some agreement, in the end no such accommodation could be found and the whole project remained stillborn.

The Mahler Legacy

'Dear friend, on second thoughts I have made some *important* revisions. Please send me your score so that I can enter them *in red ink.* They are all *very* important for the performance', Mahler wrote to Mengelberg in October 1905, following it with a further request to send '*your* score of the *Fifth* Symphony. I have planned some alterations to it which I should like to enter in red ink and have transcribed into the orchestra parts by your copyist.'[30]

On looking at Mengelberg's scores of Mahler's symphonies (a real 'legacy'—being part of the archives of the Mengelberg bequest at the Gemeentemuseum in The Hague), one can still see these revisions, written in either Mahler's hand or Mengelberg's. Immediately noticeable on the flyleaves of the scores of the Fourth and Fifth Symphonies are the words written repeatedly by Mengelberg and heavily underlined: '*This was told to me by Mahler himself*', or, '*Those were Mahler's very own words.*' And what these 'own words' tell us provide clues to the hidden programmes behind the symphonies.

---

[28] Ibid. 79–83.   [29] Ibid. 87.   [30] Reeser, *Gustav Mahler*, 59.

'Guaranteed! All revisions made *in red ink* are by Gustav Mahler in his own hand. Word of honour! All those in red pencil are by me', Mengelberg has written on the score of the Fourth Symphony. And again: 'All these remarks were made by *Mahler himself* during the rehearsals in Amsterdam before the first performance of the Symphony here.' Particularly striking is the tempo marking reiterated three times on the first page of the score, '♩ = 69 exactly, metronome'—which leaves no doubt about the 'Bedächtig, Nicht eilen' ('Slowly, don't hurry') Mahler indicates for the opening of the first movement. The second movement bears the subtitle 'Death takes us by the hand, very diabolical', followed at Fig. 2 by: 'Dance of Death by Holbein, solo violin and solo horn continually dominating, all *ppp*, ghostly, light dance rhythm. Solo violin: Death always comes in very wildly *fff*.' Fig. 3 shows us 'a beautiful landscape', and Fig. 9, 'a delightful meadow, very lovely and beautiful'. The third movement tells us 'where Death has taken us'. At Fig. 12 we find: 'when heaven opens itself we see God's glory and splendour'.

Even more revealing is the flyleaf of the Fifth Symphony, which provides a detailed programme for all the movements and documents the well-known struggle of so much of Mahler's music—*per aspera ad astra*:

First movement: deepest sorrow, melancholy, sadness—tears, tears!—a face distorted by constant weeping—worn out by violent outbreaks of despair, fury, frenzy close to madness (laughing!!!!!!!). The end: half delirious with sorrow, gruesome, ghostly.

Second movement: forced gaiety—wants to get over suffering—but it can't be yet; sounds forced, sad undertone—here and there a Dance of Death.

Third movement: *Love, love comes into his life*! return to nature, motif of nature d c♯ b a first motif. Then comes the fourth's entry *d a, a b c♯ d*—

Fourth movement: friendly—exuberant gaiety, starts with a mood of happiness and contentedness—more and more 'exuberant'. The end: mad with joy and happiness.

At almost every figure in the first movement remarks are made—mostly by Mengelberg—on the prevailing mood. For instance: at Fig. 4 he has written 'melancholy'; at Fig. 5, 'comfort and sorrow'; at Fig. 6, 'comfort'; at Fig. 7, 'outburst of despair, explosive sorrow, deep sorrow'; at Fig. 8, 'fanatic'; at Fig. 12, 'melancholy'; at Fig. 14, 'comfort', and at Fig. 15, 'sorrow'. At Fig. 9 'pesante' appears, written in red ink and in Mahler's hand.

But the most famous entry of all, and perhaps the most important—because it reveals the true character of the movement, which has been falsely represented as a lamentation (partly on account of the film *Death in Venice*)—is that made by Mengelberg on the opening page of the Adagietto:

This Adagietto was Gustav Mahler's *declaration of love* to Alma! *Instead of* a letter he sent her *this* in manuscript, *without an extra word. She understood and wrote to him: He should come*!!! (*Both of them told me this!*)

In the margin beside the first violins, Mengelberg has written this poem:

Wie ich dich liebe,   [How I love you,
Du meine Sonne,   You my Sun,
Ich kann mit Worten Dir's nicht sagen I cannot tell you in Words
Nur meine Sehnsucht   I can only lament
Kann ich Dir klagen   my Longing
Und meine Liebe   And my Love for you
Meine Wonne!   My Happiness!]

And at the foot of the page he has noted: 'If music is a language then it is one here—"He" tells her *everything* in *"Tones"* and *"Sounds"* in: Music.'[31]

---

[31]   These annotations have now been published in Mitchell and Straub (eds.), *New Sounds, New Century*, 83–4. For comprehensive information about the Amsterdam Mahlerfeest of 1995, a culminating event in the history of Mahler reception in the twentieth century, readers should consult *GMWL*.

Additional note: What to date has been almost entirely overlooked—and we gladly take the opportunity to make amends—is the important contribution that took place only a few years later in another location altogether: this time in Edinburgh, in the Usher Hall, where on 13 November 1924 Donald Francis Tovey conducted the Reid Symphony Orchestra, which he himself had founded, and the soloist George Parker in a performance of Mahler's *Kindertotenlieder*. For his concerts Tovey provided his own programme notes (of which the British Library holds a collection), which later formed the substance of his *Essays in Musical Analysis*. On this occasion he wrote: 'As for the *Kindertotenlieder*, there is nothing for it but to bow the head. The setting of these sometimes almost Euripidean and always typically German words has disciplined the composer's invention of forms and melodies, until his simplicity becomes as accurate as anything Greek'; his themes 'reflect every shade of meaning in the words, and what perfect declamation does not comprehend is supplied by perfect orchestration'. This must count among the earliest performances of Mahler's song cycle in England; we have to remind ourselves that the composer died only in 1911 and that the First World War had intervened. But this was not Tovey's only Mahler performance: on 22 October 1936, same place, same orchestra, he conducted the Fourth Symphony with Marie Thomson as soloist. This time his programme note was an extensive essay on the symphony and included numerous music examples. Given the prevailing critical judgement of the early 1930s in England, it surely stands as one of the most remarkable perceptions of the composer: 'The musical culture of Great Britain will probably be the better for the rise of a vogue for Bruckner and Mahler; and perhaps Mahler will do us more good than Bruckner, because his mastery will discourage the cult of amateurishness, which keeps us contented with ignorance and ready to believe that ineptitude is noble in itself; and the good taste which is ready to take offence at Mahler's sentimentality will be all the better for being shocked.' Strong words in 1936 which still have a resonance in 2002, when the 'vogue' that Tovey so presciently anticipated has become a torrential reality.

13

The Rückert Lieder

STEPHEN E. HEFLING

> After *Des Knaben Wunderhorn* I could not compose anything but Rückert—this is lyric poetry from the source, all else is lyric poetry of a derivative sort.
>
> Mahler to Anton von Webern, 3 February 1905[1]

Like the poet Rückert, who claimed that 'I never think without poetizing, and never poetize without thinking', Mahler often acknowledged that personal experience provided the occasion or impulse for his compositions. 'It is always thus for me', he once declared; 'only when I experience do I "compose", and only when I compose do I experience'.[2] It has long been recognized that the emergence of Mahler's second maturity as a composer largely coincides with his farewell to the world of the *Wunderhorn* in the summer of 1901. Indeed, the final poem he drew from that collection, which had inspired him for more than a decade, seems rather like the rogue's march for his *Wunderhorn* persona: 'Der Tamboursg'sell' ('The Drummer Boy') is the narrative of a soldier, formerly a humble drummer-boy, who is now being led to the gallows by night for crimes unspecified. It was during the same composing holiday that Mahler launched the Fifth Symphony and set his first Rückert lyrics—three *Kindertotenlieder* (ultimately incorporated into a cycle of five), plus four of the five 'separate' Rückert songs, with which we are chiefly concerned here.

The unmistakable contrast between the *Wunderhorn* and Rückert lieder is that inherent between stock characters and the individuated personality, as Paul Bekker observed long ago.[3] The *Wunderhorn* folk are representatives of their types; accordingly, much of the music these poems elicited from Mahler is stylistically generic. Of the twelve orchestrated songs, for example, six are marches and four are Ländler. Beyond this, as Adorno and other

---

[1] From Webern's diary, printed in Hans Moldenhauer and Rosaleen Moldenhauer, *Anton von Webern: A Chronicle of his Life and Work* (New York: Alfred A. Knopf, 1979), 75.

[2] Rückert, 'Mußt Du denn immer dichten?' in the collection 'Pantheon', *Friedrich Rückert's gesammelte Poetische Werke* (Frankfurt am Main: Sauerländer, 1868–9), vii. 159; Mahler, letter to Arthur Seidel, 17 Feb. 1897, in *Briefe* (1982), no. 216 (*Selected Letters*, no. 205).

[3] Bekker, *Gustav Mahlers Sinfonien*, 175–8, esp. 177; cf. also Reinhard Gerlach, *Strophen von Leben, Traum und Tod: Ein Essay über Rückert-Lieder von Gustav Mahler* (Taschenbücher zur Musikwissenschaft, ed. Richard Schaal, no. 83; Wilhelmshaven: Heinrichshofen's Verlag, 1982), 52–3, and E. Mary Dargie, *Music and Poetry in the Songs of Gustav Mahler* (European University Studies, ser. 1, vol. 401; Bern: Peter Lang, 1981), 269.

writers have observed, the tension between folkish verse animated by dance and march rhythms and the urbane sophistication of Mahler's musical settings overall frequently suggests that the composer has assumed an ironic, critical stance, emotionally detached from the text.[4] Indeed, he himself thought of the first five orchestral *Wunderhorn* lieder as 'humoresques'.[5] All the Rückert lieder, however, are essentially lyrical and assume a first-person perspective that, with one exception, is intimately introspective. And as we shall see, Mahler's selection and interpretation of Rückert's poetry was a strong artistic projection of his own world of feeling.

The switch to Rückert marks both a personal and an artistic turning point for Mahler. Between 1888 and 1900 his *Wunderhorn* project had evolved into much more than the setting of two dozen folkish lieder. The Second, Third, and Fourth Symphonies all contain movements based on *Wunderhorn* poems, and each of those 'symphonic worlds' was influenced by 'Das himmlische Leben' ('Heavenly Life')—the lied that brought Mahler out of his 'Budapest stagnation' (as he dubbed it) in 1892.[6] Here at last was an answer to the despair of 'Todtenfeier', the shattering first movement of his Second Symphony, beyond which he had been unable to advance for nearly four years. The child's vision of paradise manifest in the song is a naive reversal of the Fall and a return to Eden, where delicious food is everywhere, the music is incomparable, martyrs dance, and saints symbolically slaughter for the feast. 'What roguishness intertwined with the deepest mysticism is hidden in it!', Mahler exclaimed; 'It is everything turned on its head . . .'.[7] Musically, of course, a strophic lied could not properly balance the vast C minor sonata movement with which the Second was to open. Eventually 'Das himmlische Leben' became the crowning jewel of the Fourth Symphony, the gem for which the first three movements were crafted as a setting. As the conclusion of that symphony, it is to be sung (according to the score) 'with childlike, serene expression, entirely without parody', and Mahler explained to Natalie Bauer-Lechner that here 'the child, which already belongs to this higher world [of heavenly life], although in a chrysalis state, clarifies what it all means'.[8] This is the same naive expression of faith he had sought to achieve in 'Urlicht', the prelude to the vast finale of the 'Resurrection' Symphony: 'the soul is in heaven, where, in a chrysalis-like state it must begin everything anew as a child'.[9] Such was also the final fate of Goethe's Faust, whose soul had been received as a child, in chrysalis state (*im Puppenstand*) into the celestial choir of youths. Although Mahler would not dare to set the famous final scene of *Faust* until his Eighth Symphony (1906), it seems clear that, from a different perspective, he had envisaged a similar ending for the hero of his symphonies as early as 1892. Mahler himself regarded his first four symphonies as a self-contained tetralogy, to which the Fourth forms

[4] E.g. Adorno, *Mahler*, 56–7 and 74–7, as well as 'Zu einer imaginären Auswahl von Liedern Gustav Mahlers', in *Impromptus: Zweite Folge neu gedruckter musikalischer Aufsätze* (Frankfurt: Suhrkamp, 1968), 32–3; cf. also Peter Russell, *Light in Battle with Darkness: Mahler's 'Kindertotenlieder'* (Bern: Peter Lang, 1991), 113.

[5] 'Fünf Humoresken' is the title on the orchestral autograph manuscript (Vienna, Gesellschaft der Musikfreunde, A316).
[6] NB-L, *Erinnerungen*, 172 (not in *Recollections*).
[7] Ibid. 184 (not in *Recollections*).
[8] Ibid. 198 (*Recollections*, 178).
[9] Ibid. 168 (not in *Recollections*).

the conclusion; as the finale of the Fourth, the child's vision of heaven functions as 'the tapering spire of the structure'.[10]

The Fourth was essentially finished in the summer of 1900, and during the ensuing winter season Mahler worked out details of the orchestral score. Meanwhile, as usual, he drove himself relentlessly as a conductor: during the Christmas season of 1900 he performed the entire *Ring* cycle; in January and February of 1901 he introduced a new production of Wagner's *Rienzi*, gave the première of his own *Das klagende Lied*, and led three concerts of the Vienna Philharmonic (including a special performance of Beethoven's Ninth).[11] On 24 February he conducted a Philharmonic concert in the afternoon as well as an evening performance of *Die Zauberflöte* at the Opera—and that night he collapsed. The composer who had frequently struggled with the mysteries of death and eternity suffered a haemorrhoidal haemorrhage so severe that 'I thought my last hour had come.'[12] He survived, and within a year completely transformed his existence: the 40-year-old bachelor became engaged to the enchanting young Alma Schindler in December 1901, and the couple conceived a child prior to their marriage. As Stuart Feder has persuasively argued, Mahler's rapid move to participate in the renewal of life was probably a direct reaction to his recent brush with death.[13] But during the summer of 1901, months before he had ever met Alma, Mahler made that sobering moment the subject of artistic utterance; as Feder observes,

immediately following surgery and a brief period of convalescence in a nursing home . . . the relevant fears and conflicts intensified and unconsciously alternatives and potential solutions were beginning to take shape. It must have seemed to him as if he had been catapulted into middle age. The end lay before him, and time, ever a preoccupation of Mahler the composer and conductor, became all the more precious.[14]

That summer he composed three of the *Kindertotenlieder*, which memorialize the theme of the bereaved parent stricken by the loss of a child. Mahler's identification with this sorrowful subject was probably multifaceted: eight of his own siblings had died in childhood, and now he himself had nearly perished; doubtless too, he realized more urgently than ever that he might well die without issue. As Feder suggests, 'to symbolize the wish *to have* a child in the *form* of a parent in mourning would be entirely consistent with Mahler's character. Its relationship to his identification with his own parents—both mother as well as father—is also apparent'.[15] But viewed from the perspective of Mahler's

[10] NB-L, *Erinnerungen*, 162, 164, and 172 (*Recollections*, 151 and 154; third passage lacking).

[11] See HLG(E) i. 605–12 and ii. 316–36 (HLG(F) ii. 45–65).

[12] Natalie Bauer-Lechner, 'Mahleriana' (original MS of her memoire), quoted in HLG(E) ii. 334 (HLG(F) ii. 66; paraphrased in HLG(E) i. 614); a full account of Mahler's illness and recovery is found in HLG(E) ii and HLG(F) ii. Bruno Walter visited Mahler shortly after his illness, and reported as follows: 'He had become older, milder, and softer, and a deadly silence had spread across his nature. I told him years later how moved I had been by this change.

"Yes, I learnt something then", he replied, "but it belongs to those matters that one cannot talk about" ' (Walter, 'Mahlers Weg, ein Erinnerungsblatt', *Der Merker*, 3/5 (1912), 166–71, cited in Lebrecht, *Mahler Remembered*, 127 ff.

[13] Stuart Feder, 'Gustav Mahler, Dying', *International Review of Psychoanalysis*, 5 (1978), 125–48, esp. 130–3.

[14] Stuart Feder, 'Gustav Mahler um Mitternacht', *International Review of Psychoanalysis*, 7 (1980), 11–26 at 18.

[15] Feder, 'Gustav Mahler, Dying', 130–1; quotation from p. 131.

previous works, the dead children of the *Kindertotenlieder* would seem to represent an end to the simple, collective faith and hope that dominate the earlier tetralogy of symphonies.[16] In 'Um Mitternacht', another of the Rückert lieder from the summer of 1901, it seems that Mahler confronts his personal crisis more directly. Rückert's poetry commences with imagery of nocturnal desolation punctuated by the throb and pain of a single heart—all of which is much akin to Mahler's terrifying experience of the preceding February. The song concludes in exultant grandeur of religious affirmation, musically reminiscent of the Second Symphony's finale, as Bauer-Lechner observed.[17] By contrast, 'Der Tamboursg'sell', the last of the *Wunderhorn* songs, reflects another reaction of one condemned to die: the soldier acknowledges his guilt, and laments that 'had I remained a drummer, I would not have been imprisoned'. As Feder suggests, Mahler may well have felt similar guilt for various reasons, such as the neglect of his health in service of his overwhelming ambition, or the misfortunes of siblings and rivals during his extraordinary rise to eminence.[18] Indeed the morning after the February haemorrhage, the composer half-humorously outlined his obituary to Natalie Bauer-Lechner: 'Gustav Mahler has finally met the fate he deserved for his many misdeeds'.[19]

Two of the Rückert songs are lighter in character: the witty 'Blicke mir nicht in die Lieder'—in Mahler's view the least significant of the set—and 'Ich atmet' einen linden Duft', which he characterized as 'filled with the kind of quiet happiness you feel in the presence of someone dear, of whom you are entirely sure, without even a word needing to be spoken between the two souls'.[20] The last of the summer's harvest, however, stands apart from all the others, and indeed from anything Mahler had written: 'Ich bin der Welt abhanden gekommen' creates an extraordinary atmosphere of suspended time and meditative withdrawal from mundane commotion, concluding with the lines 'I am dead to the worldly throng, and rest in a peaceful domain. I live alone in my heaven, in my love and in my song.' Precisely this turning inward, away from the world's course, summarizes Mahler's change of allegiance from *Wunderhorn* poetry to Rückert.

But why specifically Rückert? Much of Rückert's enormous output is less than great poetry, as Mahler must have realized. Yet as is well known, Mahler considered it 'a profanity when composers ventured to set perfect poems to music; it was as if a sculptor chiselled a statue from marble and a painter came along and coloured it'.[21] In 1901, as today, Rückert was widely recognized as an orientalist whose immersion in Eastern literature strongly influenced his original poetry, such as the *Östliche Rosen* of 1819–20. In that collection Rückert assumes the identity of the fourteenth-century Persian poet Hafiz, in *ghazals* that idolize love, wine, and beauty; interspersed among these odes are grim lamentations on the

[16] Cf. also Carl E. Schorske, 'Mahler and Klimt: Social Experience and Artistic Evolution', in *Gustav Mahler Kolloquium 1979. Beiträge '79–81 der Österreichischen Gesellschaft für Musik* (Kassel: Bärenreiter, 1981), 16–28 at 25–6, and Feder, 'Gustav Mahler um Mitternacht', 15.

[17] 'Mahleriana', cited in HLG(E) ii. 368–9 (HLG(F) ii. 103).
[18] Feder, 'Gustav Mahler um Mitternacht', 14.
[19] 'Mahleriana', cited in HLG(E) ii. 335 (HLG(F) ii. 67).
[20] NB-L, *Erinnerungen*, 193–4 (*Recollections*, 173–4).
[21] Alma Mahler, *Memories*, 93.

transitoriness of all being.[22] But he also wrote more than 450 love lyrics for his fiancée Luise Wiethaus, among which is 'Ich bin der Welt abhanden gekommen' from 1821, subsequently published in *Liebesfrühling*, one of Rückert's most popular collections. Equally successful in his day were the *Haus- und Jahreslieder* (*Poems of Home and Season*), a celebration of everyday life and bourgeois domesticity that the poet himself characterized as 'home-baked'.[23] As Peter Russell has noted, Rückert's popularity reached a peak during his middle years, but by the end of his life (1866) he felt neglected by the literary world. A second collected edition of the poems appeared in 1881–2, followed by a lull in publication of his work. Then between 1895 and 1900 Rückert's reputation rose rapidly to its zenith; numerous editions were issued both for the bookshop and the classroom. This striking upsurge may have stemmed from widespread sentimentalist reaction to the increasingly impersonal materialism of bourgeois life in industrialized urban society.[24]

Mahler was disappointed that his *Wunderhorn* songs had not become more widely known and performed;[25] thus it is not surprising that he should consider setting more popular poetry, provided that it met his artistic purpose. And Rückert's did; whatever the shortcomings of many a verse, we can discern much in the poet's world-view that resonates with the composer's. Mahler himself provided the most important clue to this in a letter to his wife written in 1903, two years after his 'Rückert' summer, but a year before the *Kindertotenlieder* were complete: 'Remarkable how close in feeling Fechner is to Rückert: they are two nearly related people and one side of my nature is linked with them as a third.'[26] Through the influence of his long-time friend and mentor Siegfried Lipiner, a student of Gustav Theodor Fechner's, Mahler had been familiar with Fechner's panpsychic philosophy since his student days, and there now seems little doubt that it substantially affected the making of Mahler's symphonic worlds—especially the Second, Third, and *Das Lied von der Erde*.[27] For Fechner, the entire universe is an organic spiritual hierarchy leading up to the deity. Such is also the underlying metaphor of Mahler's Third Symphony (1896). Rückert, too, sees all-encompassing unity manifest both in the simplest aspects of existence and also in the complex systems of languages and cultures; his Romantic projection of feeling into nature is much akin to that of Fechner and Mahler.[28] Fechner is a universalist; in his view there is no distinction between saved and damned, but the soul continues to develop after death. Mahler, doubtless influenced by Lipiner, presents virtually the same vision of resurrection in the finale of his Second Symphony (1894), wherein we soar above death on wings won in the fervent striving of love. And for Rückert,

[22] See Manfred Grosser, 'Friedrich Rückerts "Östliche Rosen" ', *Rückert Studien*, 1 (1964), 45–108, esp. 63 ff. and 78–80; Helmut Prang, *Friedrich Rückert: Geist und Form der Sprache* (Schweinfurt and Wiesbaden: Otto Harrassowitz, 1963), 87 ff.; Arthur F. J. Remy, *The Influence of India and Persia on the Poetry of Germany* (Columbia University Germanic Studies, 4; New York: Columbia University Press, 1901), 38–56; Annemarie Schimmel, *Friedrich Rückert: Lebensbild und Einführung in sein Werk* (Freiburg: Herder, 1987), *passim* (see also references below to this work).

[23] Schimmel, *Friedrich Rückert*, 42.
[24] Russell, *Light in Battle*, 30–1 and 35–7.
[25] Mahler, *Briefe* (1982), no. 341 (*Selected Letters*, no. 319).
[26] Alma Mahler, *Memories*, 226.
[27] See below, Ch. 19, pp. 442–3.
[28] Schimmel, *Friedrich Rückert*, 41, 55, 129; Gerlach, *Strophen*, 33–4; Russell, *Light in Battle*, 49.

dying in love leads to eternal life. In the *Kindertotenlieder* Rückert is convinced that his two dead children are in heaven, and that he will join them there. Overall, he regards death as a kernel inherent in each being, which eventually becomes the fruit of that life; the after-life that follows is the realm of eternal light.[29] This is closely akin to Fechner's belief that death is merely the transition to the third stage of being, that of eternal waking, in which we are merged as one with waves of light and sound. Similarly, in Mahler's own poetry for the 'Resurrection' finale, we ascend 'to the light that no eye has penetrated', while four of the five *Kindertotenlieder* he set to music contain Rückert's metaphor of afterlife as eter-nal light.[30] It is also noteworthy that in *Das Lied von der Erde* (1908), composed the sum-mer after Mahler became aware of his heart disease, Fechner's rapturous description of eternal waking seems to have served as an inspiration for the seemingly endless close—'Ewig, ewig...'—of the final movement, 'Der Abschied' (see below, Ch. 19). Thus Mahler's abandonment of the *Wunderhorn* anthology represents not so much a fundamental change in ideals as a shift in the perspectives from which he addresses them. The 'hidden treas-ures' of folk wisdom and childlike naiveté largely vanish from his work; so, too, for the moment, does the epic approach to eschatology. Mahler's new artistic persona is more sophisticated, introverted, and personal. As he said of 'Ich bin der Welt abhanden gekom-men', the conclusion of his work during the summer of 1901 and, in the view of many, his finest lied: 'It is my very self.'[31]

The subtle and introverted quality of this music is reflected in its instrumentation as well. These are, to be sure, dual-purpose lieder: like all (save one) of Mahler's songs from 1892 on, they were conceived for performance with either orchestra or piano.[32] But in the orchestral versions, the instrumental forces are handled with chamber-music delicacy; solo winds are particularly prominent, and such overall transparency of texture is scarcely approached in Mahler's earlier works. For the first performances—in Vienna, 29 January and 3 February 1905, and Graz, 1 June of the same year—Mahler insisted on both a small hall and a reduced string section (apparently 10 first violins, 8 second violins, 6 each of vio-las and cellos, and 4 basses).[33] The Graz performance was part of the annual composers' festival sponsored by the Allgemeiner Deutscher Musikverein, of which Richard Strauss was then president; as Mahler wrote to Strauss prior to the opening of the festival, 'I do not desire a "special position"! . . . Only a *small hall* for my songs that would be performed in the manner of *chamber music*. . . . Here [i.e. in Vienna], for artistic reasons (despite all the

[29] Schimmel, 125, 129–30; Gerlach, 31–4; Russell, 51–2.

[30] See esp. Russell, *Light in Battle*, 45, 51–3, 56–7, and *passim*.

[31] The sum of these observations should constitute suffi-cient rebuttal to the objections concerning interpretation founded upon Mahler's own utterances and experiences that are briefly raised by Elisabeth Schmierer in *Die Orchesterlieder Gustav Mahlers*, 173.

[32] See Stephen E. Hefling, 'The Composition of "Ich bin der Welt abhanden gekommen" ', in Danuser (ed.), *Gustav Mahler*, 96–158, esp. 103–8, and id., '*Das Lied von der Erde*:

Mahler's Symphony for Voices and Orchestra—or Piano', *Journal of Musicology*, 10 (1992), 293–341, esp. 293–303. Mahler himself performed the four separate Rückert lieder of 1901 at the keyboard with the Dutch baritone Johannes Messchaert, well after the orchestral première had taken place; see Reeser (ed.), *Gustav Mahler und Holland*, nos. 35–8 and 42.

[33] See Renate Hilmar-Voit, 'Symphonic Sound or in the Style of Chamber Music? The Current Performing Forces of the *Wunderhorn* Lieder and the Sources', *News about Mahler Research*, no. 22 (Oct. 1992), 8–12.

pressure of "commercial" considerations), I have put on these songs only in the *small* hall, and they were only appropriate there'.[34]

The precise chronology of these songs remains uncertain. On 10 August, near the close of his composing holiday, Mahler played 'Der Tamboursg'sell' plus six new Rückert lieder for Natalie Bauer-Lechner, whose chronicle tells us that each was composed in one day and orchestrated the next. 'Ich bin der Welt abhanden gekommen' followed as an inspired coda to the summer's efforts, and the second draft of it is dated 16 August. Three of the eight songs just noted must have been *Kindertotenlieder*, while the remainder (except for 'Der Tamboursg'sell') were the single Rückert lieder that, apparently, Mahler never intended to unite into a cycle. (For convenience, these will hereafter be called 'the Rückert lieder' or 'songs'.) Dates are found on three additional song manuscripts from the summer of 1901: 'Sonntag 9. Juni' on a sketch for 'Ich atmet' einen linden Duft'; '14. Juni 1901' on a sketch of 'Blicke mir nicht in die Lieder'; and 12 July on the piano version of 'Der Tamboursg'sell'.[35] Mahler had arrived at his new summer home in Maiernigg on 5 June; given that he usually required several days to settle into his composing routine, it seems likely that 'Ich atmet' einen linden Duft' was the first of the songs to be written, probably followed by 'Blicke mir nicht'.[36] Thus it would appear that Mahler launched rather boldly into the setting of Rückert's poetry and the concomitant change in his own musical style.

Ich atmet' einen linden Duft

In ancient Persian and Turkish lyrics, repetitions and word-plays frequently create a floating, opalescent quality hovering between the sensual and the spiritual. This was among the strongest influences Rückert absorbed from his long immersion in Oriental poetry,[37] and 'Ich atmet' einen linden Duft' is a notable case in point. The recurring liquescent 'l'— *linden, lieber, Linden, lieblich, leis*, etc.—as well as the plays on *linden Duft* (delicate fragrance), *Lindenduft* (fragrance of the lime), and *gelinde* (gently), plus the generally bright vowels and frequent alliteration, all contribute to the sensuous sonority and fluid motion

---

[34] *Gustav Mahler–Richard Strauss: Correspondence*, 78–9.

[35] The sketches for 'Ich bin der Welt abhanden gekommen' are in the Pierpont Morgan Library, New York City (see Hefling, 'The Composition of "Ich bin der Welt abhanden gekommen" '). The date on the sketch for 'Ich atmet' einen linden Duft' is published in HLG(E) ii. 361 (kindly verified by Prof. Henry-Louis de La Grange, pers. comm.). The dated sketch for 'Blicke mir nicht in die Lieder' is located in Vienna, Österreichische Nationalbibliothek, Musiksammlung, S.m. 4365, reproduced in Rudolf Stephan (ed. and

comp.), *Gustav Mahler: Werk und Interpretation* (Cologne: Arno Volk Verlag, 1979), 44–5; it is discussed by Colin Matthews, *Mahler at Work*, 75–100, and also by Danuser, *Gustav Mahler und seine Zeit*, 60–5. The piano-vocal autograph of 'Der Tamboursg'sell', cited in HLG(E) ii. 361, is located in the Moldenhauer Archive: see p. 436 below. (Prof. Edward R. Reilly kindly verified the date, pers. comm.)

[36] HLG(E) ii. 358 and 361 (HLG(F) ii. 92 and 95); cf. also NB-L, *Erinnerungen*, 188 (*Recollections*, 168).

[37] Schimmel, *Friedrich Rückert*, 76 and 114–15; cf. also Gerlach, *Strophen*, 35–41.

of these verses.[38] Their subject could not be simpler—the gift of a lime branch—yet it yields a rich and subtle matrix of associations, reflections, and sensations.

The inspiration provided by these features of the text is readily apparent in the delicate musical atmosphere the composer provided for it—in Adorno's view, the poem 'has been hardly composed, but, one may indeed say, redesigned by Mahler as a musical graphic, in a truly heartbreaking way'.[39] The more notable of two revisions Mahler made in the text also reveals his affinity for its sonorous quality; Rückert's original concludes thus:

Ich atme leis	I breathe softly
Im Duft der Linde	in the fragrance of the lime
Der Herzensfreundschaft linden Duft.	the delicate fragrance of close friendship.

Mahler dropped the ungainly Biedermeier word *Herzensfreundschaft* and substituted *Liebe* (love), which, though altering the syllabic symmetry of Rückert's rhyme scheme, highlights the alliterative 'l' once more. As Reinhard Gerlach observes, through this masterly change the fragrance of the lime sprig becomes an all-encompassing symbol: 'nature, plant, man, and art are one in the ethereal element of love . . .'.[40]

But love is more passionate than close friendship, and its intensity informs an earlier textual alteration as well. The lines of Rückert's first stanza were originally ordered thus:

[1] Ich atmet' einen linden Duft.	I breathed a delicate fragrance.
[2] Im Zimmer stand	In the room stood
[3] Ein Angebinde	a gift
[4] Von lieber Hand,	from a beloved hand,
[5] Ein Zweig der Linde;	a sprig of lime;
[6] Wie lieblich war der Lindenduft!	how lovely was the fragrance of lime!

Mahler puts the fifth line in third place, whereby lines 3 and 4 of the original become 4 and 5 respectively; the resulting rhyme scheme is a palindrome (abccba; cf. 'Um Mitternacht'), although that scarcely matters. Much more striking is that mention of the 'beloved hand', the most intimate image of the first strophe, is delayed until the penultimate line: the music warms noticeably with these words, both harmonically and melodically, only to cool in the final line, as though emerging fantasy were quietly suppressed. The same musical gesture, gently intensified, recurs during the second stanza from the end of the second line ('brachst du gelinde' (you plucked gently)) until the onset of its final thought, altered by Mahler (as noted above) to read 'Der Liebe linden Duft' ((in) the delicate fragrance of love). Then unexpectedly an almost wrenching return to the tonic quells the subliminal passion that had again arisen during the preceding eight bars. Well and good for Mahler to describe the song to Bauer-Lechner as 'filled with the kind of quiet happiness you feel in the presence

---

[38] Theodor W. Adorno, 'Zu einem Streitgespräch über Mahler', in Richard Baum and Wolfgang Rehm (eds.), *Musik und Verlag: Karl Vötterle zum 65. Geburtstag am 12. April 1968* (Kassel: Bärenreiter, 1968), 123–7 at 126; Dargie, *Music and Poetry*, 274–6; Gerlach, *Strophen*, 41–2; HLG(F) ii. 1111–12.

[39] Adorno, 'Zu einem Streitgespräch', 126.
[40] Gerlach, *Strophen*, 42; he also suggests Mahler understood the poem better than the poet himself.

of someone dear, of whom you are entirely sure'[41]—yet beneath the surface of this fragile arabesque is an unmistakable current of concealed longing such as he was never to feel for Natalie.

That notwithstanding, the ethereal fluidity of the poem predominates, from the basic kernel of the song's musical substance to the chamber-like transparency of its scoring. The oriental overtones of the text are reflected in Mahler's adoption of the anhemitonic ('lacking semitones') pentatonic scale, the most common mode of Eastern pitch organization, for both the main melodic idea and its ostinato counter-melody. The resultant gentle blurring of tonal focus, culminating in the 'added sixth' chord on which the lied closes, adds to its impressionistic serenity. The title line is indeed almost fragrant in its wafting contours, leisurely pace, and pointillistic richness of accompaniment. Only mention of the 'beloved hand' (as noted above) slightly agitates this placid atmosphere: as the violin ostinato flows calmly on, motion by third to the dominant of B minor hints briefly at more varied musical discourse—an option brushed aside, however, by resumption of the tonic (D major) during the final line of the stanza.

The concluding syllable of the first stanza gives way to an oboe obbligato (derived from earlier vocal material) that apparently opens an interlude between strophes. Yet within less than a bar the voice re-enters, almost casually, as though accompanying the oboe (the singer's line is, however, a repetition of bars 5–9). Thus begins the second stanza, through musical elision entirely in keeping with the fluidity of the verse. Again, thoughts of the beloved, this time in the act of plucking the lime sprig, draw the singer's fancy away from the meditative calm of the tonic; the third-related tonality of B (here major) evoked by the penultimate line of the first stanza now opens into distant E flat, 'an effect of pure magic', as La Grange observes (see Ex. 13.1).[42] Now the line 'Ich atme leis im Duft der Linde' (I breathe softly in the fragrance of the lime) ushers in a moment of melancholy 'so brief that

Ex. 13.1. 'Ich atmet' einen linden Duft', bb. 23–5

---

[41] NB-L, *Erinnerungen*, 193–4 (*Recollections*, 173–4).

[42] HLG(E) ii. 790 (HLG(F) ii. 1112). Mahler makes no effort to disguise the parallel fifths that arise from this pro-gression; he allows himself such effects at various points in his middle- and late-period works.

Ex. 13.2. 'Ich atmet' einen linden Duft', bb. 23–36, analytical sketch

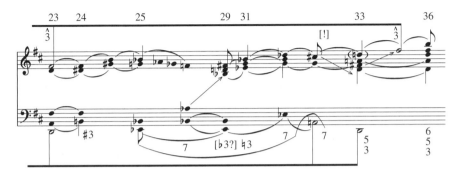

it is virtually cruel, as often happens with Webern'.[43] Musically speaking, this is the result of suspended lower neighbours (d, $f\sharp'$) to the tonic and third scale degrees (Ex. 13.2, bb. 29–30); the $f\sharp'$ ($g\flat$?) strongly suggests the minor mode. Resolution seems to entail further harmonic digression, via the dominant of A flat (b. 31); just as it sounds that A flat is certain to ensue ('der Liebe . . .'), the 'cruel' enharmonic reinterpretation of D♭ as C♯ forces a return to D. The flute echoes the oboe interlude in cool, silvery tones, unaccompanied by the voice, and the piece fades away in the gentle irresolution of the pentatonic 'added sixth' chord scored for upper winds.

Such music indeed marks a new beginning; it differs in nearly all respects from what one finds in the *Wunderhorn* lieder. Moreover, from our current vantage point, the delicate yet tensile textures and use of the pentatonic scale in 'Ich atmet' einen linden Duft' adumbrate not only the musical language of the summer's concluding masterpiece, 'Ich bin der Welt abhanden gekommen', but also foreshadow significant aspects of Mahler's late compositional style, particularly as manifested in *Das Lied von der Erde*.[44] The rippling quavers beneath slow-moving melodic lines recur in the second movement of *Das Lied* ('Der Einsame im Herbst'), while the ethereal gesture of the pentatonic closing sonority is taken over in the third and fourth songs ('Von der Jugend' and 'Von der Schönheit'), as well as in the dissolution of the cycle as a whole ('Der Abschied').[45]

[43] See ibid.

[44] Cf. also ibid. and Mitchell, *SSLD*, 57–68.

[45] How Mahler became aware of pentatonicism remains uncertain; in later years he admired and conducted Debussy's music, but we do not know when he first came to know it (see HLG(F) ii. 953 and iii. 1003 and *passim*). He may have heard original oriental music at the Paris Exhibition of 1900, while visiting that city with the Vienna Philharmonic (HLG(F) i. 879; cf. also Judith Gautier, *Les Musiques bizarres à l'Exposition de 1900* (Paris: Société d'Éditions littéraires, 1900)). Further on this issue see below, Ch. 19 n. 46.

Blicke mir nicht in die Lieder

This is certainly the shortest and simplest of the Rückert lieder, and also the most closely related to the world of the *Wunderhorn*;[46] thus it may have served Mahler as something of a transition into the more subtle and complex works of the summer. As Natalie tells us, 'the text is as characteristic of Mahler as if he himself had written the poem',[47] because Mahler could not abide others' eavesdropping while his works were in progress: 'To me it is as if a mother would undress herself and expose to the world the child in the womb before it is born', he once exclaimed exasperatedly.[48]

In 'Blicke mir nicht' the central poetic image that Mahler highlights is Rückert's homely metaphor of composition as the work of busy bees: they buzz throughout the song, sporadically swarming closer to keep us at a distance, as in the introductory passage shown in Ex. 13.3. Such imitation of natural sounds is characteristic of earlier Romantic lieder, and in keeping with the tradition Rückert's two six-line stanzas would ordinarily be set strophically. For the opening five lines of poetry, it appears that norm is to be followed: each of the first four lines is, typically, allied with a distinct musical phrase, while the fifth is sung to a sequential variant of the fourth. Then the pattern goes awry. By repeating two lines and

Ex. 13.3. 'Blicke mir nicht in die Lieder', bb. 1–7

---

[46] Cf. also Mitchell, *SSLD*, 74.   [47] NB-L, *Erinnerungen*, 194 (*Recollections*, 174).
[48] Ibid. 34 (*Recollections*, 39); July–Aug. 1893.

Table 13.1. STRUCTURE OF 'BLICKE MIR NICHT IN DIE LIEDER'

Tonal centre	Phrase no.	Text	Translation
F	Introduction, 7 bars		
F	1	Blicke mir nicht in die Lieder!	Do not look at my songs!
	2	Meine Augen schlag' ich nieder,	I turn my eyes away
	3	wie ertappt auf böser Tat.	as though caught in a naughty deed.
(F minor)	4	Selber darf ich nicht getrauen,	I can't even trust myself
(to V/F)	4'	ihrem Wachsen zuzuschauen.	to observe their growing.
A flat	1	*Blicke mir nicht in die Lieder!*	Do not look at my songs!
F	2	Deine Neugier ist Verrat, ist Verrat!	Your curiosity is betrayal, betrayal!
F	1	Bienen, wenn sie Zellen bauen,*a*	Bees, when they build their cells,
	2	lassen auch nicht zu sich schauen,	likewise do not let themselves be watched,
	3	schauen selbst auch nicht zu.	nor watch their work themselves.
(F minor)	4	Wenn die reichen Honigwaben	When the rich honeycombs
(to V/F)	4'	sie zu Tag befördert haben,	are brought by them to light of day,
A flat	1	*dann vor allen nasche du,*	then you shall be the first to taste,
F	2	dann vor allen nasche du! Nasche du!	then you shall be the first to taste!
F	Postlude, 7 bars		

a Rückert's second stanza begins here.

obscuring the original division of stanzas, Mahler creates what might best be described as 'strophic confusion', illustrated schematically in Table 13.1.

The recurrence (italicized) of the title line and the unexpected shift to A flat yield the impression that a new strophe has begun; the ensuing motion back to the tonic of F for the second phrase, although a bit like patchwork, seems plausible at first. But the return of the first phrase with new text ('Bienen, wenn sie Zellen bauen') sweeps aside all sense of strophic pattern. In fact, the music is now following the course of the first strophe; but this will be broken off, as before, by what turns out to be the song's last line, 'Dann vor allen nasche du', which is rather bumptiously repeated. Then, after a few more bars of the bees, the scene vanishes.

In short, the song seems unfinished, still in gestation. The ceaseless ostinato provides no distinct beginning, but holds our focus *in medias res* throughout—even the final cadence is inconclusive. The strophic articulation is in disarray, and certain features of the declamation, such as 'nasche du! Nasche du!', lack polish. (By contrast, the treatment of 'wie ertappt auf böser Tat' is wonderfully evocative of caught-in-the-act surprise.)[49] Most notably, the abrupt modulations by third reinforce neither structure nor affect of the poem. 'Blicke mir nicht' is a charming and witty vignette of the creative process in progress—a process Mahler himself described thus:

[49] Dargie, *Music and Poetry*, 273–4; Mitchell, *SSLD*, 74.

It happens in a hundredfold different ways. Sometimes the poem provides the impetus, sometimes it is the melody. Often I begin in the middle, often at the beginning, occasionally at the end, and the rest subsequently fits itself together here, there, and all around.[50]

Mahler's surviving preliminary manuscripts for various works show that all manner of patching, reweaving, retouching, and readjustment of the relation between melody and text—just the sort of revisions suggested by 'Blicke mir nicht'—were indeed carried out before he was ready to reveal his compositions to the light of day.

Um Mitternacht

The traditional Western association of the midnight hour with profound moments of solitary personal crisis, insight, and resolve dates back at least to the biblical story of Jesus in the Garden of Gethsemane; Goethe's *Werther* and *Faust*, and especially Nietzsche's *Zarathustra*, were literary works well known to Mahler in which such moments are crucial.[51] It was of course the middle of the night when Mahler faced the threat of death in February 1901; his most direct artistic response is the most dramatic and problematic of the Rückert lieder, 'Um Mitternacht' (At Midnight). Mahler recounted his personal reaction during the crisis of the haemorrhage as follows:

You know, last night I nearly passed away. When I saw the faces of the two doctors (Singer and Hochenegg), I thought my last hour had come. While they were putting in the tube, which was frightfully painful but quick, they kept checking my pulse and my heart. Fortunately it was solidly installed in my breast and determined not to give up so soon. . . . While I was hovering on the border between life and death, I wondered whether it would not be better to have done with it at once, since everyone must come to that in the end. Besides, the prospect of dying did not frighten me in the least, provided my affairs are in order, and to return to life seemed almost a nuisance.[52]

There is a curious touch of sang-froid in these remarks: serious, yet subdued, they lack any trace of fear, regret, or hope of transcendence. In the first four stanzas of Rückert's 'Um Mitternacht', Mahler found precisely the verses he needed for the musical manifestation of his own midnight hour; its resolution is addressed in his extraordinary treatment of the final strophe, to be discussed presently.

The formal aspects of the poem—short lines, palindromic rhyme scheme (aabbaa), and the framing of each strophe by the refrain 'Um Mitternacht'—lend it an air of restrained composure; in addition, the repetitions of the refrain and its rhyming '-acht' produce a constricted fluidity that seems austere and unrelenting. For four stanzas none of the awakened protagonist's anxious efforts—heavenward gaze, far-ranging thought, anguished pulse,

---

[50] NB-L, *Erinnerungen*, 29 (*Recollections*, 33).
[51] See Jeffrey Thomas Hopper, 'The Rückert Lieder of Gustav Mahler' (Ph.D. diss., Rutgers University, 1991), 121–4.

[52] Bauer-Lechner, 'Mahleriana', quoted in HLG(E) ii. 334–5 (HLG(F) ii. 66–7).

Ex. 13.4. Basic motives in 'Um Mitternacht' (and related passages): (*a*) b. 1; (*b*) b. 2; (*c*) bb. 3–4; (*d*) *Das klagende Lied*, recurring refrain, here excerpted from 'Waldmärchen' (1st movt.), Fig. 17^{-4} (text: 'cursing'); (*e*) bb. 7–8 (text: '[At midnight] I kept watch'); (*f*) bb. 15–16 (and 63–4) (text: 'At midnight'); (*g*) bb. 17–18; (*h*) Fourth Symphony, 3rd movt., bb. 89–90; (*i*) Third Symphony, 4th movt., 'O Mensch! Gib' Acht!', bb. 102–4, 'Der Vogel der Nacht!' (The bird of the night!)

and struggle over suffering—brings relief or solace. Yet neither does his solicitude increase. Mahler embodies all this in music that is sombre, economical to the verge of bleakness, inventively yet inexorably repetitious, and scored only for sparse combinations of solo winds, generally in low registers. As Stuart Feder has observed, the song grows out of three basic motivic kernels, which are displayed in Ex. 13.4(*a*) to (*c*): these distinctive fragments are continuously varied, reordered, and recombined in the developmental manner Mahler first mastered in his Fourth Symphony.[53] The 'Mitternacht' motto, which Feder likens to the ticking rhythm of a pendulum clock 'slowed down to surrealist proportion', emerges as shown in Ex. 13.4(a) and (b). This is immediately answered by the tread of the Phrygian scale motive (4(c)), foreboding in its grim descent and vaguely disorienting modality; as Feder also points out, this is related to a prominent refrain-motive of woe from the first movement of *Das klagende Lied*, shown in Ex. 13.4(d). At the close of the first strophe the singer takes up this line to announce that 'kein Stern vom Sterngewimmel hat mir gelacht um Mitternacht' (no star from all the starry throng smiled on me at midnight); varied, this is also the motive allied with the fruitless conclusions of the ensuing three strophes. The recurring material in Ex. 13.4(e) and (f) is derived from the rhythm of 13.4(a) and (b) plus the contour, inverted, of 13.4(c). Following the first and fourth strophes, motive 13.4(f) leads to a gesture of collapse, 13.4(g), borrowed from the slow movement of Mahler's Fourth, and also closely related to the 'bird of the night' call in Third Symphony's setting of Zarathustra's midnight drunken song (Ex. 13.4(h) and (i)).[54]

The perpetual permutations, repetitions, and phrase overlappings of the motivic materials combine with continually shifting metric groupings to underscore the constricted fluidity of the poetry; time is the great concern in this lied, yet time seems to be going nowhere. The strophic articulations are musically blurred, and although local nuances of each stanza are highlighted by such techniques as brightening of mode, temporary modulation, smoothing of contour and texture, melisma, etc., the haunting bleakness of the A minor opening and its low descending scalar tread always returns.

—Until the *deus ex machina*: 'hab' ich die Macht in deine Hände gegeben!' (I gave my strength into Thy hands!) releases blinding brightness, completely unexpected either from Rückert's final stanza in itself or from the foregoing musical context. Trumpets, trombones, tuba, and timpani accompanied by dazzling harp-and-piano glissandos peal forth a major-mode chorale, an apotheosis of faith that all but swamps the voice. As noted above, Bauer-Lechner immediately recognized its affinity with Mahler's 'Resurrection' chorus.[55] But here the jubilant outburst lasts scarcely more than a minute; it is a hymn sung by one mere mortal, accompanied by a military wind ensemble—as though the Lord were perhaps indeed a man of war.[56] Nor is the singer's existential surrender entirely harmonious: the vocatives 'Herr' (Lord) and 'Du!' (Thou!) in bars 78 and 88–9 are bellowed against gnashing dissonances.[57] As Hopper has also suggested, the entire final strophe brings to mind Mahler's earlier commentary on Jacob and the angel:

[53] Cf. also Feder, 'Gustav Mahler um Mitternacht', 20, and HLG(E) ii. 793–6 (HLG(F) ii. 1115–16).

[54] Feder, 'Gustav Mahler um Mitternacht', 20; Kravitt, 'Mahler's Dirges', 330–1; Mitchell, *SSLD*, 56–8 and 124 n. 6; and Constantin Floros, *Gustav Mahler*, ii: *Mahler und die Symphonik des 19. Jahrhunderts in neuer Deutung* (Wiesbaden: Breitkopf & Härtel, 1977), 204–6 and 386 (Table 36). The inscription 'Der Vogel der Nacht!' over

music closely related to Ex. 13.4(i) occurs four times in the autograph full score of the Third Symphony's fourth movement (New York, Pierpont Morgan Library), at bars 32, 71, 102, and 132.

[55] See above, n. 17.

[56] Cf. Feder, 'Gustav Mahler um Mitternacht', 21–2.

[57] Cf. also Hopper, 'The Rückert Lieder', 147–8.

A splendid example for creative people is Jacob, who struggles with God until He blesses him. If the Jews had discovered nothing else but that, they had to have been colossal people. — God also does not want to bless me; only in frightful struggle over the existence of my works do I wrest it from Him.[58]

While many commentators have accepted the conclusion of 'Um Mitternacht' at face value, others find this music ridden with irony and hyperbole. La Grange regards its optimism as 'more decorative than profoundly convinced and convincing', and compares it with the resplendent aureoles above Austrian Baroque altars.[59] In Feder's view, 'A desperately massive optimism spelling denial in its very force seems the aim of the form of the work itself'.[60] Adorno observes, with regard to 'the fanfare of the breakthrough' in the second movement of Mahler's Fifth Symphony, that 'Impotence attends manifested power; were it the promised and no longer the promise, it would not need to assert itself as power'.[61] The same might be said of 'Um Mitternacht'. But Reinhard Gerlach regards the lied as one in a series of artistic usurpations inspired by Nietzsche that includes the contemporaneous Fifth Symphony and culminates in the Eighth: 'The goal, from which Mahler spared neither the piety of the Brucknerian chorale nor the dignity of Christian hymns, is the Man of the Future, the "Overman" in a world without God'.[62] What does seem certain is that Mahler has, in Harold Bloom's sense, deliberately misread Rückert's final stanza, thereby transferring the problem of ambiguous resolution directly to his listeners.

Ich bin der Welt abhanden gekommen

Mahler had just completed this year's vacation work so as to devote the last couple of days to relaxation, when the composition of the last Rückert poem gripped him: 'Ich bin der Welt abhanden gekommen', which he had originally planned to set, but had let go in favour of the [Fifth] symphony. He himself said of the unusually full and restrained nature of this song: 'It is feeling that rises to the lips but does not pass beyond them!' And: 'It is my very self!'[63]

'It is my very self': more than in any of his previous music, Mahler here turns away from the 'thousand things of the world' to a realm of deeply serene contemplation, 'alone, in my love, in my song', according to the final line of Rückert's poetry (slightly retouched by the composer himself). 'One knows', he had told Bauer-Lechner the previous summer, 'that our second self [zweites ich] is active during sleep, that it grows and wills and brings about that which the real self longed for and willed in vain'—notwithstanding the winter season's 'frightful dreams of bustling theatrical life'.[64] Just as his first composing holiday following

---

[58] NB-L, *Erinnerungen*, 76 (*Recollections*, 76); cf. Hopper, 'The Rückert Lieder', 121.

[59] HLG(E) ii. 796 (HLG(F) ii. 1116).

[60] Feder, 'Gustav Mahler um Mitternacht', 21.

[61] Adorno, *Mahler*, 11 (German edn., 20); cf. also HLG(E) ii. 796 (HLG(F) ii. 1116).

[62] Gerlach, *Strophen*, 96 ff., here at 103.

[63] NB-L, *Erinnerungen*, 194 (*Recollections*, 174), Aug. 1901.

[64] Ibid. 151 (*Recollections*, 150).

the crisis of 1901 was about to end, Mahler was drawn irresistibly back to his *Häuschen*, where, as he told Ernst Decsey, this lonely piece in fact arose in deepest isolation.[65] According to Alma Mahler, while composing it he had in mind 'the monuments of the cardinals in Italy—where the bodies of the holy ones lie with folded hands in the churches'.[66]

Meditative withdrawal from worldly hubbub was of course a familiar theme to the orientalist Rückert. For Mahler, however, it also resonated with another school of thought: the philosophy of Schopenhauer, which had deeply influenced him since his student days. According to Schopenhauer it is essential to 'still the wheel of Ixion', the perpetual cycle of striving and dissatisfaction that man brings upon himself through egocentric manifestation of the individual will. Only such self-suppression of the will, as in Buddhist or Christian religion, can lead to reduction of suffering and mystical rebirth. Great works of art offer temporary relief, because the artist is concerned with contemplative, 'will-less' perception rather than action. And in Schopenhauer's view, music is the highest of all arts because it 'gives the innermost kernel of all form, or the heart of things'.[67] For this reason, Schopenhauer claims that when words and music are united, music remains the more meaningful component[68]—a view Mahler specifically endorsed. As he told Bauer-Lechner, '. . . with songs . . . one can express so much more than the words directly say. . . . The text actually constitutes only a hint of the deeper content that is to be drawn out of it, of the treasure that is to be hauled up.'[69]

To draw forth the treasure of 'Ich bin der Welt abhanden gekommen', Mahler turned once again to the anhemitonic pentatonic scale; both its mild exoticism and its capacity to diffuse goal-oriented Western tonal process are exploited more extensively than in 'Ich atmet' einen linden Duft'. Yet, almost paradoxically, it is precisely the hybrid mixture of tonality and pentatonicism that infuses this piece with concentrated organic coherence such as Mahler had previously approached only in passages of the Fourth Symphony. Pentatonic melodies and chords derived from them were of course already prominent in Debussy's music, particularly from the time of *Prélude à l'Après-midi d'un faune* (1892–4) on. But there is little of impressionistic imprecision in 'Ich bin der Welt'; the song's contrapuntal strands and integrated motivic contours are quite clearly delineated, particularly in its orchestral setting. Following the second performance of the Rückert lieder in 1905, Webern recorded the following comments Mahler had made:

[65] ' "Ich bin der Welt abhanden gekommen", dieses einsame Stück war, wie er sagte, tatsächlich in der tiefsten Einsamkeit "vor sechs Jahren" oben im Tannenwald von Meierling [*recte*: Maiernigg] entstanden'. Decsey, 'Stunden mit Mahler', 144; trans. in Lebrecht, *Mahler Remembered*, 261.

[66] Alma Mahler-Werfel, *Mein Leben*, 32. Mahler had used a similar metaphor for the serenity of the slow movement in his Fourth Symphony; see Bruno Walter, *Briefe*, 52.

[67] Schopenhauer, *The World as Will and Representation*, trans. E. F. J. Payne, 2 vols. (1958; repr. New York: Dover

Books, 1966), i. 263; see also below, Ch. 19, pp. 440–1. In the finale of his Third Symphony, for example, Mahler felt that 'everything is resolved into peace and being; the Ixion-wheel of illusion is finally brought to a standstill' (NB-L, *Erinnerungen*, 68; *Recollections*, 67); cf. Schopenhauer, i. 196: 'Thus the subject of willing is constantly lying on the revolving wheel of Ixion, is always drawing water in the sieve of the Danaids, and is the eternally thirsting Tantalus'.

[68] Schopenhauer, i. 260–3.

[69] NB-L, *Erinnerungen*, 27 (*Recollections*, 32).

... The discussion turned to counterpoint. ... Mahler ... admitted only Bach, Brahms, and Wagner as the greatest contrapuntalists. ... 'Nature is for us the model in this realm. Just as in nature the entire universe has developed from the primeval cell, from plants, animals, and men beyond to God, the Supreme Being, so also in music should a larger structure develop from a single motive in which is contained the germ of everything that is yet to be'.[70]

This is by no means Mahler's first utterance on organic continuity in his music, but it is particularly germane to what he had achieved in 'Ich bin der Welt abhanden gekommen'. And the surviving sketches for the song, more extensive than those preserved for any of his other lieder, allow us to observe many facets of just such a developmental process from primeval cell to larger structure.[71] Mahler composed the lied in F major, the key in which it is discussed below; only later, for the first performances in 1905 sung by the baritone Friedrich Weidemann, was it transposed down to E flat (in which key it is most often heard today).[72]

The cell itself—the motto line of the song—had probably been jotted down earlier that summer, before (as Bauer-Lechner tells us) Mahler had abandoned this lied in favour of working on his Fifth Symphony. In the second stave of Ex. 13.5(*a*), Greek letters identify the principal motivic components of the basic cell, while analytic notation (stems, slurs, flags) indicates the linear relationships among the pitches. Broadly speaking, the melodic contour of the motto comprises two arches: $c'-a'-f'$, followed by $f'-c''-a'$. Similar arching gestures characterize nearly all melodic phrases of the song.[73] The undulating primary motive is based on a pentatonic scale form, *Zhi*, which is labelled α^1. The thirds and sixth contained within this five-note division of the octave outline both a major tonic triad and its relative minor, as shown in Ex. 13.5(*b*). Combined, these triads yield the 'added sixth' chord, which almost sounds consonant, yet strictly speaking is not (Ex. 13.5(*c*)): this is one of the most characteristic sonorities in 'Ich bin der Welt abhanden gekommen'. Another is the triad in $^6_4$ position—harmonically the least stable of its inversions—which is emphasized by *Zhi*, the specific pentatonic form of the motto ($c'-f'-a'$). Both these sonorities mitigate the polar dynamism of functional tonality and contrapuntal motion. For convenience, Ex. 13.5(*d*) tabulates the motives bracketed in 13.5(*a*), and also identifies the several varieties of fourths (ϵ) and fifths (θ) contained within the basic pentatonic matrix. We shall refer to these motives briefly in what follows; a more comprehensive analysis than can be presented here, however, would reveal that the cell indeed comprises all essential elements, both local and large-scale, of the song's pitch structure.[74]

The nine-bar introduction is a condensed overview of the composition as a whole. It begins hesitantly, as will most of the ensuing phrases; the arching motto is presented in full,

[70] Moldenhauer, *Anton von Webern*, 75.

[71] See Hefling, 'The Composition of "Ich bin der Welt abhanden gekommen" ', 96–158.

[72] Further on this issue, see the editor's report to vols. 13 and 14 of the Mahler *Kritische Gesamtausgabe*. The E flat version is the more authoritative of the orchestral scores because it includes a number of alterations, presumably made by Mahler in preparing it for the first performances, that were inexplicably omitted from the F major orchestral score. Both orchestral versions are included in the *Gesamtausgabe*.

[73] Cf. also Hopper, 'The Rückert Lieder', 88–90.

[74] Hefling, 'The Composition of "Ich bin der Welt abhanden gekommen" '.

Ex. 13.5. 'Ich bin der Welt abhanden gekommen': (*a*) basic cell, with principal motivic components; (*b*) triads in the pentatonic scale; (*c*) combined triads forming 'added sixth' chord (α^1 verticalized); (*d*) motives of the basic cell

supported by floating $\frac{6}{4}$ and pentatonic sonorities, while pure root-position tonic harmony is avoided. And bars 7 to 9 distinctly adumbrate the penultimate vocal phrase of the piece, 'in meinem Lieben [in my love]' (bb. 55–7), which will then shortly yield to the final instrumental variant on the principal idea. Contemplative, open-ended, lacking specific direction, these initial bars of 'Ich bin der Welt' introduce and summarize simultaneously. Just how to usher in the voice cost Mahler a good bit of trouble in the sketches; what he eventually arrived at is mild pentatonic heterophony (b. 12) that further diffuses the dominant tendency of the bass C (which is now sustained rather than softly struck and released as it had been in bars 1–2), and dovetails the vocal line onto the repeated presentations of the motto phrase (c–d–f–a). The first and second lines of poetry are quietly declaimed in characteristically arching gestures of three and two bars' duration, respectively. The third statement is longer, owing in part to the slight metrical irregularity occasioned by Mahler's retouching of the poetry.[75] Musically, the listless ascent of the voice is answered by an ornamented instrumen-

[75] Rückert's 'Sie hat so lange von mir nichts vernommen' has been changed to 'Sie hat so lange nichts von mir vernommen', which breaks the tetrameter; cf. also Dargie, *Music and Poetry*, 283. Dargie's discussion of Rückert's poem begins with the assertion that 'This is a poem which has very little to commend it' (p. 281), and becomes increasingly critical; as already noted by La Grange (HLG(F) ii. 1114 n. 50), such severity seems excessive in view of what Mahler produced with this text; cf. also Russell, *Light in Battle*, 54–5 and 59.

tal descent floating upon fauxbourdon-like harmonies—a gesture that foreshadows the song's quiet climax in bars 38–9. Such 'leitmotivic' premonition and recollection in the orchestral and keyboard writing is more pronounced here than in any of Mahler's earlier lieder; it becomes a hallmark of his late style, culminating in *Das Lied von der Erde*.

The instrumental descent just noted leads to the firmest confirmation of the tonic thus far in the song, and also to the varied return of the basic cell (bb. 22–3, anticipating the third stanza's opening). This, to be sure, is a strophic interlude—except that the first strophe has yet to be completed. More artfully than in the summer's earlier harvest, Mahler adopts the technique of strophic obfuscation, here to evoke contemplative withdrawal from ordinary boundaries of space and time. 'Sie mag wol glauben, ich sei gestorben' (it [the world] might well believe that I am dead) precipitates a quietly lamenting melisma on *gestorben*, echoed in the accompaniment (b. 27); but this gives way to a delicate warming of harmony, rhythm, and pace, which slowly increases as the new strophe unfolds. Its fourth line—'denn wirklich bin ich gestorben, gestorben der Welt' (for truly I am dead, dead to the world) is the high point of the song in all respects—yet its subdued rapture is projected chiefly in the instrumental writing, as 'feeling that rises to the lips but does not pass beyond them'. The onset of D major in these bars provides bright contrast to the central tonic (F), and is also an organic outgrowth of the basic cell—a major-mode inflection of the second triad (D minor) contained within the pentatonic matrix (cf. Ex. 13.5(*b*)).

Indeed, the climax and ensuing retransition to tonic and the third strophe is perhaps the most extraordinarily artful passage of the entire song. Example 13.6 draws upon analytical notation to sum up these bars, which contain the longest span of contiguous linear motion in the piece, beginning with the inner-voice *a'* in bar 36; at bars 38 ff., this strand of texture supports the upper-voice descent in parallel motion. The latter span, commencing with the high *d'''*, will conclude on *f♮* (via register transfer to *f'*) in bar 45: as the bracket labelled 'ᾱ' suggests, this is a composed-out inversion of the major sixth, α, that is so highly characteristic of the basic cell (cf. Ex. 13.5(*a*)). Yet this long descent of a sixth is also delicately blurred—by the register transfer just noted, but even more strikingly by the

Ex. 13.6. 'Ich bin der Welt abhanden gekommen', bb. 36–46, analytical sketch

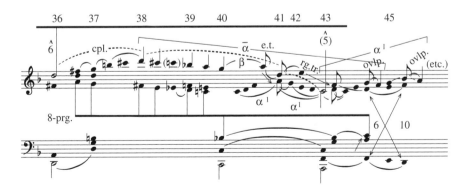

overlapping return of the cell itself (α^1), beginning on c' in bar 43, as the accumulated momentum is reduced (*Wieder zurückhaltend*). Now two arching gestures are intertwined, just as in the basic cell; but the return of the 'motto' motive is itself varied in rhythm and harmony, adding new colour and subtle tension to this moment of recapitulation, which presses gently into the final strophe. In that section the appoggiatura D–C (motive $\bar{\beta}^1$) is allied to several crucial words of the text: *gestorben, stillen, Lieben* (dead, still, love); this melodic kernel, so prominent in the concluding instrumental postlude (bb. 59, 60, 62–3), is also the final gesture of the lied (bb. 66–7)—again, 'feeling that rises to the lips but does not pass beyond them', and also organically linked to 'a larger structure develop[ed] from a single motive in which is contained the germ of everything that is yet to be'.

'It is my very self': this remarkable song was not Mahler's final utterance on the concerns that gripped him in 1901. Commentators have long noted the close connection between 'Ich bin der Welt abhanden gekommen' and his best-known composition, the Adagietto of the Fifth Symphony. While the Rückert lied is a study in serenity, the symphonic Adagietto, although intimate in character and scoring, is suffused with yearning that reaches passionate culmination just prior to the movement's conclusion (Ex. 13.7). Here both its affin-

Ex. 13.7. Fifth Symphony, Adagietto (4th movt.), bb. 94–103

attacca Rondo-Finale

ity with and contrast to 'Ich bin der Welt' are readily apparent: the expression is scarcely restrained, yet the climactic high a''' and the descending pentatonic bass line (bb. 95–101) are clearly related to the vocal close of the song—'in meinem Lieben, in meinem Lied'.

The conductor Willem Mengelberg, one of Mahler's favoured interpreters of his music who was a friend of both Mahler and his wife Alma, left the following annotation in his score of the Adagietto:

N. B. This Adagietto was Gustav Mahler's declaration of love to Alma! Instead of a letter he sent it to her in manuscript; there was no further word of explanation. She understood it and wrote to him: He should come!!! (both of them told me this!) W. M.[76]

There seems no reason to doubt the essence of Mengelberg's testimony;[77] once again, as in all Mahler's previous work, the link between song and symphony is hardly fortuitous.

[76] Reproduced in Stephan, *Gustav Mahler: Werk und Interpretation*, 86–8, and Gilbert Kaplan's facsimile edition of the Adagietto.

[77] See Gilbert E. Kaplan, 'From Mahler with Love', in *Gustav Mahler: Adagietto*, 26–9, as well as Hefling, 'The Composition of "Ich bin der Welt abhanden gekommen"', 157 n. 75.

He had met Alma Schindler in November 1901; his Fifth Symphony lay incomplete. Literally overnight, it became Mahler's most fervent hope to unite his innermost being with the stunningly beautiful, 23-year-old musician—'in meinem Lieben, in meinem Lied', but no longer 'allein'. As he wrote to her on 11 December 1901: 'If notes, if waves of sound had as much force as my longing for you, you would perforce hear them ringing all this morning. To you, for you, shall everything be that lives in me! My beloved Alma!'.[78]

Liebst du um Schönheit

The last of the single Rückert lieder was composed explicitly for Alma. In *Gustav Mahler: Erinnerungen und Briefe* she assigned this song to the summer of 1903 and described its genesis as follows:

I used to play a lot of Wagner, and this gave Mahler the idea of a charming surprise. He had composed for me the only love-song he ever wrote—*Liebst du um Schönheit*—and he slipped it in between the title-page and the first page of the *Valkyrie*. Then he waited day after day for me to find it; but I never happened to open the volume, and his patience gave out. 'I think I'll take a look at the *Valkyrie* today', he said abruptly. He opened it and the song fell out. I was overwhelmed with joy and we played it that day twenty times at least.[79]

Two telling fabrications of detail are woven into this well-known account (for reasons that emerge below): according to Alma's personal diary, the Wagner score in question was *Siegfried*, and the date she received the song was 10 August 1902 (not 1903). That evening, Alma confided her reactions more explicitly in her diary than she would later reveal them in print: 'the song is so indescribably moving ... it almost brought me to tears. What ardour there is in such a man! And how poor in spirit am I! I feel so often how little I am and have—in comparison with his immeasurable richness!'[80]

Never orchestrated by Mahler, this 'privatissimum' for Alma remains the sole exception to the dual-purpose song writing of his later years; unlike Mahler's previous and future efforts to bring the traditionally private genre of the lied into the broader forum of orchestral concerts, 'Liebst du um Schönheit' was intended to remain an intimate musical

[78] Alma Mahler, *Gustav Mahler: Erinnerungen und Briefe* (Amsterdam: Allert de Lange, 1949), 262; Alma Mahler, *Memories*, 209.

[Professor Edward R. Reilly has kindly informed us that the autograph full score of 'Ich bin der Welt abhanden gekommen' reappeared in Vienna in 2000, but that its ownership to date remains disputed. Ed.]

[79] Alma Mahler, *Memories*, 60–1.

[80] Alma Mahler, typescript for her autobiography *Mein Leben* prepared from her diaries (University of Pennsylvania, Van Pelt Library), p. 3/4 (the pages bear two sets of numbering): '... das Lied ist so ~~unnennbar~~ rührend, dass ich ... fast geweint habe. Die Innigkeit eines solchen Menschen! Und meine Seelenlosigkeit! Oft fühle ich, wie wenig ich bin und habe — im Vergleich zu seinem unermässlichen Reichtum!' The typescript confirms that 'Liebst du um Schönheit' dates from the summer of 1902 (not 1903, as Alma states in *Memories*, 60–1), and according to HLG(E) ii. 538 (HLG(F) ii. 277), Alma's autograph diary entry indicates that the Wagner score in question was *Siegfried* (rather than *Die Walküre*). An edited version of the passage is found in the published version of *Mein Leben*, 33.

utterance.[81] And it differs from the earlier Rückert songs in other significant respects as well. Save for the buzzing *perpetuum mobile* 'Blicke mir nicht in die Lieder', this is the shortest of the group, as well as the most homophonic, and also the most overtly strophic. In addition, every strophe, particularly the last, contains passages of 'composed-out rubato'—frequent changes in metre and note values that mirror the effect of a simple, beloved song rendered with slightly extravagant yet sincerely felt rhythmic liberty. *In toto*, the features just named give 'Liebst du um Schönheit' a somewhat nostalgic, old-fashioned character; it harks back to earlier nineteenth-century lieder rather than pointing forward to the second maturity of Gustav Mahler. There are of course distinctive Mahlerian touches. One is the foreboding turn towards the minor tonic at the beginning of the second strophe, 'Liebst du um Jugend, o nicht mich liebe!' (If you love youth, oh then don't love me!)— a very personal allusion, as we shall see. Another is the ubiquitous 'Ewigkeit' motive, the stepwise ascent followed by a leap to an appoggiatura that is central to the 'Resurrection' chorus of the Second Symphony, and crops up in many other movements as well (see Ex. 13.8).[82] Most characteristic of all is the final strophe—

Liebst du um Liebe,	If you love for Love's sake,
o ja mich liebe!	Oh yes, love me!
Liebe mich immer,	Love me forever,
dich lieb' ich immer, immerdar!	I love you ever, evermore!

—in which the subdued intensity of the music utterly transforms all that has been heard up to that point. The repetition of 'immer' in the last line (Ex. 13.8(*e*)), according to Alma's diary, always moved her deeply.[83] Adorno rightly finds this moment extraordinary both in its own right and as a harbinger of Mahler's later style:

the singing voice closes on an A [b. 31], the submediant, forming a discord with the tonic triad, as if the feeling found no outlet but suffocated in its excess. What is expressed is so overwhelming as to render the phenomenon, the language of music itself, indifferent. It does not finish its utterance; expression becomes a sobbing. What befalls it in such details takes hold of it entirely in the last pieces. Experience tinges all of the words and configurations of the music of the late Mahler.[84]

[81] ' "Ein Privatissimum an Dich", sagte er.' Typescript for *Mein Leben*, p. 3/4. The orchestration performed and recorded today was made by Max Puttmann (1864–1935), apparently in 1910. Mitchell, *SSLD*, 123–4, and HLG(E) ii. 797–8 (HLG(F) ii. 1117–18) provide interesting commentaries by Deryck Cooke and Harold Byrns concerning the ways in which Puttmann's style of orchestration differs from Mahler's. Mahler's original contract with C. F. Kahnt for the publication of the Rückert songs and *Kindertotenlieder*, which is dated 15 Apr. 1905, did not include 'Liebst du um Schönheit'; only on 8 Dec. 1906 did he sign an agreement for its publication 'with piano accompaniment' (see HLG(F) ii. 689 n. 24). The piano version was performed publicly in Vienna in 1907, Mahler's final year there (see Zoltan Roman, 'Revisionsbericht' to vol. 13 of the *Kritische Gesamtausgabe*, p. vi).

[82] See Philip T. Barford, 'Mahler: A Thematic Archetype', *Music Review*, 21 (1960), 297–316; Floros, *Gustav Mahler*, ii. 259–60 and 408 (Table 58); and Henry-Louis de La Grange, 'Music about Music in Mahler: Reminiscences, Allusions, or Quotations?', in Hefling (ed.), *Mahler Studies*, 143–4 and 167–8.

[83] Typescript for *Mein Leben*, p. 3/4; cf. also HLG(E) ii. 538 (HLG(F) ii. 277) and the published version of *Mein Leben*, 33.

[84] Adorno, *Mahler*, 146–7 (German edn., 189). As Peter Franklin points out, this melodic phrase appears, without poetic text, in a facsimile reproduction of Adorno's hand on the dedication page (to his wife Gretel) of *Mahler: Eine musikalische Physiognomik* (omitted from the English trans.); see Franklin, ' ". . . his fractures are the script of truth."—Adorno's Mahler', in Hefling (ed.), *Mahler Studies*, 274–5.

Ex. 13.8. The 'Ewigkeit' (Eternity) motive: (a) Second Symphony, finale, bb. 696 ff. (text: 'I shall die in order to live!'); (b) Fourth Symphony, 3rd movt., bb. 66 ff.; (c) 'Ich bin der Welt abhanden gekommen', bb. 51–3 (text: '[I live alone] in my heaven, in my love'); (d) 'Liebst du um Schönheit', bb. 5–6 (text: '[If you love for Beauty's sake,] oh then don't love me, love the sun'); (e) 'Liebst du um Schönheit', bb. 29–31 (text: 'I love you ever, ever-more!')

All these aspects of the song reflect the impulse and occasion for its composition. As we have seen, both Mahler's musical engagement with the poetry of Rückert and his marriage to Alma were in part reactions to the brush with death in February 1901 that stunned him into acknowledging his advancing age and vulnerable mortality. Alma, the mother-to-be of his children, represented the 'gateway to immortality', as Feder has suggested.[85] Their whirlwind courtship, procreation, and marriage between November 1901 and March 1902 brought Mahler contented fulfilment, and during the summer of 1902 he was able to compose more easily and for longer periods of time than ever before.[86] The prevalence of Mahler's 'Ewigkeit' motive in the song is therefore hardly surprising (he would adopt it for

[85] Feder, 'Gustav Mahler, Dying', 131–3.

[86] Typescript for *Mein Leben*, p. 2/3 (13 July 1902): 'Er hat mir gestern gesagt, dass er NOCH NIE SO LEICHT UND ANHALTEND GEARBEITET HABE ALS JETZT . . .' ('Yesterday he told me that NEVER BEFORE HAS HE WORKED SO EASILY AND PERSISTENTLY AS NOW . . .'); cf. also HLG(E) ii. 537 (HLG(F) ii. 276).

Ex. 13.9. 'Alma's theme' (opening), Sixth Symphony, 1st movt., bb. 77 ff.

the 'Alma' theme of the Sixth Symphony as well—see Ex. 13.9).[87] But for Alma, nearly twenty years younger than he, matters were different. At the time she met Mahler, Alma was on the verge of consummating an affair with her composition teacher, Alexander von Zemlinsky, for whom her passion did not cool immediately; not surprisingly, her attraction to Mahler was less intense and unwavering than his for her.[88] In addition, both Alma and those close to her had doubts about the suitability of such a match; her stepfather, the painter Carl Moll, approached her with the following summary objections:

'He's not young. To my certain knowledge, he's in debt. He's not strong. And then, it's all up with his job at the Opera.' (This was common talk in Vienna for ten years before he went. . . .) 'He's certainly no beauty. Composes, too, and they say it's no go.'[89]

Moreover, Alma herself was far from certain about the value of Mahler's music.[90] Worse, Mahler had demanded that she herself give up composing; and if she played the piano in the Maiernigg villa it disturbed his work in the nearby *Häuschen*. Newly married, pregnant, living in unfamiliar surroundings, and deprived of her favourite endeavours, Alma was often miserable during the summer of 1902, as her diary entries reveal in some detail. And Mahler was aware of it:

13 July. I was alone all morning and all afternoon—and when Gustav came down—still so filled with his work and happy about it, I could not share his good humour, and tears came to my eyes again. He became serious—my Gustav—terribly serious. And now he doubts my love. And how often have I myself doubted. Sometimes I'm dying of love for him—and then, a moment later, I feel nothing—nothing—! . . . If only I could find my inward equilibrium![91]

The situation was further complicated by Anna von Mildenburg, the Wagnerian soprano with whom Mahler had had a long affair during his Hamburg years. Although he had not concealed the fact from Alma, it seems he had revealed to her neither the passionate intensity of his involvement, which emerges distinctly form his 180-odd surviving letters to Mildenburg, nor the rather unresolved state of the liaison when he left Hamburg for

[87] Alma Mahler, *Memories*, 70: 'After he had drafted the first movement he came down from the wood to tell me he had tried to express me in a theme. . . . This is the great soaring theme of the first movement of the Sixth Symphony'.

[88] See HLG(E) i (HLG(F) ii), ch. 36 (HLG(E) ii, ch. 12).

[89] Alma Mahler, *Memories*, 23.

[90] Ibid. 3, 24, and 26.

[91] Typescript for *Mein Leben*, p. 2/3 (13 July 1902): 'Ich war den ganzen Vor- und Nachmittag allein — und wie Gustav herunterkam — noch so voll und glücklich von seiner Arbeit, da konnte ich nicht mit und mir kamen wieder die Tränen. Er wurde ernst — mein Gustav — furchtbar ernst. Und nun zweifelt er an meiner Liebe! — Und wie oft habe ich selbst gezweifelt. Jetzt vergehe ich vor Liebe zu ihm — und im nächsten Moment empfinde ich nichts — nichts! Wenn ich nur mein inneres Gleichgewicht fände!' Cf. also HLG(E) ii. 537 (HLG(F) ii. 275).

Vienna.[92] Only when Mildenburg herself was offered a position at the Vienna Court Opera in the latter part of 1897 did Mahler insist that their personal relations be restricted to an absolute minimum.[93] And while she outwardly accepted Mahler's conditions, there seems no doubt that in the privacy of her mind Mildenburg denied the break between them. She owned a residence near Mahler's villa and, despite his marriage, frequently dropped in unexpectedly during the summer of 1902. Mildenburg deployed a variety of unsavoury tactics to humiliate Alma, her junior by several years; at one point Mahler was determined to ban Mildenburg from the house, but Alma, fearing the appearance of scandal, suggested instead that her next visit be turned into a musical occasion:

We played and sang the whole of the last act of *Siegfried* together. Her voice that afternoon was truer and her singing more beautiful than they had ever been on the operatic stage; and as our concert carried right down to the lake, there was a crowd of boats in front of our house by the time we had done, and an outburst of enthusiastic applause.[94]

In the event, this proved to be the last of Mildenburg's vindictive visitations. But it can hardly have been a reassuring occasion for Alma, whose musical voice had been largely muted by marriage to Mahler. Near the end of this harrowing summer, when he had nearly completed the Fifth Symphony, which he would dedicate to Alma, Mahler created 'Liebst du um Schönheit' as an extraordinary token of consolation and hope for renewed love—and placed it, significantly, in the score of *Siegfried*. Yet more significantly, the little song is neither Wagnerian in tone nor a work in Mahler's own most recent style, which Alma did not yet find altogether pleasing. Rather, it is conceived especially for her in a retrospective, nostalgic, and intimate manner subtly different from anything else he had written, or would. The Rückert poem Mahler selected lists and dismisses three of the concerns that distressed the couple—his appearance, his age, and his disdain for material goods. The final stanza, which Mahler set to music of such simple transcendent beauty, is a quiet apotheosis of the idealistic love he had always hoped for and wanted to believe in—'God is Love and Love is God. This idea returned in his conversations thousands of times', as Alfred Roller reports.[95]

But the fundamental dissonances between the domineering, self-made composer-conductor in his forties and the highly gifted, impetuous, seductive young woman of 23 were never to be fully resolved. Alma's diary shows that the birth of their first child in November 1902 did not lessen her discontent:

It is as though my wings had been clipped. Gustav, why have you bound me to yourself, me, a glittering bird who delights in flight, when you would certainly have been better served by a gray, ponderous one! When there are so many ducks and geese who are dull and ignorant of flight.

---

[92] See HLG(E) i (HLG(F) i), chs. 21–5, as well as Stuart Feder, 'Before Alma . . . Gustav Mahler and "Das Ewig-Weibliche" ', in Hefling (ed.), *Mahler Studies*, 78–109, esp. 91–101.

[93] Mahler, *Briefe* (1982), no. 251 (July 1897; not in *Selected Letters*).

[94] Alma Mahler, *Memories*, 45.

[95] Alfred Roller, *Die Bildnisse von Gustav Mahler* (Leipzig: E. P. Tal & Co., 1922), 26; trans. in Lebrecht, *Mahler Remembered*, 164.

... Gustav lives HIS life—My child doesn't need me. I CANnot occupy myself <u>ONLY</u> with <u>that</u>! I am learning Greek—But my God—where is <u>MY</u> goal—<u>my magnificent goal</u>? My bitterness is great. I am constantly on the verge of tears. . . . God help me![96]

And the subsequent history of the marriage is well known. It is difficult to believe that Alma actually forgot that 'Liebst du um Schönheit' was given to her in the summer of 1902 during her first pregnancy, or that it was hidden in the score of *Siegfried*: a more plausible explanation is that when she prepared her carefully coloured portrait of Mahler for publication in the late 1930s, these highly charged memories were, for various reasons, among those she chose to conceal. Only in her autobiography of 1960 did she reveal the correct date and 'presentation wrapper' of the lovesong Mahler composed for her.[97]

In the summer of 1904 Mahler wrote two additional *Kindertotenlieder* to complete the Rückert cycle begun in 1901; in *Gustav Mahler: Memories*, Alma claims she found this 'incomprehensible. . . . I exclaimed at the time: "For heaven's sake, don't tempt providence!" '[98] But in the light of all that influenced the making of the Rückert lieder, it is perhaps less incomprehensible than Alma suggests. In any case, 'Liebst du um Schönheit' was the last completely joyous song Mahler wrote. His final efforts in that genre, the symphonic cycle *Das Lied von der Erde*, are tinged with the irony and autumnal glow characteristic of his late style—including the unfinished Tenth Symphony, his ultimate artistic utterance to Alma.[99]

[96] Typescript for *Mein Leben*, pp. 4/5–5/6 (13–15 Dec. 1902): '13 DEC. Mir ist, als ob man mir die Flügel beschnitten hätte. Gustav, warum hast Du mich, flugfrohen, glänzenden Vogel an Dich gebannt, so Dir doch mit einem grauen, schweren besser geholfen gewesen wäre! So es doch so viele Enten und Gänse gibt, schwer und flugunkundig.

'15 DEC. . . . Gustav lebt SEIN Leben — Mein Kind braucht mich nicht — Ich KANN auch nicht, <u>NUR</u> mich <u>damit</u> beschäftigen! Ich lerne griechisch — Aber mein Gott — wo ist <u>MEIN</u> Ziel — mein herrliches Ziel — Meine Erbitterung ist gross. Unaufhörlich stecken mir die Tränen im Halse. . . . Gott helfe mir!' Cf. also HLG(F) ii. 279; an edited version of this passage is found in *Mein Leben*, 33–4.

[97] Alma Mahler-Werfel, *Mein Leben*, 33.

[98] Alma Mahler, *Memories*, 70.

[99] See *Mein Leben*, 49, and Henry-Louis de La Grange, 'The Tenth Symphony: Purgatory or Catharsis?', in *Fragment or Completion?*, ed. Paul Op de Coul, 154–64.

14

The Sixth Symphony

DAVID MATTHEWS

The often quoted disagreement between Mahler and Sibelius on the nature of the symphony is misleading insofar as it implies a diametric difference of approach between the two composers. Mahler's symphonies, especially his early ones, are indeed all-embracing worlds; but this is not to say that he was not just as concerned as his Finnish contemporary with 'the profound logic that create[s] an inner connection between all the motives'.[1] Nowhere is this more apparent than in the Sixth Symphony, the most classical of all Mahler's works. Sibelius a few years later in his own Fourth Symphony in the same key, A minor, may have been sparer, but he was certainly not more strict. Both symphonies are unequivocally 'tragic'—the title by which Mahler's Sixth is often known.[2]

The classicism of the Sixth is most clearly evident in its basic formal plan. It is the only one of Mahler's symphonies to have the traditional four movements in their traditional order, and to follow a classical key sequence, with three movements in the tonic minor and the slow movement in E flat major. All other Mahler symphonies, except the Eighth, end in a different key from that in which they began, and his only other four-movement symphonies, the Fourth and the Ninth, do not follow an orthodox movement scheme. But on this one occasion Mahler found that what he wanted to say could best be expressed within a classical frame. His previous two symphonies, in which he had drawn closer to the Viennese Classical archetype than he had in his first three, had prepared him for this work in which he placed himself firmly in the line of Beethoven, Brahms, and Bruckner.

The first movement's sonata form could not be more clearly delineated. The exposition presents self-contained first and second subject groups, separated by a chorale which serves as a transition. The first group emphasizes A minor with tremendous—and as it will eventually prove, inescapable—power; but at the same time the music is continually striving to evade its grip. The main theme, for instance, attempts in its fifth bar (b. 11 in the score) to leap into D minor, but is clawed back into A minor two bars later (see Ex. 14.1).

[1] See Tawaststjerna, *Sibelius*, ii. 77.

[2] Bruno Walter says that the title was Mahler's own (*Gustav Mahler*, trans. James Galston (London: Kegan Paul, Trench, Trübner, 1937), 49). It does not appear in the score, but it did appear, for instance, on the progamme for the third and last performance Mahler conducted, in Vienna on 4 Jan. 1907 (see p. 371).

Ex. 14.1. Sixth Symphony, 1st movt., bb. 6–13

The reprise of Ex. 14.1 at bar 25 follows the same pattern: this time the relative major, F, is grasped securely at bar 29, but again relinquished two bars later. Mahler is already aiming at what will eventually be the key of his second subject. At bar 47 the music reaches a strong dominant pedal, which prepares us for the first appearance of the A major/minor motto (bb. 57–60). So the first great paragraph of the Symphony has ended as it began, firmly in the grip of A minor.

The chorale transition does not modulate, but stays in A minor. When it reaches a dominant chord at bar 76, the music simply makes a leap, and this time a successful one, into F major for the second subject group (Ex. 14.2).

It is curious that there are virtually no A minor Symphonies before Mahler's Sixth; the only well-known exception is Mendelssohn's 'Scotch' Symphony which, however, ends in A major. (I shall touch on the parallels that can be drawn with Beethoven's A major Seventh Symphony later.) *The* great classical A minor work is Beethoven's String Quartet, Op. 132, and it is interesting to find that the second subject of its first movement is, like

Ex. 14.2. Sixth Symphony, 1st movt., bb. 76–80

Ex. 14.3. Beethoven, String Quartet Op. 132, 1st movt., second subject

Mahler's, in F major, and begins with a rather similar idea (see Ex. 14.3). Alma Mahler relates how Mahler had told her that Ex. 14.2 was intended as a portrait of her: 'Whether I've succeeded, I don't know; but you'll have to put up with it.'[3] Its contours follow a pattern we can trace throughout Mahler's symphonies, with an opening phrase that rises aspiringly towards a point of release. Many of these themes are associated with the idea of redemption; and from the Adagietto of the Fifth onwards, Mahler associated redemption with Alma, most clearly in the Eighth Symphony, where she becomes identified with Goethe's *Ewig-Weibliche* (eternal feminine). Example 14.4 shows an assortment of these themes, from the Fifth Symphony (Ex. 14.4(*a*)), the Seventh (Ex. 14.4(*b*): the equivalent theme in the first movement to Ex. 14.2), the Eighth (Ex. 14.4(*c*)) and the Tenth (Ex. 14.4(*d*)).

The true source of all these themes, however, lies not so much in Beethoven but rather in a motive of redemption from *Parsifal*, which first appears in the Prelude to the opera (Ex. 14.5). Mahler had first heard *Parsifal* in 1883, when he attended the second series of performances at Bayreuth. He wrote to his friend Fritz Löhr: 'When I walked out of the Festspielhaus, incapable of uttering a word, I knew I had come to understand all that is greatest and most painful and that I would bear it within me, inviolate, for the rest of my life.'[4] Mahler did indeed bear *Parsifal* within him for the rest of his life. As I suggest in my chapter on the Tenth Symphony (Ch. 22), *Parsifal* played a crucial part in determining the character of that work, both at its moments of greatest anguish, and in its climax of redemption, which is marked by the triumph of an Alma-inspired, *Parsifal*-derived theme (Ex. 14.4(*d*)).

Although Ex. 14.2 may sound quite new, it is, as is all the material of the second subject group, a refashioning of material from the first subject group. Even the three-note rising phrase (marked x in Ex. 14.2) has been anticipated in the rising entries of the first violins in the introduction (bb. 2–5). The phrase marked y in Ex. 14.2 is a reformulation of phrase b in Ex. 14.1, and z in Ex. 14.2 corresponds to a in Ex. 14.1. Phrase y has already appeared in its proper second-subject guise at bar 22 of the first subject group. The falling and rising phrase in bars 11–12 forms the climax of the reprise of Ex. 14.2 (see bb. 111–13), while the semiquavers that accompany it in bars 11–12 are the climax of the first statement of the theme (see bb. 89–90). Here is a logical 'inner connection between all the motives' to match anything in Sibelius.

The second subject group having reached a protracted cadence in its own F major, Mahler asks for the exposition to be repeated. On the face of it, this is rather astonishing.

---

[3] Alma Mahler, *Memories*, 70.   [4] Mahler, *Selected Letters*, 74.

Ex. 14.4. 'Redemption' themes: (*a*) Fifth Symphony, 4th movt., bb. 2–6; (*b*) Seventh Symphony, 1st movt., bb. 118–21; (*c*) Eighth Symphony, 2nd movt., bb. 219–26; (*d*) Tenth Symphony, 5th movt., bb. 353–8

Ex. 14.5. Redemption motive in Wagner, *Parsifal*, Prelude, bb. 95–6

What other symphonist, let alone a 'progressive' one, was still using the repeated exposition convention as late as 1904? The only one who comes readily to mind is the 'conservative' Rachmaninov, whose Second Symphony of 1907 asks for a repeat of the exposition, perhaps rather unnecessarily. Brahms had already given up the convention in his Fourth Symphony, as had Tchaikovsky in his Sixth. Dvořák, having written a superbly deceptive false reprise in the first movement of his Eighth,[5] returned to the repeat convention in his last symphony. Sibelius never used the convention, and Nielsen only in his First Symphony. Mahler too (again somewhat surprisingly) had repeated the first movement exposition in his First Symphony, but not since. Here, however, the repeat both emphasizes the Sixth's classical stance and also helps balance the first movement against the enormous length of the Finale.

There is no space here for a full-length analysis of the whole Symphony. I would refer the reader to Norman Del Mar's very thorough analysis in his monograph on the Sixth.[6] For the remainder of this essay I wish to deal with two particular areas of controversy this Symphony raises. First, the problem of the order of the middle movements. As far as Mahler's own intentions are concerned, this cannot be solved conclusively. The facts are briefly as follows. Mahler composed the Symphony with the Scherzo placed second and the Andante third, and the full score was published in this form in 1906 before the first performance. At the première, however, he changed the order of the two middle movements, and a note indicating the new order was inserted into the score. Later in 1906 a new full score was issued with the Andante placed second and the Scherzo third, and with many revisions to the orchestration. No other editions appeared until 1963, when the International Gustav Mahler Society published a score edited by Erwin Ratz, who reverted to the original order, claiming in his preface that it represented Mahler's final wish, though offering no documentary evidence to support his claim.

Mahler conducted the Sixth Symphony only four times, the last occasion being in Vienna on 4 January 1907, six months after the Essen première. The programme for this concert announced that the Andante would be played second and the Scherzo third, as in the two previous performances he had conducted (see Pl. 14). At least five of the reviews in the Vienna press confirm that this was so, but one writer, 'H.R.' (almost certainly the music critic and operetta composer Heinrich Reinhardt), in the *Neues Wiener Journal* of 6 January 1907 stated that the Scherzo was played second. Reinhardt's review, however, is flippant and full of invective: he uses the confusion about the movement order as an excuse to try to ridicule Mahler; furthermore his description of the second movement, which he says was the Scherzo, is so vague and inaccurate that it could equally well be a description of the Andante (and he says that it ends with 'a loud bang', which is untrue of either movement). In contrast, the reviewer for the *Neue Zeitschrift für Musik* of 17 January 1907, Theodor Helm, makes it quite clear that the Andante was played second: he mentions that this contradicts the published study score and notes that Mahler's timings for the movements at the final rehearsal and at the performance corresponded precisely with those given in the correction slip to this score. So there can be no real grounds for taking

---

[5] See bars 127–44: Dvořák repeats the whole of his G minor introduction, but the violin and viola entry at bar 144 is half a bar later than before, and *tremolo*, telling us this is in fact the start of the development, which is properly con-firmed by the horn's entry on F (a marvellous moment) at bar 147.

[6] Norman Del Mar, *Mahler's Sixth Symphony—A Study* (London: Eulenburg Books, 1980), 34–64.

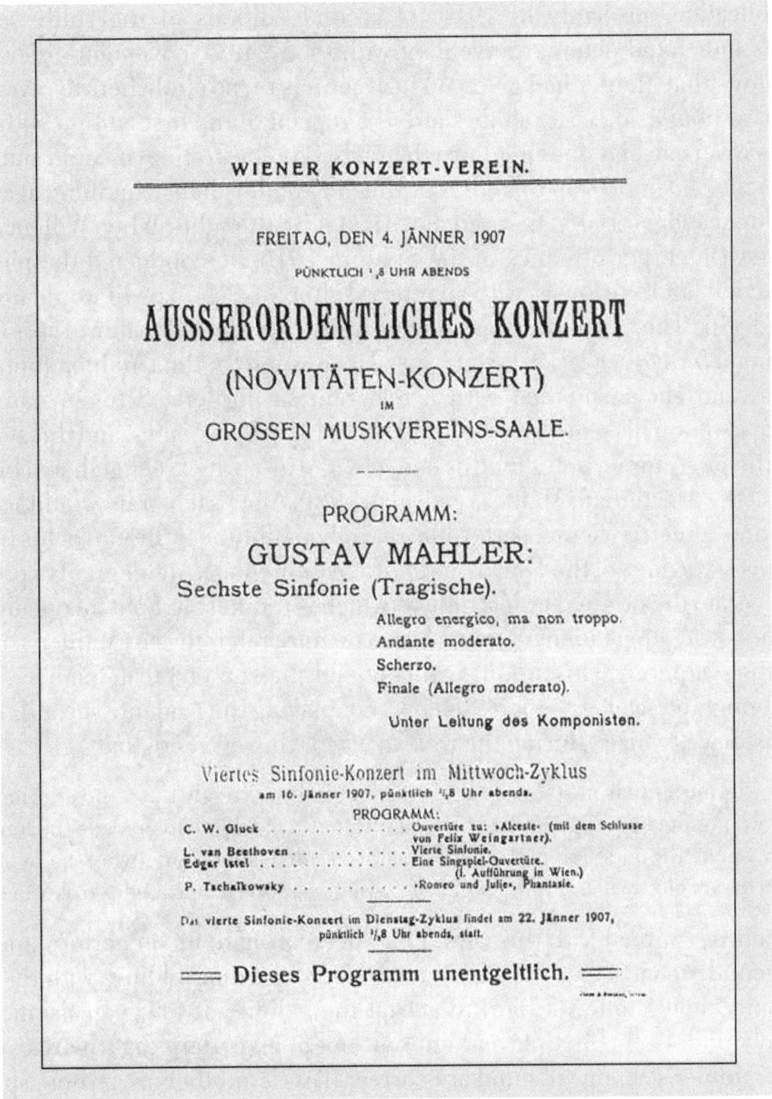

WIENER KONZERT-VEREIN.

FREITAG, DEN 4. JÄNNER 1907

PÜNKTLICH ¹⁄₂8 UHR ABENDS

AUSSERORDENTLICHES KONZERT

(NOVITÄTEN-KONZERT)

IM

GROSSEN MUSIKVEREINS-SAALE.

PROGRAMM:

GUSTAV MAHLER:

Sechste Sinfonie (Tragische).

Allegro energico, ma non troppo.

Andante moderato.

Scherzo.

Finale (Allegro moderato).

Unter Leitung des Komponisten.

Viertes Sinfonie-Konzert im Mittwoch-Zyklus
am 16. Jänner 1907, pünktlich ¹⁄₂8 Uhr abends.

PROGRAMM:

C. W. Gluck . . . . Ouvertüre zu: »Alceste« (mit dem Schlusse
                                                 von Felix Weingartner).
L. van Beethoven . . . . Vierte Sinfonie.
Edgar Istel . . . . Eine Singspiel-Ouvertüre.
                                                 (I. Aufführung in Wien.)
P. Tschaïkowsky . . . . »Romeo und Julie«, Phantasie.

Das vierte Sinfonie-Konzert im Dienstag-Zyklus findet am 22. Jänner 1907,
pünktlich ¹⁄₂8 Uhr abends, statt.

=== Dieses Programm unentgeltlich. ===

Pl. 14.1. The programme for the first Vienna performance of the Sixth Symphony
under Mahler on 4 January 1907

Reinhardt seriously or for doubting that Mahler conducted this performance also with the
Andante placed second and the Scherzo third.[7]

---

[7] For much of the information in this paragraph and the following one I am indebted to Donald Mitchell and Paul Banks, and to pioneering research in Vienna by Morten Solvik. The critical sentence by Theodor Helm runs as fol-lows: 'It may be mentioned finally that the timings of the individual movements, already given in the full score, were absolutely correct both at the final rehearsal and at the per-formance itself: 1st movement: 22 minutes; Andante (played

The publication, probably in 1910, of second editions of the study score and of Zemlinsky's four-hand piano arrangement with the revised movement order, Andante—Scherzo, shows that Mahler had given no instructions to his publishers to revert to the original order, although since the study score is a reprint of the first edition with the middle movements reversed, and does not have the revised orchestration, it could simply indicate that Mahler took no interest in this edition. But did Mahler change his mind again? Another piece of evidence suggests that he might have had third thoughts. When Willem Mengelberg gave the first Dutch performance of the Sixth in 1916, he conducted the piece with the Andante second (and, curiously, with an interval after the Scherzo—it would not have been possible to do this if he had played the Andante third). But when he came to perform the symphony again on 5 October 1919, he addressed a question to Alma Mahler about the movement order, and she responded with a telegram saying 'erst Scherzo dann Andante'. Mengelberg wrote on his score that this represented Mahler's wishes, and this statement was printed in the programme notes for this concert, and also when Mengelberg conducted the symphony at the Amsterdam Mahler Festival in 1920. Alma's telegram would seem to imply that, some time after the Vienna performance, and possibly near the end of his life (when he worked on new versions of the Fourth and Fifth Symphonies), Mahler had expressed to her a wish to revert to the original order; unless (which is unlikely but not inconceivable) Alma had made her own independent decision based on her preference for Mahler's original conception of the symphony. This original conception I shall now try to defend.

In his monograph, Del Mar argues in favour of playing the Andante second. He says that Mahler must have realized during the rehearsals for the première that

the Scherzo was too similar in style and dynamism to follow directly upon the enormously strenuous twenty-two minute opening movement. Equally, for the Andante to precede the long slow introduction that opens the monumental Finale was not really satisfactory, whereas by reversing the order the necessary contrast and relief on both counts was solved at a single stroke.[8]

Until recently, I agreed with this view. I had been brought up on performances with the Andante second, in particular the fine old recording by Eduard Flipse with the Rotterdam Philharmonic,[9] and I found it hard to accept the validity of Ratz's decision. But I have changed my mind. In the first place, I am now not at all certain that the reasons Del Mar adduces for Mahler's change of mind are correct. This is another area where speculation is our only resort. It is quite possible to argue that the chief, perhaps even the only reason why Mahler reversed the order of the two movements was the same as that which led him to remove the third hammer blow in the Finale: fear of the Symphony's prophetic power, and

as the 2nd, not as the 3rd movement, in contradistinction to the full score and piano score): 14 minutes; Scherzo: 11 minutes; Finale: 30 minutes. In total, therefore, without the breaks between the movements—77 minutes.' One further text describes the Scherzo in second place. This was contributed to the *Wiener Allgemeine Zeitung* on 7 Jan. by Carl Lafite but it is clear that this *feuilleton* must have been based on a consideration of the first published edition of the

orchestral score. Moreover, further confirmation has reached us by the kindness of Edward R. Reilly in the shape of a review by Ernst Decsey in the *Grazer Tagepost* of 10 Jan. which makes clear that the Andante was played as the second movement.

[8] Del Mar, *Mahler's Sixth Symphony*, 90.
[9] Recorded live at the Holland Festival in 1955 (Philips ABL 3103-4).

an instinctive wish to diminish it. For we know that Mahler was terrified by what he had written. As Alma writes:

None of his works moved him so deeply at its first hearing as this . . . When [the dress rehearsal] was over, Mahler walked up and down in the artists' room, sobbing, wringing his hands, unable to control himself . . . On the day of the concert Mahler was so afraid that his agitation might get the better of him that out of shame and anxiety he did not conduct the Symphony well. He hesitated to bring out the dark omen behind this terrible last movement.[10]

There are two ways in particular in which the tragic argument of the Symphony is more powerful if the Scherzo is placed second. First, we should note just how carefully Mahler has avoided A minor in the second half of the first movement. Much of the recapitulation of the first subject group takes place over a dominant E pedal: the full A minor chord with A in the bass appears only in two bars, 304–5. Even the motto is presented over an E and thus temporarily loses some of its finality. The chorale is lightened by its pizzicato accompaniment and by the presence of the celesta.[11] At bar 344 the music modulates away from A minor, and there is no more A minor in the remaining 137 bars of the movement. Indeed, the final thirty-eight bars are in A major, with the 'Alma' theme triumphant, so that the plunge back into A minor at the beginning of the Scherzo comes as a shock. We had temporarily forgotten that A major must turn irrevocably to the minor, as it does here with sudden and dreadful impact.

The second point is perhaps even more clinching. The Andante's E flat major, and the whole idyllic character of the movement, 'lost to the world', like Mahler's Rückert song, has once again caused us to forget the fundamental tonal conflict between A major and A minor. E flat was the key to which the 'visionary interlude' of the first movement (bb. 196–250) aspired (see bb. 225–50), and the Andante is full of reminiscences of this interlude, particularly in its scoring (compare the horn solos in bars 225–33 of the first movement and bars 28–32 of the Andante, and the use of cowbells and celesta). The ultimate haven of tranquillity in the Andante is reached in *A major* (bb. 124–45), before the music returns, via a passionate climax in E major, to E flat. The Finale opens in C minor, the relative minor of E flat major, but at bar 9 there is a sudden and quite unexpected return to A major/minor for the reappearance of the motto, like the spectre at the feast (see Ex. 14.6). Note especially the chilling clash between C natural in the melody line and C sharp in the motto (b. 10). The devastating power of this reappearance depends almost entirely on our

[10] Alma Mahler, *Memories*, 100.
[11] Mahler's use of the celesta could be the subject of a whole essay. He had first used the instrument in the Rückert song 'Ich atmet' einen linden Duft' and in the final song of *Kindertotenlieder*, in both of which it is symbolic of innocence and other-worldliness. In the Sixth it has both these connotations; it may be said to represent the other world of the symphony, that of aspiration and of identification with nature. Accordingly it first appears in the opening movement's 'Alma' theme (where, it has to be said, it is largely inaudible, despite Mahler's optimistic instruction in the original score that it should be doubled in *forte* passages), then in the 'visionary interlude' (b. 199 f.). The symbolic associations it acquires in the first movement and the Andante make some of its appearances in the Finale especially poignant, in particular on the last two occasions when it is heard: at Fig. 164, at the collapse of the last passage of exultant A major, and at bar 782 immediately before the third hammer blow, when its presence symbolizes the final extinction of hope. Both these celesta moments were added at the revision stage. (See also Mitchell, *SSLD*, 139 n. 31 and 497 n. 153.)

Ex. 14.6. Sixth Symphony, Finale, bb. 9–12

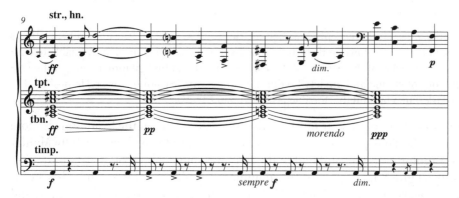

not having heard A minor since the Scherzo, but it makes very little impact if we have just heard the Scherzo. The C minor of the introduction again makes little sense as a bridge from A minor back again to A minor in a few bars.[12]

Other arguments can be advanced to support the original movement order. Karl Heinz Füssl describes the Scherzo as 'a "developing variation" on the first movement'.[13] Mahler had tried out such an idea in the Fifth Symphony, where the Allegro takes up and develops the material of the preceding Funeral March. The Sixth's first movement and Scherzo have a similar, intended interrelation; so it seems very curious to separate them. The conductor John Carewe has pointed out the similarity between the tonal plan of the Sixth and that of Beethoven's Seventh.[14] Beethoven's four movements are in A major, A minor, F major, and A major (the Finale beginning with eleven bars on the dominant). Mahler's third movement is in the more remote key of E flat, but we should note again his use of F major both for the second subject of the first movement and for the 'innocent' trio of the Scherzo (where the key is gradually undermined and finally destroyed by the Scherzo's fierce A minor). Like Beethoven's, Mahler's overall tonal scheme is deeply satisfying and logical. And just as one could not switch round the middle movements of Beethoven's Seventh without damaging the structure of the Symphony, so I believe the same is true of Mahler's Sixth. Paul Banks has argued that Mahler's indecision over the order of the movements leaves us with no alternative but to think of two separate versions of the Symphony.[15] In one respect this is true, for as I have shown, there is no way of knowing absolutely Mahler's final wishes. Yet I think that from a musical point of view there can be no doubt that the original version is far superior.

The other notorious problem about the Sixth concerns the third hammer blow in the Finale. In a famous passage of her memoirs, Alma Mahler wrote: 'In the last movement he

[12] In this connection, cf. Adorno: 'his [Mahler's] last arrangement of the movements, with the E-flat major Andante before the Finale, should be respected, if only for the modulation scheme; E-flat major is the relative of C minor, with which the Finale begins, only to decide, after long preparation, on A minor as its principal key' (*Mahler*, 85).

[13] Karl Heinz Füssl, 'On the Order of the Middle Movements in Mahler's Sixth Symphony', *News about Mahler Research*, no. 27 (Mar. 1992), 3–7 at 6.

[14] Pers. com.

[15] Pers. com.

described himself and his downfall or, as he later said, that of his hero: "It is the hero, on whom fall three blows of fate, the last of which fells him as a tree is felled." Those were his words.'[16] In the original score, Mahler marked these 'three blows of fate' by the inclusion of a hammer at three crucial places in the Finale.[17] The blows fall, respectively, in bar 336 at the collapse of the second statement of the exultant D major second subject; in bar 479, at the similar collapse of a still more glowing version of this theme in A major; and finally at bar 783, at the entrance of the motto following Mahler's last and most desperate attempt to sustain an exultant A major. In his revision of the score after the first performance, Mahler removed the third hammer blow, as well as lightening the orchestration at this point: the trombones, which originally reinforced the horns and trombones on the motto chords, were replaced by bassoons; timpani and side drum were marked *gedämpft*; dynamics were reduced.[18] There is programmatic justification for a less powerful sound here, which Alma Mahler realized; though, as so often, what she says is not strictly accurate. Strauss, she reports (in one of her many passages criticizing his insensitivity), was puzzled as to why Mahler 'gets his *fortissimo* and then damps it down'. 'Anyone who understands the symphony at all', she comments, 'understands why the first blow is the strongest, the second weaker and the third—the death-blow—the weakest of all.'[19] The second hammer blow, however, even if marked *ff* rather than *fff* as is the first, is not less powerful than the first (as Del Mar points out), nor was the third in the original version. Nonetheless, Alma makes a psychologically perceptive point about the third blow, and if it is played together with the revised orchestration, what she says about it is borne out. Removing the third blow altogether, however, makes no musical or programmatic sense, for it was merely superstition that caused Mahler to delete it. In reproducing Mahler's revised score, Ratz left out the third hammer blow, so most conductors today do not include it. But I think there is no question that it should be restored. As Del Mar, a strong advocate for restoration, succinctly puts it: 'Fate cannot still be felt to stand threateningly over the composer who has been dead and beyond her menace, real or imaginary, for over sixty years. Superstition must play no further part in what is now primarily an artistic decision.'[20]

Following the same argument, Del Mar would also restore the original orchestration at this point, which I would contest, both for the reason suggested above, and because a reduced sound here strengthens the impact of the very end of the Symphony, where the A minor triad alone is hurled out by the full orchestra over the motto's timpani rhythm. The tragedy is over. I have always been astonished that audiences can bring themselves to applaud this ending, to which silence would seem the only appropriate response.

---

[16] Alma Mahler, *Memories*, 70.

[17] At its first appearance Mahler has an explanatory footnote: 'Kurzer, mächtig, aber dumpf hallender Schlag von *nicht* metallischen Charakter (wie ein Axthieb)' ('short blow, powerful, but dull in resonance, with a *non*-metallic character (like an axe-stroke)'). The parenthetical words were added at the revision stage. The practical problems this instruction poses for the conductor are discussed by Del Mar, *Mahler's Sixth Symphony*, 127–8.

[18] Del Mar devotes the largest section of his book to a detailed examination of the changes Mahler made in his revisions to the instrumentation, which affect almost every page of the score. They offer considerable insight into Mahler's perfectionist approach to orchestral sound.

[19] Alma Mahler, *Memories*, 100.

[20] Del Mar, *Mahler's Sixth Symphony*, 152.

15

The Seventh Symphony

PETER REVERS

According to Wolf Rosenberg, the Seventh was Webern's favourite Mahler symphony: 'What seems to have attracted him most was the innovative orchestral colouring, especially in the two *Nachtmusiken*.'[1] It was a performance of the Seventh Symphony that decisively reversed Schoenberg's earlier adverse reaction to Mahler. In a letter to Mahler of 29 December 1909, he wrote of the strong and permanent impressions the work had made on him and assured Mahler: 'I am now really and entirely yours. I know that for a certainty.'[2] His unconditional devotion to Mahler, well documented in this letter, seems to have been more than a superficial gesture of respect. However, he did not refer to any concrete principles of composition—nor was he to do so in his Prague lecture (1913).

Mahler's Seventh Symphony, despite the enthusiasm of Webern and Schoenberg, is undoubtedly one of the most controversial of all his symphonies. The Rondo-Finale in particular has become the object of strongly conflicting aesthetic judgements. Paul Bekker characterized it as the 'climax of optimistic affirmation' and an expression of the 'harmony of the individual with the universe'; whereas Adorno criticized it as demonstrating a 'disproportion between the splendid exterior and the meager content of the whole'.[3] As Hermann Danuser has pointed out, the confrontation between 'polemic and apologetic music criticism of Mahler's Seventh' was especially significant in the early reviews of the piece.[4] He convincingly demonstrates how, despite the reviewers' ideological prejudices, their differing evaluations resulted from particular aspects of the work itself. The affinity of the Rondo-Finale with Wagner's *Meistersinger* Overture, for instance—one of the main issues in Adorno's criticism of the symphony—suggests a play of striking tableaux.[5] The

[1] Wolf Rosenberg, 'Mahler und die Avantgarde: Kompositionstechnisches Vorbild oder geistige Sympathie?', in Otto Kolleritsch (ed.), *Gustav Mahler: Sinfonie und Wirklichkeit* (Graz: Universal Edition for the Institut für Wertungsforschung, 1977), 81–92 at 82.

[2] Alma Mahler, *Memories*, 325.

[3] Adorno, *Mahler*, 137.

[4] Hermann Danuser, 'Erkenntnis oder Verblendung?

Zum Problem des Sachgehaltes polemischer und apologetischer Musikkritik—am Beispiel einiger früher Rezeptionszeugnisse zu Mahlers Siebenter Symphonie', in James L. Zychowicz (ed.), *The Seventh Symphony of Gustav Mahler: A Symposium* (Cincinnati: University of Cincinnati, 1990), 107–23 at 123.

[5] Adorno, *Mahler*, 137.

theatrical 'idea of play'[6] is an issue that constantly arises in the critical literature on this Finale. While some reviews of the first performance praised the movement for its *Meistersinger*-like serenity, and others condemned it as a demeaning mockery of Wagner's opera, in more recent times the 'idea of play' has been criticized as a kind of Divertissement wholly inappropriate to the form of the symphony at the beginning of the twentieth century. In his book *Logik des Zerfalls*, Bernd Sponheuer characterizes the Rondo-Finale as a type of failed attempt at a restoration of a past aesthetic convention (the type of affirmatory Finale).[7] In this view, mainly inspired by Adorno's idea of 'Gebrochenheit' (the breaking with the traditional affirmative type of formal design and aesthetic demand), Mahler's Rondo-Finale seems to fall below the standard he achieved most convincingly at the end of his Sixth Symphony.

In the Rondo-Finale the apparently superficial splendour is undoubtedly part of the musical intention and serves a compositional purpose. Mahler's direction at the final bars, 'etwas feierlich. Prachtvoll' ('somewhat solemnly. Magnificent'; two bars after Fig. 290), suggests a pompous attitude, the latent irony of which affects the individual expression of the instruments more than the musical structure itself. A good example of this can be found in the brilliant, virtuoso-like reintroduction of the timpani (Ex. 15.1). The use of wooden sticks ('Holzschlägel') had already been described by Berlioz in his *Treatise on Instrumentation* as suitable 'only for single violent blows or to accompany a tremendous noise in the orchestra'.[8] Thus Mahler emphasizes an apparently vulgar sound in contrast to the ideal of a well-disposed and homogeneous colouring represented most strikingly in the works of Richard Strauss. Mahler's Seventh is in some ways a study in the extreme diversity of what music might be—a multiplicity of sounds which occupies a spectrum from the sublimely romantic to the grotesquely deformed. It is hardly surprising that performance interpretations (such as Michael Gielen's) that focus strictly on these aspects of colouring highlight the modern and progressive approach to Mahler's Seventh. In fact, the heterogeneous musical vocabulary erupts in unexpected clashes.[9] One can find 'second-hand music' in, for instance, the

Ex. 15.1. Seventh Symphony, Rondo-Finale, Fig. 290[+2] (timpani)

[6] 'Die Idee des Spiels': Bekker, *Gustav Mahlers Sinfonien*, 16.

[7] Sponheuer, *Logik des Zerfalls*, 357 ff.

[8] Hector Berlioz and Richard Strauss, *Treatise on Instrumentation*, trans. Theodore Front (repr. New York: Dover 1991), 380. In a letter of 17 Oct. 1909 to Johann Jongkindt, Alphons Diepenbrock (the composer and friend of Mahler) wrote of the first Dutch performances of the Seventh: 'Exceedingly long but grandiose is this movement [the Rondo-Finale], although sometimes too noisy.' See Reeser, *Gustav Mahler und Holland*, 32.

[9] I agree here with Peter Davison, who also emphasizes the 'forces of disruption' and the principle of discontinuity 'which disturb the flow of the music'. See Peter Davison, 'Nachtmusik II: "Nothing but Love, Love, Love"?', in Zychowicz (ed.), *The Seventh Symphony*, 89–97 at 92.

Janissary march in the Rondo-Finale (Fig. 269), as well as extremely fractured and distorted musical material in, for example, the Scherzo (Fig. 161) (see Ex. 15.2).

Of course, the indiscriminate use of musical material (employed in Mahler's day most notably by Charles Ives) contradicts the idea of structural coherence and 'profound logic' that creates 'an inner connection between all the motives as the highest ideal of symphonic writing'.[10] Although the juxtaposition of different levels of musical expression seems to be strongly marked not only within the movements but also in the general design of the symphony as a whole, there are subtle techniques of musical integration. The first ritornello in the Rondo-Finale (in C major) ends with a stretto-like final cadence. An abrupt return to the key of the first episode in bar 53 (A flat major) takes place without even a hint of modulation. The anticipation of the new key in bar 51 intrudes quite unexpectedly. This sudden clash of two very different keys is intensified by the change in orchestral colouring: from a virtuoso and agitated tutti to a disjunct, immobile A flat major triad played by the woodwinds (see Ex. 15.3). The following episode, in the character of a simple folk tune,

Ex. 15.2. Seventh Symphony: (a) Rondo-Finale, Fig. 269; (b) Scherzo, Fig. 161[+4]

[10] Lionel Pike, *Beethoven, Sibelius and the 'Profound Logic': Studies in Symphonic Analysis* (London: Athlone, 1978), 2.

^k) So stark anreißen, daß die Saiten an das Holz anschlagen

refers to the former ritornello only in so far as in both we can find an arpeggio-like melodic shape as well as a two-bar motivic nucleus with a trill at the second bar (bb. 2 and 54); in fact, juxtaposition pervades nearly all levels of musical organization. At the very end of the Rondo-Finale the stretto reappears. In the penultimate bar, the rapid movement is suspended and the C major chord changes to an augmented triad (C–E–G♯; see Ex. 15.4). Although there is no real collision of two different keys, the musical context strongly suggests a close relation to the situation in bars 51 ff. Thus the principle of contrast constitutes musical coherence and makes clear the ambivalent nature of what seems, at first sight, to be a structural break. These compositional procedures might suggest why Schoenberg perceived so many formal subtleties when he heard the Seventh for the first time.[11]

As I mentioned earlier, the Rondo-Finale is perhaps Mahler's most controversial composition. Adorno's verdict is not a unique or exaggerated one. James Zychowicz, for example, comes to the conclusion that the 'layers of meaning, both musical and programmatic, overlap such that it becomes difficult to follow the work on any one level consistently throughout'.[12] Deryck Cooke also criticized the Finale as an isolated example of 'Kapellmeistermusik' in Mahler's work, and concluded: 'there can be no question that the finale is largely a failure'.[13] In terms of integral symphonic form and structural coherence the Rondo-Finale maintains the illusion of the traditional finale by emphasizing the

[11] 'And it was all so transparently clear to me. In short, at first hearing I felt so many subtleties of form, and yet could follow a main line throughout.' See Alma Mahler, *Memories*, 326.

[12] James L. Zychowicz, 'Ein schlechter Jasager: Considerations on the Finale to Mahler's Seventh Symphony', in id. (ed.), *The Seventh Symphony*, 98–106 at 105.
[13] Cooke, *Gustav Mahler*, 90 and 91.

Ex. 15.3. Seventh Symphony, Rondo-Finale, bb. 50–6

*) Den Akkord in allen Instrumenten scharf abreißen

Ex. 15.4. Seventh Symphony, Rondo-Finale, bb. 586–90

conventional aspects of its formal design: well-defined musical periods, simple tunes, and 'a stable—almost static—diatonic harmony'.[14] Whereas in the last movement of the Fifth Symphony (an analogous example) the expression of affirmation is part of the coherent structural design, the conventional elements in the Finale of the Seventh appear unfamiliar, dislocated, and therefore unsettling. However, this seems to be the very intention of the movement, as if Mahler were saying: 'The time of the traditional finale is over.' After the Eighth, a work of unusual ambition avoiding any kind of dualism and lacking a true finale (since the entire symphony might be regarded as a hybrid finale), any affirmation is thwarted. The dying away in the last bars of the Ninth Symphony constitutes a radically new type of ending, anticipated perhaps only by Tchaikovsky's Sixth Symphony.

Among the most outstanding phenomena in Mahler's symphonic output are the two *Nachtmusiken* (the second and fourth movements). The use of guitar and mandolin (suggesting a nocturnal serenade) prompted descriptions of these movements as unalloyed idylls. Alma's remark that Mahler was beset by 'Eichendorff-ish visions—murmuring springs and German romanticism'[15] while writing the second *Nachtmusik*, seems to confirm this characterization. In fact, the *topos* of 'Night' in German literature changed around the middle of the eighteenth century. Edward Young's poem *The Complaint, or Night Thoughts on Life, Death and Immortality* (1742–5) was among the first important examples of a new poetic genre which dwelt on night, death, the tomb, melancholy, and aspects of the emotions hardly explored before. German translations of Young's poem were published in 1752; from 1760 onwards they enjoyed enormous popularity and had a considerable influence on early Romanticism in Germany. Gotthilf Heinrich Schubert's *Ansichten von der Nachtseite der Naturwissenschaft* (1808) and *Die Symbolik des Traumes* (1814) intensified discussion about the unconscious attributes of night. E. T. A. Hoffmann, in particular, was influenced by Schubert's philosophical thoughts. Hoffmann emphasized the dual aspect of night as being a time of calmness and inner peace, as well as belonging to the powers of darkness and supernatural forces. Thus the idea of night (especially during the nineteenth century) was more or less characterized by ambivalence—which can also be found in Eichendorff's poems. Both Hoffmann and Eichendorff were among Mahler's favourite authors and one can hardly doubt their influence on him. From the literary point of view, then, a positive interpretation of Mahler's Seventh as depicting the harmonious coexistence of man with his surroundings seems to be a misleading and partial one—at least as far as the *Nachtmusiken* are concerned. Paul Bekker advanced the idea of 'from dark to light' as a metaphor for understanding the progression from Mahler's Sixth to Seventh Symphony: 'The soul is stirred in its depth; it has proclaimed its joy and pain; and now it simply wants to sing again. The lonely one returns to nature, to the world, to man. This is the origin of the Seventh Symphony.'[16]

Bekker's interpretation was for long discredited—possibly because it was no longer of interest. Hence Hans Heinrich Eggebrecht's more recent evaluation of the second

---

[14] Zychowicz, 'Ein schlechter Jasager', 104.   [15] Alma Mahler, *Memories*, 89.
[16] Bekker, *Gustav Mahlers Sinfonien*, 233.

Nachtmusik seems all the more remarkable: 'Mahler walks through the town, in the evening, at night, and takes in all the music he can hear: happy violins, quivering mandolins, guitars and clarinets, the sounds of other instruments, Schrammel music, strummed pianos—and then he walks on, happy, filled with beauty. There is also the opera house, music from the Volkstheater; and at the end, the coffee houses close, the music fades, the lights go out, night falls.'[17] There is no question that Eggebrecht's impressions are evocative; yet they contradict the immanent musical structure of the movement. The opening of the first *Nachtmusik* consists of horns echoing to each other, which evokes the idea of space as a kind of 'Naturlaut' (sound of Nature). Parallels with the third movement of Berlioz' *Symphonie fantastique*, 'Scène aux champs', are obvious. However, the basic idea of 'call' and 'answer' develops into a turmoil which results at the climax in a temporary breakdown (two bars before Fig. 72)—a rapid falling from a light to a dark timbre, combined with a sudden change from C major to C minor. The music is no longer able to resist its own inner dynamic. This pattern is repeated twice: in the middle of the movement (Fig. 91), and in the final bars. Thus we find a situation similar to the contrast of different keys and timbres in the Rondo-Finale noted above. The end of the first *Nachtmusik* exemplifies this ambivalence: horn, clarinet, and flute create a mingled texture of rudimentary motives suggesting bird calls ('Wie Vogelstimmen'; flute 1, two bars after Fig. 108), fanfare-like fragments, and even elements of a march-like character (oboe 1, two bars before Fig. 110). The major–minor contrast (see Ex. 15.5: trumpets and woodwind, Fig. 111) is combined with an abrupt change from a rising to a falling progression (first violins), resulting in an extreme contrast of orchestral timbres in the final three bars. Of course, the combination of cymbals (*pp*, with soft sticks), tam-tam (*pp*),[18] and the low C of two horns blurs any impression of a distinct pitch, and contrasts with the sustained trill on *g″* in the second violins and the same pitch on the harp and the flageolet note of the cellos. Although the tam-tam often functions as a symbol of death in the symphonic tradition of the nineteenth century (as well as in Mahler's symphonies),[19] the juxtaposition of orchestral timbres seems to take priority here, giving the impression of wide, almost infinite space. The refining of contrasts and ambivalence of timbre becomes a significant compositional principle. Berlioz, who used a similar combination of very high and very low registers (flutes and pedal notes in the trombones) in the 'Hostias' of his *Requiem*, drew attention to the special effect produced by the 'immense interval' between these two groups of instruments.[20] György Ligeti's 'Atmosphères', 'Lux aeterna', 'Lontano', and 'San Francisco Polyphony' are the more recent examples of exploiting such 'intervals' or gaps as a means of creating musical space.

Ambiguity penetrates even the basic musical material, especially the thematic structure. The impression of perpetual unrest through the intrusion of disturbing interjections often displays conventional elements of syntax. A good example of this can be seen in the second

---

[17] Hans Heinrich Eggebrecht, *Die Musik Gustav Mahlers* (Munich: Piper, 1982), 50.

[18] In his *Treatise*, Berlioz describes cymbals struck with soft sticks as producing 'a long, vibrant and sinister sound',

and the *pp* strokes of the tam-tam as 'frightening' and 'lugubrious' in character (p. 395).

[19] Floros, *Gustav Mahler*, ii. 311–17.

[20] Berlioz, *Treatise*, 300.

Ex. 15.5. Seventh Symphony, end of first *Nachtmusik*

Ex. 15.6. Seventh Symphony, second *Nachtmusik*, bb. 84–92

Nachtmusik (Ex. 15.6). Antecedent and consequent phrases no longer correspond but oppose one another. The notion of the period as an overall framework (eight-bar sentences) is preserved and yet broken: most significant is the part of the solo violin marked *melancolisch* (melancholically). Bars 89 and 90 may easily be understood as the beginning of the consequent phrase. From bar 91 onwards, however, it becomes evident that it cannot be a consequent phrase in the traditional sense. The second sequential figure disturbs the idea of a theme, and the evaporation of the *veloce* ending is the logical consequence of the preceding material: the theme remains open. Moreover, the extreme contrast between the antecedent and consequent phrases is interrupted by the underlying harmonies. The folk-song-like diatonic accompaniment of the antecedent phrase stands in direct contrast to the pizzicato chords of the cellos in the consequent phrase, which form a chromatic progression. Undoubtedly this contrast is related to the expression mark in bar 89. The term *melancolisch* refers to the melancholy reality of life which intrudes on the dreamlike atmosphere of folklore that characterizes an untroubled idyll. As in some of Eichendorff's poems, Mahler seems to envisage a poetic idyll in which the ideal state of being is withdrawal from the immediate reality of life. The threat permanently endangering a 'secure' world, or the illusion of a 'safe existence resting in itself'[21] (as represented by simple and regular procedures of musical structure), is also a significant phenomenon in the first and third movements.

The Scherzo, characterized by Mahler as 'schattenhaft' (shadowy), slowly develops from an extremely distorted structure. At the very beginning, separate notes on the strings and timpani gradually join together in an unstable pulse. The genesis of musical context itself becomes a main idea of these first bars. In bar 11, the flutes (*sf*) signal the change from purely metrical to motivic organization, which is continued in the triplets of the violins (bb. 13 ff.). However, a continuous thematic outline is more or less suspended. Rising motivic fragments fail to constitute a coherent thematic entity. Thus emergence and dissociation of motivic or thematic structures are closely related—as in the Scherzo of the Second Symphony, as well as in, for instance, Ravel's 'La Valse'. The description 'schattenhaft' seems to be more than fanciful. Constantin Floros points out that it suggests a ghost-like, frightening, and gloomy atmosphere, as well as danger and incomprehensibility.[22] From a less imaginative point of view, it reflects to the last detail the narrative potential of the movement. As in some surreal scene, motivic fragments are whirled about, and whole segments of more complex thematic unities are often suddenly cut off. Restless haste and frequent collapse are characteristic of this movement. Indeed, the Scherzo offers paradigms of Adorno's concept of 'Zusammenbruch' (the 'breakdown' or 'collapse' of musical structure) as a basic formal principle, especially in Mahler's late symphonies.[23] The distortion of orchestral colouring, mentioned earlier, is an integral part of these 'breakdowns': two passages, for instance, are marked *kreischend* (screaming); 5 bars after Fig. 130, and at Fig. 161 (see Ex. 15.7). Whereas these episodes in the *Nachtmusiken* hardly affect the continuity of the music, in the Scherzo they precipitate violent and piercing departures from the dominating principle of a restless perpetuum mobile. The collapse of musical energy in Fig. 161 leads to an act of violence (*fffff* in the cellos and double basses) as well as paving the way for a new beginning. Thus the entire form of this movement emphasizes its fragmentary nature. The end of the Scherzo (Fig. 171 f.) consists more or less of motivic splinters, pure accentuation of the metre, and the remnants of two dance-like themes. Bruno Walter's characterization of the second movement of Mahler's Ninth Symphony ('The dance is over')[24] might well be applied to this Scherzo. In both movements an assembly of disconnected fragments leads to the total disintegration of musical structure.

---

[21] Jens Tismar, *Gestörte Idyllen* (Munich, 1973), 7.
[22] Floros, *Gustav Mahler*, iii. 199.
[23] Adorno, *Mahler*, esp. ch. 2.

[24] Walter, *Gustav Mahler*, trans. Lotte Walter Lindt (London: Quartet Books, 1990), 110.

Ex. 15.7. Seventh Symphony, Scherzo, bb. 394–409

*) So stark anreißen. daß die Saiten an das Holz anschlagen

Ex. 15.8. Seventh Symphony, 1st movt., bb. 1–2

Mahler's well-known description of the introduction to the first movement ('here nature roars') and the source for its inspiration ('oars of a boat rising and falling') may give us more than a merely metaphorical clue to its composition. Mahler himself apparently pointed out that the initial rhythm inspires and permeates the musical material of the entire exposition. Thus the repeated rhythmic cell shown in Ex. 15.8 is not a subordinate idea—a kind of background from which the theme of the tenor horn emerges: on the contrary, it has an integral function and serves as a structural nucleus and generator of different thematic and/or motivic elements. It is most instructive to pursue the variety of shapes which emerge from this punctuated rhythm (see Ex. 15.9). Beethoven was amongst the first who extensively exploited the dramatic potential of such repeated rhythmic modules. In the first movement of his Seventh Symphony the slow introduction ends on a single note (E), played in different registers, which is then gradually transformed from repeated semiquavers to a punctuated pattern that serves as a fundamental structure in the following 'Vivace'

Ex. 15.9. Seventh Symphony, rhythmic cell in 1st movt.: (*a*) bb. 1–4; (*b*); bb. 14–18

Ex. 15.9. (c) bb. 49–55; (d) bb. 193–4; (e) bb. 258–63; (f) bb. 455–64

Ex. 15.10. Beethoven, Seventh Symphony, 1st movt., bb. 58–68

(see Ex. 15.10). The main theme evolves from the basic rhythm, and thus it is hard to define the point where it actually begins. Some analysts claim at bar 67: but in fact there it receives a distinct melodic shape whose origin can be clearly traced back to the purely rhythmic pattern in bar 63.

Mahler employed this technique as well. In the first movement of his Third Symphony, for instance, themes often evolve from basic rhythmic models (especially marches). Paul Bekker, drawing attention to its 'forward progression . . . and generation in the process of permanent transformation', concluded: 'Thus the most large-scale movement of the "Wunderhorn" Symphonies, the first movement of the Third, is characterized by a musical and formal representation of "generation". The musical symbolization of this process could not be expressed more clearly than in Mahler's heading "Marching. Without stopping" as an implicit motto to the entire movement.'[25]

Whilst Adorno dwells on the colouring of the orchestral technique in the first movement of the Seventh Symphony, 'from the most luminous super major to the darkest shadows',[26] Floros points to its wide range of musical forms, from funeral march to visionary chorale.[27]

[25] Bekker, *Gustav Mahlers Sinfonien*, 212.
[26] Adorno, *Quasi una Fantasia*, 91; for Adorno's definition of a 'super major' see ibid. 137.
[27] Floros, *Gustav Mahler*, iii. 189.

Ex. 15.11. Seventh Symphony, 1st movt., bb. 309–19

Ex. 15.11 (*cont.*)

Ex. 15.11 (*cont.*)

The shifting contexts, varying tempi, and contrasts in orchestral timbre, all generated by
the initial rhythmic figure, have obviously contributed to ambivalent responses to this
movement. As a recurring element, the rhythm reconciles contrasting musical expressions,
thus serving a crucial function in providing structural coherence. One of the most striking
episodes of contrast is the B major passage marked 'Sehr breit' (very broad), beginning at
bar 317 and introduced by a significant glissando on the harp (see Ex. 15.11). It is an extraordinary moment in the symphony which attracted special attention even in the reviews of
the first performance. One reason for this might be the sudden widening of the orchestral
texture, suggesting an unexpected brightening of musical colour. As Hermann Danuser
has shown, several early reviewers described the atmosphere of this episode in metaphorical terms of light, beauty, heaven, and peace.[28] The entirely different musical world of this
B major section and its transcendental characterization afford us considerable insight into
the contemporary habits of listening. In spite of the contrasts, however, this passage reveals
many structural connections with its preceding parts. Danuser draws attention to the fact
that it is prepared by a gradual reduction in tempo (Fig. 37) and a chorale-like brass passage (bb. 310 ff.). Considered in its entire context, then, the association of this episode with
light, peace, and heaven becomes more understandable. Danuser's interpretation of the B
major section as a synthesis of contrasting ideas also clarifies the role of the very opening
punctuated rhythm: again it functions as a generator of context. Having introduced the
symphony in sober and gloomy hues, the rhythmic module is here first transformed into a
fanfare on the trumpets (Fig. 37), and then taken up by the oboes, flutes, and first clarinet
alternating with chorale-like fragments in the bassoons (Fig. 38). Only seven bars later
(and three bars into the B major episode), the rhythmic cell reappears in more or less its
original colouring (trumpets in b. 319; oboes, flutes, and clarinet in b. 320; two horns and
two flutes in b. 321). Thus the evidence of contrast is offset by a concise and comprehensible texture of motivic and rhythmic relations—a feature most clearly perceived by
Schoenberg.[29] It is this also that underwrites the fascinating coherence of a 'world' which
Mahler claimed to build by means of music.

---

[28] Danuser, 'Erkenntnis oder Verblendung?', 109–10.   [29] See above, n. 11.

16

Mahler in Prague (1908)

DONALD MITCHELL

To Herta Blaukopf

One of the most remarkable accounts of any première of a Mahler symphony was that written by the French-speaking Swiss critic and writer William Ritter (1867–1955), who had attended the rehearsals and first performance (on 19 September) of the Seventh in Prague in 1908. I used extensive excerpts from Ritter's vivid recollections in the commentary on the reception of the Seventh when I contributed to the publication of the facsimile of the autograph of the symphony, one of the many publications that marked the occasion of the Mahler Festival held in Amsterdam in 1995, seventy-five years on from the first great international Mahler festival of 1920, when Mengelberg conducted a complete cycle of the symphonies and song-cycles. It was indeed to Mengelberg in 1920 that Alma was to make a gift of the autograph of the Seventh.[1]

One passage in Ritter's text claimed my attention especially, where he describes the sometimes bizarre circumstances amid which Mahler was obliged to hold his rehearsals, 'taking place as they did in a hall which doubled as a banqueting hall'.[2] Ritter continues:

Here, while the Master and orchestra were making strenuous efforts to rehearse on a very steep platform, the waiters would be laying the tables. Some of them were no more than young rapscallions, inattentive either to music or to any kind of discipline, and for whom music was just another form

I am much indebted to the following for their assistance in assembling the information, textual and graphic, that I have put together in this chapter: Herta Blaukopf (Vienna), who set me off on this trail of investigation; Graham Melville-Mason (London and Prague), without whose unrivalled knowledge and collaboration I would have made little headway; Knud Martner (Copenhagen), who contributed some vital pieces to the jigsaw; Dr Jitka Ludvová (Prague), who generously shared with me the results of her own inquiries into the circumstances surrounding the première of the Seventh (see also below, n. 3); Dr Jan Hozák, Chief Archivist of the National Technical Museum of Prague; Dr Zdeněk Míka, Director of the Prague City Museum; and Mr Jiří Štilec (Prague). Finally, two sources which have proved invaluable: Vladimir Lébl's note of 1981 that accompanies Václav Neumann's CD of the Seventh, with the Czech Philharmonic (Supraphon 11 1978-2 912), and a new publication from Dr Ludvová, *Gustav Mahler a Praha* (Prague: Ustar pro Hudební vědu Akademie věd ČR, 1996) (text in Czech and German).

[1] *Gustav Mahler: Facsimile Edition of the Seventh Symphony*, Bernard Haitink, Donald Mitchell, and Edward R. Reilly (Amsterdam: Rosbeek Publishers, 1995).

[2] Ibid., 'Reception', 34.

of excitement. The restaurant manager, meanwhile, a very rich and very coarse type of Czech indus-
trialist, evidently regarded himself more the master of the house than the wretched conductor . . .[3]

What sort of concert hall *was* this?, I wondered; and in hastening to come up with an
answer, came up with the wrong one. In short, the hall I both mention and illustrate in the
commentary on the facsimile (pp. 34–5)—the 'Obecní dům' (Civic Hall), a magnificent
example of Art Nouveau built between 1905 and 1911—was *not* where the Seventh was
given its first performance.[4] To be sure, it must have been under construction in 1908,
when it is more than probable that Mahler passed it by on one of those patrols through the
streets of Prague, when indeed he was often in Ritter's company. In any event, he must have
felt thoroughly at home in Prague, a city that must have constantly reminded him of Vienna
and his friends and acquaintances among the *Secession* group of artists and designers.[5]

While, as it turns out, we have long been able to enjoy a glimpse of the *interior* of the hall
where the Seventh was given its première—the photograph of a rehearsal there under

[3] Ritter continues, later: 'It sometimes even became necessary, when some banquet or other took precedence over a particular rehearsal at the last minute, to move into town, to the Merkur Society's hall, much too small a venue for the orchestra of the Seventh, which requires a very large number of players.' This wholly correct observation raises an issue with regard to the photograph reproduced in the facsimile edition, p. 41, where, besides getting the location wrong, I—along with virtually everybody else—refer to it as the occasion of a rehearsal of the Seventh. But a count of the players assembled on the platform, even a necessarily imperfect one, given the quality of the photograph, shows us an orchestra of between 65 and 70 players, well below the strength of resources required for the Seventh. In 1908, Mahler conducted *two* Philharmonic concerts in Prague, one on 23 May, the opening of the Exhibition series, the other on 19 Sept. (the Seventh's première), closing the series; and Dr Jitka Ludvová has confirmed in a private communication that the photograph in question was taken when Mahler was rehearsing for the *first* of the two concerts, when the programme (Beethoven's Seventh (!), and overtures by Smetana and Wagner) could have been undertaken by an orchestra of the size we see before us. In her important article, 'Gustav Mahler im Prag im Mai 1908', published (in German) in *Hudební věda*, 23/3 (1986), 255–62, with 8 pp. of plates (including a different shot from Pl. 16.6 of the exterior of the Concert Pavilion), Dr Ludvová refers to the make-up of what, in the Mahler literature, is generally referred to as the Czech Philharmonic Orchestra. In fact, however, the orchestra was recruited from two sources, i.e. the fifty players of the Czech Philharmonic, strengthened by the addition of sixteen players from the German community in Prague (drawn, other commentators have suggested, from the orchestra of the Neues Deutsches Theater). These figures give us a total of 66, something surely very close to the orchestra in the May 1908 photograph. But there must have been strenuous further recruitment before September, for the first performance of the Seventh, when, it is reported, Mahler requested that the orchestra be expanded to 100, if

his new symphony were to be undertaken. (One wonders how on earth an orchestra of that size was accommodated on what seems to have been a platform area of relatively modest dimensions.)

Also of exceptional interest in Dr Ludvová's article is the brief account she gives of the clash of nationalist zeal reflected respectively in the German press, the leading paper of which ignored the presence of the Czech Philharmonic, while the Czech press made no reference to the additional resource provided by German musicians: the resulting hybrid was named 'Exhibition Orchestra' [*Ausstellungsorchester*], occupying, as it were, neutral territory. In fact, politically coloured controversy was stimulated by the choice of Mahler to conduct the first Exhibition concert. One is reminded of course of the rise of potent nationalisms at the beginning of the new century and the proximity of the First World War. Interesting too that in the 1990s we witness an upgrading of the importance of the 'Bohemian' dimension in Mahler's music, a dimension long undervalued and underexplored, recognition of the musical significance of which is long overdue.

[4] The concert hall on the upper floor is known today as the 'Smetana Hall'. It was my recollection of that hall—the interior of which offers yet another example of Art Nouveau (as I write the whole building is undergoing comprehensive restoration and conservation)—and my confusing it with the photograph of Mahler rehearsing in the hall where the première *did* take place, that led to my erroneous description, for which I now attempt to make amends.

[5] As Ritter himself writes (see the facsimile edn., p. 37), 'Mahler seemed to take a genuine pleasure in accompanying us on several walks across the old parts of Prague which he knew so well and were associated with so many memories of the time when (between 1885 and 1888) he was also director [*recte*, chief conductor] of the German Theatre [Deutsches Theater]. Photographs from this time transport us back to some of these walks and our route under the Prašná brána [a medieval gate-tower adjoining [NB] the Obecní dům]'.

Pl. 16.1. The Concert Pavilion in the Exhibition grounds in which Mahler's Seventh Symphony was given its première in Prague on 19 September 1908

Mahler has been widely reproduced in the Mahler literature (see the facsimile edition of the Seventh; Gilbert E. Kaplan; Jitka Ludvová; Henry-Louis de La Grange, *et al.*)—there has been a conspicuous absence, in any generally accessible publication, of a photograph of the *exterior* of the hall. With the help of many friends and colleagues and institutions in Prague I am able to reproduce as Pl. 16.1 in my dossier of illustrations a photograph of the Koncertní síň (Concert Pavilion)[6] where the Seventh was launched.

This handsome timber hall, apparently with good acoustics, the architect of which was Josef Zasche, was built in the grounds of the Exhibition mounted by the Prague Chamber of Commerce and Crafts to mark the Jubilee of Franz Josef I (1830–1916), the ruler of the Austro-Hungarian Empire: 1908 was the sixtieth year of his accession to the throne. The Concert Pavilion, designed to accommodate an accompanying series of concerts and with a seating capacity of 1,500, is now demolished, hence the importance of the photographic

---

[6] Therefore this designation should replace all other named descriptions of the hall throughout the facsimile.

Pl. 16.2. The Jubilee Exhibition buildings (1908) as they stand today. Photographs: Donald Mitchell, 1996

documentation. It was an addition to the existing buildings in the exhibition grounds in Hološovice (Prague, 7), imposing edifices originally constructed in 1891 and still standing today. They are again magnificent examples, within and without, of architecture and decoration conceived in the spirit and style of Art Nouveau. Photographs taken in the summer of 1996 (see Pl. 16.2) I hope give some indication of the design of these remarkable buildings, the centenary of which was itself celebrated with an exhibition in 1991. Pl. 16.3, a ground plan of the 1908 Jubilee Exhibition, shows exactly where the Concert Pavilion (No. 42) was sited in relation to neighbouring buildings and halls, while Pl. 16.4

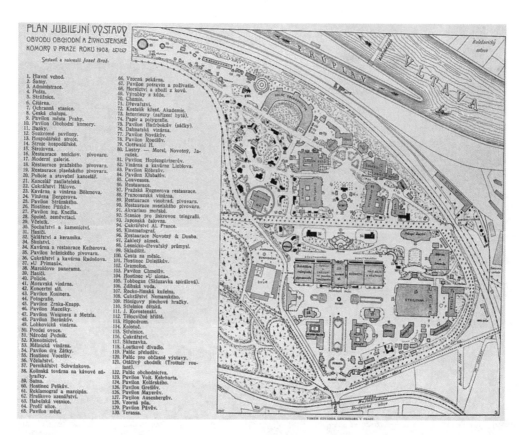

Pl. 16.3. A ground plan of the Jubilee
Exhibition of 1908, showing the exact
location of the Concert Pavilion (No. 42
'Koncertní síň')

Pl. 16.4. The title-page of a guide to the
Jubilee Exhibition of 1908

Pl. 16.5. Stereophotograph of the interior of the Concert Pavilion, showing the hall laid out for dining

Pl. 16.6. Stereophotograph of the exterior of the Concert Pavilion, showing some of the staff (waiters?) remarked upon by William Ritter

reproduces the title-page of a Guide to the Jubilee Exhibition: the photograph on the title-page shows the main Exhibition buildings for 1891 and features the Palace of Industry (cf. also Pl. 16.2).

Plate 16.5 returns us to the interior of the hall, and brings incontrovertible confirmation that what Ritter wrote was astonishingly accurate. We can see for ourselves how the Concert

Pavilion, in stereophotographic form (a photographic technique of the period), doubled as a restaurant and concert hall. Interestingly, the interior shot with which we have been familiar for many years[7] reveals how the hall looked when the seating was in place for a performance. There is a useful reproduction of it in the *Mahler Album*,[8] though for reasons I have already outlined, there can now be no doubt that it was not a rehearsal of the Seventh that Mahler was taking. (The Concert Pavilion, incidentally, was the only new building commissioned from a *German* architect. I owe this information to Herta Blaukopf, the distinguished Viennese scholar to whom this chapter is dedicated, who, in a private communication, went on to point out that the Jubilee Exhibition of 1908 was an 'eminently political event' organized by the 'Prager Handelskammer [Prague Chamber of Commerce], maybe the last society with Czech *and* German members. [...] A few weeks after the first performance of the Seventh the situation became so critical that martial law was imposed over Prague. I am sure that Mahler was aware that he conducted on top of a volcano.')

Finally, for good measure, Pl. 16.6 shows a stereophotograph of the façade of the hall, a view that supplements the information provided by Pl. 16.1. Might it be that some members of the standing group, both young and old, seemingly attired as waiters, and holding what?—napkins? table linen?—represent the bustling, noisy banqueting staff who got on Mahler's nerves during the rehearsals of his new symphony in Prague, in September 1908?

---

[7] See above, n. 3.   [8] Edited by Gilbert Kaplan (New York: The Kaplan Foundation, Harry N. Abrams, Inc., 1995).

Pl. 16.7. Decorative stamp produced for the Jubilee Exhibition of 1908. (Courtesy of Knud Martner)

17

The Eighth Symphony

JOHN WILLIAMSON

Mahler's Eighth Symphony presents the greatest possible contrast to its immediate predecessor. The use of vast choral forces (and consequently of literary texts) is the most obvious aspect of this departure. No less notable is the peculiar layout of the work. Whereas the Seventh followed a recognizable Mahlerian pattern of two weighty movements enclosing a group of shorter intermezzi, the Eighth simply presents two long movements set to texts whose relationship functions on several levels. Stylistically, there are points of contact between the Seventh and the Eighth, notably in the use of march rhythms in the first movements, and in the types of harmony and counterpoint employed. Both works tend to grow more markedly diatonic as they progress to their conclusion. But against these features, there is a wide spectrum of stylistic divergence, especially if the second part of the Eighth is contrasted with the more brittle aspects of the Seventh. Tonally the Seventh 'progresses' (to use a tendentious term) from B minor and E minor to C major; the Eighth remains firmly anchored to E flat major. Most problematically, the Eighth diverges from the Seventh and all Mahler's symphonies in its approach to form, particularly in the second part. Traditionally this has been described as a conflation of Adagio, Scherzo, and Finale: but in retrospect this notion is so foolish as to leave the Mahlerian marvelling at the longevity which bad ideas may possess.[1] Superficially the Eighth seems to renew the manner of the Second Symphony, particularly in its ending, but even this comparison leads to a number of stylistic differences.

If precedents for the Eighth in earlier composers are to be sought, it is difficult to find works which may have influenced it (apart from the often-cited *Faust-Symphonie* of Liszt and Schumann's *Szenen aus Goethes Faust*). It is possible to detect the influence of individual genres but this is not the same as placing the work in a genre. Inasmuch as several later works seem to reflect the precedent of the Eighth, it is tempting to regard it as the beginning of a new genre. It is not quite enough to say that this is a different type of choral symphony. Alongside later vocal symphonies by Szymanowski, Britten, Shostakovich,

---

[1] The origin of this description of the Eighth Symphony is Richard Specht, *Gustav Mahlers VIII. Symphonie: Thematische Analyse* (Leipzig and Vienna: Universal Edition, 1912), 4 and 33.

Havergal Brian, and others, there are cantatas—such as Pfitzner's two works of the 1920s, *Von deutscher Seele* and *Das dunkle Reich*[2]—that seem to have similarities of approach to the Eighth Symphony. But many of these works do not simply stem from the Eighth. It would be truer to say that the Eighth and *Das Lied von der Erde*, taken together, constitute the biggest single reservoir of ideas about blending symphonic and vocal elements outside Wagner's music dramas. While *Das Lied von der Erde* is usually viewed alongside the Ninth and Tenth Symphonies as part of a late trilogy, it would be unwise to disregard the many relationships between it and the Eighth (as is evidenced by Donald Mitchell's decision in his multi-volume study of Mahler to consider the two works together in the same volume).[3]

From the musicologist's point of view, difficulties with the Eighth begin with the scant-iness of sources for its composition and revision. Although the situation with regard to sketches and revisions is not quite so bad as it was some years ago, there is still compara-tively little material available to reinforce the various accounts of the Eighth's composition that can be gleaned from letter and memoir sources. Traditionally, Mahler's work on the Eighth Symphony was a single outburst of inspiration in the summer of 1906. As sketched by Alma, this picture has a double significance. Mahler's most positive work represented a last oasis of triumph and peace before the disasters of 1907, the black year from which stemmed the much more introspective works of Mahler's final period. Alongside that went a rather more symbolic appropriateness. According to Alma's account, Mahler arrived at Maiernigg to begin his summer's composing only to be afflicted (as happened 'nearly every year') by 'the spectre of failing inspiration'.[4] That he should have been rescued from this by the words of the hymn *Veni creator spiritus* (attributed then to Hrabanus Maurus but now relegated to 'author unknown') seemed a peculiarly apt stroke of fortune. Even more appropriate was the 'superhuman energy' with which he worked on his symphony, in spite of the need to break off at one point to conduct Mozart's *Figaro* in Salzburg. Even there the obsession would not leave him as Julius Korngold noted: Mahler carried his 'much-thumbed' copy of Goethe's *Faust* in his pocket. The closing scene of that most celebrated of German dramas supplied the text for Part II of the symphony as *Veni creator spiritus* shaped Part I.

From various other witnesses there is evidence to support Alma's picture. Mahler himself speaks of the work as the product of eight weeks from the moment that 'the *Spiritus Creator* took hold of me'.[5] In his examination of the various accounts of the work's genesis, Constantin Floros expands that period to ten weeks, from the middle of June to the end of August.[6] The various dates given in Mahler's correspondence suggest very strongly that the sketching of the work was essentially complete when Mahler set out for Salzburg in

[2] For the relationship of *Von deutscher Seele* to the Eighth Symphony, see Rudolf Stephan, 'Hans Pfitzners Eichendorff-Kantate *Von deutscher Seele*', *Mitteilungen der Hans-Pfitzner-Gesellschaft*, 50 (1989), 5–21.

[3] See Mitchell, *SSLD*.

[4] Alma Mahler, *Memories*, 102.

[5] Ibid. 328. In fact Mahler had long been seized by Goethe's German translation of 'Veni Creator'; this, indeed, was how Mahler first became acquainted with it. Thus in a

very real and unifying sense the conjunction of the two texts—the hymn and *Faust*—has its origins in Goethe. See Mitchell, 'Mahler: Symphony No. 8', in *GMWL*, 2.89, n. 12; Dieter Borchmeyer, 'Gustav Mahler's Goethe and Goethe's Holy Ghost', *News about Mahler Research*, no. 32 (Oct. 1994); and the programme book of the 1920 Mahlerfeest in Amsterdam, pp. 210–11.

[6] Floros, *Gustav Mahler: The Symphonies*, 216.

mid-August. What remained to be done on his return was to elaborate the sketch into a more sophisticated (presumably short) score. Richard Specht gives an even shorter time for the sketching of the work; according to Mahler's conversation with him, three weeks was all the time required to sketch 'eine ganz neue Sinfonie'.[7] The various estimates of the exact number of weeks are immaterial; what is common to all is that a massive work was brought forth as though the *creator spiritus* spoke through Mahler in one spontaneous burst. The most amusing reflection of this is the preservation by Alban Berg of a piece of toilet paper on which Mahler had sketched the first four bars of the 'Chorus mysticus' from Part II!

One detail which slightly alters our perception of this composition process is the list of titles provided by Paul Bekker for the initial stages of the work.[8] In these, the first movement is familiar enough from the completed work; what follows, however, requires some interpretation to fit into the final scheme:

1. *Hymne Veni creator*
2. *Scherzo*
3. *Adagio Caritas*
4. *Hymne: die Geburt des Eros*

A second version of this reverses the order of the middle movements (if we must think of them as such) and refers to the titles as:

1. *Veni creator*
2. *Caritas*
3. *Weinachtspiele mit dem Kindlein*
4. *Schöpfung durch Eros. Hymne*[9]

The idea of a slow movement entitled *Caritas* had already surfaced in some movement titles connected with the Fourth Symphony. That it had a connection with Mahler's concept of the closing scene of *Faust* will become evident later. The notion of 'games with the [Christ]child' is not impossible to square with the role that the younger angels have in the same scene. Even the reference to Eros seems to belong in Mahler's picture of Goethe's famous scene, though not quite in the way that either of the titles suggests. This famous draft has rightly attracted the attention of commentators searching for the key to the work, and in particular to what connection Mahler saw between his two disparate sources, an anonymous mediaeval hymn and Goethe. But it also suggests at a very tentative level that the genesis of the Symphony was not quite so spontaneous as the traditional picture allows. If we are to accept that somewhere in titles two to four a Goethean setting lies hidden, they still do not suggest a complete setting of the closing scene of *Faust II*; a Faustian movement is not necessarily the equivalent of the mighty Part II of Mahler's final conception. The titles also suggest that the traditional picture of Part II as a conflation of movements is a distortion of a diachronic process: the traditional three movements gave way to Part II, and a certain ideological substratum was retained from them.

[7] Cited in Gustav Mahler, *Sämtliche Werke*, viii: *Symphonie Nr. 8*, ed. Karl Heinz Füssl (Vienna: Universal Edition, 1977), p. iv.

[8] Bekker, *Gustav Mahlers Sinfonien*, 273.
[9] For the history of this second list of titles, see Mitchell, *SSLD*, 529–30, and HLG(F) iii. 1079–80.

The second version of the titles was originally associated with some thematic sketchings, the fullest account of which is provided by Alfred Rosenzweig.[10] From what can be deduced about these now lost sketches, it is possible to conclude that the opening of *Caritas* may have been the opening of Part II. It also appears that the whole work was based on a theme originally conceived in F sharp major (not E flat major). Donald Mitchell has further suggested that the real origin of the 'Games' scherzo was a pair of 'Wunderhorn' poems which appear on the reverse of a leaf on which Mahler arranged some strophes of 'Veni creator spiritus'.[11] So convincing does this seem that it is possible now to see the origin of the work rather more clearly than is apparent in the earliest accounts. Most of Mahler's symphonies had rather complicated geneses. The Eighth Symphony is quite consistent with this; where it differs would appear to be in the speed with which Mahler reorientated himself from one conception to another. That sketches which were known to Rosenzweig in 1933 should have disappeared is a yardstick for how little is still known about the Eighth's creation. To Alma, the work ended a period of uncertainty:

From the Fifth onwards he found it impossible to satisfy himself; the Fifth was differently orchestrated for practically every performance; the Sixth and Seventh were continually in process of revision. It was a phase. His self-assurance returned with the Eighth, and although *Das Lied von der Erde* is posthumous I cannot imagine his altering a note in a work so economical in its means of expression.[12]

Yet thanks to the researches of Donald Mitchell and Paul Banks, it is now clear that Mahler did revise the Eighth at a late stage.[13] The history of the symphony remains sketchy, a paradoxical state for a work that seems almost overpowering in its certainty.

Perhaps the best-known incident in the Eighth's early history is the affair of the missing stanzas, as related by Alma Mahler and the musicologist Ernst Decsey. In the course of the flood of inspiration which produced *Veni creator spiritus*, Mahler discovered that 'music and words did not fit in—the music had overlapped the text'.[14] Further evidence for this comes in Mahler's letters to Friedrich Löhr demanding an authentic text (as well as a good translation and advice on scansion).[15] When the missing stanzas arrived, Mahler discovered that 'the complete text fitted the music exactly', or (in Decsey's words), 'to his boundless astonishment, that the words fitted the music exactly, that he had composed too much from a sense of form: each of the new words slotted into the whole without effort'.[16] As wonderful as this story is, it is not immune to scepticism (witness Donald Mitchell's interpretation of it in his account of the symphony).[17] This story assumes a slightly different aspect, however, when another factor is taken into account; both texts of the work were set by Mahler with

---

[10] Rosenzweig's account is reproduced in Mitchell, *SSLD*, 635–7. A remarkable collection of writings by Rosenzweig and related documents surfaced in London in 1998. Enquiries should be addressed to the Librarian of the Guildhall School of Music and Drama.

[11] Ibid. 531–2.

[12] Alma Mahler, *Memories*, 143.

[13] See e.g. Mitchell, *SSLD*, 569.

[14] Decsey, 'Stunden mit Mahler', 353–4; Alma Mahler, *Memories*, 102.

[15] Mahler, *Selected Letters*, 291–2.

[16] Decsey, 'Stunden mit Mahler', 353–4; Alma Mahler, *Memories*, 102.

[17] Mitchell, *SSLD*, 524–5.

some licence in the form of reordering, inclusion, and omission. For some commentators, this aspect is so drastic as to demand explanation, not all of it favourable to Mahler.

The most pungent criticism of Mahler's approach to his texts in the Eighth Symphony comes in Hans Mayer's article 'Musik und Literatur'.[18] His target is not so much the Eighth Symphony as the significance of Mahler's literary taste as a whole, which seemed to be in as piteous a condition as the ghost in *Hamlet*. To wish to combine the two texts of the Eighth Symphony seemed an 'absurdity—both theologically and poetically', but was of a piece with Mahler's approach to literature in general.[19] Central to his argument was Mahler's own attempt to explain *Faust* to Alma. This account (in a letter of 1908) described Goethe's poetic drama in terms remarkably similar to those in which Mahler sometimes spoke of his own symphonies; *Faust* was a pyramid, 'a world . . . fashioned step by step' and leading to the final scene.[20] According to Mahler, 'the rational element' in artworks did not as a rule correspond to their 'true reality'. *Faust* emerges in his account as a mixture of the spontaneous (the operation of the *creator spiritus*, though Mahler does not specifically invoke the term) and the rational (at points where the poet was not clear as to his relationship to his goal). In the final scene, Goethe presents an allegory of 'the intransitory' as 'indescribable', with the Mater gloriosa as 'the personification of the eternal feminine'. The eternal feminine is in turn 'the resting-place' as opposed to masculine 'striving and struggling towards the goal'. In the closing lines, the 'Chorus mysticus', 'Goethe in person addresses his listeners' employing the 'beautiful and sufficient mythology' of Christianity. In the light of this letter, it is possible to speculate that Part I of the Eighth Symphony was viewed by Mahler as an invocation of that reality in art which only becomes fully attained at the apex of Goethe's pyramid in *Faust*. What is invoked is then revealed in Part II, if only in symbols.

Mayer attacked this passage as a mangling of at least four elements: Mahler's conception of *Faust* depended on viewing it as a theatre piece with an address to the spectators at the end (though Goethe hardly discouraged this partial view by beginning his drama with a 'prelude in the theatre'); he 'disowned' all Christian interpretation of the ending; he then used Christian motives to construct a profane message in which he also managed to identify himself with Goethe; the profane message thus created sat ill with a setting of *Veni creator spiritus*.[21] It is arguable that there is a fair amount of tendentious reading in Mayer's own interpretation, as has been suggested by other notable interpreters of Mahler such as Constantin Floros. As the latter points out, Mahler's vision of the 'Chorus mysticus' has as much to do with 'the meaning of the world (symbolically expressed)' as with an address to the spectators.[22] The remark about Mahler's renunciation of a Christian view of the end was something of a misreading. Yet Mahler's use of Christianity as mythology does leave the way open for readings of the Eighth Symphony according to other world-views (most obviously those of Schopenhauer and Nietzsche). And his invocation of 'the force of love'

---

[18] Hans Mayer, 'Musik und Literatur', in *Gustav Mahler* (Tübingen: Rainer Wunderlich, 1966), 142–56.

[19] Ibid. 149.

[20] Alma Mahler, *Memories*, 320–1.

[21] Mayer, 'Musik und Literatur', 146–9.

[22] Floros, *Gustav Mahler*, i. 52–3.

for the eternal feminine does leave open the question as to how far *eros* and *caritas* (to mix languages for the moment with Mahler's drafts) go together to make up this force.

The most sustained attempt to judge how far the notion of 'the birth of Eros' survived into the Eighth Symphony has been made by Constantin Floros, who suggested that Mahler probably derived the concept from the Classical *Walpurgisnacht* in Part II of *Faust*. When the scene is examined, however, the evidence seems decidedly slender, merely a chorus of sirens proclaiming the rule of Eros. While the connection should not automatically be dismissed, there is a more direct invocation of Eros in another letter from Mahler to Alma (this time from June 1910 and thus contemporary with the rehearsals for the first performances of the Eighth Symphony).[23] In this Mahler defined the nature of 'Platonic love' as 'Goethe's idea that all love is generative, creative, and that there is a physical and spiritual generation which is the emanation of this "Eros"'. Furthermore, this was 'presented symbolically' at the close of *Faust*: 'Eros as Creator of the world!' Whatever the role of the Classical *Walpurgisnacht* in shaping Mahler's reading of the whole work, the connection between creation (of life and the work of art), Eros, and the close of *Faust* seems clearly set out. This seems to offer a confirmation of the profane spirit in which Mahler may have read Goethe, though Floros has a further telling point, that Mahler abandoned his original antithesis of a *caritas* movement and a hymn to Eros because *Veni creator spiritus* and the humanistic *Faust* poem together offered the possibility of a comprehensive statement about love.[24]

Such a statement, however, was conditional on music's ability to bridge the gap between two seemingly antithetical poetic elements. Thematic unification had always been part of Mahler's vision of the symphony. Hardly any of his works lack some element of thematic transference between movements or parts. The Eighth was to be no exception, and in its final form reveals a multitude of thematic links. Two themes were to be of particular importance: the opening cry of *Veni creator spiritus* (Ex. 17.1) with its prominent fourths (an echo perhaps from the first movement of the Seventh but completely transformed), and the theme associated with the words 'Accende lumen sensibus' (Ex. 17.2). Each was to have a slightly different emphasis. The full thematic implications of the first idea were to be realized in Part I; thereafter it would function as a remembrance motive in Part II. 'Accende lumen sensibus' would be introduced in Part I but grow to full stature in Part II, where

Ex. 17.1. Eighth Symphony, Part I, bb. 1–4

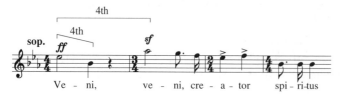

[23] Floros, *Gustav Mahler*, i. 130; Alma Mahler, *Memories*, 332.   [24] Floros, *Gustav Mahler*, i. 131.

Ex. 17.2. Eighth Symphony, Part I, bb. 262–5

aspects of it would infiltrate other themes and melodies (Ex. 17.3). In their relationship to each other, there would be little tension; the second theme would be an intensification of the first, growing out of the same motivic fourth. It is essential to stress that the relationship between these themes is not that of the conventional first and second subjects. While the first theme is indeed a first subject, the 'Accende' theme is not a second subject but rather a new idea introduced in mid-development. It belongs to a tradition of reserving important thematic contrasts until the development section that goes back at least as far as the 'Eroica' Symphony's first movement. Composers like Schumann and Mahler turned this into something approaching a distinct formal type. This in turn had quite a striking effect on the way sonata form was conceived. Here the issue serves as a useful introduction

Ex. 17.3. Eighth Symphony, Part II, themes related to 'Accende lumen sensibus': (*a*) bb. 4–7; (*b*) bb. 219–22; (*c*) bb. 780–3; (*d*) bb. 1249–52

to one of the major problems of the Eighth, how it relates to the traditional picture of the symphony.

Most of the controversy about how to describe the Eighth has centred on Part II. It has been fairly generally assumed that Part I is a sonata-form first movement, with the usual formal divisions. One or two commentators have noticed oddities in the movement. Schoenberg was impressed with the manner in which Mahler flouted conventional harmonic teaching by frequently landing on a second-inversion chord (of the tonic in particular) at important moments (such as the start of the recapitulation).[25] The passage of time has made this insight perhaps less startling. Among Mahler's contemporaries, Richard Strauss is a noted example of a composer who launches major tonal events on the second inversion (as at the start of the presentation of the rose sequence in *Der Rosenkavalier*), and other examples could doubtless be found, also in Mahler's music. More striking is the fact that the second subject first appears in D flat major, then in the subdominant, A flat major. Traditionally second subjects appear in the dominant, though from Beethoven onwards composers imported tonal strategies from the sphere of the minor mode and used key relationships with roots a third apart. The subdominant's place was usually episodic in the dominant or confirmatory in the coda. For better or worse, a fairly simple hermeneutic rule operates in music theory, equating the dominant with the active side of the tonal circle, the subdominant with the passive. Whether we follow this metaphor or not, Mahler's procedure is striking though not unprecedented in his own output. In the finale of the Sixth, a subdominant second subject is employed (D major in an A minor context), and passivity is hardly the most marked trait of that movement. It is essential then to approach the question of the key relationships of Part I of the Eighth with an open mind. In other respects, the subject groups seem conventionally divided into active motivic elements (the 'masculine' side of the work in the deplorable terminology that musicology has inherited from the nineteenth century) and more sustained melodic paragraphs.

Mahler's exposition of subject groups is far from conventional in other respects, embracing a return to E flat for more reference to the tonic, an excursion to D minor for something that might be development, and finally the return of the second subject in E flat with an overpowering cadence towards the tonic of that key: the 'towards' is important since Mahler wrenches away the final tonic in preparation for the true development section. It must be conceded that Mahler very seldom wrote a conventional exposition (and when he did in the opening movements of the First and Sixth Symphonies, he signalled strongly to this effect by adding conventional repeat marks). His attitude to sonata form was rather similar to his approach to literary texts. If Mayer's description of Mahler as a literary 'usurper' is to be retained, it might as well be extended to his use of form. Movement after movement in his oeuvre fragments, rebuilds, and cross-breeds formal types. In the Eighth, the most spectacular example of this is the incorporation of a lengthy fugue into the development section. The result of so cavalier an approach to form is inevitably that each Mahler

---

[25] Schoenberg, *Style and Idea*, 460.

first movement is unique in the manner in which it is constructed, thus generating uncertainty in commentators. It is hardly surprising that Mahler had little time for many analytical descriptions of his work when writers persistently tried to force his music into the old straitjacket.

To discuss Part I with any degree of confidence, it is essential to recognize that the shell of sonata form is secondary to the recurring appearance of E major, the key of the 'Accende lumen sensibus' theme. This happens in all three times, always with a degree of ceremony. At bar 262, the theme is presented first in an overpowering vocal unison; at bar 366, the earlier moment is recreated in the fugue (which is not just development, but a kind of double to the movement so far, replaying earlier events in new formal and contrapuntal contexts); and at bar 494, the key returns, this time without its associated theme, as part of a tonal motion, E flat major, A flat major, E major. The three most noticeable tonal areas of the movement are thus placed in close proximity; by contrast, the key of the dominant (B flat major) is hardly prominent, though it serves to prepare the final return of the tonic in the coda. The importance of A flat in this passage seems simple enough; through the enharmony A♭ = G♯ it mediates between E flat major and E. It is idle to think of such a tonal scheme in terms of conflict (a favoured metaphor for the sonata in much musical writing). Rather, a process of intensification seems to be at work. To set a hymn of praise, static and timeless, Mahler used a procedure which circles obstinately round certain fixed points. This is then amplified in Part II, where E major is associated with the Mater gloriosa and her herald, the Doctor Marianus (though she eventually sings in E flat; the two keys are not to be crudely separated—they adhere to the same idea). A consequence may be the slight feeling of irrelevance which haunts the more active, 'developmental' moments such as the orchestral interlude at Fig. 23. This music means business, in Mahler's most aggressively brittle manner, and it immediately evokes the atmosphere of the Sixth and Seventh Symphonies; but its function is unclear save as a reflection of the infirmity of human bodies as they perform a Mahlerian quick march in a confusing succession of time signatures. Otherwise, this music is not 'about' events; it invokes and praises in a way that is almost irrelevant to the sonata form it seems to resemble.

It is hardly surprising that Donald Mitchell interprets Part I more as a Bachian motet than a sonata (citing the specific example of 'Singet dem Herrn ein neues Lied', which Franz Schalk conducted in the concert of 7 December 1905 at which Mahler introduced his Fifth Symphony to Viennese audiences).[26] No other movement in his output conjures up such an impression of an elevated communal rite. When the Universe sang in earlier Mahler symphonies, it possessed a double significance that is lacking in Part I of the Eighth. The voices of creation were predominantly instrumental (save for those moments when the clinching or characterizing word was virtually unavoidable); and those voices embraced inarticulate Nature as landscape. Part I, by contrast, dwarfs the listener with the

---

[26] Mitchell, *SSLD*, 533–4; other writers have followed Hans F. Redlich in comparing the Eighth to the 17th-c. Salzburg Mass now attributed to Heinrich Ignaz Franz von Biber (formerly to Orazio Benevoli; see H. F. Redlich, *Bruckner and Mahler* (London: Dent, 1955), 213.

voices of humanity and excludes Nature entirely. Only at the start of Part II (as Isabelle Werck has noted) is Nature, with its gorges, caverns, and cliffs, granted a place.[27] It is in this opening that Mahler makes a transition from the 'music as message' defined by Floros to his own more recognizably all-embracing type of symphony.[28] Part II, then, becomes a kind of microcosm of the problems of Mahler reception in general. Its formal elusiveness holds a mirror up to the bewildering diversity of his output as a whole. Although the more 'symphonic' part in Mahlerian terms (in that it resembles a 'world'), it is the least 'symphonic' in the terms with which audiences are familiar. The argument that it conflates traditional movements in a sense is a desperate attempt to cover over the heterogeneity of Mahler's sources, among which music for the theatre figures prominently. Although Part II seems to offer another elevated message, its musical language owes considerably less than the superficially similar *Faust* music of Robert Schumann to communal rites such as distinguish mass and motet settings. Nor does it speak exclusively in terms of Wagnerian through-composition, since there are 'numbers', such as the 'arias' for the fathers, the music for the three penitents, and the Italianate 'operatic intermezzo' which announces the Mater gloriosa.

Mahler's type of symphony always did owe something to the theatre, as can be gauged by the number of theatrical metaphors that have been employed to describe it. The vehicle by which they were imported into the symphony was the cantata *Das klagende Lied*. Part II of the Eighth is about as far from being a cantata as *Das klagende Lied* is from being a symphony; what they have in common is their peculiarly hybrid condition. *Das klagende Lied* is symphonic in retrospect because of its premonitions of melodic, orchestral, and tonal features of Mahler's symphonies; also in a more general sense, since the listener may experience the same kind of symphonic sensations that possessed Nietzsche when listening to Wagner. Part II is symphonic because the listener has encountered so many of Mahler's gestures before in a symphonic context. That it also has traits of a cantata or a theatrical tableau merely points to the enormous acquisitive instinct of the Mahlerian symphony. Part I reminds us that Mahler's symphonies fed voraciously on many different forms, but Part II also underlines the manner in which different genres and media contributed to the 'universality' of the Mahlerian symphony. A wash of through-composition conceals the recognizable outlines of arias, trios, and choruses, which are the defining points in a digressive re-enactment of the tonal scheme of Part I.

This is reflected in the roles of B♭ and E in Part II, and also in the large-scale references to Part I. A good instance is the parallel between bars 135–68 of Part I and 540–79 of Part II. The latter is a fairly close recapitulation of the former, both beginning with plunges into D minor. In Part I, the music frames the text 'Infirma nostri corporis / Virtute firmans perpeti', growing in strength from the 'bodily infirmity' of D minor to the 'eternal strengthening' of the cadence towards E flat major mentioned above. Goethe's words stress the

---

[27] Isabelle Werck, 'Cosmogony of the Eighth Symphony', in *A 'Mass' for the Masses*, 89.

[28] Constantin Floros, 'Die "Symphonie der Tausend" als Botschaft an die Menschheit', in *A 'Mass' for the Masses*, 121–30.

residue of earth which clings to the soul being borne aloft by the angels; soul and earth can only be divided by eternal love. The progression of thought is similar, but only in the lengthy discursiveness of Part II is the cadence (considerably lessened in dynamic and forces) allowed release into E flat (albeit minor). What followed in Part I seemed oddly dissonant with the overall structure; in Part II, the cadence is merely one of many returns to E flat which mark the ascent to the close.

As in Part I, the recurrence of E flat gives the Goethe setting a static feeling in spite of the larger number of tonal digressions. The companion key of E major occurs twice, both times during music associated with the Mater gloriosa. On each occasion, its entry is less emphatic than at 'Accende lumen sensibus'. Alongside this less trenchantly expressed underlying structure goes a softening of Mahler's style. This is partly a question of a greater diatonicism than was the norm in the period of the instrumental symphonies. Echoes of their language can be found in Part II, but the places isolated by commentators, notably from Fig. 188 onwards, tend to employ chromaticism in a more conventional way than the Sixth and Seventh Symphonies; it is used for enhancement of, rather than as a substitute for, more traditional tonal resources.[29] As such, the feeling persists that Mahler's ascent towards the inexpressible belongs as much with Puccini and Massenet as with Goethe. Against such moments of saccharine ecstasy, Mahler provides sounds for celesta, piano, harp, harmonium, and mandolin that seem to prefigure *Das Lied von der Erde*'s orientalisms (e.g. Figs. 187 and 199). Mahler had made an equation between such music and angelic hosts before in the fifth movement of the Third Symphony, but the passages in the Eighth seem to look forward to an aspect of music that is just as 'progressive' as the chromatic developments of Schoenberg and early Stravinsky; as in Debussy, Bartók, and some Stravinsky, diatonicism is used as a kind of sonorous backcloth, purged of the traditional structural pillars. In Part I, the two fourths of Ex. 17.1 encouraged similar passages in which diatonic harmony seemed robbed of momentum. It is easy to overestimate such passages, which take up little space in relation to the rather conventional harmonic language of the whole. Yet justice dictates that these moments be recognized as essential to Mahler's developing musical language. In *Das Lied von der Erde*, polyphonic complexities arise from diatonic and chromatic material alike.

In the last resort, however, the mildness of Part II's harmonic language seems inseparable from the subject. A comparison with Schoenberg's *Jakobsleiter* brings this out forcefully. Whereas the latter is an agonized search undertaken with all the most extreme melodic and chromatic inflections at its composer's command, the Eighth Symphony progresses serenely towards its eternity. Mahler, in offering his 'message' to humanity, for a time attempts to speak clearly in a kind of late nineteenth-century musical *lingua franca*. his style blurs into the mildly chromaticized diatonicism that was common to most of his contemporaries. That is why his description of the work, 'a gift to the entire nation', seems so pregnant with meaning.[30] No work of its time is less imbued with a sense of nationality

---

[29] Marius Flothuis, 'Einige kritische Bemerkungen zu Mahlers Achter Symphonie', in *A 'Mass' for the Masses*, 180–4.
[30] Specht, *Gustav Mahlers VIII. Symphonie*, 6.

or nationalism. (It is not irrelevant in this context to remember that Mahler disagreed violently with the nationalist Pfitzner about how to interpret the conclusion of Goethe's *Faust*; unfortunately Alma, in all probability the real reason for this quarrel, did not specify the exact nature of their disagreement.)[31] That is part of the gift and the message, which attempts to be as timeless as that which Beethoven offered in his Ninth. As a result, paradoxes accumulate around the Eighth Symphony. The timeless is depicted in a style which is more easily located in time and place than any other music by Mahler. A present to a nation shuns the nationalist. A symphony embraces motet, theatre, and cantata.

A related situation arises in reception. The doubts which critics have felt towards the work are drowned in the chorus of applause with which audiences greet it. There is an element of the artful here, in that Mahler, unlike Schumann at a similar point in his *Faust*, guaranteed his ovation with a vision of 'Das Ewig-Weibliche' almost crushing in its splendour. If we compare this close with the rapt visionary ecstasy of the ending of Stravinsky's *Symphony of Psalms*, it is difficult not to be aware of the consummate but shameless materialism with which Mahler marshals his huge forces. But those huge forces conceal the final guarantee. A 'Symphony of a Thousand' will never be a regular visitor to the concert hall. The blaze of E flat major at the end was designed to be heard only on special occasions. Mahler's message, which involved an element of talking-down quite distinct from the 'popular' music of his earlier works, should be heard rarely. Otherwise its timelessness may reveal its artifice a little too clearly.

[31] Alma Mahler, *Memories*, 82.

APPENDIX.
THE EIGHTH SYMPHONY: AN UNPUBLISHED LETTER

ANDREW NICHOLSON

In her recollections of Mahler during the summer of 1910 Alma recalls:

One night I was awakened by an apparition by my bed. It was Mahler standing there in the darkness. 'Would it give you any pleasure if I dedicated the Eighth to you?' Any pleasure! All the same I said: 'Don't. You have never dedicated anything to anybody. You might regret it.' 'I have just written to Herzka now—by the light of dawn', he said.[1]

We publish here for the first time that letter which Mahler wrote to Emil Hertzka 'by the light of dawn' requesting him to print on a separate sheet of paper the dedication 'To my dear wife Alma Maria' and to send him a proof of it without delay (see Pl. 17.1). The letter bears the stamped date '12 Aug. 1910'—which might be that on which Mahler wrote it or when Hertzka received it. Two filing-holes which do not affect the text appear in the left-hand margin, and the curlicue doodle between them—not being in Mahler's ink—is very probably Hertzka's. The stamped number '0010' remains an enigma.

Alma continues: 'A long correspondence with Hertzka followed. Mahler was not satisfied with the type and spacing of the page of dedication, to which he wished to have every honour done.'[2] Nonetheless, arriving in Munich in early September for rehearsals for the première of the Eighth (which took place on 12 September 1910), Mahler was delighted to find the piano reduction with the dedication awaiting him and immediately wrote ecstatically to Alma—who had remained behind at their summer home at Toblach:

I found the piano reduction waiting for me with the dedication, and hope Hertzka had the sense to send one to Toblach too. It gave me a peculiar and exciting feeling to see the sweet, beloved name on the title-page for all the world to read as a joyful acknowledgement. Oh, what joy to engrave it in all my piano scores. But that would be calf-love once more. And I want it taken seriously, as a token meaning far more to me than a lover's extravagance. Does it not make the impression rather of a betrothal? Doesn't it seem more like the announcement of an engagement?[3]

Emil Hertzka (1869–1932) was the Director of Universal Edition (the music publishing house in Vienna founded in 1901)[4] from 1907 to his death. As such, he was to be the last and most important of Mahler's numerous publishers.[5] Mahler contracted with him for the Eighth on 26 June 1909,[6] enjoyed friendly relations with him ('of whose good manners I have the most pleasant evidence')[7] and was very impressed with Universal Edition under his directorship—notably its efficiency and accuracy—whilst regretting its not having been the publisher of his works from the outset ('I must sincerely compliment your company (or its management). What a pity that my other things were not published by you.')[8]

The original manuscript of this letter is in the possession of Graham Lloyd and Ian Venables (England). We gratefully acknowledge their permission to publish this reproduction.

[1] Alma Mahler, *Memories*, 178.

[2] Ibid.

[3] Ibid. 334–5. Alma joined him for the première itself, however (ibid. 178).

[4] Universal Edition was formed by an amalgamation of various privately owned companies, and gradually absorbed others as the century progressed. It published the works of Zemlinsky, Schoenberg, Berg, and Webern.

[5] Mahler. *Selected Letters*, 443–4.

[6] Ibid. 336 and n. 3. The vocal score was eventually published in Apr. 1910 (ibid. 352 and n. 4; also 369).

[7] Ibid. 338.

[8] *MDS*, 263; but cf. also Mahler, *Selected Letters*, 444 n. 392.

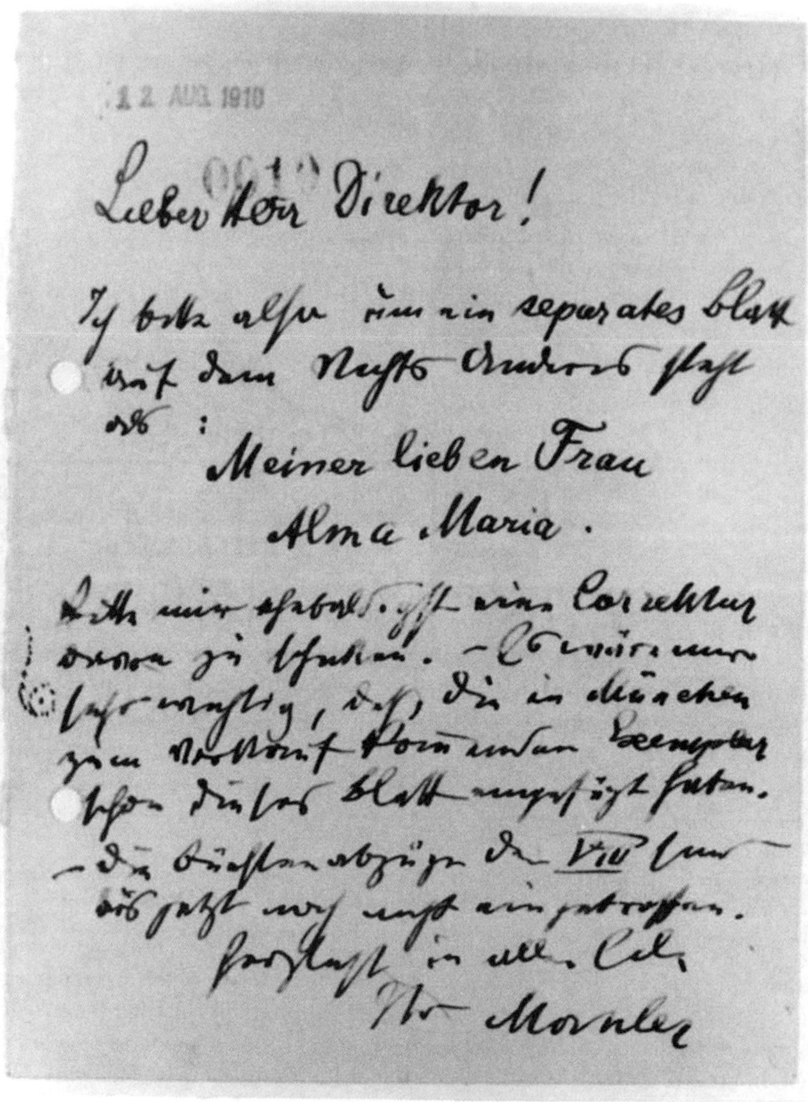

Pl. 17.1. Mahler's autograph manuscript letter of August 1910 to Emil Hertzka sending the dedication of his Eighth Symphony to Alma

[Transcription]

Lieber Herr Direktor!
Ich bitte also um ein separates Blatt auf dem Nichts Anderes steht als:

Meiner lieben Frau

Alma Maria.

Bitte mir ehebaldigst eine Correktur davon zu schicken. — Es wäre mir sehr wichtig, daß die in München zum verkauf kommenden Exemplare schon dieses Blatt eingefügt haben. — Die Bürstenabzüge der VIII sind bis jetzt noch nicht eingetroffen.

Herzlichst in aller Eile

Ihr

Mahler

[Translation]

Dear Herr Director,
I would kindly ask you to print a separate sheet with just these words:

To my dear wife

Alma Maria.

Please send me a proof of it as quickly as possible. — It would be most important to me that this sheet is added in the copies when they become available for sale in Munich. — The first proofs of the VIIIth have not yet arrived.

Kindest regards in all haste,

Yours

Mahler

18

Mahler in America

EDWARD R. REILLY

Reviewing the first New York performances of Mahler's Ninth Symphony (19 November 1931 and 9 January 1932), the well-known composer and critic Deems Taylor (1885–1966) made the following comments:

Prune it down until nothing is left save Mahler's musical ideas and the amount of development that they are worth, and the Ninth Symphony would last about twenty minutes. — Some day, some real friend of Mahler's will do just that . . . take a pruning knife and reduce his works to the length that they would have been if the composer had not stretched them out of shape; and then the great Mahler war will be over.[1]

These deliberately provocative and bizarre remarks by a highly literate musician who was himself a composer give some idea of the intensity of the reactions generated by Mahler and his music in America during roughly the first sixty years of the twentieth century. Although Taylor's views were by no means universal—Mahler always had his defenders as well as adversaries—they were shared by many, and at times probably the majority, of musicians in the North American hemisphere. The differing reactions that his music engendered and the changes in those responses as the century progressed constitute a fascinating and complex record of shifting attitudes and tastes.

Mahler's interest in America preceded by many years the first performances of his works in this country. In a single tantalizing reference, Mahler, then in Leipzig, mentioned the possibility of accepting a position in New York, in a letter to his friend Friedrich Löhr dated 18 February 1887: '. . . I have received an offer from New York, an invitation to replace Anton Seidl—perhaps I shall end up by accepting it!'[2] The offer seems to have been premature, however, since Seidl (1850–98) remained in New York, where he was highly regarded, up to the time of his early death.[3] Only twenty years later did Mahler arrive in America.

---

[1] Quoted in *Chord and Discord*, 1/1 (Feb. 1932), 23.
[2] Mahler, *Selected Letters*, 107; *Briefe* (1982), 62.
[3] On two other possible invitations to come to America,

one to Boston, one to New York, see Zoltan Roman, *Gustav Mahler's American Years: 1907–1911. A Documentary History* (Stuyvesant, NY: Pendragon Press, 1989), 2–8.

Although Mahler's reputation as a composer was far from equal to that of Richard Strauss at the time, the way for his appearance in this capacity had been prepared shortly beforehand by Walter Damrosch's performances of the Fourth Symphony in 1904, and Frank van der Stucken and Wilhelm Gericke's of the Fifth in 1905 and 1906.[4] The fact that Mahler was hired as a conductor at the Metropolitan Opera, and that he was (as he had been in Europe) still better known as a performer than as a composer, complicated the critical response to him. Damrosch was the first to perform a Mahler symphony in America. Later he summarized what he saw as the impact of Mahler's conducting on his composing, and added other elements to the litany of criticisms that were to remain standard for many decades: derivativeness, pseudo-philosophical extra-musical associations, and lack of cohesiveness.

[Mahler] was a profound musician and one of the best conductors of Europe, and it is possible that, in the latter capacity, he occupied himself so intensely and constantly in analyzing and interpreting the works of the great masters that he lost the power to develop himself as a composer on original lines. All his life he composed, but his moments of real beauty are too rare, and the listener has to wade through pages of dreary emptiness which no artificial connection with philosophic ideas can fill with real importance. The feverish restlessness characteristic of the man reflects itself in his music, which is fragmentary in character and lacks continuity of thought and development. He could write cleverly in the style of Haydn or Berlioz or Wagner, and without forgetting Beethoven, but was never able to write in the style of Mahler.[5]

Although not as extreme as the two passages quoted above, negative criticism of Mahler's works was not uncommon before and during Mahler's American seasons from 1907 to 1911. The reactions to his compositions were almost invariably mixed from the time of the first performances of the Fourth Symphony by Damrosch. Reviews of Mahler's works from this period, and of his performances of operas and symphonic works, may now be seen in considerable detail in the works of Marvin Lee Von Deck and Zoltan Roman.[6] Both act as correctives to many earlier views that depict Mahler as working in an almost totally hostile, unsympathetic, and unappreciative environment. These more recent and more detailed studies show, together with the work of Henry-Louis de La Grange, that this interpretation was far from the truth. One should, however, separate reactions to his work as a conductor from responses to his compositions. In the former sphere, although he had some major detractors, he also had many advocates and defenders. Much of his work at the

[4] For further details, see Mahler, *Unknown Letters*, 35–45 and 59–63.

[5] Walter Damrosch, *My Musical Life* (New York: Charles Scribner & Sons, 1923), 354–5. In a paper on 'The Truth behind the Legend of Mahler's American Career', given on 19 Nov. 1994 at the Mahler in America 1907–1911 symposium in New York, Henry-Louis de La Grange made a convincing case for the proposition that from the time that Mahler was given the leadership of the New York Philharmonic, Damrosch saw him as a dangerous rival in competition with his own New York Symphony Orchestra

and with himself as a conductor, and did his best to undermine him. See also La Grange's 'Mahler in the New World', *Muziek & Wetenschap*, 5 (1995–6), 225–44, and 'Mahler and the New York Philharmonic: The Truth behind the Legend', in *On Mahler and Britten*, ed. Reed, 56–77.

[6] See Marvin L. von Deck, 'Gustav Mahler in New York: His Conducting Activities in New York City, 1908–1911' (Ph.D. diss., New York University, 1973), and Roman, *Gustav Mahler's American Years*. Of course, reference to the fundamental work of Henry-Louis de La Grange (i.e. HLG(F)) is assumed throughout this chapter.

Metropolitan Opera was highly regarded, and he was even offered the directorship during his first season when it became clear that Heinrich Conried (1848–1909), the man who had hired him, was too ill to continue.[7] Mahler's refusal and the subsequent hiring of Giulio Gatti-Gasazza (1869–1940), who was closely allied to Toscanini, almost inevitably guaranteed a lessening of his activity at the opera house.

At the same time, the major reorganization of the New York Philharmonic, begun the following year with the specific goal of providing Mahler with a concert orchestra, reaffirms the high regard in which he was held. This kind of support, as well as Mahler's own varying responses to musical life in the 'New World',[8] must be kept in mind as well as journalistic records. In fact, much of the criticism of Mahler's performances in America is very similar to that of his performances in Europe. Against praise for the freshness, vitality, and intensity of his readings of well-known works, he was sometimes criticized for interpretations that differed too radically (in tempo, for example) from those familiar to the critics. As might be expected, some critics were more open to new perspectives; others were disturbed by departures from familiar traditions. Again, as in Europe, some critics were highly exercised by Mahler's 'retouchings' of the scores of classic works, such as the symphonies of Beethoven. Foremost among Mahler's opponents in this regard was Henry E. Krehbiel (1854–1923), the highly regarded critic of the *New York Tribune*, author of many books, programme annotator for the New York Philharmonic, and editor of Thayer's great *Beethoven* (published in English in 1921). Krehbiel's famous (some say infamous) obituary of Mahler[9] has so distorted the view of Mahler's reception in New York that one must be reminded that Krehbiel was only one critic, even if an important one, among many; that others held very different views of Mahler's accomplishments; and that even Krehbiel himself could admire certain performances by Mahler.[10] Perusal of reviews of Richard Aldrich for the *New York Times* or those of Henry T. Finck for the *Post* will help dispel the notion that there was any single consistently negative reaction to Mahler's work as a conductor. And a still broader spectrum can be found in the reviews cited by Roman and Von Deck.

Early responses to Mahler the composer during the period from 1907 to 1911 were generally much more negative than those to Mahler the conductor, but still offer quite a mixed picture. In New York he conducted performances of his Second Symphony (with

---

[7] Roman, *Gustav Mahler's American Years*, 16 and 63.

[8] On the reorganization of the Philharmonic, see Howard Shanet, *Philharmonic: A History of New York's Orchestra* (Garden City, NY, 1975), 207–20. On Mahler's shifting reactions to musical life in America during the years in question, see especially Mahler, *Selected Letters* and *Briefe* (1982).

[9] See Roman, *Gustav Mahler's American Years*, 483–6, where it is quoted with a few deletions, and Mitchell, *WY*, 407–13, where it is quoted in full.

[10] That there was deep friction between Krehbiel and Mahler is undeniable, but one should not imagine that Krehbiel was musically ignorant or lacking in experience. He had seen and heard some of the best Wagnerian singers under Seidl in New York in the 1880s and 1890s, and had

seen too many European musicians come to America with the exclusive goal of making money. Joseph Horowitz, in several works, has tried to give a clearer idea of Krehbiel's background and his perspective. The tone of his obituary for Mahler still seems too violently rancorous to avoid sensing a personal animus behind it, but it is not characteristic of most of Krehbiel's work. In a totally different sphere, it is perhaps worth remembering that he was a close friend of the author Lafcadio Hearn (1850–1904). See Joseph Horowitz, 'Adding Insult to Improvement', *New York Times*, 25 Oct. 1992; the same author's article 'Anton Seidl and America's Wagner Cult', in Barry Millington and Stewart Spencer (eds.), *Wagner in Performance* (New Haven: Yale University Press, 1992), 168–81; and also his *Understanding Toscanini* (New York: Alfred A. Knopf, 1987), 13–77.

Damrosch's New York Symphony Society in 1908); the First Symphony (New York Philharmonic, 1909); the Fourth Symphony (1911); *Kindertotenlieder*, with Ludwig Wüllner as soloist (1910); and 'Ging heut' Morgen übers Feld' from *Lieder eines fahrenden Gesellen* and 'Rheinlegendchen', with Alma Gluck (1910).

According to Mahler himself,[11] the New York Symphony was inadequate for the performance of his Second Symphony on 8 December 1908. The response of the audience, however, seems to have been most enthusiastic.[12] As had been the case with the New York performances of the Fourth and Fifth, a generally sympathetic background article, probably by Aldrich, appeared two days earlier in the *New York Times*. In this article Mahler's expressed antipathy to 'programmes' and his seeming ambivalence in this area are noted, with some well-chosen quotations from Mahler himself.[13] The matter of the implied programmes in his symphonies, and the composer's refusal to elucidate them, became the cause of frequent comment by reviewers, and in the case of Krehbiel, downright irritation. Reviews of the Second Symphony were generally lukewarm or dismissive. But it is worth noting that the editor of the *Musical Courier* used the occasion to praise the *Sun* review as the only accurate one (largely negative) and to blast the article in the *New York Tribune*, Krehbiel's paper.[14] Thus Krehbiel was not immune to criticism from his colleagues, and the beginnings of a pattern were already present in reactions to Mahler's own performances: divided critical opinion—with a number of the major critics opposed, but with a defender at times also speaking out—and a public response considerably more favourable than that of the critics.

With the exception of the critic of the *Musical Courier* and of Herbert F. Peyser in *Musical America*, Mahler's First Symphony met with almost total incomprehension among the critics, and apparently only dutiful applause from the audience. Krehbiel chose the occasion to vent his spleen by printing a note in the Philharmonic's concert handbook reporting Mahler's opposition to both programmes and analytical guides to his work. The business of the absence of a programme was also a constant source of discussion in the reviews.[15]

Critical comment on Mahler's performance of his Fourth Symphony on 17 and 20 January 1911 was again almost entirely negative, with the important exception of the critic of the *New York Times*, who sensed its humour even if he did not understand it. Even the normally supportive *Musical Courier* joined the chorus of opposition, and the American composer Arthur Farwell (1872–1952) expressed his hostility in *Musical America*.[16] The critic of the *Post*, however, noted that the audience had reacted quite differently: 'Mr. Mahler has reason to be proud of the reception given to his symphony. After the first movement he was called out four times, and similar demonstrations followed after the other divisions.'[17]

[11] See Roman, *Gustav Mahler's American Years*, 179.
[12] Ibid. 180.
[13] Ibid. 177–9.
[14] See ibid. 180–3, and von Deck, 'Gustav Mahler in New York', 153–4, for a sampling of reviews.

[15] See Roman, 311–16, for Krehbiel's disclaimer and a sampling of reviews. See also von Deck, 192–3.
[16] See Roman, 435–41 for reviews. That of Farwell appears on p. 441.
[17] Quoted in Von Deck, 250.

Critical reaction to the songs was generally more favourable than to the symphonies, once more suggesting a pattern that remained very common until well after the Second World War. In a surprising turn of events, the critic of the *New York Tribune*, presumably Krehbiel, was one of the appreciative reviewers of *Kindertotenlieder*. The songs 'are weighted with grief of such poignant sincerity that one must conclude that they have an autobiographic significance. We have not heard any music by Mr. Mahler which has so individual a note, or which is so calculated to stir up the imagination and the emotions.'[18] And although qualified in a backhanded way, Krehbiel also has positive things to say about the two songs already mentioned which Alma Gluck sang:

> though of a character which never before had a place in a Philharmonic programme, [the songs] were accepted as a delightful intermezzo by the audience. . . . Mr. Mahler . . . has a strong feeling toward the romantic element in music which such songs exemplify, and his utterances are of a singular eloquence when not too sophisticated by the harmonic and instrumental habiliments with which he is prone to clothe them.[19]

Krehbiel showed not a jot's worth of sympathy or understanding when he penned his obituary of Mahler, which appeared on 21 May 1911. In it no aspect of his work is spared denigration: Mahler deserved none of his reputation as an operatic and symphonic conductor or as a composer. In the last capacity 'he tried to out-Strauss Strauss and out-Reger Reger, and not having the native force of either of them he failed. We cannot see how any of his music can long survive him. There is no place for it between the old and new schools.'[20]

History's current verdict hardly bears out that of Krehbiel, but it is important also to recognize that many of Krehbiel's contemporaries did not agree with him. Ossip Gabrilovich wrote an eloquent defence of Mahler and attack on Krehbiel; and none of the other obituaries that I have seen share the latter's strictures.[21]

The two decades following Mahler's death remain the least thoroughly explored with regard to the documentation of the actual performances of his works in the United States and the critical and popular reactions to them. Nevertheless, several events stand out as being of considerable significance. In 1913 G. Schirmer published the first book in English about Mahler, a translation by T. E. Clark of Paul Stefan's *Gustav Mahler, eine Studie über Persönlichkeit und Werk* (first published in Munich in 1910). The translator, apparently an Englishman, in his preface suggests a quite different fate for Mahler's work than that prophesied by Krehbiel: 'The future of Mahler's compositions is as certain as that his ideals will live . . .'.[22] While in New York, Mahler had met Rudolf Schirmer (1859–1919) and his

---

[18] Quoted in Roman, 334.

[19] Quoted ibid. 411–12.

[20] Quoted ibid. 485.

[21] Gabrilovich's rebuttal is reproduced in full in Roman, 486–9. Gabrilovich had met Mahler in Essen in 1906, when the Sixth Symphony was given its première. As a token of her appreciation of Gabrilovich's friendship and his posthumous defence, Alma Mahler gave him the draft full score of the Adagio of the Ninth Symphony. It remained in the pos-

session of his widow, Clara Clemens Gabrilovich, the daughter of Mark Twain, after his death in 1936. In 1987 it was acquired by Henry-Louis de La Grange for his Bibliothèque Musicale Gustav Mahler in Paris. For a useful summary of the general responses of the various New York critics to Mahler, see von Deck, 293–8.

[22] Paul Stefan, *Gustav Mahler: A Study of his Personality and Work*, trans. T. E. Clark (New York: G. Schirmer, 1913), p. v.

wife, and the firm had published Mahler's arrangements of movements from Bach's suites in 1910. Thus Schirmer may well have been an enthusiastic admirer.[23] Stefan's sympathetic portrait of Mahler remained for many years the only general study of his life and works in English.

Unquestionably the most successful performance of a work by Mahler in the decade following his death was the American première of the Eighth Symphony by the Philadelphia Orchestra, directed by Leopold Stokowski, on 2 March 1916. This was followed by eight more performances in Philadelphia, and one in New York City at the Metropolitan Opera House. The ambition of performing the work had been close to Stokowski's heart ever since he had heard Mahler himself conduct the symphony in Munich in 1910, and he took enormous pains to prepare it carefully. The difference between the reactions of the audiences and those of the critics was again obvious. Popular response was overwhelmingly positive; that of the critics was much more mixed.[24]

The performances constituted a milestone in the history of the orchestra and were remembered long afterwards. On the occasion of the New York performance on 9 April, 1916, the group calling itself 'The Society of the Friends of Music', which sponsored the concert, published a pamphlet containing some valuable laudatory reports and reminiscences by many people who knew the composer, entitled *Gustav Mahler—The Composer, the Conductor and the Man. Appreciations by Distinguished Contemporary Musicians*.[25] Perhaps most strikingly, the sixty-nine testimonials are preceded by a poem in German, entitled 'Mahler's Achte Symphonie', by no less a figure than the pioneer American music historian Oscar Sonneck (1873–1928), then still Chief of the Music Division of the Library of Congress. Some of the admirers included were the American composers Mrs H. H. Beach, George Chadwick, Arthur Foote, and Daniel Gregory Mason. Among the many others were Percy Grainger, Pablo Casals, Ossip Gabrilovich, Carl Friedburg, Arthur Hutchinson, Josef Stransky, and Arthur Whiting, to say nothing of the many singers and players who had performed under Mahler. The academic world was represented by Cornelius M. Rubner of Columbia University and Walter R. Spaulding, Head of the Music Department at Harvard University.

Stokowski was also responsible for the American première of *Das Lied von der Erde*, again with the Philadelphia Orchestra. It took place on 15 December 1916, with the

[23] On Mahler's relationship with Rudolf Schirmer, see Alma Mahler, *Memories*, 154–5 and 161–2. The identification of the Schirmer family member on p. 353 as Ernest Charles Schirmer is mistaken. The date of the Bach Suite is given on p. 155 as 1910. 1909 is the date given by La Grange (HLG(F) i. 921), but the contract, reproduced in Mitchell, *WY*, 351–2, is dated 22 Dec. 1909, and thus the Suite probably appeared in the following year, as the copyright date indicates.

[24] See Oliver Daniel, *Stokowski: A Counterpoint of View* (New York: Dodd Mead & Co., 1982), 156–66, with pictures on pp. 159 and 160, for further details about the performances. See also Herbert Kupferberg, *Those Fabulous Philadelphians: The Life and Times of a Great Orchestra* (New York: Charles Scribner's Sons, 1969), 40–6, with a picture among the illustrations following p. 86. For Stokowski's own comments about the emotional impact of the work on the audiences who heard it, see William Parks Grant, 'Mahler's Art: A New Survey', *Chord and Discord*, 1/5 (Mar. 1934), 14–19 at 15.

[25] On the Friends of Music, see Olga Samaroff Stokowski, 'The "Peace Conference of Amsterdam" ', *Chord and Discord*, 2/1 (Jan. 1940), 30–1, which is taken from her *An American Musician's Story* (New York: W. W. Norton, 1939). See also the anonymous editorial statement in *Chord and Discord*, 2/2 (Nov. 1940), 1.

soloists Tilly Koenen and Johannes Sembach, but apparently created no such stir as that aroused by the Eighth Symphony. The New York première took place only six years later at Carnegie Hall on 1 February 1922, with Arthur Bodansky conducting the Metropolitan Opera Orchestra and Mme Charles Cahier and Orville Harrold as soloists. The event was once more sponsored by the Friends of Music, and was apparently successful enough for a repeat performance on 17 February.

The patterns already apparent during Mahler's years in America and in the period up to the First World War continued in the decades between the two wars. Performances were rather infrequent; some, but not all, critics were strongly opposed to Mahler's works; a devoted popular following existed, though its size is impossible to estimate; and an intrepid group of conductors continued to perform his works in spite of the critics and many of their colleagues.

The three conductors most closely associated with Mahler, Bruno Walter, Willem Mengelberg, and Otto Klemperer, all played active roles in American music and promoted Mahler's compositions despite continuing negative reactions from many of the critics. Of the three, Mengelberg was the most energetic in Mahler's cause in the 1920s. From 1921 to 1930 he conducted regularly in New York, first with the National Symphony Orchestra, and later with the New York Philharmonic. During that period he conducted the first five symphonies, the Seventh, and *Das Lied von der Erde*. These performances included the New York première of the Third Symphony, and the first New York performance of the Seventh. The newspaper critics, with some significant exceptions, were antagonistic, but enthusiastic audience responses were often noted.[26] The one work that aroused more favourable reactions among the critics was *Das Lied*—a pattern of reception which continued for some years to come. Krehbiel lived to review the Third in 1922; and in 1924 a formidable new anti-Mahler critic, Olin Downes (1886–1955), joined the staff of the *New York Times*. Like other critics, Downes excepted *Das Lied* from his general scorn, but up to the time of his death he more or less consistently attacked Mahler's other works. In a review of Mengelberg's performance of the Fifth Symphony on 3 December 1926, Downes made the following typical comments about Mahler: 'His spirit, not his music, commands respect and admiration, while he seeks vainly, by means of funeral marches, battle fanfares, Vienna waltzes, rondos, fugues, and what not, and with the aid of an immensely enlarged orchestra, to find the creative goal. But he is helpless, and certainly his music will perish.'[27] Downes had already reached a similar conclusion at an earlier stage in his career, when he reviewed Karl Muck's performance of Mahler's Second Symphony in Boston on 22 January 1918: 'But we believe the music will be shelved long before the memory of the man and his potent services to his art will be forgotten.'[28]

---

[26] For information on Mengelberg's performances in New York, I am indebted to Aarnout Coster, 'Mengelberg's Mahler Performances in America', in *Das Gustav-Mahler-Fest Hamburg 1989: Bericht über den Internationalen Gustav-Mahler Kongreß*, ed. Matthias Theodor Vogt (Kassel: Bärenreiter, 1991), 279–89.

[27] For the full review, which includes an interesting comparison of Mengelberg's performance with that of Muck, see *Olin Downes on Music*, ed. Irene Downes (New York: Simon and Schuster, 1957), 116–18.

[28] Ibid. 63.

Although Klemperer came to the United States, and conducted the Symphony Society of New York in 1926 and 1927, he changed his mind about performing Mahler's Ninth at that time.[29] The activities of both Klemperer and Bruno Walter in the cause of Mahler became more significant during the 1930s, and are recorded to a considerable extent in a journal that appeared for the first time in February 1932, entitled *Chord and Discord*. It was published by the Bruckner Society of America, and in spite of the name of the sponsoring group, was designed from the beginning to propagandize equally for the works of Bruckner and Mahler. Its editor, Gabriel Engel (1892–1952), an Hungarian-born but American-educated violinist and composer, was the author of monographs on both composers. *The Life of Anton Bruckner* was published by the Society in 1931, and *Gustav Mahler—Song Symphonist* in 1932.[30] He remained the editor of the journal until his death, and was followed first by Charles L. Eble, who continued in the role up to and including the last issue in 1969, and then by Jack Diether, who in fact died before the publication of a further issue was achieved.[31]

Through *Chord and Discord* the Bruckner Society, founded in 1931, encouraged performances of works by Bruckner and Mahler with articles on both composers and their compositions, and by reporting on performances that took place all across the country. Reviews of these performances were frequently excerpted and reprinted, and were by no means limited to those of a laudatory nature (as the quotation at the beginning of this chapter illustrates). Recordings and radio broadcasts and books were also announced and reviewed. Thus the student of today can obtain a quite vivid sense of the place of Mahler in the musical life of America (and not just in a few of the major cities like New York and Boston) from the pages of this journal, especially in the 1930s.

The Bruckner Society also encouraged performances by awarding Bruckner and Mahler medals to those conductors who programmed their works. A few non-performers were also honoured for their services. Many of the conductors so honoured were predictable names like Mengelberg, Walter, Klemperer, and Gabrilovich; but others such as Eugene Ormandy, Dimitri Mitropoulos, Artur Rodzinski, and Hans Kindler were also singled out for their active support of the Mahler cause. Perhaps most surprising, however, was Serge Koussevitzky, who in fact gave the American première of the Ninth Symphony in 1931 (16 October), but who is not often thought of as a Mahler conductor, perhaps because he did

---

[29] See Peter Heyworth, *Otto Klemperer, his Life and Times*, i: *1885–1933* (Cambridge: Cambridge University Press, 1983), 227–9. The powerful influence of a few concert managers in shaping programmes should also be recognized.

[30] The Mahler volume was reprinted by David Lewis in New York in 1970, with a new preface by Jack Diether and a list of 'First Performances of Mahler in America' which corrects and extends the list of 'Pioneer Mahler Performances in America' found in *Chord and Discord*, 2/2 (Nov. 1940), 59. In his Foreword, Engel himself drew attention to the fact that his work was the first to draw upon the German edition of Mahler's *Briefe* published in 1924.

[31] Hermann Danuser has some perceptive things to say about the role of *Chord and Discord* in promoting Mahler's works in America in the chapter 'My Time Will Yet Come: Die amerikanische Mahler-Rezeption im Spiegel der Zeitschrift "Chord and Discord"', in *Gustav Mahler und seine Zeit*, 275–85. His arguments were challenged, however, by the late Erich Leinsdorf in the *Neue Zürcher Zeitung*, 19/20 May 1990, 67–8. From my own experience, however, I can attest the influence of the journal in stimulating interest in the works of Mahler, and in providing support for conductors and record companies who sought to advance what was then the 'cause' of Mahler.

not record any of the symphonies. The Mahler medal awarded to the Hungarian conductor Erno Rapee (1891–1945) in 1942 serves as a reminder of the growing importance of radio in the dissemination of Mahler's works. Far in advance of his time, Rapee mounted the first American Mahler festival, with a series of radio concerts with the Radio City Music Hall Orchestra between 4 January and 12 April 1942, in the course of which he performed the first five symphonies, the Eighth and the Ninth, and *Das Lied von der Erde*.

The journal did not appear during the War years from 1942 to 1945. When publication was resumed in 1946 it was issued less frequently, but more articles were included by a wider range of authors. Many substantive essays, however, appeared during the existence of the journal and helped prepare the way for the remarkable new and widespread acceptance of Mahler's works that emerged in the 1960s. It may come as a surprise, for example, to find as early as 1950 (Vol. 2, no. 6) a discussion of 'The Songs of Alma Mahler' by Warren Storey Smith, and in the December 1941 (Vol. 2, no. 3) issue an article on 'Mahler's Tenth' by Frederick Block, concerning the complete five-movement form of that work and his own preparation of a four-hand piano edition of it.[32]

In that same issue William Parks Grant surveyed 'Mahler on Records',[33] drawing attention to another major development in the 1930s: the slow appearance of some of Mahler's major works on phonograph discs. Undoubtedly the most important of these were the performances by Bruno Walter and the Vienna Philharmonic of *Das Lied von der Erde* and the Ninth Symphony, recorded live in 1936 and 1938 respectively.[34] A whole generation of young people, including myself, were first drawn to Mahler through these recordings. Although Oskar Fried's recording, probably made in 1924, of the Second Symphony appears not to have been familiar in the United States, a performance by Eugene Ormandy and the Minneapolis Symphony Orchestra recorded live on 6 January 1935 was well known, and in spite of less than satisfactory soloists, made it possible for many to hear the work for the first time. The same orchestra, under Dimitri Mitropoulos, made the first recording of the First Symphony in 1941. Of the middle symphonies only the Adagietto from the Fifth was available, in recordings by Bruno Walter and the Vienna Philharmonic, and Mengelberg and the Amsterdam Concertgebouw. Just a handful of the *Wunderhorn* and Rückert songs could be heard, but a complete *Kindertotenlieder* sung by Heinrich Rehkemper was available.

The Second World War and the years that followed brought no major change in the widely held critical views of much of Mahler's music (with the songs and *Das Lied von der*

---

[32] See pp. 74–8 for the first article, 43–5 for the second. Block reports that he knew that Ernst Krenek had edited full scores of the first and third movements of the symphony shortly after the publication of the Zsolnay facsimile edition of Mahler's sketches and drafts in 1924. From the facsimile Block prepared four-hand piano versions of the second, fourth, and fifth movements. These remained unpublished, and were unknown to Deryck Cooke when he first prepared his Performing Version of the entire symphony. On other performing versions see the article by Jack Diether cited below, n. 49.

[33] See pp. 63–8.

[34] The Ninth Symphony was apparently not released in the United States until 1940 or very early in 1941. Plans for the release are mentioned in *Chord and Discord*, 2/1 (Jan. 1940), 34, and two reviews from Jan. 1941 are quoted in 2/3 (Dec. 1941), 21–2. For reissues of these and the other recordings mentioned here, see the discographies cited below, n. 48.

Erde often excepted). These views also extended into the academic world, where students in many colleges and universities were rarely encouraged to explore Mahler's works. Textbooks, such as *Music in History: The Evolution of an Art* (1940)[35] by Howard D. McKinney and W. R. Anderson, gave Mahler mixed notices, praising *Das Lied von der Erde*, but with many qualifications and questions about the future of the other symphonies. German émigré scholars, like Paul Bekker, Alfred Einstein, and Curt Sachs, however, did include more favourable brief accounts of the composer in their works.[36] And an increasing number of recordings between 1945 and 1960 gradually made all the symphonies available, some in a variety of different performances. Although the First, Second, Fourth, Fifth, Ninth, and *Das Lied* tended to remain the most favoured symphonies, even the less familiar works were gradually being heard. Mahler's Sixth finally had its first American performance in 1947 (11–13 December) with Mitropoulos conducting the New York Philharmonic. The same forces performed the Seventh Symphony the following year (11–12 November), eliciting a notable attack on the work by Olin Downes, and a strong response to it by Arnold Schoenberg.[37]

If Downes's views were still shared by many, a number of critics now voiced quite different reactions. Notably Virgil Thomson, the critic of the *New York Herald Tribune* from 1940 to 1954, offered thoughtful and sometimes thought-provoking ideas about several of Mahler's works. For example, in a review on 14 March 1941 of a performance of the Ninth Symphony by Koussevitsky and the Boston Symphony Orchestra, Thomson includes an unusual comparison of Strauss and Mahler which, rare at that time, treats them equally, and even shows a preference for Mahler's scoring. He then goes on to a still more striking suggestion, a French connection in Mahler's work:

The Ninth Symphony . . . is beautifully made and beautifully thought. It is utterly German and Viennese and strangely not so at the same time. In reviewing *Das Lied von der Erde* some time back, I opined that there were some French influences in the particular contrapuntal approach Mahler employed. Naturally, I pulled down on my head a flood of abusive correspondence from the

---

[35] New York: American Book Company; see pp. 674–8.

[36] See Paul Bekker, *The Story of Music: An Historical Sketch of the Changes in Musical Form*, trans. M. D. Herter Norton and Alice Kortschak (New York: W. W. Norton, 1927), 251–3; Alfred Einstein, *A Short History of Music* (3rd American edn.; New York: Alfred A. Knopf, 1947), 247, 250; Curt Sachs, *Our Musical Heritage: A Short History of Music* (2nd edn., Englewood Cliffs, NJ: Prentice-Hall, Inc., 1955), 307–8; Hugo Leichtentritt, *Music, History and Ideas* (Cambridge, Mass.: Harvard University Press, 1950), 247–8. Of these, Leichtentritt has the most to say, and he notes that 'It is difficult to write on Mahler for American readers because the art of this great musician . . . is not adequately known in this country; the little that has been performed in America has been misunderstood and underrated, for in essence it is too far from the current American spirit. An atmosphere favorable to Bruckner and Mahler still has to be created here.' Leichtentritt had previously written an article

on the composer entitled 'Gustav Mahler: His Aims and Achievements', *Musical Courier*, 101/21 (1930), 6 and 8.

[37] See Egbert M. Ennulat, *Arnold Schoenberg Correspondence: A Collection of Translated and Annotated Letters Exchanged with Guido Adler, Pablo Casals, Emanuel Feuermann and Olin Downes* (Metuchen, NJ: The Scarecrow Press, 1991), 241–58. The original review appeared in the *New York Times* of 12 Nov. 1948, and is reproduced on pp. 253–4. Schoenberg's reply and Downes's response to it also appear in *Olin Downes on Music*, 368–72. These documents are preserved among the Downes papers at the University of Georgia. I am indebted to Prof. Kenneth Roberts of Williams College for the information that the first university course on Mahler in the United States appears to have been given by Royal B. MacDonald at New York University in the 1960–1 academic year. Thus once again the centenary year was a turning point.

Mahlerites . . . Nevertheless, as I listened to the Ninth Symphony last night, I was still aware of French influences. Certain of these are technical, like the no-doubling orchestration. Others are aesthetic. I know the protest mail I shall get for saying this, but I must say it. Mahler has a great deal in common with the French impressionists. As an Italian musician to whom I mentioned the matter put it, 'He comes as near being an impressionist as a German could.'[38]

Aaron Copland, who had already had some positive things to say about Mahler in 1925 and 1929,[39] elaborated on them in a 1941 article in *Modern Music*, excerpted from his forthcoming volume *Our New Music*. Since it is one of the most perceptive assessments of Mahler from that period, and is also a reminder that the reactions of a number of composers differed from those of the negative critics, it merits extended quotation:

Mahler's faults have been thoroughly exploited. He is admittedly long-winded, trite, bombastic; he lacks taste, he unblushingly plagiarizes, filching his material from Schubert, Mozart, Bruckner, or any other of a half dozen favorites. His music is full of human frailty. But when all is said, there remains something extraordinarily touching about it, which compensates for the weaknesses. This may be because his music is so Mahler-like in every detail. All the nine symphonies abound in personality—he had his own way of saying and doing everything. The irascible scherzi, the heaven-storming calls in the brass, the special quality of his communings with nature, the gentle melancholy of a transition passage, the gargantuan Ländler, the pages of incredible loneliness—these together with an inevitable histrionics, an inner warmth and the will to evoke the largest forms and grandest musical thoughts, build up one of the most fascinating composer-personalities of modern times.

But Mahler would be an important figure even if his music were not so engrossing. Two facets of his musicianship were years in advance of their time—one, the curiously contrapuntal fabric of the musical texture; the other, more obvious, his strikingly original instrumentation. Viewed properly, these two elements are really connected. It was because his music was so contrapuntally conceived, without the typical nineteenth century underpinning of the melodies by blocked-out harmonies such as we find continuously in Rimsky-Korsakoff or Franck, because he worked primarily with a maze of separate strands independent of all such chordal underpinning, that his instrumentation has the sharply etched and clarified sonority which is to be heard again and again in the music of later composers. Mahler's was the first orchestra to play *without pedal*, to borrow a phrase from piano technic. The use of the orchestra as a many-voiced body in this particular way was typical of the age of Bach and Handel. So far as orchestral practice is concerned, Mahler bridges the gap between the early eighteenth century and the neo-classicists of our own time.

The timbre of Mahler's orchestra is, of course, entirely his own. His scores are full of *trouvailles*. The many years he spent conducting gave him complete assurance with unusual combinations of

[38] See Virgil Thomson, *The Musical Scene* (New York: Alfred A. Knopf, 1945), 94. For reviews of other Mahler performances, including Stokowski's presentation of the Eighth Symphony on 6 Apr. 1950, which shows more reservations about that work than about the Ninth, see Thomson's *Music Reviewed 1940–1954* (New York: Vintage Books, 1967), 310–11, 362–3, and 394–5.

[39] I have recently discovered a quite remarkable letter by Copland, dated 2 Apr. 1925, 'To the Editor of the *New York Times*', written in response to the attacks on Mahler in the press after one of Mengelberg's performances of the Second Symphony. Copland strongly condemns the critics on the one hand, and vigorously defends the composer on the other. In the process, he shows considerable familiarity with many of Mahler's works. The letter was later reprinted in the programme book of the Boston Symphony Orchestra for 16 and 17 Oct. 1931 (the first performances of the Ninth in America), 100–2. For the 1929 reference, see 'From a Composer's Notebook', *Modern Music*, 6/4 (May–June 1929), 16–17.

instruments, sudden unexpected juxtapositions of sonorities, or thinly scored passages of instruments playing far apart in their less likely registers—all such effects as are to be found again in the orchestral works of Schönberg or Honegger or even of very recent composers like Shostakovitch or Benjamin Britten.

Speaking generally, Mahler appears to be a late romantic who made use of an eighteenth century technic. However one may regard him as a composer, it is impossible to deny his influence, direct or indirect, on the present day.[40]

The small number of books about Mahler, which had been increased in 1941 by the first American edition of Bruno Walter's study of the composer, with an added biographical essay by Ernst Krenek,[41] was augmented in 1946 with the appearance of Alma Mahler's *Gustav Mahler: Memories and Letters*,[42] the most distinctive (if problematic) source document connected with the composer. Other volumes concerning Mahler, however, were still rare. Dika Newlin's pioneering *Bruckner, Mahler, Schoenberg* was published in 1947,[43] but Donald Mitchell's *Gustav Mahler: The Early Years* first appeared only a decade later in 1958,[44] the same year as the American edition of Alma Mahler's autobiography *And the Bridge is Love*, written with the assistance of E. B. Ashton.[45] Both Newlin's and Mitchell's works provided foundations for the extraordinary growth in serious Mahler research that was to come.

If one were to pick a year which marked the advent in the USA of a new appreciation and evaluation of Mahler—the time to which Mahler himself had looked forward—it would be 1960, the centenary of his birth. From January through April of that year the New York Philharmonic mounted a Mahler festival conducted by Bruno Walter, Dimitri Mitropoulos and Leonard Bernstein, by then the director of the orchestra. The First, Second, Fourth, Fifth, and Ninth Symphonies, and the first movement of the Tenth were presented, together with *Das Lied von der Erde*, *Kindertotenlieder*, two Rückert, and two *Wunderhorn* songs. In a sense these concerts marked a changing of the guard, with the young and ardent Bernstein representing a new generation of Mahlerites who recognized their indebtedness to the pioneers who preceded them, but carried their work forward with a new enthusiasm, and a new appreciation of the previously less performed works.

1960 also marked the important pioneering effort by William Malloch in Los Angeles to preserve on tape the memories of surviving musicians who had known or played under Mahler. Malloch's 'Mahlerthon' broadcast on KPFK-FM preserves a remarkable record that vividly brought Mahler's presence to life, and reflects the strong reactions that his personality produced among those who played for him.[46]

[40] See Aaron Copland, 'Five Post-Romantics', *Modern Music*, 18 (1941), 218–20, and also, with slight variants, *Our New Music* (New York: Whittlesey House, 1941), 29–34.

[41] Trans. James Galston (New York: Greystone Press, 1941; repr. New York: Da Capo Press, 1970).

[42] Trans. Basil Creighton. The first American edition was published by Viking Press in New York.

[43] New York: King's Crown Press. Rev. edn. New York: W. W. Norton, 1978.

[44] London: Rockliff. Rev. edn., ed. Paul Banks and David Matthews, Berkeley: University of California Press, 1980.

[45] New York, Harcourt, Brace & Co. The subsequent German edition, under the title *Mein Leben* (Frankfurt am Main: S. Fischer, 1960), did not involve Ashton, and differs in some respects from the English version.

[46] See the unsigned article, 'The William Malloch Tapes', *News about Mahler Research*, no. 9 (Sept. 1981), 8. See also Lebrecht, *Mahler Remembered*, p. xxviii, who gives the date of the first broadcast as 7 July 1960, and notes several later ones. Excerpts from the broadcast are included in his volume. A shorter version of the reminiscences, ed. Deryck Cooke, was included in the fourth side of Leonard

434 Edward R. Reilly

In the Sixties the rapidly developing acceptance of all Mahler's works was reflected by the new series of complete recordings of all his symphonies by Bernstein, Abravanel, Solti, Haitink, and Kubelik. Thereafter, few conductors could resist the challenge of doing their own Mahler cycles.

What brought about this extraordinary new popularity? One cannot overestimate the powerful impact of Bernstein. His immense popularity, his self-identification with Mahler, and his effectiveness as a teacher all helped enormously to further the cause of Mahler in America (as well as abroad).[47] But many other factors also enter the picture. And one must remember that the very articles of critical detractors provide a record that suggests that there had been quite substantial favourable popular reaction to Mahler's music from the very beginning. Certainly the growing number of recordings that appeared after the Second World War, and especially after the advent of long-playing discs in 1948, played a significant role.[48] And undoubtedly the continuing efforts of the Bruckner Society of America up to 1969, the date of the last issue of *Chord and Discord*, had an important effect. (After an interval of twenty-nine years, the 'Final issue' of *Chord and Discord* [vol. 3/2], edited by Charles Eble and Himie Voxman, was published in 1998.) That organization coexisted with, and was followed by, several others: The Gustav Mahler Society of America, founded in 1957 by Dr Eric Simon, and reactivated for a time in 1976; the California Mahler Society, founded in 1963–4 by Avik Gilboa and a circle of friends, and active since 1982 under the name the Gustav Mahler Society USA; and the New York Mahlerites (now renamed The Gustav Mahler Society of New York), formed in 1976 by Jack Diether (1919–87),[49] for many years a leading figure among American Mahlerites.

Bernstein's 1967 recording of the Sixth Symphony (CBS 77215). A 26.30 minute excerpt of the original tape is also included on the 1993 CD *Mahler Plays Mahler: The Welte-Mignon Piano Rolls* (GLRS 101). A more complete version of the programme has been issued in *New York Philharmonic: The Mahler Broadcasts 1948–1982* (c.1998), discs 11 and 12.

[47] For Bernstein's published views about Mahler, see his article 'Mahler: His Time has Come', originally published in *High Fidelity*, 17/9 (Sept. [not Apr., as indicated in the reprint] 1967), 51–4, and reprinted in his book *Findings* (New York: Simon and Schuster, 1982), 255–64. He also discussed Mahler in the fifth of his 1973 Norton Lectures at Harvard, entitled 'The Unanswered Question', published in recorded form, together with a performance of the Adagio from the Ninth Symphony, on Columbia Masterworks M3X 33208, vol. 5. (See also Leonard Bernstein, *The Unanswered Question* (Cambridge, Mass. and London: Harvard University Press, 1976), 312–21.) For a thoughtful recent review of Bernstein's role as an educator, see Joseph Horowitz, 'Professor Lenny', *New York Review of Books*, 40/11 (10 June 1993), 39–44. The recent biography by Humphrey Burton, *Leonard Bernstein* (New York: Doubleday, 1994), amply documents Bernstein's growing involvement with Mahler over the years.

One should also remember that strong adverse views of

Mahler were still not uncommon. In the 2 Mar. 1969 issue of the *New York Times*, Harold C. Schonberg gave heated expression to his antipathy in an article entitled 'With Malice Toward Mahler'. Acknowledging the Mahler 'renaissance', he noted: 'No matter where I turn, I seem to run into Mahler symphonies, most of which irritate me like sand in ice cream; and no matter what review I pick up, I read that Mahler (who died in 1911) was a symbol of the present day. I cannot understand the reasoning, just as I cannot respond to most of Mahler's music. To me, Mahler was a futile figure who looked back rather than forward, and who was an eternal emotional adolescent of a postromantic.'

[48] Several lengthy discographies of Mahler's works have been published. See J. F. Weber, *Mahler* (Discography Series IX; Utica, NY: self-published, 1971; 2nd edn., 1975); Peter Fülöp, *Mahler Discography* (New York: The Kaplan Foundation, 1995); Lewis M. Smoley, *The Symphonies of Gustav Mahler: A Critical Discography* (New York: Greenwood Press, 1986); id., *Gustav Mahler's Symphonies: Critical Commentary on Recordings since 1986* (New York: Greenwood Press, 1996).

[49] Diether's passionate involvement with Mahler is reflected in a considerable range of publications, including liner notes for many recordings of the composer's works. His 'A Personal History of Mahler's Tenth', in *Fragment or Completion?*, 97–105, is in my view a fine memorial to that involvement.

Other historical and social developments, however, may well have affected the response to Mahler in the United States. The rise of the Nazis in Germany brought a new wave of often highly cultured émigrés to this country in the 1930s and early 1940s. These included not only Alma Mahler Werfel and well-known conductors like Walter and Klemperer, but many other performers, composers, and critics as well as musically cultivated men and women of letters.[50] These people formed a significant new element in American musical and cultural life, and included many individuals who were sympathetic to Mahler's music. A number of outstanding scholars found new homes in American colleges and universities. Composers such as Erich Wolfgang Korngold (whom Mahler had met and admired as a nine-year-old prodigy in 1906) and Max Steiner in the 1930s and 1940s created film scores, using styles heavily influenced by Mahler and Strauss, which accustomed even totally untrained members of viewing audiences to a rich and elaborate symphonic idiom.

The fact that one of the most widespread and popular musical institutions in the United States is the marching band, and that virtually everyone is exposed to the march idiom, may also have provided fertile ground for a favourable response to Mahler's use of march themes. Up to the Second World War and to some degree thereafter, most towns (even quite small ones) had their own bands, which presented outdoor concerts during the warmer months of the year. The music performed comprised a wide range of works, including dances, overtures (such as von Suppé's *Light Cavalry*), and virtuoso solo works, especially those for trumpet or cornet. Even the eclectic character of American musical life, with the immense diversity created by numerous immigrant groups, each with their own music, may provide a more natural background for Mahler's eclecticism, since diversity of idiom and the use of popular materials are not necessarily seen as negative qualities. It is perhaps not surprising that the growth of interest in the music of Charles Ives, who also drew on a wide range of different styles, coincided with the new popularity of Mahler's works.

Whether the gradual decline in anti-Romantic aesthetic views, common in the United States from the 1920s through the 1950s,[51] prepared for or was the result of the new enthusiasm for Mahler, remains uncertain.

The aftermath of the emergence of Mahler as a popular composer in the 1960s has been the acceptance of virtually all his works into the 'standard' repertoire, and an explosion of live and recorded performances. New generations of teachers and scholars began to explore his works from almost every conceivable angle, and the slow trickle of books and articles in the early years has now become a flood. The work in Europe of Donald Mitchell, Henry-Louis de La Grange, and Kurt and Herta Blaukopf has provided an enormous stimulus to students in America. Dika Newlin's isolated 1945 dissertation (which became the foundation for her book) remained exceptional until the 1970s, when substantial numbers

---

[50] Many early friends, supporters, and colleagues of Mahler were among the émigrés; to mention only a few: Paul Stefan, Paul Bekker, Alexander Zemlinsky, Thomas Mann, and Franz Werfel.

[51] McKinney and Anderson, *Music in History*, 678, note in 1940 that 'In the world-turned-anti-Romantic of the past decades there is no doubt that it [Mahler's music] has fared badly . . .'. See also Danuser, *Gustav Mahler*, 276.

of Mahler doctoral studies began to appear.[52] At the 1973 meeting of the American Musicological Society at Dallas, Texas, a Mahler study session found a place on the programme for the first time. And now his works are discussed with some frequency in the scholarly community.

Providing significant resources for Mahler studies is the substantial body of Mahler manuscripts and other documents found in American libraries. The richest single group of Mahler's musical autographs is now in the Pierpont Morgan Library in New York City. These came to the library through a bequest by the Trustees of the Mary Flagler Cary Charitable Trust in 1968, a later bequest by Mrs Wolfgang Rosé, and the deposit by Robert Owen Lehman of his very substantial collection of Mahler manuscripts, many of which had been owned by Alma Mahler. Recently, the manuscript of the Second Symphony has also been placed on deposit at the same library by its owner, Gilbert E. Kaplan.[53] A substantial number of Mahler's letters are also in the Pierpont Morgan Library. Some of the other libraries with important Mahler holdings are the Library of the Performing Arts in New York City, the Yale University Library (the Osborn Collection), Harvard University Library, and Stanford University Library. At the University of Western Ontario in Canada, a Mahler–Rosé Room was formally opened in 1986 to house the collection of Mrs Marie Rosé, the widow of Mahler's nephew Alfred Rosé (the son of Arnold Rosé and Justine Mahler). In addition to several important musical manuscripts, a substantial body of family letters is in this collection.[54] The Mahler holdings of the Moldenhauer Archives are now housed in the Bayerische Staatsbibliothek in Munich.[55]

The new appreciation and admiration for Mahler is also reflected in the work of a number of composers. Copland's evaluation of Mahler has been quoted earlier, and although many of his own works betray little, if any, trace, of Mahler's influence, certain compositions, such as the Third Symphony, do suggest his admiration for Mahler's textures and scoring. Leonard Bernstein, in his 'serious' works, such as the *Age of Anxiety* and certain sections of the *Mass*, echoes Mahler's thematic and harmonic material, as do some of the later works of George Rochberg. George Crumb actually quotes motives from the 'Abschied' movement of *Das Lied von der Erde* in his *Ancient Voices of Children* (1970). A more complex use of Mahler's song 'Des Antonius von Padua Fischpredigt' appears in the third section of Luciano Berio's *Sinfonia* (1968). Although technically not the work of an

---

[52] Space is too limited to cite individual works here. For a comprehensive listing of North American and European doctoral dissertations, see Cecil Adkins and Alis Dickinson, *Doctoral Dissertations in Musicology*, 7th North American Edition, 2nd International Edition (n.p.: American Musicological Society and International Musicological Society, 1984), and 2nd series, first cumulation of the same work, 1990, with annual supplements thereafter. Since 1976 the Internationale Gustav Mahler Gesellschaft in Vienna has published *Nachrichten zur Mahler-Forschung/News about Mahler Research* in German and English, providing valuable current information about all kinds of research on the composer. The library of the Society in Vienna has also proved a

mecca for American as well as European Mahler scholars.

[53] A facsimile of this manuscript was published by the Kaplan Foundation in New York in 1986.

[54] See Stephen McClatchie, 'The Gustav Mahler–Alfred Rosé Collection at the University of Western Ontario', *Notes: Quarterly Journal of the Music Library Association*, 52 (1995–6), 385–406.

[55] See J. Newsom and A. Mann (eds.), *Music History from Primary Sources: A Guide to the Moldenhauer Archives* (Washington, DC: Library of Congress, 2000), 301–12 and 613–15; esp. 301–12: Edward R. Reilly, 'Gustav Mahler Sketches in the Moldenhauer Archives', a scrutiny of sketches for the Sixth and Seventh Symphonies.

American, the *Sinfonia* was 'written for (and commissioned by) [the] New York Philharmonic and dedicated to Leonard Bernstein',[56] and received its first hearing in the United States. With neo-Romantic styles now popular again, it seems more than likely that Mahler's influence will continue to grow in increasingly diverse ways. And if Mahler's star seems now to have reached its zenith, one must remember that criticism does not (and should not) cease. The future may well bring a reaction. Few composers escape shifting critical assessments and fluctuations in popularity, and it is hardly likely that Mahler will be an exception.

[56] Dedication page in the score (London: Universal Edition, 1969).

19

Das Lied von der Erde

STEPHEN E. HEFLING

To Robert Bailey—teacher, mentor, friend

— If I am to find the way back to myself again, I must surrender to the terrors of loneliness . . . you do not know what has been and is going on in me, but it is certainly not that hypochondriac fear in the face of death that you suppose. I had already realized that I must die. — But without attempting here to explain or describe to you something for which there are perhaps no words at all, I will just tell you that in one stroke I have simply lost all the clarity and reassurance I ever achieved; and that I stood vis à vis de rien and now at the end of a life I must learn to stand and move again as a beginner.

Mahler to Bruno Walter during the composition of *Das Lied von der Erde*[1]

Just seven months after he had penned the celestial conclusion of the Eighth Symphony, Mahler faced the first of the well-known crises that darkened his life during 1907. After a decade of strenuous efforts to transform the Vienna Court Opera into an ensemble that regularly achieved his ideals, he finally relinquished his grip on the directorship. Although the circumstances surrounding this decision were complex, Mahler's own assessment of them was essentially accurate: grasping a chair and tilting its legs backward, he explained to Bruno Walter, 'You see, that's what they are now doing to me: if I wanted to remain seated, all I would have to do is lean back firmly and I could hold my place. But I am not offering any resistance, and so I shall finally slide off'.[2] The terms of Mahler's resignation were agreed in March, and by mid-May he was seriously negotiating for a new post in the New World, at the Metropolitan Opera in New York.[3]

In late June the Mahler family retreated as usual to their summer home in Maiernigg on the Wörthersee, where the Fifth, Sixth, Seventh, and Eighth Symphonies, the Rückert songs, and *Kindertotenlieder* had been composed. Within days, Mahler's elder daughter Maria, his

---

[1] Mahler, *Briefe* (1982), no. 396 (*Selected Letters*, no. 375), 18 July 1908.

[2] Bruno Walter, *Gustav Mahler* (Vienna: Herbert Reichner Verlag, 1936), 41; trans. Galston (1973 edn.), 52.

[3] Details concerning the events of 1907 will be found in HLG(F) iii. chs. 49–50, and Alma Mahler, *Memories*, 116–27; cf. also Roman, *Gustav Mahler's American Years*, 1–40.

favourite child, showed symptoms of scarlet fever; a fortnight later she died. Alma Mahler collapsed from grief and exhaustion, and the doctor summoned to her aid also examined Mahler: he discovered a potentially serious heart condition, which was confirmed a few days later by a specialist in Vienna. Within four months, Mahler's life had been radically transformed.

According to Alma, 'this . . . was the beginning of the end for Mahler'.[4] But as La Grange has pointed out, the rate and extent of his decline has been exaggerated: only in the wake of Alma's affair with Walter Gropius during the summer of 1910 was Mahler's psychological balance completely shaken, while his physical health remained essentially stable until the following February, when infection resulted in bacterial endocarditis, for which there was then no cure.[5] Still, there seems little doubt that the events of 1907 deeply affected his whole way of life;[6] in particular, his lifelong habit of vigorous physical activity, including long walks almost daily, had to be curtailed. Nevertheless, he threw himself into professional activity during his New York years, and needed to do just that 'to avert my eyes and close my ears'[7] from what had occurred before his arrival in America. Indeed, such immersion in work was one of his characteristic responses to crisis.

Another, deeper response was to make his personal circumstances the occasion or impulse for composition; years earlier he had declared that 'it is always thus for me: only when I experience do I "compose", and only when I compose do I experience!'[8] Mahler's letters to Bruno Walter from the summer of 1908 clearly reveal that while his existential situation was not one of 'hypochondriac fear', it was none the less serious—justifying Walter's subsequent summary assessment: 'Death, towards whose mysteries his thought and perception had so often taken their flight, had suddenly come in sight'.[9] This was not the first time: during a severe haemorrhage in February 1901, Mahler believed 'that my last hour had struck'[10]—and out of this brush with mortality grew *Kindertotenlieder* and 'Ich bin der Welt abhanden gekommen', works related in many respects to *Das Lied von der Erde*.[11] But now the crucial difference—central to the nature of *Das Lied*—was that there seemed no hope of reprieve: the next work might well be his last, and was therefore to be a most singular utterance. It now seems certain that Mahler did no creative work during the summer of 1907; at some point after he had returned to Vienna in September for his final weeks at the Opera, he was given a copy of *Die chinesische Flöte*, the collection of paraphrase-poems (*Nachdichtungen*) Hans Bethge had recently made from earlier French and German translations of Chinese lyrics.[12] Out of eighty-three poems by thirty-eight authors on a wide variety of topics, Mahler selected and gradually modified a group of seven that

[4] Alma Mahler, *Memories*, 122.

[5] See below, Ch. 20, n. 4.

[6] See Mahler's letters to Bruno Walter from the summer of 1908, *Briefe* (1982), nos. 394, 396, and 400 (*Selected Letters*, nos. 372, 375, and 378); see also HLG(F) iii, ch. 50.

[7] Mahler to Walter, 18 July 1908; *Briefe* (1982), no. 396 (*Selected Letters*, no. 375).

[8] *Briefe* (1982), no. 167 (*Selected Letters*, no. 158), 26 Mar. 1896.

[9] Walter, *Gustav Mahler* (1937 edn.), 42–3 (Eng. trans., 54).

[10] Natalie Bauer-Lechner, 'Mahleriana' (original MS of her memoirs), quoted in HLG(F) ii. 66; pp. 66–75 provide a full account of Mahler's illness and recovery in 1901.

[11] See above, Ch. 13, pp. 340–1 and 347.

[12] Although Alma Mahler states that work on *Das Lied* began in the summer of 1907 (*Memories*, 123), according to the *Börsenblatt für den Deutschen Buchhandel* (Leipzig, 1907), p. 10130, Bethge's *Die chinesische Flöte: Nachdichtungen chinesischer Lyrik* (Leipzig, Inselverlag) was first published around 5 Oct. 1907. Mahler had left Schluderbach for Vienna on 24 Aug. that year (HLG(F) iii. 94). The dated

constitute a poignant allegory of life and death, culminating in 'Der Abschied', the moment of spiritual departure from the world of time and space.[13]

It seems astonishing that he should have found texts so admirably suited to his purpose in the centuries-old literature of the T'ang dynasty, but we can discern a number of mediating factors in this fortunate coincidence. To be sure, since the seventeenth-century French Jesuit missions to China, Western interest in Oriental culture had been both widespread and eclectic—from scholarly tomes and journals, to the Paris Exhibitions, to the art of the Viennese secessionists.[14] Among the German poets affected by this current were Rückert and Goethe, whose work Mahler knew thoroughly. Both had composed important collections of lyrics inspired by ancient Persian poetry, and Goethe in his last years again turned towards the East in his *Chinese–German Book of Hours and Seasons* (1827), a precedent Mahler may have had in mind when selecting the texts of *Das Lied*. Bethge's *Chinesische Flöte* stands somewhere between the earlier German poets' creative assimilation of Eastern influence and the vogue for straightforward translation of Asian literature: twice removed from the original sources, Bethge's versification expands and vitalizes the delicately disjunct and (for Western ears) seemingly timeless imagery of the ancient Chinese poets, accentuating the personal responses of the nameless protagonists, and bringing both style and content closer to the German Romantic tradition. And Mahler's own revisions of Bethge, which were made both before and during the composition of *Das Lied*, carry this trend even further in the service of the particular work he was creating.

Spiritual rebirth is the principal concern of *Das Lied von der Erde*, and also the root of its orientalism. Mahler had long been aware of Eastern views on the matter, and not only from Rückert and Goethe. Since his student days he had been immersed in the philosophy of Arthur Schopenhauer, for whom the Buddhistic stilling of the individual will is the only path to the reduction of suffering and to mystical rebirth.[15] Moreover, Schopenhauer

manuscripts from the gestation of *Das Lied von der Erde* also suggest that the entire work was composed during the summer of 1908 (see Hefling, '*Das Lied von der Erde*: Mahler's Symphony', 298–9, as well as Edward R. Reilly, 'The Manuscripts of *Das Lied von der Erde*', App. A in Mitchell, *SSLD*, 617–19). I am especially grateful to Knud Martner for providing me with the citation from the *Börsenblatt*. This publication was quite rigorous in monitoring the publication dates of new materials, as outlined in the issue of 2 Jan. 1907; as a rule new books were listed within two days of their arrival at the *Börsenblatt* offices.

[13] The sources of Bethge's texts and Mahler's adaptations of them are discussed in Zoltan Roman, 'Mahler's Songs and their Influence on his Symphonic Thought' (Ph.D. diss., University of Toronto, 1970), 106–23; Arthur Wenk, 'The Composer as Poet in *Das Lied von der Erde*', *19th Century Music*, 1 (1977), 33–47; HLG(F) iii. 1121–64; Mitchell, *SSLD*, 162–432; Kii-Ming Lo, 'Chinesische Dichtung als Text-Grundlage für Mahler's "Lied von der Erde"', in *Das Gustav-Mahler-Fest Hamburg 1989*, 509–28; and Hefling, '*Das Lied*', 316 ff.; and Fusako Hamao, 'The Sources of the Texts in Mahler's *Lied von der Erde*', *19th Century Music*, 19

(1995), 83–95; see also below, n. 36.

[14] See e.g. Adolf Reichwein, *China and Europe: Intellectual and Artistic Contacts in the Eighteenth Century* (New York: Alfred A. Knopf, 1925); Edward W. Said, *Orientalism* (New York: Pantheon Books, 1978); and Nicolas Powell, *The Sacred Spring: The Arts in Vienna 1898–1918* (Greenwich, Conn.: New York Graphic Society, 1974), esp. 137 ff.

[15] A concise summary concerning Mahler and Schopenhauer will be found in Hefling, 'Mahler: Symphonies 1–4', in *The Symphony, 1825–c. 1900*, ed. D. Kern Holoman (Studies in Musical Genres and Repertoires; New York: Schirmer Books, 1997), 369 ff.; see also McGrath, *Dionysian Art and Populist Politics*, esp. chs. 2–4; Floros, *Gustav Mahler*, i. 150–7 and *passim*; L. J. Rather, *The Dream of Self-Destruction: Wagner's Ring and the Modern World* (Baton Rouge: Louisiana State University Press, 1979), esp. ch. 3; Malcolm Budd, *Music and the Emotions: The Philosophical Theories* (London: Routledge & Kegan Paul, 1985), ch. 5; and Peter Franklin, *The Idea of Music: Schoenberg and Others* (London: Macmillan Press Ltd, 1985), ch. 1.

accords particular significance to the role of art in overcoming the *principium individua-tionis*, because art prompts contemplative, 'will-less' perception rather than material action.[16] And in his view, music is endowed with a special characteristic: whereas the other arts objectify the will indirectly, through ideas, music, like the will itself, 'gives the inner-most kernel preceding all form, or the heart of things'.[17] It was the contemplative with-drawal of oriental mysticism that Mahler sought to capture in 'Ich bin der Welt abhanden gekommen', the Rückert lied he composed the summer after his serious illness in 1901. To this end he used anhemitonic (i.e. lacking semitones) pentatonic scales, the most common mode of Eastern pitch organization, to diffuse and complement the goal-directed processes of traditional Western tonality; the result is an extraordinary atmosphere of suspended ani-mation. Mahler said of this song when it was finished, 'It is myself';[18] and in seeking 'to find the way back to myself again' in 1908,[19] he developed and transformed both the mood and techniques of 'Ich bin der Welt' in *Das Lied von der Erde*.

Schopenhauer's philosophy had been embraced and expounded by Wagner, and was subsequently extended by the young Nietzsche in *The Birth of Tragedy*. In this book the darker side of the will, its intoxicated collective instinctuality, is conceptualized as Dionysian, the antipode of Apollonian restraint and individuation.[20] Dionysian abandon becomes topical in the two drinking songs of *Das Lied* (movements 1 and 5), whereas 'Von der Jugend' (Of Youth) might well be characterized as Apollonian. From a broader per-spective, such dynamic polarity, the interplay between syzygial opposites, had long been recognized in the oriental doctrine of contrast between *Yin* and *Yang* (as Schopenhauer had noted);[21] it is central to Goethe's thought, culminating in the celebrated allegory of Faustian striving and the eternal feminine (as Mahler interpreted it);[22] and it became a basic feature of Mahler's new symphony for voices and instruments, which reflects so many facets of his wide-reaching world-view.

Mahler had envisaged the moment of the soul's departure from earth in three of his earl-ier symphonies—the Second, Fourth, and Eighth. From these works and his comments about them, it is evident that he did not regard that moment of liminal transition as the end of spiritual development. Rather, 'the soul is in heaven, where, in chrysalis-like state, it must begin everything anew as a child'.[23] This was his description of 'Urlicht', the lied for alto solo that introduces the vast finale of the 'Resurrection' Symphony. The 'chrysalis-like state' is an allusion to the *Schlußszene* of *Faust* (later set in the finale of the Eighth), and he made a similar observation about 'Das himmlische Leben', the child's vision of paradise that is the conclusion of the Fourth Symphony and the culmination of his early symphonic

[16] Schopenhauer, *The World as Will and Representation*, i. 179, 184–5, 195–8.

[17] Ibid. i. 257 and 263.

[18] See above, Ch. 13.

[19] Letter to Bruno Walter cited at the head of this chapter.

[20] See the sources cited in n. 15 as well as Floros, *Gustav Mahler*, i. 72–6; Hefling, 'Mahler's "Todtenfeier"', 28–9; and Nikkels, '*O Mensch! Gib Acht!*'.

[21] *The World as Will and Representation*, i. 143–4.

[22] See e.g. L. A. Willoughby, 'Unity and Continuity in Goethe', in Elizabeth M. Wilkinson and L. A. Willoughby, *Goethe: Poet and Thinker* (New York: Barnes and Noble, 1962), 214–28; Mahler's reading of *Faust* appears in a long letter to his wife written in June 1909, in Alma Mahler, *Memories*, 319–21.

[23] NB-L, *Erinnerungen*, 168 (not in *Recollections*).

tetralogy as a whole.[24] Like the Fourth, *Das Lied* turns away from the grandeur of the choral symphonies, adopting instead the perspective of a single being who stands at the threshold of life as we know it: 'it is the most personal thing I have yet created', as Mahler wrote to Bruno Walter.[25]

His views on immortality were deeply influenced by Goethe: *Faust*, the conversation with Falk (1813), and poems such as 'Eins und Alles' (one and all) are notable cases in point.[26] But in Mahler's selection and reworking of the texts for *Das Lied von der Erde*— and especially 'Der Abschied'—we can discern a strong resonance with the religious philosophy of Gustav Theodor Fechner, which he had read 'with engrossing interest; it comes home to me with the intimacy of what I have long known and seen and experienced myself. Remarkable, how close in feeling Fechner is to Rückert'.[27] Fechner also seems steeped in Goethe's views, yet develops several distinctive notions as well.[28] His thinking is rooted in quasi-gnostic nature religion: the entire universe is an organic spiritual hierarchy, leading upwards to the deity. This he calls the *Tagesansicht* ('daylight view'), as contrasted to materialism, the *Nachtansicht* ('night view'). Human existence consists of three stages: seemingly endless sleep before birth, alternate waking and sleeping on earth, and finally, eternal waking. Death is the transition to the third stage, and we really have no reason to fear it any more than the trauma of birth from the womb.[29] A universalist, Fechner rejects the division between saved and damned (as had Mahler in the 'Resurrection' Symphony). But he believes that people make for themselves the conditions of their future lives, and that the soul continues to develop after death 'according to the unalterable law of nature upon earth'[30] (a view Mahler reflected in conversation with Richard Specht).[31]

The moment of transition to the third stage of existence is described by Fechner in rapturous terms:

. . . our future life will merge as one with waves of light and sound. . . .

The spirit will no longer wander over mountain and field, or be surrounded by the delights of spring, only to mourn that it all seems exterior to him; but, transcending earthly limitations, he will feel new strength and joy. . . .

Stilled is all restlessness of thought, which no longer needs to seek in order to find itself. . . .

---

[24] NB-L, *Erinnerungen*, 198 and 164 (*Recollections*, 178 and 154).

[25] Mahler, *Briefe* (1982), no. 400 (*Selected Letters*, no. 378), early Sept. 1908.

[26] Walter, *Gustav Mahler*, 95 (Eng. trans., 137). Adorno surely alludes to Goethe's poem when he claims that in the close of *Das Lied von der Erde*, 'No one-and-all [*Kein Ein und Alles*] is conjured up as consolation' (*Mahler*, 154; German edn., 199). But as Donald Mitchell has already noted, 'it seems to me that Adorno's metaphysic is chillier than Mahler meant *his* to be, and not wholly borne out by the musical experience' (*SSLD*, 452).

[27] Letter to Alma, 2 Apr. 1903; *Memories*, 226.

[28] Fechner's most extensive work is the *Zend-Avesta* . . .

(1851), but the basic ideas of his philosophy are expressed in *Das Büchlein vom Leben nach dem Tode* (1836), which dates from early in his career (repr. with a preface by Wilhelm Wandt (Leipzig: Insel-Verlag, n.d.); trans. Mary C. Wadsworth as *Life after Death* (New York: Pantheon Books, 1943)). See also *The Encyclopedia of Philosophy* s.v. 'Fechner', by Arnulf Zweig; Reinhard Liebe, *Fechners Metaphysik* (Greifswald: Julius Abel, 1903), esp. 23–6; and Floros, *Gustav Mahler*, i. 111–13. Mahler's long-time friend and mentor Siegfried Lipiner had been a student of Fechner's.

[29] *Life after Death*, 23–4 (*Das Büchlein*, 9–10).

[30] Ibid. 33–5 (*Das Büchlein*, 16–17).

[31] Specht, *Gustav Mahler*, 38–9.

... when man dies, ... as the waves roll forth into the sea of ether and the sea of air, he will not merely feel the blowing of the wind and the wash of the waves against his body, but will himself murmur in the air and sea; no more wander outwardly through verdant woods and meadows, but himself consciously pervade both wood and meadow and those wandering there.[32]

The affinity of these passages with the conclusion of 'Der Abschied' (The Farewell), the final movement of *Das Lied*, is wholly striking when the Fechner text is compared with the last five lines of the poetry cited below, which are Mahler's own:

> I will never more wander on the horizons.
> Still is my heart, and awaits its hour!
>
> The beloved earth all over everywhere
> Blossoms forth in spring and greens up anew!
> Everywhere and ever blue brightly the horizons,
> Eternally ... ever. ...

From the perspective of these diverse influences on Mahler's world in 1908, we can gain insight into several unusual aspects of *Das Lied von der Erde*. The title itself is slightly enigmatic: when the work was drafted, Mahler wrote to Bruno Walter that 'I myself do not know what the whole thing could be called',[33] and he variously revised both the title of the entire work and the headings of individual movements.[34] While there is reliable evidence that for superstitious reasons he avoided calling it his Ninth Symphony—the last such work for Beethoven and Bruckner[35]—it is equally clear that *Das Lied* stands apart from his other symphonies in many respects.[36] It is a 'Song of the Earth', not only because it concerns man's life on this planet, but also because it culminates in transfiguration of the relationship between Nature and the soul, which, according to the *Tagesansicht*, will henceforth pervade the elements. The prospect of this final dissolution of the individual will may arouse human anxiety, but ultimately it will be a moment of ecstatic release. Thus, colours can indeed become verbs in Mahler's final lines of 'Der Abschied'; spatio-temporal distinctions no longer obtain.

Such considerations also illuminate the ubiquitous natural imagery in the poems preceding the final moment—imagery that, within the context of the whole, projects the dualistic nature of the human spirit: night and day, autumn and spring, youth and death,

---

[32] *Life after Death*, 66, 25, 63, 65–6 (*Das Büchlein*, 40, 10, 38, 39–40).

[33] Mahler, *Briefe* (1982), no. 400 (*Selected Letters*, no. 378), early Sept. 1908.

[34] See Reilly, 'The Manuscripts', in Mitchell, *SSLD*, and Hefling, '*Das Lied*'; see also p. 463 n. 69 below.

[35] See Specht, *Gustav Mahler*, 355; Alma Mahler, *Memories*, 115, 124, and 139; Walter, *Gustav Mahler*, 46 (Eng. trans., 58–9); and William Ritter, review of the première in *La Vie musicale*, 5/7 (1 Dec. 1911), 136 ff., cited in Hermann Danuser, *Gustav Mahler: Das Lied von der Erde* (Meisterwerke der Musik, 25; Munich: Wilhelm Fink Verlag, 1986), 24 and 113.

[36] Among the most notable differences is that Mahler initially conceived the work for performance with either orchestra or piano and voices, as discussed briefly below; see also Hefling, '*Das Lied*', and id. (ed.), Supplement Band II of the Kritische Gesamtausgabe, *Das Lied von der Erde, für eine hohe und eine mittlere Gesangstimme mit Klavier* (Vienna: Universal Edition, 1989), which also compares the poetic texts of both Bethge's first edition (Leipzig, 1907) and Mahler's autograph keyboard version with the text of the published orchestral score (pp. xii–xvi).

intoxication and meditation—and, in the division of the vocal material, male and female.[37] The tenor sings of Dionysian revelry (no. 5), coupled with despair (no. 1), and of the carefree chatter of sophisticated youth (no. 3). The alto—the same voice that renders 'Urlicht' in the Second Symphony—is concerned with introspective autumnal reflection upon the transitory (no. 2), *Sehnsucht* (no. 4), and the moment of departure—overall, with 'that which draws us by its mystic force, . . . the centre of its being, . . . the resting-place, the goal, in opposition to the striving and struggling towards the goal'—to paraphrase Mahler: the eternal feminine.[38] These are not the utterances of separate characters (much less of a narrator), but reflections of the dynamic polarities of a single human spirit.[39] Thus we can begin to grasp how Mahler could discover in Bethge's *Nachdichtungen* a group of poems appropriate to the work he needed to create. The songs that prepare for 'Der Abschied' are a series of vignettes, recollections, and present meditations on earthly life: vanity, loneliness, and intoxicated foolishness on the one hand; on the other, cheerful (if superficial) cameraderie of the young, plus nostalgia for the bitter-sweet longing of youth's erotic awakening.[40]

How all this becomes manifest as a musical work is quite simply magnificent. *Das Lied von der Erde* is Mahler's culminating synthesis of song and symphony, an ideal that had occupied him since the time of *Lieder eines fahrenden Gesellen* and the First Symphony (1884–8); its nearest predecessors are his Fourth and *Kindertotenlieder*. 'Symphony for a Tenor and an Alto Voice and Orchestra' was one provisional subtitle for the work;[41] more-

---

[37] Certain of the preliminary manuscripts for *Das Lied von der Erde* suggest that in the early stages of the work's gestation Mahler was undecided about the distribution of the vocal parts; thus, for example, both the *Particell* (short score) and the autograph keyboard version of the third song (ultimately entitled 'Von der Jugend') indicate that it is for tenor or soprano; the keyboard manuscript assigns the first song to the tenor, but the second is designated simply 'Singstimme' (voice), and in numbers 4, 5, and 6 the solo voice remains unspecified (see Hefling, '*Das Lied*', 295 and 322–3; Reilly, 'The Manuscripts', in Mitchell, *SSLD*, 617; and Kritische Gesamtausgabe, Supplement Band II; cf. also below, n. 42). By the time of the autograph full score (New York, Pierpont Morgan Library, Lehman Deposit), Mahler had clearly indicated that numbers 1, 3, and 5 were for 'Tenorstimme' (tenor voice), while 2, 4, and 6 were for 'Alt-Solo', 'Alt-St[imme]', and 'Alt' respectively (i.e. all for alto). Similarly, in a list of titles for 'Das Lied von der Erde / aus dem Alt-Chinesischen' and '9. Symphonie von 4 Sätzen' that Mahler drew up at the Hotel Savoy in New York, probably during the 1909–10 season, the second, fourth, and sixth movements of *Das Lied* are for 'Alt' (Vienna, Stadt- und Landesbibliothek; cf. also HLG(F) iii. 1123). But in the *Stichvorlage* of the work (printer's manuscript in the hand of a copyist; Vienna, Stadt- und Landesbibliothek, on loan from Universal Edition), at the first entrance of the *Alt-Stimme* in the second song, Mahler marked '(kann eventuell auch von Baryton übernommen werden)', ('(could possibly also be taken over by baritone)'); he did not, however, change the designations 'Alt-Stimme' and 'Alt' in movements 4 and 6. This provisional annotation in the second

movement has given rise to the occasional practice of performing the entire cycle with two male voices, tenor and baritone. Mahler had entrusted the world première of *Das Lied* to Bruno Walter, who, after the composer's death, initially performed it (Munich, 20 Nov. 1911) with tenor and alto; for the first Viennese performance (4 Nov. 1912) he substituted the baritone Friedrich Weidemann, one of Mahler's favourite singers, for the alto soloist: '*Never again*', Walter wrote near the end of his life; '. . . from then on I have always used an alto voice. . . . two male voices do the work no good. Mahler never heard Das Lied von der Erde—in my firm conviction, based on practical experience, he himself would have realized the error of giving the three songs to a baritone'. (Walter, *Briefe*, 355, letter to Wolfgang Stresemann dated 5 Dec. 1957; see also HLG(F) iii. 1131.)

[38] See the remarkable commentary Mahler wrote to Alma in June 1909, about the conclusion of *Faust* and the eternal feminine: Alma Mahler, *Memories*, 319–21, esp. 321 (German text in Henry-Louis de La Grange and Günther Weiß (eds.), *Ein Glück ohne Ruh': Die Briefe Gustav Mahlers an Alma* (Berlin: Siedler Verlag, 1995), no. 276.

[39] Cf. also Mitchell, *SSLD*, 370–3 and 424–31.

[40] Cf. also ibid. 217–18.

[41] 'Das Trink=Lied von der Erde / nach dem Chinesichen [*sic*] der 8. Jahrhundert [*sic*] n. Ch.* / Symphonie für eine Tenor= und eine Altstimme / und Orchester. / von / Gustav Mahler / *dem Text ist die deutsche Übertragung von H. Bethgen zu Grunde gelegt' ('Trink=' and 'deutsche' are later additions made with insert signs); Vienna, Gesellschaft der Musikfreunde, A 315.

over, one of the orchestral draft scores specifies 'Orchestra or Piano',[42] and in fact Mahler made a complete keyboard score of the work, just as he had for all but one of his songs from 1892 on.[43] Thus, although *Das Lied von der Erde* is more symphonic in structure than the *Kindertotenlieder* or *Gesellen* cycles, Mahler originally planned that it too could be performed either with orchestra or in the more intimate ambiance of a *Liederabend* with piano. And this reveals something fundamental about the hybrid nature of this music: whereas opera and symphony were traditionally large-scale, public musical genres, the lied cycle emerged from the more private, personal realm of musical activity (Schubert's *Winterreise* and Schumann's *Dichterliebe* were undoubtedly among Mahler's models).[44] Just as Wagner in *Tristan und Isolde* had focused the full resources of musical theatre inward, to illuminate the private psychological world of two characters united through fateful love, so Mahler draws upon all the available techniques of symphonic and lieder composition—with or without the orchestra—to manifest the inward being of one persona through two voices.

On the broadest scale, *Das Lied* is divided into two parts, reminiscent of the *Abteilungen* into which Mahler had grouped movements of the Fifth, Third, and (originally) the First Symphonies, according to the scheme of tonalities shown in Diagram 19.1.[45]

1.	2.	3.	4.	5.		6.
Das Trinklied vom Jammer der Erde	Der Einsame im Herbst	Von der Jugend	Von der Schön-heit	Der Trunkene im Frühling		Der Abschied
a	d	B♭/(G)	G	A ‖ c	ǀ c	C–a/C

Diagram 19.1. Overall structure of *Das Lied von der Erde*

The five 'vignette' movements are the first part, while 'Der Abschied', which lasts nearly as long as the first five songs together, constitutes the second. And as in most Mahler symphonies, the first and last movements are the cornerstones: they establish and resolve the main issues of the whole, and are structurally more complex than the inner interludes (which, in *Das Lied*, grow progressively brighter in character).

---

[42] 'Der Pavillon aus Porzellan / aus dem Chinesichen [*sic*] des / Li-Tai-Po / übersetzt von Bethgen [*sic*] / für Tenor oder Sopran / und Orchester oder Clavier / 1. August 1908 Gustav Mahler / Nro 3'; Vienna, Gesellschaft der Musikfreunde, A 315.

[43] See above, n. 36; the exception was 'Liebst du um Schönheit', written especially as a gift for Alma, and never orchestrated by Mahler (see above, Ch. 13, pp. 360–1).

[44] Cf. also Adorno, *Mahler*, 148 (German edn., 192).

[45] The analytical observations in this chapter owe much to Robert Bailey, '*Das Lied von der Erde*: Tonal Language and Formal Design', unpublished paper read at the Forty-Fourth Annual Meeting of the American Musicological Society, Minneapolis, Oct. 1978. Much of what I present here was first developed for lectures at Stanford and Yale Universities between 1981 and 1985; additional details on all aspects of the work will be found in Donald Mitchell's extensive discussion in *SSLD*, 161–500.

Ex. 19.1. Pentatonic scale forms and triadic derivations: (*a*) octave species of anhemitonic ('Chinese') pentatonic scales; (*b*) triads of C and A within *Gong*; (*c*) the 'added sixth' mixture of C and A that closes 'Der Abschied'

(*a*)

Gong   Shang   Kio   Zhi   Yu

(*b*)   (*c*)

C

A

As is well known, the entire work is suffused with (Chinese) anhemitonic pentatonicism, which generates a web of motivic continuity spanning the whole.[46] Characteristically, Mahler subjects these pentatonic kernels to virtuosic developmental variation—inversion, transposition, fragmentation, augmentation, etc.—and they are both integrated into and highlighted against the controlling background of structural tonality. For our purposes, it will be most convenient to identify the various octave species or 'modes' of anhemitonic pentatonicism by the Chinese names of the scale degrees that constitute their finals, using C as the basic level of transposition (see Ex. 19.1(*a*)). As Ex. 19.1(*b*) shows, the pentatonic scale on C contains within it the third-related triads of C (major) and A (minor), which are the principal, paired tonal centres of the work as a whole, while Ex. 19.1(*c*) displays the vertical combination of these two triads, which yields the unresolved 'added sixth' sonority that closes 'Der Abschied'.

[46] On Mahler and pentatonicism see also above, Ch. 13, n. 45. In his last years Mahler admired Debussy's works and performed several with the New York Philharmonic, although it remains uncertain when he first came to know the French master's music (see HLG(F) ii. 953 and iii. 1003 and *passim*). There is some evidence that Mahler may have heard cylinder recordings of Chinese music near the time he was composing *Das Lied von der Erde* (see HLG(F) iii. 341 and 1128). Various studies of pentatonicism had been published at the time, including a long article in the *Musikalisches Conversations-Lexikon*, ed. Hermann Mendel (Berlin: L. Heimann, 1870–9), s.v. 'China', by C. Billert; A. Dechevrens, 'Etude sur le système musical chinois', *Sammelbände der Internationalen Musikgesellschaft*, 2 (1900–1), esp. 526–47 (with numerous musical examples); and Otto Abraham and Erich M. von Hornbostel, 'Studien über das Tonsystem und die Musik der Japaner', *Sammelbände der Internationalen Musikgesellschaft*, 4 (1902–3), 302–60. It is unlikely that Mahler spent much time perusing musicological literature, but his circle of friends included Guido Adler, Professor of Music History at the University of Vienna; curiously, however, in his monograph *Gustav Mahler* of 1916, Adler describes the pentatonicism of *Das Lied* as 'only an incidental attendant phenomenon' (Eng. trans. in Reilly, *Gustav Mahler and Guido Adler*, 68).

Das Trinklied vom Jammer der Erde (The Drinking Song of Earth's Sorrow)

Diagram 19.2 presents a schematic overview of *Das Lied*'s opening movement as analysed by Robert Bailey.[47] From this we can grasp how Mahler has synthesized strophic song procedures (similar to those embodied in the first song of *Kindertotenlieder*) with tonal modulation and large-scale deployment of thematic materials more characteristic of a binary sonata form.[48] The original Bethge text consists of four stanzas, each concluding with the refrain 'Dunkel ist das Leben, ist der Tod' (dark is life, dark is death). Mahler compressed Bethge's last two stanzas into one, such that the three occurrences of the refrain R now punctuate the close of both expositions (i.e. the first two strophes) and the recapitulation in a sonata-form schema. The third strophe, however, bisects the development section and overlaps with the recapitulation, in conjunction with mounting musical tension that bursts forth into the reprise. Tonally, both expositions modulate, albeit to different keys.[49] Yet just this feature enables Mahler to raise the refrain by a semitone with each repetition (G–A♭–A), which intensifies the pathos of the text (an instance of Wagnerian 'expressive' tonality,[50] which Mahler uses frequently); in conjunction with the rising refrain, the piece also reaffirms the tonic in the recapitulation.[51]

Pentatonicism is active at various levels in this opening movement. The basic cell, A–G–E, is crucial to the head-motive of the piece (X), and appears in many other guises as well. Ex. 19.2 shows occurrences of this cell that coincide with large-scale tonal articulations. Harmonic juxtapositions of A and C (the central tonal foci of the work overall) mark the opening of both expositions and the recapitulation: these stem from the pentatonic matrix (cf. Ex. 19.1), as do the numerous V–IV–I cadence patterns (e.g. Figs 3 through 4, Fig. 10^{-2} ff., Fig. 16^{-4} ff., etc.), which undermine the dominant–tonic polarity of traditional Western tonality. (Scale forms *Shang*, *Zhi*, and *Yu* contain this potential sequence of harmonic roots.)

The movement's exceptionally cogent formal background stands in stark and ironic contrast to the bitter, half-drunken, nihilistic anxiety projected against it: before we drink the wine, the song of sorrow should burst laughing into our souls, whose gardens lie wasted,

---

[47] Bailey, '*Das Lied von der Erde*'; Diagram 19.2 is reproduced by courtesy of *The Journal of Musicology* from Hefling, '*Das Lied*', 304.

[48] Analysis of the first movement with respect to sonata form dates at least to the work of Ernest W. Mulder, *Gustav Mahler: 'Das Lied von der Erde', een critisch-analytische studie* (Amsterdam: Uitgevers Maatschappij, 1951), 9–26, and has more recently been pursued by Danuser, *Gustav Mahler: Das Lied von der Erde*, 37 ff. For a discussion of literature on the work see Vill, *Vermittlungsformen verbalisierter und musikalischer Inhalte*, 155–90, and HLG(F) iii. 1136–8.

[49] The first movements of Mahler's Second and Fourth Symphonies are additional examples of sonata form with a varied second exposition (beginning at bb. 64 and 72 respectively); for further on this issue see Hefling, '*Das Lied*', 303 ff.

[50] See Robert Bailey, 'The Structure of the *Ring* and its Evolution', *19th Century Music*, 1 (1977), 48–61 at 51–2.

[51] The surviving manuscripts suggest that Mahler initially planned to set the text strophically, with expanding instrumental interludes, but without structural modulation away from the centrality of A, much as he had done in the first song of *Kindertotenlieder*; see Hefling, '*Das Lied*', 305–8.

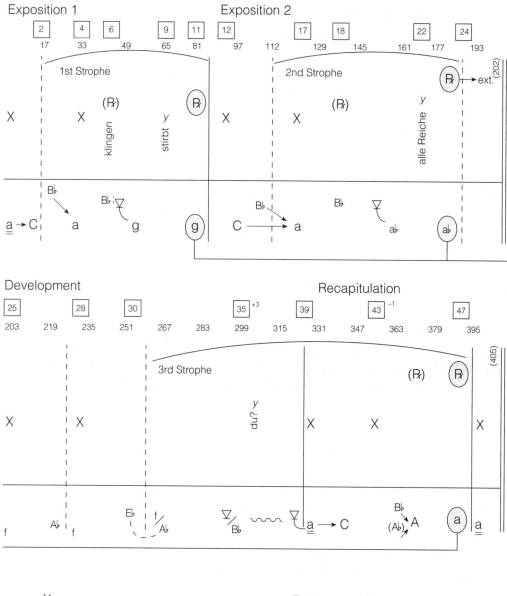

Diagram 19.2. Formal scheme of first movement of *Das Lied von der Erde*. Reproduced by courtesy of *The Journal of Musicology*.

Ex. 19.2. Occurrences of the basic pentatonic cell coinciding with significant tonal articulations in 'Das Trinklied vom Jammer der Erde'

whose joy is dried up; hence the brimming cup is worth more than all the kingdoms of the earth! Metre and tempo at the beginning of both expositions suggest a waltz gone awry; melodic lines surge hectically upwards, only to collapse in arpeggiations derived from the basic cell, while the tonal orientation lurches unsteadily through A minor, C, and B flat. The upper winds shriek and chatter, accentuated by flutter-tonguing flutes: only in the third strophe is this tone-painting fully identified as the shrill voice of Death, a phantom monkey howling on the gravestones. Dark, indeed, as the refrain exclaims—and in its second appearance, Mahler underscores the personification of the phantom by stressing the article, '*der* Tod', through chromatic inflection (Fig. 24^{-1}).

Each of the first two refrains is preceded by another recurring component, *y* (see Diagram 19.2): this short phrase culminates in a nearly atonal sonority, which is a verticalization of elements from the Japanese (hemitonic) pentatonic scale form *Hirajoshi*, as shown in Ex. 19.3.[52] This dissonance stresses particularly biting moments in the poetry— 'dries up and *dies* the joy', and 'is worth more than *all* the kingdoms'. Such, of course, is a fortunate result of strophic procedure; later in the movement, however, *y* becomes a pivotal element in Mahler's fusion of sonata procedure with the third stanza of the text.

At the close of the second strophic exposition (Fig. 24), the refrain is extended by the orchestra; this involves a local shift to the major mode, and ushers in a period of uneasy calm, which is largely maintained during the purely instrumental first half of the development. And this orchestral interlude is itself bipartite (see Diagram 19.2), with each half seeming to approach a gesture of climax not fully realized (Fig. 27^{+5} and Fig. 30). These two passages are at once subtly developmental and premonitory (the technique is Wagnerian, and Mahler deploys it frequently in *Das Lied*): as with the shrill wind texture, their full import emerges only in conjunction with the recapitulatory process.

[52] The scale *Hirajoshi* is discussed by Abraham and von Hornbostel, 'Musik der Japaner', 325. The sonority of element *y* is pitch-class set 4-Z29, one of two forms of the all-interval tetrachord; it is common in the works of Schoenberg, Webern, Berg, Stravinsky, and Ives (see Allen Forte, *The Structure of Atonal Music* (New Haven: Yale University Press, 1973), 21, 218, and *passim*).

Ex. 19.3. Hemitonic ('Japanese') pentatonic scale forms: (*a*) *Hirajoshi*, followed by element *y* verticalized from the scale; (*b*) *Kumoijoshi*

(*a*)   (*b*)

(4-Z29)

The entrance of the voice (Fig. 31⁻²) restores the uncertain calm. Here the text alludes to the ageless duration of sky and earth: this is the principal imagery of 'Der Abschied', and Mahler secures the connection by interpolating 'und aufblüh'n im Lenz' (and bloom forth in spring) into the text. (There is a notable motivic relation as well; cf. Fig. 58 ff. in the final movement.) Now a third appearance of element *y* punctuates the question, 'Du aber, Mensch, wie lang lebst denn *du*?' (but you, man, how long then live *you*?). This precipitates a sequential shift from B flat to A flat; the harmonic fabric then verges on chaos, shot through with atonal and whole-tone sonorities (Fig. 38⁻⁴ ff.), and the voice lurches wildly in the declamation of 'morschen Tande dieser Erde' (rotten trifles of this earth): this is the climactic moment adumbrated by the 'premonitory' passages of the development. Then quite literally at a stroke, tonal order is re-established by the glockenspiel's high *e″/e‴* octave—the dominant of A—and the recapitulation is at hand, altogether unexpectedly (Fig. 39).

As noted above, the third strophe overlaps this moment; it carries the voice immediately into the reprise, thus cutting short the instrumental preambles heard in both expositions. The singer now spies the loathsome monkey, and for the first time voices the orchestral head-motive of the movement (X), thereby identifying what this oft-recurring fanfare her-alds: 'Hear you, how his howling shrieks forth into the sweet scent of *Life!*' (*Lebens!*) 'Lebens' (Fig. 44) is the movement's frenetic high point, which quickly collapses in bitter futility: the tenor howls on the high B♭ (his highest pitch in the song), only to slide down a ninth as the orchestra tumbles yet further, through pentatonic and whole-tone scales, to dominant preparation of A—the last of the tipsy B flat–A juxtapositions in this movement (but not the work). Now follows a modified return of the original vocal material (Fig. 45⁻² ff.), soon combined with reference to the refrain (Fig. 46⁻⁴); but there is little energy in this, and the exhortation to drink is apathetic and resigned.

The last refrain is again twofold (orchestra first, then the voice), and its characteristic major–minor inflection is poignantly redoubled. But the final declamation of 'Tod' (Fig. 48) provokes a parting shriek that recalls the earlier lunge into the second exposition (—might it all transpire again?). The ensuing thirteen-bar coda ceases, however, with an echo of 'das Le-ben ...' from the refrain (scale degree 6̂ to 5̂), abruptly terminated by a tonic thud in the lowest register. Thus the atmosphere remains highly charged at the end of this opening *Trinklied*, and what has been set in motion here will be resolved only at the con-clusion of the cycle.

Der Einsame im Herbst ('The Lonely One in Autumn')

The second movement leaves the raging nocturnal drinking bout behind. The protagonist stands alone on the edge of a lake in autumn, there to meditate upon Nature's withdrawal from blossoming summer warmth into hibernal slumber. The contrast between those two seasons, contemplated during the slow yet inexorable transition between them, forms the basis of this song; musically, this is manifest in two delicately intertwined elements.

The first captures the mood projected onto the landscape, in the tradition of so many Romantic lieder: the listless undulations of the violin ostinato, the unpredictable play of light and shade in the oboe, and the static pedal-points evoke the chilly haze wafting over the gently rippling lake, with withered lotus blossoms waving on the bank, reflected on the placid surface of the water. This music is mildly exotic, owing both to occasional appearances of the pentatonic motive (D–C–A) and to interpolation of the Chinese heptatonic scale (see Ex. 19.4(*a*); the pattern is like the Lydian mode, without octave duplication[53]). Typically, the heptatonic kernel is subject to manifold variation, yet Mahler frequently highlights its characteristic tritone and whole-tone tetrachord, and roots the scale on a pitch that does not coincide with the local tonic (e.g. Ex. 19.4(*b*)). The first instance of this is at Fig. 1 in the instrumental ritornello (Ex. 19.5(*a*)), where elements of the heptatonic scale also suffuse the harmonic texture in a sonority prolonged through Fig. 2 (see Ex. 19.5(*b*)).

Ex. 19.4.   Heptatonic scales: (*a*) on F (= Lydian mode); (*b*) on B♭

(*a*)   (*b*)

This oriental matrix also influences the initial vocal gesture—a pair of curves outlining a concave arc—which recurs frequently in the movement. Specifically heptatonic at Figs. 7 and 9, this line is modally transformed in other appearances. At Fig. 6 it gives rise to breezy, hollow-sounding parallelism in the winds; it is cast, on the whole, in harmonic contexts that skirt the leading-note and root-function directedness of Western tonality. Texturally, this autumnal music frequently approaches heterophony,[54] while the large orchestra has become an intimate chamber ensemble. Overall, this first principal element of 'Der Einsame im Herbst' is subtly unsettling in its Eastern shading; the landscape is not quite familiar, and it is indeed as though 'an artist had sifted a powder of jade' over the whole.

The contrasting music first emerges briefly at Fig. 5⁻² (see Ex. 19.6). Marked 'flowing, very expressive, nobly sung, warm', it manifests inner longing, replete with late-Romantic

---

[53] Cf. e.g. *Musikalisches Conversations-Lexikon*, s.v. 'China', by C. Billert, 405.
[54] Concerning heterophony in *Das Lied von der Erde*, see also Mitchell, *SSLD*, 62, 125–7, 373–4, and *passim*.

Ex. 19.5. 'Der Einsame im Herbst': (*a*) heptatonic passage from ritornello (Fig. 1 ff.); (*b*) heptatonic sonority in the accompaniment (also contained in *Hirajoshi*)

Ex. 19.6. 'Der Einsame im Herbst', contrasting thematic material (Fig. 5⁻² ff.)

chromaticism. The semitones of the cool Eastern scale pattern become inflections of major–minor wistfulness, and the timbre shifts to the richness of cellos and horn. Here again, in 'leitmotivic' manner, the music distinctly adumbrates the poetic feeling of the text with which it is later united: 'the autumn in my heart endures too long' is sung only in the final strophe (Fig. 17 ff.). The singer's longing is for final peace, joyous renewal in the 'beloved resting place' which lies ahead—yet also, nostalgically, for the warm summer sun of love, whose time is past. And this inner conflict culminates in the poignant dénouement of the finale strophe.

The developmental interplay between the song's two central poetic-musical images is both complex and continual, yet readily accessible because the formal background of the movement is exquisitely simple. The strophic structure of the poem and the central tonality of D minor frame the whole. The first two stanzas modulate indecisively through third-relations to B flat and G minor, only to yield again to the tonic and the present reality of autumn (Figs. 7 and 11). The bright parallel major of the third strophe is ephemeral; the ostinato returns. And in the final couplet, following an ecstatic semitone surge to E flat, the singer implores, 'Sun of love, will you never more shine, that my bitter tears might gently dry up?' But D minor returns before the line is finished; wordlessly, the violins sing 'covered with frost is all the grass' (Fig. 19⁺³), and the ritornello wafts quietly towards the final *morendo*.

Von der Jugend (Of Youth)

'Von der Jugend' (Of Youth) is Mahler's own title for the third movement ('The Porcelain Pavilion' in Bethge's collection), and the change suggests the song's role in the allegorical scheme of the whole. Once again, the scene shifts radically, from reflection on the current season to bitter-sweet recollection of the past, in the form of a delicate and highly stylized miniature. This shortest movement of *Das Lied von der Erde* is also structurally the simplest: seven strophes of text are grouped 2+3+2 into an ABA format, tonally articulated by the third-related keys of B flat and G (major/minor, with a brief venture into E).

The poem presents a carefree world of stylish young people chatting over tea, occasionally writing down a bit of verse, while sitting in a little pavilion on a pond, connected to the bank only by an arching jade footbridge. Mahler captures this atmosphere in musical *chinoiserie* far more obvious than the oriental overtones of the previous pieces. Pentatonic and whole-tone configurations fill the immediate foreground; the texture is exceptionally homophonic and treble-dominated, animated by continuously chattering quavers, and coloured by high oriental flutes, fleeting trills, and triangle strokes.

The arching shape of the jade bridge, one of the poem's principal images, becomes the arch form of the song, as Arthur Wenk has noted.[55] And Mahler emphasizes the semicircularity by switching the order of Bethge's last two stanzas (i.e. the sixth and seventh were originally seventh and sixth). As a result, the little piece closes with the image of the young folk endlessly sipping and chatting away, just as they were in the beginning; and this also enables the composer to make light of the only serious reflection in the song, which occurs at the end of the B section (see below). The arch is again manifest in the modulations by third (B flat–G–E/E minor–G minor–B flat); and as Wenk also notes, this curve prevails in the melodic material, as illustrated in Ex. 19.7: (*a*) shows the basic pattern in the introduction, while (*b*) and (*c*) present arching lines from the second and third stanzas.

Ex. 19.7. Arching contours in 'Von der Jugend': (*a*) bb. 3–4; (*b*) Fig. 3 ff.; (*c*) Fig. 6 ff.

---

[55] Wenk, 'The Composer as Poet', 36–8.

All this is charming, almost rococo in its delicate artifice. Yet from the perspective of the first two movements, this exotic, superficial good humour borders on parody: such is the protagonist's reflection on youthful insouciance. The submerged seriousness begins to surface in the fifth strophe, where, in the minor mode, the singer quietly observes that 'on the small pond's still surface everything shows up wonderfully in mirror image'. In the orchestral response, the characteristic perpetual motion drags nearly to a standstill, accompanied by offbeats of a Viennese waltz gone awry—what, exactly, does the inverted reflection reveal? But the potential significance of this moment is denied before it can be taken seriously. The gaity returns, and everything seems rather funny 'standing on its head' in the pond; the friends gossip on, and the vignette fades away on a high-pitched $\frac{6}{4}$ chord. As Adorno observes, 'the song on the pavilion, which ends like a transparent mirage, calls to mind the Chinese tale of the painter who vanishes into his picture . . . '.[56]

Von der Schönheit (Of Beauty)

The fourth movement continues the reflective review of time past at the water's edge; the key, the pentatonic lines, and the light, high texture of its opening, flow naturally from what has passed before. But the voice has changed, and as Adorno notes, the commingled tenderness and uncertainty of the girl picking flowers seems almost Proustian.[57] Yet there is also a tinge of irony in the song: the springtime innocence of her longing for love is intertwined with sensuality and primitive power uncharacteristic 'Of Beauty' in the stereotypical Romantic sense. This Apollonian–Dionysian polarity is central to the formal conception of the movement, and Mahler underscores it by extending the poem's middle section—the episode of the young man's horse tearing up the turf. Moreover, the movement is highly stylized throughout, even in its most touching moments; like reflections on the water, it remains intangibly remote, enticing yet illusive.

Mahler reworked the text into five strophes of unequal length, which are set in a broad ABA' format, with instrumental interludes preceding the third and fourth stanzas. The tonal modulations that articulate the form all arrive unexpectedly, accentuating the growing excitement and ensuing wistfulness of the poem's reminiscence; ultimately the music circles back to the tonic, yet only after the thematic reprise is under way. The scheme can be summarized as in Diagram 19.3. The 'A' material, *dolicissimo commodo*, is fresh and supple in its flexible metre and delicately irregular phrasing. As the girls gather flowers into their laps, the violins' gently rocking accompaniment recalls both the closing lullaby of *Kindertotenlieder* and the nostalgic slow movement of the Sixth Symphony. And as the

[56] Adorno, *Mahler*, 152 (German edn., 197); Adorno continues: 'Diminution, disappearance is the guise of death, in which music still preserves the vanishing.'

[57] Ibid. 145–6 (German edn., 187–8); Adorno acknowledges, however, that the two artists knew nothing of each other and would probably not have understood one another.

	Form	Tonality	Strophe	Text
A		G		Introduction
	a	G	1	Junge Mädchen pflücken Blumen
	b	G		Zwischen Büschen und Blättern sitzen sie
	a′	G	2	Gold'ne Sonne webt um die Gestalten
	c	E; to V/$_E$ //		Sonne spiegelt ihre schlanken Glieder
B		G to C		Interlude, developmental
	d	C	3	O sieh, was tummeln sich für schöne Knaben
		A♭/c		Interlude, wildly developmental
	d	F; D //	4	Das Roß des einem wiehert fröhlich auf
A′	a′	B♭	5	Gold'ne Sonne webt um die Gestalten
	c′	G		Und die schönste von den Jungfrau'n sendet
	b	G		In dem Funkeln ihrer großen Augen
		G		Postlude

Diagram 19.3. Formal scheme of third movement of *Das Lied von der Erde*

Zephyr lifts their sleeves with 'coaxing caresses' (Mahler's words), and wafts their scent through the air, the music is suffused with a sensuous atmosphere comparable only to that of 'Ich atmet' einen linden Duft' among Mahler's other works.

This idyll is lustily invaded by the lads on horseback: parodistic in its martial splendour (bb. 49–51/Fig. 8^{-1} ff. cite Tchaikovsky's '1812'), yet serious in its wild strength, this is arguably 'the best horse-music ever written', as David Lewin has put it.[58] The transformation of previous thematic material is transparent, indeed almost a caricature of the Lisztian procedure Mahler in fact adopted only sparingly in his oeuvre (see Ex. 19.8); however, it clinches his point about the dual nature of *Sehnsucht*.

The second orchestral interlude (Fig. 12^{-3} ff.) is among the most uproarious passages in all of Mahler: frenzy and parody effect a curiously Straussian rawness, yet even this seeming chaos is developmental. Both linearly and vertically, the syntax is controlled by a tonal mixture of A flat and C minor, which in turn is derived from the hemitonic (Japanese) pentatonic scale *Hirajoshi* (see Ex. 19.3(*a*) above). Verticalizations of pitches from *Kumoijoshi* (see Ex. 19.3(*b*)) are also frequent, as are whole-tone and 'ordinary' pentatonic fragments; in context, the alienating capacity of the work's exotic elements has been pressed to new extremes.

By the end of the fourth strophe (the last four lines are Mahler's) the singer is almost as breathlessly excited as the horse she sings about, when suddenly the throng vanishes—and

[58] Pers. comm.; quoted by permission.

Ex. 19.8. Thematic transformation in 'Von der Schönheit': (a) bb. 1–3 and 7–9; (b) Fig. 8⁺¹ ff.

the reprise has begun. Thematic transformation and a quick third-modulation (by now characteristic of the piece) make this kaleidoscopic shift possible; still, it is a shock, forcefully underscoring that the equestrian episode is recollection in fantasy, not action in the present. But the girl's ardent longing remains, unrequited, intensified, and now linked through musical reminiscence to the caress of the Zephyr. (And once again, Mahler has touched up the poetry to highlight her feelings.) As in Schumann's *Dichterliebe*, the instrumental postlude is nearly as expressively arresting as the song proper; both singer and audience are held fast in suspended, wistful reflection on the nature of what remains unresolved.[59] Like 'Von der Jugend', the lied simply fades ethereally in the instability of the tonic $\frac{6}{4}$.

---

[59] For Adorno, 'the clarinet entry in the epilogue, a passage the like of which is granted to music only every hundred years, rediscovers time as irrecoverable' (*Mahler*, 146; German edn., 188).

Der Trunkene im Frühling (The Drunkard in Spring)

. . . I am realizing something curious. I can do nothing but work; I have forgotten everything else over the years. I am like a morphine addict or a drunkard who is suddenly forbidden his vice.[60]

Although Mahler actually drank but sparingly, these lines point to an element of personal insight in the theme of intoxication that frames the first half of *Das Lied von der Erde* and re-emerges at crucial moments in 'Der Abschied' as well. While the search for solace in wine only intensifies the singer's bitterness in the opening movement, for 'The Drunkard in Spring' it is the source of defiant yet farcical denial that rejects even natural beauty. The song's eerie cheeriness calls to mind Schubert's 'Täuschung' in *Die Winterreise*—'deception is my only prize'; but in the context of *Das Lied*, such levity is also a sardonic representation of Dionysian impotence: the reawakening of spring is indeed at hand, but the orgiastic cortège comprises only a single Bacchant—and an ebullient buffoon at that, who falls asleep on his doorstep every night. Yet here again, as in the previous two songs, stylization distances us from the scene described, even as the singer is separated from himself by intoxication. The piece remains a vignette, and its irony amusing; this drinker, like the flower maiden and the chattering youths, is a static projection of inner reflection.[61]

The broad ABA′ outline of 'Der Trunkene' is related in form to the two preceding movements, and its musical imagery is frequently a recoloration of material we have already heard. *Chinoiserie* in the upper winds is by now commonplace, and here evokes the birds of spring—a telling image in the text; more specifically, the pentatonic horn calls mingled with accented trilling hark back to the 'Trinklied vom Jammer der Erde', as do the lurching tonal shifts (especially A to B flat in the 'A' sections) and the reeling melodic contour associated with drinking to the limit of endurance (cf. Figs. 1 and 10).

This last idea, however, is subsequently transformed into the bird's mellifluous proclamation of spring in the 'B' section (Fig. 6 ff.). As a result, the interplay between two principal elements—the opening seven bars and the 'drinking/spring' motive first occurring at Fig. 1—spans the movement as a whole; and this recalls the more profound developmental process of 'Der Einsame im Herbst'. But here thematic contrast is linked with a notable feature of the overall form: the onset of the 'B' section is not tonally articulated. Structural modulation occurs only as the singer sobers up sufficiently to wonder whether the bird's message is significant; and then there is a move to D flat (Fig. 8), an entirely fresh tonal region for both the movement and the work. As in 'Von der Jugend', the mid-point of the song brings a moment of serious reflection—'Aus tiefstem Schauen lauscht' ich auf' (in deepest gazing I took careful note) (Mahler's text). And as in the earlier movement, it is quickly dismissed: D flat gives way to C, the wineglass is refilled and drained, and the thematic transformation associated with spring is reversed. The tonal reprise, decisive for the movement's structure and import, follows shortly. 'What does spring matter to me?! Let me

---

[60] Mahler to Bruno Walter, June–early July 1908; *Briefe* (1982), no. 394 (*Selected Letters*, no. 372).
[61] Cf. also Adorno, *Mahler*, 152–3 (German edn., 197–8).

be drunk!' is the singer's parting shot (Fig. 14⁻³ ff.), and the piece concludes with a bois-
terous flourish of A major—the brightest sound in the entire first half of *Das Lied von der
Erde*, which rings in the ear well after the performers have stopped.

Der Abschied (The Farewell)

He turned the manuscript over to me for study; for the first time, it was not from himself that I
became familiar with a new work. When I brought it back to him, almost unable to utter a word, he
turned to the *Abschied* and said: 'What do you think? Is that to be endured at all? Will not people do
away with themselves after hearing it?' Then he pointed out the rhythmic difficulties and asked jok-
ingly: 'Have you any idea how one is supposed to conduct this? I haven't!'[62]

A stroke of the gong abruptly disperses the echoes of 'Der Trunkene im Frühling'; suddenly, C minor in low register, an uncertain pulse, and haunting oriental *broderie* in the
oboe conjure forth all that the drinker would deny. The second half of the work is come,
and with it the time of departure, alternately loathed and embraced across the forty-year
span of Mahler's oeuvre.

Two poems by two different poets form the basis of this movement: they are entitled 'In
Expectation of the Friend' and 'Departure of the Friend' in Bethge's edition, and according to him the two poets were writing to each other.[63] Mahler's treatment of these texts
divides 'Der Abschied' into two parts—as the whole of *Das Lied von der Erde* is divided—
the anticipation of departure, and the moment itself. The 'friend' who is expected here is
none other than Freund Hein, the spectre of Death who has appeared as a shrieking monkey in the first movement.[64] This phantom had long haunted Mahler's inner world, and not
only musically. In 1901, just after his near-fatal haemorrhage, he recounted a vivid dream
to Natalie Bauer-Lechner; as the two of them talked, they were walking in the moonlight
beside a mountain lake, which is virtually the setting of 'Der Abschied':

He found himself in the midst of a large gathering in a brightly lit room, when the last of the guests
entered—a large man of stiff bearing, faultlessly dressed, and with the air of a man of affairs. But he
[Mahler] knew: that is Death.... The stranger seized him by the arm with an iron grip and said, 'You
must come with me!' [*Du mußt mit mir!*] . . . he could not tear himself loose until, by expending all
his forces, he threw the nightmare off.[65]

---

[62] Walter, *Mahler*, 46 (Eng. trans., 59).

[63] Bethge, *Die chinesische Flöte: Nachdichtungen chinesischer Lyrik* (Leipzig: Inselverlag, 1920), 112.

[64] Cf. also Mitchell, *SSLD*, 390. 'Freund Hein strikes up
the dance' was Mahler's description of the Fourth
Symphony's Scherzo; see Walter, *Briefe*, 52, and Reeser
(ed.), *Gustav Mahler und Holland*, 105, as well as NB-L,

Erinnerungen, 179 (*Recollections*, 162). Freund Hein is an
archetypal German folk figure of Death whose origins date
to medieval legend, and who had been portrayed by numerous 19th-c. artists; see Mitchell, *WY*, 237 and 303.

[65] NB-L, *Erinnerungen*, 185–6 (not in *Recollections*); the
dream actually took place in 1891 (see also HLG(F) ii.
72–3).

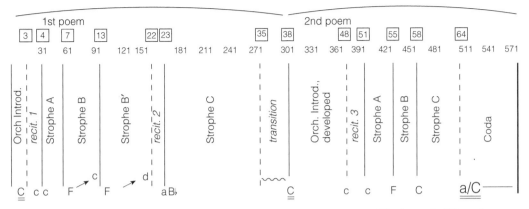

Diagram 19.4. Overall structure of 'Der Abschied'. Reproduced by courtesy of *The Journal of Musicology*

Mahler's intense psychological involvement with this symbolic figure is apparent through-out this movement, but especially at its mid-point, as we shall see.

The binary structure of 'Der Abschied' is outlined in Diagram 19.4, which is once again based on Robert Bailey's analysis.[66] As the diagram shows, the two halves are closely related through the recurrence of several musical segments: the introductory instrumental material, the recitatives, and three *musical* strophes (i.e. not poetic stanzas). As we have already noted, A and C are the structural tonalities of *Das Lied* as a whole, and this third-pairing is central to the nature of its finale. The first part begins in C minor (the key of 'Todtenfeier'), shifts to F for Strophes B and B', and then proceeds to A minor—the tonal-ity of the first movement—for the second recitative; Strophe C follows this in an unex-pected move to B flat. A chilling return of C minor inaugurates the second half, which then replicates the overall tonal motion of the first, up until the close of Strophe B. At this point Strophe C re-emerges, now in C major, and the movement dissolves in the ethereal penta-tonic blend of A minor and C (cf. Ex. 19.1(*c*) and Diagram 19.4).

Once grasped, the symmetry and coherence of the form is compelling, but it is not imme-diately obvious. The relation between structure and detail in this finale is in telling contrast to the work's opposite cornerstone, the opening 'Trinklied vom Jammer der Erde'. There, all is tightly wrought in dynamic sonata style, building towards the bitter climax before the reprise. In 'Der Abschied', gradually yet inexorably, time and space are dissolving; so, too, is all striving towards definite musical goals. No previous movement by Mahler is so fully and extensively focused on the immediate flow of inner feeling—what remains of the pre-sent even as it slips away.

[66] See above, n. 45; cf. also Mitchell, *SSLD*, 363 ff., esp. 383–6. Diagram 19.4 is reproduced by courtesy of *The Journal of Musicology* from Hefling, '*Das Lied*', 329. It is noteworthy that in Bruno Walter's last recording of *Das Lied* *von der Erde*, these two sections last 14′ 35″ and 14′ 40″ respectively (performed with Ernst Haefliger, Mildred Miller, and the New York Philharmonic; CBS Masterworks MK 42034).

This dissolution of spatio-temporal orientation is musically manifest through several recurrent, interrelated procedures, which can be sketched out as follows:

1. *Blurring of local pulse.* This is obvious in the free recitatives; heterophonic textures and cross-rhythms (e.g. 5, 4, or 3 against 2, sometimes in multiple combinations) also diffuse the rhythmic motion. In addition, periodic phrasing is either avoided or subsequently obfuscated.

2. *Blurring of tonal direction.* This results chiefly from pentatonicism, yet is also brought about through whole-tone configurations and sonorities that approach those of atonal style. Dominant preparation and overt cadence are rare; and in Schenkerian terms, goal-oriented middleground linear motion is often avoided or interrupted, without subsequent closure.

3. *Local repetitions.* Ostinato elements are repeatedly recycled; at length they seem no longer to maintain distinct identity, but rather create the impression of a slightly undulating yet essentially static, and endless, background. The ostinatos are linked by a web of subtle motivic interrelationships that only rarely (but then, significantly) develop into distinctive musical events.

4. *Large-scale repetitions.* All three of the movement's large segments (Strophes A, B, and C) recur as broad, static units that make little or no headway within themselves; as they return, it remains uncertain where they are leading.

Mahler greatly prized the Austro-Germanic tradition of 'organic' interrelation between musical structure and detail; that, he knew, was the foundation of development and drama in symphonic music. But he had also discovered that such organicism could be pressed towards formal liquidation through a surfeit of integrated detail that swamps the semblance of larger structural design; such 'development in reverse' is central to the expressive import of 'Der Abschied'. Into and out of the musical procedures just outlined Mahler weaves a great deal of suggestive nature imagery, which abounds in the two poems of this movement as in several of the others. Chilly darkness, wind, water, and birds all surface and fade from perception, yet this collage of stylized imitations does not seem out of place in the hazy atmosphere of the whole; moreover, it never disrupts the deeper flow of inner consciousness, which is manifest through the extraordinary treatment of time and tonality.

Part 1: Anticipation

The brief orchestral introduction gradually reveals the kernels of three principal ostinato types, which will be deployed throughout much of the movement (see Ex. 19.9). Just as a regular pulse begins to emerge from the sombre opening, the first minor–major modal shift takes place—a recurrent symbol of transition from darkness to light (and vice versa) throughout 'Der Abschied'. At this point (b. 13) the oboe foreshadows the singer's description of the moon as a silver ship (Fig. 4^{+6} ff.), one of many 'leitmotivic' references in a movement where the orchestra 'sings' as much as the voice. But the major mode collapses

Ex. 19.9. Ostinato figures in 'Der Abschied'

in a chromatic cascade of high winds (Fig. 5^{+6} f.): this figure, *x*, will punctuate many crucial moments, and is directly linked to the flute accompaniment in the first two recitatives; inevitably, it recalls the 'Bird of Death' from the finale of the Second Symphony.[67]

The ensuing stillness yields to the recitative, its concave arcs derived from the introduction (Ex. 19.9, 2(*a*) and (*b*)). Following this acknowledgement of nightfall, the ostinatos resume, and the poetic reference to the moonlight is reflected in the tonic major (Fig. 4^{+6}). The mode is reversed again, however, as attention shifts from the celestial sea to the dark pines, stirred by a foreboding breeze and echoing an eerie bird call; then, as in the introduction, all motion again ceases.

At the beginning of Strophe B (Fig. 7) the ostinato figures merge into the listless current of the brook; the key is a relaxed subdominant of C, the mode major. Here we learn that it is spring, a fact utterly incidental to the flow of inner emotion: the orchestra brings forth music (Fig. 11^{-3} ff.) that will shortly be linked with the words 'all longing [*Sehnsucht*] will now only dream'; this is one of many lines Mahler interpolated into the poetry to highlight the broader issues of the work. Ecstatic and tinged with exotic harmony, this gesture also plummets back towards C minor (Fig. 13^{-3}), and thence to F for Strophe B′ (Fig. 13^{+4}).

This section begins as a condensation of Strophe B. The 'Sehnsucht' music soon arrives with text (Fig. 14), but then the tonality slips into C sharp minor and the pulse becomes

[67] Mahler, Symphony No. 2 in C minor ('Resurrection'), fifth movement, Fig. 30^{+5} ff., esp. Fig. 31^{-5} ff.; cf. NB-L, *Erinnerungen*, 40 (*Recollections*, 44).

increasingly blurred. 'Die müde Menschen' (the tired men) (Fig. 15⁺³ ff.) is a musical quotation of 'Mein Herz ist müde' (my heart is tired) from 'Der Einsame im Herbst', while the ensuing two lines of text allude to Mahler's own passionate youthful poetry from the days of the *Gesellen-Lieder* ('um im Schlaf vergess'nes Glück . . .' (So in sleep to learn anew forgotten happiness and youth)).[68] An all-too-noisy chorus of birds breaks into this nostalgia, to be silenced by the recurrence of *x*—a marked sort of bird call, now in the lower register. As the world falls asleep, the musical motion once again comes to rest, underscoring the traditional symbolic association of sleep and death.

The A-minor recitative (Fig. 22⁻¹) is a return to the movement's opening, but in the other polarity of the work's third-related tonal pairing (A/C). Here the singer reveals the reason for this nocturnal vigil, and we realize what is so ominous about the pine grove: thence will come the friend for the last farewell. But in the ensuing orchestral interlude (the beginning of Strophe C, Fig. 23 ff.), key, metre, and mood effect a delicate yet definite contrast to all that has gone before. The ostinatos (3 (*b*) and (*c*) in Ex. 19.9) become lilting, the texture is gently suffused with pentatonicism, and a broad melody emerges, which is later fully associated with 'Die liebe Erde', the ecstatic release of spirit into the cosmos (see Ex. 19.10). Anxiety is temporarily forgotten and the music literally quivers in anticipation of the coming encounter with eternity.

But this expectancy is still mingled with passionate attachment to the present, which surges forth in a minor–major thrust towards C: 'O Schönheit, o ewigen Liebens-, Lebens

Ex. 19.10. 'Der Abschied': the 'Erde' or 'ewig' motive in first and subsequent appearances (texts: 'The beloved earth'; 'blue brightly the horizons'; 'Eternally, ever')

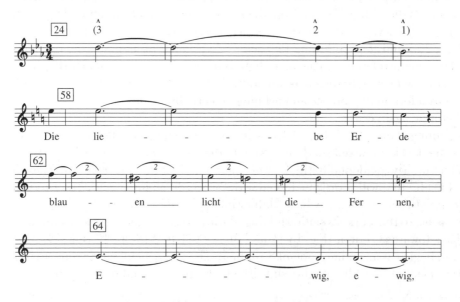

<hr/>

[68] See HLG(E) i. 826–7 and 831–2 (HLG(F) i. 1070–1 and 1075–7).

trunk'ne Welt!' (O Beauty, O World drunken of eternal love-and-life!). The line is Mahler's, yet also nearly Faust's—'Then to the moment could I say: Linger you now, you are so fair!' It embraces all that was richest in the world of individuated willing reviewed in the previous songs of *Das Lied von der Erde*. But none of this is to remain as it is, and the ensuing musical collapse precipitates a decisive regression to the state of the movement's opening.

Part 2: Departure

'Grabgeläute' (death knell) is Mahler's annotation to himself at the return of C minor in the *Particell* draft of 'Der Abschied'[69]—explicit confirmation, if such were needed, of what is imminent. Here the ostinatos (2 (*a*) and (*b*)) recur endlessly, combined with a contour from the recitatives (Ex. 19.11) and spun out in a long funereal march, coloured by wailing wind-band texture. Broadly 'developmental', it makes little headway; the only striking motivic evolution is the twofold appearance of material later allied to the words 'einsam Herz' (lonely heart) (Figs. 42^{-1}, and 44^{-2} f.; see Ex. 19.12). The harmonies grow searingly dissonant, yet the whole episode never moves far from C minor. Relentlessness is the chief characteristic of this inner vision of a march—funereal indeed, but not for a funeral.

Ex. 19.11. Ostinato motif prominent in the instrumental interlude of 'Der Abschied', Fig. 39 ff., and its derivation from the first recitative (Fig. 3^{-1} f.) (text: 'The sun departs behind [the mountain]')

As the processional music comes to a grim halt, the gong continues to toll, and we know who has arrived on a pale horse, bearing the cup of departure. In the stanza of poetry beginning with the third recitative (Fig. 48 ff.). Mahler has reduced the characters of the confrontation to a single pronoun—'Er'—which underscores that Death is an archetypal figure of the psyche, as in a dream, and that protagonist and phantom are no longer adversaries, but united.[70] As Fechner had put it, dying is but the transition to the third stage of existence.

The modified reprise of Strophe A, which initially set the scene in anticipation of departure, now presents an enigmatic account of 'why it had to be': 'Fate was not favourable to me in this world' (Fig. 51 ff.). Mahler chose not to alter this line in Bethge, which, in context, seems like a cryptic, personal cipher; nevertheless, he left several hints about its veiled

[69] In the Gemeentemuseum, The Hague, Mengelberg Stichting; photofacsimile in Mitchell, *SSLD*, 476. These manuscripts (the Mengelberg collection) are now in the possession of the Dutch Music Institute which forms part of the Royal Library in The Hague.

[70] Cf. also Mitchell, *SSLD*, 370–3 and 424–31.

Ex. 19.12. The 'einsam Herz' motive in 'Der Abschied': (*a*) Fig. 42⁻¹; (*b*) Fig. 44⁻²; (*c*) Fig. 54⁻¹ f. (text: 'Peace for my lonely heart')

meaning. One thinks again of Faust, striving proudly and blindly to the very end: such labour had become Mahler's opiate, as he revealed to Walter ('O ewigen Liebens-, Lebens trunk'ne Welt!'). And earlier in this movement, alluding to his own past, he had written that tired men will learn anew in sleep their forgotten fortune (*Glück*) and youth. Now the singer is about to close Strophe A' (Fig. 53⁺⁴ ff.) with an unmistakable reference to the first song of *Kindertotenlieder* (see Ex. 19.13). The misfortune of the night in 'Nun will die Sonn' so hell aufgeh'n' was the death of a child—symbolically, the death of childlike love and trust (such as that revealed in 'Das himmlische Leben'). Thus this curious moment in 'Der Abschied' would appear to be an expression of mourning at the end of life for innocence corrupted and utopian hope unfulfilled.

The reprise of Strophe B (Fig. 55 ff.) is condensed, which balances the binary form following the long orchestral interlude that has opened the second half. The voice enters at once, and the first line of poetry is Mahler's: here is the final homeland for the wanderer who declared that he was thrice without a country. Just as the 'Sehnsucht' music appears in the orchestra (Fig. 57⁻⁴), the singer's words counter it: 'I will nevermore roam on the horizons. Still is my heart and waits its hour!' Then time and tonality seem almost to evaporate; exotic scales ascend through a tritone up to E, slower in each recurrence, and wholetone ambiguity suffuses the harmony.—

The onset of C major is the last outcome to be suspected at such a moment. The ethereal *e♮'''*, which affirms the major mode, is the sole connecting fibre from what has just transpired. Now the third strophe is transformed into undisturbed ecstasy of light, as temporal definition gradually vanishes in the radiant pulsing of cross-rhythms and arpeggiation. The music of 'O Schönheit, o ewigen Liebens-, Lebens trunk'ne Welt' becomes 'und ewig, ewig blauen licht die Fernen' (and ever, eternally, blue brightly the horizons), and from Fig. 63 the texture is saturated with pentatonicism. Linearly, *Yu* (on E) ascends repeatedly until at

Ex. 19.13. (a) *Kindertotenlieder*, no. 1, 'Nun will die Sonn' so hell aufgeh'n' (Now the sun will rise just as brightly), bb. 10–14, transposed (orig.: D minor) (text: 'as though no misfortune the night [had seen]'); (b) *Das Lied von der Erde*, 'Der Abschied', Fig. 53^{+3} ff. (text: 'I go, I wander into the mountains. I seek peace, peace [for my lonely heart]')

length B♮, leading-note to the tonic, is lost (after Fig. 67^{-5}); vertically, the fusion of A and C is fully established, and all other fleeting sonorities only highlight its permanence. The singer cadences briefly at Fig. 65, but the last three utterances of 'ewig' (*e′–d′*) never descend to C. For the first and final time, Mahler does not resolve, but simply merges the poetic-musical polarities of his art, releasing the work in the moment of liminal transition: as Benjamin Britten observed, 'it goes on for ever, even if it is never performed again—that final chord is printed on the atmosphere'.[71]

---

[71] Britten, letter to Henry Boys postmarked 29 June 1937, in *Letters from a Life: The Selected Letters and Diaries of Benjamin Britten, 1913–1976*, ed. Donald Mitchell *et al.* (Berkeley: University of California Press, 1991), i. 493–4; cf. also Mitchell, *SSLD*, 340. The quotation from Britten's letter is copyright ©1985 The Britten Estate and reproduced by kind permission of the Trustees. Not to be further reproduced without written permission.

DIE EINSAME IM HERBST

TSCHANG-TSI

Herbstnebel wallen bläulich überm Strom,
Vom Reif bezogen stehen alle Gräser,
Man meint, ein Künstler habe Staub von Jade
Über die feinen Halme ausgestreut.

Der süsse Duft der Blumen ist verflogen,
Ein kalter Wind beugt ihre Stengel nieder;
Bald werden die verwelkten goldnen Blätter
Der Lotosblüten auf dem Wasser ziehn.

Mein Herz ist müde. Meine kleine Lampe
Erlosch mit Knistern, an den Schlaf gemahnend.
Ich komme zu dir, traute Ruhestätte, —
Ja, gib mir Schlaf, ich hab Erquickung not!

Ich weine viel in meinen Einsamkeiten,
Der Herbst in meinem Herzen währt zu lange;
Sonne der Liebe, willst du nie mehr scheinen,
Um meine bittern Tränen aufzutrocknen?

The text of 'Die Einsame im Herbst'

HANS BETHGE—DIE
CHINESISCHE
FLÖTE

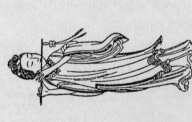

LEIPZIG—IM INSELVERLAG
MDCCCCXIX

The title-page of Hans Bethge's *Die chinesische Flöte* (tenth impression, 1919)

20

The Ninth Symphony

STEPHEN E. HEFLING

The earliest interpreters of Mahler's oeuvre were convinced that his last completed work grew directly from the world of *Das Lied von der Erde*. According to Bruno Walter, 'the title of the last song, *Der Abschied*, could stand at the head of the Ninth'.[1] Willem Mengelberg regarded the work as 'Departure [*Abschied*] from all that he loved—and from the world—! and from his art, his life, his music.'[2] Alban Berg, writing to his wife about the first movement, declared that 'it is the expression of an unheard-of love for this earth, the longing to live in peace upon her, Nature, still to enjoy her utterly, even to her deepest depths—before Death comes. For it comes irresistibly. This entire movement is based upon a presentiment of death'.[3] Although the validity of such readings has recently been challenged,[4] much

[1] Walter, *Gustav Mahler* (1936 edn.), 87; trans. Galston (repr. 1973), 124; see also Adler, *Gustav Mahler*, trans. Reilly, *Gustav Mahler and Guido Adler*, 69; Floros, *Gustav Mahler*, iii. 267–70.

[2] These remarks from Mengelberg's conducting score are published in Peter Andraschke, *Gustav Mahlers IX. Symphonie: Kompositionsprozeß und Analyse* (Beihefte zum Archiv für Musikwissenschaft, 14; Wiesbaden: Franz Steiner Verlag, 1981), 81.

[3] Alban Berg, *Briefe an seine Frau*, ed. Franz Willnauer (Munich: Langer-Müller, 1965), 238; see also *Letters to his Wife*, ed. and trans. Bernard Grun (New York: St. Martin's Press, 1971), 147. Both collections suggest the date of this letter to be autumn 1912, but Floros points out (iii. 269) that it appears to contain references to Mahler's orchestral draft score, the first three movements of which were given to Berg in 1923 (see also Erwin Ratz, preface to Mahler, *IX. Symphonie: Partiturentwurf der ersten drei Sätze, Faksimile nach der Handschrift* (Vienna: Universal Edition, 1971)).

[4] In a number of articles and lectures dating from 1969, La Grange has suggested that Alma Mahler deliberately exaggerated the extent to which Mahler's heart disease affected his last years (see the bibliography in HLG(E) i. 959 (HLG(F) i. 1090)); see also HLG(F) iii. 80–90, 99–100, 478–9, 537–41, 754–63, and *passim*, as well as id., '"Ma Musique est vécue": La biographie comme outil d'analyse', in *Colloque international Gustav Mahler 25. 26. 27. janvier*

1985 (Paris: L'Association Gustav Mahler, 1986), 36–8; ' "Meine Musik ist 'gelebt' ": Mahler's Biography as a Key to his Works', *Opus*, 3/2 (Feb. 1987), 16–17; 'Auf der Suche nach Gustav Mahler: Eine Bilanz', in Danuser (ed.), *Gustav Mahler*, 30–68 at 56 ff; and 'Mahler and the New York Philharmonic'. Influenced by this view, Vera Micznik and Anthony Newcomb both claim that Mahler's personal circumstances are not relevant to an interpretation of the Ninth Symphony; see Micznik, 'Is Mahler's Music Autobiographical? A Reappraisal', *Revue Mahler Review*, 1 (1987), 47–63; ead., 'Meaning in Gustav Mahler's Music: A Historical and Analytical Study Focusing on the Ninth Symphony' (Ph.D. diss., State University of New York at Stony Brook, 1989), *passim*; ead., 'The Farewell Story of Mahler's Ninth', *19th Century Music*, 20 (1996), 144–66; Newcomb, 'Narrative Archetypes and Mahler's Ninth Symphony', in Steven Paul Scher (ed.), *Music and Text: Critical Inquiries* (Cambridge: Cambridge University Press, 1992), 118–36, esp. 120.

Part of the difficulty in assessing this issue is that we do not know precisely what Mahler's physicians told him about the prognosis of his heart condition. But it had long been established that patients with valvular defects often developed bacterial endocarditis (as Mahler ultimately did), a disease that was fatal until the discovery of antibiotics years later. (See e.g. Fredrick A. Willius and Thomas J. Dry, *A History of the Heart and the Circulation* (Philadelphia:

evidence stands in support of them. To be sure, as La Grange has shown, in 1909 Mahler was not merely a sick man obsessed by death; indeed, early in that year he had declared to Bruno Walter that 'I am thirstier for life than ever, and find the "habits of existence" sweeter than ever'.[5] Throughout his American years (1907–11) Mahler fulfilled a rigorous musical schedule, and was to conduct forty-six concerts (ninety-seven works) with the New York Philharmonic during the 1909–10 season.[6] Nonetheless, in the letter to Walter just cited, Mahler notes that 'these days of my life are in fact like the Sibylline Books'—an allusion to ancient Roman oracles to be consulted in time of crisis, which became more costly as their number decreased.

In the same letter to Walter, Mahler also reveals that 'I cannot help thinking very often of Lipiner. . . . I would like to know whether he still thinks the same about death as he did 8 years ago, when he gave me the particulars of his so very remarkable views (at my somewhat importunate request—I was just convalescing from my haemorrhage)'. As outlined in Chapter 13, this serious illness in February 1901 brought Mahler face to face with the limits of his mortality, and his response was manifold: personal participation in the renewal of life through marriage to Alma within a year, and artistic reflection on the nature of death in the lieder he composed that summer. Also during July of 1901 he began the Fifth Symphony,[7] whose opening movements—a funeral march and a rondo 'stormily agitated, with greatest vehemence'—contain the most dejected and acrid moments Mahler had then yet composed, which are reflected in the Ninth Symphony in several respects. At this time the poet-philosopher Siegfried Lipiner had been Mahler's close friend and mentor for over twenty years; but with Mahler's marriage to Alma, who quickly came to despise Lipiner,[8] the relationship between the two men was suspended. Now in 1909, just months before he returned to Toblach to compose the symphony bearing the number he had feared to commit to paper, Mahler again wished to consult Lipiner about his views on death; accordingly, Bruno Walter arranged a meeting for shortly after Mahler's arrival in Austria that spring.[9] Earlier in 1909 Mahler had acquired a plot for a grave in Grinzing cemetery, and in July the body of his elder daughter, who had died in July 1907, was transferred to the tomb that would ultimately be Mahler's as well.[10]

Thus, if not morbidly obsessed by death in 1909, Mahler was nevertheless aware of its relentless approach. A number of private inscriptions in the orchestral draft score of the

W. B. Saunders Co., 1948), 135–223; James B. Herrick, *A Short History of Cardiology* (Springfield, Ill.: Charles C. Thomas, 1942), 176–86; and William Osler's influential Gulstonian Lectures, 'Malignant Endocarditis', *British Medical Journal*, 1 (1885), 467–70, 522–6, 577–9. Cf. also Nicholas P. Christy, Beverly M. Christy, and Barry G. Wood, 'Gustav Mahler and his Illnesses', *Transactions of the American Clinical and Climatological Association*, 82 (1970), 200–17; Feder, 'Gustav Mahler, Dying'; David Levy, 'Gustav Mahler and Emanuel Libman: Bacterial Endocarditis in 1911', *British Medical Journal*, 293 (1986), 1628–31; and Susan M. Filler, 'Mahler in the Medical Literature', *News about Mahler Research*, no. 23 (Mar. 1990), 8–13.)

[5] Mahler, *Briefe* (1982), no. 404 (*Selected Letters*, no. 382).

[6] See Roman, *Gustav Mahler's American Years*, 252–3.

[7] See NB-L, *Erinnerungen*, 192–3 (*Recollections*, 172) and HLG(F) ii. 95–6.

[8] Alma Mahler, *Memories*, 25–6; HLG(E), i. 697–8.

[9] Walter, *Theme and Variations*, 148; cf. also Mahler's letter to Alma of 13(?) June 1909 in La Grange and Weiß (eds.), *'Ein Glück ohne Ruh'*, no. 268; abridged text in Alma Mahler, *Memories*, 319; cf. also HLG(F) iii. 501–3.

[10] HLG(F) iii. 83 and 541.

Ninth also suggest as much: 'O Jugendzeit! Entschwundene! O Liebe! Verwehte!' (O days of youth! Vanished! O Love! Scattered!) and 'Leb' wol! Leb' wol!' (Farewell! Farewell!) in the first movement, 'O Schönheit! Liebe! Lebt wol! Lebt wol! Welt! Lebe wohl!' (O Beauty! Love! Farewell!Farewell! World! Farewell!) at the end of the finale.[11] In earlier years Mahler had often allowed a large work to occupy him for two summer holidays. No longer: the finale of the orchestral draft for the Ninth is dated 2 September 1909, confirming that the entire symphony was composed in a single summer. When it was finished Mahler wrote to Walter that 'on account of the mad hurry and rush the score is quite mangled, and probably altogether illegible to unfamiliar eyes. And so I most fervently wish that it may be granted me to produce a fair copy this winter'.[12] The urgent haste of composition is apparent in the draft as well as the fair copy, both of which contain many more revisions and corrections than one finds in the corresponding manuscripts for Mahler's earlier works.[13]

Mahler frequently declared that his life and work were intertwined. For the works composed in the summer of 1901, as well as for the *Gesellen* lieder, the first four symphonies, and *Das Lied von der Erde*, his personal circumstances had served as the 'occasion' or 'impulse'—to use his words—for composition. This was probably the same in the case of the Ninth; it was none other than Lipiner who had written that 'Art is a symbolic abbreviation of life'.[14] Yet as Mahler himself pointed out, 'All understanding between the composer and the listener is based on convention'.[15] And heard from the perspective of his previous works, Mahler's Ninth presents an extraordinary musical profile: gone are the epic-heroic struggles that culminate in the affirmative breakthroughs and apotheosis-finales of the First, Second, Third, Fifth, and Eighth Symphonies; gone too is the Sixth's seemingly final shattering of heroic illusion.[16] The Ninth begins and ends with slow movements—a broad and nostalgic Andante comodo and a hymnic Adagio—both full of suggestive musical allusions to his earlier works as well as music by other composers. In between are two extraordinary Mahlerian parodies—the Ländler-waltz second movement, and the virtuosically sarcastic Rondo-Burleske. Compared with Mahler's earlier symphonic worlds, each of the Ninth's movements is relatively independent; no overarching symphonic drama compels the work to move through its cycle.[17] The symphony's overall tonal progression, from D to

---

[11] The first three movements of the orchestral draft are published as *IX. Symphonie: Partiturentwurf*, ed. Erwin Ratz; the draft of the finale has been acquired by the Bibliothèque Musicale Gustav Mahler in Paris, to which I am grateful for the opportunity to examine a photocopy. This document is described in some detail by James Zychowicz, 'The *Partiturentwurf* of the Adagio of Mahler's Ninth Symphony', *Revue Mahler Review*, 1 (1987), 77–101; photofacsimiles of two pages bearing some of the inscriptions cited here are found in *GMWL*, pt. 4, p. 25. A sketchbook containing ideas for the Ninth Symphony is discussed by Colin Matthews, *Mahler at Work*, 105–24.

[12] Mahler, *Briefe* (1982), no. 423 (undated; early Sept. 1909) (*Selected Letters*, no. 399).

[13] The autograph fair copy of the full score is in the possession of the Pierpont Morgan Library, New York, Lehman Deposit.

[14] Lipiner, *Über die Elemente einer Erneuerung religiöser Ideen in der Gegenwart. Vortrag gehalten im Lesevereine der deutschen Studenten Wiens am 19. Januar 1878* (Vienna: Leseverein der deutschen Studenten Wiens, 1878), 9.

[15] Natalie Bauer-Lechner, 'Aus einem Tagebuch über Mahler', *Der Merker*, 3/5 (1912), 184–8 at 188 (NB-L, *Recollections*, 234, Apr. 1896; not in *Erinnerungen*).

[16] Cf. also Adorno, *Mahler*, 135 (German edn., 178).

[17] Dieter Schnebel, 'Das Spätwerk als Neue Musik', in *Gustav Mahler* (Tübingen: Rainer Wunderlich Verlag, 1966), 157–88 at 162–3, suggests that as much transpires in a single movement like the opening Andante of the Ninth as in one of the entire earlier symphonies.

D flat, is recessive rather than progressive:[18] it reverses the expressive rise in the Fifth, which moves from an opening C sharp minor funeral march to a joyous D major rondo. And as we shall see, in the Ninth the associative connotations of the two tonal areas, D and D flat, are deployed at various points of the musical discourse. Moreover, like the 'Abschied' of *Das Lied von der Erde*, the Ninth's finale does not so much conclude as stop on the threshold—'looking questioningly into uncertainty' as Adorno puts it[19]—'ersterbend' (dying).[20]

I: Andante comodo

'The splendor of immediate life reflected in the medium of memory' is Adorno's perceptive characterization of the first movement: 'Yet as the movement . . . involves itself with time, it becomes entangled in immediacy, in a second life, blooming as if it were the first. . . . The music develops by losing the detachment with which it began'.[21] As noted above, his teacher Berg sensed in the Ninth's Andante

a premonition of death . . . that registers itself again and again. Everything earthly that has been dreamt away culminates in it (hence the climaxes breaking forth like new ebullitions after the sweetest passages)—strongest, naturally, at the uncanny place where this premonition of death becomes *certainty*, where in the midst of the deepest, most painful lust for life, *mit höchster Gewalt* [with greatest power, Fig. 15⁻² ff.] Death announces his arrival.[22]

Whether or not one accepts Berg or Adorno at face value, their metaphorical descriptions emphasize that the unusual interplay of materials in the movement tends to confute traditional formal categorizaton; rather, as Adorno notes, 'The technical procedures exactly fit the content. The conflict with the schemata is decided against the latter'[23]—hence the variety of formal descriptions to be found in the Mahler literature.[24]

[18] See e.g. David Rivier, 'A Note on Form in Mahler's Symphonies', *Chord and Discord*, 2/7 (1954), 29–33 at 32, as well as Reilly, *Gustav Mahler and Guido Adler*, 49, and Jack Diether, 'The Expressive Content of Mahler's Ninth Symphony', *Chord and Discord*, 2/10 (1963), 94–7.

[19] Adorno, *Mahler*, 138 (German edn., 181–2).

[20] This is Mahler's indication, written over the last note. While the Italian term *morendo* is common in his scores, Mahler uses the German *ersterbend* or *gänzlich ersterbend* only rarely: other instances are the conclusion of 'Urlicht' in the Second Symphony, the half-cadential conclusion of the third movement in the Fourth Symphony (which leads directly to 'Das himmlische Leben'), and the final bars of *Das Lied von der Erde*: in each of these cases the poetic texts relate to the transition from life to eternity. (See also Andraschke, *Gustav Mahlers IX. Symphonie*, 48, and NB-L, *Erinnerungen*, 163 (*Recollections*, 152–3).)

[21] Adorno, *Mahler*, 155 (German edn., 201).

[22] Berg, *Briefe an seine Frau*, 238.

[23] Adorno, *Mahler*, 156 (German edn., 202).

[24] See e.g. Erwin Ratz, 'Zum Formproblem bei Gustav Mahler: Eine Analyse des ersten Satzes der IX. Symphonie', *Musikforschung*, 8 (1955), 169–77, repr. in Danuser (ed.), *Gustav Mahler*, 276–88; Carl Dahlhaus, 'Form und Motiv in Mahlers neunter Symphonie', *Neue Zeitschrift für Musik*, 135 (1974), 286–9, repr. in Danuser (ed.), *Gustav Mahler*, 289–99; Andraschke, *Gustav Mahlers IX. Symphonie*, 11–70 (including a useful review of literature); Diether de la Motte, 'Das komplizierte Einfache: Anmerkungen zum 1. Satz der 9. Sinfonie von Gustav Mahler', in Kolleritsch (ed.), *Gustav Mahler*, 52–67; Friedhelm Krummacher, 'Struktur und Auflösung: Über den Kopfsatz aus Mahlers IX. Symphonie', *Studier och essäer tillägnade Hans Eppstein* (Stockholm: Kungl. musikaliska akademien, 1981),

Exposition

In addressing this issue it should be recalled that Mahler's conception of sonata form was congruent with the form's historical development: tonality, not thematic contrast, is the defining factor. Whatever else occurs, there will be large-scale modulation away from established tonic centrality, and one principal return thereto, constituting a clearly defined reprise.[25] That the first movement of Mahler's Ninth should present three thematic 'groups' or fields is not unusual for a post-Brucknerian symphony, but that the first two should stand in parallel major–minor relation to each other (D major in the opening, D minor at Fig. 3^{-9} ff.) reduces the dynamic tonal polarity that is typically a driving force in sonata form.[26] As many commentators have pointed out, these two thematic areas are in fact closely interrelated motivically, which diminishes the potential for forceful thematic contrast. And after the second of them is introduced, the first returns twice in the major mode (Fig. 4^{-10} and Fig. 5^{-5}), flanking a temporary move towards B flat. As regards sonata form, B flat, the flat submediant (or lower third-relation) in D, is ultimately established as the secondary tonal area (Fig. 5^{+12}). The music that follows, as Ratz and others have noted, functions like a closing section and results in a bright B flat cadence (Fig. 6^{+9} ff.), a break in momentum, and a double bar that had been a repeat sign in Mahler's draft score.[27] Thus these first 107 bars, tonally, function like an exposition (which is symmetrically balanced by the 108 bars of the reprise and coda). Thematically, however, the B flat closing group draws heavily from both the previous thematic fields, particularly the second. (Adorno goes so far as to suggest that the entire movement is *durchmelodisiert* (through-melodized).[28]) Thus the goal-oriented action of traditional sonata procedure is obscured by procedures more characteristic of double-variation and rondo movements, both in the 'exposition' and later: Mahler had experimented with such hybrid forms since the time of the First Symphony's finale and the 'Todtenfeier' movement of the Second, but not to the degree we encounter in the Ninth.[29]

Other features of the exposition hint that this movement may not culminate in a traditional development and resolution of the issues seemingly latent in it. The opening six bars

133–49, repr. in Danuser (ed.), *Gustav Mahler*, 300–23 (Krummacher's n. 2 contains extensive bibliographic information); Christopher Orlo Lewis, *Tonal Coherence in Mahler's Ninth Symphony* (Studies in Musicology, 79; Ann Arbor: UMI Research Press, 1984), ch. 2; Peter Revers, *Gustav Mahler: Untersuchungen zu den späten Sinfonien* (Hamburg: Karl Dieter Wagner, 1985), 79–135; Vera Micznik, 'Meaning in Gustav Mahler's Music', 128–251; and HLG(F) iii. 1183–200, wherein various analytic viewpoints are summarized.

[25] It should be recalled that major-minor mixture of the tonic centre, common from Schubert on, is taken for granted by post-Wagnerian composers; see Robert Bailey (ed.), *Wagner: Prelude and Transfiguration from 'Tristan and Isolde'* (Norton Critical Scores; New York: W. W. Norton &

Co., 1985), 116.

[26] Cf. also Adorno, *Mahler*, 156–8 (German edn., 202–7).

[27] Ratz, 'Zum Formproblem', in Danuser (ed.), *Gustav Mahler*, 278–82; see also Ratz (ed.), *IX. Symphonie: Partiturentwurf*, p. I/12, and Andraschke, *Gustav Mahlers IX. Symphonie*, 41.

[28] Adorno, *Mahler*, 155 (German edn., 200); Adorno's play on words refers to a through-composed (*durchkomponiert*) song, as opposed to a strophic one.

[29] See Hefling, 'Mahler's "Todtenfeier" and the Problem of Program Music', 39; id., 'Mahler's Symphonic Worlds', 382–3; Jack Diether, 'Notes on Some Mahler Juvenilia', *Chord and Discord*, 3/1 (1969), 3–100, pls. V and VI; see also above, Ch. 19 nn. 48 and 49.

Ex. 20.1. (*a*) Ninth Symphony, motivic fragments in the opening of the first movement, bb. 1–6; (*b*) *Das Lied von der Erde*, 'Der Abschied', Fig. 31⁻⁹ ff., followed by pentatonic scale form *Yu* (text: 'I wander to and fro [with my lute]')

are diffused with fragments that will reappear almost obsessively (see Ex. 20.1);[30] yet as presented at the beginning, they establish neither connectedness nor momentum—the syncopations, rests, and muted chamber-music colours make this brief introduction seem static, yet also strangely charged. (Writers who view Mahler as a precursor of the Second Viennese School invariably point to these bars.)[31] As Ex. 20.1 shows, the harp motive i² introduced in bars 3–4 (and later taken over by violas) harbours a contour inversion of the pentatonic cell from *Das Lied von der Erde*;[32] this emphasizes the sixth scale degree ($\hat{6}$), as does the stopped horn fragment (i³) in bar 5. The resulting 'added sixth' sonority, a mixture of D (major) and B (minor), evokes the close of 'Der Abschied' both syntactically and affectively. At the broadest level of structure, as Lewis points out, the tonal plot of the Ninth's first movement is based on the structural pairing of D and its lower third-relations, B and B flat.[33] Just as the minor mode of D is about to arrive for the first time (Fig. 2⁺⁹), the pitch B♭ (the 'lowered' sixth of the minor scale) linearly replaces B, and subsequently becomes the secondary key centre of the exposition. (As we shall see, B major will be prominent later in the tonal scheme.)

The ever-changing main theme (hereafter identified as 'A') first emerges among the fragments of the introduction as the anacrusis to bar 7. Halting for rests in nearly every bar, it proceeds unhurriedly in one-bar pulses, its goal uncertain—and such short-breathed phrases become characteristic of the entire movement.[34] It is a lyrical melody, suffused with nostalgia; and as de la Motte observes, for a symphonic work of 1909 it is also a fairly old-fashioned theme, not far removed from nineteenth-century 'popular' music in its sim-

---

[30] Cf. Ratz, 'Zum Formproblem', in Danuser (ed.), *Gustav Mahler*, 277, and Andraschke, *Gustav Mahlers IX. Symphonie, passim*.

[31] Schnebel, 'Das Spätwerk als Neue Musik', 169–71; Adorno, *Mahler*, 157–8 (German edn., 203–4). Floros suggests that the syncopated rhythm of motive i¹ is a symbol of death (*Gustav Mahler*, ii. 267 ff. and 416–18; iii. 277).

[32] See also Bekker, *Gustav Mahlers Sinfonien*, 339; Diether, 'The Expressive Content', 72–81; and Revers, *Untersuchungen*, 89–95. The line shown with text in Ex.

20.1(*b*) becomes very prominent in the close of 'Der Abschied', Fig. 63 ff.

[33] Lewis, *Tonal Coherence*, 13–22. Pursuing Robert Bailey's concept of the double-tonic complex, Lewis posits such a tonal scheme for the first movement of the Ninth, but claims that 'B and B-flat assume equivalent functions in relation to D, and are therefore interchangeable at some levels' (p. 15).

[34] Cf. also Adorno, *Mahler*, 155 (German edn., 201).

ple shape and phrasing.[35] Like the introductory bars, theme A also emphasizes the sixth scale degree, and stresses even more an incomplete descent, $\hat{3}$–$\hat{2}$, which again seems to recall 'Der Abschied' from afar. (Indeed, only in the movement's final high d''', softly plucked and whistled by string harmonics and piccolo, does one sense full—and rather

Ex. 20.2. 'Lebewohl' motive in (a) Beethoven, Sonata in E♭, Op. 81a, opening; (b) bb. 7–8; (c) bb. 227–35; (d) Mahler, Ninth Symphony, 1st movt., bb. 245–50

[35] 'Das komplizierte Einfache', 52–7. De la Motte's argument and music examples support Adorno's assertions that this is a movement 'telling of the past' (*Mahler*, 155; German edn., 201). Dieter Schnebel suggests that these measures are rather like 'an arsenal for a lied' ('Das Spätwerk', 172).

chilling—closure from $\hat{2}$ to $\hat{1}$.) Many commentators have suggested that in both the Ninth and *Das Lied* this gesture alludes to Beethoven's explicitly programmatic 'Lebewohl' Sonata, Op. 81a (see Ex. 20.2(*a*), (*b*), and (*c*)), and Mahler's annotation 'Leb' wol! Leb' wol!' over its surfacing on the penultimate page of his draft score for the first movement of the Ninth would seem to support this interpretation.[36] As Floros has noted, the thematic affinity between the Beethoven passage in Ex. 20.2(*c*) and bars 245–50 of Mahler's first movement (Ex. 20.2(*d*)) is striking indeed.[37] (The music in Ex. 20.2(*d*) also includes the so-called 'motto' harmonic progression, prominent in the second, third, and fourth movements of the symphony, which may stem from the second phrase of the 'Lebewohl' sonata shown in Ex. 20.2(*b*); see also below, especially Ex. 20.9.)[38] In any case, the downbeat repetitions of non-tonic scale degrees $\hat{6}$ and $\hat{2}$ occasioned by the main theme produce the predominating sonority of the first thematic area (Ex. 20.3)—a clouded tonic D strongly reminiscent of the fading close of 'Der Abschied'.[39] Overall, the opening twenty-six bars of the Ninth seem more like music recalled in memory and quietly hummed over in short segments rather than material with the capacity to launch a thirty-minute symphonic first movement.

Ex. 20.3.

The arrival of the second thematic area (B, bar 29/Fig. 3^{-7}) is notably more characteristic of a double-variation movement than of a sonata. The transition into it comprises merely two bars of the first theme's $\hat{3}$-$\hat{2}$ head-motive ('Leb' wol') in the minor, and as noted, the change of mode is substituted for structural modulation, whereby the first and second themes are bound together as brighter and darker polarities of the same tonic centre.[40] The second group stresses not only scale degrees $\hat{2}$ and $\hat{6}$ (e.g. bb. 32 and 36), which were prominent at the opening, but also more acerbic non-harmonic leading-notes (C♯, G♯) in both the melody and agitated accompanying arpeggiations (which gradually supplant the ostinato sextuplets carried over from the A area). Such emphasis of neighbour and passing notes (whose resolution is often considerably delayed) marks the overall tone of the movement (and Mahler's late style generally). In addition, the inner voices of this secondary material frequently intone the halting, incomplete descent of the main theme, and expand

[36] Ratz (ed.), *IX. Symphonie: Partiturentwurf*, p. I/52.

[37] Floros, *Gustav Mahler*, iii. 276–7.

[38] See Lewis, *Tonal Coherence*, 50; Diether, 'The Expressive Content of Mahler's Ninth', 83–4; and Deryck Cooke, 'Mahler's Melodic Thinking', in id., *Vindications: Essays in Romantic Music* (London: Faber, 1982), 103–5.

[39] Cf. also Krummacher, 'Struktur und Auflösung', in Danuser (ed.), *Gustav Mahler*, 306.

[40] Cf. also Adorno, *Mahler*, 157 and 158 (German edn., 202–4). I take it that from *Das klagende Lied* and *Lieder eines fahrenden Gesellen* on, the expressive contexts of the major and minor modes in Mahler's music are sufficiently clear to justify their characterization as 'brighter' and 'darker'.

upon the rhythmic complexity latent in its accompaniment.[41] All these features characterize B as the darker counterpart of A: the two thematic areas are strongly linked, like the
components of a syzygial pair—and throughout the course of the movement they function
as paired, interrelated opposites in rondo-like juxtaposition.

The melodic line of the second theme rises in range and dynamic level, leading (Fig. 3^{+4})
to the first of the 'climaxes breaking forth like new ebullitions' noted by Berg. But within
half a dozen bars a trumpet fanfare (Ex. 20.4) dispels this grim recollection, transforms the
mode back to major, and ushers in a new, ecstatic presentation of A material (Fig. 4^{-10}),
which is intensified by the wide leaps and octave displacement of intervals typical in late
Mahler. Precisely as Adorno suggests, the music seems to become 'entangled in immediacy, in a second life, blooming as if it were the first', and the remainder of the exposition
largely continues thus. But the move to B flat through a deceptive cadence in this passage
(Fig. 4^{-3}) effects diversion rather than new direction; a distinct allusion to the trio section
(bb. 58–9) of the scherzo from the Fourth Symphony invokes the aura of memory once
more; and with the recurrence of D major (bb. 64 ff./Fig. 5^{-5}) the material of the first theme
gradually fragments, with the head-motive coming to rest on a single (and rather ominous)
stopped-horn $c\#'$ (Fig. 5^{+11}).

Ex. 20.4. Ninth Symphony, 1st movt., bb. 44–5

Reinterpreted as $d\flat'$, that note serves as very brief transition to the closing group, which
arrives by way of B flat minor. The beginning of the second theme and its accompanying
arpeggiations appear (though strangely ill-suited to the new key), only to be swept aside
again by the fanfare that had re-established the tonic major earlier (Ex. 20.4). Now the
music suddenly sounds like an episodic passage from a mature Mahler development section: a collage of motives from both previous thematic groups intertwines and juxtaposes
the materials with unexpected intricacy and energetic intensity. The dissynchronous
rhythms latent in the A material and expanded in B are here given free reign; the swirling
ebullience peaks first in a derivative phrase (Fig. 6^{-4}, Ex. 20.5) of great import for later
events, and then again in the gleaming B flat close of the section (heightened by the now-
motivic added sixth; Fig. 6^{+9} ff.). Yet there seems something slightly forced in this music—
both structurally, as the unprepared closing of an unsettled exposition, and affectively, in
its hyper-jubilant yet rhythmically fluctuating gestures, which vaguely resemble the agitated inebriation of *Das Lied* (nos. 1 and 5).

---

[41] As Mitchell points out (*SSLD*, 373–4), Mahler's use of such strong dissynchronization in all parts first emerges in the
final movement of *Das Lied von der Erde*.

Ex. 20.5. Ninth Symphony, 1st movt., Fig. 6⁻⁴ ff.

Development

'Joy flares high at the edge of horror', as Adorno puts it:[42] the closing group vanishes into near silence more suddenly than it appeared. A soft B flat pedal articulated only by the irregular syncopation of the movement's first bars opens the development; two measures later the drop of a third to G flat sounds like a pale echo of 'vor Gott!' in another Ninth Symphony.[43] Motivic fragments previously drawn into musical continuity now stand isolated and static. The shift to a mixture of G minor and B flat (Fig. 7⁻⁶ ff.) inverts the exposition's B flat added-sixth close, and the horns repeat the syncopated B♭'s, *fortissimo* (whereby there seems little doubt that this curiously dull motivic shard portends something sinister). Such brokenness continues for more than a dozen bars, drifting into a rather pathetic recollection of the first theme's close, which is counterpointed by its head-motive (Fig. 7⁺⁶ ff.). Then gradually, almost surreptitiously, the music begins to resume momentum, first in D minor, then major; 'pianissimo, but very expressively, sweetly sung, very intimately sung', a lyrical variant of the first theme emerges (Fig. 8⁻⁴ ff.). Yet its sweetness is delicately tinged with ironic reminiscence: this is the widely recognized quotation of a waltz tune by Johann Strauss jun., 'Freuet Euch des Lebens' ('Enjoy Life'), which Mahler probably knew from his student days (see Ex. 20.6).[44] As in the exposition, the tonality shifts to B flat (Fig. 8⁺⁹), then ventures forth to E flat, and the thickening motivic interplay begins to resemble the exposition's closing group. Quietly approaching fanfares

Ex. 20.6. Johann Strauss jun., 'Freuet Euch des Lebens', Op. 340

[42] Adorno, *Mahler*, 126 (German edn., 166).

[43] 'Sensuality was given to the worm, and the cherub stands before God.' Beethoven, Ninth Symphony, finale, just before the 6/8 *alla marcia* interlude in B flat.

[44] Philip Barford, *Mahler Symphonies and Songs* (BBC Music Guides; Seattle: University of Washington Press, 1971), 55–6, was apparently the first to observe this striking resemblance, which has been noted by many later writers. 'Freuet Euch des Lebens' was composed for the inaugural

ball celebrating the new 'Golden Hall' of the Gesellschaft der Musikfreunde on 15 Jan. 1870, and is dedicated to the Gesellschaft (see Franz Grasberger and Lothar Knessel, *Hundert Jahre Goldener Saal: Das Haus der Gesellschaft der Musikfreunde am Karlsplatz* (Vienna: Gesellschaft der Musikfreunde, n.d.), 14–17). The same building housed the Vienna Conservatory, where Mahler studied from 1875 to 1878.

grow increasingly prominent, precipitating another episode of varied A material (Fig. 9 ff.): this is music in frenzied heroic style ('*Mit Wut*') intensified by a chromatic rise in tonality from C to D flat to the main key of D (Fig. 10). D then serves as dominant of G,[45] and the music becomes overblown and shrill; such hyper-energy seems even less sustainable here than in the exposition's closing section. But now the outcome is different: the motive shown in Ex. 20.5 rings *fortissimo* over a progression leading to E flat—another half-step ascent, up from D—and then without warning the entire musical substance collapses into low-register, atonal sonorities (Fig. 11^{-4} through 11^{+2}).[46]

Out of the chaos emerges the arpeggiating accompaniment of the B material, in D minor, and we expect the theme itself. It duly arrives (Fig. 11^{+10}), but in the acrid setting of B flat minor that, in the exposition's closing section, was shunted aside; the texture of the material grows darker and thicker, while linear resolutions and local harmonic relations become more tenuous. When it seems as though this grim passage might be endless, the dominant of D major arrives unexpectedly and the tempo becomes 'suddenly slower' (Fig. 13^{-9} ff.): in earlier Mahler such a gesture could well signal the moment of 'breakthrough'— the unexpected transcendence of negative affect that previously had seemed overwhelming. But the mode shifts; the head-motive of the first theme appears in the minor (Fig. 13^{-6}), as does the fanfare that had twice forced an energetic return to major-mode exuberance (Ex. 20.4). The texture fragments, and muted trombones render the fanfare impotent; the tonal centre rambles by thirds, D minor to B flat to G flat to E flat minor; the pulse weakens, and Mahler marks this music 'schattenhaft' (shadowy, Fig. 13^{+12}): the breakthrough was an illusion. Then once again the music rises phoenix-like from fragments, just as it had near the beginning of the development (Fig. 7^{+12} ff.). Substance and momentum increase, and the tonality reverts to D major; the waltz-variant of the first theme reappears, again 'very sweetly but expressively' (it was here in the draft score that Mahler wrote 'Oh days of youth! Vanished! O Love! Scattered!'[47]). This nostalgically bitter-sweet reminiscence of banal but happy music would seem to be all that has survived intact, all that remains to cling to, from the unfolding of the symphonic narrative.

In retrospect, the outcome of the movement would seem to be inevitable at this point, even though the engrossed first-time listener is unlikely to anticipate it. The next build-up is the most extensive and most intense. The tonal focus moves from D through the dominant of E flat to the new area of B major (Fig. 14^{-8} ff.)—the other of the third-related pairings to D, which is implied by the added-sixth sonority of the movement's opening (see above, p. 472). Now the motive of Ex. 20.5 is heard twice, first in the winds (Fig. 14^{+3}), then tutti (Fig. 15^{-8}); but the crisis ensues just when complete transformation seems within reach. Against an F♯ pedal, triple-*forte* trombones sound the tritone, *diabolus in musica*, C♮—the same pitch in the same colour that had announced the arrival of the rider on horseback in 'Der Abschied'—and in the syncopated rhythm of the movement's opening bars: it is as though, Adorno notes, the catastrophe 'secretly . . . had always been known and

[45] The horn call here would not be out of place in Strauss's *Don Juan* or *Ein Heldenleben*.
[46] Pitch-class sets 4–12 (Fig. 11^{-1}) and 4–19 (Fig. 11^{+1}).   [47] Ratz (ed.), *IX. Symphonie: Partiturentwurf*, p. I/29.

nothing else were expected'.[48] This seems to be confirmed, as the trombones fade, by muted violas quoting the 'pathetic' transformation of the main theme's close from the first portion of the development (as though to emphasize: *there* was the reason for its enervation), and by the bass ostinato on the harp motive (i^2) from the opening bars, at the original pitch level. 'Wie ein schwerer Kondukt' (like a slow funeral cortège), Mahler notes: it is as though the long march of 'Der Abschied' now led beyond the trombone summons and the arrival of the horseman, rather than towards that moment. For Adorno, 'The almost labored one-measure steps of the narrative carry the burden of the symphony's momentum at the start of the Funeral March like a coffin in a slow cortège. The bells here are not Christian ones: with such malign pomp a mandarin is buried.'[49]

Reprise

Mahler's sketches reveal that he considered the movement's climax to be part of the retransition to the reprise,[50] as indeed structurally it is: the orientation of the bass ostinato towards B will yield, by third relation, to D (Fig. 16^{-19}). Yet such an approach to the tonic generates no urgency to move ahead; the introductory fragments recur in full voice over the continuing bass pattern, which is doubled by the exotic-sounding bells and heterophonic tremolos; in addition, the head-motive of the main theme sounds repeatedly before matters actually get under way (Fig. 16^{-9}). Although the reprise is virtually equal to the exposition in number of bars (and slightly longer in playing time), it invariably seems shorter: this is the outcome of its function in relation to all that has transpired thus far. Owing to the episodic, rondo-like nature of the thematic fields in both exposition and development, there is little tonal polarity to be resolved, and still less need to rehearse the themes themselves. Rather, this reprise will focus on discharging the accumulated affective tension that has been generated through the music's 're-engagement with immediacy': it does so by diffusing the thematic materials back into the sort of fragmentary recollections from which they arose (cf. p. 472 above). From the standpoint of dramatic musical narrative, there would seem to be no other rationale for a reprise in this movement, because had the catastrophe transpired in present time rather than memory, the movement would logically end shortly thereafter (as does, for example, the finale of Mahler's Sixth).[51] Such

[48] Adorno, *Mahler*, 160 (German edn., 208). As Floros points out (*Gustav Mahler*, iii. 277), the climax is the last time the syncopated rhythm of motive i^1 is heard in this movement. In German the equivalent of 'the last trumpet' is 'die letzte Posaune', i.e. literally 'the last trombone'.

Among Mahler's predecessors who employ similar juxtapositions of immediacy and memory is Schubert, e.g. in the first movements of his String Quartets in A minor, D. 804 and G major, D. 887; see Stephen E. Hefling and David S. Tartakoff, 'Schubert's Chamber Music', in *Nineteenth-Century Chamber Music*, ed. Hefling (New York: Schirmer Books, 1998), 79–81 and 94–7, as well as Carl Dahlhaus, 'Sonata Form in Schubert: The First Movement of the

G-major String Quartet, Op. 161 (D. 887)', trans. Thilo Reinhard, in Walter Frisch (ed.), *Schubert: Critical and Analytical Studies* (Lincoln, Nebr.: University of Nebraska Press, 1986), *passim*.

[49] Adorno, *Mahler*, 155 (German edn., 201).

[50] See the short-score page reproduced by Andraschke as Fig. 2 (p. [96]), which is labelled 'Rückgang' (retransition) and contains the climax as well as the note 'folgt Reprise' (reprise follows).

[51] This is not to suggest that the reprise is truncated in the Sixth, but only that once the final blow falls (Fig. 165^{-7}) there is virtually nothing left to hear.

a recapitulatory process produces the most musically unified portion of the movement, precisely because everything is now oriented towards one goal—dispersion—which thus seems to be achieved much more quickly than the exposition's unfolding of interrelated yet conflicting material.

The end of the funeral march overlaps with the reprise of the main theme, and continues to resonate in its counterpoint as the material grows louder, brassier, almost coarse; thus is its fundamental lyricism spurned. The predictable move to B flat (Fig. 16^{+10}) continues in this vein, leading sooner than expected to the minor-mode second group. It arrives over an uncharacteristically consonant A pedal, combined already with the fanfare that had previously dispelled it: within five bars this shadow-motive has lost all power, its rhythmic complexities dispersed in the dialogue of the high winds, and then in the extraordinary cadenza-duet for horn and flute. (Such exposed, asymmetric, dissynchronous textures once again recall similar passages in 'Der Abschied'.) A final outburst of passionate energy leads to a recollection of the exposition's major-mode rejection of the second theme (b. 398; cf. Fig. 3^{+9} ff.); this is dispersed in D minor by a variant of the fanfare motive shown in Ex. 20.4. Then follow fifty measures of exquisitely bitter-sweet release into D major (delicately coloured by its Neapolitan, E flat, and the third-relation of B, bar 419 ff.). Fanfare, head-motive ('Leb' wol!'), and waltz-variant are all fragmented and fade into the chamber-music texture; the movement evaporates on a final high d'''.

II: Ländler and Waltz

The first movement of the Ninth is almost self-contained; the ensuing scherzo and Rondo-Burleske turn all but completely away from the domain of the long opening Andante, and these two inner movements are affectively linked by the rising levels of ironic bitterness and distorted tonal syntax. Rustic Ländler and sophisticated waltz had been frequent topoi in Mahler's earlier symphonies; in the second movement of the Ninth he juxtaposes the two dances, parodying each to an unusually disorienting degree.[52] Bekker and Adorno regard this movement as a 'Totentanz', akin to the scherzo of the Fourth Symphony;[53] whether or not one accepts that reading, when the piece has run its course, 'one feels that "the dance is over" ', as Bruno Walter observes.[54] The underlying formal scheme is fairly simple, as shown in Diagram 20.1: two Ländler and two waltzes mingle in rondo-like manner.[55] Although its

[52] Lewis, *Tonal Coherence*, 54 and 43.

[53] Bekker, *Gustav Mahlers Sinfonien*, 345; Adorno, *Mahler*, 161 (German edn., 209); cf. also Floros, *Gustav Mahler*, iii. 280.

[54] Walter, *Mahler*, 88 (Eng. trans., 125).

[55] The formal scheme in Diagram 20.1 is similar to that presented by Lewis, *Tonal Coherence*, 44; the main differences are as follows: (i) Lewis believes Waltzes 1 and 2 constitute a refrain; yet in context it seems just as reasonable to regard the waltz pair as a distinct, independent formal component; (ii) following Mahler's marking 'Langsamer Menuett' in the orchestral draft score (p. II/23), Lewis labels the 'C' material 'Menuet'. But as Floros has shown (ii. 175 and 379), the principal theme of this music is clearly in the style of a slow Ländler; moreover, in the autograph full score Mahler marks it 'Tempo III. (Ländler, ganz langsam)'.

Bar:	1	90		218	261	333	369	404		523	
Theme:	A	B1	B2	// C	B1′	C′	// A′	B2″	B1″	A″	//
		Ländler 1 | Waltz 1	Waltz 2	// Ländler 2	| Waltz 1	| Ländler 2	// Ländler 1	| Waltz 2	Waltz 1	| Ländler 1	//
Tonality:	C	| E	E♭	// F	| D	| F	// C	| E♭	B♭	| C	//

Diagram 20.1. Formal plan of the second movement of the Ninth Symphony

design retains vestiges of the scherzo-trio plan and also of the old waltz suite, the movement's musical materials interact in complex and unexpected ways that contradict more traditional formal categorization.

'Somewhat clumsy and very coarse' is Mahler's characterization of the opening section. It owes much of its clumsiness to a relentless tonic–dominant and diatonic emphasis on C major, plus the avoidance of cumulative, goal-directed periodic phrasing and directionality; this music proceeds by repetition and seemingly random phrase groupings for eighty-nine bars, driven chiefly by the droning triple time of the peasant dance.[56] The $\hat{3}$-$\hat{2}$-$\hat{1}$ span of the introductory gesture, which echoes the shape of the first movement's principal theme, is also embedded in the first waltz (B1) and slow-Ländler (C) sections (see Ex. 20.7),[57] while the 'cumbersome' (*Schwerfällig*) main idea is actually a contrapuntal combination of two thematic lines (violins and violas, bb. 9 ff.) in the manner of Bruckner's Ländler movements.[58] Adorno regards this opening section as a significant early example of 'musical montage . . . a collage picture made from deformed clichés: it pillories reified, petrified forms'.[59] However artful, the material is of deliberately limited interest; just as it seems as if nothing more can happen, the first waltz appears.

Arriving without warning or transition, this sudden swirl from the world of Johann Strauss and Lehár is both a relief and a surprise; as Adorno notes, it 'shocks through the reeling, overenergetic harmony of "Der Trunkene im Frühling" and by its wild vulgarisms'.[60] The key—mediant major—was hardly to be anticipated, and neither recurs nor is otherwise rationalized to the overall tonal plan. Moreover, within a dozen bars the acute listener knows that normal tonal processes will not always prevail; as Lewis points out, while the passage shown in Ex. 20.8 prolongs E major, it seems inexplicable in conventional harmonic or contrapuntal terms.[61] Cadential references to the 'Fischpredigt' scherzo of the Second Symphony (e.g. horns, bb. 101–3) remind us of a movement in which 'the world seems crazy and confused, as though deformed by a concave mirror',[62] and during the course of the next forty bars melodic, harmonic, and contrapuntal relations become increasingly distorted as the dance swings on with abandon.

[56] Schnebel, 'Das Spätwerk', 176, describes it as music of 'dissociated continuity, from which the form has already shrunk away—these are composed ruins'.

[57] See also Lewis, *Tonal Coherence*, 49–50, as well as Diether, 'The Expressive Content of Mahler's Ninth', 83.

[58] See Floros, ii. 172–6, esp. 175.

[59] Adorno, *Mahler*, 161–2 (German edn., 209–10).

[60] Ibid. 162 (German edn., 210).

[61] See Lewis, *Tonal Coherence*, 52–4, and *passim* for further details of unusual tonal procedures.

[62] Mahler in conversation with Natalie Bauer-Lechner, Jan. 1896 (NB-L, *Erinnerungen*, 40; *Recollections*, 43–4); cf. also Floros, iii. 282.

Ex. 20.7. Ninth Symphony, 2nd movt.: (*a*) opening; (*b*) bb. 95–7; (*c*) bb. 218–21

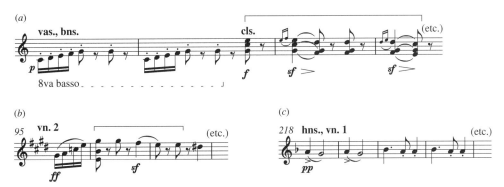

Ex. 20.8. Ninth Symphony, 2nd movt., bb. 96–102

The first waltz presses directly into the second (in E flat, Fig. 20⁻¹¹), where the music becomes truly grotesque: trombones, tuba, and contrabasses introduce a banal, bloated dance tune with continuous oom-pah accompaniment by the full orchestra.[63] Shortly thereafter (Fig. 20⁺²) violins and flutes present a lamenting chromatic descent that will become increasingly prominent as it crops up in subsequent thematic sections of the piece. In the midst of this quick-paced, sophisticated ill-humour the introductory Ländler tune appears in horns and woodwind, sounding almost breathless and distinctly out of place. This yields to further contrapuntal virtuosity and syntactical stretching, until at length the energy begins to subside, the tonal focus becomes a mixture of F and D (b. 204/Fig. 21⁺¹⁸ ff.), and a genuine transition, the first in the piece, ushers in the slow Ländler ('C') in clearly defined F major, subdominant of the main key.

This serene and refreshingly normal music seems at first to function as a trio section; the close connection to the main theme of the first movement lends it a somewhat retrospect-ive, nostalgic quality. A cheerful A major variant for winds (bb. 230 ff.) provides a purer exemplar of the pastoral Ländler than the movement's opening. Yet the ensuing B flat minor version (b. 243) is tinged with the complexity of what has transpired earlier in the work; one begins to suspect that music of relative simplicity will not long predominate, and

---

[63] In a footnote Adorno identifies this passage as one of the waltz section's 'wild vulgarisms' (*Mahler*, 162).

indeed the return of the slow Ländler in F quickly dissolves into circling harmonies anticipating later twentieth-century cocktail-piano clichés (bb. 256–9). Waltz 1 intervenes,
now in D major (key of the opening Andante), reharmonized by the 'motto progression'
that will be distinctly recalled both in the third movement and in the opening of the symphony's finale (Ex. 20.9). The three, almost symmetrical, 15-bar strophes of the waltz grow
progressively more effusive, culminating in the chromatic lament noted above (bb. 305–9).
Meanwhile the tonal focus has moved from D (via B and E minor) to a C pedal, while texture and phrasing become more fragmentary—all of which prepares the return of the slow
Ländler in F (b. 333). Formally, this rounds out the middle section, but affectively the innocence of the material is lost; outbursts of lament seem barely suppressed during the ritardando bars that twice disrupt the regular phrasing (bb. 344–5, 357–9). As before, the music
falters in wandering progressions of fifths, ending on the dominant of E.

The opening Ländler in C is hardly expected here, yet its rustic stolidity seems almost
welcome. But this material has also lost the immediacy of its original character; new harmonic directions, refined chamber-like textures, and the recurring chromatic wail seem to

Ex. 20.9. The 'motto progression': (*a*) 2nd movt., bb. 261–4; (*b*) 3rd movt., bb. 109–11; (*c*) 4th movt., opening
(cf. Ex. 20.2)

(*a*)

(*b*)

(*c*)

undermine its strength, and within less than forty bars the Ländler begins to yield to the tempo and figurations of a waltz; the transitional gestures that had formerly introduced the slow Ländler now usher in Waltz 2, commencing in C minor and moving to E flat (bb. 423 ff.). As this music seems to approach the level of its original ferocity, the tonality shifts unexpectedly (G flat, Fig. 24) and a shrieking counter-melody in the winds intensifies the waltz parody further.[64] A yet more raucous chorus in E flat follows (Fig. 25), leading directly into two strophes of Waltz 1, first in B flat, then moving to G.

G serves as the dominant transition for the final return to the opening Ländler (Fig. 26⁻¹⁹). But now the dance has lost its stalwart droning on C major; as though groping for tonal identity, the consequent phrases sound in E flat, F, and G before yielding to tonic minor (Fig. 26⁻⁴). Additional tonal wandering precipitates C minor once again (Fig. 27), now combined with the chromatic lament; one senses that the dance may indeed be over. The texture thins to chamber-music proportions while the collective energy level wanes, as though small groups and individuals are exchanging parting remarks before the end. By the time the major mode returns (b. 599) the music is clearly fading; following further dispersion, the final motivic ascent to C is taken in widely spaced octaves by double bassoon and piccolo (the lowest and highest voices of the company)—and the movement evaporates inconclusively, much as the opening Andante had done.

The parody of musical topoi—peasant Ländler and dapper waltz—as well as their interaction in this movement suggests that while neither yokel nor false sophisticate achieves artistic utopia, each may corrupt the other, leaving both bereft of integrity: ultimately, there is neither waltz nor Ländler, only dispersion. Accordingly, one may well agree with Adorno that

Through its irreconcilable and obtrusive negativity, the movement, despite the traditional dance forms, is miraculously ahead of its time. And all the while it splits hairs even in hell, like Karl Kraus. . . . The Scherzo remains dynamic, does not take delight in the mere montage of senselessly ossified, immobile elements, but carries these with it in symphonic time. . . . only symphonic time makes legible the horror of what time has lost, like Peter Schlemihl his shadow.[65]

III: Rondo-Burleske

But Mahler's compositional tour de force of negativity is the Rondo-Burleske. Originally dedicated 'To my brothers in Apollo',[66] it is the most syntactically untraditional, contrapuntally complex, and riotously sardonic movement in all Mahler's oeuvre—as La Grange

---

[64] The wind counter-melody is briefly adumbrated at Fig. 21⁺⁶ f.

[65] Adorno, *Mahler*, 161–2 (German edn., 209–10).

[66] Adler, *Gustav Mahler* (Reilly, *Gustav Mahler and Guido Adler*, 54; cf. also 59). The inscription is not found in any manuscript known today, but Adler's close acquaintance with Mahler and his circle plus his scrupulous attitude towards musical scholarship make it unlikely that the dedication is a fabrication.

comments, Mahler never ventured further into nihilism than here.[67] Not surprisingly, several writers regard the Rondo-Burleske as Mahler's most 'modern' utterance.[68] Both motivically and tonally it recalls the A minor second movement of the Fifth Symphony—a 'stormily agitated' outburst, 'with greatest vehemence', following (and intertwined with) that work's imposing opening funeral march; A minor is also the key of tragedy in the Sixth Symphony, and of nihilistic despair in 'Das Trinklied vom Jammer der Erde', which opens *Das Lied von der Erde*. Formally, this third movement of the Ninth is even more straightforward than the second (see Diagram 20.2); the complexity lies in the musical language of the principal material.

Bar:	1	79	109	180	209	262	311	346	522	617
		fugato			fugato		fugato			
Theme:	A		B (1st episode)	A′		B′	(A″)	C (2nd episode)	A‴	Coda
Tonality:	a̱	d	F	a♭–a–d (a)	A		(A)	D	⌇⌇ d a d	a̱

Diagram 20.2. Formal plan of the Rondo-Burleske of the Ninth Symphony

To date, the best analysis of the movement is that by Lewis, who rightly observes that while the techniques Mahler deploys here are not new, their intensification results in an extraordinary accumulation of surface dissonance, which contributes to the apparent modernity of the music. Among the specific procedures are (i) superimposition of triads having different functions, and likewise of melodic strands implying different tonics; (ii) the metric displacement of conventional harmonic and contrapuntal motions, which is related to the triadic and melodic superimposition just noted; (iii) very fast changes of local triadic centre; (iv) complex cross-relations.[69] As a result of such techniques, the clear articulations of tonal centricity marking the form of the movement function as framing devices—points of arrival and departure—that often exert only tangential influence upon what transpires between them. Such complex ambiguity is apparent from the very opening of the movement, shown in Ex. 20.10, which gives little hint that it will arrive in A minor; the unusual progression marked x in the example (D♭–B♭ augmented sixth–A minor) will be invoked frequently to articulate the tonic during the course of the Rondo-Burleske. The movement's texture is dense and complicated from the outset, but in the fugato passages, based on pairs of subjects in the manner of double fugues, Mahler's contrapuntal dexterity becomes truly virtuosic.[70] Yet as Adorno suggests, just such virtuosity in the dissonant context of the piece effects an iconoclastic parody of fugal style, which Mahler had treated

[67] HLG(F) iii. 1209.
[68] e.g. Cooke, *Gustav Mahler*, 117; Lewis, *Tonal Coherence*, 65.
[69] Lewis, *Tonal Coherence*, ch. 4, esp. 65–7.
[70] Mahler very likely had in mind as a precedent

Beethoven's *Große Fuge*, Op. 133, a contrapuntal extravaganza of high surface dissonance that Stravinsky has characterized as an 'absolutely contemporary piece of music that will be contemporary forever…' (Igor Stravinsky and Robert Craft, *Dialogues and a Diary* (London: Faber, 1968), 124.)

Ex. 20.10. Ninth Symphony, 3rd movt., opening

nobly in his Fifth and Eighth Symphonies (the Eighth especially)—'The mature master of counterpoint stumbles on the fact that fugues can no longer be written'.[71]

The episodes of the rondo scheme create strong contrasts through their lighter textures and relative tonal clarity. The first ('B', b.109 ff.) is distinctly popular in tone; Adorno's notion that 'It saunters to the rhythm of the "Women" song in the *Merry Widow* [by Lehár], which at that time squeaked from the brass horns of phonographs' has been accepted by nearly every subsequent commentator.[72] Its harmonic scheme is shown in Ex. 20.8—the so-called 'motto progression' that opens the finale as well. The second episode ('C') is the longest section of the movement, and initially the most stable in tonality, focusing on D major for its first 100 bars. The rather severe first motivic idea (bb. 348–52) comes from the subjects of the two previous fugato sections;[73] this gives way to a graceful turn motive recurring throughout the section, and anticipating the pervasive turns of the Adagio finale. D major was the tonic of the first movement, and in both key and character this music sounds somewhat nostalgic; indeed, the climactic passage at Fig. 38 ff. recalls the warmer moments of the opening Andante, in which a positive breakthrough seemed imminent. But neither there nor here is such transcendence to be attained;[74] the clarinets shrilly and abruptly dismiss D (Fig. 39^{-2}), and each of the four short episodes that follow seeks to establish another key centre previously prominent in the first movement—B flat (minor) (Fig. 39^{+3}/b. 448), G (minor) (b. 458), B (minor) (b. 469), and B (major) (b. 480)—none of which prevails.[75] An increasingly agitated transitional passage ushers in the final refrain of the rondo (b. 522), at first in D minor (modal transformation of the potential break-through), then in the tonic A minor. The biting rawness of the material becomes even more pronounced, and the twofold acceleration of tempo in the coda drives the piece to its end with frenzied abandon.

[71] Adorno, *Mahler*, 162 (German edn., 210).

[72] Ibid. 162–3 (German edn., 211); Kurt von Fischer, 'Die Doppelschlagfigur in den zwei letzten Sätzen von Gustav Mahlers 9. Symphonie: Versuch einer Interpretation', *Archiv für Musikwissenschaft*, 32 (1975), 99–105 at 100; HLG(F) iii. 1209; Schnebel, 'Das Spätwerk', 16 and 183; Floros, *Gustav Mahler*, iii. 285. The 'Women Song' is the March-Septet in the second act (no. 9); it would seem that Adorno was thinking especially of the Trio in this piece,

which is repeated as the finale (no. 16) of the operetta. On Mahler's acquaintance with Lehár's *Merry Widow* see Alma Mahler, *Memories*, 120.

[73] At bars 348 ff. this material sounds distinctly like the opening of the second thematic area (G flat) in the first movement of Beethoven's Op. 130 quartet.

[74] Cf. also Adorno, *Mahler*, 163 (German edn., 212).

[75] Cf. also Lewis, *Tonal Coherence*, 89–90.

IV: Adagio

Perhaps none of the countless surprises and contrasts in the Ninth Symphony is so unexpected or so touching as the onset of its finale: the octave sweep, turn, and scalar descent of the unison violins (all playing on the dark fourth string) is a singing gesture of an intensely expressive character;[76] its focus on A♭ (G♯), heard just after the close of the Rondo-Burleske, seems to lead back to A minor until the very moment the broad hymnic Adagio theme arrives in sombre D flat major.[77] As noted above, both the harmony of the main theme's opening phrase and its omnipresent turn figures have been adumbrated in the previous movements; here these elements are utterly transformed in affective import. In the eighth bar we hear a distinct reference to the 'Urlicht' movement (also in D flat) of Mahler's 'Resurrection' Symphony—'Je lieber möcht' ich *im Himmel sein*' (I would so much rather *be in heaven* [italics indicate the specific musical phrase])—the first of several allusions to his earlier works, which yield strong hints, if such were needed, of the occasion for this hymn. The next bar sounds the first of numerous harmonic leanings towards D major; vaguely foreshadowed by the third chord of the theme (A major, b. 3), these yearning gestures surface frequently, even in the last page of the work,[78] yet none is fulfilled—a striking aspect of tonal association spanning all four movements of the symphony.

It is generally observed that Mahler's inspiration for this movement came from the monumental slow movements of Bruckner, especially that of his (incomplete) Ninth

---

[76] See von Fischer, 'Die Doppelschlagfigur', esp. 103.

[77] The subdued quality of D flat is owing both to its lower-neighbour relation to D, and to the relative lack of sympathetic open-string overtone resonance in this key among the stringed instruments, which dominate the texture for most of the movement.

Both Jack Diether ('The Expressive Content', 100) and Deryck Cooke ('Mahler's Melodic Thinking', 103–5) have noted the strong resemblance between the opening bars of the main theme and the English hymn 'Abide with Me' as sung to the tune 'Eventide' by William Henry Monk. The similarity may not be accidental: this hymn was extremely popular in both England and America. It was included in all editions of the Church of England's widely used *Hymns Ancient and Modern* from 1861 onwards (also published in Philadelphia in 1865), which had achieved a worldwide circulation of 60,000,000 copies by 1912. 'Abide with Me' was also adopted by many other denominations; the text was frequently associated with the end of earthly life. (See John Julian (ed.), *A Dictionary of Hymnology* (2nd edn., London: J. Murray, 1907), 7; Henry Wilder Foote, *Three Centuries of American Hymnody* (Cambridge, Mass.: Harvard University Press, 1940), 220–1; Robert G. McCutchan, *Our Hymnody: A Manual of the Methodist Hymnal* (2nd edn., New York: Abingdon-Cokesbury Press, 1937), 502–3; Maurice Frost (ed.), *Historical Companion to Hymns Ancient and Modern* (London: W. Clowes, 1962), 479 and *passim*.) Alma Mahler (*Memories*, 161–2) tells of an extraordinary tour she and

Mahler made of New York's Chinatown, which ended thus: 'Finally, on the outskirts of this district we came on the habitat of a religious sect. There was a large hall at the far end of which sat a man with the face of a fanatic playing hymns on a harmonium in a pronouncedly whining style. The benches were occupied by a starving congregation. We were given the explanation. For listening to the hymns and joining in—a cup of coffee and a roll.' Alma's book ascribes this incident to the autumn of 1909 (i.e. after the Ninth was completed); yet she is sometimes inaccurate in her chronology, and she and Mahler may have undertaken similar excursions during their earlier American years (1907 ff.). It will be recalled that the funeral cortège of a New York fireman inspired the famous drum strokes in the fourth and fifth movements of the unfinished Tenth Symphony (see *Memories*, 135).

However, six bars of sketching closely related to the opening of the Ninth's finale are found in Mahler's sketchbook for the Seventh Symphony, which probably dates from the summer of 1905; thus, aspects of the finale's first phrase may have 'rattled about in my head', as he put it, for two years prior to his first visit to New York. (See Stephen E. Hefling, ' "Ihm in die Lieder zu blicken": Mahler's Seventh Symphony Sketchbook', in Hefling (ed.), *Mahler Studies*, 191–4.)

[78] Cf. bb. 19, 32–3, 63, 121–2 (brass), 127–8, 155–6, 161, 166 (fourth crotchet)–167; cf. also Lewis, *Tonal Coherence*, 107 ff.

Symphony;[79] perhaps more significantly, Mahler had concluded his own Third Symphony with an Adagio, 'with a higher as opposed to a lower form', as he put it.[80] That finale, originally entitled 'War mir die Liebe erzählt' (What Love tells me), was intended as the liberating resolution of a symphonic world tracing the inner evolution of being, from raw nature to the divine; in the closing movement of the Third Mahler believed that 'everything is resolved into peace and being; the Ixion-wheel of appearance is finally brought to a standstill'[81]—an allusion to Schopenhauer's doctrine of overcoming the Will's relentless cyclical quest for satisfaction. 'Over and above all, eternal love moves within us—as rays come together in a focal point', he wrote his friend Fritz Löhr. 'Now do you understand?'[82] To his confidante Natalie Bauer-Lechner Mahler spoke about the Third more boldly: 'Can a spirit that ponders the eternal creative thought of the godhead in a symphony such as this, die? No, one gains trust: everything is eternally and intransitorily well born; as Christ teaches, "In my Father's house are many dwellings"; and here human sorrow and misery no longer has a place'.[83] In the final pages of the Third Mahler deploys his full orchestral resources 'not with raw power' but rather with 'saturated, noble tone' in the superabundantly bright D major close of the work.[84]

But the concluding Adagio of the Ninth offers no such confident fulfilment. Externally it resembles the Third's finale: the formal scheme is rondo-like, with thematic materials varied as the movement proceeds; focus on the principal tonal centre is strong, with little tonicization of other key areas; and the texture is dominated by rich contrapuntal string writing (see Diagram 20.3).[85] Yet there the similarities end, and the differences are most

Bar:	1	11	13	17	28		49	56	60	64	73		88	
Theme:	A1	(B)	A2	A1 var.	B		A1 var.	A2 var.	A2 var.	A1 var.			B var.	
					+ counter-melodies						'3rd movt.'		'Abschied'	
Tonality:	D♭	d♭	(V)	D♭	c♯		D♭	D♭		D♭	⁀ D♭		c♯(A–F♯)	

							(Coda)				
	107	118	126	136	138	153	159		169	173	178	(185)
	A2 var.		A1 var.	A2 var.	A1 var.		(B→A2)					
	'1st movt'							('ersterbend')	[liquidation]		('ppp ersterbend')	
	F♯	V/D♭	D♭		D♭		V/D	V/D♭ D♭: ⁀ IV — I				

Diagram 20.3.   Formal scheme of the finale of the Ninth Symphony

[79] Eberhardt Klemm, 'Über ein Spätwerk Gustav Mahlers', *Deutsches Jahrbuch der Musikwissenschaft für 1961*, ed. W. Vetter (Leipzig: Edition Peters, 1962), 19–32; repr. in Danuser (ed.), *Gustav Mahler*, 324–43 (see p. 330); Adorno, *Mahler*, 165 (German edn., 214–15); von Fischer, 'Die Doppelschlagfigur', 103; Sponheuer, *Logik des Zerfalls*, 424–5; HLG(F) iii. 1213. Concerning Mahler's familiarity with Bruckner's Ninth, see HLG(F) ii. 299–300 and 907.

[80] NB-L, *Erinnerungen*, 68, Aug. 1896 (*Recollections*, 67).

[81] Ibid.

[82] Mahler, *Briefe* (1982), no. 146 (*Selected Letters*, no. 137), 29 Aug. 1895.

[83] NB-L, *Erinnerungen*, 59, 4 July 1896 (*Recollections*, 62).

[84] Instructions from Fig. 32 of the score.

[85] Like the finale of the Third, the texture here may well have been influenced by the celestial slow movements in Beethoven's last quartets, especially that of Op. 135 (in D flat major). See (*inter alia*) Bekker, *Gustav Mahlers Sinfonien*, 352, and von Fischer, 'Die Doppelschlagfigur', 103–4.

telling: despite frequent articulations of D flat, the harmony of the Ninth's finale is heavily steeped in chromaticism, non-harmonic notes, irregular resolutions, etc.—the sort of musical language heard in more acerbic form during the second and third movements. As a result, the music seems ever prepared to slip linearly away from D flat (to D for example, although that goal is never fulfilled). In addition, the fullness and expressivity of the primary material is radically countered by the bleak, hollow secondary theme—a prosaic, low-register scale first foreshadowed *pianissimo* beneath a tonic pedal (b. 11), then later sounding more than four octaves below a listless counter-melody, as though hinting at the musical disintegration to come. And indeed, far from resolving in 'saturated, noble' D major brightness, this movement dissolves, quite literally dying away in short-breathed motivic fragments liquidated slowly over a span of thirty bars, marked 'Äußerst langsam *ppp ersterbend*' (extremely slow, *pianissimo*, dying).

Mahler's habit of adopting motives, phrases, or even complete strophes from his earlier music and introducing them into related expressive contexts of new works dates from the time of *Das klagende Lied* (1880), his 'Opus 1'; to the listener familiar with this process, his self-quotations in the finale of the Ninth are striking indeed.[86] We have already noted the 'Urlicht' reference; the next is a specific, rather flippant turn gesture, familiar from the Rondo-Burleske (e.g. Fig. 39^{-2} f.), that becomes fully absorbed into the character of the finale's first refrain (b. 24), and recurs (b. 134) just prior to the last full presentation of the 'A' material. In the counterpoint to the secondary theme ('B', bb. 30–1 and 36–7) we hear a slow-motion quotation from the scherzo of the Third Symphony—'Was mir die Thiere im Walde erzählen' (What the Animals in the Forest tell Me) in the original scheme of titles.[87] This allusion is really twofold, because the main material of the Third's scherzo is itself based on Mahler's grimly humorous *Wunderhorn* song 'Ablösung im Sommer' (Changing the Guard in Summer), which concerns a nightingale replacing a dead cuckoo as the lead singer in the forest. Mahler described the symphonic movement that grew from this scion as 'the most scurrilous and yet the most tragic that ever was—as only music can mystically lead us from the one to the other in a single turn. This piece is truly as though all of Nature made a face and stuck out her tongue. Yet there is such a ghastly Panic humour in it that shock overcomes one more than laughter'.[88] Such tragi-comic horror was one of Mahler's idiosyncratic achievements as a composer, and is abundantly in evidence throughout the preceding Rondo-Burleske. But in the finale of the Ninth this languid recollection from the Third seems to suggest that the animals of the forest no longer have much to tell us.

The third variant of 'A1' material (bb. 64 ff.) is the most intense passage yet heard in the movement—through full textures, complex rhythms, and a strong gesture of modulation (bb. 70–2), the music seems to become 'entangled in new immediacy' as the first movement had done. This energy suddenly vanishes in the unexpected drop back to D flat, *pp subito*

[86] See also Tibbe, *Lieder und Liedelemente* (1st edn.), 119–24; Schnebel, 'Das Spätwerk', esp. 166 ff.; HLG(F) iii. 1212 ff.; and Floros, *Gustav Mahler*, iii. 288–92.

[87] Third Symphony, third movement, bb. 184–7/Fig. 9^{+9} ff.

[88] NB-L, *Erinnerungen*, 136 (*Recollections*, 120), June–July 1899.

(b. 73) that introduces a four-bar interpolation from the second episode of the Rondo-Burleske (Fig. 38⁻¹⁰ ff.).[89] As already observed, in the scherzo this D-major material leads towards recollection of a passage from the first movement that hints at positive resolution; here, in D flat, it is slow-moving, subdued, and insubstantial in tone. Moreover, it leads to another explicit quotation: the prominent ostinato figure from 'Strophe B' of 'Der Abschied', beneath which the 'B' theme of the Adagio is subsumed (bb. 88 ff.). In the first half of 'Der Abschied' (Fig. 7 ff.) this ostinato is associated with the beauty and peace of the earth—'The brook sings melodiously through the darkness . . .', 'The earth breathes full of rest and sleep . . .'—and it is twice interrupted by the 'Sehnsucht' motive—ecstatic music identified with the line 'Alle Sehnsucht will nun träumen' (all longing will now dream) (Fig. 14; see also above, pp. 461–2). The second half of *Das Lied*'s finale combines this ostinato with a verse Mahler himself contributed to the text, 'I wander to the homeland, my abode! . . .' (Fig. 55 ff.): then the 'Sehnsucht' music blossoms with the lines 'I shall never more roam on the horizons' and (Mahler's text again) 'Still is my heart and awaits its hour!' In the finale of the Ninth the ostinato is also twice interrupted (at bb. 92 and 97), but there is no 'Sehnsucht'—merely more listless, wide-spaced 'B' material. The recollection of departure from *Das Lied* is devoid of that moment's ecstatic yearning.

Passion returns in the passage that follows (bb. 107 ff.), driving towards a direct reference (bb. 118 ff.) to the first movement's first eruption of immediacy (first movement, bb. 44 ff.—cf. Ex. 20.4); but the mounting climax falls away, leaving violins alone in a searing augmentation of the first syncopated fragment heard at the symphony's opening (i¹).[90] Yet again no breakthrough ensues; the seemingly inevitable return of the main idea, however embellished, prepares for the movement to close without resolution. At the onset of the coda (b. 159) Mahler wrote in the orchestral draft, 'O Schönheit! Liebe!' (O Beauty! Love!); this is followed by 'Lebt wol' (Farewell) (twice, bb. 162 ff.), 'Welt!' (World!) (b. 178) and again 'Lebe wohl!' (bb. 180–2). These exclamations of farewell distinctly recall Mahler's poetry for the rapturous climax of 'Der Abschied': 'O Schönheit! o ewigen Liebens-, Lebens trunk'ne Welt!' (O Beauty! O World drunken of eternal love-and-life!). But the last of his musical quotations (bb. 163–71: Ex. 20.11) confounds any such hopefulness: this is a slow-motion citation from the fourth of the *Kindertotenlieder*, 'Oft denk' ich, sie sind nur ausgegangen' (Often I think they've merely gone out). In the lied a feigned optimism would deny the tragedy of the children's death:

> Wir holen sie ein auf jenen Höh'n
> Im Sonnenschein! Der Tag ist schön auf jenen Höh'n!
>
> We'll go and fetch them up on the hills
> In the sunshine! It's a beautiful day up on the hills!

---

[89] It is intriguing to note that in the orchestral draft score of the finale Mahler actually marks 'siehe Scherzo mit Skizze' (see scherzo with sketch) over the passage that quotes the Rondo-Burleske (at what is now b. 75); cf. also Żychowicz, 'The *Partiturentwurf*', 89.

[90] Floros, *Gustav Mahler*, ii. 282 and 418.

Ex. 20.11. (*a*) Ninth Symphony, 4th movt., bb. 163–71; (*b*) *Kindertotenlieder*, no. 3, 'Oft denk' ich, sie sind nur ausgegangen', bb. 62–9

At the close of the Ninth, the meagreness of the musical substance and its gradual deterioration, abetted by a curious tonal instability drawing towards D for the last time (bb. 166–7), seem to tell a different story: there is no further denial, and no further reminiscence.

Thus the closing of the Ninth's Adagio constitutes a subdued counterpart to the end of 'Der Abschied'—an isolated, meditative utterance, a fading away rather than a paean to eternal Nature 'printed on the atmosphere'. Since the première of the Ninth in 1912, critics have been divided over the significance of such a leave-taking.[91] For Adorno, philosopher of negative dialectics, it means that

> Music admits that the fate of the world no longer depends on the individual, but it also knows that this individual is capable of no content except his own, however fragmented and impotent. Hence his fractures are the script of truth. In them the social movement appears negatively, as in its victims. . . . Bereft of promises, his [Mahler's] symphonies are ballads of the defeated, for 'Nacht ist jetzt schon bald'—soon the night will fall.[92]

Yet for Floros, 'With the celestial dying away of the Ninth Symphony Mahler confessed himself renewed in his belief in a continuation of existence after death'.[93] Perhaps Kurt von Fischer best sums up the existential ambiguity of the moment: 'intimations of a possible that is no more and also is not yet. . . . Here perhaps music could once again begin'.[94] And the drafts of the unfinished Tenth Symphony bring to mind what Mahler wrote of himself the winter before he began the Ninth: 'I see everything in such a new light—I am so in motion; I sometimes wouldn't be surprised if I suddenly noticed a new body on me. (Like Faust in the last scene) . . .'.[95]

---

[91] See HLG(F) iii. 1212–21 for a useful summary.
[92] Adorno, *Mahler*, 166–7 (German edn., 216).
[93] Floros, iii. 292.

[94] von Fischer, 'Die Doppelschlagfigur', 104 and 105.
[95] Mahler, *Briefe* (1982), no. 404, early 1909 (*Selected Letters*, no. 382).

21

The Tenth Symphony

COLIN MATTHEWS

> The author inclines to the view that precisely someone who senses the extraordinary scope of the conception of the Tenth ought to do without adaptations and performances. The case is similar with sketches of unfinished pictures by masters: anyone who understands them and can visualize how they might have been completed would prefer to file them away and contemplate them privately, rather than hang them on the wall.[1]

This author adheres firmly to the view that such an opinion is little short of monstrous. It is debatable whether Adorno had even heard Deryck Cooke's partially realized performing version of the Tenth in 1963 when he wrote the introduction to the second edition of his study of Mahler; it is less open to question that his few words on the subject reveal that he misunderstood the nature of the symphony's textural differences from the earlier symphonies: his implication that the fabric of the Adagio is only sketched, and would have been elaborated contrapuntally, is totally misconceived. But I can best counter his argument with some words of my own, written for a radio talk given not long after Deryck Cooke's death. Speaking of Erwin Ratz's implied prohibition of any 'realization' of the Tenth, I said:

Would the president of an International Michelangelo Society go to great lengths to prevent the exhibition of the unfinished Rondanini *Pietà*? Should we be deprived of Shelley's *The Triumph of Life*—one of the poet's greatest achievements—because it is only a draft, written on the backs of letters and bills, and left unfinished as a result of his sudden death? In both cases we are properly grateful for what has survived, and at the same time fascinated by the incompleteness itself.[2]

Of course the parallels between music and the visual arts or literature cannot be drawn precisely: the primary difference, in the case of unfinished musical works, is that the work in question has to be 'finished' by another hand, so that for the non-literate (although where a composer's sketches are concerned the literate constitute a very small band indeed) there can be no first-hand experience of the music. Yet this is surely all the more reason for a 'realization' of the work to be attempted. I can think of few things less

---

[1] Adorno, *Mahler*, p. x.   [2] Colin Matthews, 'Deryck Cooke's Achievement', London, BBC Radio 3 Magazine, 1978.

attractive than the prospect of a handful of concerned musicologists hugging to themselves the knowledge of a major work.

The pros and cons of performing music which has been left incomplete by its composer can be argued indefinitely. Though I shall return to the subject later, this chapter does not depend on a resolution of the argument, since it is concerned with the actual *state* of this particular unfinished work. But I start from the premise that the state of the Tenth Symphony is such that performances of the work can only enhance our understanding of Mahler; and I should make it clear that I regard Deryck Cooke's 'performing version' of the draft at 'the stage the work had reached when Mahler died'[3] (which is the only adequate description) as the real measure of the work as it stands.[4]

Mahler's superstitious fear of writing a ninth symphony is well known, although it has perhaps been exaggerated. Even the fateful circumstances of the summer of 1907 did not prevent him from composing; and once he had completed *Das Lied von der Erde* there was no delay in embarking on the 'real' Ninth. That the Tenth was begun at all is remarkable in view of the intensity of Mahler's preparations for the first performance of his Eighth Symphony in the summer of 1910. In fact, it was completed in sketch during the summer, just as all the other symphonies had been, and only his ill health during the winter of 1910–11 and, apparently, his undertaking further revisions of the Ninth, prevented the Tenth from being near to completion at the time of his death.

Mahler's working methods by and large remained the same throughout his life, although the description that follows is more or less specific to the Tenth. Initial sketches—from a few bars to whole sections—sometimes in sketchbooks (several of which have survived) were quickly expanded to a rough draft of a whole movement, written out on three or four (or occasionally only two) staves, with hardly any indications of instrumentation. This preliminary stage involved the most changes of mind: individual bars or groups of bars might be ringed round for possible deletion, transposition of extended passages could be contemplated, the structure of the movement was by no means fixed. This stage—the composition sketch—reflects the great speed at which Mahler composed: from 1899, and the Fourth Symphony, all the symphonies were composed (that is, sketched out) during one or two summer holidays, each of which amounted to at most three months.

After the composition sketch, Mahler moved on to the short score, the handwriting of which indicates a more relaxed frame of mind, although here, too, many changes were possible. The short score is generally written on four or five staves (occasionally only three), with more details of instrumentation.[5] There is much more attention to detail—notational as well as contrapuntal—and the structure is more settled. Virtually all of the Tenth Symphony manuscript is written in ink, with only a handful of pencil sketches; the few

---

[3] Deryck Cooke, *Gustav Mahler: A Performing Version of the Draft for the Tenth Symphony* (2nd edn., New York and London: AMP/Faber, 1989), p. xvii.

[4] For a discussion of the merits of other versions of the Tenth see David Matthews's Preface to the second edition of the published performing version (1989).

[5] Although still not many: the fourth movement, for instance, has only fifteen indications of instrumentation in 578 bars, the finale twelve in 400.

markings in blue pencil, however, are of great significance—possibly Mahler's last thoughts on the symphony. The manuscript paper used for sketching is almost exclusively 22-stave 'landscape' (horizontal) format, with 20-stave used for the draft score and some sketches; one sketch page only, for the beginning of the Adagio, is on upright 24-stave paper, a format Mahler usually reserved for the fair copy.

The next stage (with other symphonies this would have extended into the rest of the year, in the time that Mahler could spare from conducting and administration) was the elaboration into draft score ('Partitur'). Here the details of the instrumentation would begin to be defined and refined, and the structure pinned down. But radical revisions could still take place, as in the Ninth, where the draft orchestral score[6] is still a very long way from the final version, especially in the first and second movements, and the orchestration is far from definitive—sometimes only first thoughts. Whereas the draft is in 'open' score—each page allows for the full orchestra to be deployed—the fair copy (of which none exists for the Tenth) only includes those instruments actually playing. But even this is not definitive, not only because Mahler would continue to make changes to his final manuscript, but because the published scores as well were subject to a process of continuous revision. In one of his last letters he speaks of having just 'finished my Fifth'.[7]

What is unique to the Tenth is that the entire manuscript (with the possible exception of the blue-pencil markings) almost certainly belongs to the summer months alone. Mahler returned from New York to Paris towards the end of April 1910, but probably did not begin extensive work on the Tenth for two months. He left Munich, where preliminary rehearsals for the Eighth were already under way, for his summer retreat at Toblach, on 26 June. As the first two weeks of September were devoted to the final rehearsals and performances of the Eighth, it seems likely that the bulk of the Tenth was composed in July and August. His state of mind during those months was made even more precarious by the discovery that his wife was having an affair with the architect Walter Gropius. Mahler returned to New York at the end of October.

The surviving 165 pages[8] of manuscript sketches for the Tenth (a number of pages—five at the very least[9]—are missing) include all the above categories except for the fair copy (there is, however, no sketchbook, although a sketchbook for the Ninth contains unused sketches which have a very tenuous relationship to the Tenth). A detailed description of the manuscript can be found in the score of the Performing Version; but although I was partly responsible for this description, I have to say that I do not now agree with the distinctions that it makes between 'sketch page', 'preliminary short score', and 'short score'. This attempt to codify the different stages of composition is in some respects misleading, since,

[6] Erwin Ratz (ed.), *Mahler, IX. Symphonie: Partiturentwurf der ersten drei Sätze, Faksimile nach der Handschrift* (Vienna: Universal Edition, 1971).

[7] To Georg Göhler, 8 Feb. 1911; Mahler, *Selected Letters*, 372.

[8] Strictly speaking, 166, as one sketch page for the Adagio has a few notations on the reverse; all the other

sketches are written on one side of the paper only, whereas the draft orchestral scores use both sides.

[9] Pages 6 and 7 of the Adagio short score and 1–3 of the composition sketch of the fourth movement; this is deduced simply from the numbering, but many more pages are undoubtedly missing, of which the second page of the third movement's composition sketch is the most obvious.

in the first place, there are only one or two 'sketch pages' which can be definitely identified as such: even the roughest sketches are probably part of what I have called above the composition sketch—either inserts into it, or workings which were not sketched independently. In the case of the second movement, and possibly also the fifth, what the Performing Version calls the short score is really the composition sketch.

It needs to be stressed that it is not possible to say in what order Mahler composed the work, and that, during the composition, the position of the individual movements remained in a state of flux. However, it cannot be entirely accidental that, proportionately, there is less material for each succeeding movement, and it is unlikely that all the preliminary sketching was done before Mahler started elaborating any of the individual movements. Thus he may even, for instance, have been working at the draft score of the Adagio at the same time as composing the Finale, although that, too, is unlikely (but see below, pp. 502–3). What can be said is that the final decision about the ordering of the movements was a very late one, even though with hindsight, of course, it is the only logical way the symphony could have been put together.

Before summarizing the material for the Tenth Symphony, a word about the two facsimile editions of the manuscript. The first, published in 1924 by the Paul Zsolnay Verlag, Vienna, must be one of the most perfect facsimiles ever produced: when in 1968 Deryck Cooke had the opportunity to compare a copy directly with the manuscript he found the two virtually indistinguishable. However, by including only 116 pages of the manuscript, it omitted a great deal of the sketch material, most notably the composition sketches of both the first movement and all but one page of the second. The arbitrary inclusion of eight pages from the other movements, out of a possible total of at least fifty-five, as 'Skizzenblätter' is inexplicable. In 1967 the manuscript was republished by the Verlag Walter Ricke, under the auspices of the International Mahler Society, and edited by Erwin Ratz. It included a further forty-four pages of sketches, but although the quality of reproduction is good, it is no match for the 1924 original.[10] A further five pages which came to light subsequently were published for the first time in 1975 in the Performing Version. Both facsimiles follow the format of the manuscript: all the movements and the short score of the Adagio are enclosed within folders (double sheets of 20- or 22-stave paper).

I. Adagio

The seventeen[11] surviving composition sketch pages for the first movement do not give the whole picture of how the first movement was put together, even when taken in conjunction with the short score. There are too many seemingly missing pages to establish a clear

---

[10] The general clarity is markedly inferior, and the photographic process used has caused some of the blue-pencil markings to shift very slightly.

[11] Or fourteen: three pages of sketches for bars 217 ff. may be contemporary with the short score.

sequence, but one fact that emerges clearly is that the movement was initially much shorter. No sketches survive for the opening fifteen bars, and it is likely that the upright format page numbered 'II' was originally the first page, and that the movement began with the Adagio (i.e. without the violas' introduction). The subsequent development is much abbreviated, and one of two pages numbered 'VII'—altered from either 'V' or 'VI'—contains the first very rough draft of the ending, in which the final ninety-eight bars of the orchestral draft are encapsulated within a mere forty-seven bars.

However, inserts and rewritten pages bring the composition sketch much closer to the short score. This consisted initially of eight pages (of which pages 6 and 7 are missing), with a redrafted page 8 extending to page 9, and a further unnumbered page which expands the final sixteen bars of page 9 into twenty-three bars which are almost identical with the orchestral draft. Thus nine pages of short score survive. It is the missing pages that are the most intriguing aspect of the short score, for they correspond to bars 159–212 of the orchestral draft, and thus the crux of the whole symphony—the monumental A flat minor outburst and the ensuing nine-note chord. In the composition sketch this is almost entirely absent: on the first page VII (the page which continues to the end of the movement) the high violin lines, which in the draft score precede the A flat minor episode, simply stop in mid-air, and the music slips calmly back into F sharp major (see Ex. 21.1). However, an insert is marked between the second and third bars, which, although not present in either facsimile edition, has survived (the pencil sketch is reproduced as pl. 2 in the Performing Version); and this is found *in situ* on the other page VII of the composition sketch (Ex. 21.2). This is an extraordinary conception, with a massive *pianissimo* chord of E minor (or just possibly E flat minor—the accidentals on both the insert page and the sketch are very difficult to determine)[12] above which a high (presumably) violin line floats. But bars 3–7 of this example are crossed out, with the word 'Einlage' (insert) above them; and by a lucky chance a pencil sketch for this insert has survived as well, marked 'Einlage zu VII' (it is reproduced as pl. 3 in the Performing Version); see Ex. 21.3. Here at last is something approaching the draft score: the first four bars are in A flat minor, and are very close to bars 199–202; but there is no dynamic, and the music subsides harmlessly in the first bar into B major (this bar has been encircled, an indication that Mahler intended to reconsider it). The subsequent five bars, written in ink, are very lame, although the A natural clearly prefigures the seven-bar sustained A of the trumpet in the draft score.

Leaving aside for the moment the question of the missing pages, the short score is very close to the draft orchestral score, the main differences being the switching of the first two statements of the Adagio (already indicated in the short score, in fact), and several bars pitched a semitone lower in the coda. And because the draft score itself can be played as it stands—and has, of course, been performed regularly since 1924—it has generally been assumed that, structurally, it represents Mahler's definitive thoughts.

---

[12] In bar 6 the insert sketch seems to imply a chord of C major, but the composition sketch has naturals only to the E, implying C sharp minor.

Ex. 21.1. Tenth Symphony, composition sketch, first page VII

Ex. 21.2. Tenth Symphony, composition sketch, second page VII and insert

But even if the climactic passage of the draft score was present on the missing pages (and, as David Matthews suggests on pp. 512–14 below, it may well be that Alma Mahler removed them because they contained exclamations even more personal than those present elsewhere in the manuscript), it was clearly a late addition to the music. It is even just possible—and the comparative untidiness of the manuscript here does not contradict it—that it was virtually composed in full score. It seems that, although Mahler knew that *some-*

Ex. 21.3. Tenth Symphony, composition sketch, insert to page VII

thing was needed at this point, he could not establish what it should be until a very late stage. Possibly the large number of sketches and insertions that relate to the coda imply that he felt that what was necessary was to extend the coda; and the duly extended coda, which is disproportionately long in relation to the whole movement, did not take account of the impact that the A flat minor outburst was to make on the course of the movement.

There is a compelling parallel in the climax of the first movement of the Ninth Symphony, where, in the draft orchestral score, the trombones' terrifying enunciation of the motto rhythm (bb. 312 ff.) is only added as a pencilled afterthought in the margin; and instead of moving straight into the 'funeral march' section (marked 'wie ein schwerer Kondukt' in both the draft and the fair copy) the music seems to lose all sense of direction in a rambling episode of some twenty bars.

This particular passage, and others, in the draft first movement of the Ninth—not to mention the wholesale restructuring of the second movement which took place between the draft and the fair copy—certainly provide food for thought as to how 'finished' the first movement of the Tenth actually is. It seems to me that the structure may in fact be less sure than the orchestration—contradictory though this is to the received opinion that Mahler pinned down the structure first, and then worried endlessly about the details of the instrumentation. Although he would, of course, have greatly refined the orchestration, and there are clearly details missing (the most obvious being the chordal accompaniment to the final statement of the Adagio before the climax, where the lower strings are omitted in his haste to move on), the draft of the Adagio is playable in a way that the draft of the first movement of the Ninth is not. Whatever changes Mahler might have made, there would have been none of the contrapuntal elaboration that Adorno implied is missing. At most there would have been no more than extra counterpoint of the kind that Deryck Cooke suggested in bars 162–4. However, these considerations are minor when compared with the problems to which the rest of the symphony gives rise.

II. Scherzo

I have already suggested that what the Performing Version calls the short score of the second movement is in fact the composition sketch, so that the twelve pages of 'short score' and eleven 'sketch pages' constitute twenty-three pages which are all part of the same stage of the composition. Although there were no doubt some preliminary sketches which have not survived, the relatively chaotic state of these twenty-three pages clearly implies that much of the music constitutes Mahler's first thoughts. The sketch was transferred straight into an orchestral draft, and there can be no question of a missing short score, since the draft matches the sketch more or less bar for bar. In his haste to put the music into score, however, Mahler occasionally missed out details that are present in the sketch; and a further indication of haste is that the sketch—in what is by far the most metrically complex of any Mahler movement, with innumerable changes of time signature in 522 bars of music— contains no more than seven indications of time signature, while the draft score has only one! (Apart, that is, from the opening '/4', amplified by the ambiguous marking '4/4 Alla breve'.)

The draft score does, nevertheless, get off to a good start; and although the opening horn motive is difficult to decipher without the composition sketch,[13] the first two pages are more or less complete. But subsequently the texture becomes increasingly spare, and there is no real attempt at orchestration as such, except in the first F major trio (bb. 76–130) and in the E flat major Ländler (bb. 165–245), which, while by no means fully scored, contain much detail and several particularly felicitous touches of orchestration. Unfortunately, this is far from the case with the rest of the draft: in his haste to complete it, Mahler simply copied out his composition sketch into the most convenient instrumental parts, with the result that a great deal of the score consists of a continuous first violin line, with sometimes only a single trombone or double bass to keep it company. It can hardly be denied that much of the material is weak, and its weakness is compounded by being presented in unrepresentative and sometimes even inappropriate orchestral colours. Thus the entire centre of the movement (bb. 246–415) labours under a double handicap: the areas which

---

[13] And, in the fourth bar, in spite of it: although the upper part is clearly in 5/4, the horns have six beats in the sketch, and seven in the score.

need most structural reparation are also those where Mahler has made the least effort to orchestrate the music. This presents a serious problem for any performing version, since remaining faithful to the draft score (the case for which does not need to be argued) means forgoing the opportunity to make any substantive improvements to the orchestration, even where it is obvious that Mahler himself would have done so. Whereas in the first and fourth movements the progression from composition sketch to short score is a major part of the compositional process, here the transfer of the composition sketch directly into the draft score simply clarifies the sketch without greatly changing or improving it. The draft score is *not* a blueprint for the orchestration, as Ex. 21.4—a transcription of bars 469–83 in both the score and the sketch—makes clear. (For the sake of clarity and to save space the transcription of the score diverges from the original in a few insignificant details; in the sketch it should be noted that bar 481 is an insert into what appears originally to have been a 7/4 bar incorporating bars 480 and 482.)

In writing of the problem of this music elsewhere[14] I have made the mistake of interpreting the title on the second movement's folder—a blue-pencilled 'II' with underneath in ink '2. Scherzo — Finale' ('Finale' clearly added later), and 'Partitur'—to mean that Mahler was at some stage thinking of a two-movement symphony. This might have explained the haste with which the second movement was put into the draft score. But '2.' is the German abbreviation for 'Zweite', so that the title should be interpreted as '2nd Scherzo, possibly Finale', and needs to be taken in conjunction with one of the (many) titles to be found on the fourth movement's folder: '1. Scherzo (I. Satz)', that is '1st Scherzo (1st movement)'. The implications of this will be considered a little later. As far as the second movement is concerned, it has to be assumed that Mahler put the movement into score as the most convenient way of putting the sketch in order. But it is very revealing of the urgency with which he was working in the summer of 1910.

III. Purgatorio

The unequivocal 'Nro 3.' is followed by the title 'Purgatorio oder Inferno', with 'Inferno' crossed out. The lower half of the title-page has been cut away, probably by Alma (as David Matthews suggests; see pp. 512–14 below). There is one page of composition sketch, for bars 1–81 (though encapsulated within only sixty-one bars). Since it covers more than half the music, it is clearly one of originally only two pages. The short score is written on three pages, with numerous details of instrumentation; the recapitulation (bb. 127–53) is indicated by 'Da Capo'. The thirty bars of draft score are written on two sides of a double sheet, although there are only five bars on the second side. The score is, surprisingly, laid out as if it were the fair copy, using only those instruments actually playing.

---

[14] Colin Matthews, *Mahler at Work*, pp. i and 139.

Ex. 21.4. Tenth Symphony, bb. 469–83: (a) score; (b) sketch

The short score presents few problems, but as Deryck Cooke puts it in his introduction to the Performing Version: 'The Da Capo . . . would no doubt have been realised by Mahler with a varied and possibly extended repeat, rather than with an exact one; but nothing can be done about that.'[15]

---

[15] Cooke, *Mahler: A Performing Version*, p. xxv.

IV. [Scherzo]

Identifying the composition sketch for the fourth movement is not easy: thirteen pages have survived of which six are numbered IV–VIII (confusingly, the short score also has roman numerals, whereas those for the other movements have arabic numbers). Apart from one page, which contains isolated workings for various sections, the six unnumbered pages form a sequence with the composition sketch, and would seem on the face of it to be part of it—there is only one short gap after page VIII, between bars 383 and 410, although the unnumbered pages become very sketchy towards the end. But in the short score as well the end is hardly more detailed, so probably not many pages are missing.

Indeed, the short score of twelve pages is throughout untidy and hasty, with a great deal of crossing out and a number of insertions, suggesting perhaps that it is more an advanced composition sketch than a short score, as the roman numerals perhaps also imply: certainly there are many signs of Mahler 'thinking on his feet'. Two extended passages in the short score (bb. 410–31 and 452–504) are written out as little but melodic line with occasional single bass notes (in one place, figured bass). But since both of these are varied recapitulations of earlier material, there is no difficulty in understanding Mahler's intentions. By contrast, the opening four bars are a minefield for the interpreter, with more notes crossed out than remaining, and the definitive reading established by heavy blue-pencil deletions. In this movement alone there are blue-pencil markings to the music as well as on the folder, and they may well represent Mahler's final work on the symphony. If so, they probably reflect his feeling that this is the least advanced of the five movements, even though its conception is one of the strongest.

V. Finale

The short score for the Finale comprises fourteen pages; the movement is complete on ten pages, but the first version ended, in B flat major (resolving the B flat minor of the Purgatorio), on pages 8 and (unnumbered) 9, with the rewritten F sharp major ending, written in a relaxed and flowing hand, on the definitive pages 8–10. There are two rejected pages, numbers 5½ and 6; and there is one separate unnumbered page which is not part of the short score, but a composition sketch for the transition from B flat major to F sharp major, and thus probably the last music that Mahler composed.

The absence of a composition sketch can hardly mean that the short score *is* the composition sketch: some preliminary sketches at least must have existed. Furthermore, the score is, with one exception, free from the indecision that evidently plagued the fourth movement. The exception is the resumption of the Allegro after the central (slower) section, which seems to lack much sense of direction on the rejected page 5½, and then, on the rejected page 6, tries to rework in 2/2 the A major waltz episode (bb. 312 ff.) from the fourth movement.[16] This survives to appear on the definitive page 6, but is there crossed out, leaving only the rather drastically foreshortened Allegro episode of twenty-four bars before the climactic return of the first movement's nine-note chord. This is sketched so hastily that it would be virtually unintelligible were it not for its previous appearance. It is even just feasible that it was actually *composed* here, and then transferred back to the Adagio.

According to Richard Specht,[17] Mahler spoke of the Tenth Symphony as being 'fully prepared in the sketch', and the evidence of the manuscript confirms this: for all its shortcomings there is not a single gap in the musical argument. Yet there remains one particularly puzzling aspect: even when the work had been completed in outline, Mahler had still not made up his mind about the order of the movements. Although the blue-pencil numbering on the title-pages is definitive, even at that stage Mahler was hesitating. The Adagio's folder had no number on it at all before the pencilled 'I'; the second movement's ambiguous 'Scherzo-Finale' has already been noted; the Purgatorio was always the third movement. But, while the Finale's folder has a straightforward 'V. Finale' (the 'V' overwritten in blue), the fourth movement is a complete enigma.

In Pls. 21.1–4 I have endeavoured to reconstruct how the title-page of this movement may have appeared at each stage of its revision.[18] The original of the no less than seven titles on this folder appears to have been 'Finale', since it is in the centre of the page, and is the only title crossed out in ink. This has been taken to imply that the Adagio was the only other movement that had been sketched at this time, but I do not believe that there is any implication that Mahler was thinking of a two-movement symphony: it is more likely that the other scherzo was under way, but was as yet untitled, and that Mahler thought that this movement would be the finale. The title that replaced 'Finale' is presumably '1. Scherzo (I. Satz)'—'1st scherzo (1st movement)'—together with the first line of the inscription 'Der Teufel tanzt es mit mir' (Pl. 21.1), and this does seem to imply a three-movement symphony: first Scherzo—Adagio—second scherzo: Finale (the hesitancy with which 'Finale' is written on that folder suggests, perhaps, that Mahler was not sure of its place, or was aware of the need for other movements). Although there is nothing to prove that the Purgatorio did not exist at this stage, and that thus a four-movement symphony was already in embryo, the only logical sequence seems to be that Mahler next crossed out the first-movement title with blue pencil, and wrote 'Finale (3. Satz)' (Pl. 21.2). So we definitely seem to have a three-movement symphony, but with the order of the scherzos reversed—or perhaps the Adagio first, followed by two scherzos. (It is particularly puzzling that all this change of order is reflected only on one of the folders, and not in any way on the others.)

---

[16] Including the sketches for the fourth movement, this passage was reworked no less than six times, but still remains curiously unfinished.

[17] Quoted in Cooke, *Mahler: A Performing Version*, p. xv.

[18] The following three paragraphs are based on my earlier article, 'The Tenth Symphony and Artistic Morality', in *Muziek & wetenschap, Dutch Journal for Musicology*, 5/3 (1995/1996), 303–19.

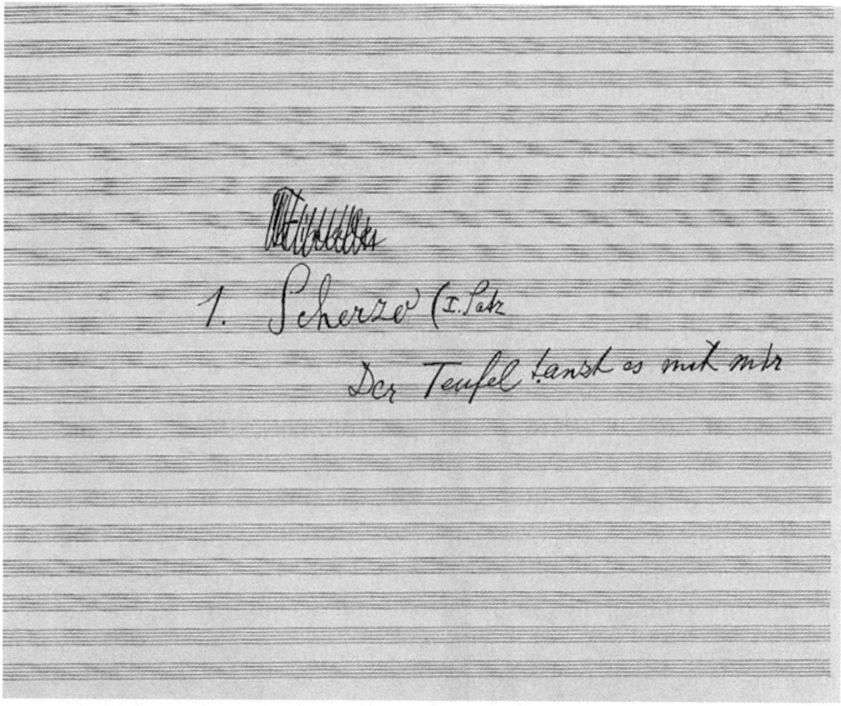

Pl. 21.1. Tenth
Symphony, reconstruction
of title-page of fourth
movement, first stage

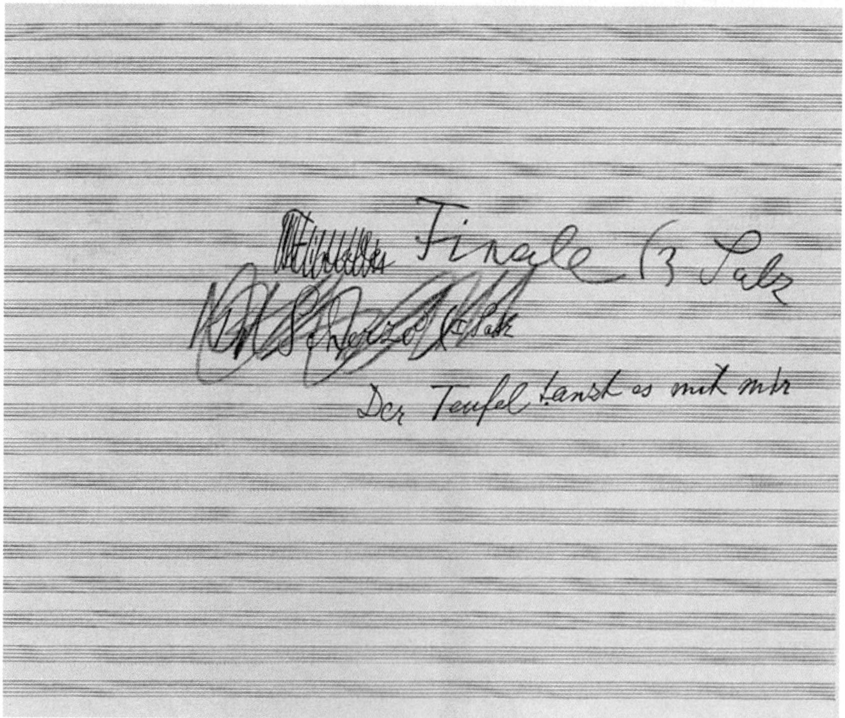

Pl. 21.2. Tenth
Symphony, reconstruction
of title-page of fourth
movement, second stage

The next stage on this title-page that has to be accounted for is the unexpected appearance (in ink) of '2. Satz' at the top of the page, without any cancelling out in ink of any of the other titles. It is possible that this '2. Satz' title preceded the blue-pencilled 'Finale (3. Satz)', but unless Mahler crossed out the previous '1st movement' in pencil and then wrote '2. Satz' in ink, which seems unlikely, we end up with a title-page that simultaneously calls itself first movement and second movement. (Yet any attempt to establish a sequence that makes sense without contradictory titles has to depend upon Mahler alternately picking up pen and pencil—rather too fastidious an act, we may feel, for a composer in such a hurry!). The '2. Satz' title allows a four-movement symphony, in the sequence Adagio—Scherzo—Purgatorio—Scherzo-Finale; but it is not until the only other addition in ink, the overwriting of the '3' of 'Finale (3. Satz)' with a rather tentative '4', that we can be sure that the Purgatorio has been composed, and that the order of movements must be as we know it, but without the fifth movement. The second part of the inscription, written much more untidily, may well have been added now (Pl. 21.3). The penultimate stage is a forcefully blue-pencilled roman 'II': yet this cannot be taken to imply that the fifth movement now exists, since before writing 'II', Mahler seems to have picked up his blue pencil with the intention of crossing out the '2. Satz' title by writing 'Finale', but abandoning it after the 'F', and crossing everything else out except the inscription. Finally the pencilled 'II' is changed into a 'IV' (Pl. 21.4: the title-page as Mahler left it). At this point, and not earlier, we can assume that he added the blue-pencil numbers to the other folders.

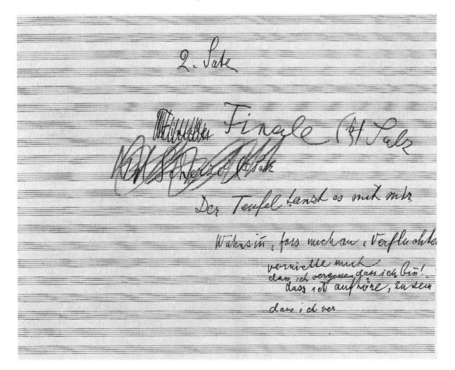

Pl. 21.3. Tenth Symphony, reconstruction of title-page of fourth movement, third stage

Colin Matthews

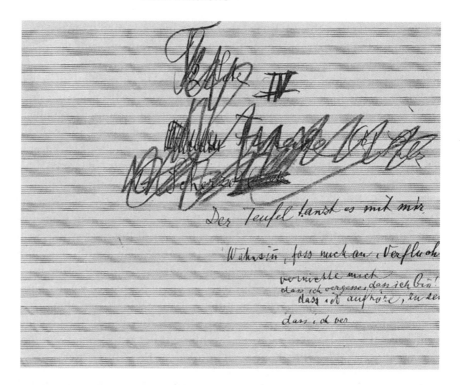

Pl. 21.4. Tenth Symphony, title-page of fourth movement, final stage

The deductions that can be made from this detective work depend crucially upon the timing of the blue-pencil markings. For a long time I thought myself that they represented Mahler's last thoughts on the symphony, perhaps even when looking through it in New York in the winter of 1910/11, making a few changes to the music of the fourth movement as well—since it is the only movement which has blue-pencil markings on the music itself. But clearly some, if not all, of the pencil markings were *not* made earlier: otherwise it needs a very tortuous logic to establish how this title-page can have evolved. I can suggest at least two possible readings which confuse the issue further—one, that the isolated ink '4' predates the blue-pencilled '3', which is tenable if pencil and ink were never used simultaneously; and the other, that the original 'Finale' title belonged to another symphony altogether, and had been crossed out before Mahler used it for this one. Every time one looks at this page one seems to see something new, and there are surely other possibilities before its wealth of information is exhausted.

Fortunately for us, Mahler *did* make a final decision, leaving us only with the moral problem of what to do with an unfinished work. For although the symphony, and its several realizations, will not go away, there remains a strong body of opinion that the work should not be performed.[19] Is the implication that the music is not good enough? Deryck Cooke's answer to this was that 'Mahler's actual music, even in its unperfected and unelaborated

[19] See e.g. *Fragment or Completion?*, ed. Op de Coul.

state, has such significance, strength, and beauty, that it dwarfs into insignificance [any] uncertainties.'[20] He implied that the musical reality of the symphony far outweighs any question of artistic morality; and this seems to me to be indisputable. The alternative is to pretend that the work does not exist, or to reserve it for the use of musicologists (which amounts to much the same thing). How else can we understand the significance of the Tenth Symphony, and the light it throws on what we now know to be a final trilogy, other than by *listening* to it—albeit in a state which is remote from what it might have been. This is, after all, what Alma Mahler did, for the first time, in 1963, and having listened to it, immediately lifted the ban she had imposed on performance of it. Or rather, not quite immediately—for she was so moved by the music that she asked at once to hear it a second time.

[20] Cooke, *Mahler: A Performing Version*, p. xvii.

Additional note Part of the Mahler phenomenon that characterizes the latter half of the twentieth century has been the intensity of interest in the Tenth Symphony which has led, since Cooke's unique achievement, to various performing versions by, among others, Rudolf Barshai, Clinton Carpenter, and Remo Mazzetti. A pioneer in this field was Joseph H. Wheeler (1927–77). This interest continues to reveal itself in the increasing number of recordings, particularly of Cooke's version which maintains its classic status. Ed.

22

Wagner, Lipiner, and the 'Purgatorio'

DAVID MATTHEWS

The highly emotional superscriptions that occur at various places in the manuscript of the third, fourth, and fifth movements of the Tenth Symphony bear witness to Mahler's troubled state of mind when he was composing this music. The reason for their presence is well known: Mahler's discovery of his wife's infidelity, his horrified feelings of betrayal, and his desperate attempts to win back her love, resulting, in the Tenth, in the passionate string music of the Finale, which so much recalls the Adagietto of the Fifth, the first music Mahler had written for Alma.

The manuscripts of the first two movements do not contain any superscriptions, and the second movement is the most confident music that Mahler had written since his discovery of his heart illness in 1907. As Henry-Louis de La Grange has pointed out, this strongly suggests that these movements were composed, or at any rate sketched, before the marital crisis occurred, and that the short third movement, 'Purgatorio', was his immediate response to it.[1] Colin Matthews (p. 499) has described the mutilated state of the title-page of this movement. This must surely be Alma's doing; for it is almost impossible to imagine that Mahler would have carefully cut away the lower half of the cover: had he wished to replace it, he would have provided a new one. We must suppose that Mahler wrote something on the lower half of the title-page that Alma did not wish posterity to see when she had the manuscript published in facsimile in 1924. It is even possible that she crossed out 'Inferno' herself, as the thick pen strokes are unlike any others in the manuscript.

What had Mahler written here? We shall never know for certain, but Knud Martner has gone a considerable way towards elucidating the problem, and I am very grateful to him for allowing me to publish the results of his research here. In a volume of poetry called *Buch der Freude*,[2] by Mahler's old friend Siegfried Lipiner (1856–1911), there appears a sequence of nineteen poems called 'Il Purgatorio'. As we know from his letters to Lipiner,

---

[1] La Grange, 'The Tenth Symphony', 162. Colin Matthews's description of the title-page implies that the fourth movement was composed at least in part before the crisis (see below).

[2] Leipzig: Breitkopf & Härtel, 1880.

Mahler had always been very impressed by his friend's poetry, and Bruno Walter tells us that he reread much of it during the last years of his life. Mahler had used the title of one of Lipiner's translations of the Polish poet Adam Mickiewicz, *Todtenfeier*, for the original first movement of the Second Symphony. That 'Purgatorio' refers to Lipiner and not to Dante seems almost certain, especially when one looks at the content of Lipiner's poems. There is much that would have disconcerted Alma, if Mahler, as is reasonable to deduce, had written some lines from 'Il Purgatorio' on the manuscript. (Incidentally, Alma disliked Lipiner intensely, as she makes clear in her recollections of Mahler.[3]) Exactly what he wrote, we cannot of course say, but Mr Martner suggests that it may have been poem no. XII (it is the shortest poem in the sequence, so there would have been room for the whole of it):

> Ich kann dir nicht in's Auge seh'n,
> Ich müsste ja vor Scham vergeh'n;
> Vor Scham? Und hab' doch Nichts gethan!
> Ach, wer's gethan, was liegt daran?
>
> Wer's auch gethan, es ist gescheh'n!
> Ich kann dir nicht in's Auge seh'n; —
> Du schämst dich nicht — drum schäm' ich mich;
> Weh' mir, noch immer lieb' ich dich!

I cannot look you in the eye, as I would perish in shame. In shame? When actually I have done no wrong! So what; whoever he was, does it matter? Whoever did it—it's a thing of the past. I cannot look you in the eye, as *you* are not ashamed, it is *I* who am: alas, I still love you.[4]

Mr Martner comments: 'What he did write was no doubt some sort of an accusation against Alma, and I could imagine that poem no. XII could be the one in question. We know from Alma that when Mahler found out that she had betrayed him with Gropius, she began to accuse Mahler for not loving her. In other words, she was not ashamed ("Du schämst dich nicht — drum schäm ich mich").'[5] This is indeed very plausible; another possibility is the opening stanza of the first poem, which would explain why Mahler wrote 'Purgatorio oder Inferno':

> Die Hölle lieben: kannst du Das versteh'n?
> Nach Leben dürsten und mit Lust vergeh'n,
> Voll Todessehnsucht Leben doch erfleh'n:
> Die Hölle fühlen — und die Hölle lieben![6]

To love Hell: can you understand why? To thirst for life and die in raptures, longing for death, yet clamouring for life: to suffer Hell—and yet love it!

---

[3] Alma Mahler, *Memories*, 26.

[4] The English translations of this and the next poem are by Berthold Goldschmidt.

[5] Letter from Knud Martner to the author, 22 Apr. 1993.

[6] A line from the fourth stanza of this poem reads 'Dem goldnen Wein im goldenen Pokal'. The similar line in Bethge's 'Das Trinklied vom Jammer der Erde' is not to be found in the poem by Li-Tai-Po on which it is based (see Mitchell, *SSLD*, 163): such lines were no doubt German Romantic clichés of the period.

Ex. 22.1. Wagner, *Parsifal*, Act I, Amfortas' lament

Ex. 22.2. Tenth Symphony, 'Purgatorio', bb. 106–15

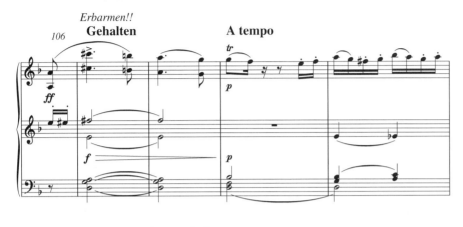

Two of the superscriptions in the 'Purgatorio' manuscript, 'Tod!Verk!' and 'Erbarmen!', refer to Wagner. 'Erbarmen!' (have mercy) is the cry of the wounded Amfortas in Act I of *Parsifal*, the climax of his lament when he is called upon by Titurel to perform the grail ritual (see Ex. 22.1). Mahler's music (Ex. 22.2) quite clearly refers to *Parsifal* here, especially in bars 113–14,[7] where he has written on the manuscript 'Dein Wille geschehe!' (Thy will be done). There is the same progression from the dominant of F sharp minor to D (compare the last two bars of Ex. 22.1). Below 'Erbarmen!' Mahler has also written 'O Gott! O Gott! Warum hast du mich verlassen?' (O God, O God, why has thou forsaken me?): Christ's words from the cross. This outburst perhaps marks the climax of Mahler's lifelong tendency towards self-dramatization in his music; it certainly reveals the depth of his anguish.

I shall return to *Parsifal* a little later. The second Wagner reference 'Tod!Verk!' almost certainly refers to the so-called *Todesverkündigung* (Annunciation of Death) scene in Act II of *Die Walküre*, in which Brünnhilde appears to Siegmund to tell him be must die, rather than, as some have thought, to Strauss's *Tod und Verklärung*. The relevant passage in the

---

[7] Bar numbering refers to Deryck Cooke's Performing Version (2nd edn., 1989).

Ex. 22.3. Tenth Symphony, 'Purgatorio', bb. 91–7

'Purgatorio', which occurs shortly before the 'Erbarmen' passage and is part of the same D minor central episode, is shown in Ex. 22.3. Compare the beginning of the *Todesverkündigung* (Ex. 22.4). The motive on the tubas at the start (*x*) is usually called the 'fate' motive, and that which follows it on the brass (*y*—which incorporates *x*) the 'death' motive. While I do not like labelling Wagner's leitmotifs, it will be a convenient way of referring to them here (and these particular labels are not misleading). Mahler's 'Tod!Verk!' chord (see Ex. 22.3) is not literally to be found in the *Todesverkündigung*, though if the D is flattened it then becomes identical with the second chord in the 'fate' motive. But it is more relevant to relate the *Todesverkündigung* music to the A flat minor episode in the first movement, the beginning of which is shown as Ex. 22.5. We should note that this is an A flat minor episode within an F sharp minor/major movement. So it is rather extraordinary that the first two statements of the 'death' motive in the *Todesverkündigung* are in F sharp minor and A flat minor respectively. There are also strong similarities between Mahler's brass chorale and Wagner's 'death' motive (also on the brass). It would not be wrong to suggest, then, that this A flat minor passage, which culminates in the famous and terrifying nine-note dissonance (see below, Ex. 22.7(*c*)), is also intended as an annunciation of death. A similar annunciation had marked the climax of the first movement of the Ninth Symphony, the passage that Colin Matthews refers to on p. 497. This, as he points out, was an afterthought. Could the A flat minor episode also have been an afterthought, inserted into the first movement at the time the 'Purgatorio' was written?[8] The evidence from the sketches is inconclusive (see p. 496). Mahler's thinking was clearly moving towards something like what we have in the draft score, but the brass chorale is not sketched, nor is there any hint of the dissonant chord. We shall never know, as the relevant pages 6 and 7 of the composition sketch have disappeared. It is curious that this crucial passage should be the only substantial omission from the manuscript, and I am at least tempted to link this with the missing lower half of the 'Purgatorio' title-page. If Alma felt constrained to cut this out because she did not want us to see what Mahler had written there, then could the composition sketch of the A flat minor episode (if indeed it was present on pp. 6 and 7 of the

---

[8] And note Colin Matthews's suggestion (p. 503) that it is even possible that the dissonance was first sketched for the Finale, and then transferred back to the first movement.

Ex. 22.4. Wagner, *Die Walküre*, Act II, sc. 4, *Todesverkündigung*

(Brünnhilde, ihr Roß am Zaume geleitend, tritt aus der Höhle und schreitet langsam und feierlich nach vornen.)
(*Brünnhilde, leading her horse by the bridle, comes out of the cave, and comes slowly and solemnly to the front.*)

Sehr feierlich und gemessen
Molto solenne e misurato

(Sie hält an und betrachtet Siegmund von fern)
(*She pauses and contemplates Siegmund from afar*)

(Sie schreitet wieder langsam vor)
(*She again advances slowly*)

(Sie hält in größerer Nähe an.)
(*She again pauses, nearer.*)

Ex. 22.5. Tenth Symphony, 1st movt., bb. 194–8

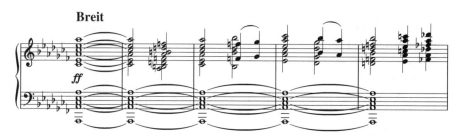

composition sketch) have also contained superscriptions that she found embarrassing, and therefore destroyed?

If we look again at the 'Erbarmen' passage, we may find in it the origin of the nine-note dissonance.[9] For the chord over which Mahler has written 'Dein Wille geschehe!' (b. 113) is the dissonance in embryo, at the same pitch (and adding the D minor triad from b. 115 to it brings it much closer). As I have noted, this chord appears in the parallel passage in *Parsifal*; and the chord immediately before Amfortas first cries out 'Erbarmen' (see Ex. 22.1) is a more intense form of it. At the climactic moment of Act II, when Parsifal, after Kundry's kiss, cries out 'Amfortas! Die Wunde!', we hear the same chord, at the same pitch, in a more exposed and forceful version (see Ex. 22.6). Transposed up a major third (Ex. 22.7(a)), this passage reveals the whole of Mahler's dissonance, except for the C♯, which is

Ex. 22.6. Wagner, *Parsifal*, Act II

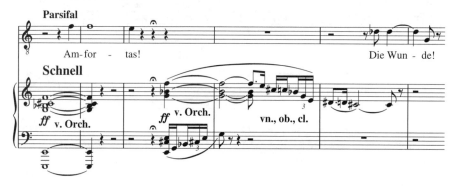

At the risk of undermining my own argument, I should point out that the dissonance is also prefigured by a chord in *Götterdämmerung*, Act III, at the point where Gutrune cries out 'O Hilfe!' after being told by Hagen of Siegfried's death (I am indebted to Lewis M. Smoley for pointing this out to me) and, even more closely, by a chord in *Salome* (at Fig. 299) which has six of Mahler's notes at the same pitch, plus an F♯ (see Robin Holloway, '*Salome*: Art or Kitsch?', in *Richard Strauss: Salome*, ed. Derrick Puffett (Cambridge

Opera Handbooks; Cambridge: Cambridge University Press, 1989), 145–60 at 146). Mahler of course knew *Salome* well, and this chord is even closer to his than the one in *Parsifal* (from where I dare say Strauss obtained his chord); nevertheless I would maintain that *Parsifal* is the chief source of the dissonance, though very likely Mahler's unconscious memories of *Götterdämmerung* and *Salome* played their part in its formation. With Mahler nothing is ever straightforward!

Ex. 22.7. Comparison of (*a*) Ex. 22.6 transposed up a major third, and (*b*) chord at 'Dein Wille geschehe' (cf. Ex. 22.2); (*c*) nine-note dissonance

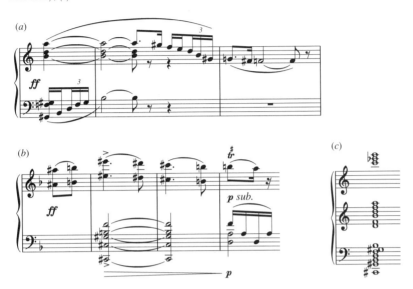

present in the 'Dein Wille geschehe!' chord (Ex. 22.7(*b*)), and the additional C minor triad at the top (Ex. 22.7(*c*)). Ex. 22.7 shows the whole sequence.

Is all, or some of this conscious? Mahler's frequent references to other composers in his music are, I think, almost always unconscious; yet the fact that he wrote 'Erbarmen' on his manuscript near a passage that parallels the 'Erbarmen' music in *Parsifal* suggests that this at least was conscious. We cannot say precisely how Mahler arrived at this potent symbol of pain and anguish, the nine-note chord; but we can infer a psychological link between *Parsifal* and the Tenth Symphony. For Mahler, surely, felt wounded by Alma's betrayal, and cried out for his wound to be healed.

It is significant, however, that the 'Erbarmen' passage from the 'Purgatorio' also contains the seed of redemption.[10] The melodic line at bars 112–15 of Ex. 22.2 (marked *z*) is a variant of the motive that initiated the D minor central episode; this is the form in which it is found in the Introduction to the Finale, also in D minor, a slow upward groping from darkness to light, whose progress is abetted by Mahler's last and most chilling symbol of death, the muffled drum stroke he had heard at a fireman's funeral in New York.[11] At the end of the Introduction, motive *z* leads directly into the flute theme, which emerges out of it (Ex. 22.8). It is this flute theme that marks the true beginning of the redemptive process that culminates in the great statement of renewed faith in love with which the Tenth Symphony ends.

[10] As indeed does the 'Erbarmen' passage from *Parsifal*: the motive marked *a* in Ex. 22.1 is a motive of redemption (and see above, Ch. 14, for a further discussion of Mahler and *Parsifal*).

[11] See Alma Mahler, *Memories*, pp. xvi and 135.

Ex. 22.8. Tenth Symphony, 5th movt., bb. 28–33

23

Mahler and Russia

INNA BARSOVA

Mahler was interested in Russia long before he visited either of its capitals. For years there had been close cultural connections between Germany, Austria, and Russia in which musicians played an important part. In 1877, when the St Petersburg Chamber Music Society announced a competition for a chamber work open to composers of all nations, Mahler entered a quartet—which must have been his Piano Quartet in A minor, of which only the first movement and a sketch for the opening twenty-four bars of a Scherzo have survived. Luck was against him, however; for, as he told Natalie Bauer-Lechner: 'I sent it to a competition in Russia, and somehow it was lost.'[1]

Mahler's cousin and friend from student days, the engraver Gustav Frank (1859–1923), lived in Russia from 1890 to 1911, having accepted an invitation from the State Papers Office in St Petersburg to help improve the artistic quality of its work.[2] Frank made portraits in crayon of the Emperors Alexander III and Nicholas II, and etchings of Leo Tolstoy and Eleonora Duse, and in 1899 became a member of the Royal Academy of Arts. The cousins frequently met when Mahler stayed in St Petersburg with Alma in 1902 and on his own in 1907.[3]

Russia also had literary attractions for Mahler. In his imagination, St Petersburg was closely associated with Dostoyevsky, for whom the Mahlers as a family were immensely enthusiastic. Mahler himself had a thorough knowledge of his writings and especially

---

[1] NB-L, *Recollections*, 57. However, there is no reference to Mahler, or to any work submitted by him, in the archives of the St Petersburg competition of 1877 or any other year. The first movement of the Piano Quartet in A minor (1876) has been edited by Peter Ruzicka and published by Hans Sikorski (Hamburg: Edition Sikorski 800, 1973). In his 'Editorial Remarks' (p. 31), Ruzicka argues that this movement most probably was part of the quartet submitted for the 1877 contest, but that it 'cannot have any connection with the one performed on 12 September 1876 in Jihlava (Iglau) with Mahler himself at the keyboard (because the programme there shows an instrumental setting of *piano, two violins, and viola*)', nor with 'either of the prize-winning

quintet movements of 1876 and 1878 at the Vienna Conservatory'. For further discussion on this matter, see Mitchell, *EY*, 34–5, 123–9, and 278–80, *WY*, 54, and NB-L, *Recollections*, 200. See also the most recent edition of the movement in *Klavierquartett, 1. Satz*, ed. Manfred Wagner-Artzt, Reinhold Kubik, and Renate Hilmar-Voit (Sämtliche Werke, Suppl. III; Vienna: Universal Edition, 1997). And see Barham, Ch. 29, pp. 597–603 below.

[2] Letter dated 14 Mar. 1899 from Sergey Witte to Emperor Nicholas II, *Muzykal'naya akademiya*, 1 (1994), 204.

[3] For Gustav Frank and his hospitality to Mahler and Alma in St Petersburg, see Alma Mahler, *Memories*, 34, 296, and 300, and HLG(E) ii. 489–90.

valued *Crime and Punishment* and *The Brothers Karamazov*. His interest was stimulated by his close friend Nina Hoffmann-Matscheko (1844–1914) who was Dostoyevsky's German translator and first German biographer.[4] It was at her house, after a discussion of Dostoyevsky's 'tragic sense of life',[5] that Mahler's favourite and gifted younger brother Otto (b. 1873) committed suicide on 6 February 1895.[6]

In Dostoyevsky Mahler found his own ethical outlook formulated: 'How can one be happy while a single being on earth still suffers?', Alma reports him often saying,[7] which sentiment is a sort of summary of Ivan's argument with Alyosha in *The Brothers Karamazov*.[8] Dostoyevsky's impact on Mahler can also be traced in his music, which similarly dwells on critical moments in the life of the spirit, seeking answers to the eternal questions of existence. Moreover, like Dostoyevsky, Mahler makes use of borrowed materials, reminiscences, allusions, and mixtures of high and low styles.[9]

Mahler's acquaintance with Russian musicians took place early in his career. As a student, he heard the pianist-composer Anton Rubinstein (1829–94) perform in Vienna, and from then on considered him the greatest interpreter of Beethoven. In 1886 he met him in person at the composer-conductor Karl Reinecke's house in Leipzig; and although he did not wish to be regarded as just another of the 'admiring nobodies', he remarked that Rubinstein had, unfortunately, 'never heard of me, so I could only "look and not do" '.[10] He was to meet him again in Hamburg in 1893, and later summed him up as 'a "man of the Steppes" [eine "Steppennatur"] by which he meant to indicate the elemental force, the boundless power and the lack of cultivation—in the sense of nature, which needs no cultivation—of that magnificent artist'.[11] Mahler was also familiar with Rubinstein's opera *The Demon* (1895), which he performed in Hamburg in 1891, and of which he gave the Vienna première at the Hofoper on 23 October 1899.[12]

On 19 January 1892 Mahler conducted Tchaikovsky's music for the first time: the German première of *Eugene Onegin* in Hamburg. Tchaikovsky had been expected to conduct the opera himself; but after the dress rehearsal, he yielded the baton to Mahler—of whom he wrote to his nephew: 'The conductor here is not a mediocrity but a versatile genius who keenly desires to conduct the first performance' (which was 'magnificent' and 'a considerable success').[13] On 3 January 1893 Mahler gave the first production outside Russia of Tchaikovsky's *Iolanta*; and on 7 September he conducted the opera again in the composer's

[4] Nina Hoffmann-Matscheko's biography of Dostoyevsky, *Th. M. Dostoyevsky: Eine biographische Studie*, was published in Berlin in 1899. For her meeting with Dostoyevsky's widow, Anna Grigorievna, in St Petersburg in 1898 during its preparation, see *Muzykal'naya akademiya*, 1 (1994), 209–10. Mahler had been introduced to Nina by Friedrich Löhr, and dedicated his *Wunderhorn* song 'Lied des Verfolgten im Turm' to her. See Mitchell, *WY*, 140, and Mahler, *Selected Letters*, 414–15.

[5] HLG(E) i. 325.

[6] See Michael Kennedy, *Mahler* (2nd edn., London: Dent, 1990), 34 and 44. Otto left a suicide message 'saying that life no longer pleased him, so he "handed back his ticket" ' (ibid. 44)—a phrase echoing Ivan Karamazov's at the close of Book V, ch. 4 of *The Brothers Karamazov*.

[7] Alma Mahler, *Memories*, 20.

[8] See *The Brothers Karamazov*, Book V, chs. 3 and 4.

[9] For a fuller discussion of Mahler and Dostoyevsky, see Inna Barsova, 'Mahler and Dostoyevsky', in *Gustav Mahler Kolloquium 1979*, ed. Klein, 65–76.

[10] Undated letter of [Oct.?] 1886 to Friedrich Löhr; Mahler, *Selected Letters*, 101.

[11] NB-L, *Recollections*, 174.

[12] See Mahler, *Selected Letters*, 101 n; HLG(E) ii. 70 and 190–4, and *GMWL*, 3.41 and 3.45.

[13] See Lebrecht, *Mahler Remembered*, 65.

presence, when they met for the last time. On 18 November 1893, twelve days after Tchaikovsky's death, Mahler gave a memorial concert for him at the Hamburg Theatre, the programme for which included the Letter Scene from *Eugene Onegin*, *Iolanta*, and the *Romeo and Juliet* Fantasy-Overture.[14] In succeeding years, Mahler conducted Tchaikovsky's works on many occasions; and, despite his initial disapproval of the Sixth Symphony as 'a shallow, superficial, distressingly homophonic work—no better than salon music',[15] in his last concert seasons in New York he chose to perform it six times—this *last* of Tchaikovsky's symphonies—which may suggest a kind of kinship between the two composers.

Mahler particularly admired *The Queen of Spades*. When he was preparing it for its Vienna première, which took place on 9 December 1902, the score was constantly before him and he felt the impact of Tchaikovsky's intense lyricism. In a letter of 22 June 1901 to the critic Max Kalbeck, the German translator of the libretto, he wrote of the opera as 'Tchaikovsky's most mature and artistically solid work';[16] and Alma records that Mahler 'took me to many of the rehearsals and was always playing bits of it to me. For weeks we lived with no other music in our ears.'[17] It is understandable, therefore, to find echoes of the 'love theme' from *The Queen of Spades* (Ex. 23.1) in the third movement of Mahler's Fourth Symphony (Ex. 23.2) and in the Adagietto of his Fifth (Ex. 23.3).

Mahler's final production of *The Queen of Spades* (and the very last opera he was to conduct)—the American première at the Metropolitan Opera on 5 March 1910—seems symbolic. Leo Slezak (1873–1946), the Czech tenor who sang the part of Hermann, recalled: 'At the rehearsals it was usually he and I alone. The others often did not turn up. He rarely had the whole company together. He sat there with me, frustrated and depressed—a changed man. I looked sadly for the fiery genius of yester-year. He had become mild and melancholy.'[18]

Mahler in Russia

Mahler made three conducting tours in Russia: in 1897, 1902, and 1907. On his first visit, to Moscow in 1897, he found 'the city quite *intoxicating*! Everything is so different, so exotically beautiful!'[19] To Anna von Mildenburg he wrote: 'Moscow makes a weird and wonderful impression. First impression: no clatter of wheels—nothing but sledges.'[20] He gave one concert in the Blagorodnoye Sobranie Hall on 15 March, the programme for which included Beethoven's Fifth Symphony, Wagner's *Siegfried Idyll* and Overture to *Rienzi*, the Piano Concerto in A flat major by the Moscow composer Anton Simon (pianist Victor

---

[14] See *GMWL*, 3.41 and 3.42, and Martner, *Gustav Mahler im Konzertsaal*.

[15] NB-L, *Recollections*, 166.

[16] Mahler, *Selected Letters*, 251.

[17] Alma Mahler, *Memories*, 50.

[18] Lebrecht, *Mahler Remembered*, 122 (translation adapted); see also Mahler, *Unknown Letters*, 179.

[19] Letter dated 13 Mar. 1897 to Max Marschalk; *Selected Letters*, 215.

[20] Ibid.

Ex. 23.1. Tchaikovsky, 'love theme' from *The Queen of Spades*: (*a*) Introduction, Fig. 2, bb. 1–7 (strings); (*b*) close of Sc. 2, Fig. 60, bb. 16–21 (text: 'Forgive me, heavenly creature, for having disturbed your peace')

(*a*)

Staub), and the Waltz from Gounod's opera *Romeo and Juliet*. One newspaper critic claimed without hesitation that Mahler was a 'confirmed Wagnerian'.[21]

However, it was neither in Moscow nor the provinces but in St Petersburg that Mahler established a real contact with the Russian public. During his first visit there with Alma in 1902, he conducted three concerts with the Mariinsky Theatre Orchestra in the hall of 'Assembly of Nobles' (now the auditorium of the St Petersburg Philharmonic). On 18

---

[21] 'Filarmonicheskoe sobranie', review signed 'A.G.', *Russkoe slovo*, no. 61 (15 Mar. 1897).

March the programme included Beethoven's 'Eroica', Mozart's Symphony in G minor (no. 40), and the Prelude and 'Liebestod' from *Tristan und Isolde*. The second concert, on 22 March, comprised Beethoven's Egmont Overture, Tchaikovsky's Manfred Symphony, Wagner's *Eine Faust-Overtüre*, and the Piano Concerto No. 1 in E minor by Emil von Sauer (1862–1942), one of Liszt's last pupils, who was himself the pianist on the occasion. In the final concert, on 27 March, Mahler performed Haydn's 'Drumroll' Symphony in E flat (no.

Ex. 23.2. Mahler, Fourth Symphony, 3rd movt., bb. 195–8 (strings)

Ex. 23.3. Fifth Symphony, Adagietto: (*a*) bb. 2–5 (1st violins); (*b*) bb. 73–8 (2nd violins)

103), the Overture to *Der Freischütz*, Tchaikovsky's Violin Concerto (solo violinist Alexander Petchnikov), the Overture to *Die Meistersinger*, and the Funeral March from *Götterdämmerung*.

On the whole, Mahler had a very favourable reception in the Russian press, although comparisons were inevitably made (sometimes to his advantage, sometimes not) between his conducting and that of Arthur Nikisch and Hans Richter.[22] As one anonymous critic in the *Russian Musical Gazette* put it: 'In Mahler we have seen a powerful and mature artist, who places a work of art above his own personality'; 'his passionate nature is tempered by the intellectual insights into the music he performs—which results in something ascetic, not so much emotionally experienced and expressed as contemplated'.[23]

In 1907 Mahler was back in Russia (on his own, without Alma), dividing his time between St Petersburg and Helsinki—Finland then being part of the Russian empire. He gave two concerts in the Grand Hall of the St Petersburg Conservatoire with the Mariinsky Theatre Orchestra. In the first, on 26 October, the programme consisted of Berlioz's *Carnaval romain*, Beethoven's Seventh Symphony and '*Ah! Perfido!*', the songs 'Hymnus' (Op. 33, No. 3) by Richard Strauss, 'Die Musikantin' by Max Fiedler, and 'Er ists's' by Hugo Wolf (sung by the Dutch contralto Tilly Koehnen), and the Overture to *Die Meistersinger*.

---

[22] See HLG(E) ii. 493 and 494.

[23] 'Tretiy Kontsert Malera', unsigned review, *Russkaya muzykal'naya gazeta*, no. 12 (23 Mar. 1902), 374.

The second, on 9 November, included Mahler's own Fifth Symphony, Beethoven's Coriolan Overture, and the Overture to *Die Meistersinger*. Stravinsky, who was in the audience, was struck by his 'super-intense power' and later recalled: 'I remember seeing Mahler in St. Petersburg, too. His concert there was a triumph'; he 'played some Wagner fragments and, if I remember correctly, a symphony of his own. Mahler impressed me greatly, himself and his conducting.'[24] Mahler's gift as a conductor made itself felt to the Russian orchestra as well, not only at the concerts themselves but even more so during rehearsals. Viktor Walter, leader of the orchestra, recorded in his memoir written for Richard Specht: 'From the very first Mahler's numerous directions concerning tempi, dynamics, and phrasing struck the members of the orchestra as new and interesting. When I asked him how he achieved these new effects in such familiar works he said: "The notes don't tell you the most important things about the music." ' However, Walter added that Mahler 'had a cold, even hostile reception amongst critics and musicians that became even worse when he performed his Fifth Symphony, which was not a success'.[25] (It was concerning the preparation of parts for the second rehearsal of his Fifth Symphony that Mahler wrote to Karl Köhler in a hitherto unknown letter, reproduced here in facsimile; see Pl. 23.1.)[26]

Between these two concerts, Mahler travelled to Helsinki, where, on 1 November, he conducted the Helsinki Philharmonic Orchestra at the Universitetets Solennitetssal in a performance of Beethoven's Fifth Symphony and Coriolan Overture, the Overture to *Die Meistersinger*, and the Prelude and 'Liebestod' from *Tristan und Isolde*. It was on this occasion that Mahler and Sibelius had their famous meeting and exchanged views about the symphony. Mahler, who had heard Sibelius's *Spring Song* and *Valse triste* at a concert on the very evening of his arrival (by which he was far from impressed),[27] wrote somewhat laconically to Alma on 2 November 1907: 'Sibelius paid me a call this morning. I found him extremely sympathetic, as all Finns are.'[28] Sibelius, on the other hand, writing quarter of a century later, recalled their meeting rather more spaciously:[29]

Mahler and I were together a great deal. . . . We came on good terms during a number of walks together, where we discussed all of music's problems in deadly earnest. When our conversation touched on the symphony, I said that I admired its style and severity of form, and the profound logic that created an inner connection between all the motives. This was my experience in the course of my creative work. Mahler's opinion was just the opposite. 'No!' he said, 'The symphony must be like the world. It must be all-embracing.'

Sibelius also noted that the orchestra 'did not particularly warm to him, which may have been due to the fact that during his Helsinki visit, Mahler was not in the best of health.'

[24] Igor Stravinsky and Robert Craft, *Conversations with Igor Stravinsky* (London: Faber, 1959), 38.

[25] Undated letter to Richard Specht; see Inna Barsova, 'Novoe v russkoy Maleriane', *Sovetskaya muzyka*, 3 (1990), 98–102 at 100.

[26] Karl Khristianovich Köhler was the solicitor of the keyboard company K. M. Schröder and the proprietor of a concert agency, K. Kh. Köhler & Co., in Nevsky Prospekt 65. See Barsova, 'Novoe v russkoy Maleriane', 99. The letter is in St Petersburg, Department of Manuscripts, Russian Art History Institute, fond 56, opis' I, ed. khr. 3.

[27] See Tawaststjerna, *Sibelius*, ii. 75–6.

[28] Alma Mahler, *Memories*, 297–8.

[29] See Tawaststjerna, *Sibelius*, ii. 76–7.

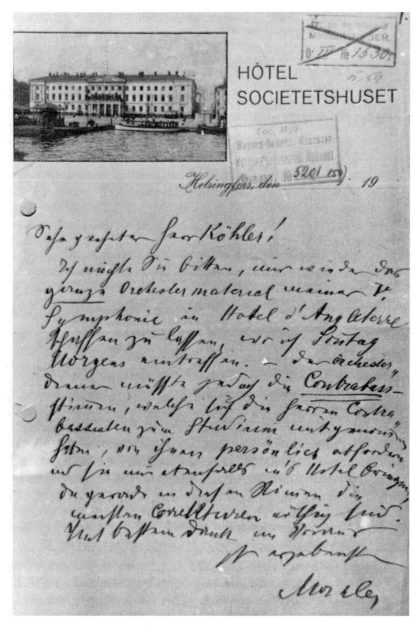

Pl. 23.1. Mahler's autograph manuscript letter to Karl Köhler concerning arrangements for rehearsals of his Fifth Symphony in St Petersburg in 1907

Undated letter (*circa* early November 1907) from Mahler to Karl Köhler concerning his Fifth Symphony.

[Transcription]

Sehr geehrter Herr Köhler!

Ich möchte Sie bitten, mir wieder das *ganze* Orchestermaterial meiner V. Symphonie in Hotel d'Angeleterre schaffen zu lassen, wo ich Sontag Morgens eintreffen [*sic*]. — der Orchesterdiener müsste jedoch die *Contrabass*-stimmen, welche sich die Herren Contrabassisten zum Studium mitgenommen haben, von ihnen persönlich abfordern und sie mir ebenfalls in's Hotel bringen, da gerade an diesen Stimmen die meisten Correkturen nöthig sind.

Mit bestem dank im Voraus
Ihr ergebenster
Mahler

[Translation]

Dear Herr Köhler,

I would kindly ask you to send all the orchestral material of my Fifth Symphony to me at the Hotel d'Angleterre where I shall arrive on Sunday morning. The orchestra's porter, however, must personally ask the *Bass* players for their parts—which they have taken away with them to study—and bring them to me at the hotel, because it is those parts in particular that are most in need of correction.

With best thanks in advance
Yours faithfully
Mahler

Russia's Mahler

Recognition of Mahler's music was slow to develop in Russia. For one reason, his works were virtually unknown there. During his lifetime, only two of his symphonies were performed in St Petersburg: the Second Symphony, under Oskar Fried on 28 October 1906, and the Fifth, as we have seen, under Mahler himself on 9 November 1907. Hence the earliest responses were made after a single hearing and 'without so much as a look at the score'.[30] In the thirteen seasons preceding the First World War, a little over twenty articles on Mahler appeared in the St Petersburg press, and ignorance of his works did not prevent critics from expressing very decided opinions. Many—such as Nikolay Rimsky-Korsakov, Vyacheslav Karatygin, and Nikolay Miaskovsky—described his symphonies as 'formless', 'cumbersome', and 'unduly prolonged', and his musical material as 'vulgar', 'hackneyed', and 'unoriginal'.[31] Others were more broad-minded. Viktor Kolomiytsev, for example, after enumerating the various weaknesses he found in the Second Symphony, nevertheless went on to say that Mahler's 'individuality' would always attract those who could 'break through

[30] Ivan Sollertinsky, *Gustav Maler* (Leningrad: Gosudarstvennoe muzikal'noe izdatel'stvo, 1932), 15.
[31] See Nikolay Rimsky-Korsakov, *Vospominaniya*, ed. Vasily Yastrebtsev (Leningrad: Muzgiz, 1960), ii. 439;

Vyacheslav Karatygin, *Izbrannie stat'i* (Moscow: Muzyka, 1965), 60; and Nikolay Miaskovsky, *Pis'ma iz Peterburga . . . Sobranie materialov v dvukh tomakh* (Moscow: Muzyka, 1964), ii. 106–7.

the charmed circle of one-sided ideas about music'.[32] The World War, and the Russian Revolution and Civil War account for the period of silence on Mahler and his music which lasted for the next seven years.

In the 1920s informed interest in Mahler grew rapidly. In the musical circles of what was then Petrograd the Mahler movement was particularly strong. The eminent Russian conductor Emil Cooper (1877–1960) began a series of performances which opened with the Fifth Symphony on 29 November 1922. Thereafter, throughout the decade and the 1930s, Mahler's symphonies and songs were performed in Leningrad and (less frequently) Moscow by Heinz Unger, Fritz Stiedry, Hans Steinberg, Albert Coates, Bruno Walter, Otto Klemperer, Alexander Zemlinsky, Joseph Rosenstock, Václav Talich, Eugen Szenkar and Jascha Horenstein, and by such Soviet conductors as Aleksandr Gauk, Karl Eliasberg, Natan Rakhlin, Nikolay Rabinovich, and Evgeny Mravinsky.[33] Not all the performances got off to a smooth start with the concert officials, however. Bruno Walter, for instance, who conducted the Fourth Symphony in Moscow in 1923, recalled:

I had Mahler's Fourth Symphony on one of my concert programmes and had given the text of its last movement, which deals with ' the heavenly Life', to the organizers to have translated and printed in the programme notes. It was returned to me with a request to alter the words; in the new Russia one did not sing of Heaven and angels, St Peter, and other saints. Naturally, I refused to change a thing, and finally made my case by explaining to the pedantic representative of Atheism that the poem was intended to be understood 'symbolically'.[34]

Otto Klemperer, on the other hand, who visited the Soviet Union annually between 1924 and 1929 and gave what appears to have been the first performance 'in Russian' of *Das Lied von der Erde*, found 'the musical atmosphere' there 'absolutely free'.[35]

During the 1920s and 1930s, students and professional musicians in Leningrad studied and performed Mahler's music in piano reductions and scores. The Bruckner–Mahler Society held regular meetings at which piano eight-hand arrangements of Bruckner's and Mahler's works were played—'thirteen movements per evening';[36] and the Society for New Music and Culture, formed by the young composer Gavriil Popov (1904–72) at the Central Professional School of Music in the academic year 1929–30, met to discuss the latest symphonic ideas in the works of Bruckner, Strauss, and Mahler.[37] Ivan Sollertinsky was its heart and soul. Enthusiasts were also keenly interested in Western ideas about Mahler. When Paul Bekker's study, *Die Sinfonie von Beethoven bis Mahler* (first published in

[32] Viktor Kolomiytsev, 'Gustav Maler i ego simfoniya', *Oko*, 31 Oct. 1906 (repr. in id., *Stat'i i pis'ma*, ed. July Kremlev (Leningrad: Muzyka, 1971), 32). See also e.g. A. Iliaschenko, 'Vos'maya simfoniya Gustava Malera, korrespondentiya iz Myunkhena', *Russkaya muzykal'naya gazeta*, no. 4 (1910), cols. 854–6.

[33] Fuller details can be found in Sollertinsky's 'Khronograf ispol'neniya proizvedeniy Malera i Bruknera v SSSR', in *Pamyati I. I. Sollertinskogo, vospominaniya, materialy, issledovaniya*, ed. Ludmila Mikheyeva (Leningrad and Moscow: Sovetskiy kompozitor, 1974), 232–4.

[34] Bruno Walter, *Thema und Variationen* (Frankfurt am Main: S. Fischer Verlag, 1967), 333 (trans. Ed.).

[35] *Conversations with Klemperer*, ed. Peter Heyworth (rev. edn., London: Faber, 1985), 65–6.

[36] Sollertinsky, 'Nikolay Malko: Vospominaniya', in *Pamyati I. I. Sollertinskogo*, 107.

[37] Letter dated 19–22 Oct. 1939 from Gavriil Popov to Pavel Nazarevsky; see Gavriil Popov, *Iz literaturnogo naslediya*, ed. Zarui Apetyan (Moscow: Sovetskiy kompozitor, 1986), 123. Amongst the society's members were Boris Asaf'ev and Vladimir Shcherbachev (1889–1952).

Berlin in 1918), was translated into Russian by Roman Gruber in 1927, it was avidly read.

The two most outstanding interpreters of Mahler in Russia in the inter-war years were Boris Asaf'ev (1884–1949), who wrote much of his musical criticism under the pseudonym of Igor Glebov, and Ivan Sollertinsky (1902–44). Asaf'ev, who was a composer as well as a critic and musicologist, saw Mahler's music as reflecting the 'St Petersburg myth'—the phantasmagoria in which the writings of Dostoyevsky, Gogol, and E. T. A. Hoffmann, and Pushkin's and Tchaikovsky's *The Queen of Spades* came together. 'In the grip of delusion himself, Mahler too knew the power of invocation: like Byron's Manfred, he could command spirits and summon Death; like Dostoyevsky's Ivan Karamazov, he carried in his soul a terrifying image of the Demon; and like Hoffmann's Medardus, he was constantly fleeing from his double, seeking support in religious meditation.'[38] Since 1918 Asaf'ev had been occupied with trying to interpret the phenomenon of development in Mahler's music as a 'process'—a method he later elaborated in his book *Musical Form as Process* (1930–47). In this he compares musical development—movement, 'the wave-like rises and falls', the 'swelling' and 'thinning' of musical texture in the works of Schubert, Brahms, Bruckner, and especially Mahler—to 'demonstrations of organic life' in terms of Bergson's, Lossky's, and Ernst Kurth's philosophical ideas.[39]

The years 1929 to 1943, however, can be described as the Sollertinsky epoch in Russian musicology. Sollertinsky had a brilliant intellect and a formidable memory. He knew twenty languages, and had a keen sense of humour and an inexhaustible social drive. He accepted some of the ideas propagated by contemporary artistic policy, above all the maxim that 'Art should be useful to the people'—which derived from the Russian Enlightenment of the 1860s. He could memorize a score with precision; and the conductors Kyril Kondrashin (1914–81), Nikolay Malko (1883–1961), and Nikolay Rabinovich (1908–72) have testified that 'Sollertinsky prided himself particularly on knowing all Bruckner's and Mahler's symphonies by heart.'[40] Although a theatre critic who turned to music late in his career, Sollertinsky's treatment of material was professional. As one contemporary put it: 'Malko is introducing him to the secrets of the art of conducting; his friendship with Shostakovich is broadening his musical vision.'[41] Sollertinsky lectured extensively on Mahler and wrote the first book on him in Russian (*Gustav Mahler*, Leningrad, 1932), which marked a watershed in Russian Mahler studies. In this he argues that Mahler was a 'genius' as a composer, but a 'failure' in philosophical and cultural matters—thus epitomizing Sollertinsky's Beethoven-orientated thesis, the 'death of European

---

[38] 'Mahler (1860–1911)', *Programma k akademicheskomu simfonicheskomu orkestru 1922/23*, Petrograd; cited from Boris Vladimirovich Asaf'ev, *O muzyke XX veka*, ed. Tat'yana Dmitrieva-Mey (2nd edn., Leningrad: Muzyka, 1982), 126.

[39] Boris Asaf'ev, *Muzykal'naya forma kak protsess*, ed. E. M. Orlova (Leningrad: Muzyka, 1971), 140. The most thorough introduction to Kurth's work in English is Lee A. Rothfarb's *Ernst Kurth as Theorist and Analyst* (Philadelphia:

University of Pennsylvania Press, 1988). Rothfarb points out that Kurth's *Grundlagen des linearen Kontrapunkts: Bachs melodische Polyphonie* (1917) was translated into Russian by Asaf'ev in 1931, and suggests that Asaf'ev's *Musical Form as Process* 'shows strong links to Kurth's ideas' (p. 234 n. 60).

[40] 'Nikolay Malko: Vospominaniya', 107.

[41] Mikhail Druskin, 'Vospominaniya: Drug', *Issledovaniya, vospominaniya* (Leningrad and Moscow: Sovetskiy kompozitor, 1977), 231.

symphonism in the Beethovenian sense of the word'.[42] Nonetheless Mahler's music remained 'inseparable from the social and ideological *Weltanschauung* problems which humanity has to solve'.[43] The clue to his work was the image of St Anthony of Padua preaching in vain to the fish—the subject of his *Wunderhorn* song 'Des Antonius von Padua Fischpredigt', which reappeared, without the words, as the Scherzo of his Second Symphony. Sollertinsky interprets this as a sermon on the renunciation of 'universal evils' which it was Mahler's mission in life to undertake. Such renunciation was achieved musically by means of the 'grotesque' in which genuine emotion was masked by irony, parody, the grimace of the jester—'Chaplinesque' humour. (Another example Sollertinsky cites is the third movement of the First Symphony, 'Todtenmarsch "in Callots Manier" ', with its parody of 'Bruder Martin' in the minor key introduced by the muted solo double bass.) Ultimately, in Mahler Sollertinsky heard 'a musical renunciation of the capitalist inferno— the modern version of Dante's Hell',[44] and he includes him in the same typological stratum as Dante himself, Hieronymus Bosch, Goya, Pieter Bruegel the elder, Félicien Rops, and, in this century, Georg Grosz. Amongst his surviving papers there are plans for further essays or lectures on Mahler, such as 'Mahler and the Chaplinesque use of indirect lyricism' and 'Mahler and pre-war Don Quixotic humanism (cf. Gandhi, Stefan Zweig)'.[45] One can only regret that he did not live to complete them.

Sollertinsky's book was enormously influential in determining the perception and appreciation of Mahler's works by numerous musicians and music-lovers in Russia. All the same, many prominent figures—Heinrich Neuhaus, Maria Yudina, and Shostakovich, for example—found their own way to Mahler. Mahler's impact on Shostakovich can already be seen in the grotesque Scherzo of his First Symphony, and in later works—including the Fourteenth Symphony, which, like *Das Lied von der Erde*, can be described as a 'Symphony of Songs': Mahler 'penetrated into the innermost secrets of human consciousness', Shostakovich wrote in 1964.[46]

During the Second World War and throughout the Stalin Terror, Mahler and his music were neglected in Russia. This was due to the unofficial ban on his compositions, both in the concert hall and in educational institutions, which began in 1949 with the notorious 'anti-cosmopolitan' campaign. A few people, however, managed to keep his music and memory alive amongst their students and followers: the composers Aleksandr Lokshin (1920–87) and Yuri Fortunatov, and the conductors Nikolay Anosov of the Moscow Conservatoire and Nikolay Rabinovich of the Leningrad Conservatoire. The latter conducted the only performance of a Mahler work during the war—the First Symphony, in Novosibirsk on 8 May 1943.

After the war, and with the political thaw of the post-Stalin years, Mahler gradually experienced a renaissance in Russia. While in the 1940s one learned his music from piano

[42] Sollertinsky, *Gustav Maler*, 61 and 4.
[43] Ibid. 13.
[44] Ibid. 27.
[45] 'Tezisi, plani, zametki', in *Pamyati I. I. Sollertinskogo*, 216.

[46] Shostakovich, *Gustav Maler: Pis'ma, vospominaniya*, trans. Sergey Osherov, ed. and intro. Inna Barsova, with a Foreword by Dmitri Shostakovich (Moscow: Muzyka, 1964; 2nd edn., 1968), 7.

four-hand arrangements, after the 'iron curtain' had been lifted, recordings of his works began to be imported from abroad, the earliest of which was that of the Fourth Symphony conducted by Karel Šejna with the Czech Philharmonic Orchestra. The rare live performances of his works were remarkable events—despite the loss of a Mahler tradition amongst Russian orchestras. In Moscow, the First Symphony was performed by the Gosorchestr under Karl Eliasberg on 11 May 1953, under Natan Rakhlin on 25 April 1957, and under Georges Sebastian on 8 and 9 April 1961; while the Moscow Philharmonic Orchestra performed *Das Lied von der Erde* under Nikolay Rabinovich in 1958, and the Fifth Symphony under Natan Rakhlin in 1960.

The centenary celebrations of Mahler's birth in 1960 injected new blood into the Mahler movement. His works coloured the entire concert life in Leningrad and Moscow. They were performed by the Russian conductors Nikolay Rabinovich, Natan Rakhlin, David Oistrakh, Gennady Rozhdestvensky, Evgeny Svetlanov (b. 1928), Maxim Shostakovich, Yuri Temirkanov (b. 1938) and, most often, Kyril Kondrashin, as well as by such visiting conductors as Igor Markevitch (1912–83), Efrem Kurtz (b. 1900), Paul Kletzki (1900–73), and Lorin Maazel.[47] The concert season a decade later (1969–70) also featured a Mahler cycle; and Kyril Kondrashin was awarded the Gold Medal of the International Mahler Society in Vienna for his indefatigable promotion of Mahler's music in Russia. It so happened that the very last work Kondrashin ever conducted, before he died later the same day, was Mahler's First Symphony—at the Amsterdam Concertgebouw, on 7 March 1981.

Devotees of his music followed closely the developments in European Mahler studies. The première of Deryck Cooke's Performing Version of the Tenth Symphony, conducted by Berthold Goldschmidt at a promenade concert in the Albert Hall on 13 August 1964 and broadcast by the BBC, was tape-recorded by Moscow music-lovers. Eight months later, on 6 April 1965, members and musicians gathered to hear the tape in the Composers' Union Hall: it had an enthusiastic reception and was favourably reviewed in the press.

In 1973, Roland Petit choreographed the Adagietto from the Fifth Symphony for a one-act ballet *à deux*, *La Rose Malade*, which was performed by Maya Plisetskaya and Rudi Brilans and other partners at the Bolshoi Theatre in Moscow. This was a great success and remains the only instance of Mahler's music being used for a ballet by Russian choreographers.

During the 1960s and 1970s, the Mahler renaissance in the concert hall served to stimulate research and musical criticism which led to the first Russian publication of his letters.[48] Between 1960 and 1976, the Muzyka Publishing House in Moscow published a

[47] For reviews of these performances, see e.g. Edison Denisov, 'Vtoraya simfoniya Malera', *Sovetskaya muzyka*, no. 4 (1968); Ludmila Mikheyeva, 'Tret'ya simfoniya Malera v ispolnenii simfonicheskogo orkestra Leningradskoy Konservatorii', *Sovetskaya muzyka*, no. 1 (1961); Elizaveta Mnatsakanova, 'Moskovskaya prem'era devyatoy simfonii Malera', *Muzykal'naya zhizn'*, no. 13 (1962); Izrail' Nest'ev, 'Primechatel'naya prem'era. Ispolnenie pyatoy simfonii Malera', *Sovetskaya muzyka*, no. 7 (1960); David

Rabinovich, 'Simfoniya vozrozhdeniya. K ispolneniyu v Moskve Vtoroy simfonii Malera', *Muzykal'naya zhizn'*, no. 3 (1962). See also Izrail' Nest'ev's article 'Gustav Maler: Posledniy velikiy simfonist', *Na rubezhe dvukh stoletiy* (Moscow: Muzyka, 1967).

[48] For the edition of Mahler's letters, see above, n. 46. Books on Mahler were written by Ludmila Mikheyeva, *Gustav Maler, kratkiy ocherk zhizni i tvorchestva, popular-naya monografiya* (Leningrad: Muzyka, 1972); Konstantin

complete edition of the symphonies and, between 1971 and 1977, piano four-hand arrangements of the first five. In 1975 it published his *Kindertotenlieder* (translated by Viktor Kolomiytsev and M. Yurgenson), and in 1984, his *Lieder eines fahrenden Gesellen* (translated by Aleksey Mashistov). Since that time, however, one of the negative effects of 'Perestroika' has resulted in an instability in the music publishing business and a decline in concert-hall performances. Nevertheless, Dmitri Kitayenko (b. 1940) and the Moscow Philharmonic Orchestra gave the first live performance of Deryck Cooke's Performing Version of the Tenth Symphony on 29 December 1983, and the Russian première of the Eighth Symphony on 25 December 1988. More recently, during the 1995–6 season, cycles of Mahler's symphonies were conducted in Moscow by Evgeny Svetlanov and Pavel Kogan (b. 1952), and in St Petersburg by Yuri Temirkanov, Aleksandr Dmitriev (b. 1935), and Mariss Jansons (b. 1943).

Mahler's music continues to influence Russian composers, though a change in emphasis—a marked preference for the meditative atmosphere of his later works, rather than the energetic and dramatically charged emotions of his earlier symphonies—is noticeable. Mahler himself embarked on this journey, from the slow finale of his Third Symphony to 'Der Abschied' of *Das Lied von der Erde* and the Adagio of his Ninth Symphony. As he said to Natalie Bauer-Lechner: 'In the Adagio, everything is resolved into quiet "being"; the Ixion-wheel of appearances has at last been brought to a standstill.'[49] Indeed, Alfred Schnittke's *Epilogue, Peer Gynt* (1987), the one-movement symphonies of Giya Kancheli (b. 1935), and the Fifth Symphony of Valentin Silvestrov (b. 1937) testify to the fact that the Adagio has now become the highest musical expression of *Weltanschauung*.

Rosenshil'd, *Gustav Maler* (Moscow: Muzyka, 1975); and by Inna Barsova, *Simfonii Gustava Malera* (Moscow: Sovetskiy kompozitor, 1975); and dissertations were written by Loretta Agasaryan, 'Osobennosti sonatnoy formi v simfoniyakh G. Malera' (Inst. iskusstv Akademii Nauk Armjanskoj SSR, Yerevan, 1974); Larisa Nebolyubova, 'Spetsificheskie zakonomernosti dramaturgii simfonii Gustava Malera: k probleme Maler—ekspressionizm' (Inst. iskusstvovedenija, fol'klora i etnografii Akademii Nauk SSSR, Kiev, 1978); Aleksandr Guzhva, 'Zhanrovo-kompozitsionnye tipy simfonii v Avstrii i Germanii nachala XX veka/Gustav Maler i ego sovremenniki' (Moscow: Moskovskaya Gosudartvennaya Konservatoriya, 1985); Galina Timoshchenkova, 'Pozdnee tvorchestvo Gustava Malera' (Leningradskiy institut teatra, muzyki i kinematografii, 1977); and by Natal'a Dekhtyareva, 'Pozdniy period tvorchestva Gustava Malera filosofsko-esteticheskie osobennosti simfonicheskikh kontseptsiy' (Leningradskaya Gosudarstvennaya Konservatoriya, 1981).

[49] NB-L, *Recollections*, 67.

24

Mahler and Japan

KENJI AOYAGI

Background

In 1854 Japan was compelled by the United States to conclude a US–Japan Treaty of Friendship, which induced it to abandon the policy of national isolationism it had maintained for more than two hundred years. As a consequence of the Treaty, several ports were opened to foreign countries: two small ones, Shimoda and Hakodate, in 1854; and three major ones, including Yokohama, the gateway to Edo (present Tokyo), in 1859. It is of course a mere coincidence that the period in which Japan opened itself to the West coincided with Mahler's birth. However, the coincidence looks a little more symbolic when we consider the history of the reception of Mahler's music in Japan.

The Meiji Government was established in 1868. Its policy of Westernization was so radical as to introduce Western music into the army and at social gatherings. Naturally, there had been ethnic music before then (generally called *Ho-gaku*, or Japanese music); but several factors influenced the official adoption of Western music instead. One was that there were to many genres in *Ho-gaku* from which to select a single one; these ranged from *Ga-gaku* (ancient court music influenced by Chinese music), *Shoumyou* (Buddhist ritual song), to *So-kyoku* (music for Japanese harp, or Koto), each of which has a different musical structure. In addition, each genre was dominated by a different school, and thus music in Japan had no unified organization or musical system as in Western music. Another curious factor would have been that the most popular Japanese music of the time was heavily biased in subject matter towards love affairs of an adult nature, which would certainly not have been suitable for music education in primary schools! Japanese music may not have been appropriate to teach in primary and secondary schools where music was adopted for

The principal sources used in this chapter are Takashi Ogawa, *Japanese Symphony Orchestras: Documents of Regular Concerts, 1927–1981* (Tokyo: V. Minon-on Music Library, 1983); id., *Japanese Symphony Orchestras: Documents of Regular Concerts, 1982–1991* (Tokyo: V. Minon-on Music Library, 1992); Hiroshi Watanabe (ed.), *Das Bruckner-Mahler Lexicon* (Tokyo: Shoseki, 1993); and *Philharmony* [Newsletter of the NHK Symphony Orchestra] (Tokyo, 1927–).

the first time as an official subject, but this was most probably only a superficial reason. The most important one was that everyone in the nineteenth-century world believed that the only civilized culture was that of Western Europe, all other cultures being inferior and not 'modern'. This was not only the belief of Westerners themselves, but of the Japanese. For example, Amane Nishi (1829–97), a representative philosopher/thinker in the Meiji era (1868–1912), argued for the adoption of an alphabetical (romanized) writing system to replace that of Japanese; while Arinori Mori (1847–89), an influential politician, even went so far as to propose making English the official language of Japan. The Japanese were eager to introduce anything Western into their country almost indiscriminately, assuming that to be modern was to be Western. Music was just one of these aspects.

The pre-war reception of Mahler

Mahler's music was appreciated in Japan even earlier than in many Western countries. Several fortunate accidents allowed this to happen. First mention should be given to the role played by Hidemaro Konoë (1898–1973), a descendant of the highest of aristocrats (the Fujiwara family), whose genealogy can be traced back more than one thousand years. In contrast to his brother Fumimaro Konoë, who was Prime Minister at the end of the Second World War and committed suicide just after Japan's defeat, Hidemaro apparently had a happy life immersed in music. He spent two periods in Europe: the first, from 1923 to 1924, in Paris and Berlin studying composition with Vincent d'Indy, Max von Schillings, and Georg Alfred Schumann, and conducting with Erich Kleiber and Carl Muck; the second, from 1936 to 1945, in Austria and Germany conducting many first-rank orchestras such as the Berlin Philharmonic and the Vienna Philharmonic. During this latter visit he and Kleiber are said to have discussed Mahler's Fourth Symphony in detail together after Kleiber had listened to the recording of it made by Konoë with a Japanese orchestra. When the Second World War broke out, Konoë remained in Germany and was exploited by the German and Japanese governments as a symbol of their friendship.

Konoë was also a pioneering composer of Western music; his arrangement of *Etenraku* (a representative *Ga-gaku* piece) was one of the most important works in the repertoire of early orchestral music in Japan. Just how fascinated he was by Mahler's music is shown by the fact that when he returned to Japan in 1924 at the age of 26 from his first stay in Europe he chose the third movement of the First Symphony as part of the programme for his first concert. However, all the orchestras in Japan at that time were only amateur and none was well trained. Not until 1925 was a professional orchestra first heard in this country, a joint Russian–Japanese orchestra. These two events, namely Konoë's return and the joint concert, heralded the birth of real symphonic orchestras in Japan. Konoë energetically started to perform Mahler's music, conducting the New Symphony Orchestra he had just established. However, apart from vocal pieces, he could only play the First and the Fourth Symphonies (and sometimes the fifth movement of the Third) because the orchestra was still limited in technique and organization. Why did he become so enthusiastic about Mahler's music? One can only conjecture that he was moved in his youth by the latest music in Europe. However, the depth of his understanding of Mahler is evident from the articles he wrote discussing the essential characteristics of Mahler's music and its fundamental difference from Bruckner's. Indeed, we can appreciate how well he understood Mahler from his world-première recording (1930) of the Fourth Symphony, reissued in 1988 on CD (DENON/Japan Columbia 30CO-2111). Of course the quality of the sound is poor, and the technique is far from perfect, for it was only a few years since this first professional symphony orchestra had been formed.

What is puzzling, however, is why such an immature orchestra should have chosen Mahler to record. In Europe, audiences regarded Mahler's music as belonging to the long tradition of the symphony from Haydn, Mozart, and Beethoven, to Brahms and Bruckner. By contrast, in Japan—at least in those days—Mahler was seen not against the background of a long musical tradition but on a par with his predecessors. Thus, while people in Europe appreciated Mahler's music in the context of musical history, it was received in Japan as just one piece of music amongst others. It is pointless to speculate whether or not such an attitude leads to an authentic understanding of music. Western music in general was transplanted into Japan as something already established, not as it had developed throughout history. So the answer to the question why Mahler's Fourth was first recorded in Japan might simply be that Konoë happened to be acquainted with the composition. However, as two other important conductors took up Mahler seriously after Konoë, the early introduction of his music cannot be regarded merely as a whim of Konoë: other factors must have accounted for this.

Before the Second World War, orchestral pieces arranged for the piano were never popular in Japan. At that time only a few people could play the piano, for it was less than a couple generations since Western music had come to be known in this country. It was mainly through the gramophone that ordinary Japanese music-lovers listened to orchestral music, rather than attending concerts. Moreover, concert performances were few, and the only place where they were held was almost always Tokyo. So it might sometimes happen that a music-lover who had never even attended a concert was familiar with world-famous conductors such as Toscanini and Mengelberg. Records by famous conductors were always popular in Japan. Thus, the majority of Japanese were exposed to Western music primarily through the gramophone. Without a tradition of concert-going, they tended to accept orchestral music as something sacrosanct that had to be learned, not just enjoyed. Against this background, the Japanese music world welcomed Pringsheim and Rosenstock enthusiastically when they came to stay in Japan, and eagerly learned from the Mahler works they conducted. Their authority, especially concerning Mahler, was absolute for the Japanese.

Klaus Pringsheim (1883–1972) was born into a well-known family in southern Germany which produced many scholars and writers. His father was Professor of mathematics at the University of Munich and was a close friend of Wagner. His brother was a composer, and his twin sister eventually married Thomas Mann. He started his conducting career as the assistant to Mahler at the Court Opera House in Vienna. Between 1923 and 1924 he conducted all Mahler's symphonies and songs with the Berlin Philharmonic Orchestra. It is surprising that such a first-rate composer and conductor should ever have accepted a professorship in Japan, which was a backward country in Western music at the time. But it is still more astonishing that a conductor so closely acquainted with Mahler, and one of the best interpreters of his work, should have encouraged the immature orchestra of the Tokyo Conservatoire to play such music. On his arrival in 1931, Pringsheim conducted the première performances in Japan of Mahler's Fifth (1932), Second (1933), Sixth (1934), Third (1935), and Seventh (1937) Symphonies with the Conservatoire Orchestra. At the time only the New Symphony Orchestra of Konoë and the Tokyo Conservatoire Orchestra were capable of playing complete symphonies. Even so, it is amazing that the latter could ever play Mahler's symphonies at all, which were regarded as the most difficult works to perform. Some listeners were said to have complained about the standard of performances. Nevertheless, Pringsheim's enthusiasm certainly influenced Japanese audiences to whom Mahler's music was new.

We cannot tell whether Pringsheim's staying in Japan had anything to do with the fact that Konoë abruptly stopped conducting Mahler after 1932. Konoë's numerous musical essays include articles on Mahler only up until 1932, and sources close to him testify that Beethoven and Richard Strauss occupied his interest from then onwards. After 1931, Konoë only conducted Mahler's Fourth twice—in 1954 and 1968.

When he left Japan after six years, Pringsheim was succeeded by Joseph Rosenstock (1895–1985), an Austrian Jew from Poland, who came to Japan in 1936. He had escaped from Berlin where he had been persecuted by the Nazis. From 1936 to 1946, when he left Japan, he conducted the New Symphony Orchestra (renamed the New Japan Symphony Orchestra in 1942, and then the NHK Symphony Orchestra, as it is still known today), except for the last year of the war, when Jews were prohibited from conducting even in Japan. He was an excellent director and trainer of the orchestra whose contribution to Japanese musical life cannot be overestimated. It is interesting to find him advertising private lessons for piano, composition and conducting in the newsletter of the New Symphony Orchestra alongside an article introducing him as the new conductor. I am not certain whether this was because of the economic situation of the orchestra or of Rosenstock himself, or both; or whether it was merely his intention to promote Western music as widely as possible. At any rate, advertising for private lessons by the conductor of the chief orchestra was remarkable and certainly reflects the circumstances in Japan at this period. Rosenstock in fact succeeded in attracting quite a number of students. Among them was Kazuo Yamada (1912–91), who conducted the Japanese première of Mahler's Eighth just after the war. Though Mahler was not Rosenstock's main interest, he conducted Des Knaben Wunderhorn in 1938, the Japanese première of Das Lied von der Erde in 1941, and the first complete performance in Japan by a professional orchestra of the Third Symphony in 1938. Rosenstock's interpretation was highly praised for its clarity and vigour.

The post-war reception of Mahler

In pre-war Japan, then, Mahler's music was accepted by music-lovers and became part of the standard repertoire of the newly emerging professional orchestras. This is in sharp contrast to the situation in the West, where the reception of his music was slow to make headway. Moreover, in Germany and Austria, once his homelands, his work was prohibited by the Nazis as representing decadent Jewish music, whereas in Japan the government never interfered with its progress even in the midst of the war. Thus, the Fourth Symphony was played twice during the Second World War.

When the war ended, with the complete defeat of Japan, the spiritual, no less than the material, destruction of the Japanese was devastating. The old values collapsed, many people grew nihilistic or apathetic; and it may be no exaggeration to say that Mahler's music consoled and encouraged the Japanese nation in the depths of its despair. The Japanese première of Mahler's Eighth Symphony in 1949, conducted by Kazuo Yamada, was an important event both socially and musically. Just how excited people were by it can be seen from the newsreels of the time. It is moving to watch Mahler's Eighth being performed in the same film that reports severe food shortages and dire unemployment. Yamada, who studied under Pringsheim and Rosenstock and had conducted the Fourth during the fierce air raid on Tokyo in 1945, also conducted Mahler's Second Symphony in 1949.

However, it seems that the post-war revival of Mahler by Yamada did not proceed so smoothly. For example, even in 1960 (the centenary of Mahler's birth) and 1961 (the fiftieth anniversary of his death), the only piece officially recorded as having been performed was the Adagio of his Tenth Symphony—in 1960 by the Boston Symphony Orchestra conducted by Richard Burgin. Furthermore, very few articles on Mahler appeared in the music journals for those years, though there were special issues celebrating the 150th anniversary of the birth of Chopin and Schumann (both born in 1810). In the five years from 1961 to 1966, the only symphonies of Mahler to be performed were the First and the Fourth, which had been stock-in-trade since before the war. There is a reason for this apparently waning enthusiasm for Mahler. Keeping pace with the general recovery after the war, orchestras were formed in many cities besides Tokyo: Osaka, Kyoto, Sapporo, and others. Several new orchestras emerged in Tokyo itself as well. First-class foreign orchestras visited Japan from Vienna, Berlin, and Boston, and concerts of orchestral music at last became accessible to the general public—and were thus no longer the privilege of a musical elite in Tokyo. As orchestras tended to perform the works of more popular composers at the time to attract a larger audience, Mahler was relegated to second place.

However, the situation changed around 1970, by which time Japanese orchestras had digested the standard repertoire of Classical and Romantic music and were keen to explore new areas. The next nominee was Mahler, and this time, the boom or 'Mahler renaissance' which had occurred elsewhere in the world on the occasion of the centenary of his birth, was matched by a Japanese one. Every concert hall where Mahler's works were performed was almost full to capacity. Akeo Watanabe (1919–90), wishing to introduce the whole profile of Mahler to Japanese audiences, started a 'Mahler Series' with the Tokyo Metropolitan Symphony Orchestra in 1973. It was during this series that Deryck Cooke's Performing Version of the Tenth Symphony was played for the first time in Japan.

In the 1980s, the character of this Mahler boom changed somewhat: audiences were no longer satisfied with mere performances of his works, but demanded more 'authentic' interpretations of them. Nonetheless, the number of performances steadily increased (see Table 24.1), and his works have now become fixtures in concert programmes.

Since the late 1980s it is possible to say that the Japanese have shown a marked preference for a more systematic understanding of Mahler. Several Mahler cycles, exhibitions, and symposia reflect the trend of appreciation in the modern musical world of Japan. Hiroshi Wakasugi (b. 1935) regularly conducted all Mahler's symphonies—including *Das Lied von der Erde*—between 1988 and 1991; and such world-famous Mahler interpreters as Inbal, Bertini, and Sinopoli have visited Japan with their orchestras and performed Mahler cycles. There are also many younger Japanese conductors who are eager to include Mahler in their programmes; amongst these, Michiyoshi Inoue (b. 1946) and Ken Takaseki (b. 1955) are outstanding.

The Tsuyama International All-Round Music Festival, with Mahler as the 'theme composer', was held in 1987, 1990, and 1993. Tsuyama is a small city with a population of 80,000, located about 160 km. west of Osaka. The Festival itself was not very grand or big; but it is remarkable that not only Mahler concerts but also symposia about him were held there. The music director of the Festival, Akeo Watanabe (who died just before the 1990 festival), wanted to make it an occasion at which the Japanese—especially those from the provinces—could have the opportunity to experience and to think about every aspect of Mahler. Besides the First and Fifth Symphonies and *Das Lied von der Erde*, the Second, Third, and Eighth Symphonies were performed at the Festival with the choruses consisting mainly of Tsuyama citizens and those of neighbouring towns.

Coda

Over the last decade Japanese audiences have become more discerning in their appreciation of Mahler and are listening more attentively to what is expressed in his works. They have begun to accept the 'dark' side of his music—its agony and suffering, alienation and

Table 24.1. NUMBER OF PERFORMANCES OF MAHLER'S SYMPHONIES IN JAPAN BY PROFESSIONAL AND VISITING ORCHESTRAS
Note. For Japanese orchestras only performances at regular concerts have been included; concerts at festivals (e.g. the Tsuyama International All-Round Music Festival) are not included.

Symphony	1927–45 (Aug.)a	1945 (Sept.)–51	1952–6	1957–61	1962–6	1967–71	1972–6	1977–81	1982–6	1987–91
No. 1	3+0b	0	3+0	0	5+0	9+7	13+6	17+11	19+12	20+63
No. 2	0	2+0	0	0	0	2+0	5+0	5+0	8+0	13+15
No. 3	1+0	0	3+0	0	0	0	2+0	4+0	7+2	11+7
No. 4	7+0	0	1+0	1+0	3+0	4+0	12+2	8+4	16+2	15+25
No. 5	0	0	1+0	0	0	3+0	6+4	10+10	16+18	17+31
No. 6	0	0	0	0	0	0	2+0	4+1	7+0	6+11
No. 7	0	0	0	0	0	0	1+0	5+0	5+0	0+8
No. 8	0	2+0	0	0	0	1+0	2+0	2+0	1+0	2+8
No. 9	0	0	0	0	0	0+3	3+1	4+0	5+8	9+12
No. 10c	0	0	0	3+1	0	0	5+2	3+0	4+1	3+14
Das Lied von der Erde	2+0	2+0	0	3+0	2+0	4+0	5+0	0	5+2	9+4

a Japan surrendered to the Allied Powers on 15 Aug. 1945.
b The first figure means the number of performances by Japanese orchestras; the second, the number of those by foreign orchestras.
c In the case of the Tenth Symphony, the figure includes the number of performances of the Adagio only.

self-disdain, solitude and despair, and the evil and ugliness of the world it exposes. It would be wrong to see this phenomenon as merely a fleeting enthusiasm. The Japanese have discovered through Mahler that Western music as a whole relates to their own lives and experiences as human beings. We might call it, rather, the rediscovery of Western music through Mahler; or, the 'renaissance' of Western music by Mahler.

25

Mahler in London in 1892

ANDREW NICHOLSON

In memory of Nick John, 1952–96

On 2 April 1892, during his tenure in Hamburg, Mahler signed a contract with Sir Augustus Harris[1] to conduct the first German season in London at Covent Garden.[2] Writing to his friend Siegfried Rosenberg shortly after the formalities had been completed, he observed:

The engagements in London have all been settled—even before *I* had said anything. Between you and me, Harris would rather have had Hans Richter, who would of course have been a tremendous asset for the London enterprise, in view of his standing there. However, this seems to have fallen through—and so I have been engaged.[3]

The arrangements had been made by Bernhard Pollini, the impresario who had engaged Mahler at the Hamburg Opera, and included a company of twenty-four soloists, an orchestra of eighty, a chorus of fifty-five, and Mahler's assistant conductor, Leo Feld.[4] It appears that Mahler was quite right in his conjecture that Harris would have preferred Richter, whose various conducting activities had, since 1879, included his annual Richter Concerts in London. According to Christopher Fifield:

A letter from Arthur Goring Thomas in October 1891 . . . suggests that an approach may have been intended to get him [Richter] to conduct for Harris's project. 'Mr Higgins,' he wrote, 'who is on the Committee of the Royal Italian Opera, Covent Garden, is most anxious to see you before you leave

---

I am grateful to Chris Banks for reading through this chapter and making some helpful comments and observations.

[1] Sir Augustus Henry Glossop Harris (1852–96), actor, dramatist, and impresario, manager of Covent Garden from 1888 and lessee of Drury Lane from 1879; Sheriff of London (and knighted therefore) 1891. According to Henry Wood, 'He was a splendid musician', 'a man who understood *both* drama *and* music', and whose 'insight and vision for the public taste' could hardly be equalled. See Henry J. Wood, *My Life of Music* (London: Gollancz, 1938), 117–18.

[2] Until 1892, the opera house was called the Royal Italian Opera, Covent Garden. For the German season, 'Italian' was dropped from its title, and thus it has remained ever since. Other innovations introduced at the same time were electric lighting (though gas was still retained), the dimming of the auditorium during the performance, and the singing of all German operas *in German* (not, as previously, in Italian).

[3] *MDS*, 193.

[4] For the various arrangements, see Mahler, *Selected Letters*, 411–12.

England, as he has some important proposals respecting the opera season of 1892 to lay before you.'[5]

Be this as it may; the initial plan was that Mahler should conduct six operas—*Tristan, Fidelio*, and what would be the first *Ring*-cycle at Covent Garden[6]—to run between 8 June and 13 July 1892. In the event, however, the visit proved so successful that extra performances were put on at the Drury Lane Theatre, with the addition of two performances each of *Tannhäuser* and Viktor Nessler's *Der Trompeter von Säckingen*—thereby extending the tour by ten days, to 23 July, and increasing the number of performances to a total of twenty.[7]

For the purposes of this visit, Mahler undertook to learn English, his proficiency in which is rather charmingly illustrated by the letters he wrote to his friend Arnold Berliner, with whom he had studied the language. Indeed, it is from these letters that we know that Mahler stayed at two addresses: 69 Torrington Square (the house of Solomon Jacobson) and 22 Alfred Place (the lodging house of Mrs Mary A. Gusterson)—both of which are within the proximity of Covent Garden.[8] Unfortunately, these locations have since been demolished and rebuilt as part of the University College London complex. However, we have been lucky enough to discover general views of the two sketched prior to demolition, which we reproduce as Pls. 25.1 and 25.2.

Readers may be interested to know the exact date and venue of each of the operas; they are as follows:

Covent Garden		Drury Lane	
Wed. 8 June	*Siegfried*	Mon. 13 June	*Siegfried*
Wed. 15 June	*Tristan*	Sat. 18 June	*Tristan*
Wed. 22 June	*Rheingold*	Sat. 25 June	*Tristan*
Wed. 29 June	*Walküre*	Mon. 27 June	*Rheingold*
Wed. 6 July	*Siegfried*	Sat. 2 July	*Fidelio*
Wed. 13 July	*Götterdämmerung*	Mon. 4 July	*Walküre*
Sat. 16 July	*Tannhäuser*	Fri. 8 July	*Trompeter* (Feld)
Wed. 20 July	*Fidelio*	Sat. 9 July	*Tristan*
Fri. 22 July	*Tannhäuser*	Mon. 11 July	*Siegfried*
		Thurs. 14 July	*Trompeter* (Feld)
		Mon. 18 July	*Götterdämmerung*

Mahler thus conducted eighteen out of the twenty performances—right up to the evening before his return journey to Hamburg: *Tristan* and *Siegfried* four times each; *Rheingold*,

---

[5] Christopher Fifield, *True Artist and True Friend: A Biography of Hans Richter* (Oxford: Clarendon Press, 1993), 291.

[6] The *Ring* cycle had been performed for the first and *only* time in London (as Shaw was quick to point out with indignation, in *World*, 27 July 1892; see *Shaw's Music*, ed. Dan H. Laurence (2nd rev. edn., 3 vols. London: Bodley Head, 1989), ii. 681), ten years earlier, on 5, 6, 7, and 9 May 1882 at Her Majesty's Theatre, under Anton Seidl.

[7] As can be seen from the table of dates and venues,

Mahler was happy to conduct both of the performances of *Tannhäuser* at Covent Garden on 16 and 22 July, but handed over the baton to Leo Feld for those of *Der Trompeter von Säckingen* at Drury Lane on 8 and 14 July. It will be remembered that in 1884 Mahler had composed the incidental music for Scheffel's *Der Trompeter von Säckingen*, of which *Blumine*—later deployed as the second movement of his original five-movement version of the First Symphony (only to be subsequently rejected)—is all that remains.

[8] See Mahler, *Selected Letters*, 141–3; also *MDS*, 193–4.

Pl. 25.1. Torrington Square (*c*.1930), where Mahler stayed during his conducting of the Opera season at Covent Garden in 1892

Pl. 25.2. Alfred Place (*c*.1900?), where Mahler stayed during his conducting of the Opera season at Covent Garden in 1892

Walküre, Götterdämmerung, Fidelio, and *Tannhäuser* twice each—a demanding programme, and one that he fulfilled to great public and critical acclaim. As the advertised cast lists (even if extant, which is rare) frequently differ from the cast that appeared on the night itself, the singers and their roles in each opera *as performed* are given below. Many of these singers—such as Alvary, Schumann-Heink, Reichmann, and Sucher—were already established figures at Bayreuth and elsewhere, and continued to gain prominence under Mahler's direction.

Siegfried
Siegfried: Max Alvary
Brünnhilde: Rosa Sucher (8 and 13 June); Katherina Klafsky (6 and 11 July)
Erda: Ernestine Schumann-Heink
Mime: Julius Lieban
Wotan: Karl Grengg (8 and 13 June); Theodor Reichmann (6 and 11 July)
Alberich: Herr Lorent
Fafner: Herr Wiegand
Waldevogel: Sophie Traubmann

Tristan
Tristan: Max Alvary
Isolde: Rosa Sucher (15 June);[9] Frl. Erde-Andriessen (18 and 25 June); Katherina Klafsky (9 July)
Kurwenal: Herr Knapp
Brangäne: Frl. Ralph (*not* Ernestine Schumann-Heink as advertised)
Marke: Herr Wiegand
Melot: Herr Simon
Steersman: Herr Lorent
Shepherd: Herr Landau
Sailor: Julius Lieban

Rheingold
Rhinemaidens: Sophie Traubmann, Frl. Ralph, Ernestine Schumann-Heink
Alberich: Herr Lissman
Mime: Julius Lieban
Wotan: Karl Grengg
Fricka: Frl. Erde-Andriessen
Freia: Frl. Bettaque
Fasolt: Herr Wiegand
Fafner: Herr Litter
Loge: Max Alvary
Erda: Frl. Froehlich
Donner: Herr Dome
Froh: Herr Simon

Walküre
Siegmund: Max Alvary
Sieglinde: Frl. Bettaque
Hunding: Herr Wiegand
Wotan: Theodor Reichmann
Brünnhilde: Frl. Erde-Andriessen (29 June); Katherina Klafsky (4 July)

---

[9] Rosa Sucher was unexpectedly recalled to Berlin shortly after this performance to sing in *Die Walküre* on the last night of the season there.

Fricka: Ernestine Schumann-Heink
Valkyres: Sophie Traubmann, Frl. Kollar, Frl. Ralph, Frl. Froehlich, Frl. Meisslinger, Frl. Upleger, Frl.
    Simon, Ernestine Schumann-Heink [*sic*]

Götterdämmerung
Rhinemaidens: Sophie Traubmann, Frl. Ralph, Frl. Froehlich
Brünnhilde: Katherina Klafsky
Siegfried: Max Alvary
Gutrune: Frl. Bettaque
Waltraute: Ernestine Schumann-Heink
Gunther: Herr Knapp
Alberich: Herr Lissmann
Hagen: Herr Wiegand

Tannhäuser
Elizabeth: Katherina Klafsky
Tannhäuser: Max Alvary
Venus: Frl. Bettaque
Wolfram: Theodor Reichmann
Landgrave: Herr Wiegand
Shepherd boy: Ernestine Schumann-Heink

Fidelio
Leonora: Katherina Klafsky
Florestan: Herr Seidel
Marzelline: Sophie Traubmann
Jaquino: Herr Landau
Rocco: Herr Wiegand
Pizarro: Herr Lissman
The Minister: Herr Litter

The season opened with *Siegfried*, performed out of sequence at the request of Max
Alvary, who (understandably, it was generally granted) wanted to make his London début
in the role of its eponymous hero. It seems customary when considering the opinion of the
press to allude to Shaw's notice of this particular performance, which appeared in the
World (15 June 1892), as a reasonable sample of the general reaction to the season amongst
English critics.[10] However, it should not be forgotten that Shaw (despite his evident delight
and enthusiasm, and *pace* his enormous breadth of knowledge and fastidious taste) had an
axe to grind with Harris: far from 'establishing the Wagnerian music-drama in London',
Harris had merely 'sent for a German *impresario* and a German company to help him out
of the difficulty', which Shaw felt he could have done just as well had he the ready cash.[11]
That is, Harris had not employed a *native* conductor and *indigenous* company and
groomed them to the task—though, to be fair, Shaw's barb is surely directed as much

---

[10] See e.g. *MDS*, 194–5. It is true that Shaw wrote 'Herr
Mahler . . . knows the score thoroughly, and sets the *tempi*
with excellent judgment' (*World*, 15 June 1892; *Shaw's
Music*, 650); but elsewhere his comments are not entirely
complimentary. For his observations covering the whole of
the German season, see *Shaw's Music*, 645–51, 659–63,
670–1, and 680–5.

[11] *World*, 15 June 1892; *Shaw's Music*, 657. In fact, Shaw
may have been responding in an oblique way to the sentiments expressed in the passage from *The Times* (9 June)
quoted in the text below.

towards the deplorable state of the opera generally and the public's atrocious taste in England at the time, as towards Harris himself. Moreover, Shaw is not altogether representative; besides the *World*, reports also appeared in the *Morning Post, Daily Telegraph, Sunday Times, Musical Times, The Times, Illustrated London News*, and *Athenaeum* ('the stronghold of English musical conservatism', according to Max Graf)[12]—to name only the London-based press. I shall quote here various excerpts from the last four named publications—or where their opinions coincide, the best expressed of them—solely insofar as they give some idea of Mahler's impact upon critics and of the manner of his conducting.[13]

The Times (Thursday 9 June) stated:

If the rest of the Wagnerian trilogy is to receive the same justice that was accorded to *Siegfried*, the opening work of Sir Augustus Harris's German season, given last night and to be repeated, not only in its place in the cycle, but at Drury Lane on Monday next, the present year will be indeed remarkable in operatic history. The policy of bringing over a complete company, including orchestra, costumes, and scenery, from Germany was one of indisputable wisdom, and the wonderful success of last night's performance is its just reward. . . . From beginning to end scarcely a single detail, either in the orchestra or on the stage, fell short of perfection. . . . The orchestra, greatly augmented in size, is of very fine quality, and it is pleasant to see certain excellent German practices adopted. For example, Herr Mahler, the admirable conductor, sits, or rather stands, not close to the stage, but in the middle of his players.[14] The effect of the beautiful scenery was immensely enhanced by the absence of all light in the auditorium during the acts. . . . An enormous audience received the work and the performance with an amount of enthusiasm quite beyond the average, and evidently quite sincere.

The *Athenaeum* (Saturday 11 June) matched such sentiments:

It would be impossible to overpraise the efforts of the orchestra under Herr Mahler. Though the tone neither of the strings nor the wind was that to which we are accustomed from our best English orchestras, the lights and shades in Wagner's wonderful scoring were brought into the fullest prominence, and it would be well for conductors to attend these performances, if only for the purpose of watching the methods by which Herr Mahler gains the desired effects.[15]

The *Illustrated London News* (Saturday 18 June) was even more effusive:

Herr Mahler is a Wagnerian conductor of the first order. He proved this, not only by a perfect acquaintance with every detail of the wonderful score, but by the rare unity of spirit with which he inspired his mixed orchestra of ninety-six German and English executants. The difficulties of the instrumentation are almost beyond ordinary conception, but they were vanquished without apparent effort, and, from first to last, the intricate maze of *leit-motiven* was threaded with a simply extraordinary degree of clearness and accuracy.[16]

[12] Max Graf, *Composer and Critic* (London: Chapman & Hall, 1947), 292.

[13] See also Mosco Carner's chapter, 'Mahler's Visit to London', in his *Of Men and Music* (London: Joseph Williams, 1944), 106–10, and Harold Rosenthal, *Two Centuries of Opera at Covent Garden* (London: Putnam, 1958), ch. 15.

[14] This was also noted by the *Musical Times* (1 July 1892): 'Herr Mahler, who conducted *more Teutonico* from the middle of the orchestra . . .' (p. 406).

[15] *Athenaeum*, no. 3372 (Saturday, 11 June 1892), 770.

[16] *Illustrated London News*, Saturday, 18 June 1892, 747.

And again (Saturday 25 June), of *Tristan*, it remarked: 'Herr Mahler once more demonstrated all the qualities that go to make a great conductor. He had his orchestra thoroughly in hand from the "Vorspiel" down to the "Liebestod," and gave a masterly interpretation of the most complex and exacting of Wagner's scores.'[17]

Meanwhile, the *Musical Times*, which appeared monthly, carried the following notice on 1 July:

The interest and enthusiasm excited by these performances, which have been attended by crowded audiences both at Covent Garden and at the supplementary performances at Drury Lane, forms a most conclusive and convincing rejoinder to those critics who have chosen to regard the Wagnerian cult as an elaborately inflated bubble which had already collapsed.... Whatever may be the ultimate fate of Wagnerian opera there can be no doubt that, to use the cant phrase of the day, it has 'caught on' like wild-fire in the present season, and that the admirers of the Bayreuth master in this country have been doubled in number by the enterprise of Sir Augustus Harris. To this result many causes have co-operated, foremost amongst which must be reckoned the retention of the services of Herr August Mahler [*sic!*], to whose great ability and mastery of his subject the completeness of the representations have been primarily due.

And of *Tristan*, it continued:

Herr Mahler gave a much more sentimental, not to say jerky, reading of the *Vorspiel* than that with which English audiences have been familiarised by Dr. Richter; but with this exception his share of the performance was marked by rare intelligence and mastery of the score. It is worthy of note, as a characteristic indication of the tone and temper of the audience who frequent Wagnerian opera, that when a cat appeared and remained on the stage for some little time in the last act, there was not the faintest ghost of a giggle throughout the vast auditorium.[18]

Of the *Fidelio* performance 'given on Saturday [2 July], out of its advertised course in the German season, and at Drury-Lane, the reason being that Frau Klafsky, the exponent of Fidelio, desired, not unnaturally, to make her *début* in London in that part', *The Times* (Monday 4 July) noted:

Herr Mahler conducted excellently as usual; the *Fidelio* overture began the performance, and the famous 'Leonore, No. 3,' was played between the acts. The quartet in canon was taken a good deal more slowly than usual; the quartet of the second act was spoilt, as regards its climax, by the ill-restrained energy of a drummer, who made himself far too prominent in many other passages. The beautiful *finale*, with its curious foreshadowing of the Ninth Symphony, was happily given in its entirety, and the performance was, as usual, warmly received.

On this occasion, the *Musical Times* and *Athenaeum* were almost in complete accord and somewhat more critical. First, the *Musical Times* (1 August): 'Herr Mahler's reading of the latter ['Leonora No. 3'] showed marked individuality and contained some original points, some of which were decidedly effective. On the other hand, the *tempi* adopted both here and in the body of the opera were occasionally open to criticism, and the misguided

---

[17] Ibid., Saturday 25 June 1892, 802.   [18] *Musical Times*, 1 July 1892, 406–7; one wonders what the cat thought.

violence of the drummer was more than once disagreeably in evidence.'[19] And the *Athenaeum* (9 July): 'The overtures played were No. 4, in E, previous to the opera, and No. 3, in C, between the acts. The rendering of the latter was unconventional, and Herr Mahler's indulgence in the *tempo rubato* is open to question, but a more serious fault throughout the evening was the din created by the tympani. Beethoven's score is not a drum solo with orchestral accompaniment.'[20]

To draw this brief overview to a close: in its report of the *Götterdämmerung* performance on 13 July, the *Musical Times* (1 August)—noting the omission of the opening Norn scene and the curtailment of that between Brünnhilde and Waltraute—declared:

The splendid 'Rheinfahrt' music and the famous 'Trauermarsch' afforded Herr Mahler and his orchestra opportunities for distinguishing themselves, of which they availed themselves more as regards spirit and intelligence than beauty of tone. The musicianship of the Hamburg orchestra is of a high order, and the playing of the wind instruments—notably the horns—quite admirable; but the quality of the strings, especially in any sustained high notes, often left a great deal to be desired on the score of smoothness and purity of tone. . . . A word of praise is due to the exemplary conduct of *Grane, Brünnhilde's* charger. His singular gentleness of disposition may not have added to the artistic completeness of the representation, but it must certainly have been most reassuring to many ladies present.[21]

While finally, the *Illustrated London News* (23 July), writing about the same performance in nearly a full page of sustained panegyric, remarked: 'The orchestra, under Herr Mahler's inspiring guidance, was once more equal to all requirements, and furnished a worthy climax to the succession of triumphs won by it in "Der Ring des Nibelungen" '; and concluded that on Saturday 16 July, 'before a brilliant and crowded audience' at Covent Garden, it had given 'one of the best performances of "Tannhäuser" ever seen in this country.'[22]

We have come a long way from Shaw!

---

[19] *Musical Times*, 1 Aug. 1892, 475. It did, however, applaud the fact that the performance was 'given as the composer intended that it should be given—*i.e.*, with spoken dialogue, and without the clever but unnecessary additions made by Balfe and adopted in the Italian version of the opera' (p. 474).

[20] *Athenaeum*, no. 3376 (9 July 1892), 74.

[21] *Musical Times*, 1 Aug. 1892, 475. *The Times* (Saturday, 2 July) had noted that, at the performance of *Die Walküre* on 29 June at Covent Garden, it 'was no great regret that Grane and Fricka's rams were omitted'.

[22] *Illustrated London News*, 23 July 1892, 109. The *Athenaeum* (no. 3378, 23 July 1892), however, deplored the adoption of the Dresden version, and urged the adoption of the Paris version (p. 139). (For more recent considerations of the relative merits of the two versions, see Carl Dahlhaus, *Richard Wagner's Music Dramas*, trans. Mary Whittall (Cambridge: Cambridge University Press, 1992), 27–31, and Geoffrey Skelton, *Wagner in Thought and Practice* (London: Lime Tree, 1991), 143–81.)

26

The Mahler Renaissance in England: Its Origins and Chronology

DONALD MITCHELL

The Mahler Renaissance in England: when, in fact, *did* it begin? In trying to answer that question and bring to light the first manifestations and early stirrings, I am reminded of my own chronology; that I was born in 1925, was a schoolboy in 1937 and still at school in 1939, when the Second World War began, and 20 years old when it ended. These were crucial dates, as it so happened, for the history of the reception—and performance—of Mahler's music in England.

What, it may well be asked, is their particular musical significance? That question can be simply answered in the case of 1937 and 1939. In the first of those two years, in June, the Columbia Graphophone [*sic*] Company, Ltd., issued the legendary recording on seven shellac 78 r.p.m. discs of *Das Lied von der Erde*, a concert performance by the Vienna Philharmonic Orchestra under Bruno Walter, with Kerstin Thorborg and Charles Kullman as soloists, recorded live in the Musikvereinsaal, Vienna, on 24 May 1936. On 16 January 1938, again in the Musikvereinsaal, Bruno Walter conducted the Vienna Philharmonic in a concert performance of the Ninth Symphony. This was also recorded live and issued on ten shellac 78 r.p.m. discs—this time by His Master's Voice—in 1939, not long before the outbreak of war.

One cannot put too much stress on the work done for the Mahler cause by those two historic recordings of two masterpieces. I document below the impact made by one of them (*Das Lied*) on the youthful Benjamin Britten; but his response to the music was shared by many pairs of inquiring, unprejudiced English ears, mine among them. Indeed my own

This chapter is based on the following sources: D. Cox, *The Henry Wood Proms* (London: BBC, 1980); Philip Hammond, 'The Hallé Years and After', in David Greer (ed.), *Hamilton Harty: His Life and Music* (Belfast: Blackstaff, 1979); Michael Kennedy, *Adrian Boult* (London: Hamish Hamilton, 1987); Kennedy, *Mahler*; and Mitchell and Reed (eds.), *Letters from a Life: The Selected Letters and Diaries of Benjamin Britten*. All quotations from Britten's letters and diaries are © The Trustees of the Britten–Pears Foundation and not to be further reproduced without written permission.

I am indebted to the kindness of Mr Stewart Spencer, who provided me with copies of the press comments on the early performances of the First and Fourth Symphonies conducted by Henry Wood and Thomas Beecham, from which I quote extensively.

dedication to Mahler—now the dedication of a lifetime—dates from my first encounter with *Das Lied* in the shape of Walter's 1936 recorded performance; and at the earliest possible moment I was likewise immersed in the new release of the Ninth. It is not too much to say that a whole new generation of Mahler admirers was *educated* by these two remarkable recordings,[1] a fact which itself pays tribute to the power and influence of the new recording technology of the 1930s and to the extraordinary foresight and enthusiasm of the recording engineers who travelled to Vienna to capture these performances on disc.

The history of the reception of Mahler's music in England was bound up, productively, with the history of the gramophone, a history that has continued until today. With the multiplicity of Mahler recordings, the advent of CD, and the promise of new recording techniques, we witness the influence of recording on a global scale. In this connection it is interesting to recall that the first commercial recording of Mahler's Fourth Symphony was made, not in Europe, but in Japan, as early as 1930, when, on 28 and 29 May, the work was recorded by the New Symphony Orchestra of Tokyo conducted by Viscount Hidemaro Konoë, with Eiko Kitazawa (soprano), and issued on six Parlophone shellac 78 r.p.m. discs (see Ch. 24). But whereas the recordings of *Das Lied* and the Ninth issued in England represented, as I shall hope to show, a climactic point in the development of Mahler appreciation, and led to the creation of an informed opinion, the Japanese have had, as it were, to rediscover their Mahlerian past: the rise of Japanese militarism, and the Pacific war, meant that the continuity of Japan's reception of Mahler was interrupted, as it was in Central Europe.

The circulation of the two sets of discs, of *Das Lied* and the Ninth, aroused exceptional interest and undoubtedly helped stimulate those few and yet highly significant concert performances of Mahler that took place during the war years or in the years immediately post-1945. In a vocal score of *Das Lied* belonging to Peter Pears I came across a list of performances of the work in which he himself had participated as tenor soloist. As the dates suggest, these would have been performances for which an audience would have been in part created by the pre-war Walter recording:

8 November 1942	London Philharmonic Orchestra, conducted by Sir Adrian Boult. Soloists: Astra Desmond/Pears
23 April 1944	New Symphony Orchestra, conducted by Sydney Beer. Soloists: Mary Jarred/Pears
1 & 3 December 1946	Liverpool Philharmonic Orchestra, conducted by Karl Rankl. Soloists: Catherine Lawson/Pears
11 September 1947 (Edinburgh Festival)	Vienna Philharmonic Orchestra, conducted by Bruno Walter. Soloists: Kathleen Ferrier/Pears

This last performance was one of the most important of the immediate post-war performances of Mahler and had a profound influence on future public perception and reception

---

[1] A singular consequence of getting to know Mahler's oeuvre in reverse order, i.e. the late works first, meant that there were occasions when we were puzzled by features of the early symphonies for which the final masterpieces had not prepared us.

of his music in England. It also led to a new recording of the score by Walter, with Ferrier and Julius Patzak.

A novel by J. B. Priestley (1894–1984), *Three Men in New Suits*, first published in 1945, gave an account of the efforts of three demobbed servicemen to adjust to post-war life (new paperback edition, London, 1984). It clearly indicates how a work like *Das Lied von der Erde* had become during wartime (a consequence, no doubt, of the release and dissemination of the discs in mid-1937) part of the established cultural 'scene'. This is what greets Alan's ears on approaching Uncle Rodney in his upstairs room:

He could hear the gramophone inside and so he waited, leaning against the oak chest of drawers that had always been there, and staring at a large old watercolour of an incredible street scene in some Mediterranean port. The window, further along the landing, was bright with racing clouds and blue air; but here in the corner there was a warm dusk, the day already dying. But what made it so queer was the music coming from Uncle Rodney's room. A woman—a deep throbbing contralto—was crying farewell to the earth. The strings thinly soared, broke, and fled. There was a faint sweet jangling of harps. The soft silver hammering of a celesta, scattered in the deepening silences, was like some dawn, far-off, pearly, indifferent to men in its pure beauty, stealing over a scene of ruined hearths and dead cities. '*Ewig!*' cried the woman softly, out of a lost Vienna. The last instruments murmured and died. The silences grew. '*Ewig, ewig!*' The blue brightens; the earth awakes in Spring; but the last whispering farewell is heard no more, because man has gone to find his long-lost home. . . .

'Steady, boys, steady,' Alan muttered, more moved than he cared to admit even to himself. And then went in.

His uncle, wearing an old shooting jacket and tweed trousers, was attending, with the huge deliberation of the run-down elderly, to the needs of a gramophone whose giant horn dominated the room. The windows were closed, and the air was sweet and thick with the smoke of Egyptian cigarettes.

'Hello, Uncle. I waited until it was over. Last movement of Mahler's *Lied von der Erde*, eh? And rather clever of me to recognise it after all this time.' (pp. 25–6)

Uncle Rodney, albeit a somewhat exotic figure, had admirable musical taste; at the end of the novel Delius's violin concerto is added to his enthusiasm for *Das Lied* and Elgar's cello concerto. The novel itself was written before the end of the war in Europe and Priestley uses his musical idols and images (was the author also Uncle Rodney?) to reinforce his conviction that the 'old' Europe was no more:

'The fact is, my boy, the real world—the one worth living in—is finished. These fellas—Mahler, Elgar, Delius, and the rest of 'em—knew it years ago. They saw it all coming, and before it was too late, they looked about 'em, saw what was gracious and charming and beautiful and knew it was all finished. Have a whisky? I've still got a bottle or two.'

Nor is it without interest that this early perception of Mahler, sympathetic though it undoubtedly was, almost exclusively promoted him as the poet *par excellence* of nostalgia and regret for a vanished world. How radically different is the way we hear him now! But in the evolution of our understanding of Mahler the nostalgia stage was doubtless something that had to be lived through, providing as it did a basis of genuine enough appreciation from which generations younger than Uncle Rodney would advance in understanding.

Of course the nostalgia factor was itself generated by the exclusive character of the available recordings in the 1930s, a short list of which makes the point for me: the Adagietto, *Kindertotenlieder*, *Das Lied*, and the Ninth Symphony—not exactly a representation of Mahler's creative personality in its totality.

When I was looking through the scores I had collected at the start of my discovery of Mahler, I found that I had scribbled down on the flyleaf of one or two of them, details of those early performances I attended in London (and I doubt that there were others elsewhere; though see *Additional note*, p. 337 above). The details I fear are not complete, and some of the orchestras and the conductors have disappeared altogether from view. But these partial lists bring fascinating evidence that the English Mahler 'boom' was struggling to get under way even during the inauspicious wartime years, boosted not only by the Walter recordings but also by other factors. For example, it must be the case that the Fistoulari performance of the Fourth was influenced by his marriage to Anna Mahler, Mahler's surviving daughter, who was resident in England during the war.[2]

I list here the performances of the Fourth and Fifth that I attended or heard broadcast, in chronological order:

Fourth Symphony

(month not known) 1943	National Symphony Orchestra, conducted by Sydney Beer
October 1943	London Philharmonic Orchestra, conducted by Anatole Fistoulari
March 1944	London Philharmonic Orchestra, conducted by Fistoulari (BBC broadcast)
18 October 1944	BBC Symphony Orchestra, conducted by Basil Cameron (broadcast)
6 March 1945	National Symphony Orchestra, conducted by Beer
23 October 1945	National Symphony Orchestra, conducted by Beer; Elisabeth Schumann (soloist)
26 June 1946	BBC Symphony Orchestra, conducted by Adrian Boult, Schumann (soloist)

Fifth Symphony

21 October 1945	London Philharmonic Orchestra, conducted by Heinz Unger (first public performance in England of complete symphony)

Memories of these wartime and post-war performances were soon to be engulfed by the flood of Mahler performances that followed, in the 1950s and 1960s, two decades in which the Mahler 'boom' in England as it were came of age. It revealed an exceptional enthusiasm for and inquisitiveness about Mahler's music—and not only about his music but also his life—that have been sustained until the onset of the 1990s. It would be possible, of

---

[2] Ironically, this was a period when Anna preferred to detach herself from her father's music and ostensibly took little interest in it. But she must have had a hand in encouraging the 1943 performance of the Fourth. She died in London in 1988; my obituary of her appeared in the *Guardian*, 7 June. (See below, Ch. 28.)

course, but well beyond the reach of this inquiry, to analyse the myriad concert performances and broadcasts which constituted the Mahler revival at the peak of its activity;
perhaps an avalanche rather than a 'boom'. But even amid the welter of post-war performances, there were certain events that must be singled out for special attention. I mentioned above the particular cultural significance that must be accorded the 1947
performance of *Das Lied* at the first Edinburgh Festival. The same sort of status belongs to
the performance of the Second Symphony Walter gave under the auspices of the BBC on
1 October 1949, in the Proms season at the Albert Hall, a performance that movingly complemented the first English performance of the same work that he had conducted on 16
April 1931 at the Queen's Hall.

This last fact—the first English performance of the Second—must remind us that part
of the history of Mahler's reception in England can be told from a chronological account of
the first performances of his works. In some though relatively few cases, we had to wait
until after the end of the Second World War for a performance. The English première of the
Fifth is shown in my table above. Other late starters, if they may be so described, were the
Third Symphony, first heard on 29 November 1947 in a BBC broadcast (conducted by Sir
Adrian Boult)—the first concert performance (conducted by Bryan Fairfax) had to wait
until 1961—and *Das klagende Lied*, the first English performance of which, in Mahler's
revised two-part version of 1898, conducted by Walter Goehr, was given on 13 May 1956
at the Festival Hall, London. As for the Sixth, it was through BBC broadcast performances
that the public made its first acquaintance with the work. There was a broadcast from
Hamburg on 21 December 1947 and then three years later, on 28 December 1950, a
broadcast performance by the London Symphony Orchestra conducted by Walter Goehr;
and then, with the BBC Symphony Orchestra, a further broadcast on 16 October 1956,
when the conductor was Norman Del Mar (1919–94), not only a distinguished Mahler
interpreter (his performance with the London Symphony Orchestra of Mahler's Third on
26 July 1962 was to become a legend in his lifetime) but author of an analytic monograph
on the Sixth, published in 1980, which should be far better known among Mahler students
and scholars.

These performances clearly filled out—and were clearly aimed at filling out—the gaps
in public knowledge of Mahler. As the 1940s progressed and the 1950s began, the public
both knew more of Mahler and wanted to know more, especially the works that had never
before been played to an English audience. The educative process and the 'boom' walked
hand in hand in these decades.

Those are landmark performances that I have outlined above. But what strikes me, I
think, when regarding them from the point of view of 'filling out the gaps', is how *few* the
gaps were. This encourages us to look back to yet earlier years, and earlier performances.
If those historic Walter recordings were crucial to the later development of a Mahler
renaissance, were they not also a response, at the end of the 1930s, to an interest
in Mahler that had already been growing through the decades following his death in
1911?

In the performing arenas I have chosen to examine two conductors, Sir Henry Wood (1869–1944) and Sir Adrian Boult (1889–1983), both of them not only highly active and popular conductors of leading orchestras but also associated with an organization—the BBC—which in pre-war and post-war years had a major role to play in the influencing of public musical taste and judgement.

Let us take Wood first, who may not have been a conductor of the first rank but whose insatiable inquisitiveness was exemplary and constituted a marked feature of the famous series of concerts, the 'Proms', he founded in 1895. The Mahler dimension makes particularly interesting reading. Already in the 1903 season—while Mahler was still alive—Wood gave the first English performance of the First Symphony on 21 October.[3] He cannot have been much encouraged by the critical reception accorded his initiative. *The Times* critic— anonymous in those days, but the paper's Chief Music Critic from 1889 to 1911 was J. A. Fuller Maitland—wrote on the 22nd:

From time to time the name of Herr Gustav Mahler has come before those who follow the course of musical events attentively as that of a composer who had not only done great things already, but was expected to accomplish even greater. By those, however, who remember him as the 'completer' of Weber's unfinished opera *Die Drei Pintos*, which was heard in Leipzig and one or two other German towns some 15 years ago, the news of his late-developed creative faculty was received with feelings of doubt; and now that his first symphony (in D) has been heard in England—it was given at the Promenade Concert last night—the doubt is resolved into a certainty that Herr Mahler has little or no creative faculty. It is, in fact, quite impossible, however willing one may be, to find any genuinely good point in the symphony, which is a work commonplace and trite to an almost infantile degree, contains no germ of real inventive ability, and is not even well scored, but is imitative of Weber, Mozart, Wagner, and other composers, and when 'original' is naive to childishness. To English hearers some amusement was caused by *quasi* references to 'Three Blind Mice' and 'Hot Cross Buns' in the first and the slow movements; but even these were cases in a desert of incongruous and inconsecutive dullness; and at the end of the three-quarters of an hour which the symphony occupies in performance, one found oneself still wondering what the composer set out to say.

The *Musical Times* (issue of 1 November) was not much more enlightened, though the Funeral March as least seems to have provoked some sort of response:

Herr Gustave [*sic*] Mahler's Symphony (No. 1) in D was heard for the first time in England on the 21st ult. It proved to be a clever, scholarly work, but so over-developed as to frequently give rise to a sense of weariness before the hour, less eight minutes, occupied by the performance had expired. Most of the themes are couched in folk-tune phraseology, and their treatment is reminiscent of the style of Humperdinck, though less polyphonic than that composer's. The most memorable move-

---

[3] While it is certainly the case that Wood's 1903 performance of the First is the earliest documented performance of a Mahler symphony in England, there was in fact a yet earlier occasion when orchestral music by Mahler was heard in London. I am much indebted to my colleague Knud Martner (Copenhagen) for informing me of a performance of the 'Entr'acte' from Mahler's completion of Weber's opera, *Die drei Pintos*, on 22 Jan. 1889, conducted by George Henschel. Mahler's 'arrangement' of Weber had been staged at Leipzig the year before. This short orchestral interlude was actually composed by Mahler, though based on ideas by Weber.

ment of the symphony is the *Andante*, which, though more gruesome than charming, possesses distinctiveness.

As for the *Musical Standard* (24 October), 'J.H.G.B.', in the circumstances perhaps fortunately, did not 'think it necessary to write much about [the work]'. He continued:

The music struck me as utterly impossible. Nearly sixty minutes of dreadful monotony and weakness were spent listening to a composition that appeared to have more childishness than charm. There is nothing daring in the symphony beyond the fact that the composer asks us to listen to yards of stuff that seems to be of the least imaginable musical value. When the music is not coarsely loud and confused, it is generally of a baby-like simplicity. The orchestral colouring is often the composer's own, and he has certainly written a symphony that is unlike any other work in the same form. But for all that I doubt whether any rational musical being wants to become better acquainted with it. It matters not to me what 'programme' the composer had before him: for the music is bad—at least, that is my opinion. Very likely the later symphonies may be infinitely better. I cannot say.

For good measure 'J.H.G.B.' had reacted similarly to Bruckner's Seventh (its second time only in England!): 'Honestly, it is a composition of very little talent . . . No, Bruckner's music is square-toed, emotionless and dull.' The only reason for rehearsing these awful opinions here—and perhaps their sole interesting feature—is to show the embarrassingly primitive and ignorant level at which much that passed for music criticism was practised in England in the first decade of the century. There was plenty of poorly informed criticism elsewhere, but the English variety, surely, was uniquely bad?

On 25 October 1905, nothing daunted, Wood followed up his performance of the First with the first English performance of the Fourth (with Wood's wife, Olga, as soprano soloist!). On 31 August 1909, the Proms included the Adagietto from the Fifth; as we have seen, the first complete English performance of the symphony did not take place until 1945.

This Wood first performance of the Fourth was followed on 2 December 1907 by a second, conducted by (Sir) Thomas Beecham. This must have been the only occasion on which he conducted a Mahler symphony. What follows is a recollection of that performance by a member of the audience, the Hon. William Maitland Strutt (1886–1912):

The other concert was given by Mm. Blanche Marchesi, with the help of the New Symphony Orchestra, and its conductor Thomas Beecham. This remarkable musician, who a year or two later leapt suddenly into fame, was at this time practically unknown save to the critics and a very few amateurs who kept their eyes open for any concert-giver who was not afraid to try new paths. He formed the New Symphony Orchestra and gave most interesting concerts to almost empty halls, but of this I shall have more to say later. The programme on this occasion was characteristic, including the overture to 'La chasse du jeune Henri', by Méhul, which I thought rather attractive, Cyril Scott's 'Aubade', and the 4th Symphony of that fine conductor but hopeless megalomaniac Gustav Mahler. In his last symphony he wrote, if I remember right, for a thousand performers, and though in the fourth he did not go to such extreme lengths, yet the length of time, the number of players, and the amount of rehearsing required for its adequate production were quite out of proportion to the real merit of the music.[4]

No doubt Strutt's views reflected the generally received English opinion of the day, yet more forcibly expressed in the *Musical Standard* of 7 December 1907, where, under the subheading 'Mahler's Fourth Symphony', a column of editorial comment was dedicated to H.H.'s review of Beecham's concert:

J.H.G.B. wrote at some length for 'The Daily News' on October 25, 1905, concerning this preposterous composition; he ventured to doubt whether Mahler was really a talented musician. One sentence ran: 'It is almost continuously subdued and thin, and when the composer does launch out he soon becomes ashamed of himself or is it he feels he has not the strength to carry things on?' Be that as it may, here is what our H. H. reports: Mme. Blanche Marchesi in conjunction with the New Symphony Orchestra gave a concert at the Queen's Hall on Tuesday, December 3. As is usual when the New Symphony Orchestra assist, chief interest was centred on the orchestral portion. On this occasion Mahler's Symphony, No. 4, in G, was brought forward. As has already been stated in this journal this was not the 'first performance', and I was glad to see the claim withdrawn on the programme. The analytical note states that this is Mahler's shortest symphony and the one in which his ideas are expressed most clearly. If this be so, we may reasonably anticipate the others with a certain amount of dread, for there is a paucity of genuinely original matter in this work which renders it intolerably dull. It reminds one of the ponderous tomes which German professors add to their academic shelves at regular intervals; works which represent fabulous industry and correctness of detail, but which are of interest only to the academic clique. The first movement is spun out to a wearisome length and although it makes an attempt at lightness and gaiety, the whole thing is wearisome and common-place and 'weighs' as heavy as lead. The *Scherzo* is certainly better and more interesting in outline and in the *Adagio* expectation of something exceptional is raised. But the last movement in which a German folk-song is introduced is an anti-climax and is not far removed from the bathetic. The interpretation impressed me as rather dull and perfunctory at times. This was especially so in the first movement, although the grace of the *Scherzo* was well brought out and the *Adagio* was given with considerable breadth. Mme. Blanche Marchesi is a well-known vocalist and her immense interpretative range makes her always interesting. In Senta's ballad from 'The Flying Dutchman' her dramatic gifts served her well, but she assuredly had not the lightness and *coloratura* necessary for the closing *Allegretto* of Schubert's 'Der Hirt auf dem Felsen'. Her selection of vocal items included a cycle, 'Songs of the Wind', by Marie Horne, and the 'Gipsy Song' from Mr. Joseph Holbrooke's opera, 'Varenka'.[5]

[4] From his 'Musical Reminiscences', edited by his mother and privately printed in 1913, p. 96. Strutt's father had been installed as Chancellor of the University of Cambridge in 1908. As for Strutt's mention of the 'last symphony', the Eighth would have been the latest symphony of Mahler's of which he had knowledge at the time his reminiscences were written, in 1911.

There is one further, if marginal, point of interest, on pp. 66–7, where Strutt writes of a visit to London in June 1906 by the Vienna Philharmonic Orchestra, when three concerts were conducted by Franz Schalk, programmes which apparently 'made no attempt to leave the beaten track'. Thus, no

Mahler! However, they did include a performance of Elgar's 'Enigma' Variations which, in turn, reminds us that Mahler was himself to conduct a performance of the work with the New York Philharmonic four years later in 1910.

[5] There is a nice irony in the juxtaposition of this singularly obtuse notice with the review on the very same page of a biography of Smetana by William Ritter (Paris, 1907). Ritter (1867–1955) was a Swiss writer, critic, and painter who had himself attended the première of the Fourth in Munich in 1901 and reacted against it with a ferocity altogether more interesting—and more revealing of the work's originality—than the parochial condescension of the

Two details of interest emerge here. First, the date of the performance in the *Standard* is given as 3 December (not 2 December); second, the programme differs from that remembered by Strutt, who mentions Méhul and Cyril Scott, not Wagner, Schubert, Holbrooke *et al.* Were there, then, two performances of the Fourth conducted by Beecham on successive days?

In 1914, Wood had scheduled in the Proms season for that year, the first English performances of *Lieder eines fahrenden Gesellen* and *Kindertotenlieder* for 17 October. But the outbreak of war and the grotesque banning of all German music meant the cancellation of these premières. (The first English performance of *Kindertotenlieder* was eventually to be given in 1924, on 27 May, with Elena Gerhardt as soloist and the London Symphony Orchestra conducted by Fritz Reiner, while that of the *Gesellen* cycle was to be delayed until 1927 when, on 3 November, Wood conducted a performance with Maria Olczewska at the Queen's Hall, London.) It is a singular feature of the history of the reception of Mahler's music that it was interrupted by two World Wars and, in Europe, by the grievous years of Nazi oppression and plague of anti-Semitism.

But Wood's pioneering Mahler performances were not confined to the Proms' seasons. For example, on 18 January 1913—just over four years after the Prague first performance in September 1908!—Wood conducted his Queen's Hall Orchestra (augmented to 110 players) in the first English performance of the Seventh. There followed, on 31 January 1914, with the same orchestra and Doris Woodall and Gervase Elwes as soloists, the first English performance of *Das Lied von der Erde*. A remarkable record of first performances judged by any standards, one might think, performances that significantly pre-date even the first stirrings of a Mahler 'renaissance'. But the truth must be that his performances were an essential part of the laying down of the basis without which the future renaissance could never have materialized, or would have been yet longer postponed. A final Wood landmark was the first English performance of the Eighth, given on 15 April 1930, in which the BBC Symphony Orchestra and chorus participated.[6] This was a sign of the times. The assembling of such large forces could not have been done without the backing, financial and administrative, of a powerful broadcasting organization; and as we shall see, the BBC was itself to play an indispensable part in the dissemination of Mahler's works among a broad listening public. One should not forget that radio was a *new* and forceful medium in the 1920s and 1930s, especially in the promotion and circulation of music and especially when, as in the case of the BBC, it was principally a national broadcasting system, with potentially wide and widespread audiences at its command.

The BBC was eventually to play a very significant role in the career of another conductor who, like Henry Wood, exercised a quite particular influence on public concert life in

---

Standard. Ritter was to become an ardent admirer, indeed an advocate, of Mahler's and contributed to the *Festschrift* published to mark the occasion of the composer's fiftieth birthday (Munich, 1910).

[6] A later performance by Wood on 9 Feb. 1938 was attended by the youthful Benjamin Britten, who wrote in his diary on returning from the Queen's Hall: 'Execrable performance (under H. Wood)—but even then the work made a tremendous impression. I was physically exhausted at the end—& furious with the lack of understanding all around.' See also Jennifer Doctor, *The BBC and Ultra-Modern Music, 1922–1936: Shaping a Nation's Taste* (Cambridge: Cambridge University Press, 1999).

England between the wars—(Sir) Adrian Boult. Boult was certainly the better technician and more distinguished interpreter. But neither man was a virtuoso 'great' conductor in the sense that the term is used today. They were, rather, pioneer interpreters and above all sources of *information*, through their performances, about a great mass of music which they felt the public *ought* to know about, to hear. Perhaps the verdict would be adverse; but at least it would be reached on the basis of an experience of the music. It is highly interesting that the careers of both men, through the later organization and funding of the Proms in the case of Wood, and through Boult's long service as principal conductor of the BBC Symphony Orchestra and as a broadcasting administrator, were shaped decisively by the BBC, the great enabler of their ambitions to introduce the new and the unknown to the new, mass audiences that the new technology of broadcasting was itself in the process of creating. A beneficiary, of course, was Mahler. One should not underestimate the fact that the rediscovery of his music synchronized with the new technologies of radio and gramophone recording and came to be powerfully energized by them.

Boult, unlike Wood, was not responsible for a whole batch of English first performances of the symphonies: the exception was the 1947 first broadcast performance of the Third, already noted above as one of those post-war landmark events. He followed this up with a performance a year later, on 10 February, of the Eighth, a concert which formed part of the BBC Symphony Orchestra's winter season, another important and influential occasion, representing again the release of energy and resources which characterized the performing arts in Britain in the aftermath of the war. In 1949, on 28 October, Boult was to conduct the BBC Symphony Orchestra in a broadcast performance of the Adagio of the Tenth, following up the first broadcast performance of the movement that had been given a year earlier by the same orchestra, but this time conducted by Hermann Scherchen. The first concert performance, of both the Adagio and 'Purgatorio', was heard at the Festival Hall, London, on 30 November 1955, when the Royal Philharmonic Orchestra was conducted by Richard Austin. I make a point of these early performances of movements from the Tenth because, as we shall see, the work was to have a quite special place in the performance history of Mahler's music in England.

Boult was not a natural Mahler interpreter, perhaps not even an enthusiastic one, although he had taken the trouble to attend the great Amsterdam Mahler Festival of 1920, from where he wrote non-committally that Mahler 'is master of his structure'. But Boult was above all inquisitive and inquiring, and, as I see it, believed that it was his musical duty to keep his audiences informed and extend their experience. Hence his honourable record of Mahler performances post-war. Hence too a list of performances between 1914 and 1934 that reinforces his status as a pioneer.

In 1914, indeed, on 25 and 26 July, just a month or two before the outbreak of the first World War, Boult conducted at Oxford what must have been the first performances of *Das klagende Lied* in England, although with piano accompaniment only. This must take its place along with some of Wood's early performances, but it also represents one of the earliest introductions of Mahler's music to an audience outside London.

He sustained the tradition when he was appointed principal conductor of the City of Birmingham Symphony Orchestra in 1924. On 3 February 1926, Boult conducted at Birmingham the Fourth, only the third concert performance of a Mahler symphony in England, Michael Kennedy tells us, since 1913, when Wood had conducted the Seventh—although Balling's performance of the First at Manchester in 1913 (see below) must now be added to the tally. (Wood, incidentally, had also brought Mahler to the provinces. He had performed the Fourth at Liverpool in November 1922.) A. J. Sheldon, a local critic, wrote on the occasion of Boult's performance of the Fourth that more should be heard of Mahler in Britain. It was not only the public that was engaged in the process of education and information, with Wood and Boult—and others—as their guides. The critics too, however reluctantly, were changing their tune.

On 13 February 1930, again in Birmingham, Boult conducted *Das Lied von der Erde*, with Astra Desmond and Steuart Wilson as soloists. This was only the second performance of the work in England, Wood having given the first performance in 1914.

Boult was to give further performances of *Das Lied* in 1942 and 1945; but in 1934, when he had become principal conductor of the BBC Symphony Orchestra, he conducted the Ninth Symphony, the first London performance of the work, on 7 February.[7] This in fact had been preceded by the very first performance of the work in England on 27 February 1930, given in Manchester by the Hallé Orchestra under Sir Hamilton Harty. Here indeed was a landmark *regional* event of the first importance; and into the immediately ensuing seasons, 1930–3, Harty also introduced a performance of *Das Lied von der Erde*. Manchester, fascinatingly, was to become in later years a centre of Mahler interpretation. Sir John Barbirolli, the best-known principal conductor of the Hallé in post-war years, was a noted Mahlerian, and he was supported in the press by the tireless advocacy of Neville Cardus, the music critic of the *Manchester Guardian*, as it was in those days. Barbirolli was to create and, with his orchestra, to become part of the Mahler 'boom' of the 1950s and 1960s.

But the momentum and the particular association with Manchester had been initiated as far back as 1913, and not only in terms of performances: Cardus's predecessor on the *Manchester Guardian*, Samuel Langford, was one of the earliest critics in England to write with real perception about Mahler while his colleagues were still floundering in ignorance and prejudice. Langford mentions a pre-1914 performance of a Mahler symphony given by the Hallé Orchestra under Michael Balling, the German conductor (1866–1925), who was Richter's successor at Manchester from 1912 to 1914.[8] With the kind assistance of John Owen and the orchestra's archive, I have been able to identify the symphony and the

---

[7] It helps define Boult's inquisitive adventurousness when one recalls that between 21 Feb. and 14 Mar. this extraordinary man was to conduct the first broadcast of Busoni's massive piano concerto and the first complete performance in England of Berg's *Wozzeck*.

[8] Langford's writings, edited by Neville Cardus, were published after his death in one volume, *Music Criticisms* (London: Oxford University Press, 1929); for his mention of

Balling's Manchester performance, see p. 4. He wrote an obituary of Mahler in his newspaper on 19 May 1911 in which he described him as 'the greatest of present-day symphonists'. What was said in Manchester in 1911 was certainly not being said at the same time in Vienna. For further on Langford on Balling, see p. 559 below, and Michael Kennedy, *The Hallé Tradition* (Manchester: Manchester University Press, 1960), 184.

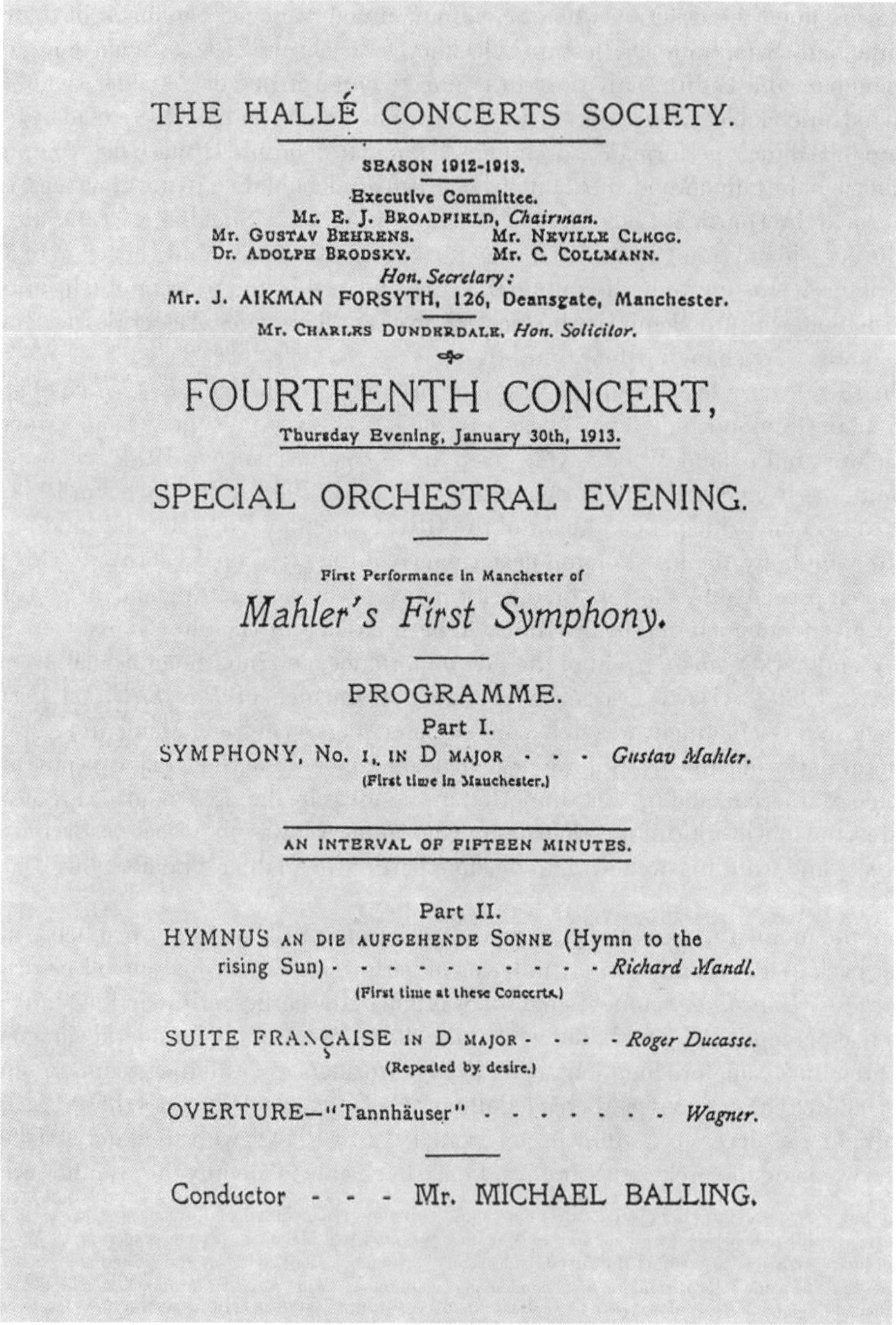

THE HALLÉ CONCERTS SOCIETY.

SEASON 1912-1913.

Executive Committee.
Mr. E. J. BROADFIELD, *Chairman.*
Mr. GUSTAV BEHRENS.   Mr. NEVILLE CLEGG.
Dr. ADOLPH BRODSKY.   Mr. C. COLLMANN.
Hon. Secretary:
Mr. J. AIKMAN FORSYTH, 126, Deansgate, Manchester.

Mr. CHARLES DUNDERDALE, *Hon. Solicitor.*

FOURTEENTH CONCERT,
Thursday Evening, January 30th, 1913.

SPECIAL ORCHESTRAL EVENING.

First Performance in Manchester of
Mahler's First Symphony.

PROGRAMME.
Part I.
SYMPHONY, No. 1, IN D MAJOR - - - *Gustav Mahler.*
(First time in Manchester.)

AN INTERVAL OF FIFTEEN MINUTES.

Part II.
HYMNUS AN DIE AUFGEHENDE SONNE (Hymn to the
rising Sun) - - - - - - - - - *Richard Mandl.*
(First time at these Concerts.)

SUITE FRANÇAISE IN D MAJOR - - - *Roger Ducasse.*
(Repeated by desire.)

OVERTURE—"Tannhäuser" - - - - - - *Wagner.*

Conductor - - - Mr. MICHAEL BALLING.

Pl. 26.1. The programme of Mahler's First Symphony, under Michael Balling, heard for the first time in Manchester, 30 January 1913

precise date of its performance. It was the First, and the concert took place on 30 January 1913. The front cover of the programme is reproduced as Pl. 26.1. It includes 'Analytical and Historical Notes' written by Ernest Newman and incorporating no fewer than twenty-six music examples! Although Langford did not himself identify the symphony, he went on to write in the report he dispatched to the *Manchester Guardian* from Amsterdam in 1920:

[Mr. Balling's] interpretation was casual, and the melody for the most part strained beyond its naive and easeful expression. The miscalculation might be ever so little, but it was sufficient to remove the composer completely from the general understanding. In that circumstance we had set before us the whole difficulty that lies in the appreciation of such composers as Mahler and Bruckner. It does not follow even that Mr. Balling's direction of the music was faulty, for the naive is made of little effect in its working by only a slight admixture of restlessness and scepticism among its interpreters.

Perhaps, then, this was something less than a convinced, committed performance of the First that was heard—'First time in Manchester'—in January 1913. It is not without interest that Newman, in his notes, makes a point of mentioning Wood's early performances of the First and Fourth, in 1903 and 1905 respectively, and his performance of the Seventh in the Queen's Hall, London, which had preceded Balling's First at Manchester by just twelve days.

January 1913 proves to have been something of a special month in the history of Mahler performances in England. Eighteen months later the First World War was under way. What one might think of as a Manchester 'school' was a vital factor in the development of Mahler's reception in England and, as the facts suggest, while it was especially influential during the years between the two World Wars and post-1945, even before 1914 signally early attention to Mahler had been paid by the Hallé.

Britten and Mahler

There is a final area of response and reception which I have yet to explore and attempt to document: the strong body of positive feeling about Mahler represented in England by a small young group of composers, musicians, and writers—almost constituting a 'cell'—whose eventual influence was to prove to be out of all proportion to their numbers.

Among them was Benjamin Britten, born in 1913; and if I choose him as the leading example of the group I have in mind, it is because his diaries, which he kept from 1928 to 1939, and his extant correspondence from the same period, document in precise detail how one preternaturally creative pair of ears received Mahler's music while still a schoolboy and how his enthusiasm for Mahler developed across the years (and was, indeed, sustained until the end of his life). As Britten himself developed as a brilliant young composer in the 1930s, so too did the power and penetration of his advocacy of Mahler increase in influence. There were undoubtedly other 'cells' of a like kind, of whose existence we have no direct knowledge but which would, of course, have vitally contributed to the public demand for performances and indeed themselves formed part of the audiences attending those still comparatively rare events. It was exactly these groups, which had parallel 'cells' in other countries—I am thinking in particular of central figures like Shostakovich in the (then) USSR (whose close friend was the early Mahler scholar, I. I. Sollertinsky) and Copland in the USA (whose teacher, Nadia Boulanger, was active in bringing Mahler to Copland's attention)—which did so much to spread the word about Mahler; and not just through the written or spoken word, but—in the case of composers—through their music, which itself exercised an educative influence on audiences, preparing as it were the way for the reception of Mahler's own music. It is paradoxical but true nonetheless that directly Mahler-influenced works, by Shostakovich, say, or Copland, or Britten, had won audiences and acclaim *in advance* of the established Mahler 'boom' in the years after 1945. There is a further paradox, this time a politico-historical one: that even while Mahler's music was suppressed and not performed at all—and only a little in territories elsewhere, outside the Fascist European/Pacific axis—it lived on, so to say, subliminally, in the works of a younger generation of composers, whose music, technically, was profoundly indebted to Mahler's example.

The advantage, of course, of composers taking up the Mahler cause was their ability to read and absorb his scores, even if they were unable to hear them in live performance (and remember, it was not until the latter half of the 1930s that gramophone records of certain works began to become more widely accessible). Britten was not only a voracious score-reader. He was also acquisitive, and in a number of cases dated his Mahler acquisitions. For example, he bought a miniature score of the Fourth in Vienna in 1934, and was given the Fifth, by his teacher, Frank Bridge, for Christmas 1936, a year in which he also added *Das Lied* to his collection. In 1938 there was another Christmas gift, this time a score of the Ninth, from Peter Pears; and I have no doubt that the remainder of his Mahler holdings (he had virtually everything that Mahler composed) was purchased early, even when undated. In one case—the *Lieder eines fahrenden Gesellen*—his diaries pinpoint the precise date on which he purchased the music, in London on 24 January 1931 (Britten was then a student at the Royal College of Music). He was to hear the songs on 6 May in the Queen's Hall, sung by Maria Olczewska, when he wrote in his diary: 'Lovely little pieces, exquisitely scored—a lesson to all the Elgars and Strausses in the world. [Elgar's] Enigma Variations a terrible contrast to these little wonders . . .'. For the rest of his life, Britten's admiration of the *Gesellen* cycle was not to diminish.

It was to be exceeded, however, by his enthusiasm for the *Kindertotenlieder* cycle, a very early recording of which—made in 1928, and issued on the Decca label in the UK, with Heinrich Rehkemper as soloist and Jascha Horenstein conducting the Berlin State Opera Orchestra—Britten acquired in 1934. His response to the work was overwhelming. Here are some characteristic entries from his diaries: 'heavenly Mahler songs' (19/20 December); the *Kindertotenlieder* cycle 'restores my faith in life' (16 January 1935); 'cheered by Mahler's glorious *Kindertotenlieder*' (6 March); 'Listen also for the 12th time to Mahler's peerless *Kindertotenlieder*' (13 October); on 9 February 1936, 'play Mahler's divine *Kindertotenlieder*. I feel it is worth having lived, if only for those little miracles'; and on 18 October, 'Music that I think I love more than any other.' And so on, and so on.

Here again we have an interesting example of the powerful influence of the circulation of early gramophone records of Mahler (Britten did not fail to conscript his circle of friends to listen to them). The *Kindertotenlieder* set may not have made the same public impact as the later sets of *Das Lied* and the Ninth, but it formed part of the same process.

Gramophone recordings were part of the new technology, and so too was radio; and it was again through the medium of broadcasting that we must imagine Britten and his companions expanding their Mahler horizons. To be sure Britten's earliest experience of Mahler was in the Queen's Hall, where, on 23 September 1930, he heard the Fourth, conducted by Henry Wood. Britten was 16 and at the College and wrote in his diary: 'Much too long, but beautiful in parts.' But a later *broadcast*—and no doubt a better interpretation: it was conducted by Webern!—began to dispel whatever youthful doubts Britten may have had. 23 April 1933: 'Listen to Webern conducting Mahler's lovely 4th Symphony from [BBC] London Regional. This work seems a mix up of everything that one has ever heard, but it is definitely Mahler. Like a lovely Spring day.'[9] Revealingly, while Britten commends the orchestra for having 'caught the spirit' of the work, he suggests an overall lack of orchestral accuracy. Here again one has to remind oneself that in England in the 1930s orchestras had to learn *how* to play Mahler. It was not only audiences that had to be educated: performers too.

By 1943, Britten's 'conversion' by the Fourth was complete, and he was to write to Peter Pears on 11 March: 'what a miracle that work is—I think I have almost more *affection* for that piece than for any I know.'[10]

His first encounter with the Seventh (though not the whole of it) was again a broadcast: performances of the two *Nachtmusik* movements conducted by Webern on 25 April 1934; and in this same year a broadcast of the Fifth, under Bruno Walter, from Hilversum. The Fifth was to become a much admired work. In 1936 he was 'revelling' in the score and—in

[9] Interestingly enough, a further performance of the Fourth that Britten was to hear, again a broadcast (from Vienna), was also conducted by a distinguished composer, Zemlinsky, on 14 Feb. 1935, when Britten wrote in his diary: 'Mahler's adorable 4th Symphony—the lovely Vienna Symphony under Zemlinsky with Annie Michaldy as a lovely soloist.' It was, it seems, a 'truly sensitive' performance. He had also heard the Fourth in Vienna in 1934, on 4 Nov., when the Vienna Philharmonic Orchestra was conducted by Mengelberg. This prompted a wry comment from Britten in his diary: 'Mengelberg doesn't impress me so much. He rescores Beethoven's lovely Pastoral Symphony in places almost out of recognition—& even Mahler's 4th Symphony (M. of all people knew to the nth degree what he wanted).... Elis. Schumann sings the lovely solo incomparably.' Schumann was a most persuasive advocate of Mahler's songs and undoubtedly her many performances in England,

as Britten's diaries witness, contributed significantly to public appreciation of Mahler's music.

[10] In 1961 Britten was himself to conduct the London Symphony Orchestra in a performance of the Fourth at the Aldeburgh Festival, the only occasion on which he conducted a complete Mahler symphony. However, he conducted performances of *Kindertotenlieder* and the *Gesellen* cycle in 1966 and 1972 respectively and the second 'Nachtmusik' from the Seventh in 1963. A landmark event was his conducting of the *first* modern performance of the discarded 'Blumine' movement from the First Symphony with the New Philharmonia Orchestra at the 1967 Aldeburgh Festival. Scarcely less of a landmark, however, was the 1966 *Kindertotenlieder* performance, though for a reason that was not fully appreciated at the time. See Ch. 10, pp. 230–1 above; see also *Additional note* on p. 564 below.

the absence of a complete recording—playing again and again all that existed of the symphony on disc, the Adagietto: 'it is indeed a miracle', he wrote in his diary on 21 June, and six days later, about the work as a whole, 'I suppose there are more beautiful bits of music than Mahler's 5th—but I don't know them.'

It was again a broadcast occasion, this time of the Ninth Symphony, that provided what was undoubtedly an event of no little historic importance. This took place in 1935, when the BBC Symphony Orchestra was conducted by Oskar Fried, who had known Mahler and performed his music in the composer's presence (for example, Mahler had heard Fried conduct the Sixth in Berlin in 1906). Thus there was some expectation of authenticity from Fried's interpretations. Britten, it seems, was not disappointed, by either the performance or the symphony. On 27 January 1935 he wrote in his diary: 'listen to what seems a fine performance by B.B.C. orch. under Oskar Fried (tho' without the suavity & rhythm of the Wien Phil) of Mahler's wonderful 9th symphony. I could listen to this for hours. The end is really very moving.'

I have seen this performance documented nowhere else; and were it not for Britten's diaries, we should have no evidence that it had ever happened. In the light of his entry, we could now doubtless locate the performance in the BBC's programmes for 1935.

Inevitably, Britten was at most public performances of Mahler. In 1936, for example, there was *Das Lied*. His diary entry for 29 October is fascinating on many counts: 'Dash up to Queen's Hall for 2nd half of [Royal Philharmonic Society] concert where Julius Harrison (with Simby (tenor) & Jarred (alto) 1. good. 2. excellent) does *Lied von der Erde*. Boyd Neel takes me & we eat after to recover from the show, which, all things considered (lack of rehearsal, lack of ability of orchestra, lack of real understanding by conductor) isn't bad. But what a work—it moves me more than any other music—certainly of this Century. *He seems to be gaining a large public here*—which is almost annoying—one doesn't want to share one's beauty spots!' [my emphasis].

Of particular interest, surely, is Britten's remark about Mahler 'gaining a large public'. As the 1930s progressed in England that was certainly the case; and it was in response to that growing, awakening public that the historic gramophone recordings that I have mentioned above, *Das Lied* first, and then the Ninth, were released.

One of the earliest purchasers of the 'Mahler Society' set of *Das Lied* was Britten, who refers in his 1937 diary on 22 June to 'my new (& very good) records of 'Das Lied von der Erde'—which is too exciting to think of much else to-day'. Thereafter he was busy listening to the records, introducing them to his friends, and on 29 June writing to one of them—Henry Boys—a letter which reveals how completely *Das Lied* had possessed the imagination of the most gifted English composer of his generation:

It is now well past mid-night & society dictates that I should stop playing the Abschied. Otherwise I might possibly have gone on repeating the last record indefinitely—for 'ewig' keit of course.

It is cruel, you know, that music should be so beautiful. It has the beauty of loneliness, & of pain: of strength & freedom. The beauty of disappointment & never-satisfied love. The cruel beauty of nature, and everlasting beauty of monotony.

And the essentially 'pretty' colours of the normal orchestral palette are used to paint this extraordinary picture of loneliness. And there is nothing morbid about it. The same harmonic progressions that Wagner used to colour his essentially morbid love-scenes (his 'Liebes' is naturally followed by 'Tod') are used here to paint a serenity literally supernatural. I cannot understand it—it passes over me like a tidal wave—and that matters not a jot either, because it goes on for ever, even if it is never performed again—that final chord is printed on the atmosphere.

Perhaps if I could understand some of the Indian [sic] philosophies I might approach it a little. At the moment I can do no more than bask in its Heavenly light—& it is worth having lived to do that.

There was much still to be achieved, especially in standards of performance—of which Britten had already shown his awareness in 1930 in his comments on Wood's performance of the Eighth—but 1937, we may well conclude, was a watershed in terms of the perception and dissemination of Mahler's music in England. If it had not been for the onset of war in 1939 we may be sure that the English Mahler 'boom' would have materialized at least a decade earlier. We were on the brink of it as the 1930s closed.[11]

There remains only a tailpiece to complete the history of the last symphony, the Tenth, and its special relationship to England, a story which is itself the tale of a completion. As we have seen, the first of its music to be heard in England was the Adagio, in 1948 (a BBC broadcast); and it was only that movement and the 'Purgatorio' that were available in performing editions until the 1960s, when Deryck Cooke, the noted post-war Mahler scholar, brought to completion his performing edition of all five movements of the Tenth. His extraordinary success in deciphering Mahler's sketches—a task that had been thought beyond the bounds of possibility by Schoenberg and Berg and other distinguished musicians approached by Alma Mahler—was revealed in stages, the first in 1960, in the shape of a BBC broadcast of substantial excerpts from the symphony's second and fourth movements, the last in 1964, on 13 August, when the Tenth was heard complete, at the Royal Albert Hall, with the London Symphony Orchestra conducted by Berthold Goldschmidt.

Much controversy has surrounded Cooke's version, and the debate will surely continue. But what cannot be denied was his exemplary skill in providing us with a meticulous and

---

[11] An important document indicating the wind of change that was beginning to blow in the critical assessment of Mahler in England is a contribution made to the *New Statesman and Nation* of 23 Aug. 1941 by Edward Sackville West. This article was prompted, it is clear, by the thirtieth anniversary of Mahler's death, an occasion, according to Sackville West, that gave the BBC the opportunity to describe most of his music as 'preposterously dull' when announcing its 'parsimonious' acknowledgement of the event. Sackville West in the 1930s and 1940s was an influential writer and critic; a little later he was to emerge as a powerful advocate of Benjamin Britten, after Britten's return from the United States (who was to dedicate his famous *Serenade* to him). Britten, indeed, along—perhaps less convincingly–with Lennox Berkeley, is mentioned as one of the young English composers unashamed 'to display practically

their admiration of and indebtedness to' Mahler. Sackville West, albeit intermittently, at least attempted a serious approach to Mahler, while his response to certain works in particular, for example the Fourth Symphony, *Kindertotenlieder*, and the Ninth, revealed a real sensibility which was by no means commonly found in public print at the time. His adverse judgements, however—of the Second for example, Mahler's 'worst, because most pretentious work', and his own (I fear) preposterous comments on the 'arch, tea-shop chinoiserie which disfigures the central portions of *Das Lied von der Erde*, and those dreadful mandolines [one mandolin, actually] in the last'—show how even a well-intentioned and sympathetic critic could be still, opinion-wise, a captive of the bad old days. Nonetheless, it is a text which represented a significant shift in the English evaluation of Mahler in the early 1940s.

continuous transcription of Mahler's sketches (the bulk of the 'Purgatorio' movement and all of the fourth and fifth movements), allowing us to perceive for the very first time the outline of the work as Mahler had left it when his death intervened. Furthermore, Cooke was scrupulous in abstaining from the attempt to make compositional decisions. His edition was 'complete' only in the sense that it presented, *in addition* to a transcription of the sketches—an invaluable source for all future Mahler research—a practical means of performing the work. Cooke enables us to *hear* the stage to which Mahler himself had taken the Tenth; he takes us no further. Whatever the final view of Cooke's work may be, and I find it hard to believe that it would be otherwise than positive, there can be no doubt that the peculiar excitement generated by his unveiling of the Tenth and its overpowering and—until then—hidden inspirations, was very much part of the intense and intensive interest in Mahler and his music that was characteristic of the 1960s.

By then, in England, the Mahler 'boom' was well and truly under way. But, as I hope the information regarding performances that I have laid out above—incomplete though it must necessarily be—suggests, the 'boom' of the 1950s and 1960s had been long prepared in England, stretching back even to the first decade of the century, when the composer was still alive. There was always, it seems, a significant interest in Mahler in England, even when Anglo-Saxon critical objections were at their height and Mahler's fortunes elsewhere in Europe, for reasons of twentieth-century history and politics, were at low ebb. With the onset of the new disseminating technologies—broadcasting and recording—and the proselytization of a highly creative group of musicians (composers and writers), Mahler's cause was won. When I look at the history of the reception of Mahler's music world-wide, it seems to me that England had an honourable and unexpectedly early role to play in the establishing of a reputation which now forms part of our everyday musical life. Who would have thought that in 1903, when the First Symphony was first heard in London?

Additional note (see p. 561, n. 10 above). Britten's performance of the Fourth in 1961 has since been released on CD by the BBC (BBCB 8004-2 (1999)) in its 'Britten the Performer' series, along with the *Lieder eines fahrenden Gesellen* (1972) and two of the orchestral *Wunderhorn* songs (1969). Another fascinating item dating from 1969, and released as a BBC 'Bonus CD' (BBCB 8016-2 (2000)), is Britten himself conducting—probably for the first time—his reduction for small(er) orchestra of the Minuet from Mahler's Third Symphony, an 'arrangement' made originally in New York in 1941. His performance of *Kindertotenlieder* (with John Shirley-Quirk) remains in the BBC Sound Archive. An off-the-air recording of the 'Blumine' movement from the First Symphony, a further unique item—Britten gave its first 'modern' performance at the Aldeburgh Festival of 1967, when he conducted the New Philharmonia Orchestra—is in the possession of the Britten–Pears Library. To date, no recording of the second 'Nachtmusik' from the Seventh Symphony has been located. Neither of these last two performances is to be found in the BBC Sound Archive.

27

Mahler and the Great Tradition: Then and Now

WILFRID MELLERS

I

A mere fifty years ago Mahler was little known in this country, and insofar as he was known was reviled as un-English, which he couldn't help, and neurotically disordered, which he might have done something about. Yet today he vies with Tchaikovsky, another disordered type, in the popularity stakes; it may even be that he is the most performed symphonist after Beethoven. I was knocked over by Mahler's Ninth Symphony during my student days in the late 1930s, when the Second World War loomed. This was not fortuitous: for Mahler's music is about ends and beginnings, and it caught on at a time when Old England's complacency had been seriously ruffled. Perhaps adversity, such as the loss of Empire, helped us to rediscover our true nature, which is that of the first Elizabeth and of Shakespeare. Certainly a Shakespearian epigraph will serve to introduce this essay. *The Winter's Tale*, Shakespeare's late, great romance of death and resurrection, is so called because the child Mamilius, son of a sick King, opined that 'a sad tale's best for winter': a view countered, however, by the comment of an Old Shepherd, stalwart representative of Old England, that 'thou mettest with things dying, I with things new born'. Today, our winter could scarcely be grimmer. No wonder we still turn to Mahler, who knew what winter meant, yet held death in balance with birth.

Although Mahler is not a composer of Bach's stature, he resembles him in standing between worlds. Bach, an axis on which Europe revolved, had roots in an ancient medieval and Renaissance past, while his feet were firmly on the ground of his Baroque Heroic Age, and his spirit prophetically soared in an undivulged future. Mahler was apex to a very long, unbroken tradition which, disintegrating in his work, in the process of decay sowed seeds. His tradition—that of Viennese sonata and symphony—represented the most crucial reorientation in Europe's musical history, for in it Western, 'Faustian' man triumphed through conflict that musically paralleled the turbulent story of Europe. Haydn, an apostle of eighteenth-century civilization, held the balance precisely between the private and the public life, between tradition and revolution, between an age of faith and an age of anxiety. He did not rebel against the Catholic faith he was born into, but unwittingly transformed it from mystical dogma into ethical humanism. Mozart reinterpreted his Catholic faith into personally emotional terms that, being related to the humane mysticism of Free Masonry, caused his Church a measure of disquiet. Beethoven rejected many aspects of the past, including Catholic dogma, but created new belief out of conflict, recognizing with Kant that 'we live in an invisible church, God's kingdom is in ourselves'. Like his exact contemporary William Blake, he knew that 'Without Contraries is no progression', and found in contrariety the precious lifeblood of the spirit annealed. Schubert turned more violently from orthodox Catholicism, but discovered nothing to take its place except a pantheistic faith in the beauty of the visible and audible world that came near to breaking the heart. Brahms reaffirmed Beethoven's middle-period Morality of Power, but made do with stoic fortitude, without resort to religious transcendence. All such inner disturbances inevitably affected the conduct of life out there in the world. Beethoven was a loner who, deafly living in the reality of his music, confessed that he could have no friends. Schubert used friends, as he used music, as a bulwark against an inimical society. Yet Beethoven created a faith through his music, whereas Schubert found only moments of illumination. This is why Schubert's late music is, except on its own musical terms, inexpressibly sad, while Beethoven's late music, also on its own terms, is inexpressibly joyful. There is no deeper experience than the joy Beethoven discovered, though conventional Romanticism came to believe that only unhappiness could be profound.

The change in the attitude to belief that evolved between Haydn and Schubert, and was consummated in agnostic Brahms, reflects the slow deterioration of Austrian Catholicism. Schubert's dismissal of the Church was echoed by most of his successors as Catholicism strayed further from the realities of the nineteenth century. By the time of Franz Josef II, the identification of the Church with oppression could not be gainsaid, and the Jesuitical spirit pervaded every aspect of life. The revolutionary stirrings of 1848 were soon suppressed; conditions returned to an even more reactionary conservatism, and the Concordat of 1855 handed over the entire educational system to the Church. Yet the fact that Austria preserved a fossilized feudalism alone made possible the strange phenomenon of Anton Bruckner: the last of the First Viennese School, and an artist who accepted the tenets of his Church with a guileless simplicity that has been compared with that of a medieval peasant. Yet a moment's reflection convinces us that such an account cannot be the whole truth: for although Bruckner composed liturgical music for his Church, we remember him less for that blissful music than for his nine symphonies, composed perhaps as hymns to God, but also as homage to Beethoven and in affection for Schubert. Since the symphony is a form geared not to faith but to strife, it would seem that, in being a symphonist, saintly Bruckner admitted to doubt, even if the point was that, through conflict, faith might be vindicated. There is point in the fact that he presented the dichotomy endemic to the symphony in its most rudimentary terms. It is also pertinent that in their final works the religious ecstatic Bruckner and the stoic humanist Brahms display close affinities: the winged yet agonized melodic leaps in the Adagio of Bruckner's Ninth Symphony are not altogether remote from the soaring vocal line in the last of Brahm's valedictory 'Serious Songs', especially at the point when the text refers to the 'faith, hope, and love' which remain after Death has taken his toll. Brahms comes to terms with Bruckner, the man regarded, during their lifetimes, as his polar opposite: reminding us that if love is the seed of creation, it does not in the long run greatly matter whether we think of it as human or divine.

II

In this context we may understand Mahler's place as an appendix to the first Viennese school, and as a lever into the second, and into music's future in a general sense. Like Beethoven, Mahler was a composer of strife; like Schubert, he equivocated between reality and dream; like Brahms, he was a composer of elegiac disillusion; like Bruckner, he exalted. But he was born later than Beethoven and Schubert, later even than Bruckner or Brahms; for him the dream was more elusive, the nostalgia more profound.

The sense of alienation that distinguishes the earlier composers becomes, in Mahler, racial as well as spiritual. Though he worked in so rich a musical tradition, he had no spiritual home, and his isolation was intensified by his family's poverty. He was not only a Jew; he was a poor boy who made good. His life was a battle, as much for other people's music as for his own. His fearsome autocracy, his tyranny as an orchestral and operatic conductor, were entirely disinterested: so the hostility he aroused only exacerbated the anguish of his mind. Beethoven could devote all his energies to his spiritual (which meant musical) salvation; even Schubert spent most of his time writing music, though not always the music he was most interested in. But for Mahler composition had to be a spare-time activity— though it was in the deepest sense the meaning of his life. Apart from his songs and orchestral song-cycles, all Mahler's music was symphonic, and he regarded his nine symphonies at once as experiments in spiritual autobiography and as extensions of and comments on the Viennese tradition. The identity between the private and the public life that Haydn and Mozart intuitively manifested becomes in Mahler a conscious testament; these fragments of a glorious but disintegrating past he has 'shored against our ruins', and he soon discovered that from crumbled dust may sprout new seeds: his first two symphonies adumbrate his dual theme. The First Symphony, in D (1884–8), is a tribute to Nature and to agrarian Austria; its melodies are permeated with the inflexions of Austrian folk song, and their simplicity suggests an Edenic ideal to which Mahler, like Schubert, recurrently returned. With him, however, the sense of estrangement, and the consequent threat to primal innocence, is more potent. Schubert oscillates so sensitively between reality and dream (and between minor and major tonality) that he is often doubtful which is which. Mahler, wishing he were a child free of adult perversities and perturbations, may expand the folk-like phrases into periods that grow nostalgically emotive, and may undermine them with enharmonies comparable with, though sometimes more extreme than, those cultivated by Bruckner. Urban popular song, no less than rural folk tunes, may be involved in this direct relationship to an environment. Café songs may be satirically, if on the whole benignly, distorted with nostalgia, while military fanfares, all too familiar to Mahler in his boyhood, may malignly hint at traumas to be released in later years.

Nightmare, as well as heroic aspiration, becomes overt in the gigantic Second Symphony (1887–95). The first movement is a conflict piece in Beethoven's strifeful C minor, with an initial theme that spurts up like a Mannheim skyrocket more apocalyptically titanic than anything in the First Symphony (which, at one stage, was entitled 'Titan'). The skyrocketing theme strives to burst the bonds of the solemn processional rhythm, which is that of a funeral march for a world defunct. Only in the fourth movement does a solo voice offer relief in a lyrical vision of innocence and light, chanting verse from the folk anthology of *Des Knaben Wunderhorn*. That the dream or vision is further from its pristine source than it is in Schubert or Bruckner may be implicit in the fact that although the quasi-folk song effects transition from death to resurrection, the final resurrection chorale, set to Mahler's own version of the aspirational and philosophical poem by Klopstock, is 'subjective' in the same sense as Beethoven's 'Eroica', albeit presented with the naive realism of Bruckner. As a Catholic by birth and instinct, Bruckner believed in a physical resurrection, as Beethoven did not. Mahler, who as a Jew was obliged to convert to Catholicism before he could be appointed Director of the Vienna Opera, related the personal quest for his Grail to his artistic pilgrimage—not only in the shape of the Viennese symphonic tradition he was heir to, but also the much older tradition of Baroque ecclesiastical polyphony, which in turn had roots in the Renaissance, and even in the Middle Ages. Mahler's inclusiveness is another reason why his music so potently haunted later generations of composers, and plumbed the hearts of so great a diversity of listeners.

Mahler's *specific* relationship to the Viennese symphony is most patent in his Fourth (1899–1901), in traditionally benedictory G major. He begins with a classical, symmetrical phrase, at once Haydnesque and folky. This evokes a vanished world. Gradually, Mahler injects into the phrase something of his own rhapsodic exaltation, with widely stretched leaps and sighing appoggiaturas. He doesn't exactly transform the theme into one of different emotional significance, as was Beethoven's wont; but he increasingly hears it from the standpoint of his own self-consciousness. As both intervals and rhythms expand, the phrase's civilized urbanity is tarnished, becoming so free in tonality, as well as in rhythm, that stable diatonicism is undermined. This tonal licence was fostered by the fact that Mahler naturally thought polyphonically; his spare textures are frequently based on two-part writing, and often on fourths and fifths rather than the triad. In this respect, as in others he looks towards Schoenberg, and 'things new born'.

Given his polyphonic bias, Mahler begins to orchestrate in chamber-music style, delineating the orchestral voices with maximum precision. The Italian element, already latent in Mozart and Schubert, is here explicit, and the wheel comes full circle. Haydn's lucent periods had clipped the free vocal phrases of seventeenth-century Italian madrigal and opera into symmetrical, diatonic, instrumental phrases typical of Viennese street music. Starting from Haydn, Mahler elongates and loosens the phrase, until he arrives once more at principles analogous to the Baroque rhetoric of early Italian opera, and to the supple line-drawing of the Italian polyphonists. This means that his conception of symphonic form changes even more radically than does Bruckner's in his attempt to create a symphony based on lyricism—though this is not fully apparent in the Fourth, which is deliberately a revocation of the past, ending, with the appearance of a human voice, in the dream-world of a child's heaven. The text is again from *Des Knaben Wunderhorn*; a folk poem inspires a folk-like directness of melodic speech, and Mahler's highly sophisticated orchestration enhances the effect of naive candour.

If Mahler's First and Fourth Symphonies reveal, in different ways, his relation to Viennese tradition, while his Second adumbrates his generic relationship to 'Europe', a fusion of the specific with the general is consummated in the last complete symphony he wrote, the Ninth (1908–9), perhaps his most fully realized work. The immense first movement is unique among his symphonic entities in that it offers a cycle of experience apparently complete in itself. It opens with subterranean murmurings from which emerges, like an act of birth, a dreamfully singing melody in D major, slowly gaining momentum from fragmentation. That this magical melody embraces both past and future is suggested by the fact that Mahler wrote on the score the words 'O vanished days of youth, O scattered loves'—as though only Proustian retrospection could be a gateway to new life. Each aspiring, at first broken, phrase droops in a sighing appoggiatura, until the dream-song is rudely swept aside by a ferocious upward-surging theme in the tonic minor. This is followed by a sinister, dislocated rhythmic motive that had been implicit in the dream-song, and by a nightmarish trumpet fanfare in dislocated march rhythm. The vast movement proceeds not in orthodox sonata form but in a repetitive process of climax, crescendo, and collapse, based on the fundamental tonal duality of major and minor—with excursions, prompted by Beethoven's late obsession with flat submediants especially between D and B flat. (Consider the 'Archduke' Trio, the 'Hammerklavier' Sonata, the Ninth Symphony, and the *Missa Solemnis*). In Mahler's Ninth each cycle of crisis and collapse exceeds the previous cycle in frenzy, the more so because generated out of polyphonic complexity. The impact of these wildly striving counterpoints changes the significance of the dream-song each time it recurs. Its components become more tumultuous, but ultimately more attenuated, to end in a widely spaced, glassily scored texture closer to 'private' chamber music than to 'public' symphonic rhetoric. Yet although the dream-song evanesces, the whole of the immense movement is enclosed within a dominant–tonic progression. Strained to breaking point, that symbol of the stability of the classical world survives, hanging on the thread of a high D on piccolo and cello harmonic.

If this complex movement is Mahler's personal re-creation of Viennese tradition, the two middle movements are in different senses public statements. The second movement is a

Ländler which is not only nostalgic, but also spectral—the ghost of the agrarian past, scary as well as, or rather than, comforting. Like the personal strife of the first movement, it disintegrates into linear fragments 'shored against our ruins'. The third movement, Rondo-Burleske, is a parody-inversion of two positives of Mahler's art—folk song and monumental polyphony. Both the simplicity of folk tune and the solemnity of the ceremonial Baroque become savagely grotesque, reminding us that the dissolution of the Austrian Empire was to release horrors dreamt of only in the imagination of artists of Mahler's neurotic sensibility. Military tattoos become a mortuary tolling of bells; nostalgia for splendours past becomes dark prophecies of chaos. Even Mahler's horn calls—deriving from heroic gestures in Beethoven, Brahms, and Bruckner—become rhythmically and tonally minatory. Shortly before the end of the movement there occurs a visionary, serio-comic anticipation of the theme of the consummatory Adagio. Hearing the work for the first time we cannot, of course, know that this is what it is, but we are perturbed by its ambiguity of effect, with its operatic turn metamorphosed into figures now ecstatic, now perkily irreverent. We suspect that for Mahler neither folk song nor dogmatic counterpoint can afford salvation. Such peace as he can find must be in communion with his own spirit: so the finale is an unabashedly subjective Adagio, carrying the vast leaps of Bruckner's exaltation and the fluidity of his (and *Parsifal*'s) enharmonies to so extreme a point that the music literally breaks in world-weariness. This Adagio is founded on the same dichotomy between major and minor as had characterized the first movement, though without that movement's latent dramatic conflict. Each harmonically enriched statement of the theme is not, as in the first movement, an evolution towards an unknown goal, but is an intensified restatement of a self-contained melody that may justifiably be called sublime. Although harmony disintegrates into linear counterpoint comparable with that of the first movement and prophetic of so much in twentieth-century music, and although the melody itself dissolves in piteous fragmentation, the ultimate quietude induces peace. Most significant is the fact that the key of this movement is not the first movement's D major, but D flat major, a semitone lower. One could not have anticipated this unprecedented tonal adventure; yet having heard it, one knows it to be inevitable. The subsidence of key is not a death; or if it is, it transports us into a new world: 'thou mettest with things dying, I with things new born.'

In the first and last movements of the Ninth, and no less in the finale of his symphonic song-cycle, *Das Lied von der Erde* (1907–9), Mahler attains a translucent texture that evokes oriental rather than occidental modes of being. The cycle sets Chinese poems with a sometimes overt (pentatonic) orientalism; but in the 'Abschied' appear strange linear arabesques, sometimes pentatonic, sometimes in chromatically inflected modes, occasionally as non-tonal and inhuman as bird calls; while in the protracted suspensions on the word 'ewig', music strains for release from both harmony and metre—the musical synonyms for space and time. Beethoven had to liberate himself from Time and the Will if he were to preserve his sanity. He found his salvation, if Europe did not. In the dying fall of Mahler's last music the madness of a world burns itself out. The obsession with Time, by which Europe had been dominated since the Renaissance, begins to dissolve into Asiatic immobility, and the process is at once a laceration of spirit and an act of birth. Mahler lingers on those sus-pended dissonances, his last hold on the life he had loved with all his richly attuned senses, while the hollow reverberations of gongs and tuned percussion sound like a world's physi-cal disintegration—even like thudding masonry, a literal collapse and catastrophe. Even so, psychological restitution counteracts physical dissolution, including that of Mahler's dying body. The chord on which the 'Abschied' fades to silence is a verticalization of the penta-tonic scale—of all melodic formulae the one most devoid of harmonic implications. So out of harmonic disintegration blooms a flower. In technical terms, the linear principle of ser-ial music is already latent in the texture of the music of Mahler's last years; and new life is not restricted to a local habitation, but illuminates the wide world. If the New Music (chro-matic serialism) emerged from Vienna, Mahler's rebirth had repercussions throughout Europe, and no less in Soviet Russia and in the American New World.

III

Mahler functions as the transition from the first to the second Viennese school. Between his late music and the splendours and miseries of the early Schoenberg of *Verklärte Nacht* (1899) and the *Gurrelieder* (1900–11) there is continuity, if little direct influence. Deeper Mahlerian affinities are observable in some of Schoenberg's 'free' atonal pieces—in for instance the quivering sonorities and flickering contrapuntal imitations of *Das Buch der hängenden Gärten*, and in the exquisite final piano piece from Op. 19, which was con-ceived as a funeral bell tolling for Mahler's death. But the link between Mahler's linear polyphony and Schoenberg's fully-fledged serialism is not deep-rooted, and imaginatively Berg, with his compromising tonality and his teetering between ecstasy and valediction, is closer to Mahler. Overtly Mahlerian is the famous 'D minor' interlude in *Wozzeck* (1917–22), which prepares us for the final catastrophe of the opera. Passages of Debussyan sensitivity and of Straussian voluptuousness occur without incongruity alongside passages of extreme atonality, just as the screwy, banal military music outside Marie's window is no more an anachronism in Wozzeck's terror-haunted world than is the near-diatonic lullaby she croons to her child. Things dying and things new born are once more contiguous: in which context we may note that Mahler's music occasionally anticipates that of Webern, the tenuousness of which would seem to be remote from Mahlerian opulence. Webern's Op. 6 orchestral pieces borrowed something of their radiance from late Mahler; there is even a mini-parallel between the last piece and the crescendo-catastrophe device in the first movement of Mahler's Ninth.

But the most direct Viennese heir to Mahler was Egon Wellesz (1885–1979), who was cre-atively associated with Schoenberg and became his pupil, while being under the spell of Mahler as composer, conductor, and Opera Director. Wellesz made his mark with theatrical works—operas and ballets on classically mythological themes—that achieved equilibrium between Schoenbergian chromaticism and tonal concepts prompted by Wellesz's scholarly research into Byzantine monody and seventeenth-century Italian and Austrian opera. Both Byzantine music and Italian opera were ritualistic arts, one ecclesiastical, the other secular. Mahler and Schoenberg were Austrian Jews whose religion was part of a struggle towards a Faustian self-awareness. Wellesz too was a divided being, a fervent Roman Catholic of half-Jewish descent, a man who deeply respected religious and cultural traditions, the more so when he was exiled from them, during the Second World War, by Nazi persecution. Having settled in England, Wellesz abandoned his association with musical theatre, sensing that in Britain it would offer him scant opportunities. Instead, he turned to liturgical music, which ought to be independent of time and place, and to the symphony, a form he had ignored during his Viennese years. He composed his First Symphony in 1945, the year the war ended, and added eight more between that date and 1971. Despite their English provenance, these symphonies stand directly in the line from Bruckner and Mahler, with long-spanned, wide-spaced, angular themes at once anguished and exalted, and with large-scale structural coherence, sometimes (as in the Fifth Symphony) serially organized, more commonly in chromaticized diatonicism. The conflict between Viennese sonata style and the kinetic motor-rhythms and counterpoint of the monumental Baroque is more Brucknerian than Mahlerian, perhaps because of the ardour of Wellesz's religious conviction; but the 'open' textures and the polyphonic scoring are potently Mahlerian, while the melismatic embroideries around the lines may owe something to the Byzantine aspects of Wellesz's scholarship. In later symphonies the contradictory elements tend to be juxtaposed rather than fused; this makes, in the works written during Wellesz's eighties, for a 'late' style that is formidably gritty and abrasive. This is understandable in view of the fact that his symphonies, written in Oxford, remain essentially Viennese and un-English. The music's anger, too, may bear on its neglect in Wellesz's adopted country, if not in Austria and Holland. This would seem to be one end to the Mahlerian legacy, were it not that native British composers contemporaneously came under Mahler's spell. (See also *News about Mahler Research*, no. 43, Special Issue: Egon Wellesz (Autumn 2000).)

IV

Between Mahler and British composers like Delius and Bax there is no kinship apart from the fact that they were all late Romantics who liked large orchestras; significantly, the Mahler influence surfaces in later composers who were preoccupied with new births, as well as deaths. The most distinctive and distinguished example is Benjamin Britten, who began, when he was a boy of 19, with a virtuoso work in the English choral tradition, appropriately called *A Boy was Born* (1933). If the boy was Jesus, he was also Britten himself who, born in 1913, belonged to the generation that needed to offset English insularity with renewed contact with 'Europe'. What more rewarding contact could there be than Mahler, who was transitional between worlds and cultures? Britten's second major work—the *Variations on a Theme of Frank Bridge* (1937)—was a deliberate break from English pastoralism, and was intentionally eclectic. Nor was it an accident that its theme was borrowed from Britten's teacher, Frank Bridge, who had been relatively impervious to Holst's and Vaughan Williams's rediscovery of our past, and eager to try his hand in fashionable Continental styles from Scriabinesque chromatics, to Ravellian polyharmony, to Stravinskian percussive dissonance, and to Schoenbergian atonality. The particular theme that Britten lighted on was in fact pastoral, and is called an *Idyll*; but if he started from what had been home, he was ready for adventure, and Bridge's stylistic eclecticism merges into the more 'European' synthesis of Mahler, whose search for a Paradise Lost anticipated Britten's essential theme. Unsurprisingly, the identities of Britten and Mahler seem to coalesce in the Introduction to the *Variations*, built on arpeggiated figures in (English) bitonal false relation, and in the first variation, wherein Mahlerian declamatory rhetoric and bitter-sweet harmonic pathos flower in a radiance that is unmistakable Britten.

After the first variation, however, the work momently ceases to be a personal testament and becomes a series of genre pieces—'March', 'Romance', 'Aria Italiana', 'Bourrée Classique', 'Wiener Walzer', and 'Moto Perpetuo'. These range from overt parody of a European stylization to the 'serious' use of a mask whereby an artist may depersonalize experience. Such pastiche and parody are themselves Mahlerian devices, for the Viennese composer's symphonic 'worlds' reflect the eclecticism of his cosmopolitan city. But Britten's work reaches its climax with a return to the pathos and the ceremonial rhetoric of the tragic, doom-laden Mahler in movements explicitly titled 'Funeral March' and 'Chant'. Britten strikes the balance between levity and *gravitas* with Mahlerian precision; the dark and the light aspects of the *Variations* are another, totally convincing, fusion of things dying with things new born. This is why accumulated tension can be resolved in the orchestral virtuosity of a brilliantly developed fugue, which makes unity out of plurality in combining the externalized vivacity of the genre pieces with the interiorized passion of the Introduction and Funeral March.

No less remarkable as a Mahlerian revocation is the *Sinfonia da Requiem* which Britten composed three years later, in 1940, on his first visit to the United States. Significantly, the work, though an official commission, is dedicated to the memory of the composer's parents: a death-consciousness that seems to have triggered a potent interior connection with Mahler's Ninth. The first movement begins with subterranean murmurings that echo the opening of Mahler's Ninth, while the fateful thumps on pentatonically tuned timpani might almost be quotations from Mahler's first movement. In the second movement the orchestral wizardry and the literal deconstruction of the thematic material are as 'realistically' alarming as Mahler's most deathly negations of burgeoning energy; while the paradisal last movement—in the D major of the first (but not last) movement of Mahler's Ninth—affects rebirth in a slowly swaying, lyrically flowering, lullaby. It is significant that Britten's *Sinfonia*, so close to Mahler's elegy on his Old World, should have been written in the New World. Ancillary to this is the fact that *Canadian Carnival* (1939), a minor, 'occasional' piece written as a tribute to his Canadian hosts, displays more or less simultaneously the influence of Old World Mahler and of New World Copland.

Both the Bridge *Variations* and the *Sinfonia da Requiem* indicate, in purely musical terms, how one must lose the self in order to find it. It is as if Britten already knew that he was destined to be an opera composer; and although the cycle of his mature operas no longer needed to be explicitly Mahlerian, Mahler remained a contributory influence over Britten's theatrical idiom, whether in the large-scale canvases of *Peter Grimes* and *Billy Budd*, or the chamber-style intimacy of *The Turn of the Screw*, or in the autobiographical inwardness of *Death in Venice*. A composer of a later generation, Peter Maxwell Davies, drew on Mahler in the parodistic satire and expressionist frenzy of such works as the *Leopardi Fragments* (1962) and the *Eight Songs for a Mad King* (1969). English late Romantics—such as Nicholas Maw and David Matthews—have profited from Mahler's elegiac lyricism and harmonic sumptuousness; David Blake, a composer of the same generation, has indulged in stylistic 'parody' of Mahler in the dream episode in his opera *The Plumber's Gift* (1988).

British composers belong to an old world in need of refurbishment hardly less than Mahler's Austria. New worlds also found succour in Mahler's simultaneous awareness of death and birth. The Soviet Union was hopefully a new, communistic society; and if Mahler seems an improbably elegiac artist to affect a future-orientated man of the Soviet, we must remember that his view of the symphony as an all-embracing world was in an obvious sense democratic. It is not fortuitous that Shostakovich, the Soviet composer most conspicuously endowed with genius, should reveal affinities with a composer who sang the swansong of Western traditions, and should have drawn on Western nineteenth-century conventions in ways closer to Mahler than to Beethoven. In Shostakovich, as in Mahler, self-contemplation leads to self-forgetfulness; subjective grief is absorbed into the vastness of the Steppes and the epic sorrow of a people. There is a hint of this even in his adolescent First Symphony, which has for its slow movement an elegy as much Mahlerian as Tchaikovskian—and therefore 'European' as well as Russian.

Mahler is more potently present in the climactic Fifth Symphony, especially in the first movement, in which the strenuous first theme is recurrently transmogrified, as is the dream-song in Mahler's Ninth. And as in the Viennese work, the heroic main theme finally disintegrates, leaving the Scherzo to turn self-forgetfulness into self-mockery, as though there were no answer except a shrug of the shoulders. Nor does the very Mahlerian Largo, hollowly scored in chamber-music style, provide a subjective 'solution', as does Mahler's Adagio to the Ninth. In *his* finale Shostakovich hopefully returns to the public world, making a triumphal apotheosis justified by the Largo's meditation. The mood is, however, ambiguous, and has been judged, by people who dislike what they believe to be Shostakovich's politics, to be ironic.

Whether or not it is ironic, there can be no doubt that Shostakovich's late works, written after his disillusion with Soviet imperialism had become palpable, are ambivalent in a Mahlerian manner. His Fourteenth Symphony is not really a symphony at all, but rather a song-cycle with orchestra which, like Mahler's *Das Lied*, wrests affirmation from an unflinching confrontation with death. There may be an autobiographical overtone in that by 1957 Shostakovich knew that he was seriously, perhaps terminally, ill; and without interpreting it in crudely political terms, we may think of his impending demise as being also the death of a world that had failed. This notion is supported by the extraordinary Fifteenth (and last) symphony, written in 1972. There seems little doubt that Shostakovich intended this as an epilogic work, riddling it with quotations from his own music—presumably of autobiographical import—and from other composers. It thus becomes a résumé of, and a threnody for, himself and Civilization: the latter embracing not merely the Soviet Union, but also 'Europe'. The concept is close to that of Mahler's Ninth, and the 'Russian toyshop' of the first movement allows a hint of Mahlerian psychological murk to intrude beneath its perky façade. Much of the movement sounds like the wry satire of Stravinsky, interspersed with ludic quotations of the march from *Guillaume Tell* of Rossini—a composer immensely popular in Vienna, in his own day and subsequently. The incompatibility of Rossini's tootling tune with Mahlerian agony and ecstasy is itself Mahlerian in equivocation. Militarism is further debunked in the second movement, which also incorporates a Mahlerian march, bony in texture and funereal in pace, while making references to the pristine First Symphony composed half a century earlier. A short Scherzo may be jokey; but again, in Mahlerian fashion, it is no longer a game. Men too may behave like puppets; we are no longer merely playing with toys.

The finale, the most substantial movement, comments on the previous three. There are many direct quotations, none of them from Mahler, though the quotation from Siegfried's 'Funeral March', intertwined with the 'Tristan' motive, emphasizes that the death that pervades the symphony is that of Europe, not merely of Russia and of Shostakovich himself. Even so, funerals are celebratory; this one is based on that ancient principle of unity, divisions on a ground bass in the rhythm of a chaconne, originally a marriage dance, so that Love and Death are again equated. The bass theme is quoted from the 'Leningrad' Symphony which, in its original wartime context, had symbolized the will of the Russian people to endure. In the Fifteenth Symphony it seems rather a riposte to the grim reaper himself: so we're not surprised that the chaconne-variations should embrace a lifetime's experience, from Tchaikovskian balletic grace, to a tremendous climax in which Siegfried's 'Funeral March' and the dotted rhythm of the first Adagio fuse in majesty and terror. Ultimately the music floats off in a tinkling and clinking of toyshop percussion, into which the celesta inserts a liquid major third. The key is A major, traditionally innocent and youthful; here the effect is as though a child's Eden were distantly glimpsed, far beyond the weary body and sorrowing soul. The symphony is strangely moving and movingly strange: an elegy of Shostakovich, Russia, and Europe which (just) ensures the spirit's survival. But the toyshop Eden of the close offers no clue as to the kind of 'real' world we shall find ourselves living in, if live we do.

Russia was a hopefully New Society that aborted; America was literally a New World, hacked out of a wilderness by death-dealing 'virtuosos of the axe, dynamiters and huntsmen', ballasted by 'an excess of military qualities, of the resourcefulness of thieves, the camaraderie of the irresponsible, and the accidental beauties of silly songs'—as W. H. Auden brilliantly put it in the libretto he wrote for Britten's first (American) opera (*Paul Bunyan*, 1941). If Soviet Russia's greatest composer, Shostakovich, made music resembling Mahler's Ninth Symphony, so did America's greatest composer, Charles Ives. He was a New Englander and Yale man who composed in high Romantic tradition, including two magnificent piano sonatas which are not unworthy successors to Beethoven's still greater 'Hammerklavier'. Yet if the sounds that went to make up Ives's music include those of 'manly' classical composers like Beethoven, they also represent a New World, democratically pluralistic in veering, like late Mahler, between traditional diatonicism, chromaticism, and various modalities as whim or experience dictates; they may also embrace evangelical hymns, parlour ditties, Civil War marches, the ragtime of shanty-town bars and honkey-tonk saloons. In the first movement of Ives's best-known because most performed orchestral work, *Three Places in New England* (1903–14), Ives presents himself as a small boy at 'General Putnam's Camp' during the Civil War years, watching and listening to the continual flux of life as bands pass him and one another on the march. It is difficult to think of any art that conveys more precisely the experience, common in childhood, rare in later years, of being at once identified with the world of appearances and detached from it, so that momentarily one discovers a New Found Land. In the second movement Ives reinvoked 'The Housatonic at Stockbridge': the sounds of murmuring river, rustling leaves, and chirruping birds as aural backcloth to a magic love song for his young bride (charmingly called Harmony Twitchell) of twenty years back. This *renouvellement* of childhood and adolescence explains why Ives's empirical techniques sound (like Mahler's Ninth) at once old and new. The ripe resonance of the texture is potently Mahlerian, whether or no Ives had ever heard the Austrian's music; and its technique likewise embraces contrarious realms of experience, democratically high and low. Again like Mahler's Ninth, this music enters the inner worlds of dream and nightmare, substituting for Mahler's European sophistications a buoyantly New World fusion of orthodox musical conventions with random acoustical phenomena—such as those marching bands, and the love song that drifts, through the mists, across the river. Multiple quotations from diverse sources (church, parade ground, parlour, bar) effect a democratic pluralism; partial recall of past experience, the mechanics and semantics of improvisation, even game-playing and problem-solving, also contribute to Ives's process rather than progress. This ultimate democratization of the symphonic principle occurs in its most extreme form in Ives's Fourth Symphony (1910–16), which he referred to as a world, precisely in Mahler's sense, though it contains no music that *sounds* as ripely Mahlerian as 'The Housatonic at Stockbridge'. Interestingly enough, Mahler the conductor was possibly intending, in the last year of his life (1911), to include an Ives symphony in his New York concert schedule. Although the plan was aborted by death, the relationship between Mahler and Ives itself affirms the interdependence of death and birth.

Mahlerian motives crop up in other American composers—in the orchestral works of Ives's contemporary Carl Ruggles, for instance, though Ruggles's immediate inspiration was the 'free' atonal music of Schoenberg. In the next generation there are Mahlerian over-tones in Copland's Third Symphony (1944–6), consciously a 'big' piece for the concert cir-cuit, though the cantor-like declamatory phrases that surface, Copland told us, from memories of his boyhood, tend to be buoyant rather than angst-ridden. In a slighter vein Barber's famous *Adagio for Strings* (1938)—taken up by Toscanini as a memorial for the Second World War dead—undeniably still communicates. The piece—which bears a clear relationship to the Adagietto from Mahler's Fifth—may be a tear-jerker, but its tears are for real; and the same may be said of passages of high Romantic Mahlerian panache in Barber's opera *Vanessa* (1957), significantly about a love experience frozen in time. An odd appendix to the American theme is provided by George Rochberg, a university composer (b. 1918) who for many years espoused Schoenbergian serialism. Since the mid-1970s, however, he has renounced serialism as a principle, on the grounds that composers of the first, not the second, Viennese school are still our musical bread and butter. In a series of string quartets and other chamber works he has regressed, usually by way of Mahler, to an idiom that refashions Brahms, Schubert, and Beethoven, sometimes in a general stylistic sense poised between tonality and atonality, but sometimes in deliberate 'parody', in the technical sense. His Sixth String Quartet (1978) reverses history in using near-quotation from Mahler as a pointer to strict (eventually quite long) quotation from Beethoven. Whilst there is a certain logic in Rochberg's case, it must surely be perverse, since we are not nine-teenth- or even twentieth-century Viennese.

V

Even so, the exercise reveals how critical is Mahler's place in music's present and in its potential future. Perhaps unsurprisingly, this is strikingly manifest in Mahler's impact on a world even newer than the United States—Australia. Peter Sculthorpe (b. 1929), Australia's leading composer, has come close to creating an Australian vernacular compa-rable with the American vernacular evolved by Copland. In so doing he too has revealed interconnections between life and death: for the Aboriginal Australians were, like the Amerindians, all but wiped out by the technology (and greed) of the white settlers—who paradoxically cannot find an identity for themselves except through a rediscovery of Aboriginal life and culture. Sculthorpe has called on native sources in evolving a contem-porary idiom, which must inevitably also involve Western traditions. Death pervades both the old and the new aspects of his art: in the Aboriginal elements because the natives were a dying race, and in the white elements because the settlers, in an immemorially ancient land, were *ipso facto* alienated. In a series of works called *Irkanda* (which means 'a remote and lonely place'), written between 1954 and 1961, Sculthorpe has made string music stemming from the 'ancient chant' of Aboriginal music, and functioning by the primitive aggregation of tiny cells, pervaded by ostinati and drones that deny temporal progression.

'Western' alienation came into his work first by way of Hungarian Bartók and of Swiss-Jewish Bloch—the former an exile, the latter a wanderer on the face of the earth. In later works, such as *Irkanda IV* (1961) for solo violin, string orchestra, and percussion, Jewish-European Mahler effaces the more overtly alienated Bloch, so that Sculthorpe's heritage from Europe and his antipodal music are more subtly intertwined. Significantly, *Irkanda IV* was written immediately after Sculthorpe, on the death of his father, had returned from study in Europe. Despite his Western affiliations, Sculthorpe makes music for the Ancestors, dedicating this work to the memory of his father. Much later he similarly dedicated another work—this time a *Requiem* (1979) for solo cello, which starts from Aboriginal techniques involving microtones and metrical ostinati, but is also a concert piece for solo cello, fusing Christian plainchant with Aboriginal lament. Although death-haunted, Sculthorpe's later music is also a rite of passage, instigating renewal.

Such life-enhancing properties, sprouting from wilderness and ruin, grow ever more powerful in Sculthorpe's recent music, as though in fulfilment of the rebirths that Mahler's Ninth had envisaged from within European catastrophe. *Kakadu*, a piece for large orchestra composed in 1988, was engendered by the human relationship of love, since it was commissioned by an American admirer of Sculthorpe's music (Dr Emanuel Pepper) as a birthday present for his wife. The title (which in German means parrot) refers to the vast National Park in northern Australia, traditional home of the nearly extinct Gagadju tribe. The opening section reanimates forgotten rituals in rapid motor rhythms and non-developing ostinati, the tune naggingly evolving by syncopated stepwise movement. What Sculthorpe calls a 'chaunt' incrementally gathers momentum through the orgiastic rhythms. That there is desperation within the joyousness testifies to the fact that for the Aborigines power can only be retrospective; and the point is given a further twist in a middle section based on an undulating melody for cor anglais—representing Dr Pepper himself, an individual white man within Nature's cosmos. His theme is as poignantly expressive as the string cries in the *Irkanda* pieces; but that *modern* man is solitary in the wilderness is manifest when the human song is disrupted by the undisputed denizens of the desert—a babel of birds and beasts imitated nor merely by freak string techniques, but by all the orchestra.

The work's positive qualities are consummated when these non-human chirpings and chitterings prove a trigger to human fulfilment. Whatever the fate of the dead or dying Aborigines, modern man learns something from Nature; for man, in the person of Dr Pepper, is purged by the birds. As one wise wit has put it, for Sculthorpe the paraclete is a parakeet! When Dr Pepper's human melody returns, it serves as a bridge to a long section in which modern man and Nature have a proleptic vision of the Dream Time redeemed. The strings sing a chant from Arnheim Land, known as 'Djilile' (or Whistling Duck)—a stepwise-flowing tune that literally enchants, in an undulating rhythm notated by Sculthorpe as a flexible 12/8. The melody faintly murmurs, as an immemorially ancient backcloth to Pepper's cor anglais tune, which is the hazardously hopeful present. This time accommodation between modern man and his remote ancestors has positive consequences: for when the fast ritual dance returns, the human chant is transferred from English horn to reverberating French horns, while the birds and beasts chaotically chatter and chortle on improvising strings. There is a tonal resolution too; for the Whistling Duck tune, originally pentatonic on F or A, is ultimately anchored to a powerful deep C as pedal, over which the work ends with riotously upsurging fanfares.

This music may not have much direct relation to Mahler; certainly it does not use, even exploit, Mahler in the way a central European and richly talented composer such as Henze does, in sundry works both instrumental and operatic. Nor does it indulge in straight 'parody' of Mahler of the kind Berio employs—most notably, by quoting material from Mahler's Second Symphony in his *Sinfonia* (1968–9). Even so, there is a sense in which Sculthorpe's *Kakadu* and other late works such as *Mangrove* (1979) reveal more radically than any other music what was latent within the dissolution and *renouvellement* of Mahler's Ninth. At a fundamental level Sculthorpe reminds us of the words of the seventeenth-century mystic Jacob Boehme:

No people understands any more the sensual language, and the birds of the air and the beasts in the forests do understand it according to their species. Therefore man may reflect what he has been robbed of, and what he is to recover in the Second Birth, for in the Second Coming all spirits will speak with one another.

(*De electionae gratiae* and *Quaestiones theosophicae*, trans. John Rolleston Earle, 1930)

Sculthorpe's fundamentally modest music glimpses that 'Second Coming', beyond however distant a rainbow; and Mahler's crucial significance surely lies in the fact that the 'death of Europe' in his Ninth Symphony hinted at what such a 'Second Coming' must entail. Between them, Mahler and Sculthorpe remind us that music's, as well as civilization's, ultimate problem is ecological.

28

Mahler's Smile:
A Memoir of his Daughter
Anna Mahler (1904–1988)

ALBRECHT JOSEPH, ANNA MAHLER, MARINA MAHLER,
& DONALD MITCHELL

Introduction

In 1997, when some of my old Mahler files were being sorted out, I came across the following text—a concise biography of Mahler's surviving daughter, Anna Justine ('Gucki'), born on 15 June 1904. Her elder sister, Maria Anna ('Putzi'), born in 1902, was to die in July 1907 of diphtheria.

The typescript I found had some minor editorial amendments in my own hand, which meant that Anna must have shown it to me and invited me to run my eye over the English before it was committed to print. I could not immediately recall the occasion, but then remembered that the biographical sketch had been written to appear in a study of her sculptures, comprising some hundred plates, *Anna Mahler: Her Work*, published by Phaidon in 1975, with an introduction by Ernst H. Gombrich. The text appeared there on pp. 114–16, and although it was unattributed, the author in fact was Anna's husband, Albrecht Joseph, who had been the secretary of Franz Werfel (Albrecht, whom Anna had married in the late Sixties, after her move to Italy (see p. 587 below), died on 28 April 1991). Anna of course would have supplied the autobiographical details, and Albrecht have written up her recollections.

Anna was a great human being and a remarkable sculptor. We should know more about her and above all about her work. The biographical sketch that Albrecht prepared was necessarily—and happily—incomplete. It was not until 1988 that Anna herself died, in London. A complete outline of her life appeared in the catalogue of the Salzburg exhibition of her sculptures that formed part of the 1988 Salzburg Festival, an exhibition that, as is recounted below, Anna was not to see. I am much indebted to Marina Mahler, Anna's daughter by Anatole Fistoulari, for supplying the continuation of Albrecht's text, which follows the asterisks and rounds off the story of Anna's life.

It seems particularly appropriate to me that this memory of Anna should serve as a postlude to the contents of this *Companion*, the more so as it includes as complete an account as is currently possible of Anna's few but vivid and infinitely touching reminiscences of her father. It is rare indeed that we read of Mahler smiling; and yet it was his smile that lived on in his surviving daughter's memory. Her memory of it should live on in ours, for which reason we include (Pl. 28.1) that marvellous photograph of a smiling Mahler taken in Holland in 1906 which came to light during the great Mahler Festival held in Amsterdam in 1995. He could never have foreseen that his only surviving daughter was to become a British citizen after her enforced exit from Austria in 1938; how ironic that at the time her father's music was only an occasional and mostly unwelcome visitor to the country which was to offer his daughter refuge!

Donald Mitchell

Anna Mahler: A Biography

Anna Mahler was born in 1904, in Vienna, the daughter of Gustav and Alma Mahler. She did not see much of her father, except when he came home from the Opera for lunch. The soup had to be on the table when he opened the door, and Anna was not permitted to talk during the meal. She did not mind, for she was a quiet child, with a round face and big blue eyes. Aside from his need for silence, the dreaded 'tyrant' of the Vienna Opera was, at home, an understanding, patient, loving father.

Anna's sister Putzi, three years older, was dark and wild, and it was not easy for the younger child to get along with her. In 1907, an infection caused her death. That same year Mahler resigned from the Opera. Anna was put in the charge of a dragon, in the shape of an English governess who insisted on making a Lady of the tiny girl. There ensued much senseless suffering, and no love was lost between the two of them.

When Anna travelled for the first time with her parents to America [in 1907] she laughed and yelled and clapped her hands as the ship cast anchor and started moving. The governess tried to stop her. A Lady should never show excitement. Mahler who stood nearby lifted the child up, sat her on his arm, and cried: 'But she *should* be excited!', and put her down on the ship's rail to give her a better look at the foaming waters.

In New York the Mahlers lived in a hotel [Hotel Majestic] on Central Park. Little Anna was bored, and she disliked the food—tough steak every day. Here, however, she saw and heard her father conduct for the only occasion in her life—Smetana's *Bartered Bride*. She

Pl. 28.1. Mahler at the Zuiderzee coast, March 1906. (Photo: H. de Booy)

was surprised because from her mother's box he seemed so small, as though seen through the wrong end of a pair of opera glasses; but she remembered the music and could sing much of it. Because she was such a quiet child she was allowed, before Mahler went to the opera house [the Metropolitan], to sit next to him at his desk where he worked on his own scores in the mornings. Sometimes he erased a note with a small, curved knife. 'I would not want to be a note', she said once. 'Why not?', her father asked. 'You would erase me.' Mahler laughed, and ran off to tell Alma about it.

Anna went to an American Kindergarten. She spoke German with an American accent, and that was the cause of an ordeal when she returned to school in Vienna, in 1911, after her father's death. She was seven years old then, one year older than her classmates. As a 'newcomer', she was an outcast. During the recess between lessons, she ran as quickly as she could to the school yard and stood there with her back against a tree. It was the best position in which to fight off the attacks of the other girls. These battles were a daily occurrence, but Anna was strong. At home she told her mother nothing about it, not from pride or stoicism, but because on the way home she had already forgotten all about it.

Anna played the piano. She had begun to play as a small child, and then had a number of teachers, quite incompetent ones it would seem, personal friends of Alma from whom the girl learned nothing. Only much later, in 1919, did she get permission to take lessons, during one winter, with Professor Richard Robert. Today she feels that all she ever learned she owes to him (who, by the way, as a music critic in Vienna had been an opponent of Mahler). During her first visit with Robert he asked her if it was easy for her to learn music by heart. Not really, she said, only Bach. He laughed and immediately took her to his heart. (Rudolf Serkin and Georg Szell were at that time also among his pupils.)

During the 1914–18 war Alma refused to send her daughter to a state school. A private tutor came to the house. Once, Anna had to submit to an official examination of her progress. The tutor brought a sock with him, knitted by his sister, and showed it to the authorities as proof of Anna's proficiency in handicraft. She liked the tutor, but when, as an exercise in calligraphy, she copied a poem by Novalis and the baffled young man did not know who Novalis was, he went to Alma and told her that he was no longer needed there, that the girl would be better off by herself; and from then on, Anna had no formal education. Like most gifted young people she absorbed the important things without consciously knowing from where they came. She already spoke English and German. French, Italian, and some Latin, she acquired without much effort. An unpleasant feature were the violin teachers, especially a friend of Arnold Rosé's, Mahler's brother-in-law and the first violin of the Opera orchestra. He himself was an excellent musician but his friend seems to have been an atrocious creature, and Anna despised him. Still, she did learn to play the violin, and later the cello.

But she never considered music as a possible career. Her healthy instinct saved her from the often sad, sometimes tragic, fate of 'famous' children. Quiet growth, undisturbed calm—these she valued above everything. The avoiding of wrong turns and dead ends was undoubtedly easier for her to achieve in the absence of an overwhelming father, but it is only fair to emphasize that the equally overwhelming mother, despite her unbridled, sometimes almost scandalous egotism, refrained from interfering with the development of her daughter in those decisive years. She did not attempt to educate her, but left her to herself, which, in those days, may have looked like neglect, but in reality was Anna's great good luck.

During the 1914–18 war and the following period of inflation there was not much money and very little to eat, but there was music—at first a blissful happiness for mother and daughter, then the source of bitterness and estrangement.

Music was Alma's element. She played the piano practically all day long, superbly, it seems, and Anna stood next to her and turned the pages. Alma played Wagner exclusively. And that became the origin of their serious, insoluble conflict during Anna's years of development: she discovered Bach and turned away from Wagner. It was a terrible blow for Alma. It was blasphemy, an outrageous contradiction of her sacred creed. For days she went to bed, weeping, and in the future, locked the music room when she played the piano. Anna's presence was no longer welcome.

The usual conflicts between parents and children have to do with money, debts, love affairs, alcohol, and all the other excesses of the age of puberty. Here it was Bach against Wagner, that alone, and nothing else. But for Anna and Alma it was deadly serious, a breach that could never be healed. At the same time Anna also discovered the Chinese philosophers. Yesterday she had been an ardent reader of Karl May's sagas of the Wild West. Now it was Lao-Tse and Tchuan-Tse, and it was not an ephemeral infatuation, either. China became for Anna the land of her dreams. Many years later she was on her way to China when the fatal illness of her young half-sister Muzi [Manon] (Alma's child by Walter Gropius, whom she had married in 1916) forced her to abandon the trip at the last moment. But the desire lives on, though there is not much hope any longer for fulfilment of it. [However, Anna was to succeed in at last visiting China more than once in the early 1980s.]

Alma had a 'salon', where she received the celebrities of Vienna. As she was a Great Lady, it was her habit to keep her guests waiting, and Anna functioned as some sort of master of ceremonies and conversed with those bright, amusing people, whose faces she sketched with pencil while talking, until Alma made her entrance. These conversations formed Anna's mind better and more decisively than any university lectures could have done. And even when there was no official reception, the adolescent Anna was almost always surrounded by important people, most of them admirers of her mother: writers and musicians, among them the composer Hans Pfitzner, and the painter Oskar Kokoschka, in whose studio the girl was allowed to sit and watch while he worked on 'Die Windsbraut', that famous monument to his stormy love affair with Alma. Kokoschka went to the war in 1914 and returned seriously wounded. Alma did not marry him, however, but the architect, Walter Gropius. That marriage did not last, and Alma fell in love with the poet Franz Werfel, who became her last husband, and also Anna's faithful friend.

Anna herself married as soon as it was legally possible, when she was sixteen years old. The bridegroom was a young man to whose parents she felt closer than to him. He was a young musician of very modest talent, and Anna went with him to Barmen-Elberfeld where he had a job at the opera house, which left Anna plenty of free time to practise the cello and draw and paint. The marriage was soon dissolved, and Anna went to Berlin to continue her painting. German Expressionism of the post-war years was at its height in the early 1920s, stimulating, controversial, and full of elemental force. Anna knew all about contemporary art but practically nothing of the classical masters.

In Berlin she met Ernst Křenek, and they decided to live together. She continued her painting and went to an art school which taught her nothing; but most of her time and attention she devoted to Křenek, who could write pages and pages of music without ever stopping and whose scores, above all his opera *Orpheus und Eurydike*, after a play by Kokoschka, she transcribed for the piano. Very important to her was the friendship of Eduard Erdmann, the pianist, and of a whole group of young, progressive musicians. Everyone was poor—it was the worst phase of the inflation in Germany—but despite that it was a rich, happy time.

Křenek had been invited to go to Switzerland for a year, and he insisted, for the sake of propriety, that Anna should go as his legal wife. Anna is capable of loving with her whole heart, while still refusing to give up her freedom. Marriage has always seemed confining to her, and the Swiss atmosphere did nothing to mitigate her uneasiness. The situation became unbearable, and there was no way of salvaging the marriage with Křenek.

Anna went to Rome, as a painter. Her teacher there was Giorgio di Chirico, who meant well, but was not a born pedagogue. When his pupil had finished something she liked, she hid it from him—to stop him from 'correcting' it. But Anna had great respect for him as an artist, and she appreciated his generosity, for he refused to accept any fees for his lessons.

A British girl, who was also a student of painting, shared a small apartment with Anna in Trastevere. This developed into a long, close friendship, and both young women set out together on adventurous voyages to other countries, with great enthusiasm and very little cash. They took a train to Yugoslavia, fled from the dirty, verminous railway carriage, and went hiking for many miles, not without incidents and surprises. Later, they were in Spain and Morocco, which was in the midst of the Berber war. Here, too, there was no lack of adventure, even of danger, sometimes; but all these experiences were full of life, unfamiliar and exciting. This friendship came to a sad end when the Englishwoman, married and the mother of a baby, had to be confined, some years later, as hopelessly insane; Anna has lost all trace of her since.

From Rome, Anna went to Venice where her mother owned a house, and from there she went on a trip through Italy with Carl Moll, the painter, a profound connoisseur of classical art, and also her step-grandfather. On this trip she became acquainted with the masterpieces of the Renaissance, but Moll restricted her in every museum to one painting only, all others being passed by at a quick march, for he contended that it was impossible to look at more than one masterpiece with complete attention. Anna stayed on in her mother's house in Venice and painted. Once she decorated the inside of a church, in partnership with a friend. This young man was better at landscape than at heads, so he painted the background, Anna the figures.

Upon Moll's insistence she went to Paris to improve her drawing and painting. She disliked the city as well as the teachers and spent two miserable winters there, almost penniless, in the icy rooms of cheap hotels. Hepatitis, chilblains, and complete exhaustion were the result, but not much artistic progress.

The publisher Paul Zsolnay, who had met her in Vienna, came to Paris. He had fallen in love with Anna and wanted to marry her. For a while Anna resisted, unwilling to give up her freedom again, but eventually she weakened before his passionate assault. She went with him to Egypt, swayed on the backs of camels, and dutifully climbed a pyramid. The acquaintance with ancient Egyptian sculpture and architecture provided full compensation for these experiences.

In Vienna, she moved with Zsolnay into the small Palais Kaunitz in Hietzing, an eighteenth-century jewel. Disappointed with her efforts as a painter, she turned to sculpture. The technique of this field of art which, thenceforth, she never quitted, and to which she devoted all her future life, she learned almost entirely by herself. Fritz Wotruba, then himself beginning as a sculptor, sometimes came to her studio to advise her. Anna regards him as her teacher, but the lessons seem to have been very sporadic and informal. From the beginning she worked in stone, preferably on big blocks, without any model. In 1937, the World Exhibition in Paris showed a more than life-size stone figure of hers, which was awarded the Grand Prix.

Anna had a daughter (Alma) by Zsolnay, but again this marriage was so unsatisfactory that she decided to escape. That would have been achieved by the carefully planned trip to China which she had to cancel because of the illness of her half-sister, Muzi Gropius [memorialized in Berg's violin concerto of 1935]. Anna stayed on in Vienna, separated from her husband, working and living in her studio, and concentrating entirely on her work. Only as the Nazi takeover became an immediate threat to the life of Austria did her interest in politics, dormant until then, awaken; and she tried, as did many others, with every means at her disposal, with the impact created by her great energy, and by marshalling her personal contacts with many influential people, to stop the catastrophe at the last minute—naturally without success. She had to flee, and went to London. All her possessions that remained in Vienna, especially her extensive library, were stolen by the Nazis. All her work, which she had to abandon, was destroyed by bombs during the war.

England meant safety, but in extremely modest circumstances. There was hardly any money at all, severe cold during the winter, and frozen waterpipes. She was not really disturbed by the difficulties, and continued working. Throughout the entire war Anna lived in London, relieved to have escaped in time from the paralysing spectre of Nazi terror. She admired the determined calm and firmness of the British and loved them more every day. She became a British subject. In these years she executed many portraits, but many sculptures were also created during the way in London.

Here, she married the conductor, Anatole Fistoulari, born a Russian. By him, she had a second daughter, Marina. Fistoulari formed a company for the production in England of Russian opera in Russian. The first venture, Mussorgsky's *Sorochintsï Fair*, was an unexpected success. Anna was hired as a coach for the singers and as a rehearsal pianist for the ballet, but her main concern was to keep an eye on her husband and the seductive ladies of the troupe. The company had a promising future, but bad management led to its premature dissolution. Fistoulari then founded an orchestra of his own in London, and conducted many concerts, but the material success was insufficient and financial collapse ensued.

Anna had to leave him, not only because external circumstances became impossible, but also for personal emotional reasons; and she went to her mother in California, still hoping to be able to provide some financial help for her husband from there. With her went her little daughter, Marina. Anna stayed in America. She had an exhibition of her work, partly created in Los Angeles, partly shipped from England after the war. She taught sculpture at the University of California and made more portraits, some of which are today in prominent locations in public buildings, but it proved impossible to provide for the child and for herself with what she was able to earn. Furthermore, she had to leave the United States and go to Canada for ten months, while waiting to obtain an immigration visa for the USA. In Montreal, she had, to start with, no money at all, and worked for a short time as a waitress in a drug store. By and by, some people heard about her and wanted their portraits done, and the situation improved so quickly that she regretted having to leave Montreal when at last the visa arrived.

Back in Los Angeles, she found an old but cosy house in a quiet, green lane among the hills of that enormous city. Here she worked without pause. There were more exhibitions, in Los Angeles, La Jolla, California, and Phoenix, Arizona, and even some sales; and there were more portraits, and eventually the big project of the Tower of Masks for the foyer of the theatres of the University of California at Los Angeles. That promised to be the occasion for the long overdue breakthrough and wide public acclaim. But her work did not conform to the extremely abstract fashion of those years, and the recognition she had so much good reason to expect, failed to materialize.

In 1964 Alma's death made her financially independent. She leased a flat with studio in London and bought in Italy an ancient Palazzo in the hills of Umbria, unpretentious on the outside but inside of very noble proportions, festive and grand. She came to realize, though, that this beautiful building was much too cold during the winter and not easily heated. So Anna decided to settle in the nearest town, Spoleto, where she spends most of the year in her town house, which is also a very old structure, now comfortably remodelled. She has given the city of Spoleto three of her stone figures which have been placed in fine situations and please the townspeople and the tourists. There is a studio on the ground floor of the house in Spoleto, and here she can continue to work in stone.

Albrecht Joseph

*   *   *

She continued to work, dividing her time between Spoleto and the house in Los Angeles which had the great advantage of a large outdoor parking lot which served her as an outdoor studio for stone carving and in which she had the most important tool for working—natural daylight. It was scattered with sculptures in all sizes and colours of stone, the accumulated work of many years and there was always a new work in progress. Because of the Californian weather she could work out of doors nearly all the year, and had the full benefit of daylight around the clock. In summer, due to the exhausting and blinding heat of the sun, she worked only in the early mornings, and the rest of the day was spent reading, resting on her bed and playing solitaire on the dining room table, this daily card game just another form of thinking and concentrating on her work. Years passed in this way. Her companion and then, from the time that she moved to Italy, her husband, was her old, close friend of many years, Albrecht Joseph, whom she had first met in Vienna during previous lives and marriages and then met again at Alma's house in Beverly Hills when she moved there from England. Albrecht had been a close friend of Werfel and also his secretary. So life passed in this way with the years spent divided into half-year periods between Los Angeles and Spoleto with short and well-loved visits to her London home where she had also an indoor studio where she mostly did clay portraits and small figures. And out of this settled and always disciplined daily life came her best work. Until, feeling suddenly bereft of ideas and feeling that her creative life was probably over and that she had perhaps reached 'old age', she revived an old dream and set out for China, returning after that journey for two further longer visits, where the astonishingly new shapes of landscapes and the sight of many unknown sculptures which she discovered in her treks by small planes to the many caves outside Peking, stimulated new ideas and brought to life again her wish to work. And she began again, and again worked as usual, until only a few days before her death. She fell down in Los Angeles while working outside on a large stone figure, hurt her leg and was taken to hospital where her strength began to fail her. But she flew in spite of this to London, accompanied by her doctor and by her daughter, Marina, determined that London should be only a resting place on her way to the long desired exhibition at the Salzburg Festival. But, in London, trying with all her considerable force to live, she lost all her strength in the last attempt to regain it and she died at midnight on 5 June 1988, just days before her 84th birthday.

Some months before her death she had embarked on two large stones, one in Spoleto, the other in Los Angeles that she was working on when she fell, undertakings that indicated a new and fascinating direction in her work. Her ideas, it was apparent, were in a state of flux and fresh, simplified shapes were emerging. Perhaps it is the happiest frame of mind in which an artist can die, but it leaves us who remain full of curiosity as to what her new works would have led to, and how those works would have looked.

Marina Mahler

Postscript

There was a later event in which I was involved which gave rise to further documentation of Anna's memories of her father. This was a TV film about *Das Lied von der Erde* I made with Barrie Gavin for BBC2 in 1986 entitled *The Jade Flute*, for which I interviewed Anna in her mews flat in 20 Kinnerton Street, London SW1. She had a studio on the ground floor. It is only very recently that I recovered from an old file a complete transcript of that interview,[1] and in looking through it after such a long interval of time—some eighteen years!— I was struck how vividly it brought back to life Anna's unique manner of reminiscing, often halting in its delivery, often ungrammatical in syntax and idiosyncratic in its choice of words, often elliptical in character, i.e. sentences interrupted or not concluded and left suspended in the air. And yet how touching and above all *immediate* these recollections are, especially if they are reproduced virtually *verbatim*, as they are here. I have here and there introduced some minimal editing, on those relatively few occasions when I thought the reader might have to work too hard to receive what it was that Anna was trying to communicate; and I have excluded the repetitions and repertory of vocal sounds that substituted for words when one was waiting for these to materialize (sometimes they didn't). But in general the gains are immense when compared with the loss of authenticity that the superimposition of an editor's hand unavoidably introduces. My own questions I have tidied up so that they help, I hope, to provide a context for Anna's answers.

DM I know Anna that you don't have a lot of recollections of your father, but I remember you telling me once that one of your memories was sitting by your father's side at a desk or something of the sort when he was . . .

AM . . . Oh yes, every morning . . .

DM . . . and what was it you remember?

AM . . . Well, children wake up early and so did he and he worked . . . It was in New York, I remember, his room, it was very small but I was allowed to stand and watch him, you know. And it was always, I know the little knife, the shape of the little knife [see also p. 583 above and p. 590 below] and that's why for instance I know exactly what his hands look like. And things like . . . I know stories, you know in my memory, but oh, very few, very funny ones. And . . . but things like the voice and the hands . . . and . . . the smile when he, you know, I mean I know that so definitely. I mean . . . I've been thinking that we'll talk today and, and something came to mind which I hadn't thought about . . . well . . . for the last hundred and twenty years [*sic*] . . . and . . . that was once he took me . . . to Central Park and in the morning—it must have been a Sunday morning or something . . . I wonder that he had the time, but that happened and I had a new pair of roller skates . . . I was . . . not very clever with things like that, so I put them on and as soon as they moved, bump—I was . . . Mahler took me and put me on my feet again. As soon as . . . they moved, I was down. He took me and put me up again. Now, I don't know how often that happened. He didn't scold . . . he didn't laugh. He just was completely serious and matter of fact . . . you know. Oh that's how things are, you know, I mean . . . And that was very strange because either

---

[1] The reference on the document reads, 'Mahler Workshop—1.LMA M257W, "Donald Mitchell and Anna Mahler" ', Reels 14 and 15. Have the reels survived, I wonder?

you laugh, you know, makes you angry—it did nothing of the sort. He just put me on my feet again. And expecting me to be down again . . . Well . . . it's not a story you know, but a sudden memory which I really didn't have for a long time.

*

AM   . . . the composer I would never say [call?] anything else but Mahler, you know? And the other one was somehow [not] Mahler, you know. And the other one was very difficult, he just ate and it was no pleasure. Only for health, so the food was awful—it was quite dreadful. And children are not asked, you know, what [they liked] to eat. I mean, I was a horrible eater and there is a story I find very interesting and that, after all one shouldn't forget. I was 6 then so, I mean . . . it was, I'm quite sure, the last year of his life and I was awful for a very long time, so suddenly he took notice of it and thought and said, Well—Gucki I was called—go out and send [in] your friend Gladys . . . and I did that, came in [returned] as Gladys . . . and sat down and said 'Gucki's very silly, this is awfully good', and ate it without any trouble whatsoever. And that worked every day. Now, that he understood . . . I was not allowed to talk, you know, and that is very disturbing for a child, I mean I shouldn't have been eating with the grown-ups you know . . . that made it impossible for me to swallow, and he must have noticed that, and the reason because that was very early—a grown-up now would easily have thought of that—but then I thought it was very, very strange because . . . it worked every day. Every day again I couldn't swallow, I was sent out, came back as Gladys . . . I think that's strange, don't you think so?

DM   I think it shows what an extraordinary psychologist your father was.

AM   Exactly.

DM   Very early on.

*

DM   Anna, I remember something else you told me once, something about a knife, scratching out a note . . . What was that?

AM   Oh that's a story I can't . . . Look I can only tell you what I remember . . .

DM   Yes, but . . .

AM   That's a story which I was told, you know, so it's no good . . .

DM   But what was the story?

AM   Well, that I, apparently, said that I would not like to be a note because then he [Mahler] would scratch me out, you know. But I mean I don't remember it, so I keep away from what I was told.

DM   That was a family memory?

AM   Yes, yes, yes. He apparently was moved by it and went and . . . but I don't remember that of course. I can't be sure, but I had a feeling that it wasn't the score, that it was a part [i.e. an orchestral part] where he had to scratch out one note for, let's say, one of the violins, because he did the same several times. That he would have done [would have had to do] that himself is terrible.

DM   It's true, though, that he often had to do that, correct the orchestral materials of his own works.

AM   Well, there you are. I mean, so it's not so silly because I have the feeling, memory ... by [from] memory of what I saw that it was not a full score, that it was parts, you know. Notes were bigger and somehow ... so that's possible, you think?

DM   It's absolutely possible.

AM   And what's always the same, you know, he took another and the same note.

DM   Yes, and that would have really caught your attention as a child ...

AM   Yes, yes.

DM   ... this 'attack', as you saw it, on one note ...

AM   On one note—yes.

DM   ... and erased under your eyes.

AM   Yes.

DM   Do you remember your sister at all?

AM   ... there I have just one glance. And I must say that it speaks very badly for me this glance. I was, still small that I was ... put up on a very high piece of furniture. I don't know, to be dressed or something of the sort, and suddenly ... the much bigger—she was smaller than I. And that must have impressed me deeply because I, she treated me abominably, yes. And she was a very wise creature and I was terrified of her.

DM   Do you remember playing with her?

AM   No, no, no. That's the only moment I remember and I think really, I mean, you know, to be able to look down on her gave me great pleasure—maybe I wouldn't have remembered it otherwise.

*

DM   Anna, do you remember at all playing at Toblach with other children ...

AM   Yes, I remember one, and that was from the other family who lived [in the Toblach country-cum-farmhouse], you know ... Trenker [the family]. And she must have been my age but just a picture [is what I have in mind], you know. I don't remember play-ing; and later on, during all my youth, I mean, I hated childen and never played with other children. I really hated them. And when my mother invited a friend of hers to bring . . . oh my heart fell when I knew that somebody was coming up with . . . very lonely, I mean I wanted to be lonely. And very silent. That's why I didn't disturb Mahler, you know, because I never said a word, no.

*

DM   Where was your room? (Here I showed Anna a photograph of the farmhouse.)

AM   On this side, I know. And there was wallpaper and a big catastrophe because I loved getting the paper off somewhere and, oh God, I mean the fuss the Trenkers made because I had ruined the awful wallpaper, you know. Dark and full of flowers. Awful.

*

DM   Do you feel you have roots, say, in Vienna?

AM   No. I have no feeling of 'Heimat', you know . . . home, home . . . I can't imagine what it means to be homesick, I mean I can't imagine it. But I think that might be because I spent three winters very early in New York, and so that cut off this belonging, you know? I mean, I then spoke very very good American. And I had an American accent in German . . . which is really funny. Well, then came the war and . . . but somehow, something [was] left, so that when I spoke English after, long after, the war, there . . . it wasn't difficult somehow . . . I feel at home in English very much. Naturally I speak better German . . .

*

DM   There you are, you really are the last Mahler, aren't you? In 1986, the only survivor of the original Mahler family. How does it feel?

AM   Which Mahler do you mean? The composer or the person [the man]?

DM   Both.

AM   Well, I mean, the person . . . very, very sad; but the other [the composer] is just not dying, you know. I mean, I don't feel that I have more to do with him than you . . . you know. Everybody who really loves him and knows so much about him, knows more about him than I do.

DM   But you're undeniably his daughter?

AM   Yes, yes. I haven't yet figured it out quite what that does to one. I mean, maybe in five years, maybe I'll know, or in ten—you know . . . we'll talk again.

We never did.

*   *   *

In the absence of a properly researched biography of Anna—and how strange it is that we still await a *serious* biography of her mother, Alma—we must be grateful for those recollections which were the result of a reluctant Anna submitting herself to inquisition, reluctant because she was always touchy about approaches made to her on the grounds of her being 'Mahler's daughter'. She had softened a bit in this respect in the 1980s, and indeed already in the 1960s, when she had talked to that pioneering Mahlerian in the United States, William Malloch. This important source, readily accessible these days in recorded form on a CD, 'Mahler Plays Mahler', *The Welte-Mignon Piano Rolls* (The Kaplan Foundation, Pickwick, GLRS101), also has the inestimable advantage of allowing us to hear Anna's own throaty voice. My brief transcriptions from that interview introduce memories—her father's gait, the story of the scissors with an independent life of their own—that did not surface in 1986. And of course once again we encounter the smile, 'that little smile . . . the most lovely smile, and so warm' that Anna remembered in the 1960s and again in the 1980s, and which generated the compilation of this chapter.

*

AM   I remember him very well, I was nearly seven when he died, but my memories are not anecdotes. I have nothing to say. They are that I remember his voice; I remember his hands; I remember his walk, his very strange walk. I know *exactly* what it was because

I walked with *him* [see Pl. 28.3]. People say it was a nervous tic; it wasn't. It *was* irregular but it was a change of pace; every few paces he just changed—

WM   He shifted gear.

AM   He shifted—yes—that was all. Why he did it I don't know. It was somehow nervous apparently but it was not a tic—it just shifted. So I walked with him as a child often so I know these things. And I remember these terrible lunches, you know. I wasn't allowed to speak and he was always absorbed and thinking about other things and we had dreadful food. Anyhow it appeared to me so. But I do remember when he suddenly took notice of me, that complete change, and as it were, a burst of warmth. That I remember so well. It didn't happen often because he didn't have time. But suddenly he took notice of me and the change in the face—these are my memories. It is so strange that I really only recognize two or three photos. That doesn't sound cold to me, you know. And there suddenly, oh! that is the memory. It is so personal. And also it is always the pictures of the very last time when he was, my God, old. He was fifty.

WM   Nothing.

AM   But he was old. In some way he was so — spent. He was really lined. It was a dramatic face in his last years. [See Pl. 28.2.]

WM   And the pictures that you recognize are the ones that dramatize that particular period.

AM   Yes. And also this little smile. I mean, he had the most lovely smile and so warm, but from this mask-like behaviour. You know, the sudden burst is maybe my main memory. For instance, one thing I always sort of, you know, fiddled about and I had a pair of scissors and I cut into something. And then Mummy said, 'Hmm, hmm, did you do that?' And I said 'No, of course not.' And I lied and I lied. And I was sitting in the sitting-room with Mummy and Mahler came in and he knelt down and he said, 'Don't you think that the scissors might have suddenly moved?' And I said (*as though crying*), 'Yes.'

WM   And you couldn't do anything to stop them.

AM   No. Well, there I confessed you know. Well—

WM   I knew there was another story—

AM   Well, there you are. But I mean, this is not a story—but it's just—how can you describe this? I mean, I can see it in front of me, I know it. But these things can't be said.

*

Anna was buried in Highgate Cemetery on 19 June 1988. My obituary had appeared in the *Guardian* on 7 June:

> Anna Mahler, sculptor and Mahler's daughter, has died just before her 84th birthday. Every encounter was an occasion. The first time I met her, not long after I had published my first book on her father, her opening volley ran something like this: 'Don't ask me about Mahler's music. I don't know all of it and some of it I don't like.'
>
> A characteristic posture that: combative, independent, uncompromising, spirited. But a moment afterwards her mood might change and one would be rewarded with one of those radiant smiles that was quite as typical of her as her pugnacity.

Pl. 28.2. Mahler and
Anna in Toblach, 1909

Pl. 28.3. Mahler and
Anna walking in Central
Park, New York City,
1910

Pl. 28.4. Anna,
Los Angeles, May
1988

In this, she was less remote from her father's music than she might have imagined, full of contradictions and yet at the same time an extraordinarily coherent and consistent personality, and creative to her fingertips, not least at the keyboard: she was an accomplished and forceful pianist.

She probably needed all the attack that she could command. There was her famous father for a
start, who died when she was six years old. Her few—though ineradicably vivid—memories of him
were deeply touching: she recalled his smile, his patience, the shape of his hands. But she had to
keep quiet and not disturb him.

Perhaps the sense of being overwhelmed by her past came later, and especially with the immense
growth in Mahler performances. She made it clear that she suffered somewhat from always being
acknowledged as 'Mahler's daughter'.

She was that too, and proud of being so: but she was also herself a creator, a sculptor of great distinction and originality, largely self-taught, though she always recognized the influence and inspiration of the Austrian sculptor, Fritz Wotruba. Perhaps because of the genius, glamour and talents
of her immediate family—her mother, Alma, an independent social and cultural phenomenon—
Anna was obliged to struggle hard to win recognition on her own merits. Her portrait busts include
many of the leading musicians of her day—Schoenberg, Berg, Klemperer, Schnabel, and others—
and these are surely among her best work.

But there are also visionary pieces, some of them conceived on a monumental scale, for the most
part studies of the female body, which must claim future attention for their serene and sometimes
classical beauty. It will further sadden her daughter Marina that Anna has died (in London on her

way from California) just before an exhibition of her work planned for Salzburg this summer, itself a sign of the slow but steadily increasing recognition of her stature.

As Anna grew older, she relaxed a little and became ever more beautiful in her looks [see Pl. 28.4]. (She was married five times, including two musicians, Ernst Křenek and Anatole Fistoulari.) She had the grandeur and nobility of her father's face, and it was perhaps his generous smile that lived on in her. I hope she would forgive me for suggesting that she was unmistakably one of her father's creations.

Donald Mitchell

29

Mahler's First Compositions: Piano Quartet and Songs

JEREMY BARHAM

Piano Quartet

If contemporary accounts of Mahler's early life are accurate, his youthful works—those produced up to his final year at the University of Vienna (1880)[1]—were both numerous and generically diverse.[2] However, almost none of this output has survived, and, together with the three songs of 1880 discussed below, Mahler bequeathed only one complete instrumental work written during this period: a movement for piano quartet in A minor which probably dates from 1877.[3] According to Bauer-Lechner, in a conversation that took place approximately twenty years later on 21 June 1896, Mahler referred to his early compositions as follows:

The best of them was a piano quartet [. . .] which was written at the end of my four years [sic] at the Conservatoire, and which provoked a very favourable response. Graedener kept it with him for months and was so pleased with it that he performed it at Billroth's. I sent the quartet to a competition in Russia where it was lost.[4]

---

[1] Mahler enrolled at the University of Vienna for the winter semester of 1877–8, the summer semester of 1878, and the winter semester of 1879–80.

[2] 'Catalogues' assembled by Donald Mitchell (EY, 116–20 and 322–4) and Henry-Louis de La Grange (HLG(F), i. 915–17), for example, refer to abortive opera projects, songs, and song fragments, as well as symphonic, chamber, and piano works.

[3] For further details of the history and provenance of this and other contemporary works see Renate Hilmar-Voit's foreword to the critical edition of the quartet (*Klavierquartett, 1. Satz*, ed. Manfred Wagner-Artzt (Sämtliche Werke, Suppl. III; Vienna: Universal Edition, 1997), pp. viii–x) and Jeremy Barham's review of this edition (*Music & Letters*, 80 (1999), 163–5). The manuscript of the quartet is

housed in the Pierpont Morgan Library, New York, as part of the Bequest of Mrs Wolfgang Rosé.

[4] NB-L, *Erinnerungen*, 55, my translation. Mahler in fact attended the Vienna Conservatory from 1875 to 1878, during which time two *quintet* movements of his won first prizes in the 1876 and 1878 Conservatory composition competitions. Theodor Billroth (1829–94), eminent Viennese surgeon, amateur musician, and close friend of Brahms, became Professor and Director of Operations at Vienna University in 1867. Hermann Grädener (1844–1929), violinist, conductor, and composer, taught harmony and counterpoint at the Vienna Conservatory from 1877 to 1913, although Mahler was not his student. See also p. 517 and n. 1 above, and Mitchell, *EY*, 279–80, for further details of the Russian competition.

If the reference here is to the surviving quartet, as now seems likely despite the loss of a copy of the manuscript, then the composer's own endorsement and the work's status as the only extant representative of a genre to which Mahler would never again return together suggest that the piece deserves serious attention.

In light of this and the scarcity of Mahler's extant juvenilia, it is almost impossible to examine the movement without searching for clues that bear upon Mahler's future compositional development and, arguably in this regard, without investing the work with undue importance. The relatively few scholars who have studied the quartet in any detail have to a certain extent all been tempted down this path.[5]

Most commentators agree that the influence of Beethoven, Schubert, Schumann, and Brahms can be traced in the movement, which is hardly surprising given the musical repertoire to which the young Mahler was exposed during his early years in Vienna, whether in his piano lessons with the Schubert aficionado and chamber-music performer Julius Epstein, through contemporary performances of the late works of Beethoven by the quartet led by the Director of the Conservatory, Josef Hellmesberger, or in the orchestral concerts of the Vienna Philharmonic.[6] Commentators disagree, however, in their assessment of, on the one hand, the relative importance of the quartet's thematic content as opposed to its formal characteristics for Mahler's future compositional practice, and, on the other hand, the intrinsic merit of the formal processes themselves.[7]

Locating thematic links may be interesting at one level,[8] but in terms of scale, general melodic character, and certain aspects of harmonic idiom, the quartet—perhaps unsurprisingly—is considerably far removed from the spirit and technique of Mahler's mature symphonic works. Moreover, no significant link can be traced to the instrumental characteristics of Mahler's later symphonic chamber-music style. It is undoubtedly the work's structural processes (whether regarded in a positive or a negative light), filtered through the composer's instinctive dramatic understanding, which offer the most interesting insights, for they give early glimpses of Mahler's ability to generate considerable emotional power through dialogue with the gestures of perceived formal conventions.

[5] Dika Newlin, 'Gustav Mahler's Piano Quartet in A minor', *Chord and Discord*, 2/10 (1963), 180–3; Peter Ruzicka, 'Editorial Remarks' in his first published edition of the work (Hamburg: Sikorski, 1973), and 'Gustav Mahlers Klavierquartett von 1876', *Musica*, 28/5 (Sept.–Oct., 1974), 454–7; HLG(F), i. 933–5; Klaus Hinrich Stahmer, 'Mahlers Frühwerk — Eine Stiluntersuchung', in id. (ed.), *Form und Idee in Gustav Mahlers Instrumentalmusik* (Wilhelmshaven: Heinrichshofen, 1980), 10–28; and Mitchell, *EY*, 123–7.

[6] For further information on aspects of this repertoire see pp. 7–11 of Herta Blaukopf, 'The Young Mahler, 1875–1880: Essay in Situational Analysis after Karl R. Popper', in Stephen E. Hefling (ed.), *Mahler Studies* (Cambridge: Cambridge University Press, 1997), 1–24,

[7] Newlin ('Gustav Mahler's Piano Quartet', 180–1) traces melodic links between the first and third themes of the quartet (bb. 3–4 and 54–5 of the critical edition) and the principal theme of the Sixth Symphony's first movement (I and II violins, bb. 8–9); Ruzicka ('Gustav Mahlers Klavierquartett', 456) compares the quartet's violin cadenza (bb. 218–21) with the melody in first violins of bars 236–7 of the Ninth Symphony's first movement. See also the divergent evaluations of the quartet's formal construction in Newlin, 'Gustav Mahler's Piano Quartet', 183, Mitchell, *EY*, 126, and Stahmer, 'Mahlers Frühwerk', 28.

[8] There may be some significance in the fact that the movement of the Sixth Symphony from which Newlin's examples are taken shares the same key as the quartet.

The sectional division of the movement by repeat signs and double bars would indicate—at least visually—that Mahler adopted an unambiguous sonata-form plan.[9] Such a plan would no doubt have been a prerequisite, either explicit or implicit, of Conservatory work, whether or not the results were intended for entry into institutional competition. Yet, given that the nineteenth century was the era in which the concept of sonata form had been subject to both its most rigorous theoretical codification and its most intensive compositional manipulation, one might expect that by the latter part of the century even a novice composer would be sensitive to the creative tensions arising from these developments. In Mahler's quartet, it is perhaps the curiously ambiguous role of the three principal themes around which the movement is built (bb. 3–4, 42–8, and 54–7) that provides evidence of such sensitivity. The subdued beginning, in which the instruments gently pass around the opening theme among themselves, suggests quiet emergence into the movement 'proper' by way of a slow introduction; but as the section progresses, the extent of the imitative repetition and development of the theme somewhat undermines this impression. By the time the second, 'determined' (*Entschlossen*) theme appears (b. 42), separated by a double bar, its 'first-subject' qualities are in doubt; the brevity of the second theme—a mere eleven bars—only contributes to this sense of doubt. Moreover, the almost immediate juxtaposition (at b. 54) of the third theme—contrapuntally combined with varied statements of the first theme in lower strings—represents a toying with the established sonata-form convention of preparing new ideas through transition and thus forces a reappraisal of the second theme's function. By shifting to a chromatically inflected C major in its last three bars and preparing (at least tonally) for the major-mode opening of the third theme (see bb. 48–54), it is the resolute second theme itself which seemingly takes on the role of a transition.

If one is seeking prophetic elements in Mahler's quartet, this kind of blurring of formal categories and thematic types, carried out so determinedly in, for example, the first movement of the Third Symphony nearly twenty years later, would be a useful starting point for discussion. Rather than embodying some vivid Beethovenian conflict of opposing tonalities and thematic ideas, the quartet's relatively monotonal 'sonata-form exposition' dominated by A minor fulfils more the function of what Adorno, in the context of Mahler's mature symphonic writing, would call a presentation of 'dramatis personae, whose musical story is then told'.[10] More than this, however, the sense of emergent drama in the movement's 'exposition' is embodied less in specific tonal and thematic oppositions than in broader fields of conflict between major and minor modes, flat and sharp keys, and fulfilled as opposed to thwarted expectations—all elements that would become central to Mahler's later idiosyncratic techniques of large-scale construction, underpinning the intense expressivity of his mature compositional 'voice'. For instance, several short-lived forays

[9] Throughout this discussion of the movement, reference is made to the critical edition by Manfred Wagner-Artzt (see n. 2 above), which I gratefully acknowledge, from which Ex. 29.1 is taken. This supersedes the first published version of the quartet (see n. 4 above) which contains a significant number of textual errors. For further details of these editions see Barham (review cited in n. 3 above).

[10] Adorno, *Mahler*, 95. Note the foreshadowing of the third theme in bb. 32–4

into major-mode tonalities during the 'exposition' occur either in, or on the flat side of, the relative major, their progress frustrated in different ways by the surrounding blanket of minor-mode harmony (see bb. 19–24, 35–42, 54–7, and 62–5). The distinctive bass line of the second of these examples, rising chromatically here to a second-inversion chord of B flat major, reappears at three important structural moments during the movement (bb. 65–7, 188–90 and 213–16) but is never again allowed, even momentarily, to reach its major-mode goal.

The 'development' section proceeds initially by way of a somewhat mechanical imitative interplay between the first and third themes, which is intensified in the section's latter stages (bb. 116–35). What is most noticeable throughout this entire section, however, is the absence of a single glimpse of a major-mode key. The arena shifts instead to a conflict between flat- and sharp-side tonalities, the former dominating the first half (D minor and G minor, both quashed by returns to the tonic) and the latter, for the first time in the movement, dominating the second half (E minor and F sharp minor) at a time when the music's texture and figuration reach their highest intensity (from b. 102). These two segments of the 'development' are separated by a passage of ten bars (bb. 92–101), constituting perhaps an early example of what Adorno would subsequently describe as a 'breakthrough' (*Durchbruch*):[11] partially unison statements in tonic and subdominant tonalities (the central harmonic axis of the movement) of a new assertive theme with little obvious link to previous material and characterized by opening octave leaps and longer note values; these statements interrupt the prevailing contrapuntal texture and are themselves separated by a series of virtuosic double octaves in the piano (Ex. 29.1).

Ex. 29.1. Piano Quartet, bb. 92–100

---

[11] Ibid., 41.

As if to confound expectations even further, the moment of 'recapitulation' is not prepared by a tension-building dominant pedal but, on the contrary, emerges enigmatically (b.
151) after an inordinately long peroration on the *tonic* (bb. 116–33, briefly interrupted by
D-minor Neapolitan harmony, bb. 129–31) which fades away to a pedal on the subdominant axis point (b. 134). After coming to a pause (b. 138), this passage is followed by the
surprising introduction of a new motive, described by Stahmer as a composite of the first
and third themes of the 'exposition' (Ex. 29.2).[12] The long peroration, which increases the
sense of artificiality engendered by Mahler's 'development', could be taken as an intriguing
foretaste of what Adorno would term 'collapsing passages' (*Einsturzpartien*),[13] an example
of which may be found in the Third Symphony's first movement whose 'development' similarly peters out through textural reduction and thematic disintegration until the disembodied sound of an off-stage side drum takes over (see bb. 626–42 of that movement). Can
it be mere coincidence that towards the end of this symphonic 'development' (b. 608)
Mahler also suddenly introduces a new theme related to previous march material? The
subtle use of Neapolitan harmony to lead into the quartet's 'recapitulation' (the dominant
seventh of the Neapolitan sixth in A minor shifts chromatically straight to the tonic in bb.
150–1, a similar progression in D minor having taken place earlier in bb. 131–2) provides
further points of contact with the Third Symphony's occasionally startling use of such harmony (as for instance in bb. 865–7 of the first movement).

Ex. 29.2. Piano Quartet, first theme, bb. 3–4; new theme, bb. 139–41; third theme, bb. 54–5. Thematic links
according to Klaus Hinrich Stahmer

It is perhaps no surprise that Mahler includes elements from the 'development' in the
'recapitulation'. This ploy was by no means unique in the historical traditions of sonata
form, but its particular qualities could in this case be understood to prefigure recognizably
Mahlerian tactics. In an additional passage (bb. 174–89), beginning in F sharp minor and
modulating via B minor to the tonic, he combines in an integrating process the imitative
interplay between the first and third themes, which was seen in both the 'exposition' and
the first half of the 'development', with the emphasis on sharp-side tonality noted in the
second half of the 'development'. After the reappearance of the second theme, virtually
unaltered (b. 190), the final occurrence of the third theme (b. 202), initially without the

[12] Stahmer, 'Mahlers Frühwerk', 20.   [13] Adorno, *Mahler*, 45.

accompanying counterpoint of the first theme, leads into the surprising cadenza; the latter together with the third theme provide the crux of the movement. Whereas the equivalent statement of the third theme in the 'exposition' (bb. 54–66) made reference to three flat-side keys (F major, G minor, and D minor) as well as the tonic, here the movement's dramatic conflict of modes and keys is encapsulated in the successive allusion to the sharp keys A major, B minor, F sharp minor and then—by way of a remarkable chromatic and obliquely Neapolitan sleight of hand involving successive chords of F sharp minor and a dominant seventh on C natural (bb. 209–10)—the flat keys F major and D minor leading to the tonic A minor. Where bar 66 prepared for the tonic and the 'development', its later equivalent (bb. 214–15) prepares for the tonic and, in the next bar, a final echo of the 'development'—a reappearance of the 'breakthrough' assertive theme in octaves (cf. bb. 92–100). The formal process has spiralled in on itself so tightly that by this stage the only recourse seems to be to the kind of structural interruption that Adorno would later call a moment of 'suspension':[14] a caesura which de-temporalizes proceedings and whose 'ungemein rubato' melodic figures introduce an unsuspected element of Schumannesque instrumental 'recitative' into the music. The coda following this cadenza (b. 223) apparently functions only to preserve in rather dejected manner the unresolved counterpoint of the first and third themes and the unchallenged dominance of A minor.[15]

There is disagreement as to whether the autograph twenty-six-bar fragment of a 6/8 scherzo-like movement in G minor for the same instruments, located on the inner cover (fos. 12ʳ and 12ᵛ) of the manuscript folder containing the A minor quartet, is related to the latter movement. For the Russian composer Alfred Schnittke (1934–98), who professed a deep affinity with Mahler's music and metaphysical concerns and whose own 'polystylistic' works have often been described as developments of similar Mahlerian attributes, the connection is clear.[16] Particularly impressed by Mahler's unusual modulation from G minor to A major in bars 7–9, Schnittke composed in 1988 a 'paraphrase' of the sketched movement in which Mahler's material (as realized in Ruzicka's 1973 edition with some additional figuration and an altered, polytonal final chord) appears as if from distant memory at the end of an allegro movement characterized by cross-rhythms and abrasive note clusters.[17]

[14] Adorno, *Mahler*, 41.

[15] Ruzicka's bare-fifth reading of the final chords is one of the few aspects of his edition which seem to reflect the composer's manuscript notation more accurately than Wagner-Artzt's critical edition. See Barham review, *Music & Letters*, 80 (1999), 164.

[16] For further information on Schnittke's relationship with Mahler see Georg Borchardt, 'Alfred Schnittke und Gustav Mahler', in Georg Borchardt, Constantin Floros, Thomas Schäfer, and Hans Christian Worbs, *Gustav Mahler 'Meine Zeit wird kommen'. Aspekte der Mahler-Rezeption* (Hamburg: Dölling und Galitz, 1996), 61–73; Alexander Ivashkin, *Alfred Schnittke* (London: Phaidon, 1996); and John Webb, 'Schnittke in Context', *Tempo*, 182 (1992), 19–22.

[17] Interestingly, Ruzicka's realization of the sketch on which Schnittke based his work contains many editorial additions in the form of accidentals. For example, the C sharp in the right-hand part of the piano's final bar is not present in Mahler's autograph manuscript. Notice was given of Enguerrand-Friedrich Lühl's completion of the 'scherzo' fragment and its première at the Paris Conservatoire on 7 March 1994 in *News about Mahler Research*, 31 (Mar. 1994), 28. I am also grateful to Donald Mitchell who brought to my attention Alexander Asteriades's arrangement of the A minor quartet movement for string orchestra made in 1999 and published by Universal Edition. More than a simple transcription, it contains registral and metric alterations, more detailed performance directions, and supplementary accompanimental figures which occasionally embellish Mahler's original harmony.

Early Songs

Bauer-Lechner reported that Mahler, while not making reference to specific works, considered the songs he wrote at this time to be 'inadequate' owing to his 'wild' and 'excessive' imagination and the difficulties of achieving something significant on such a small scale.[18] The earliest surviving complete songs comprise a group of three composed to his own texts in February and March 1880 for tenor voice and piano, dedicated to the daughter of the Iglau postmaster, Josephine Poisl, with whom Mahler was romantically linked at the time.[19] Of these, the third song, 'Maitanz im Grünen', transposed from D to F major and with a small number of textual alterations and additional chromaticisms in the accompaniment, became the song 'Hans und Grethe', the third item in Volume 1 of *Lieder und Gesänge* (later known as *Lieder und Gesänge aus der Jugendzeit*), published in 1892. This song was subsequently to be the inspiration for the 'Kräftig bewegt' second movement of the First Symphony. It is discussed elsewhere in this book and, except for the following, will not be examined further: first, 'Maitanz im Grünen', marked 'Lustig und keck. Im Zeitmaß eines Ländlers', appears to be the earliest expression of Mahler's affinity with the Austrian folk dance which was to become such an important part of his creative constitution; secondly, the instruction 'wie aus der Ferne' in the final bars of the song provides the first example of Mahler's lifelong concern with the evocation of musical space.

The texts of the other two songs ('Im Lenz' and 'Winterlied') are typically romantic expressions of unrequited or unattainable love; although they may be criticized for their literary quality,[20] they none the less give early pointers to recurrent Mahlerian themes of isolation and alienation. 'Im Lenz', in which the protagonist speaks despairingly of the long-absent object of his affection, is an example of the type of 'dialogue' song frequently found in Mahler's later *Wunderhorn* settings;[21] it is notable both for its melodic links with 'Wenn mein Schatz Hochzeit macht', the first of the *Lieder eines fahrenden Gesellen* with which it shares similar subject matter,[22] and for its somewhat diffuse harmonic construction in which certain tonal areas seem to be employed more for their localized symbolic

---

[18] See NB-L, *Erinnerungen*, 55, and NB-L, *Recollections*, 58.

[19] The manuscript is housed in the Alfred Rosé Room of the Music Library at the University of Western Ontario, London, Canada. Its title page describes the songs as '5 Lieder', but the absence of titles listed against numbers 4 and 5 suggests that the group remained incomplete, probably owing to the termination of the relationship. Two further poems written for Poisl by Mahler at this time, cited in HLG(F), i. 1068–70, may have been intended for musical treatment and inclusion in the set.

[20] See E. Mary Dargie, *Music and Poetry in the Songs of Gustav Mahler* (Bern: Peter Lang, 1981), 57 and 60, where

Mahler's verses are criticized for their structure and clichéed imagery.

[21] As with the *Wunderhorn* settings, the term 'dialogue' does not refer to the spurious performance practice of employing two singers, but rather the discourse embodied in the poem's internal characterizations. Reference throughout this discussion of the early songs is made to the critical edition: *Verschiedene Lieder für eine Singstimme mit Klavier*, ed. Zoltan Roman (Sämtliche Werke, 13/5; Mainz: Schott, 1990).

[22] Compare bb. 21–6 and 49–51 of 'Im Lenz' with bb. 14–17, 34–8, 71–4, and 85–8 of 'Wenn mein Schatz'. The textual links at these points are clear.

power than for their function within an over-arching design.[23] The ambiguous progressions at the end of the song (bb. 43–53), taking the tonality from C major via F sharp minor to an inconclusive A flat major, intensify this quality. With a keyboard accompaniment characterized by glissandos, tremolandos, and rapid repeated chords suggestive of an orchestral conception, such features sharply differentiate the song from 'Winterlied', although both songs, notably, begin and end in different keys. In 'Winterlied' itself, a pervasive *berceuse*-like rhythm provides the anchor not only for greater structural and tonal clarity but also for such interesting expressive gestures as the increasingly impassioned, arching vocal phrases of the closing lines of the second verse (bb. 44–58) and the Schumannesque use of piano introduction, interlude, and postlude. The song ends, for example, with a sixteen-bar passage for piano alone which seemingly embodies at least a partial resolution of the poem's downbeat ending—tonally in the shift to a pastoral F major, and texturally through the absorption within its restful atmosphere of the poignant, semiquaver spinning-wheel figuration which first appeared in bar 15 and which becomes a symbol of loss and displaced love.

Ex. 29.3. (*a*) 'Im Lenz', bb. 13–15; (*b*) 'Im Lenz', bb. 17–19; (*c*) *Das klagende Lied*, 'Der Spielmann', bb. 301–3, alto solo; (*d*) *Das klagende Lied*, 'Der Spielmann', bb. 305–7, alto solo; (*e*) 'Winterlied', bb. 14–16, piano right hand; (*f*) 'Winterlied', bb. 69–72, piano right hand; (*g*) *Das klagende Lied*, 'Waldmärchen', bb. 176–9, I & II violins, clarinet; (*h*) *Das klagende Lied*, 'Waldmärchen', bb. 327–30, I & II violins

---

[23] See the brief discussion of Mahler's use of C major in the third stanza as a symbol of light and release in Peter Revers, *Mahlers Lieder. Ein musikalischer Werkführer* (Munich: C. H. Beck, 2000), 51.

Both songs display melodic similarities with the original three-movement version of *Das klagende Lied* which Mahler was working on at the same time (see Ex. 29.3). Furthermore, the copy of the text accompanying the only surviving manuscript source of the complete three-movement version of the cantata contains the lines 'Es klingt wie Lachen und Weinen/doch sagen könt' ich es Keinem!'—almost identical to the end of the second verse of 'Im Lenz': 'Könnt' lachen und könnte weinen/Doch sagen könnt ich es Keinem'— crossed through as part of a revisionary process but clearly indicating the close emotional link between the cantata and the song. In the case of 'Im Lenz', Reinhold Kubik has convincingly demonstrated through detailed textual and source analysis that it was the song which cited music from the cantata and not vice versa.[24] If this is also true of 'Winterlied', could it be significant that both of the points in the narrative of 'Waldmärchen' (the original first part of *Das klagende Lied*) during which the melody cited in the song appears (bb. 177–80 and 328–31) are concerned with the search for the flower that will win the beautiful but proud and unbending Queen's hand in marriage and also with the flower's subsequent discovery by the innocent brother—a quest that will lead to personal tragedy in the short term but an eventual higher justice? Notably, the motive's appearance in 'Winterlied'—associated with similar, perhaps privately significant, textual allusions to seeking out the distant, yearned-for beloved through song (Mahler was in Vienna at the time)—initially coincides with the first use of the evocative spinning-wheel figure in the left hand of the piano accompaniment and then forms the concluding bars of the

---

[24] Foreword to the critical edition, *Das klagende Lied. Erstfassung in drei Sätzen (1880)* (Sämtliche Werke, Suppl. IV; Vienna: Universal Edition, 1997), p. x.

all-important conciliatory piano epilogue.[25] Whatever the case, these songs provide fascinating early examples of Mahler's familiar procedure of self-quotation and of the productive relationship between condensed song forms and large-scale dramatic structures demonstrated so often in the composer's subsequent working practice.

[25] The opening text of the song, leading to the first citation of the melody in b. 15, is as follows (translations taken from Dargie, *Music and Poetry*, 59 and 60): 'Über Berg und Tal/Mit lautem Schall/Tönet ein Liedchen./Durch Schnee und Eis/Dringt es so heiss/Bis zu dem Hüttchen' ('Over hill and dale/Loudly resounding/A song is heard./Through snow and ice/Its heat makes a way/Up to the cottage'). The concluding lines preceding the piano epilogue are: 'O liebliche Zeit/Wie bist du so weit!/O selige Stunden!/Ach nur ein Blick/War unser Glück/Ewig verschwunden' ('O delightful time/How far away you are!/O happy hours!/Alas, only a glance/Was our happiness/Gone for ever').

SOURCES

Abbate, Carolyn, *Unsung Voices: Opera and Musical Narrative in the Nineteenth Century* (Princeton: Princeton University Press, 1991).

Abraham, Otto, and Hornbostel, Erich M. von, 'Studien über das Tonsystem und die Musik der Japaner', *Sammelbände der Internationalen Musikgesellschaft*, 4 (1902–3), 302–60.

Adler, Guido, *Gustav Mahler* (Vienna: Universal Edition, 1916).

Adorno, Theodor W., *Mahler: A Musical Physiognomy*, trans. Edmund Jephcott (Chicago and London: University of Chicago Press, 1992).

—— 'Mahler: Centenary Address, Vienna 1960', in id., *Quasi una Fantasia.*

—— *Mahler, une physionomie musicale*, trans. J.-L. Leleu and T. Leydenbach (Paris: Éditions de Minuit, 1976).

—— *Philosophy of Modern Music*, trans. Anne G. Mitchell and Wesley V. Bloomster (London: Sheed & Ward, 1973).

—— *Quasi una Fantasia: Essays on Modern Music*, trans. Rodney Livingstone (London: Verso, 1992).

—— 'Zu einem Streitgespräch über Mahler', in Richard Baum and Wolfgang Rehm (eds.), *Musik und Verlag: Karl Vötterle zum 65. Geburtstag am 12. April 1968* (Kassel: Bärenreiter, 1968), 123–7.

—— 'Zu einer imaginären Auswahl von Liedern Gustav Mahlers', in id., *Impromptus: Zweite Folge neu gedruckter musikalischer Aufsätze* (Frankfurt: Suhrkamp, 1968).

Agasaryan, Loretta, 'Osobennosti sonatnoy formi v simfoniyakh G. Malera' (Ph.D. diss., Inst. iskusstv Akademii Nauk Armjanskoj SSR, Yerevan, 1974).

Andraschke, Peter, *Gustav Mahlers IX. Symphonie: Kompositionsprozeß und Analyse* (Beihefte zum Archiv für Musikwissenschaft, 14; Wiesbaden: Franz Steiner Verlag, 1981).

Asaf'ev, Boris, *Muzykal'naya forma kak protsess*, ed. E. M. Orlova (Leningrad: Muzyka, 1971).

—— *O muzyke XX veka*, ed. Tat'yana Dmitrieva-Mey (2nd edn., Leningrad: Muzyka, 1982).

Avenary, Hanoch (ed.), *Kantor Salomon Sulzer und seine Zeit: Eine Dokumentation* (Sigmaringen: J. Thorbecke, 1985).

Bailey, Robert, 'The Structure of the *Ring* and its Evolution', *19th Century Music*, 1 (1977), 48–61.

Banks, Paul, 'Aspects of Mahler's Fifth Symphony: Performance Practice and Interpretation', *Musical Times*, 130 (May 1989), 258–65.

—— 'Fin de Siècle Vienna, Politics and Modernism', in Jim Samson (ed.), *The Late Romantic Era* (Englewood Cliffs, NJ: Prentice-Hall, 1991), 362–88.

—— (ed.), *The Making of 'Peter Grimes'* (Woodbridge, The Britten Estate/The Boydell Press, 1996).

—— and Mitchell, Donald, 'Gustav Mahler', in Stanley Sadie (ed.), *The New Grove Dictionary of Music and Musicians*, 6th edn. (London: Macmillan, 1980), xi. 505–31.

Barford, Philip, *Mahler Symphonies and Songs* (BBC Music Guides; Seattle: University of Washington Press, 1971).

Barsova, Inna, 'Mahler and Dostoyevsky', in *Gustav Mahler Kolloquium 1979*, ed. Klein, 65–76.

—— 'Novoe v russkoy Maleriane', *Sovetskaya muzyka*, 3 (1990), 98–102.

—— *Simfonii Gustava Malera* (Moscow: Sovetskiy kompozitor, 1975).

Bauer-Lechner, Natalie, 'Aus einem Tagebuch über Mahler', *Der Merker*, 3/5 (1912), 184–8.

—— *Gustav Mahler in den Erinnerungen von Natalie Bauer-Lechner*, ed. Herbert Killian (Hamburg: Karl Dieter Wagner, 1984).

—— *Recollections of Gustav Mahler*, trans. Dika Newlin, ed. Peter Franklin (London: Faber, 1980).

Beaumont, Antony, *Zemlinsky* (London: Faber and Faber, 2000).

Bekker, Paul, *Gustav Mahlers Sinfonien* (Berlin: Schuster und Loeffler, 1921; repr. 1969).

Berg, Alban, *Briefe an seine Frau*, ed. Franz Willnauer (Munich: Langer-Müller, 1965).

—— *Letters to his Wife*, ed. and trans. Bernard Grun (New York: St. Martin's Press, 1971).

Berlioz, Hector, and Strauss, Richard, *Treatise on Instrumentation*, trans. Theodore Front (New York: Dover, 1991).

Bernstein, Leonard, *Findings* (New York: Simon and Schuster, 1982).

—— 'Mahler: His Time has Come', *High Fidelity*, 17/9 (1967), 51–4.

—— *The Unanswered Question* (Cambridge, Mass., and London: Harvard University Press, 1976).

Bethge, Hans, *Die chinesische Flöte: Nachdichtungen chinesischer Lyrik* (Leipzig: Inselverlag, 1920).

Bisanz-Prakken, Marian, *Gustav Klimt. Der Beethovenfries: Geschichte, Funktion und Bedeutung* (Salzburg: Graphische Sammlung Albertina, 1977).

Blaukopf, Kurt, *Gustav Mahler*, trans. Inge Goodwin (London: Allen Lane, 1973).

Block, Frederick, 'Mahler's Tenth', *Chord and Discord*, 2/3 (Dec. 1941), 43–5.

Block, Geoffrey, and Burkholder, J. Peter (eds.), *Charles Ives and the Classical Tradition* (New Haven and London: Yale University Press, 1996).

Bohlman, Philip V., 'Auf der Bima/auf der Bühne—zur Emanzipation der jüdischen Popularmusik um die Jahrhundertwende in Wien', in Elisabeth Th. Hilscher, Theophil Antonicek, and Ottmar Wessely (eds.), *Vergleichend-systematische Musikwissenschaft: Beiträge zu Methode und Problematik der systematischen, ethnologischen und historischen Musikwissenschaft* (Tutzing: Hans Schneider, 1994), 417–49.

Bónis, Ferenc, 'Gustav Mahler und Ferenc Erkel', *Studia musicologica*, 1 (1960), 475–85.

Borchmeyer, Dieter, 'Gustav Mahler's Goethe and Goethe's Holy Ghost', *News about Mahler Research*, no. 32 (Oct. 1994).

Botstein, Leon, 'Brahms and Nineteenth-Century Painting', *19th Century Music*, 14 (1990), 154–68.

—— 'Innovation and Nostalgia: Ives, Mahler and the Origins of Modernism', in Burkholder (ed.), *Charles Ives and his World*, 35–74.

—— *Judentum und Modernität: Essays zur Rolle der Juden in der deutschen und Österreichischen Kultur, 1848 bis 1938* (Vienna: Böhlau, 1991).

—— 'Music and its Public: Habits of Listening and the Crisis of Musical Modernism in Vienna, 1870–1914' (Ph.D. diss., Harvard University, 1985).

Britten, Benjamin, *Letters from a Life: The Selected Letters and Diaries of Benjamin Britten, 1913–1976*, ed. Donald Mitchell and Philip Reed (London: Faber, 1991; Berkeley: University of California Press, 1991).

Brod, Max, *Gustav Mahler: Beispiel einer deutsch-jüdischen Symbiose* (Frankfurt am Main: Ner-Tamid Verlag, 1961).

Budd, Malcolm, *Music and the Emotions: The Philosophical Theories* (London: Routledge & Kegan Paul, 1985).

Burkholder, J. Peter (ed.), *Charles Ives and his World* (Princeton: Princeton University Press, 1996).

Burton, Humphrey, *Leonard Bernstein* (London: Faber, 1994; New York: Doubleday, 1994).

Busoni, Ferruccio, *The Essence of Music and Other Papers*, trans. Rosamond Ley (New York: Dover, 1965).

Carner, Mosco, *Of Men and Music* (London: Joseph Williams, 1944).

Carr, Jonathan, *The Real Mahler* (London: Constable, 1997).

Charlton, David (ed.), *E. T. A. Hoffmann's Musical Writings: 'Kreisleriana', 'The Poet and the Composer', Music Criticism*, trans. Martyn Clarke (Cambridge: Cambridge University Press, 1989).

Christy, Nicholas P., Christy, Beverly M., and Wood, Barry G., 'Gustav Mahler and his Illnesses', *Transactions of the American Clinical and Climatological Association*, 82 (1970), 200–17.

Conversations with Klemperer, ed. Peter Heyworth (rev. edn., London: Faber, 1985).

Cooke, Deryck, *Gustav Mahler: An Introduction to his Music* (London: Faber, 1980).

—— *Gustav Mahler: A Performing Version of the Draft for the Tenth Symphony* (2nd edn., New York and London: AMP/Faber, 1989).

—— 'Mahler's Melodic Thinking', in id., *Vindications: Essays in Romantic Music* (London: Faber, 1982).

Copland, Aaron, 'Five Post-Romantics', *Modern Music*, 18 (1941), 218–20.

—— 'From a Composer's Notebook', *Modern Music*, 6/4 (May–June 1929), 16–17.

—— *Our New Music* (New York: Whittlesey House, 1941).

Coster, Aarnout, 'Mengelberg's Mahler Performances in America', in *Das Gustav-Mahler-Fest Hamburg 1989*, ed. Vogt, 279–89.

Cox, D., *The Henry Wood Proms* (London: BBC, 1980).

Dahlhaus, Carl, 'Form und Motiv in Mahlers neunter Symphonie', *Neue Zeitschrift für Musik*, 135 (1974), 286–9, repr. in Danuser (ed.), *Gustav Mahler*, 289–99.

—— *Ludwig van Beethoven: Approaches to his Music*, trans. Mary Whittall (Oxford: Clarendon Press, 1991).

—— *Realism in Nineteenth-Century Music*, trans. Mary Whittall (Cambridge and New York: Cambridge University Press, 1985).

—— *Richard Wagner's Music Dramas*, trans. Mary Whittall (Cambridge: Cambridge University Press, 1992).

Damrosch, Walter, *My Musical Life* (New York: Charles Scribner & Sons, 1923).

Daniel, Oliver, *Stokowski: A Counterpoint of View* (New York: Dodd Mead & Co., 1982).

Danuser, Hermann, 'Erkenntnis oder Verblendung? Zum Problem des Sachgehaltes polemischer und apologetischer Musikkritik—am Beispiel einiger früher Rezeptionszeugnisse zu Mahlers Siebenten Symphonie', in *The Seventh Symphony of Gustav Mahler*, ed. Zychowicz, 107–23.

—— *Gustav Mahler: Das Lied von der Erde* (Meisterwerke der Musik, 25; Munich: Wilhelm Fink Verlag, 1986).

—— *Gustav Mahler und seine Zeit* (Laaber: Laaber-Verlag, 1991).

—— 'My Time Will Yet Come: Die amerikanische Mahler-Rezeption im Spiegel der Zeitschrift "Chord and Discord"', in id., *Gustav Mahler und seine Zeit*, 275–85.

Danuser, Hermann, (ed.), *Gustav Mahler* (Wege der Forschung, 653; Darmstadt: Wissenschaftliche Buchgesellschaft, 1992).

Darcy, Warren, *Wagner's 'Das Rheingold'* (Oxford: Oxford University Press, 1993).

Dargie, E. Mary, *Music and Poetry in the Songs of Gustav Mahler* (European University Studies, ser. 1, vol. 401; Bern: Peter Lang, 1981).

Davison, Peter, 'Nachtmusik II: "Nothing but Love, Love, Love"?', in *The Seventh Symphony of Gustav Mahler*, ed. Zychowicz, 89–97.

Debussy, Claude, *Monsieur Croche et autres écrits* (Paris: Gallimard, 1971).

Debussy Letters, selected and ed. François Lesure and Roger Nichols, trans. Roger Nichols (London: Faber, 1987).

Dechevrens, A., 'Étude sur le système musical chinois', *Sammelbände der Internationalen Musikgesellschaft*, 2 (1900–1), 485–51.

Decsey, Ernst, 'Stunden mit Mahler: Notizen', *Die Musik* (Berlin), 10/18 (1910/11), 352–6; and 10/21 (1911), 143–53.

Dekhtyareva, Natal'a, 'Pozdniy period tvorchestva Gustava Malera (filosofsko-esteticheskie osobennosti simfonicheskikh kontseptsiy' (MS diss., Leningradskaya Gosudarstvennaya Konservatoriya, 1981).

Del Mar, Norman, *Mahler's Sixth Symphony—A Study* (London: Eulenburg Books, 1980).

Dent, Edward J., *Ferruccio Busoni* (London: Eulenberg Books, 1974).

Diether, Jack, 'The Expressive Content of Mahler's Ninth Symphony', *Chord and Discord*, 2/10 (1963), 94–7.

—— 'Notes on Some Mahler Juvenilia', *Chord and Discord*, 3/1 (1969), 3–100.

—— 'A Personal History of Mahler's Tenth', in *Fragment or Completion?*, ed. Op de Coul, 97–105.

Doctor, Jennifer, *The BBC and Ultra-Modern Music, 1922–1936: Shaping a Nation's Taste* (Cambridge: Cambridge University Press, 1999).

Dolmetsch, Carl, *'Our Famous Guest': Mark Twain in Vienna* (Athens, Ga.: University of Georgia Press, 1992).

Downes, Graeme Alexander, 'An Axial System of Tonality Applied to Progressive Tonality in the Works of Gustav Mahler and Nineteenth-Century Antecedents', (Ph.D. thesis: University of Otago, Dunedin, 1991).

Downes, Olin, *Olin Downes on Music*, ed. Irene Downes (New York: Simon and Schuster, 1957).

Druskin, Mikhail, 'Vospominaniya: Drug', *Issledovaniya, vospominaniya* (Leningrad and Moscow: Sovetskiy kompozitor, 1977).

Eggebrecht, Hans Heinrich, *Die Musik Gustav Mahlers* (Munich: Piper, 1982).

Engel, Gabriel, *Gustav Mahler—Song Symphonist* (New York: Bruckner Society of America, 1932; repr. David Lewis, 1970).

Ennulat, Egbert M., *Arnold Schoenberg Correspondence: A Collection of Translated and Annotated Letters Exchanged with Guido Adler, Pablo Casals, Emanuel Feuermann and Olin Downes* (Metuchen, NJ: The Scarecrow Press, 1991).

Feder, Stuart, 'Before Alma. . . Gustav Mahler and "Das Ewig-Weibliche"', in Hefling (ed.), *Mahler Studies*, 78–109.

—— 'Gustav Mahler, Dying', *International Review of Psychoanalysis*, 5 (1978), 125–48.

—— 'Gustav Mahler um Mitternacht', *International Review of Psychoanalysis*, 7 (1980), 11–26.

Fifield, Christopher, *True Artist and True Friend: A Biography of Hans Richter* (Oxford: Clarendon Press, 1993).

Filler, Susan M., 'Mahler in the Medical Literature', *News about Mahler Research*, no. 23 (Mar. 1990), 8–13.

Finlay, Ian F., 'Gustav Mahler in Holland and England', *Britain and Holland*, 10/4 (1958), 85–90.

Fischer, Kurt von, 'Die Doppelschlagfigur in den zwei letzten Sätzen von Gustav Mahlers 9. Symphonie: Versuch einer Interpretation', *Archiv für Musikwissenschaft*, 32 (1975), 99–105.

Floros, Constantin, *Gustav Mahler*, i: *Die geistige Welt Gustav Mahlers in systematischer Darstellung*; ii: *Mahler und die Symphonik des 19. Jahrhunderts in neuer Deutung*; iii: *Die Symphonien* (Wiesbaden: Breitkopf & Härtel, 1977–85).

—— *Gustav Mahler: The Symphonies*, trans. Vernon Wicker (Aldershot: Scolar, 1994).

—— 'Die "Symphonie der Tausend" als Botschaft an die Menscheit', in *A 'Mass' for the Masses*, ed. van Leeuwen et al., 121–30.

Flothuis, Marius, 'Einige kritische Bemerkungen zu Mahlers Achter Symphonie', in *A 'Mass' for the Masses*, ed. van Leeuwen et al., 180–4.

Förster, J. B., 'Aus Mahlers Werkstatt', *Der Merker*, 1 (1910), 921–4.

—— *Der Pilger: Erinnerungen eines Musikers* (Prague: Artia, 1955).

Forte, Allen, *The Structure of Atonal Music* (New Haven: Yale University Press, 1973).

Fragment or Completion? Proceedings of the Mahler X Symposium, Utrecht 1986, ed. Paul Op de Coul (The Hague: Nijgh & Van Ditmar/Universitaire Pers Rotterdam, 1991), 154–64.

Franklin, Peter, '"Funeral Rites"—Mahler and Mickiewicz', *Music & Letters*, 55 (1974), 203–8.

—— '". . . his fractures are the script of truth."—Adorno's Mahler', in Hefling (ed.), *Mahler Studies*, 271–94.

—— *The Idea of Music: Schoenberg and Others* (London: Macmillan Press Ltd., 1985).

—— *The Life of Mahler* (Cambridge: Cambridge University Press, 1997).

—— *Mahler: Symphony No. 3* (Cambridge: Cambridge University Press, 1991).

Fülöp, Peter, *Mahler Discography* (New York: The Kaplan Foundation, 1995).

Füssl, Karl Heinz, 'On the Order of the Middle Movements in Mahler's Sixth Symphony', *News about Mahler Research*, no. 27 (Mar. 1992), 3–7.

Gautier, Judith, *Les Musiques bizarres à l'Exposition de 1900* (Paris: Société d'Éditions littéraires, 1900).

Gerlach, Reinhard, *Strophen von Leben, Traum und Tod: Ein Essay über Rückert-Lieder von Gustav Mahler* (Taschenbücher zur Musikwissenschaft, ed. Richard Schaal, no. 83; Wilhelmshaven: Heinrichshofen's Verlag, 1982).

Graf, Max, *Composer and Critic* (London: Chapman & Hall, 1947).

Grant, William Parks, 'Mahler on Records', *Chord and Discord*, 2/3 (Dec. 1941), 63–8.

—— 'Mahler's Art: A New Survey', *Chord and Discord*, 1/5 (Mar. 1934), 14–19.

Grasberger, Franz, and Knessel, Lothar, *Hundert Jahre Goldener Saal: Das Haus der Gesellschaft der Musikfreunde am Karlsplatz* (Vienna: Gesellschaft der Musikfreunde, n.d.).

Grasberger, Renate, *Bruckner-Ikonographie. Teil I. Um 1854 bis 1924* (Graz: Akademischer Druck und Verlagsanstalt, 1990).

—— and Partsch, Erich Wolfgang (eds.), *Bruckner—skizziert: Ein Porträt in ausgewählten Erinnerungen und Anekdoten* (Vienna: Musikwissenschaftlicher Verlag BNM, 1991)

Grosser, Manfred, 'Friedrich Rückerts "Östliche Rosen" ', *Rückert Studien*, 1 (1964), 45–108.

Gülke, Peter, 'The Orchestra as Medium of Realization: Thoughts on the Finale of Brahms's First Symphony, on the Different Versions of Bruckner's Sixth Symphony, and on "Part One" of Mahler's Fifth', *Musical Quarterly*, 80 (1996).

Gustav Mahler: Facsimile Edition of the Seventh Symphony, Bernard Haitink, Donald Mitchell, and Edward R. Reilly (Amsterdam: Rosbeek Publishers, 1995).

Das Gustav-Mahler-Fest Hamburg 1989: Bericht üben den Internationalen Gustav-Mahler Kongress, ed. Matthias Theodor Vogt (Kassel: Bärenreiter, 1991).

Gustav Mahler Kolloquium 1979, ed. Rudolf Klein (Beiträge der Österreichischen Gesellschaft für Musik, 2; Kassel: Bärenreiter, 1981).

Gustav Mahler–Richard Strauss: Correspondence 1888–1911, ed. Herta Blaukopf, trans. Edmund Jephcott (London: Faber, 1984; Chicago: University of Chicago Press, 1984).

Gustav Mahler: The World Listens, the Programme Book of the 1995 Mahler Festival, Amsterdam, ed. Donald Mitchell (Haarlem: TEMA Uitgevers, 1995).

Guzhva, Aleksandr, *Zhanrovo-kompozitsionnye tipy simfonii v Avstrii i Germanii nachala XX veka/ Gustav Maler i ego sovremenniki* (Moscow: Moskovskaya Gosudasrtvennaya Konservatoriya, 1985).

Hailey, Christopher, *Franz Schreker, 1878–1934: A Cultural Biography* (Cambridge: Cambridge University Press, 1993).

Hamao, Fusako, 'The Sources of the Texts in Mahler's *Lied von der Erde*', *19th Century Music*, 19 (1995), 83–95.

Hammond, Philip, 'The Hallé Years and After', in David Greer (ed.), *Hamilton Harty: His Life and Music* (Belfast: Blackstaff, 1979).

Hanslick, Eduard, *Die moderne Oper*, viii: *Am Ende des Jahrhunderts (1895–1899). Musikalische Kritiken und Schilderungen* (Berlin, Allgemeine Verein für Deutsche Literatur, 1899).

—— *Music Criticisms 1846–99*, trans. and ed. Henry Pleasants (London: Penguin, 1963).

Harrison, Julius, *The Musical Companion*, ed. A. L. Bacharach (London: Gollancz, 1934).

Härtwig, Dieter, 'Notes on Gustav Mahler's Arrangement of Carl Maria von Weber's Opera Fragment *Die drei Pintos*', *News about Mahler Research*, no. 37 (Autumn 1997), 3–11.

Haylock, Julian, *Gustav Mahler: An Essential Guide to his Life and Works* [Classic FM Lifelines] (London: Pavilion Books, 1996).

Hefling, Stephen E., 'The Composition of "Ich bin der Welt abhanden gekommen" ', in Danuser (ed.), *Gustav Mahler*, 96–158.

—— 'Content and Context of the Sketches', in Kaplan (ed.), *Mahler: The Resurrection Chorale* 13–24.

—— ' "Ihm in die Lieder zu blicken": Mahler's Seventh Symphony Sketchbook', in id. (ed.), *Mahler Studies*, 191–4.

—— '*Das Lied von der Erde*: Mahler's Symphony for Voices and Orchestra—or Piano', *Journal of Musicology*, 10 (1992), 293–303.

—— *Mahler: Das Lied von der Erde* (Cambridge: Cambridge University Press, 2000).

—— 'Mahler: Symphonies 1–4', in *The Symphony, 1825–c. 1900*, ed. D. Kern Holoman (Studies in Musical Genres and Repertoires; New York: Schirmer Books, 1997), 369 ff.

—— 'Mahler's "Todtenfeier" and the Problem of Program Music', *19th Century Music*, 12 (1988), 27–53.

—— 'The Making of Mahler's "Todtenfeier": A Documentary and Analytical Study' (Ph.D. diss., Yale University, 1985).

—— 'Miners Digging from Opposite Sides: Mahler, Strauss, and the Problem of Program Music', in Brian Gilliam (ed.), *Richard Strauss: New Perspectives on the Composer and his Work* (Durham, NC: Duke University Press, 1992), 41–53.

—— (ed.). *Das Lied von der Erde, für eine hohe und eine mittlere Gesangstimme mit Klavier* (Kritische Gesamtausgabe, Supplement Band II; Vienna: Universal Edition, 1989).

—— *Mahler Studies* (Cambridge: Cambridge University Press, 1997).

Heller, Friedrich C., and Revers, Peter, *Das Wiener Konzerthaus: Geschichte und Bedeutung 1913–1983* (Vienna: Wiener Konzerthausgesellschaft, 1983).

Heusgen, Birgit, *Studien zu Gustav Mahlers Bearbeitung und Ergänzung von Carl Maria von Webers Opernfragment 'Die drei Pintos'* (Regensburg, 1983).

Heyworth, Peter, *Otto Klemperer, his Life and Times*, i: *1885–1933* (Cambridge: Cambridge University Press, 1983).

Hilmar-Voit, Renate, *Im Wunderhorn-Ton: Gustav Mahlers sprachliches Kompositionsmaterial bis 1900* (Tutzing: Hans Schneider, 1988).

—— 'Symphonic Sound or in the Style of Chamber Music? The Current Performing Forces of the *Wunderhorn* Lieder and the Sources', *News about Mahler Research*, no. 28 (Oct. 1992), 8–12.

Hinton Thomas, R. S., *Nietzsche in German Politics and Society, 1890–1918* (Manchester: Manchester University Press, 1983).

Holland, Dietmar, 'Gustav Mahler und die Muenchner Philharmoniker', in *Die Münchner Philharmoniker von der Gründung bis heute*, ed. Regina Schmoll Eisenwert (Munich: Wolf, 1985), 183–206.

Holländer, Hans, 'Unbekannte Jugendbriefe Gustav Mahlers', *Die Musik*, 22 (1928), 807–13.

Hollingdale, R. J., *Nietzsche* (London and Boston: Routledge and Kegan Paul, 1973).

Holloway, Robin, '*Salome*: Art or Kitsch?', in *Richard Strauss: Salome*, ed. Derrick Puffett (Cambridge Opera Handbooks; Cambridge: Cambridge University Press, 1989), 145–60.

Hopper, Jeffrey Thomas, 'The Rückert Lieder of Gustav Mahler' (Ph.D. diss., Rutgers University, 1991).

Horowitz, Joseph, 'Adding Insult to Improvement', *New York Times* (25 Oct. 1992).

—— 'Anton Seidl and America's Wagner Cult', in Millington and Spencer (eds.), *Wagner in Performance*, 168–81.

—— *Understanding Toscanini* (New York: Alfred A. Knopf, 1987), 13–77.

Jackson, Timothy L., and Hawkshaw, Paul, (eds.), *Bruckner Studies* (Cambridge: Cambridge University Press, 1997).

Jacobs, Arthur, *Henry J. Wood: Maker of the Proms* (London: Methuen, 1994).

Jankélévitch, Vladimir, *Debussy et le mystère* (Neuchâtel: Baconnière, 1949).

Jarocinski, Stefan, *Debussy, Impressionism and Symbolism*, trans. Rollo Myers (London: Eulenburg Books, 1976).

Kalbeck, Max, *Johannes Brahms* (Berlin: Deutsche Brahms-Gesellschaft, 1915).

Kandinsky, Wassily, *Concerning the Spiritual in Art*, trans. M. T. H. Sadler (New York: Dover Publications, 1977).

Kaplan, Gilbert E. (ed.), *Gustav Mahler: Adagietto: Facsimile, Documentation, Recording* (New York: The Kaplan Foundation, 1992).

Karatygin, Viacheslav, *Izbrannie statʾi* (Moscow: Muzyka, 1965).

Karbusicky, Vladimir, *Gustav Mahler und seine Umwelt* (Darmstadt: Wissenschaftliche Buchgesellschaft, 1978).

Karbusicky, Vladimir, *Mahler in Hamburg: Chronik einer Freundschaft* (Hamburg: von Bockel, 1996).

Karpath, Ludwig, *Begegnung mit dem Genius* (Vienna: Fiba, 1934).

Keegan, Susanne, *The Bride of the Wind: The Life and Times of Alma Mahler-Werfel* (London: Secker & Warburg, 1991).

Kennedy, Michael, *Adrian Boult* (London: Hamish Hamilton, 1987).

—— *The Hallé Tradition: A Century of Music* (Manchester: Manchester University Press, 1960).

—— *Mahler* (2nd edn., London: Dent, 1990).

Klemm, Eberhardt, 'Über ein Spätwerk Gustav Mahlers', *Deutsches Jahrbuch der Musikwissenschaft für 1961*, ed. W. Vetter (Leipzig: Edition Peters, 1962), 19–32; repr. in Danuser (ed.), *Gustav Mahler*, 324–43.

—— 'Zur Geschichte der Fünften Sinfonie von Gustav Mahler: Der Briefwechsel zwischen Mahler und dem Verlag C. F. Peters und andere Dokumente', in *Jahrbuch Peters 1979*, 9–116.

Knittel, K. M., ' "Ein hypermoderner Dirigent": Mahler and Anti-Semitism in Fin-de-siècle Vienna', *19th Century Music*, 18 (1995), 257–76.

Kobau, Ernst, *Die Wiener Symphoniker: Eine sozialgeschichtliche Studie* (Vienna: Böhlau, 1991).

Kolleritsch, Otto (ed.), *Gustav Mahler: Sinfonie und Wirklichkeit* (Graz: Universal Edition for the Institut für Wertungsforschung, 1977).

Kolomiytsev, Viktor, 'Gustav Maler i ego simfoniya', *Oko* (31 Oct. 1906); repr. in id., *Stat'i i pis'ma*, ed. July Kremlev (Leningrad: Muzyka, 1971).

Kramer, Lawrence, *Music as Cultural Practice, 1800–1900* (Berkeley and Oxford: University of California Press, 1990).

Kravitt, Edward F., *The Lied: Mirror of Late Romanticism* (New Haven and London: Yale University Press, 1996).

—— 'Mahler's Dirges for his Death: February 24, 1901', *Musical Quarterly*, 64 (1978), 329–53.

Kretzschmar, Hermann, *Führer durch den Concertsaal* (3rd edn., Leipzig: Breitkopf & Härtel, 1898).

Krummacher, Friedhelm, *Gustav Mahlers III Symphonie: Welt im Widerbild* (Kassel: Bärenreiter, 1991).

—— 'Struktur und Auflösung: Über den Kopfsatz aus Mahlers IX. Symphonie', *Studier och essäer tillägnade Hans Eppstein* (Stockholm, 1981), 133–49; repr. in Danuser (ed.), *Gustav Mahler*, 300–23.

Kubik, Reinhold, '*Das klagende Lied*, Sources and Versions', in *Mahler the Revisionist*, Programme Book of the Symposium held at the Bridgewater Hall, Manchester, 7 October 1997, pp. 8–16, 20.

Kupferberg, Herbert, *Those Fabulous Philadelphians: The Life and Times of a Great Orchestra* (New York: Charles Scribner's Sons, 1969).

La Grange, Henry-Louis de, 'Auf der Suche nach Gustav Mahler: Eine Bilanz', in Danuser (ed.), *Gustav Mahler*, 30–68.

—— *Gustav Mahler: chronique d'une vie*, 3 vols. (Paris: Fayard, 1973–84).

—— *Mahler*, i (London: Gollancz, 1974); *Gustav Mahler*, ii: *Vienna: The Years of Challenge (1897–1904)* (Oxford: Oxford University Press, 1995); *Gustav Mahler*, iii: *Vienna: Triumph and Disillusion (1904–1907)* (Oxford: Oxford University Press, 1999).

—— 'Mahler and the New York Philharmonic: The Truth behind the Legend', in Reed (ed.), *On Mahler and Britten*, 56–77.

—— 'Mahler in the New World', *Muziek & wetenschap*, 5 (1995–6), 225–44.

—— ' "Ma Musique est vécue": La biographie comme outil d'analyse', in *Colloque international Gustav Mahler 25. 26. 27. janvier 1985* (Paris: L'Association Gustav Mahler, 1986), 36–8.

—— ' "Meine Musik ist 'gelebt' ": Mahler's Biography as a Key to his Works', *Opus*, 3/2 (Feb. 1987), 16–17.

—— 'Music about Music in Mahler: Reminiscences, Allusions, or Quotations?', in Hefling (ed.), *Mahler Studies*.

—— 'The Tenth Symphony: Purgatory or Catharsis?', in *Fragment or Completion?*, ed. Op de Coul, 154–64.

——, Weiss, Günther, and Martner, Knud (eds.), *Ein Glück ohne Ruh'. Die Briefe Gustav Mahlers an Alma* (Berlin: Siedler Verlag, 1995).

Lange, Friedrich Albert, *History of Materialism and Criticism of its Present Importance*, 2nd edn., trans. Ernest Chester Thomas (London: Kegan Paul, Trench, Trübner & Co., 1892).

Lawford-Hinrichsen, Irene, *Music Publishing and Patronage: C F Peters, 1800 to the Holocaust* (Kenton, Middx.: Edition Press, 2000).

Lea, Henry A., *Gustav Mahler: Man on the Margin* (Bonn: Bouvier, 1985).

Lebrecht, Norman, *Mahler Remembered* (London: Faber and Faber, 1987; New York: W. W. Norton, 1988).

Leichtentritt, Hugo, 'Gustav Mahler: His Aims and Achievements', *Musical Courier*, 101/21 (1930), 6 and 8.

—— *Music, History and Ideas* (Cambridge, Mass.: Harvard University Press, 1950).

Leur, Truus de, 'Mahler's Fifth Symphony and the Royal Concertgebouw Orchestra', in Mitchell and Straub (eds.), *New Sounds, New Century*, 76–101.

Levy, David, 'Gustav Mahler and Emanuel Libman: Bacterial Endocarditis in 1911', *British Medical Journal*, 293 (1986), 1628–31.

Lewis, Christopher O., 'On the Chronology of the *Kindertotenlieder*', *Revue Mahler*, 1 (1987), 21–45.

—— *Tonal Coherence in Mahler's Ninth Symphony* (Studies in Musicology, 79; Ann Arbor: UMI Research Press, 1984).

Lichtenfeld, Monika, 'Zur Klangflächentechnik bei Mahler', in Peter Ruzicka (ed.), *Mahler: Eine Herausforderung* (Wiesbaden: Breitkopf & Härtel, 1977), 121–34.

Lichtenstein, Sabine, 'Mahler als Jood aan de Hofoper: Antesemitisme en Joodse reacties in het Wenen van 1897–1907', *Muziek & wetenschap*, 7 (2001), 271–304.

Lipiner, Siegfried, *Buch der Freude* (Leipzig: Breitkopf & Härtel, 1880).

Lockspeiser, Edward, *Claude Debussy*, trans. Léo Dilé (Paris: Fayard, 1980), 369.

Lo, Kii-Ming, 'Chinesische Dichtung als Text-Grundlage für Mahler's "Lied von der Erde" ', in *Das Gustav-Mahler-Fest Hamburg 1989*, ed. Vogt, 509–28.

Ludvová, Jitka, *Gustav Mahler a Praha* (Prague: Ustar pro Hudební vědu Akademie věd ČR, 1996).

—— 'Gustav Mahler im Prag im Mai 1908', *Hudební věda*, 23/3 (1986), 255–62.

McClatchie, Stephen, 'The Gustav Mahler–Alfred Rosé Collection at the University of Western Ontario', *Notes: Quarterly Journal of the Music Library Association*, 52 (1994–5), 385–406.

McGrath, William J., *Dionysian Art and Populist Politics in Austria* (New Haven: Yale University Press, 1974).

—— 'Mahler and Freud: The Dream of the Stately House', in *Gustav Mahler Kolloquium 1979*, ed. Klein, 41–51.

Mahler, Alma, *Gustav Mahler: Erinnerungen und Briefe* (Amsterdam: Allert de Lange, 1940; Amsterdam: Bermann-Fischer, 1949; Frankfurt: Propyläen, 1971).

—— *Gustav Mahler: Memories and Letters*, trans. Basil Creighton (New York: Viking, 1946); 3rd edn., ed. Donald Mitchell and Knud Martner (London: John Murray, 1973; Seattle: University of Washington Press, 1975); 4th edn., ed. Donald Mitchell and Knud Martner (London: Sphere Books, 1990).

Mahler[-]Werfel, Alma, *And the Bridge is Love* (New York: Harcourt, Brace & Co., 1958; London: Hutchinson, 1959).

—— *Diaries 1898–1902*, selected and trans. Antony Beaumont (London: Faber and Faber, 1998).

—— *Mein Leben* (Frankfurt: Fischer, 1960).

Mahler, Gustav, *Briefe*, ed. Herta Blaukopf (Vienna and Hamburg: Zsolnay, 1982).

—— *Briefe, 1879–1911*, ed. Alma Mahler (Berlin and Vienna: Zsolnay, 1924).

—— *Mahler's Unknown Letters*, trans. Richard Stokes, ed. Herta Blaukopf (London: Gollancz, 1986).

—— *Selected Letters of Gustav Mahler*, trans. Eithne Wilkins, Ernst Kaiser, and Bill Hopkins, ed. Knud Martner (London: Faber, 1979).

Mahler: A Documentary Study, comp. and ed. Kurt Blaukopf, with contributions by Zoltan Roman (London: Thames and Hudson, 1976).

Mahler Album, ed. Gilbert Kaplan (New York: The Kaplan Foundation, Harry N. Abrams, Inc., 1995).

Mahler a Roma (Rome: Accademia Nazionale di Santa Cecilia, 2000).

Martner, Knud, *Gustav Mahler im Konzertsaal: Eine Dokumentation seiner Konzerttätigkeit 1870–1911* (Copenhagen: privately published, 1985).

—— and Becqué, Robert, 'Zwölf unbekannte Briefe Gustav Mahlers an Ludwig Strecker', *Archiv für Musikwissenschaft*, 34 (1977), 287–97.

Marx, Joseph, *Betrachtungen eines romantischen Realisten: Gesammelte Aufsätze, Vorträge und Reden über Musik*, ed. Oswald Ortner (Vienna: Gerlach & Wiedling, 1947).

A 'Mass' for the Masses: Proceedings of the Mahler VIII Symposium Amsterdam 1988, ed. Jos van Leeuwen, Eveline Nikkels, and Robert Becqué (Rijswijk: Universitaire Pers Rotterdam, 1992).

Matthews, Colin, 'Mahler and Self-Renewal', in Reed (ed.), *On Mahler and Britten*, 85–8.

—— *Mahler at Work: Aspects of the Creative Process* (New York and London: Garland Publishing, Inc., 1989).

—— 'The Tenth Symphony and Artistic Morality', *Muziek & wetenschap*, 5 (1995–6), 303–19.

Mayer, Hans, 'Musik und Literatur', in *Gustav Mahler* (Tübingen: Rainer Wunderlich, 1966), 142–56.

Mayer, Johannes-Leopold, 'Musik als gesellschaftliches Ärgernis — oder: Anton Bruckner, Der anti-Burger. Das Phänomen Bruckner als historisches Problem', in Franz Grasberger (ed.), *Anton Bruckner in Wien* (Graz: Akademischer Druck und Verlagsanstalt, 1980), 75–160.

Miaskovsky, Nikolay, *Pis'ma iz Peterburga . . . Sobranie materialov v dvukh tomakh* (Moscow: Muzyka, 1964).

Micznik, Vera, 'The Farewell Story of Mahler's Ninth', *19th Century Music*, 20 (1996), 144–66.

—— 'Is Mahler's Music Autobiographical? A Reappraisal', *Revue Mahler Review*, 1 (1987), 47–63.

—— 'Meaning in Gustav Mahler's Music: A Historical and Analytical Study Focusing on the Ninth Symphony' (Ph.D. diss., State University of New York at Stony Brook, 1989).

Mikheyeva, Ludmila, *Gustav Maler, kratkiy ocherk zhizni i tvorchestva, popularnaya monografiya* (Leningrad: Muzyka, 1972).

Millington, Barry, and Spencer, Stewart (eds.), *Wagner in Performance* (New Haven: Yale University Press, 1992).

Mitchell, Donald, *Cradles of the New: Writings on Music, 1951–1991*, ed. Christopher Palmer and Mervyn Cooke (London: Faber, 1995).

—— *Gustav Mahler: The Early Years* (London: Rockliff, 1958); rev. and ed. Paul Banks and David Matthews (London: Faber, 1980; Berkeley: University of California Press, 1980).

—— *Gustav Mahler: Songs and Symphonies of Life and Death* (London: Faber, 1985; Berkeley: University of California Press, 1985).

—— *Gustav Mahler: The Wunderhorn Years* (London: Faber, 1975; Berkeley: University of California Press, 1980).

—— 'Mahler and Smetana: Significant Influences or Accidental Parallels?', in Hefling (ed.), *Mahler Studies*, 110–21.

—— 'Mahler's Creation Symphony', CD liner-note to the Third Symphony conducted by Kent Nagano, Teldec CD 8573–82354–2 (2000).

—— 'Mahler's Eighth Symphony: The Triumph of Eros', CD liner-note to the Eighth Symphony conducted by Riccardo Chailly, Decca CD 467 314–2 (2001).

—— 'Mahler's "Lieder-Abend": Many Songs, Many Orchestras', CD liner-note to the orchestral songs sung by Dietrich Henschel (baritone), conducted by Kent Negano, Teldec CD 8573–86573–2 (2001).

—— 'The Modernity of Gustav Mahler', in Weiss (ed.), *Neue Mahleriana*, 175–90.

—— '*Peter Grimes*: Fifty Years On', in Banks (ed.), *The Making of 'Peter Grimes'*, 125–51.

—— and Straub, Henriette (eds.), *New Sounds, New Century: Mahler's Fifth Symphony* (1901–2), *With a History of Performances by the Royal Concertgebouw Orchestra* (1906–97) (editor-in-chief, Donald Mitchell) (Bussum: THOTH/Amsterdam, Royal Concertgebouw Orchestra, 1997).

Moldenhauer, Hans, and Moldenhauer, Rosaleen, *Anton von Webern: A Chronicle of his Life and Work* (New York: Alfred A. Knopf, 1979).

Morgan, Robert P., 'Ives and Mahler: Mutual Responses at the End of an Era', *19th Century Music*, 2 (1978/9), 72–81; repr. in Block and Burkholder (eds.), *Charles Ives and the Classical Tradition*, 75–86.

Morold, Max, *Wagners Kampf und Sieg: Dargestellt in seinen Beziehungen zu Wien*, 2 vols. (Zürich: Almathea-Verlag, 1930).

Motte, Diether de la, 'Das komplizierte Einfache: Amnerkungen zum 1. Satz der 9. Sinfonie von Gustav Mahler', in Kolleritsch (ed.), *Gustav Mahler*, 52–67.

Mulder, Ernest W., *Gustav Mahler: 'Das Lied von der Erde', een critisch-analytische studie* (Amsterdam: Uitgevers Maatschappij, 1951).

Müller, Karl Josef, *Mahler: Leben, Werken, Dokumente* (Munich: Schott, Piper, 1988).

Muziek & wetenschap: Dutch Journal for Musicology, 5/3 (1995/1996): 'Gustav Mahler The World Listens' [contributors include Reeser, Mitchell, La Grange, Aoyagi, Banks, Danuser, Barsova, C. Matthews, Kaplan, Comini, Blaukopf, Reilly, D. Matthews, Pecker Berio, and Principe].

Muziek & wetenschap: Dutch Journal for Musicology, 7/1 (1999): '*Das Klagende Lied* and the Fifth Symphony' [contributors include Blaukopf, Kubik, Mitchell, Straub, and Wennekes (Nodnagel and Göhler)].

Nebolyubova, Larisa, 'Spetsificheskie zakonomernosti dramaturgii simfonii Gustava Malera: k probleme Maler—ekspressionizm' (Ph.D. diss., Inst. iskusstvovedenija, fol'klora i etnografii Akademii nauk SSSR, 1978).

Nest'ev, Izrail', 'Gustav Maler: Posledniy velikiy simfonist', *Na rubezhe dvukh stoletiy* (Moscow: Muzyka, 1967).

—— 'Primechatel'naya prem'era. Ispolnenie pyatoy simfonii Malera', *Sovetskaya muzyka*, no. 7 (1960).

Newcomb, Anthony, 'Narrative Archetypes and Mahler's Ninth Symphony', in Steven Paul Scher (ed.), *Music and Text: Critical Inquiries* (Cambridge: Cambridge University Press, 1992), 118–36.

Newlin, Dika, *Bruckner, Mahler, Schoenberg* (New York: King's Crown Press, 1947; rev. edn., New York: W. W. Norton, 1978).

Newsom, Jon, and Mann, Alfred, *Music History from Primary Sources: A Guide to the Moldenhauer Archives* (Washington, DC: Library of Congress, 2000).

Nikkels, Eveline, *'O Mensch! Gib Acht!' Friedrich Nietzsches Bedeutung für Gustav Mahler* (Amsterdam and Atlanta: Rodopi, 1989).

Nodnagel, Ernst Otto, 'Gustav Mahlers zweite Symphonie', *Die Musik*, 2 (1903), 337–53.

—— *Jenseits von Wagner und Liszt* (Königsberg: Ostpreussischen Druckerei, 1902).

Notley, Margaret, 'Brahms as Liberal: Genre, Style, and Politics in Late Nineteenth-Century Vienna', *19th Century Music*, 17 (1993–4), 107–23.

—— 'Bruckner and Viennese Wagnerism', in Jackson and Hawkshaw (eds.), *Bruckner Studies*, 54–71.

—— '*Volksconcerte* in Vienna and Late Nineteenth-Century Ideology of the Symphony', *Journal of the American Musicological Society*, 59 (1997), 421–54.

Ogawa, Takashi, *Japanese Symphony Orchestras: Documents of Regular Concerts, 1927–1981* (Tokyo: V. Minon-on Music Library, 1983).

—— *Japanese Symphony Orchestras: Documents of Regular Concerts, 1982–1991* (Tokyo: V. Minon-on Music Library, 1992).

Oltmanns, Michael Johannes, ' "Ich bin der Welt abhanden gekommen" und "Der Tamboursg'sell"—Zwei Liedkonzeptionen Gustav Mahlers', *Archiv für Musikwissenschaft*, 43 (1986), 69–88.

100 Years Remembered: A History of the Theatre and Music Publishers Josef Weinberger, comp. and pub. by Josef Weinberger Ltd (London: Weinberger, 1985).

Osthoff, Helmuth, 'Zu Gustav Mahlers Erster Symphonie', *Archiv für Musikwissenschaft*, 28 (1971), 217–27.

Overman, Rob, 'The Mahler Reception in the Netherlands', in *A 'Mass' for the Masses*, ed. van Leeuwen et al., 68–77.

Pfohl, Ferdinand, *Gustav Mahler: Eindrücke und Erinnerungen aus den Hamburger Jahren*, ed. Knud Martner (Hamburg: Musikalienverlag Karl Dieter Wagner, 1973).

Philharmony [Newsletter of the NHK Symphony Orchestra] (Tokyo, 1927–).

Pike, Lionel, *Beethoven, Sibelius and the 'Profound Logic': Studies in Symphonic Analysis* (London: Athlone, 1978).

Pollack, Michael, 'Cultural Innovation and Social Identity in *Fin-de-siècle* Vienna', in Ivar Oxaal, Michael Pollack, and Gerhard Botz (eds.), *Jews, Antisemitism and Culture in Vienna* (London and New York: Routledge and Kegan Paul, 1987).

Popov, Gavriil, *Iz literaturnogo naslediya*, ed. Zarui Apetyan (Moscow: Sovetskiy kompozitor, 1986).

Powell, Nicolas, *The Sacred Spring: The Arts in Vienna 1898–1918* (Greenwich, Conn.: New York Graphic Society, 1974).

Prange, Helmut, *Friedrich Rückert: Geist und Form der Sprache* (Schweinfurt and Wiesbaden: Otto Harrassowitz, 1963).

Pynsent, Robert B., 'Conclusory Essay: Decadence, Decay and Innovation', in id. (ed.), *Decadence and Innovation: Austro-Hungarian Life and Art at the Turn of the Century* (London: Weidenfeld and Nicolson, 1989), 128–40.

Rather, L. J., *The Dream of Self-Destruction: Wagner's* Ring *and the Modern World* (Baton Rouge: Louisiana State University Press, 1979).

Ratz, Erwin, 'Zum Formproblem bei Gustav Mahler: Eine Analyse des ersten Satzes der IX. Symphonie', *Musikforschung*, 8 (1955), 169–77, repr. in Danuser (ed.), *Gustav Mahler*, 276–88.

—— (ed.), *Mahler, IX. Symphonie: Partiturentwurf der ersten drei Sätze, Faksimile nach der Handschrift* (Vienna: Universal Edition, 1971).

Redlich, H. F., *Bruckner and Mahler* (London: Dent, 1955).

Reed, John, *The Schubert Song Companion* (London: Faber, 1993).

Reed, Philip, 'Aschenbach becomes Mahler: Thomas Mann as Film', in *Death in Venice*, ed. Donald Mitchell (Cambridge: Cambridge University Press, 1987), 178–83.

—— (ed.), *On Mahler and Britten: Essays in Honour of Donald Mitchell on his Seventieth Birthday* (Woodbridge: The Boydell Press, 1995).

Reeser, Eduard, 'Die Mahler-Rezeption in Holland, 1903–1911', in Rudolf Stephan (ed.), *Mahler-Interpretation* (Mainz: Schott's Söhne, 1985), 81–103.

—— (ed.), *Gustav Mahler und Holland: Briefe* (Bibliothek der Internationalen Gustav Mahler Gesellschaft; Vienna: Universal Edition, 1980).

Reid Orchestral Concerts [Programmes] (Edinburgh, 1917–46), 62nd Session, 9th Season, 2nd Concert (13 Nov. 1924); 74th Session, 21st Season, 1st Concert (22 Oct. 1936).

Reilly, Edward R., 'A Brief History of the Manuscripts', in Gustav Mahler, *Symphony No. 2 in C Minor 'Resurrection' Facsimile*, ed. Gilbert Kaplan (New York: The Kaplan Foundation, 1986).

—— *Gustav Mahler and Guido Adler: Records of a Friendship* (Cambridge: Cambridge University Press, 1982).

—— '*Das klagende Lied* Reconsidered', in Hefling (ed.), *Mahler Studies*.

—— 'The Manuscripts of Mahler's Fifth Symphony', in Mitchell and Straub (eds.), *New Sounds, New Century*, 58–63.

—— 'Sketches, Text Sources, Dating of Manuscripts: Unanswered Questions', *News about Mahler Research*, no. 30 (Oct. 1993), 3–9.

—— 'Die Skizzen zu Mahlers Zweiter Symphonie', *Österreichische Muzikzeitschrift*, 34 (1979), 265–85.

Remy, Arthur F. J., *The Influence of India and Persia on the Poetry of Germany* (Columbia University Germanic Studies, 4; New York: Columbia University Press, 1901).

Revers, Peter, *Gustav Mahler: Untersuchungen zu den späten Sinfonien* (Hamburg: Karl Dieter Wagner, 1985), 79–135.

Rimsky-Korsakov, Nicolay, *Vospominaniya*, ed. Vasiliy Yastrebtsev (Leningrad: Muzgiz, 1960).

Rivier, David, 'A Note on Form in Mahler's Symphonies', *Chord and Discord*, 2/7 (1954), 29–33.

Riz, Elisabeth, 'Robert Hirschfeld: Leben—Wirken—Bedeutung', in Friedrich C. Heller (ed.), *Biographische Beiträge zum Musikleben Wiens im 19. und frühen 20. Jahrhundert*, i (Vienna: Österreichischer Kunst- und Kulturverlag, 1992), 1–79.

Rolland, Romain, *Musiciens d'aujourd'hui* (Paris: Hachette, 1922).

Roller, Alfred, *Die Bildnisse von Gustav Mahler* (Leipzig, E. P. Tal & Co., 1922).

Roman, Zoltan, *Gustav Mahler and Hungary* (Budapest: Akadémiai Kiadó, 1991).

—— *Gustav Mahler's American Years: 1907–1911. A Documentary History* (Stuyvesant, NY: Pendragon Press, 1989).

—— 'Mahler's Songs and their Influence on his Symphonic Thought' (Ph.D. diss., University of Toronto, 1970).

Rosenberg, Wolf, 'Mahler und die Avantgarde: Kompositionstechnisches Vorbild oder geistige Sympathie', in Kolleritsch (ed.), *Gustav Mahler*, 81–92.

Rosenshil'd, Konstantin, *Gustav Maler* (Moscow: Muzyka, 1975).

Rosenthal, Harold, *Two Centuries of Opera at Covent Garden* (London: Putnam, 1958).

Rothfarb, Lee A., *Ernst Kurth as Theorist and Analyst* (Philadelphia: University of Pennsylvania Press, 1988).

Russell, Peter, *Light in Battle with Darkness: Mahler's 'Kindertotenlieder'* (Bern: Peter Lang, 1991).

Ryding, Erik S., and Pechefsky, Rebecca, *Bruno Walter: A World Elsewhere* (New Haven and London: Yale University Press, 2001).

Samuels, Robert, *Mahler's Sixth Symphony: A Study in Musical Semiotics* (Cambridge: Cambridge University Press, 1995).

Schaefer, Hans Joachim, *Gustav Mahler in Kassel* (Kassel: Bärenreiter, 1982).

——, Rölleke, Heinz, and Linnebach, Andrea, *Gustav Mahler: Jahre der Entscheidung in Kassel, 1883–1885* (Kassel: Stadtsparkasse Kassel, 1990).

Scharberth, Irmgard, 'Gustav Mahlers Wirken am Hamburger Stadttheater', *Musikforschung*, 22 (1969), 443–56.

Schenker, Heinrich, 'Das Hören in der Musik', in Hellmut Federhofer (ed.), *Heinrich Schenker als Essayist und Kritiker* (Hildesheim: G. Olms, 1990), 96–102 and 259–68.

Schiedermair, Ludwig, 'Gustav Mahler als Symphoniker', *Die Musik*, 1 (1901–2), 506–10, 603–8, 696–9.

Schimmel, Annemarie, *Friedrich Rückert: Lebensbild und Einführung in sein Werk* (Freiburg: Herder, 1987).

Schmierer, Elisabeth, 'Between Lied and Symphony: On Mahler's "Tamboursg'sell" ', *News about Mahler Research*, no. 33 (Mar. 1995), 15–22.

—— *Die Orchesterlieder Gustav Mahlers* (Kieler Schriften zur Musikwissenschaft, 38; Kassel: Bärenreiter, 1991).

Schnebel, Dieter, 'Sinfonie und Wirklichkeit am Beispiel von Mahlers Dritte', in *Gustav Mahler: Sinfonie und Wirklichkeit* (Graz: Universal Edition, 1977), 103–17.

—— 'Das Spätwerk als Neue Musik', in Arnold Schönberg et al., *Gustav Mahler* (Tübingen: Rainer Wunderlich Verlag, 1966), 157–88.

Schnitzler, Arthur, *Tagebuch 1909–1912* (Vienna: Österreichische Akademie der Wissenschaften, 1981).

Schoenberg, Arnold, *Style and Idea*, trans. Leo Black, ed. Leonard Stein (London: Faber, 1975).

Schopenhauer, Arthur, *The World as Will and Representation*, trans. E. F. J. Payne, 2 vols. (New York: Dover Books, 1966).

Schorske, Carl E., *Fin-de-siècle Vienna: Politics and Culture* (New York: Knopf, 1980).

—— 'Mahler and Klimt: Social Experience and Artistic Evolution', in *Gustav Mahler Kolloquium 1979*, ed. Klein, 16–28.

Schubert, Franz, String Quartet in D Minor (D. 810), arranged for string orchestra by Gustav Mahler, ed. Donald Mitchell and David Matthews (London: Josef Weinberger, 1984).

Secrest, Meryle, *Leonard Bernstein: A Life* (New York: Knopf, 1994).

The Seventh Symphony of Gustav Mahler: A Symposium, ed. James L. Zychowicz (Cincinnati: University of Cincinnati, 1990).

Shanet, Howard, *Philharmonic: A History of New York's Orchestra* (Garden City, NY: Doubleday, 1975).

Shaw's Music, ed. Dan H. Laurence (2nd rev. edn., 3 vols. London: Bodley Head, 1989).

Shmith, Michael, *Mahler—Musician of the Century* (London: Royal Philharmonic Orchestra, 1998).

Shostakovich, Dmitry, *Gustav Maler: Pis'ma, vospominaniya*, trans. Sergey Osherov, ed. and intro. Inna Barsova, with a Foreword by Dmitry Shostakovich (Moscow: Muzyka, 1964; 2nd edn., 1968).

Skelton, Geoffrey, *Wagner in Thought and Practice* (London: Lime Tree, 1991).

Small, Christopher, 'Performance as Ritual; Sketch for an Enquiry into the True Nature of a Symphony Concert', in Avron Levine White (ed.), *Lost in Music: Culture, Style and the Musical Event* (London and New York: Routledge and Kegan Paul, 1987), 6–32.

Smith, Warren Storey, 'The Songs of Alma Mahler', *Chord and Discord*, 2/6 (1950), 74–8.

Smoley, Lewis M., *Gustav Mahler's Symphonies: Critical Commentary on Recordings since 1986* (New York: Greenwood Press, 1996).

—— *The Symphonies of Gustav Mahler: A Critical Discography* (New York: Greenwood Press, 1986).

Sollertinsky, Ivan, *Gustav Maler* (Leningrad: Gosudarstvennoe muzikal'noe izdatel'stvo, 1932).

—— *Pamyati I. I. Sollertinskogo, vospominaniya, materialy, issledovaniya*, ed. Ludmila Mikheyeva (Leningrad and Moscow: Sovetskiy kompozitor, 1974).

Specht, Richard, *Gustav Mahler* (Berlin: Gose und Tetßlaff, 1905).

—— *Gustav Mahler* (Berlin: Schuster & Loeffler, 1913).

—— *Gustav Mahlers II. Sinfonie: Thematische Analyse* (Vienna: Universal Edition, 1915).

—— *Gustav Mahlers VIII. Symphonie: Thematische Analyse* (Leipzig and Vienna: Universal Edition, 1912).

Spielmann, Heinz, *Oskar Kokoschka: Die Facher für Alma Mahler* (Dortmund: Harenberg, 1985).

Sponheuer, Bernd, *Logik des Zerfalls: Untersuchungen zum Finalproblem in den Symphonien Gustav Mahlers* (Tutzing: Hans Schneider, 1978).

Stahmer, Klaus Hinrich (ed.), *Form und Idee in Gustav Mahlers Instrumentalmusik* (Wilhelmshaven: Heinrichshofen, 1980).

Stefan, Paul, *Gustav Mahler: Eine Studie über Persönlichkeit und Werk* (Munich: R. Piper, 1920).

—— *Gustav Mahler: A Study of his Personality and Work*, trans. T. E. Clark (New York: G. Schirmer, 1913).

Stein, Erwin, 'Billy Budd', in Donald Mitchell and Hans Keller (eds.), *Benjamin Britten: A Commentary on his Works* (London: Rockliff, 1952; repr. Westport, Conn.: Greenwood Press, 1971).

Stein, Erwin, *Orpheus in New Guises* (London: Rockliff, 1953).

Stephan, Rudolf, *Gustav Mahler: II. Symphonie C-moll* (Meisterwerke der Musik, 21; Munich: Wilhelm Fink Verlag, 1979).

—— 'Hans Pfitzners Eichendorff-Kantate *Von deutscher Seele*', *Mitteilungen der Hans-Pfitzner-Gesellschaft*, 50 (1989), 5–21.

—— 'Mahlers sinfonische Dichtung "Todtenfeier" ', *Nachrichten zur Mahler-Forschung*, 13 (1984), 6–7.

—— (ed. and comp.), *Gustav Mahler: Werk und Interpretation* (Cologne: Arno Volk Verlag, 1979).

Stokowski, Olga Samaroff, *An American Musician's Story* (New York: W. W. Norton, 1939).

—— 'The "Peace Conference of Amsterdam" ', *Chord and Discord*, 2/1 (Jan. 1940), 30–1.

Stravinsky, Igor, and Craft, Robert, *Conversations with Igor Stravinsky* (London: Faber, 1959).

Sulzer, Joseph, *Ernstes und Heiteres aus den Erinnerungen eines Wiener Philharmonikers* (Vienna and Leipzig: F. Eisenstein, 1910).

Tawaststjerna, Erik, *Sibelius*, ii: *1904–1914*, trans. Robert Layton (Berkeley and Los Angeles: University of California Press, 1986).

Teibler, Hermann, *Gustav Mahler: Symphonie No. 2 in c-moll* (Musikführer No. 207; Leipzig: Hermann Seemann Nachfolger, n.d. [*c.*1902]).

Thomson, Virgil, *The Musical Scene* (New York: Alfred A. Knopf, 1945).

—— *Music Reviewed 1940–1954* (New York: Vintage Books, 1967).

Tibbe, Monika, *Lieder und Liedelemente in instrumentalen Symphoniesätzen Gustav Mahlers* (Berliner Musikwissenschaftliche Arbeiten, 1; Munich: Musikverlag Emil Katzbichler, 1971; 2nd edn., 1977).

Timoshchenkova, Galina, 'Pozdnee tvorchestvo Gustava Malera' (Ph.D. diss., Leningradskiy Institut teatra, muzyki i kinematografii, 1977).

Tovey, Donald Francis, *The Classics of Music: Talks, Essays, and Other Writings Previously Uncollected*, ed. Michael Tilmouth, edn. completed by David Kimbell and Roger Savage (Oxford: Oxford University Press, 2001), 135–7.

—— *Essays in Musical Analysis*, vi (London: Oxford University Press, 1939), 73–83.

Türcke, Berthold, 'The Mahler Society', *Journal of the Arnold Schoenberg Institute*, 7/1 (June 1983), 29–93.

Vallas, Léon, *Claude Debussy et son temps* (Paris: A. Michel, 1958).

Vaughan Williams, Ralph, *National Music and Other Essays* (2nd edn., Oxford: Oxford University Press, 1987).

Vill, Susanne, *Vermittlungsformen verbalisierter und musikalischer Inhalte in der Musik Gustav Mahlers* (Frankfurter Beiträge zur Musikwissenschaft, 6; Tutzing: Hans Schneider, 1979).

Von Deck, Marvin L., 'Gustav Mahler in New York: His Conducting Activities in New York City', 1908–1911' (Ph.D. diss., New York University, 1973).

Wagner, Cosima, *Diaries*, ii: *1878–1883*, ed. Martin Gregor-Dellin and Dietrich Mack, trans. Geoffrey Skelton (New York and London: Harcourt Brace Jovanovich, 1980).

Walter, Bruno, *Briefe 1894–1962*, ed. Lotte Walter Lindt (Frankfurt am Main: S. Fischer Verlag, 1969).

—— *Gustav Mahler* (Vienna: Herbert Reichner Verlag, 1936).

—— *Gustav Mahler*, trans. Lotte Walter Lindt (London: Quartet Books, 1990).

—— *Gustav Mahler*, trans. James Galston (London: Kegan Paul, Trench, Trübner, 1937; New York: Greystone Press, 1941; repr. Vienna House, 1973; repr. New York: Da Capo Press, 1970).

—— 'Mahlers Weg, ein Erinnerungsblatt', *Der Merker*, 3/5 (1912), 166–71.

—— *Thema und Variationen* (Frankfurt am Main: S. Fischer Verlag, 1967).

—— *Theme and Variations: An Autobiography*, trans. James A. Galston (New York: Alfred A. Knopf, 1946; London: Hamish Hamilton, 1947).

Watanabe, Hiroshi (ed.), *Das Bruckner–Mahler Lexicon* (Tokyo: Shoseki, 1993).

Watkins, Glenn, *Soundings: Music in the Twentieth Century* (New York: Schirmer Books, 1988).

Weber, J. F., *Mahler* (Discography Series IX; Utica, NY: self-published, 1971; 2nd edn., 1975).

Weiss, Günther (ed.), *Neue Mahleriana: Essays in Honour of Henry-Louis de La Grange on his Seventieth Birthday* (Berne: Peter Lang, 1997).

Wenk, Arthur, 'The Composer as Poet in *Das Lied von der Erde*', *19th Century Music*, ed. van Leeuwen et al., 1 (1977), 33–47.

Werck, Isabelle, 'Cosmogony of the Eighth Symphony', in *A 'Mass' for the Masses*, ed. van Leeuwen et al., 89.

Wilkens, Sander, *Gustav Mahlers Fünfte Symphonie: Quellen und Instrumentationsprozess* (Frankfurt: C. F. Peters, 1989).

Willem Mengelberg Gedenkboek (The Hague: Martinus Nijhoff, 1920).

Williamson, John, *The Music of Hans Pfitzner* (Oxford: Oxford University Press, 1992).

Willnauer, Franz, *Gustav Mahler und die Wiener Oper* (2nd. rev. edn., Vienna: Löcker, 1993).

Wood, Henry J., *My Life of Music* (London: Gollancz, 1938).

Youens, Susan, 'Schubert, Mahler and the Weight of the Past: *Lieder eines fahrenden Gesellen* and *Winterreise*', *Music & Letters*, 67 (1986), 256–68.

Zychowicz, James L., *Mahler's Fourth Symphony* (Oxford: Oxford University Press, 2000)

—— 'The *Partiturentwurf* of the Adagio of Mahler's Ninth Symphony', *Revue Mahler Review*, 1 (1987), 77–101.

—— 'Ein schlechter Jasager: Considerations on the Finale to Mahler's Seventh Symphony', in id. (ed.), *The Seventh Symphony*, 98–106.

INDEX OF WORKS

Figures in **bold** indicate main analytical entries and figures in *italics* indicate music examples and illustrations.

GENERAL INDEX

References in *italic* type indicate illustrations or music examples.